MASTERY AND TIMING PRACTICE

Reading Comprehension

KAPLAN

TEST PREP

Special thanks to the Kaplan teams who made this LSAT course possible:

Contributing Developers: Misha Alexeef, M.F.A., Joshua Allen, M.F.A. (exp. '11), Krista Ammons, Deborah Baker, J.D., Jennifer Barta, Chris Bauer, Ph.D. (exp. '13), Kevin Bedeau, Howard Bell, J.D., Jeff Boudreau, Richard Boutcher, J.D., Aaron Brown, Robert Brown, J.D., Juliet Brownell, Zarina Burbacki, Geri Burgert, Matthew Burke, M.Div., Jack Chase, J.D., Ahn Chi, Natasha Chua Tan, J.D. (exp. '12), Christopher Combs, Christopher Cosci, Emily Cripe, Ph.D. (exp. '12), John Cummins, Jeffrey Cunningham, Erin Decker, M.A., Zach Denver, J.D. (exp. '13), Michael Durante, J.D.(exp. '12), Ian Edelson, Scott Emerson, Cailin Emmett, Jesse Evans, Ben Fierce, Paula Fleming, Joe Freimuth, John Fritschie, J.D., Darcy Galane, J.D., Devu Gandhi, M.B.A., Megan Gendell, Christopher Gomes, Joanna Graham, Raul Grau, Aaron Hammes, William Havemann, J.D., Christian Hertzog, J.D., Jeannie Ho, Gar Hong, Jonathan Hopkins, Rebecca Houck, J.D., Cinzia Iacono, Sasha Kahn, Deborah Katz, J.D., Heather M. Kenney-Nield, J.D., Stuart Kovinsky, L.L.B., Sarah Kramer, Michael Kermmoade, Ph.D. (exp. '11), Joanne L'Abbate, Dianne Lake, Julie Lamberth, J.D., Lisa Lamming, J.D., Devin Landin, Matthew Landin, Carolyn Landis, J.D., Elizabeth Ledkovsky, J.D. (exp. '13), Farrah Lehman, Jay Libou, J.D. (exp. '13), Kristin Longley, Adam Loren, Keith Lubeley, Andrew Lucas, Wesley Madison, Kalee Magnani, J.D., Eric May, Danielle Mazza, Amy McClish, Shana McCullough, Sheryl McNamee, Jason Moss, M.B.A., Maria Nicholas, Walt Niedner, M.B.A., Josh Newville, J.D. (exp. '12), Deborah Osborn, J.D., Anne Pennick, Glenn Phillips, Lisa Plante, M.B.A., Lindsey Plyler, Kate Rawsthorne, J.D., Scott Reed, J.D., Andrew Royal, J.D., Helen Sabo, J.D., Stephanie Schrauth, Eric Sepe, Rebecca Shansky, Ph.D., Jessica Smith, Murl Smith, J.D., Stephen Snyder, Richard Spoonts, J.D. (exp. '13), Jennifer Steiger, J.D., M.B.A. (exp. '10), J. Ethan Sterling, M.A., Glen Stohr, J.D., Caroline Sykes, J.D., Bruce Symaka, L.L.B., Jeff Thomas, J.D., Anthony Todd, Shaunagh Tomlin, Barry Tonoff, Martha P. Torres, Michael Vandenbrooks, Bob Verini, M.F.A., Thomas Volo, Missy Wanstall, M.S., Bryce Warwick, J.D., Shane Wesley, Emily West, M.A., Andrew Whang, J.D., Wayne Wilden, Matthew Williamson, J.D., Dan Wittich, James Yeh, Matthew Zaller, Elizabeth Zeanah, Ph.D. (exp. '12), and Heather Zezeck.

Additional Support: Advisory Panel and Brain Trust, Customer Service, Corporate Marketing, Creative Services, Production Development, Kaplan Publishing, Catalyst, Corporate Research, Territory and Regional Staff, eLearning, Live Online, Graduate Programs, Scheduling, Mailroom, Technical Support, Midwest and Canada Territory, Philadelphia, Orange County, and Washington, DC Centers.

TABLE OF CONTENTS

Timing Practice Answers and Explanations can be found in your online resources at kaplanlsat.com

Welcome to Reading Comprehension Mastery and Timing Practice

Mastery Practice

Material in the first half of this book is organized specifically to prepare you for dealing with the individual multiple-choice questions you will see on Test Day. The content is structured to facilitate practicing the skills you have learned against specific question types and along progressive levels of difficulty. This should be done after you have worked though specific topics in your teaching sessions and have gained an understanding of those areas in which you need additional practice.

All of the material presented in this book is content from PrepTests released by the LSAC. We have selected questions that are representative of what you will see on Test Day and that best illustrate (and build on) skills learned in the classroom.

You will work on question mastery throughout the program. Until you gain basic proficiency, worry less about how quickly you are doing a problem and more about whether you are getting it correct. For every question, review the included explanations to ensure that you are getting the right answers for the right reasons (rather than "lucky guesses") and that you will not repeat the mistakes you made on those you got wrong. Once you are able to do question types at various levels of difficulty, you will be ready to move on to your "Timing" and "Endurance" practice material.

LSAT Extreme – EX

LSAT Extreme will cover some of the material presented in this book in their additional in-class practice workshop sessions. Material used in these sessions is marked with the "EX" label. Extreme students should refer to the "What to Bring to Class" guide in the front of the Extreme Lesson Book to determine when to bring this book to in-class practice workshop sessions.

LSAT Advanced – ADV

LSAT Advanced will cover some of the material presented in this book in their additional in-class practice workshop sessions. Material used in these sessions is marked with the "ADV" label. Advanced students should refer to the "What to Bring to Class" guide in the front of the Advanced Lesson Book to determine when to bring this book to in-class practice workshop sessions.

In addition, LSAT Advanced student should avoid Stratosphere questions contained in this book.

Stratosphere Questions – ST

Students scoring 158+ on any practice test are encouraged to supplement their studies by viewing the Stratosphere sessions online and downloading the Stratosphere Student Piece available online. Questions used in whole or in part in these sessions are marked with the "ST" label. If you anticipate that you will be using the Stratosphere sessions, you may want to skip over any questions in this book that will be covered in these sessions.

Advanced students should avoid these questions which will be covered in class.

Review Exercises – $\frac{R}{E}$

Portions of questions or passages in this book are also presented in the Review Exercises in your Lesson Book, which are assigned as required homework. This material has been marked with the "RE" label so that you can choose to skip these questions until you have completed the applicable Review Exercise assignment.

Online Tutorials – $\frac{O}{T}$

Portions of questions or passages in this book are also presented in the Online Tutorials in your online resources. This material has been marked with the "OT" label so that you can choose to skip these questions until you have completed the applicable Online Tutorial.

Timing Practice

Material in the latter half of this book is organized specifically to prepare you for dealing with the individual multiple-choice sections you will see on Test Day. As you know, it pays to think of (and practice) the LSAT as five 35-minute multiple-choice sections (plus one 35-minute writing section) rather than one 3.5-hour exam. Continue to develop your section-management (which we call Timing) by working through and grading the sections contained in this book.

When doing Timing sections, make sure you are timing yourself (or having someone time you) as you do each section so that you can practice working with the clock. The LSAT is designed as a time-pressured exam—only through consistent practice will you learn to perform the skills you have mastered in class in the time allotted for each section. Make sure to view Kaplan's online section management tutorials. Use Kaplan's section-management tips as you work through each section.

Developing your timing assumes a certain level of mastery of the content being tested. Timing practice should be integrated into your preparation just before Test 2, when you have begun to really master the skills tested in the specific questions. If there is an area that you are unfamiliar with or are weak in, refer to the Mastery material in this book for additional training.

If needed, material from these section lengths can be used for additional mastery practice. Specific question types and difficulties can be located by referencing the Q-Finder, available in your online resources.

This book contains sections of PrepTests 47, 45, 44, 43, 39, 38, 36, 34, 30, B, 25, February 1997, 19, 16, 15, and 18.

Note for LSAT Extreme students: The following sections of this book will be covered in the additional in-class practice workshop and attack sessions: Reading Comprehension 2, 3, and 5. Refer to the "What to Bring to Class" guide to determine when you should bring this book to in-class practice workshop sessions.

Note for LSAT Advanced students: The following sections of this book will be covered in the additional in-class practice workshop sessions: Reading Comprehension 13. Refer to the "What to Bring to Class" guide to determine when you should bring this book to in-class practice workshop sessions.

Mastery Practice

Humanities Passages

Directions: Each passage in this section is followed by a group of questions to be answered on the basis of what is <u>stated</u> or <u>implied</u> in the passage. For some of the questions, more than one of the choices could conceivably answer the question. However, you are to choose the <u>best</u> answer; that is, the response that most accurately and completely answers the question.

For decades, there has been a deep rift between poetry and fiction in the United States, especially in academic settings; graduate writing programs in universities, for example, train students as poets or as

(5) writers of fiction, but almost never as both. Both poets and writers of fiction have tended to support this separation, in large part because the current conventional wisdom holds that poetry should be elliptical and lyrical, reflecting inner states and

(10) processes of thought or feeling, whereas character and narrative events are the stock-in-trade of fiction.

Certainly it is true that poetry and fiction are distinct genres, but why have specialized education and literary territoriality resulted from this distinction?

(15) The answer lies perhaps in a widespread attitude in U.S. culture, which often casts a suspicious eye on the generalist. Those with knowledge and expertise in multiple areas risk charges of dilettantism, as if ability in one field is diluted or compromised by

(20) accomplishment in another.

Fortunately, there are signs that the bias against writers who cross generic boundaries is diminishing; several recent writers are known and respected for their work in both genres. One important example of

(25) this trend is Rita Dove, an African American writer highly acclaimed for both her poetry and her fiction. A few years ago, speaking at a conference entitled "Poets Who Write Fiction," Dove expressed gentle incredulity about the habit of segregating the genres.

(30) She had grown up reading and loving both fiction and poetry, she said, unaware of any purported danger lurking in attempts to mix the two. She also studied for some time in Germany, where, she observes, "Poets write plays, novelists compose libretti, playwrights

(35) write novels—they would not understand our restrictiveness."

It makes little sense, Dove believes, to persist in the restrictive approach to poetry and fiction prevalent in the U.S., because each genre shares in the nature of

(40) the other. Indeed, her poetry offers example after example of what can only be properly regarded as lyric narrative. Her use of language in these poems is undeniably lyrical—that is, it evokes emotion and inner states without requiring the reader to organize

(45) ideas or events in a particular linear structure. Yet this lyric expression simultaneously presents the elements of a plot in such a way that the reader is led repeatedly to take account of clusters of narrative details within the lyric flow. Thus while the language is lyrical, it

(50) often comes to constitute, cumulatively, a work of narrative fiction. Similarly, many passages in her fiction, though undeniably prose, achieve the status of lyric narrative through the use of poetic rhythms and

elliptical expression. In short, Dove bridges the gap

(55) between poetry and fiction not only by writing in both genres, but also by fusing the two genres within individual works.

1. Which one of the following most accurately expresses the main point of the passage?

   (A) Rita Dove's work has been widely acclaimed primarily because of the lyrical elements she has introduced into her fiction.

   (B) Rita Dove's lyric narratives present clusters of narrative detail in order to create a cumulative narrative without requiring the reader to interpret it in a linear manner.

   (C) Working against a bias that has long been dominant in the U.S., recent writers like Rita Dove have shown that the lyrical use of language can effectively enhance narrative fiction.

   (D) Unlike many of her U.S. contemporaries, Rita Dove writes without relying on the traditional techniques associated with poetry and fiction.

   (E) Rita Dove's successful blending of poetry and fiction exemplifies the recent trend away from the rigid separation of the two genres that has long been prevalent in the U.S.

2. Which one of the following is most analogous to the literary achievements that the author attributes to Dove?

   (A) A chef combines nontraditional cooking methods and traditional ingredients from disparate world cuisines to devise new recipes.

   (B) A professor of film studies becomes a film director and succeeds, partly due to a wealth of theoretical knowledge of filmmaking.

   (C) An actor who is also a theatrical director teams up with a public health agency to use street theater to inform the public about health matters.

   (D) A choreographer defies convention and choreographs dances that combine elements of both ballet and jazz dance.

   (E) A rock musician records several songs from previous decades but introduces extended guitar solos into each one.

Source: PrepTest June 2007, Section 4, Passage 1, Questions 1–8

3. According to the passage, in the U.S. there is a widely held view that

    (A) poetry should not involve characters or narratives
    (B) unlike the writing of poetry, the writing of fiction is rarely an academically serious endeavor
    (C) graduate writing programs focus on poetry to the exclusion of fiction
    (D) fiction is most aesthetically effective when it incorporates lyrical elements
    (E) European literary cultures are suspicious of generalists

4. The author's attitude toward the deep rift between poetry and fiction in the U.S. can be most accurately described as one of

    (A) perplexity as to what could have led to the development of such a rift
    (B) astonishment that academics have overlooked the existence of the rift
    (C) ambivalence toward the effect the rift has had on U.S. literature
    (D) pessimism regarding the possibility that the rift can be overcome
    (E) disapproval of attitudes and presuppositions underlying the rift

5. In the passage the author conjectures that a cause of the deep rift between fiction and poetry in the United States may be that

    (A) poets and fiction writers each tend to see their craft as superior to the others' craft
    (B) the methods used in training graduate students in poetry are different from those used in training graduate students in other literary fields
    (C) publishers often pressure writers to concentrate on what they do best
    (D) a suspicion of generalism deters writers from dividing their energies between the two genres
    (E) fiction is more widely read and respected than poetry

6. In the context of the passage, the author's primary purpose in mentioning Dove's experience in Germany (lines 32–36) is to

    (A) suggest that the habit of treating poetry and fiction as nonoverlapping domains is characteristic of English-speaking societies but not others
    (B) point to an experience that reinforced Dove's conviction that poetry and fiction should not be rigidly separated
    (C) indicate that Dove's strengths as a writer derive in large part from the international character of her academic background
    (D) present an illuminating biographical detail about Dove in an effort to enhance the human interest appeal of the passage
    (E) indicate what Dove believes to be the origin of her opposition to the separation of fiction and poetry in the U.S.

7. It can be inferred from the passage that the author would be most likely to believe which one of the following?

    (A) Each of Dove's works can be classified as either primarily poetry or primarily fiction, even though it may contain elements of both.
    (B) The aesthetic value of lyric narrative resides in its representation of a sequence of events, rather than in its ability to evoke inner states.
    (C) The way in which Dove blends genres in her writing is without precedent in U.S. writing.
    (D) Narrative that uses lyrical language is generally aesthetically superior to pure lyric poetry.
    (E) Writers who successfully cross the generic boundary between poetry and fiction often try their hand at genres such as drama as well.

8. If this passage had been excerpted from a longer text, which one of the following predictions about the near future of U.S. literature would be most likely to appear in that text?

    (A) The number of writers who write both poetry and fiction will probably continue to grow.
    (B) Because of the increased interest in mixed genres, the small market for pure lyric poetry will likely shrink even further.
    (C) Narrative poetry will probably come to be regarded as a sub-genre of fiction.
    (D) There will probably be a rise in specialization among writers in university writing programs.
    (E) Writers who continue to work exclusively in poetry or fiction will likely lose their audiences.

The autobiographical narrative *Incidents in the Life of a Slave Girl, Written by Herself* (1861), by Harriet A. Jacobs, a slave of African descent, not only recounts an individual life but also provides, implicitly and
(5) explicitly, a perspective on the larger United States culture from the viewpoint of one denied access to it. Jacobs, as a woman and a slave, faced the stigmas to which those statuses were subject. Jacobs crafted her narrative, in accordance with the mainstream literary
(10) genre of the sentimental domestic novel, as an embodiment of cherished cultural values such as the desirability of marriage and the sanctity of personal identity, home, and family. She did so because she was writing to the free women of her day—the principal
(15) readers of domestic novels—in the hopes that they would sympathize with and come to understand her unique predicament as a female slave. By applying these conventions of the genre to her situation, Jacobs demonstrates to her readers that family and domesticity
(20) are no less prized by those forced into slavery, thus leading her free readers to perceive those values within a broader social context.

Some critics have argued that, by conforming to convention, Jacobs shortchanged her own experiences;
(25) one critic, for example, claims that in Jacobs's work the purposes of the domestic novel overshadow those of the typical slave narrative. But the relationship between the two genres is more complex: Jacobs's attempt to frame her story as a domestic novel creates a
(30) tension between the usual portrayal of women in this genre and her actual experience, often calling into question the applicability of the hierarchy of values espoused by the domestic novel to those who are in her situation. Unlike the traditional romantic episodes in
(35) domestic novels in which a man and woman meet, fall in love, encounter various obstacles but eventually marry, Jacobs's protagonist must send her lover, a slave, away in order to protect him from the wrath of her jealous master. In addition, by the end of the
(40) narrative, Jacobs's protagonist achieves her freedom by escaping to the north, but she does not achieve the domestic novel's ideal of a stable home complete with family, as the price she has had to pay for her freedom is separation from most of her family, including one of
(45) her own children. Jacobs points out that slave women view certain events and actions from a perspective different from that of free women, and that they must make difficult choices that free women need not. Her narrative thus becomes an antidomestic novel, for
(50) Jacobs accepts readily the goals of the genre, but demonstrates that its hierarchy of values does not apply when examined from the perspective of a female slave, suggesting thereby that her experience, and that of any female slave, cannot be fully understood without
(55) shedding conventional perspectives.

9. The author of the passage displays which one of the following attitudes toward the position of the critics mentioned in line 23?

(A) complete rejection
(B) reluctant rejection
(C) complete neutrality
(D) reluctant agreement
(E) complete agreement

10. According to the passage, Jacobs's narrative departs from the conventions of a typical domestic novel in which one of the following ways?

(A) Jacobs's protagonist does not ultimately achieve her freedom.
(B) Jacobs's protagonist does not wish for the same ideals as the protagonists of domestic novels.
(C) Jacobs's protagonist does not encounter various obstacles in her quest for love.
(D) Jacobs's protagonist does not ultimately achieve the ideals of home and family.
(E) Jacobs's protagonist does not experience the stigmas to which women and slaves were subject.

11. It can most reasonably be inferred from the passage that the critics mentioned in line 23 hold which one of the following views?

(A) The mixture of literary genres in a single narrative often creates a useful tension that adds value to the narrative.
(B) The mixture of literary genres in a single narrative tends to cause the goals of both genres to be compromised.
(C) The mixture of literary genres in a single narrative tends to favor the genre having the greater degree of realism.
(D) The mixture of literary genres in a single narrative tends to favor the genre having the lesser degree of sentimentality.
(E) The mixture of literary genres in a single narrative can sometimes cause the goals of one of the genres to be compromised.

Source: PrepTest 33, Section 2, Passage 2, Questions 8–14

KAPLAN

12. Which one of the following, if true, would most support the position of the critics mentioned line 23?

   EX

   (A) Most readers of Jacobs's narrative when it was first published concluded that it was simply a domestic novel and were thus disinclined to see it as an attempt to provoke thought.

   (B) Many reviewers of Jacobs's narrative included passionate statements in their reviews calling for the immediate abolition of slavery.

   (C) Most scholars believe that Jacobs's narrative would not have been able to communicate its message effectively if it had not adopted the conventions of the domestic novel.

   (D) Jacobs's narrative was modeled not only after domestic novels of the period but after realistic novels whose goal was to point out social injustices.

   (E) Jacobs's goal in crafting her narrative was not only to preach against the injustices of slavery but also to tell a powerful story that would make those injustices vivid to readers.

13. The author describes Jacobs's narrative as an "antidomesic novel" (line 49) for which one of the following reasons?

   EX

   (A) Jacobs's protagonist does not lament her separation from her family.

   (B) Jacobs's protagonist is disinclined toward stereotypical domestic aspirations.

   (C) Jacobs's narrative reveals the limitations of the hierarchy of values espoused by the domestic novel genre.

   (D) Jacobs's narrative implicitly suggests that the desire for domestic ideals contributes to the protagonist's plight.

   (E) Jacobs's narrative condemns domestic values as a hindrance to its protagonist's development of personal identity.

14. With which one of the following statements would the author of the passage be most likely to agree?

   EX

   (A) Some authors of slave narratives allowed the purposes of the genre to overshadow their own experiences.

   (B) The slave narrative, no less than the domestic novel, constitutes a literary genre.

   (C) Authors who write in a particular genre must obey the conventions of that genre.

   (D) An autobiography, no less than a novel, should tell a powerful story.

   (E) Autobiographies should be evaluated not on their literary merit but on their historical accuracy.

15. Which one of the following principles most likely governs the author's evaluation of Jacobs's narrative?

   EX

   (A) Those autobiographical narratives that capture the mood of a particular period are thereby more valuable.

   (B) Those autobiographical narratives that focus on accurately depicting the events in the individual's life are thereby more valuable.

   (C) Those autobiographical narratives that force readers to view certain familiar cultural values in a wider context are thereby more valuable.

   (D) Those autobiographical narratives that are written from a perspective familiar to the majority of their readers are thereby more valuable.

   (E) Those autobiographical narratives that employ the conventions of another literary genre are thereby more valuable.

It has recently been discovered that many attributions of paintings to the seventeenth-century Dutch artist Rembrandt may be false. The contested paintings are not minor works, whose removal from the
(5) Rembrandt corpus would leave it relatively unaffected: they are at its very center. In her recent book, Svetlana Alpers uses these cases of disputed attribution as a point of departure for her provocative discussion of the radical distinctiveness of Rembrandt's approach to
(10) painting.

Alpers argues that Rembrandt exercised an unprecedentedly firm control over his art, his students, and the distribution of his works. Despite Gary Schwartz's brilliant documentation of Rembrandt's
(15) complicated relations with a wide circle of patrons, Alpers takes the view that Rembrandt refused to submit to the prevailing patronage system. He preferred, she claims, to sell his works on the open market and to play the entrepreneur. At a time when Dutch artists were
(20) organizing into professional brotherhoods and academies, Rembrandt stood apart. In fact, Alpers' portrait of Rembrandt shows virtually every aspect of his art pervaded by economic motives. Indeed, so complete was Rembrandt's involvement with the
(25) market, she argues, that he even presented himself as a commodity, viewing his studio's products as extensions of himself, sent out into the world to earn money. Alpers asserts that Rembrandt's enterprise is found not just in his paintings, but in his refusal to limit
(30) his enterprise to those paintings he actually painted. He marketed Rembrandt.

Although there may be some truth in the view that Rembrandt was an entrepreneur who made some aesthetic decisions on the basis of what he knew the
(35) market wanted, Alpers' emphasis on economic factors sacrifices discussion of the aesthetic qualities that make Rembrandt's work unique. For example, Alpers asserts that Rembrandt deliberately left his works unfinished so as to get more money for their revision and
(40) completion. She implies that Rembrandt actually wished the Council of Amsterdam to refuse the great *Claudius Civilis*, which they had commissioned for their new town hall, and she argues that "he must have calculated that he would be able to get more money by
(45) retouching [the] painting." Certainly the picture is painted with very broad strokes but there is no evidence that it was deliberately left unfinished. The fact is that the look of a work like *Claudius Civilis* must also be understood as the consequence of
(50) Rembrandt's powerful and profound meditations on painting itself. Alpers makes no mention of the pictorial dialectic that can be discerned between, say, the lessons Rembrandt absorbed from the Haarlem school of painters and the styles of his native Leiden.
(55) The trouble is that while Rembrandt's artistic enterprise may indeed not be reducible to the works he himself painted, it is not reducible to marketing practices either.

16. Which one of the following best summarizes the main conclusion of the author of the passage?

E X

(A) Rembrandt differed from other artists of his time both in his aesthetic techniques and in his desire to meet the demands of the marketplace.

(B) The aesthetic qualities of Rembrandt's work cannot be understood without consideration of how economic motives pervaded decisions he made about his art.

(C) Rembrandt was one of the first artists to develop the notion of a work of art as a commodity that could be sold in an open marketplace.

(D) Rembrandt's artistic achievement cannot be understood solely in terms of decisions he made on the basis of what would sell in the marketplace.

(E) Rembrandt was an entrepreneur whose artistic enterprise was not limited to the paintings he actually painted himself.

17. According to the passage, Alpers and Schwartz disagree about which one of the following?

E X

(A) the degree of control Rembrandt exercised over the production of his art

(B) the role that Rembrandt played in organizing professional brotherhoods and academies

(C) the kinds of relationships Rembrandt had with his students

(D) the degree of Rembrandt's involvement in the patronage system

(E) the role of the patronage system in seventeenth-century Holland

Source: PrepTest 23, Section 4, Passage 1, Questions 1–5

KAPLAN

18. In the third paragraph, the author of the passage
EX discusses aesthetic influences on Rembrandt's work
most probably in order to

   (A) suggest that many critics have neglected to study
        the influence of the Haarlem school of painters
        on Rembrandt's work
   (B) suggest that *Claudius Civilis* is similar in style to
        many paintings from the seventeenth century
   (C) suggest that Rembrandt's style was not affected
        by the aesthetic influences that Alpers points out
   (D) argue that Rembrandt's style can best be
        understood as a result of the influences of his
        native Leiden
   (E) indicate that Alpers has not taken into account
        some important aspects of Rembrandt's work

19. Which one of the following, if true, would provide the
EX most support for Alpers' argument about
   Claudius Civilis?

   (A) Rembrandt was constantly revising his prints and
        paintings because he was never fully satisfied
        with stylistic aspects of his earlier drafts.
   (B) The works of many seventeenth-century Dutch
        artists were painted with broad strokes and had
        an unfinished look.
   (C) Many of Rembrandt's contemporaries eschewed
        the patronage system and sold their works on the
        open market.
   (D) Artists were frequently able to raise the price of a
        painting if the buyer wanted the work revised in
        some way.
   (E) Rembrandt did not allow his students to work
        on paintings that were commissioned by public
        officials.

20. It can be inferred that the author of the passage and
EX Alpers would be most likely to agree on which one of
the following?

   (A) Rembrandt made certain aesthetic decisions
        on the basis of what he understood about the
        demands of the marketplace.
   (B) The Rembrandt corpus will not be affected if
        attributions of paintings to Rembrandt are found
        to be false.
   (C) Stylistic aspects of Rembrandt's painting can
        be better explained in economic terms than in
        historical or aesthetic terms.
   (D) Certain aesthetic aspects of Rembrandt's art are
        the result of his experimentation with different
        painting techniques.
   (E) Most of Rembrandt's best-known works were
        painted by his students, but were sold under
        Rembrandt's name.

Painter Frida Kahlo (1910–1954) often used harrowing images derived from her Mexican heritage to express suffering caused by a disabling accident and a stormy marriage. Suggesting much personal and
(5) emotional content, her works—many of them self-portraits—have been exhaustively psychoanalyzed, while their political content has been less studied. Yet Kahlo was an ardent political activist who in her art sought not only to explore her own roots, but also to
(10) champion Mexico's struggle for an independent political and cultural identity.

Kahlo was influenced by Marxism, which appealed to many intellectuals in the 1920s and 1930s, and by Mexican nationalism. Interest in Mexico's culture and
(15) history had revived in the nineteenth century, and by the early 1900s, Mexican *indigenista* tendencies ranged from a violently anti-Spanish idealization of Aztec Mexico to an emphasis on contemporary Mexican Indians as the key to authentic Mexican culture.
(20) Mexican nationalism, reacting against contemporary United States political intervention in labor disputes as well as against past domination by Spain, identified the Aztecs as the last independent rulers of an indigenous political unit. Kahlo's form of *Mexicanidad*, a romantic
(25) nationalism that focused upon traditional art uniting all *indigenistas*, revered the Aztecs as a powerful pre-Columbian society that had united a large area of the Middle Americas and that was thought to have been based on communal labor, the Marxist ideal.
(30) In her paintings, Kahlo repeatedly employed Aztec symbols, such as skeletons or bleeding hearts, that were traditionally related to the emanation of life from death and light from darkness. These images of destruction coupled with creation speak not only to
(35) Kahlo's personal battle for life, but also to the Mexican struggle to emerge as a nation—by implication, to emerge with the political and cultural strength admired in the Aztec civilization. *Self-Portrait on the Border between Mexico and the United States* (1932), for
(40) example, shows Kahlo wearing a bone necklace, holding a Mexican flag, and standing between a highly industrialized United States and an agricultural, preindustrial Mexico. On the United States side are mechanistic and modern images such as smokestacks,
(45) light bulbs, and robots. In contrast, the organic and ancient symbols on the Mexican side—a blood-drenched Sun, lush vegetation, an Aztec sculpture, a pre-Columbian temple, and a skull alluding to those that lined the walls of Aztec temples emphasize the
(50) interrelation of life, death, the earth, and the cosmos.

Kahlo portrayed Aztec images in the folkloric style of traditional Mexican paintings, thereby heightening the clash between modern materialism and indigenous tradition; similarly, she favored planned economic
(55) development, but not at the expense of cultural identity. Her use of familiar symbols in a readily accessible style also served her goal of being popularly understood; in turn, Kahlo is viewed by some Mexicans as a mythic figure representative of
(60) nationalism itself.

21. Which one of the following best expresses the main point of the passage?

(A) The doctrines of Marxist ideology and Mexican nationalism heavily influenced Mexican painters of Kahlo's generation.

(B) Kahlo's paintings contain numerous references to the Aztecs as an indigenous Mexican people predating European influence.

(C) An important element of Kahlo's work is conveyed by symbols that reflect her advocacy of indigenous Mexican culture and Mexican political autonomy.

(D) The use of Aztec images and symbols in Kahlo's art can be traced to the late nineteenth-century revival of interest in Mexican history and culture.

(E) Kahlo used Aztec imagery in her paintings primarily in order to foster contemporary appreciation for the authentic art of traditional Mexican culture.

22. With which one of the following statements concerning psychoanalytic and political interpretations of Kahlo's work would the author be most likely to agree?

(A) The psychoanalytic interpretations of Kahlo's work tend to challenge the political interpretations.

(B) Political and psychoanalytic interpretations are complementary approaches to Kahlo's work.

(C) Recent political interpretations of Kahlo's work are causing psychoanalytic critics to revise their own interpretations.

(D) Unlike the political interpretations, the psychoanalytic interpretations make use of biographical facts of Kahlo's life.

(E) Kahlo's mythic status among the audience Kahlo most wanted to reach is based upon the psychoanalytic rather than the political content of her work.

Source: PrepTest 22, Section 1, Passage 1, Questions 1–8

23. Which one of the following stances toward the United States does the passage mention as characterizing Mexican nationalists in the early twentieth century?

    (A) opposition to United States involvement in internal Mexican affairs

    (B) desire to decrease emigration of the Mexican labor force to the United States

    (C) desire to improve Mexico's economic competitiveness with the United States

    (D) reluctance to imitate the United States model of rapid industrialization

    (E) advocacy of a government based upon that of the Marxist Soviet Union rather than that of the United States

24. In the context of the passage, which one of the following phrases could best be substituted for the word "romantic" (line 24) without substantially changing the author's meaning?

    (A) dreamy and escapist

    (B) nostalgic and idealistic

    (C) fanciful and imaginative

    (D) transcendental and impractical

    (E) overwrought and sentimental

25. The passage mentions each of the following as an Aztec symbol or image found in Kahlo's paintings EXCEPT a

    (A) skeleton

    (B) sculpture

    (C) serpent

    (D) skull

    (E) bleeding heart

26. Which one of the following best describes the organization of the third paragraph?

    (A) contrast of opposing ideas

    (B) reconciliation of conflicting concepts

    (C) interrelation of complementary themes

    (D) explication of a principle's implications

    (E) support for a generalization by means of an example

27. The passage implies that Kahlo's attitude toward the economic development of Mexico was

    (A) enthusiastic

    (B) condemnatory

    (C) cautious

    (D) noncommittal

    (E) uncertain

28. The main purpose of the passage is to

    (A) critique an artist's style

    (B) evaluate opposing theories

    (C) reconcile conflicting arguments

    (D) advocate an additional interpretation

    (E) reconsider an artist in light of new discoveries

Many literary scholars believe that Zora Neale Hurston's *Their Eyes Were Watching God* (1937) has been the primary influence on some of the most accomplished Black women writing in the United
(5) States today. Indeed, Alice Walker, the author of the prize-winning novel *The Color Purple*, has said of *Their Eyes*, "There is no book more important to me than this one." Thus, it seems necessary to ask why *Their Eyes*, a work now viewed by a multitude
(10) of readers as remarkably successful in its complex depiction of a Black woman's search for self and community, was ever relegated to the margins of the literary canon.

The details of the novel's initial reception help
(15) answer this question. Unlike the recently rediscovered and reexamined work of Harriet Wilson, *Their Eyes* was not totally ignored by book reviewers upon its publication. In fact, it received a mixture of positive and negative reviews both from
(20) White book reviewers working for prominent periodicals and from important figures within Black literary circles. In the *Saturday Review of Literature*, George Stevens wrote that "the narration is exactly right, because most of it is dialogue and the
(25) dialogue gives us a constant sense of character in action." The negative criticism was partially a result of Hurston's ideological differences with other members of the Black literary community about the depiction of Black Americans in literature. Black
(30) writers of the 1940s believed that the Black artist's primary responsibility was to create protest fiction that explored the negative effects of racism in the United States. For example, Richard Wright, the author of the much acclaimed *Native Son* (1940),
(35) wrote that *Their Eyes* had "no theme" and "no message." Most critics' and readers' expectations of Black literature rendered them unable to appreciate Hurston's subtle delineation of the life of an ordinary Black woman in a Black community,
(40) and the novel went quietly out of print.

Recent acclaim for *Their Eyes* results from the emergence of feminist literary criticism and the development of standards of evaluation specific to the work of Black writers; these kinds of criticism
(45) changed readers' expectations of art and enabled them to appreciate Hurston's novel. The emergence of feminist literary criticism was crucial because such criticism brought new attention to neglected works such as Hurston's and alerted readers to Hurston's
(50) exploration of women's issues in her fiction. The Afrocentric standards of evaluation were equally important to the rediscovery of *Their Eyes*, for such standards provided readers with the tools to recognize and appreciate the Black folklore and
(55) oral storytelling traditions Hurston incorporated within her work. In one of the most illuminating discussions of the novel to date, Henry Louis Gates, Jr., states that "Hurston's strategy seems to concern itself with the possibilities of representation of the
(60) speaking Black voice in writing."

29. The passage suggests which one of the following about Harriet Wilson's novel?

(A) It was written at the same time as *Their Eyes Were Watching God*, but it did not receive as much critical attention.

(B) It greatly influenced Black women writing after the 1940s.

(C) It was widely read when it was published, but it has not received attention from literary critics until recently.

(D) It was not formally published, and the manuscript has only recently been discovered by literary critics.

(E) It did not receive critical attention when it was published, but it has recently become the subject of critical study.

30. The passage offers support for which one of the following statements about literary reviewers and *Their Eyes Were Watching God*?

(A) *Their Eyes* was widely acclaimed by reviewers upon its publication, even though it eventually went out of print.

(B) The eventual obscurity of *Their Eyes* was not the result of complete neglect by reviewers.

(C) Some early reviewers of *Their Eyes* interpreted the novel from a point of view that later became known as Afrocentric.

(D) *Their Eyes* was more typical of the protest fiction of the 1940s than reviewers realized.

(E) Most early reviewers of *Their Eyes* did not respond positively to the book.

Source: PrepTest 17, Section 4, Passage 1, Questions 1–8

31. Which one of the following best states the main idea of the passage?

   (A) Hurston's *Their Eyes Were Watching God* had little in common with novels written by Black authors during the 1940s.
   (B) Feminist critics and authors such as Alice Walker were instrumental in establishing Hurston's *Their Eyes Were Watching God* as an important part of the American literary canon.
   (C) Critics and readers were unable to appreciate fully Hurston's *Their Eyes Were Watching God* until critics applied new standards of evaluation to the novel.
   (D) Hurston's *Their Eyes Were Watching God* was an important influence on the protest fiction written by Black writers in the mid-twentieth century.
   (E) Afrocentric strategies of analysis have brought attention to the use of oral storytelling traditions in novels written by Black Americans, such as Hurston's *Their Eyes Were Watching God*.

32. According to the passage, which one of the following is true of Black folklore traditions as used in literature written in the United States?

   (A) They are an aspect of Black American literature first recognized and written about by Henry Louis Gates, Jr.
   (B) They were not widely incorporated into novels written by Black Americans until after the 1940s.
   (C) They were first used by a novelist in Zora Neale Hurston's *Their Eyes Were Watching God*.
   (D) They were not incorporated into novels published by Black Americans in the 1940s.
   (E) They are an aspect of Black literature that some readers did not fully appreciate until relatively recently.

33. The passage suggests that *Native Son* differs from *Their Eyes Were Watching God* in which one of the following ways?

   (A) It received fewer positive reviews at the time of its publication than did *Their Eyes*.
   (B) It is less typical of literature written by Black Americans during the 1940s than is *Their Eyes*.
   (C) It is less focused on an ordinary individual's search for self within a Black community than is *Their Eyes*.
   (D) It depicts more aspects of Black American folklore than does *Their Eyes*.
   (E) It has received more attention from feminist and Afrocentric literary critics than has *Their Eyes*.

34. Which one of the following provides the clearest example of the kind of fiction that many Black writers of the 1940s, as their views are described in the passage, believed should be written?

   (A) a novel that focuses on the interrelationships among four generations of Black women
   (B) a historical novel that re-creates actual events that occurred as Black people suffered from oppression and racial injustice in a small town
   (C) a novel, based on biographical stories orally relayed to the author as a child, that describes the development of traditions in a Black family
   (D) a novel that explores the psychological aspects of a relationship between a White man and a Black man as they work together to organize protests against unjust working conditions
   (E) a novel that examines the different ways in which three Black children experience their first day of school in a rural community

35. The author would be most likely to agree with which one of the following statements about the relationship between art and literary criticism?

   (A) The long-term reputation of a work of art is less dependent on the response of literary critics than on the response of readers and authors.
   (B) Experimental works of fiction are usually poorly received and misunderstood by literary critics when they are first published.
   (C) The response of literary critics to a work of art can be determined by certain ideological perspectives and assumptions about the purpose of art.
   (D) Literary critics do not significantly affect the way most people interpret and appreciate literature.
   (E) The ideological bases of a work of art are the first consideration of most literary critics.

36. The primary purpose of the passage is to

   (A) correct a misconception
   (B) explain a reassessment
   (C) reconcile two points of view
   (D) criticize a conventional approach
   (E) announce a new discovery

Countee Cullen (Countee Leroy Porter, 1903–1946) was one of the foremost poets of the Harlem Renaissance, the movement of African American writers, musicians, and artists centered in the
(5) Harlem section of New York City during the 1920s. Beginning with his university years, Cullen strove to establish himself as an author of romantic poetry on abstract, universal topics such as love and death. Believing poetry should consist of "lofty thoughts
(10) beautifully expressed," Cullen preferred controlled poetic forms. He used European forms such as sonnets and devices such as quatrains, couplets, and conventional rhyme, and he frequently employed classical allusions and Christian religious imagery,
(15) which were most likely the product both of his university education and of his upbringing as the adopted son of a Methodist Episcopal reverend.

Some literary critics have praised Cullen's skill at writing European-style verse, finding, for example, in
(20) "The Ballad of the Brown Girl" an artful use of diction and a rhythm and sonority that allow him to capture the atmosphere typical of the English ballad form of past centuries. Others have found Cullen's use of European verse forms and techniques unsuited to treating
(25) political or racial themes, such as the themes in "Uncle Jim," in which a young man is told by his uncle of the different experiences of African Americans and whites in United States society, or "Incident," which relates the experience of an eight-year-old child who hears a
(30) racial slur. One such critic has complained that Cullen's persona as expressed in his work sometimes seems to vacillate between aesthete and spokesperson for racial issues. But Cullen himself rejected this dichotomy, maintaining that his interest in romantic
(35) poetry was quite compatible with his concern over racial issues. He drew a distinction between poetry of solely political intent and his own work, which he believed reflected his identity as an African American. As the heartfelt expression of his personality
(40) accomplished by means of careful attention to his chosen craft, his work could not help but do so.

Explicit references to racial matters do in fact decline in Cullen's later work, but not because he felt any less passionately about these matters. Rather,
(45) Cullen increasingly focused on the religious dimension of his poetry. In "The Black Christ," in which the poet imagines the death and resurrection of a rural African American, and "Heritage," which expresses the tension between the poet's identification with Christian
(50) traditions and his desire to stay close to his African heritage, Cullen's thoughts on race were subsumed within what he conceived of as broader and more urgent questions about the suffering and redemption of the soul. Nonetheless, Cullen never abandoned his
(55) commitment to the importance of racial issues, reflecting on one occasion that he felt "actuated by a strong sense of race consciousness" that "grows upon me, I find, as I grow older."

37. Which one of the following most accurately states the main point of the passage?

(A) While much of Cullen's poetry deals with racial issues, in his later work he became less concerned with racial matters and increasingly interested in writing poetry with a religious dimension.

(B) While Cullen used European verse forms and his later poems increasingly addressed religious themes, his poetry never abandoned a concern for racial issues.

(C) Though Cullen used European verse forms, he acknowledged that these forms were not very well suited to treating political or racial themes.

(D) Despite the success of Cullen's poetry at dealing with racial issues, Cullen's primary goal was to re-create the atmosphere that characterized the English ballad.

(E) The religious dimension throughout Cullen's poetry complemented his focus on racial issues by providing the context within which these issues could be understood.

38. Given the information in the passage, which one of the following most closely exemplifies Cullen's conception of poetry?

(A) a sonnet written with careful attention to the conventions of the form to re-create the atmosphere of sixteenth-century English poetry

(B) a sonnet written with deliberate disregard for the conventions of the form to illustrate the perils of political change

(C) a sonnet written to explore the aesthetic impact of radical innovations in diction, rhythm, and sonority

(D) a sonnet written with great stylistic freedom to express the emotional upheaval associated with romantic love

(E) a sonnet written with careful attention to the conventions of the form expressing feelings about the inevitability of death

Source: PrepTest 41, Section 4, Passage 2, Questions 7–13

39. Which one of the following is NOT identified by the author of the passage as characteristic of Cullen's poetry?

    (A) It often deals with abstract, universal subject matter.
    (B) It often employs rhyme, classical allusions, and religious imagery.
    (C) It avoids traditional poetic forms in favor of formal experimentation.
    (D) It sometimes deals explicitly with racial issues.
    (E) It eventually subsumed racial issues into a discussion of religious issues.

40. The passage suggests which one of the following about Cullen's use of controlled poetic forms?

    (A) Cullen used controlled poetic forms because he believed they provided the best means to beautiful poetic expression.
    (B) Cullen's interest in religious themes naturally led him to use controlled poetic forms.
    (C) Only the most controlled poetic forms allowed Cullen to address racial issues in his poems.
    (D) Cullen had rejected the less controlled poetic forms he was exposed to prior to his university years.
    (E) Less controlled poetic forms are better suited to poetry that addresses racial or political issues.

41. The references to specific poems in the second paragraph are most likely intended to

    (A) contrast some of Cullen's more successful poems with some of his less successful ones
    (B) serve as illustrations of Cullen's poetry relevant to the critics' claims
    (C) demonstrate that Cullen's poetic persona vacillates from poem to poem
    (D) summarize the scope of Cullen's treatment of racial issues in his poetry
    (E) illustrate the themes Cullen used in expressing his concern about racial matters

42. Based on the passage, the literary critics mentioned in line 18 would be most likely to hold which one of the following views of Cullen's poetry?

    (A) It demonstrates that European verse forms can be successfully adapted to different contexts.
    (B) It is most notable for the ways in which its content reflects Cullen's upbringing and education.
    (C) It is more successful when it does not attempt to capture the atmosphere of previous poetic styles.
    (D) Its reliance on European verse forms is best suited to dealing with racial concerns.
    (E) Its focus is divided between aesthetic and racial concerns.

43. Which one of the following most accurately describes the organization of the passage?

    (A) Biographical information about Cullen is outlined, his artistic development is traced through several of his poems, and a critical evaluation of his later work is offered.
    (B) Biographical information about Cullen is outlined, criticism of his use of European verse forms is presented, and the success of this use is evaluated.
    (C) Biographical information about Cullen is outlined, his approach to writing poetry is described, and the relationship between his poetry and his life is discussed.
    (D) Cullen's approach to poetry is described, certain poems are characterized as his most notable, and a claim about the religious focus of his work is made.
    (E) Cullen's approach to poetry is described, differing opinions about the success of his poetry are presented, and thematic developments in his later work are discussed.

Published in 1952, *Invisible Man* featured a protagonist whose activities enabled the novel's author, Ralph Ellison, to explore and to blend themes specifically tied to the history and plight of African
(5) Americans with themes, also explored by many European writers with whose works Ellison was familiar, about the fractured, evanescent quality of individual identity and character. For this thematic blend, Ellison received two related criticisms: that his
(10) allegiance to the concerns of the individual prevented him from directing his art more toward the political action that critics believed was demanded by his era's social and political state of affairs; and that his indulging in European fictional modes lessened his
(15) contribution to the development of a distinctly African American novelistic style.

Ellison found these criticisms to voice a common demand, namely that writers should censor themselves and sacrifice their individuality for supposedly more
(20) important political and cultural purposes. He replied that it demeans a people and its artists to suggest that a particular historical situation requires cultural segregation in the arts. Such a view characterizes all artists as incapable of seeing the world—with all its
(25) subtleties and complications—in unique yet expressive ways, and it makes the narrow assumption that audiences are capable of viewing the world only from their own perspectives.

Models for understanding *Invisible Man* that may
(30) be of more help than those employed by its critics can be found in Ellison's own love for and celebration of jazz. Jazz has never closed itself off from other musical forms, and some jazz musicians have been able to take the European-influenced songs of U.S. theater and
(35) transform them into musical pieces that are unique and personal but also expressive of African American culture. In like manner, Ellison avoided the mere recapitulation of existing literary forms as well as the constraints of artistic isolation by using his work to
(40) explore and express the issues of identity and character that had so interested European writers.

Further, jazz, featuring solos that, however daring, remain rooted in the band's rhythm section, provides a rich model for understanding the relationship of artist
(45) to community and parallels the ways the protagonist's voice in *Invisible Man* is set within a wider communal context. Ellison's explorations in the novel, often in the manner of loving caricature, of the ideas left him by both European and African American predecessors are
(50) a form of homage to them and thus ameliorate the sense of alienation he expresses through the protagonist. And even though *Invisible Man's* protagonist lives alone in a basement, Ellison proves that an individual whose unique voice is the result of
(55) the transmutation of a cultural inheritance can never be completely cut off from the community.

44. It can be inferred from the passage that the author most clearly holds which one of the following views?

EX

(A) The possibility of successfully blending different cultural forms is demonstrated by jazz's ability to incorporate European influences.

(B) The technique of blending the artistic concerns of two cultures could be an effective tool for social and political action.

(C) Due to the success of *Invisible Man*, Ellison was able to generate a renewed interest in and greater appreciation for jazz.

(D) The protagonist in *Invisible Man* illustrates the difficulty of combining the concerns of African Americans and concerns thought to be European in origin.

(E) Ellison's literary technique, though effective, is unfortunately too esoteric and complex to generate a large audience.

45. Based on the passage, Ellison's critics would most likely have responded favorably to *Invisible Man* if it had

EX

(A) created a positive effect on the social conditions of the time

(B) provided a historical record of the plight of African Americans

(C) contained a tribute to the political contributions of African American predecessors

(D) prompted a necessary and further separation of American literature from European literary style

(E) generated a large audience made up of individuals from many cultural backgrounds

Source: PrepTest 37, Section 1, Passage 3, Questions 14–21

46. The expression "cultural segregation in the arts" (lines 22–23) most clearly refers to

    (A) a general tendency within the arts whereby certain images and themes recur within the works of certain cultures

    (B) an obvious separation within the art community resulting from artists' differing aesthetic principles

    (C) the cultural isolation artists feel when they address issues of individual identity

    (D) the cultural obstacles that affect an audience's appreciation of art

    (E) an expectation placed on an artist to uphold a specific cultural agenda in the creation of art

47. The primary purpose of the third paragraph is to

    (A) summarize the thematic concerns of an artist in relation to other artists within the discipline

    (B) affirm the importance of two artistic disciplines in relation to cultural concerns

    (C) identify the source of the thematic content of one artist's work

    (D) celebrate one artistic discipline by viewing it from the perspective of an artist from another discipline

    (E) introduce a context within which the work of one artist may be more fully illuminated.

48. Which one of the following statements about jazz is made in the passage?

    (A) It is not accessible to a wide audience.
    (B) It is the most complex of modern musical forms.
    (C) It embraces other forms of music.
    (D) It avoids political themes.
    (E) It has influenced much of contemporary literature.

49. It can be inferred from the passage that Ellison most clearly holds which one of the following views regarding an audience's relationship to works of art?

    (A) Audiences respond more favorably to art that has no political content.

    (B) Groundless criticism of an artist's work can hinder an audience's reception of the work.

    (C) Audiences have the capacity for empathy required to appreciate unique and expressive art.

    (D) The most conscientious members of any audience are those who are aware of the specific techniques employed by the artist.

    (E) Most audience members are bound by their cultural upbringing to view art from that cultural perspective.

50. The primary purpose of the passage is to

    (A) make a case that a certain novelist is one of the most important novelists of the twentieth century

    (B) demonstrate the value of using jazz as an illustration for further understanding the novels of a certain literary trend

    (C) explain the relevance of a particular work and its protagonist to the political and social issues of the time

    (D) defend the work of a certain novelist against criticism that it should have addressed political and social issues

    (E) distinguish clearly between the value of art for art's sake and art for purposes such as political agendas

51. The passage provides information to answer each of the following questions EXCEPT:

    (A) Did Ellison himself enjoy jazz?
    (B) What themes in *Invisible Man* were influenced by themes prevalent in jazz?
    (C) What was Ellison's response to criticism concerning the thematic blend in *Invisible Man*?
    (D) From what literary tradition did some of the ideas explored in *Invisible Man* come?
    (E) What kind of music did some jazz musicians use in creating their works?

James Porter (1905–1970) was the first scholar to identify the African influence on visual art in the Americas, and much of what is known about the cultural legacy that African-American artists inherited
(5) from their African forebears has come to us by way of his work. Porter, a painter and art historian, began by studying African-American crafts of the eighteenth and nineteenth centuries. This research revealed that many of the household items created by African-American
(10) men and women—walking sticks, jugs, and textiles— displayed characteristics that linked them iconographically to artifacts of West Africa. Porter then went on to establish clearly the range of the cultural territory inherited by later African-American
(15) artists.

An example of this aspect of Porter's research occurs in his essay "Robert S. Duncanson, Midwestern Romantic-Realist." The work of Duncanson, a nineteenth-century painter of the Hudson River school,
(20) like that of his predecessor in the movement, Joshua Johnston, was commonly thought to have been created by a Euro-American artist. Porter proved definitively that both Duncanson and Johnston were of African ancestry. Porter published this finding and thousands of
(25) others in a comprehensive volume tracing the history of African-American art. At the time of its first printing in 1943, only two other books devoted exclusively to the accomplishments of African-American artists existed. Both of these books were written by Alain
(30) LeRoy Locke, a professor at the university where Porter also taught. While these earlier studies by Locke are interesting for being the first to survey the field, neither addressed the critical issue of African precursors; Porter's book addressed this issue,
(35) painstakingly integrating the history of African-American art into the larger history of art in the Americas without separating it from those qualities that gave it its unique ties to African artisanship. Porter may have been especially attuned to these ties because
(40) of his conscious effort to maintain them in his own paintings, many of which combine the style of the genre portrait with evidence of an extensive knowledge of the cultural history of various African peoples.

In his later years, Porter wrote additional chapters
(45) for later editions of his book, constantly revising and correcting his findings, some of which had been based of necessity on fragmentary evidence. Among his later achievements were his definitive reckoning of the birth year of the painter Patrick Reason, long a point of
(50) scholarly uncertainty, and his identification of an unmarked grave in San Francisco as that of the sculptor Edmonia Lewis. At his death, Porter left extensive notes for an unfinished project aimed at exploring the influence of African art on the art of the Western world
(55) generally, a body of research whose riches scholars still have not exhausted.

52. Which one of the following most accurately states the main idea of the passage?

(A) Because the connections between African-American art and other art in the Americas had been established by earlier scholars, Porter's work focused on showing African-American art's connections to African artisanship.

(B) In addition to showing the connections between African-American art and African artisanship, Porter's most important achievement was illustrating the links between African-American art and other art in the Americas.

(C) Despite the fact that his last book remains unfinished, Porter's work was the first to devote its attention exclusively to the accomplishments of African-American artists.

(D) Although showing the connections between African-American art and African artisanship, Porter's work concentrated primarily on placing African-American art in the context of Western art in general.

(E) While not the first body of scholarship to treat the subject of African-American art, Porter's work was the first to show the connections between African-American art and African artisanship.

53. The discussion of Locke's books is intended primarily to

(A) argue that Porter's book depended upon Locke's pioneering scholarship

(B) highlight an important way in which Porter's work differed from previous work in his field

(C) suggest an explanation for why Porter's book was little known outside academic circles

(D) support the claim that Porter was not the first to notice African influences in African-American art

(E) argue that Locke's example was a major influence on Porter's decision to publish his findings.

54. The passage states which one of the following about the 1943 edition of Porter's book on African-American art?

(A) It received little scholarly attention at first.

(B) It was revised and improved upon in later editions.

(C) It took issue with several of Locke's conclusions.

(D) It is considered the definitive versions of Porter's work.

(E) It explored the influence of African art on Western art in general.

Source: PrepTest 26, Section 4, Passage 2, Questions 6–13

55. Given the information in the passage, Porter's identification of the ancestry of Duncanson and Johnston provides conclusive evidence for which one of the following statements?

(A) Some of the characteristics defining the Hudson River school are iconographically linked to West African artisanship.

(B) Some of the works of Duncanson and Johnston are not in the style of the Hudson River school.

(C) Some of the work of Euro-American painters displays similarities to African-American crafts of the eighteenth and nineteenth centuries.

(D) Some of the works of the Hudson River school were done by African-American painters.

(E) Some of the works of Duncanson and Johnston were influenced by West African artifacts.

56. Which one of the following can most reasonably be inferred from the passage about the study that Porter left unfinished at his death?

(A) If completed, it would have contradicted some of the conclusions contained in his earlier book.

(B) If completed, it would have amended some of the conclusions contained in his earlier book.

(C) If completed, it would have brought up to date the comprehensive history of African-American art begun in his earlier book.

(D) If completed, it would have expanded upon the project of his earlier book by broadening the scope of inquiry found in the earlier book.

(E) If completed, it would have supported some of the theories put forth by Porter's contemporaries since the publication of his earlier book.

57. Which one of the following hypothetical observations is most closely analogous to the discoveries Porter made about African-American crafts of the eighteenth and nineteenth centuries?

(A) Contemporary Haitian social customs have a unique character dependent on but different from both their African and French origins.

(B) Popular music in the United States, some of which is based on African musical traditions, often influences music being composed on the African continent.

(C) Many novels written in Canada by Chinese immigrants exhibit narrative themes very similar to those found in Chinese folktales.

(D) Extensive Indian immigration to England has made traditional Indian foods nearly as popular there as the traditional English foods that had been popular there before Indian immigration.

(E) Some Mexican muralists of the early twentieth century consciously imitated the art of native peoples as a response to the Spanish influences that had predominated in Mexican art.

58. The passage most strongly supports which one of the following inferences about Porter's own paintings?

(A) They often contained figures or images derived from the work of African artisans.

(B) They fueled his interest in pursuing a career in art history.

(C) They were used in Porter's book to show the extent of African influence on African-American art.

(D) They were a deliberate attempt to prove his theories about art history.

(E) They were done after all of his academic work had been completed.

59. Based on the passage, which one of the following, if true, would have been most relevant to the project Porter was working on at the time of his death?

(A) African-American crafts of the eighteenth and nineteenth centuries have certain resemblances to European folk crafts of earlier periods.

(B) The paintings of some twentieth-century European artists prefigured certain stylistic developments in North American graphic art.

(C) The designs of many of the quilts made by African-American women in the nineteenth century reflect designs of European trade goods.

(D) After the movement of large numbers of African Americans to cities, the African influences in the work of many African-American painters increased.

(E) Several portraits by certain twentieth-century European painters were modeled after examples of Central African ceremonial masks.

Musicologists concerned with the "London Pianoforte school," the group of composers, pedagogues, pianists, publishers, and builders who contributed to the development of the piano in London
(5) at the turn of the nineteenth century, have long encountered a formidable obstacle in the general unavailability of music of this "school" in modern scholarly editions. Indeed, much of this repertory has more or less vanished from our historical
(10) consciousness. Granted, the sonatas and *Gradus ad Parnassum* of Muzio Clementi and the nocturnes of John Field have remained familiar enough (though more often than not in editions lacking scholarly rigor), but the work of other leading representatives, like
(15) Johann Baptist Cramer and Jan Ladislav Dussek, has eluded serious attempts at revival.

Nicholas Temperley's ambitious new anthology decisively overcomes this deficiency. What underscores the intrinsic value of Temperley's editions
(20) is that the anthology reproduces nearly all of the original music in facsimile. Making available this cross section of English musical life—some 800 works by 49 composers—should encourage new critical perspectives about how piano music evolved in
(25) England, an issue of considerable relevance to our understanding of how piano music developed on the European continent, and of how, finally, the instrument was transformed from the fortepiano to what we know today as the piano.
(30) To be sure, the concept of the London Pianoforte school itself calls for review. "School" may well be too strong a word for what was arguably a group unified not so much by stylistic principles or aesthetic creed as by the geographical circumstance that they worked at
(35) various times in London and produced pianos and piano music for English pianos and English markets. Indeed, Temperley concedes that their "variety may be so great as to cast doubt on the notion of a 'school.'"

The notion of a school was first propounded by
(40) Alexander Ringer, who argued that laws of artistic survival forced the young, progressive Beethoven to turn outside Austria for creative models, and that he found inspiration in a group of pianists connected with Clementi in London. Ringer's proposed London
(45) Pianoforte school did suggest a circumscribed and fairly unified group—for want of a better term, a school—of musicians whose influence was felt primarily in the decades just before and after 1800. After all, Beethoven did respond to the advances of the
(50) Broadwood piano—its reinforced frame, extended compass, triple stringing, and pedals, for example—and it is reasonable to suppose that London pianists who composed music for such an instrument during the critical phase of its development exercised no small
(55) degree of influence on Continental musicians. Nevertheless, perhaps the most sensible approach to this issue is to define the school by the period (c. 1766–1873) during which it flourished, as Temperley has done in the anthology.

60. Which one of the following most accurately states the author's main point?

(A) Temperley has recently called into question the designation of a group of composers, pedagogues, pianists, publishers, and builders as the London Pianoforte school.

(B) Temperley's anthology of the music of the London Pianoforte school contributes significantly to an understanding of an influential period in the history of music.

(C) The music of the London Pianoforte school has been revived by the publication of Temperley's new anthology.

(D) Primary sources for musical manuscripts provide the most reliable basis for musicological research.

(E) The development of the modern piano in England influenced composers and other musicians throughout Europe.

61. It can be inferred that which one of the following is true of the piano music of the London Pianoforte school?

(A) The nocturnes of John Field typify the London Pianoforte school style.

(B) The *Gradus ad Parnassum* of Muzio Clementi is the best-known work of these composers.

(C) No original scores for this music are extant.

(D) Prior to Temperley's edition, no attempts to issue new editions of this music had been made.

(E) In modern times much of the music of this school has been little known even to musicians.

Source: PrepTest 21, Section 4, Passage 2, Questions 1–8

62. The author mentions the sonatas of Muzio Clementi and the nocturnes of John Field as examples of which one of the following?

    (A) works by composers of the London Pianoforte school that have been preserved in rigorous scholarly editions
    (B) works that are no longer remembered by most people
    (C) works acclaimed by the leaders of the London Pianoforte school
    (D) works by composers of the London Pianoforte school that are relatively well known
    (E) works by composers of the London Pianoforte school that have been revived by Temperley in his anthology

63. Which one of the following, if true, would most clearly undermine a portion of Ringer's argument as the argument is described in the passage?

    (A) Musicians in Austria composed innovative music for the Broadwood piano as soon as the instrument became available.
    (B) Clementi and his followers produced most of their compositions between 1790 and 1810.
    (C) The influence of Continental musicians is apparent in some of the works of Beethoven.
    (D) The pianist-composers of the London Pianoforte school shared many of the same stylistic principles.
    (E) Most composers of the London Pianoforte school were born on the Continent and were drawn to London by the work of Clementi and his followers.

64. It can be inferred that the author uses the word "advances" (line 49) to refer to

    (A) enticements offered musicians by instrument manufacturers
    (B) improvements in the structure of a particular instrument
    (C) innovations in the forms of music produced for a particular instrument
    (D) stylistic elaborations made possible by changes in a particular instrument
    (E) changes in musicians' opinions about a particular instrument

65. It can be inferred from the passage as a whole that the author's purpose in the third paragraph is primarily to

    (A) cast doubt on the usefulness of Temperley's study of the London Pianoforte school
    (B) introduce a discussion of the coherency of the London Pianoforte school
    (C) summarize Ringer's argument about the London Pianoforte school
    (D) emphasize the complex nature of the musicological elements shared by members of the London Pianoforte school
    (E) identify the unique contributions made to music by the London Pianoforte school

66. The author of the passage is primarily concerned with

    (A) explaining the influence of the development of the pianoforte on the music of Beethoven
    (B) describing Temperley's view of the contrast between the development of piano music in England and the development of piano music elsewhere in Europe
    (C) presenting Temperley's evaluation of the impact of changes in piano construction on styles and forms of music composed in the era of the London Pianoforte school
    (D) considering an alternative theory to that proposed by Ringer concerning the London Pianoforte school
    (E) discussing the contribution of Temperley's anthology to what is known of the history of the London Pianoforte school

67. It can be inferred that Temperley's anthology treats the London Pianoforte school as

    (A) a group of pianist-composers who shared certain stylistic principles and artistic creeds
    (B) a group of people who contributed to the development of piano music between 1766 and 1873
    (C) a group of composers who influenced the music of Beethoven in the decades just before and just after 1800
    (D) a series of compositions for the pianoforte published in the decades just before and just after 1800
    (E) a series of compositions that had significant influence on the music of the Continent in the eighteenth and nineteenth centuries

The career of trumpeter Miles Davis was one of the most astonishingly productive that jazz music has ever seen. Yet his genius has never received its due. The impatience and artistic restlessness that characterized
(5) his work spawned one stylistic turn after another and made Davis anathema to many critics, who deplored his abandonment first of bebop and then of "cool" acoustic jazz for ever more innovative sounds.

Having begun his career studying bebop, Davis
(10) pulled the first of many stylistic surprises when, in 1948, he became a member of an impromptu musical think tank that gathered in a New York City apartment. The work of this group not only slowed down tempos and featured ensemble playing as much as or even
(15) more than solos—in direct reaction to bebop—it also became the seedbed for the "West Coast cool" jazz style.

In what would become a characteristic zigzag, Davis didn't follow up on these innovations himself.
(20) Instead, in the late 1950s he formed a new band that broke free from jazz's restrictive pattern of chord changes. Soloists could determine the shapes of their melodies without referring back to the same unvarying repetition of chords. In this period, Davis attempted to
(25) join jazz phrasings, harmonies, and tonal qualities with a unified and integrated sound similar to that of a classical orchestral piece: in his recordings the rhythms, no matter how jazz-like, are always understated, and the instrumental voicings seem muted.

(30) Davis's recordings from the late 1960s signal that, once again, his direction was changing. On *Filles de Kilimanjaro*, Davis's request that keyboardist Herbie Hancock play electric rather than acoustic piano caused consternation among jazz purists of the time. Other
(35) albums featured rock-style beats, heavily electronic instrumentation, a loose improvisational attack and a growing use of studio editing to create jagged soundscapes. By 1969 Davis's typical studio procedure was to have musicians improvise from a base script of
(40) material and then to build finished pieces out of tape, like a movie director. Rock groups had pioneered the process; to jazz lovers, raised on the ideal of live improvisation, that approach was a violation of the premise that recordings should simply document the
(45) musicians' thought processes in real time. Davis again became the target of fierce polemics by purist jazz critics, who have continued to belittle his contributions to jazz.

What probably underlies the intensity of the
(50) reactions against Davis is fear of the broadening of possibilities that he exemplified. Ironically, he was simply doing what jazz explorers have always done: reaching for something new that was his own. But because his career endured, because he didn't die
(55) young or record only sporadically, and because he refused to dwell in whatever niche he had previously carved out, critics find it difficult to definitively rank Davis in the aesthetic hierarchy to which they cling.

68. Which one of the following best states the main point of the passage?

(A) Because the career of Miles Davis was characterized by frequent shifts in styles, he never fulfilled his musical potential.

(B) Because the career of Miles Davis does not fit neatly into their preconceptions about the life and music of jazz musicians, jazz critics have not accorded him the appreciation he deserves.

(C) Because the career of Miles Davis was unusually long and productive, he never received the popular acclaim generally reserved for artists with more tragic life histories.

(D) The long and productive career of Miles Davis spawned most of the major stylistic changes affecting twentieth-century jazz.

(E) Miles Davis's versatility and openness have inspired the admiration of most jazz critics.

69. According to the passage, which one of the following is true of the "West Coast cool" jazz style?

(A) It was popularized by Miles Davis.
(B) It was characterized by a unified and integrated sound.
(C) It was played primarily by large ensembles.
(D) It introduced a wide variety of chord change patterns.
(E) It grew out of innovations developed in New York City.

Source: PrepTest 20, Section 2, Passage 1, Questions 1–6

70. The passage suggests which one of the following about the kind of jazz played by Miles Davis prior to l948?

(A) It was characterized by rapid tempos and an emphasis on solo playing.
(B) It equally balanced ensemble and solo playing.
(C) It was a reaction against more restrictive jazz styles.
(D) It is regarded by purist jazz critics as the only authentic jazz style.
(E) It was played primarily in New York City jazz clubs.

71. Which one of the following best describes the author's attitude toward Miles Davis's music?

(A) uneasy ambivalence
(B) cautious neutrality
(C) grudging respect
(D) moderate commendation
(E) appreciative advocacy

72. Which one of the following creative processes is most similar to Miles Davis's typical studio procedure of the late 1960s, as described in the fourth paragraph of the passage?

(A) The producer of a television comedy show suggests a setting and general topic for a comedy sketch and then lets the comedians write their own script.
(B) An actor digresses from the written script and improvises during a monologue in order to introduce a feeling of spontaneity to the performance.
(C) A conductor rehearses each section of the orchestra separately before assembling them to rehearse the entire piece together.
(D) An artist has several photographers take pictures pertaining to a certain assigned theme and then assembles them into a pictorial collage.
(E) A teacher has each student in a writing class write an essay on an assigned topic and then submits the best essays to be considered for publication in a journal.

73. Which one of the following, if true, would most undermine the author's explanation for the way Miles Davis is regarded by jazz critics?

(A) Many jazz musicians who specialize in improvisational playing are greatly admired by jazz critics.
(B) Many jazz musicians whose careers have been characterized by several radical changes in style are greatly admired by jazz critics.
(C) Several jazz musicians who perform exclusively on electronic instruments are very highly regarded by jazz critics.
(D) The jazz innovators who are held in the highest regard by jazz critics had brief yet brilliant careers.
(E) Jazz critics are known to have a higher regard for musicality than for mere technical virtuosity.

Innovations in language are never completely new. When the words used for familiar things change, or words for new things enter the language, they are usually borrowed or adapted from stock.
(5) Assuming new roles, they drag their old meanings along behind them like flickering shadows. This seems especially true of the language of the contemporary school of literary criticism that now prefers to describe its work simply and rather
(10) presumptuously as "theory" but is still popularly referred to as poststructuralism or deconstruction.

The first neologisms adopted by this movement were *signifier* and *signified*, employed to distinguish words from their referents, and to illustrate the
(15) arbitrariness of the terms we choose. The use of these particular terms (rather than, respectively, *word* and *thing*) underlined the seriousness of the naming process and its claim on our attention. Since in English "to signify" can also mean "to
(20) portend," these terms also suggest that words predict coming events.

With the use of the term *deconstruction* we move into another and more complex realm of meaning. The most common use of the terms *construction*
(25) and *deconstruction* is in the building trades, and their borrowing by literary theorists for a new type of criticism cannot help but have certain overtones to the outsider. First, the usage suggests that the creation and critical interpretation of literature are
(30) not organic but mechanical processes; that the author of any piece of writing is not an inspired, intuitive artist, but merely a laborer who cobbles existing materials (words) into more or less conventional structures. The term *deconstruction*
(35) implies that the text has been put together like a building or a piece of machinery, and that it is in need of being taken apart, not so much in order to repair it as to demonstrate underlying inadequacies, false assumptions, and inherent contradictions.
(40) This process can supposedly be repeated many times and by many literary hard hats; it is expected that each deconstruction will reveal additional flaws and expose the illusions or bad faith of the builder. The fact that deconstructionists prefer to
(45) describe their activities as *deconstruction* rather than *criticism* is also revealing. *Criticism* and *critic* derive from the Greek *kritikos*, "skillful in judging, decisive." *Deconstruction*, on the other hand, has no overtones of skill or wisdom; it merely suggests
(50) demolition of an existing building. In popular usage *criticism* suggests censure but not change. If we find fault with a building, we may condemn it, but we do not carry out the demolition ourselves. The deconstructionist, by implication, is both judge and
(55) executioner who leaves a text totally dismantled, if not reduced to a pile of rubble.

74. Which one of the following best expresses the main idea of the passage?

(A) Implicit in the terminology of the school of criticism known as *deconstruction* are meanings that reveal the true nature of the deconstructionist's endeavor.

(B) The appearance of the terms *signifier* and *signified* in the field of literary theory anticipated the appearance of an even more radical idea known as *deconstruction*.

(C) Innovations in language and the relations between old and new meanings of terms are a special concern of the new school of criticism known as *deconstruction*.

(D) Deconstructionists maintain that it is insufficient merely to judge a work; the critic must actively dismantle it.

(E) Progress in the field of literary theory is best achieved by looking for new terms like *signifier* and *deconstruction* that might suggest new critical approaches to a work.

75. Which one of the following is a claim that the author passage makes about deconstructionists?

(A) Deconstructionists would not have been able to formulate their views adequately without the terms *signifier* and *signified*.

(B) Deconstructionists had no particular purpose in mind in choosing to use neologisms.

(C) Deconstructionists do not recognize that their own theory contains inherent contradictions.

(D) Deconstructionists find little interest in the relationship between words and their referents.

(E) Deconstructionists use the terms *signifier* and *signified* to stress the importance of the process of naming.

Source: PrepTest 14, Section 3, Passage 2, Questions 7–13

KAPLAN

76. Which one of the following generalizations about inventions is most analogous to the author's point about innovation in language?

   (A) A new invention usually consists of components that are specifically manufactured for the new invention.
   (B) A new invention is usually behind the times, never making as much use of all the available modern technology as it could.
   (C) A new invention usually consists of components that are already available but are made to function in new ways.
   (D) A new invention is most useful when it is created with attention to the historical tradition established by implements previously used to do the same job.
   (E) A new invention is rarely used to its full potential because it is surrounded by out-of-date technology that hinders its application.

77. The author of the passage uses the word "*criticism*" in lines 46–56 primarily in order to

   (A) give an example
   (B) introduce a contrast
   (C) undermine an argument
   (D) codify a system
   (E) dismiss an objection

78. Which one of the following best describes the function of the second paragraph within the passage as a whole?

   (A) It introduces a hypothesis that the author later expands upon.
   (B) It qualifies a claim made earlier by the author.
   (C) It develops an initial example of the author's general thesis.
   (D) It predicts a development.
   (E) It presents a contrasting view.

79. The passage suggests that the author most probably holds the view that an important characteristic of literary criticism is that it

   (A) demonstrate false assumptions and inherent contradictions
   (B) employ skill and insight
   (C) be carried out by one critic rather than many
   (D) reveal how a text is put together like a building
   (E) point out the superiority of conventional text structures

80. The passage suggests that which one of the following most accurately describes the author's view of deconstructionist thought?

   (A) The author is guardedly optimistic about the ability of deconstruction to reveal the intentions and biases of a writer.
   (B) The author endorses the utility of deconstruction for revealing the role of older meanings of words.
   (C) The author is enthusiastic about the significant neologisms that deconstruction has introduced into literary criticism.
   (D) The author regards deconstruction's tendency to focus only on the problems and faults of literary texts as too mechanical.
   (E) The author condemns deconstruction's attempts to define literary criticism as a creative act.

Robin D. G. Kelley's book *Hammer and Hoe* explores the history of communism in the U.S. state of Alabama. Kelley asks not whether the Communist Party was ideologically correct, but how it came to
(5) attract a substantial number of African-American workers and how these workers could embrace and use the Communist Party as a vehicle for organizing themselves. He insists on measuring communism not by its abstract tenets but by its ability to interact with a
(10) culture to generate bold class organization.

Most scholarship that has offered a defense of the Communist Party in the 1930s and 1940s (a period known as the party's Popular Front) has tended to emphasize its attempts to draw on democratic political
(15) traditions, and to enter meaningful political alliances with liberal political forces. While this is an understandable viewpoint among historians searching for models of unity between radicals and liberals, Kelley's interest is in African-American organizing.
(20) From that point of view the Popular Front appears as much less of a blessing.

Indeed Kelley argues that the wild, often sectarian Third Period that preceded the Popular Front better undergirded organization among African-American
(25) farmers and industrial workers. The extreme rhetoric of the Third Period communists was not taken seriously by African-American party members, who avoided posturing and confrontation whenever possible. But on another level, rhetoric regarding a "new world"
(30) resonated among African-Americans, whose traditions emphasized both a struggle for survival and the transcendent hope of deliverance. Help from a powerful ally, even one as far away as Moscow, seemed a source of power and possibility. The
(35) worldwide efforts of the communist-led International Labor Defense in mobilizing against lynch law in the United States helped to establish the party's image as such an ally.

The Popular Front saw African-American
(40) participation in the Communist Party decline. A retreat from attacks on white chauvinism and a tendency to de-emphasize, however slightly, involvement in local African-American issue-oriented politics made the party seem less an instrument of deliverance. The
(45) party's increasing cautiousness, born of a desire to appeal to moderates, doubtless made it a less attractive alternative in interracial conflicts.

Even so, Kelley is far from claiming that the change to a Popular Front line was the sole reason for
(50) the decline of African-American communism. The Popular Front initially appealed to African-American communists because it seemed to open new strategies for blunting repression. Kelley's rounded portrait of the decline emphasizes not the absence of a "correct line"
(55) but the presence of factional battles and of transformations in the agriculture industry caused by market changes and U.S. federal government intervention.

81. Which one of the following most accurately characterizes the passage's main point?

(A) By spending little time discussing ideological controversies, *Hammer and Hoe* fails to fully explicate the relationship between the Communist Party and African-American workers during the 1930s and 1940s.

(B) The relationship between the Communist Party and African-American workers during the 1930s and 1940s makes it clear that ideological purity and consistency are not essential to effecting political change.

(C) *Hammer and Hoe* constitutes a valuable tool for the modern historian who is attempting to search for models of unity between radicals and liberals.

(D) The true measure of the success of the Communist Party at organizing African-American workers was not its ability to change people's thinking but to interact with their culture.

(E) *Hammer and Hoe* offers new insights into the nature of the relationship, in the 1930s and 1940s, between the Communist Party and African-American workers.

82. The passage's characterization of the Communist Party in Alabama before the 1930s includes each of the following EXCEPT that the party

(A) refrained from attacking white chauvinism

(B) benefited from the goodwill created by the actions of the International Labor Defense

(C) inspired some African Americans with its rhetoric

(D) failed to convince some of its African-American members that confrontation was an acceptable political stance

(E) was involved in local African-American political issues

Source: PrepTest C, Section 4, Passage 3, Questions 16–20

KAPLAN

83. The primary purpose of the second paragraph is to

(A) contrast Kelley's viewpoint on the Popular Front with that of previous historians

(B) defend the Popular Front from Kelley's attacks on it

(C) question the political usefulness of searching for common ground between radicals and liberals

(D) enumerate the differences between the Popular Front and the Third Period

(E) argue that one valid way to approach the study of communism in the United States is to discuss its impact on African-American workers

84. It can be inferred from the passage that Kelley would most likely agree with which one of the following assertions about the Popular Front?

(A) The Popular Front introduced factors that hampered the political appeal of communism for African Americans.

(B) The Popular Front was inherently inimical to African-American interests from its inception.

(C) The increasing cautiousness of the Popular Front appealed to most African-American party members.

(D) The Popular Front was viewed by African Americans as an improvement over the rhetoric of the Third Period.

(E) The extreme posturing and confrontation of the Popular Front alienated many African Americans.

85. Based on the passage, which one of the following statements is more likely to have been made by a Communist Party organizer during the Third Period than during the Popular Front?

(A) African Americans and whites must join together under the common banner of communism.

(B) Workers everywhere must revolt to bring about the final global victory over capitalist oppression.

(C) African Americans should strive to overcome racism in the highest levels of government.

(D) The goals of communism have much in common with those of more liberal causes.

(E) One should not expect too much progress too quickly when attempting to change the prevailing social order.

A fake can be defined as an artwork intended to deceive. The motives of its creator are decisive, and the merit of the object itself is a separate issue. The question mark in the title of Mark Jones's *Fake? The*
(5) *Art of Deception* reveals the study's broader concerns. Indeed, it might equally be entitled *Original?*, and the text begins by noting a variety of possibilities somewhere between the two extremes. These include works by an artist's followers in the style of the master,
(10) deliberate archaism, copying for pedagogical purposes, and the production of commercial facsimiles.

The greater part of *Fake?* is devoted to a chronological survey suggesting that faking feeds on the many different motives people have for collecting
(15) art, and that, on the whole, the faking of art flourishes whenever art collecting flourishes. In imperial Rome there was a widespread interest in collecting earlier Greek art, and therefore, in faking it. No doubt many of the sculptures now exhibited as "Roman copies" were
(20) originally passed off as Greek. In medieval Europe, because art was celebrated more for its devotional uses than for its provenance or the ingenuity of its creators, the faking of art was virtually nonexistent. The modern age of faking began in the Italian Renaissance, with
(25) two linked developments: a passionate identification with the world of antiquity and a growing sense of individual artistic identity. A patron of the young Michelangelo prevailed upon the artist to make his sculpture *Sleeping Cupid* look as though it had been
(30) buried in the earth so that "it will be taken for antique, and you will sell it much better." Within a few years, however, beginning with his first masterpiece, the *Bacchus*, Michelangelo had shown his contemporaries that great art can assimilate and transcend what came
(35) before, resulting in a wholly original work. Soon his genius made him the object of imitators.

Fake? also reminds us that in certain cultures authenticity is a foreign concept. This is true of much African art, where the authenticity of an object is
(40) considered by collectors to depend on its function. As an illustration, the study compares two versions of a *chi wara* mask made by the Bambara people of Mali. One has pegs allowing it to be attached to a cap for its intended ceremonial purpose. The second, otherwise
(45) identical, lacks the pegs and is a replica made for sale. African carving is notoriously difficult to date, but even if the ritual mask is recent, made perhaps to replace a damaged predecessor, and the replica much older, only the ritual mask should be seen as authentic,
(50) for it is tied to the form's original function. That, at least, is the consensus of the so-called experts. One wonders whether the Bambaran artists would agree.

86. The passage can best be described as doing which one of the following?

(A) reconciling varied points of view
(B) chronicling the evolution of a phenomenon
(C) exploring a complex question
(D) advocating a new approach
(E) rejecting an inadequate explanation

87. Which one of the following best expresses the author's main point?

(A) The faking of art has occurred throughout history and in virtually every culture.
(B) Whether a work of art is fake or not is less important than whether it has artistic merit.
(C) It is possible to show that a work of art is fake, but the authenticity of a work cannot be proved conclusively.
(D) A variety of circumstances make it difficult to determine whether a work of art can appropriately be called a fake.
(E) Without an international market to support it, the faking of art would cease.

88. According to the passage, an artwork can be definitively classified as a fake if the person who created it

(A) consciously adopted the artistic style of an influential mentor
(B) deliberately imitated a famous work of art as a learning exercise
(C) wanted other people to be fooled by its appearance
(D) made multiple, identical copies of the work available for sale
(E) made the work resemble the art of an earlier era

Source: PrepTest 24, Section 1, Passage 4, Questions 21–27

89. The author provides a least one example of each of the following EXCEPT:

    (A) categories of art that are neither wholly fake nor wholly original
    (B) cultures in which the faking of art flourished
    (C) qualities that art collectors have prized in their acquisitions
    (D) cultures in which the categories "fake" and "original" do not apply
    (E) contemporary artists whose works have inspired fakes.

90. The author implies which one of the following about the artistic merits of fakes?

    (A) Because of the circumstances of its production, a fake cannot be said to have true artistic merit.
    (B) A fake can be said to have artistic merit only if the attempted deception is successful.
    (C) A fake may or may not have artistic merit in its own right, regardless of the circumstances of its production.
    (D) Whether a fake has artistic merit depends on whether its creator is accomplished as an artist.
    (E) The artistic merit of a fake depends on the merit of the original work that inspired the fake.

91. By the standard described in the last paragraph of the passage, which one of the following would be considered authentic?

    (A) an ancient Roman copy of an ancient Greek sculpture
    (B) a painting begun by a Renaissance master and finished by his assistants after his death
    (C) a print of a painting signed by the artist who painted the original
    (D) a faithful replica of a ceremonial crown that preserves all the details of, and is indistinguishable from, the original
    (E) a modern reconstruction of a medieval altarpiece designed to serve its traditional role in a service of worship

92. Which one of the following best describes how the last paragraph functions in the context of the passage?

    (A) It offers a tentative answer to a question posed by the author in the opening paragraph.
    (B) It summarizes an account provided in detail in the preceding paragraph.
    (C) It provides additional support for an argument advanced by the author in the preceding paragraph.
    (D) It examines another facet of a distinction developed in the preceding paragraphs.
    (E) It affirms the general principle enunciated at the beginning of the passage.

Law Passages

<u>Directions</u>: Each passage in this section is followed by a group of questions to be answered on the basis of what is <u>stated</u> or <u>implied</u> in the passage. For some of the questions, more than one of the choices could conceivably answer the question. However, you are to choose the <u>best</u> answer; that is, the response that most accurately and completely answers the question.

The jury trial is one of the handful of democratic institutions that allow individual citizens, rather than the government, to make important societal decisions. A crucial component of the jury trial, at least in serious
(5) criminal cases, is the rule that verdicts be unanimous among the jurors (usually twelve in number). Under this requirement, dissenting jurors must either be convinced of the rightness of the prevailing opinion, or, conversely, persuade the other jurors to change their
(10) minds. In either instance, the unanimity requirement compels the jury to deliberate fully and truly before reaching its verdict. Critics of the unanimity requirement, however, see it as a costly relic that extends the deliberation process and sometimes, in a
(15) hung (i.e., deadlocked) jury, brings it to a halt at the hands of a single, recalcitrant juror, forcing the judge to order a retrial. Some of these critics recommend reducing verdict requirements to something less than unanimity, so that one or even two dissenting jurors
(20) will not be able to force a retrial.

But the material costs of hung juries do not warrant losing the benefit to society of the unanimous verdict. Statistically, jury trials are relatively rare; the vast majority of defendants do not have the option of a jury
(25) trial or elect to have a trial without a jury—or they plead guilty to the original or a reduced charge. And the incidence of hung juries is only a small fraction of the already small fraction of cases that receive a jury trial. Furthermore, that juries occasionally deadlock
(30) does not demonstrate a flaw in the criminal justice system, but rather suggests that jurors are conscientiously doing the job they have been asked to do. Hung juries usually occur when the case is very close—that is, when neither side has presented
(35) completely convincing evidence—and although the unanimity requirement may sometimes lead to inconclusive outcomes, a hung jury is certainly preferable to an unjust verdict.

Requiring unanimity provides a better chance that a
(40) trial, and thus a verdict, will be fair. Innocent people are already occasionally convicted—perhaps in some cases because jurors presume that anyone who has been brought to trial is probably guilty—and eliminating the unanimity requirement would only
(45) increase the opportunity for such mistakes. Furthermore, if a juror's dissenting opinion can easily be dismissed, an important and necessary part of the deliberation process will be lost, for effective deliberation requires that each juror's opinion be given
(50) a fair hearing. Only then can the verdict reached by the jury be said to represent all of its members, and if even

one juror has doubts that are dismissed out of hand, society's confidence that a proper verdict has been reached would be undermined.

1. Which one of the following most accurately states the main point of the passage?

(A) Because trials requiring juries are relative rare, the usefulness of the unanimity requirement does not need to be reexamined.

(B) The unanimity requirement should be maintained because most hung juries are caused by irresponsible jurors rather than by any flaws in the requirement.

(C) The problem of hung juries is not a result of flaws in the justice system but of the less than convincing evidence presented in some cases.

(D) The unanimity requirement should be maintained, but it is only effective if jurors conscientiously do the job they have been asked to do.

(E) Because its material costs are outweighed by what it contributes to the fairness of jury trials, the unanimity requirement should not be rescinded.

Source: PrepTest 37, Section 1, Passage 1, Questions 1–7

2. Which one of the following most accurately describes the author's attitude toward the unanimity requirement?

   (A) cursory appreciation
   (B) neutral interest
   (C) cautious endorsement
   (D) firm support
   (E) unreasoned reverence

3. Which one of the following principles can most clearly be said to underlie the author's arguments in the third paragraph?

   (A) The risk of unjust verdicts is serious enough to warrant strong measures to avoid it.
   (B) Fairness in jury trials is crucial and so judges must be extremely thorough in order to ensure it.
   (C) Careful adherence to the unanimity requirement will eventually eliminate unjust verdicts.
   (D) Safeguards must be in place because not all citizens called to jury duty perform their role responsibly.
   (E) The jury system is inherently flawed and therefore unfairness cannot be eliminated but only reduced.

4. Which one of the following sentences could most logically be added to the end of the last paragraph of the passage?

   (A) It is not surprising, then, that the arguments presented by the critics of the unanimity requirement grow out of a separate tradition from that embodied in the unanimity requirement.
   (B) Similarly, if there is a public debate concerning the unanimity requirement, public faith in the requirement will be strengthened.
   (C) The opinion of each juror is as essential to the pursuit of justice as the universal vote is to the functioning of a true democracy.
   (D) Unfortunately, because some lawmakers have characterized hung juries as intolerable, the integrity of the entire legal system has been undermined.
   (E) But even without the unanimity requirement, fair trials and fair verdicts will occur more frequently as the methods of prosecutors and defense attorneys become more scientific.

5. Which one of the following could replace the term "recalcitrant" (line 16) without a substantial change in the meaning of the critics' claim?

   (A) obstinate
   (B) suspicious
   (C) careful
   (D) conscientious
   (E) naive

6. The author explicitly claims that which one of the following would be a result of allowing a juror's dissenting opinion to be dismissed?

   (A) Only verdicts in very close cases would be affected.
   (B) The responsibility felt by jurors to be respectful to one another would be lessened.
   (C) Society's confidence in the fairness of the verdicts would be undermined.
   (D) The problem of hung juries would not be solved but would surface less frequently.
   (E) An important flaw thus would be removed from the criminal justice system.

7. It can be inferred from the passage that the author would be most likely to agree with which one of the following?

   (A) Hung juries most often result from an error in judgment on the part of one juror.
   (B) Aside from the material costs of hung juries, the criminal justice system has few flaws.
   (C) The fact that jury trials are so rare renders any flaws in the jury system insignificant.
   (D) Hung juries are acceptable and usually indicate that the criminal justice system is functioning properly.
   (E) Hung juries most often occur when one juror's opinion does not receive a fair hearing.

Medievalists usually distinguished medieval public law from private law: the former was concerned with government and military affairs and the latter with the family, social status, and land transactions.

(5) Examination of medieval women's lives shows this distinction to be overly simplistic. Although medieval women were legally excluded from roles thus categorized as public, such as soldier, justice, jury member, or professional administrative official,

(10) women's control of land—usually considered a private or domestic phenomenon—had important political implications in the feudal system of thirteenth-century England. Since land equaled wealth and wealth equaled power, certain women exercised influence by

(15) controlling land. Unlike unmarried women (who were legally subject to their guardians) or married women (who had no legal identity separate from their husbands), women who were widows had autonomy with respect to acquiring or disposing of certain

(20) property, suing in court, incurring liability for their own debts, and making wills.

Although feudal lands were normally transferred through primogeniture (the eldest son inheriting all), when no sons survived, the surviving daughters

(25) inherited equal shares under what was known as partible inheritance. In addition to controlling any such land inherited from her parents and any bridal dowry— property a woman brought to the marriage from her own family—a widow was entitled to use of one-third

(30) of her late husband's lands. Called "dower" in England, this grant had greater legal importance under common law than did the bridal dowry; no marriage was legal unless the groom endowed the bride with this property at the wedding ceremony. In 1215 Magna

(35) Carta guaranteed a widow's right to claim her dower without paying a fine; this document also strengthened widows' ability to control land by prohibiting forced remarriage. After 1272 women could also benefit from jointure: the groom could agree to hold part or all of

(40) his lands jointly with the bride, so that if one spouse died, the other received these lands.

Since many widows had inheritances as well as dowers, widows were frequently the financial heads of the family; even though legal theory assumed the

(45) maintenance of the principle of primogeniture, the amount of land the widow controlled could exceed that of her son or of other male heirs. Anyone who held feudal land exercised authority over the people attached to the land—knights, rental tenants, and

(50) peasants—and had to hire estate administrators, oversee accounts, receive rents, protect tenants from outside encroachment, punish tenants for not paying rents, appoint priests to local parishes, and act as guardians of tenants' children and executors of their

(55) wills. Many married women fulfilled these duties as deputies for husbands away at court or at war, but widows could act on their own behalf. Widows' legal independence is suggested by their frequent appearance in thirteenth-century English legal records. Moreover,

(60) the scope of their sway is indicated by the fact that some controlled not merely single estates, but multiple counties.

8. Which one of the following best expresses the main idea of the passage?

E X

(A) The traditional view of medieval women as legally excluded from many public offices fails to consider thirteenth-century women in England who were exempted from such restrictions because of their wealth and social status.

(B) The economic independence of women in thirteenth-century England was primarily determined not by their marital status, but by their status as heirs to their parents' estates.

(C) The laws and customs of the feudal system in thirteenth-century England enabled some women to exercise a certain amount of power despite their legal exclusion from most public roles.

(D) During the thirteenth century in England, widows gained greater autonomy and legal rights to their property than they had had in previous centuries.

(E) Widows in thirteenth-century England were able to acquire and dispose of lands through a number of different legal processes.

9. With which one of the following statements about the views held by the medievalists mentioned in line 1 would the author of the passage most probably agree?

E X

(A) The medieval role of landowner was less affected by thirteenth-century changes in law than these medievalists customarily have recognized.

(B) The realm of law labeled public by these medievalists ultimately had greater political implications than that labeled private.

(C) The amount of wealth controlled by medieval women was greater than these medievalists have recorded.

(D) The distinction made by these medievalists between private law and public law fails to consider some of the actual legal cases of the period.

(E) The distinction made by these medievalists between private and public law fails to address the political importance of control over land in the medieval era.

Source: PrepTest 23, Section 4, Passage 2, Questions 6–13

10. Which one of the following most accurately expresses the meaning of the word "sway" as it is used in line 60 of the passage?

    (A)   vacillation
    (B)   dominion
    (C)   predisposition
    (D)   inclination
    (E)   mediation

11. Which one of the following most accurately describes the function of the second paragraph of the passage?

    (A)   providing examples of specific historical events as support for the conclusion drawn in the third paragraph
    (B)   narrating a sequence of events whose outcome is discussed in the third paragraph
    (C)   explaining how circumstances described in the first paragraph could have occurred
    (D)   describing the effects of an event mentioned in the first paragraph
    (E)   evaluating the arguments of a group mentioned in the first paragraph

12. According to information in the passage, a widow in early thirteenth-century England could control more land than did her eldest son if

    (A)   the widow had been granted the customary amount of dower land and the eldest son inherited the rest of the land
    (B)   the widow had three daughters in addition to her eldest son
    (C)   the principle of primogeniture had been applied in transferring the lands owned by the widow's late husband
    (D)   none of the lands held by the widow's late husband had been placed in jointure
    (E)   the combined amount of land the widow had acquired from her own family and from dower was greater than the amount inherited by her son

13. Which one of the following is mentioned in the passage as a reason why a married woman might have fulfilled certain duties associated with holding feudal land in thirteenth-century England?

    (A)   the legal statutes set forth by Magna Carta
    (B)   the rights a woman held over her inheritance during her marriage
    (C)   the customary division of duties between husbands and wives
    (D)   the absence of the woman's husband
    (E)   the terms specified by the woman's jointure agreement

14. The phrase "in England" (lines 30–31) does which one of the following?

    (A)   It suggests that women in other countries also received grants of their husbands' lands.
    (B)   It identifies a particular code of law affecting women who were surviving daughters.
    (C)   It demonstrates that dower had greater legal importance in one European country than in others.
    (D)   It emphasizes that women in one European country had more means of controlling property than did women in other European countries.
    (E)   It traces a legal term back to the time at which it entered the language.

15. The primary purpose of the passage is to

    (A)   explain a legal controversy of the past in light of modern theory
    (B)   evaluate the economic and legal status of a particular historical group
    (C)   resolve a scholarly debate about legal history
    (D)   trace the historical origins of a modern economic situation
    (E)   provide new evidence about a historical event

(The following passage was written in 1986.)

The legislature of a country recently considered a bill designed to reduce the uncertainty inherent in the ownership of art by specifying certain conditions that must be met before an allegedly stolen work of
(5) art can be reclaimed by a plaintiff. The bill places the burden of proof in reclamation litigation entirely on the plaintiff, who must demonstrate that the holder of an item knew at the time of purchase that it had been stolen. Additionally, the bill creates a
(10) uniform national statute of limitations for reclamation of stolen cultural property.

Testifying in support of the bill, James D. Burke, a citizen of the country and one of its leading art museum directors, specifically praised the inclusion
(15) of a statute of limitations; otherwise, he said, other countries could seek to reclaim valuable art objects, no matter how long they have been held by the current owner or how legitimately they were acquired. Any country could enact a patrimony
(20) law stating that anything ever made within the boundaries of that country is its cultural property. Burke expressed the fear that widespread reclamation litigation would lead to ruinous legal defense costs for museums.
(25) However, because such reclamation suits have not yet been a problem, there is little basis for Burke's concern. In fact, the proposed legislation would establish too many unjustifiable barriers to the location and recovery of stolen objects. The
(30) main barrier is that the bill considers the announcement of an art transaction in a museum publication to be adequate evidence of an attempt to notify a possible owner. There are far too many such publications for the victim of a theft to survey,
(35) and with only this form of disclosure, a stolen object could easily remain unlocated even if assiduously searched for. Another stipulation requires that a purchaser show the object to a scholar for verification that it is not stolen, but it is
(40) a rare academic who is aware of any but the most publicized art thefts. Moreover, the time limit specified by the statute of limitations is very short, and the requirement that the plaintiff demonstrate that the holder had knowledge of the theft is
(45) unrealistic. Typically, stolen art changes hands several times before rising to the level in the marketplace where a curator or collector would see it. At that point, the object bears no trace of the initial transaction between the thief and the first
(50) purchaser, perhaps the only one in the chain who knowingly acquired a stolen work of art.

Thus, the need for new legislation to protect holders of art is not obvious. Rather, what is necessary is legislation remedying the difficulties
(55) that legitimate owners of works of art, and countries from which such works have been stolen, have in locating and reclaiming these stolen works.

16. Which one of the following most accurately summarizes the main point of the passage?

(A) Various legal disputes have recently arisen that demonstrate the need for legislation clarifying the legal position of museums in suits involving the repossession of cultural property.

(B) A bill intended to prevent other governments from recovering cultural property was recently introduced into the legislature of a country at the behest of its museum directors.

(C) A bill intended to protect good-faith purchasers of works of art from reclamation litigation is unnecessary and fails to address the needs of legitimate owners attempting to recover stolen art works.

(D) Clashes between museum professionals and members of the academic community regarding governmental legislation of the arts can best be resolved by negotiation and arbitration, not by litigation.

(E) The desire of some governments to use legislation and litigation to recover cultural property stolen from their counties has led to abuses in international patrimony legislation.

17. The uncertainty mentioned in line 2 of the passage refers to the

(A) doubt that owners of works of art often harbor over whether individuals have a moral right to possess great art

(B) concern that owners of works of art often have that their possession of such objects may be legally challenged at any time

(C) questions that owners of works of art often have concerning the correct identification of the age and origin of their objects

(D) disputes that often arise between cultural institutions vying for the opportunity to purchase a work of art

(E) apprehension that owners of works of art often feel concerning the possibility that their objects may be damaged or stolen from them

Source: PrepTest 14, Section 3, Passage 3, Questions 14–20

18. Which one of the following is an example of the kind of action that Burke feared would pose a serious threat to museums in his country?

    (A) the passage of a law by another country forbidding the future export of any archaeological objects uncovered at sites within its territory

    (B) an international accord establishing strict criteria for determining whether a work of art can be considered stolen and specifying the circumstances under which it must be returned to its country of origin

    (C) the passage of a law by another country declaring that all objects created by its aboriginal people are the sole property of that country

    (D) an increase in the acquisition of culturally significant works of art by private collectors, who are more capable than museums of bearing the cost of litigation but who rarely display their collections to the public

    (E) the recommendation of a United Nations committee studying the problem of art theft that all international sales of cultural property be coordinated by a central regulatory body

19. According to the passage, Burke envisaged the most formidable potential adversaries of his country's museums in reclamation litigation to be

    (A) commercial dealers in art
    (B) law enforcement officials in his own country
    (C) governments of other countries
    (D) private collectors of art
    (E) museums in other countries

20. The author suggests that in the country mentioned in line 1, litigation involving the reclamation of stolen works of art has been

    (A) less common than Burke fears it will become without passage of a national statute of limitations for reclamation of stolen cultural property

    (B) increasing as a result of the passage of legislation that aids legitimate owners of art in their attempts to recover stolen works

    (C) a serious threat to museums and cultural institutions that have unwittingly added stolen artifacts to their collections

    (D) a signal of the legitimate frustrations of victims of art theft

    (E) increasing as a result of an increase in the amount of art theft

21. Which one of the following best describes the author's attitude toward the proposed bill?

    (A) impassioned support
    (B) measured advocacy
    (C) fearful apprehension
    (D) reasoned opposition
    (E) reluctant approval

22. Which one of the following best exemplifies the sort of legislation considered necessary by the author of the passage?

    (A) a law requiring museums to notify foreign governments and cultural institutions of all the catalogs and scholarly journals that they publish

    (B) a law providing for the creation of a national warehouse for storage of works of art that are the subject of litigation

    (C) a law instituting a national fund for assisting museums to bear the expenses of defending themselves against reclamation suits

    (D) a law declaring invalid all sales of cultural property during the last ten years by museums of one country to museums of another

    (E) a law requiring that a central archive be established for collecting and distributing information concerning all reported thefts of cultural property

In a recent court case, a copy-shop owner was accused of violating copyright law when, in the preparation of "course packs"—materials photocopied from books and journals and packaged as readings for
(5) particular university courses—he copied materials without obtaining permission from or paying sufficient fees to the publishers. As the owner of five small copy shops serving several educational institutions in the area, he argued, as have others in the photocopy
(10) business, that the current process for obtaining permissions is time-consuming, cumbersome, and expensive. He also maintained that course packs, which are ubiquitous in higher education, allow professors to assign important readings in books and journals too
(15) costly for students to be expected to purchase individually. While the use of copyrighted material for teaching purposes is typically protected by certain provisions of copyright law, this case was unique in that the copying of course packs was done by a copy
(20) shop and at a profit.

Copyright law outlines several factors involved in determining whether the use of copyrighted material is protected, including: whether it is for commercial or nonprofit purposes; the nature of the copyrighted work;
(25) the length and importance of the excerpt used in relation to the entire work; and the effect of its use on the work's potential market value. In bringing suit, the publishers held that other copy-shop owners would cease paying permission fees, causing the potential
(30) value of the copyrighted works of scholarship to diminish. Nonetheless, the court decided that this reasoning did not demonstrate that course packs would have a sufficiently adverse effect on the current or potential market of the copyrighted works or on the
(35) value of the copyrighted works themselves. The court instead ruled that since the copies were for educational purposes, the fact that the copy-shop owner had profited from making the course packs did not prevent him from receiving protection under the law.
(40) According to the court, the owner had not exploited copyrighted material because his fee was not based on the content of the works he copied; he charged by the page, regardless of whether the content was copyrighted.
(45) In the court's view, the business of producing and selling course packs is more properly seen as the exploitation of professional copying technologies and a result of the inability of academic parties to reproduce printed materials efficiently, not the exploitation of
(50) these copyrighted materials themselves. The court held that copyright laws do not prohibit professors and students, who may make copies for themselves, from using the photoreproduction services of a third party in order to obtain those same copies at lesser cost.

23. Which one of the following most accurately states the main point of the passage?

(A) A court recently ruled that a copy shop that makes course packs does not illegally exploit copyrighted materials but rather it legally exploits the efficiency of professional photocopying technology.

(B) A court recently ruled that course packs are protected by copyright law because their price is based solely on the number of pages in each pack.

(C) A court recently ruled that the determining factors governing the copyrights of material used in course packs are how the material is to be used, the nature of the material itself, and the length of the copied excerpts.

(D) A recent court ruling limits the rights of publishers to seek suit against copy shops that make course packs from copyrighted material.

(E) Exceptions to copyright law are made when copyrighted material is used for educational purposes and no party makes a substantial profit from the material.

Source: PrepTest 41, Section 4, Passage 1, Questions 1–6

24. In lines 23–27, the author lists several of the factors used to determine whether copyrighted material is protected by law primarily to

    (A) demonstrate why the copy-shop owner was exempt from copyright law in this case
    (B) explain the charges the publishers brought against the copy-shop owner
    (C) illustrate a major flaw in the publishers' reasoning
    (D) defend the right to use copyrighted materials for educational purposes
    (E) provide the legal context for the arguments presented in the case

25. The copy-shop owner as described in the passage would be most likely to agree with which one of the following statements?

    (A) The potential market value of a copyrighted work should be calculated to include the impact on sales due to the use of the work in course packs.
    (B) Publishers are always opposed to the preparation and sale of course packs.
    (C) More copy shops would likely seek permissions from publishers if the process for obtaining permissions were not so cumbersome and expensive.
    (D) Certain provisions of copyright law need to be rewritten to apply to all possible situations.
    (E) Copy shops make more of a profit from the preparation and sale of course packs than from other materials.

26. The information in the passage provides the most support for which one of the following statements about copyright law?

    (A) Copyright law can be one of the most complex areas of any legal system.
    (B) Courts have been inconsistent in their interpretations of certain provisions of copyright law.
    (C) The number of the kinds of materials granted protection under copyright law is steadily decreasing.
    (D) New practices can compel the courts to refine how copyright law is applied.
    (E) Copyright law is primarily concerned with making published materials available for educational use.

27. Which one of the following describes a role most similar to that of professors in the passage who use copy shops to produce course packs?

    (A) An artisan generates a legible copy of an old headstone engraving by using charcoal on newsprint and frames and sells high-quality photocopies of it at a crafts market.
    (B) A choir director tapes a selection of another well-known choir's best pieces and sends it to a recording studio to be reproduced in a sellable package for use by members of her choir.
    (C) A grocer makes several kinds of sandwiches that sell for less than similar sandwiches from a nearby upscale café.
    (D) A professional graphic artist prints reproductions of several well-known paintings at an exhibit to sell at the museum's gift shop.
    (E) A souvenir store in the center of a city sells miniature bronze renditions of a famous bronze sculpture that the city is noted for displaying.

28. Which one of the following, if true, would have most strengthened the publishers' position in this case?

    (A) Course packs for courses that usually have large enrollments had produced a larger profit for the copy-shop owner.
    (B) The copy-shop owner had actively solicited professors' orders for course packs.
    (C) The revenue generated by the copy shop's sale of course packs had risen significantly within the past few years.
    (D) Many area bookstores had reported a marked decrease in the sales of books used for producing course packs.
    (E) The publishers had enlisted the support of the authors to verify their claims that the copy-shop owner had not obtained permission.

Until about 1970, anyone who wanted to write a comprehensive history of medieval English law as it actually affected women would have found a dearth of published books or articles concerned with specific
(5) legal topics relating to women and derived from extensive research in actual court records. This is a serious deficiency, since court records are of vital importance in discovering how the law actually affected women, as opposed to how the law was
(10) intended to affect them or thought to affect them. These latter questions can be answered by consulting such sources as treatises, commentaries, and statutes; such texts were what most scholars of the nineteenth and early twentieth centuries concentrated on whenever
(15) they did write about medieval law. But these sources are of little help in determining, for example, how often women's special statutory privileges were thwarted by intimidation or harassment, or how often women managed to evade special statutory limitations. And,
(20) quite apart from provisions designed to apply only, or especially, to women, they cannot tell us how general law affected the female half of the population—how women defendants and plaintiffs were treated in the courts in practice when they tried to exercise the rights
(25) they shared with men. Only quantitative studies of large numbers of cases would allow even a guess at the answers to these questions, and this scholarly work has been attempted by few.

One can easily imagine why. Most medieval
(30) English court records are written in Latin or Anglo-Norman French and have never been published. The sheer volume of material to be sifted is daunting: there are over 27,500 parchment pages in the common plea rolls of the thirteenth century alone, every page nearly
(35) three feet long, and written often front and back in highly stylized court hand. But the difficulty of the sources, while it might appear to explain why the relevant scholarship has not been undertaken, seems actually to have deterred few: the fact is that few
(40) historians have wanted to write anything approaching women's legal history in the first place. Most modern legal historians who have written on one aspect or another of special laws pertaining to women have begun with an interest in a legal idea or event or
(45) institution, not with a concern for how it affected women. Very few legal historians have started with an interest in women's history that they might have elected to pursue through various areas of general law. And the result of all this is that the current state of our
(50) scholarly knowledge relating to law and the medieval Englishwoman is still fragmentary at best, though the situation is slowly improving.

29. It can be inferred from the passage that the author believes which one of the following to be true of the sources consulted by nineteenth-century historians of medieval law?

(A) They are adequate to the research needs of a modern legal historian wishing to investigate medieval law.

(B) They are to be preferred to medieval legal sources, which are cumbersome and difficult to use.

(C) They lack fundamental relevance to the history of modern legal institutions and ideas.

(D) They provide relatively little information relevant to the issues with which writers of women's legal history ought most to concern themselves.

(E) They are valuable primarily because of the answers they can provide to some of the questions that have most interested writers of women's legal history.

30. Which one of the following best describes the organization of the first paragraph of the passage?

(A) The preparations necessary for the production of a particular kind of study are discussed, and reasons are given for why such preparations have not been undertaken until recently.

(B) A problem is described, a taxonomy of various kinds of questions relevant to its solution is proposed, and an evaluation regarding which of those questions would be most useful to answer is made.

(C) An example suggesting the nature of present conditions in a discipline is given, past conditions in that discipline are described, and a prediction is made regarding the future of the discipline.

(D) A deficiency is described, the specific nature of the deficiency is discussed, and a particular kind of remedy is asserted to be the sole possible means of correcting that deficiency.

(E) The resources necessary to the carrying out of a task are described, the inherent limitations of those resources are suggested by means of a list of questions, and a suggestion is made for overcoming these limitations.

Source: PrepTest 29, Section 2, Passage 4, Questions 22–27

31. According to the passage, quantitative studies of the kind referred to in line 25 can aid in determining

    (A) what were the stated intentions of those who wrote medieval statutes
    (B) what were the unconscious or hidden motives of medieval lawmakers with regard to women
    (C) what was the impact of medieval legal thought concerning women on the development of important modern legal ideas and institutions
    (D) how medieval women's lives were really affected by medieval laws
    (E) how best to categorize the masses of medieval documents relating to women

32. According to the passage, the sources consulted by legal scholars of the nineteenth and early twentieth centuries provided adequate information concerning which one of the following topics?

    (A) the intent of medieval English laws regarding women and the opinions of commentators concerning how those laws affected women
    (B) the overall effectiveness of English law in the medieval period and some aspects of the special statutes that applied to women only
    (C) the degree of probability that a women defendant or plaintiff would win a legal case in medieval England
    (D) the degree to which the male relatives of medieval Englishwomen could succeed in preventing those women from exercising their legal rights
    (E) which of the legal rights theoretically shared by men and women were, in practice, guaranteed only to men

33. As used in lines 37–38, the phrase "the relevant scholarship" can best be understood as referring to which one of the following kinds of scholarly work?

    (A) linguistic studies of Anglo-Norman French and Latin undertaken in order to prepare for further study of medieval legal history
    (B) the editing and publication of medieval court records undertaken in order to facilitate the work of legal and other historians
    (C) quantitative studies of large numbers of medieval court cases undertaken in order to discover the actual effects of law on medieval women's lives
    (D) comparative studies of medieval statutes, treatises, and commentaries undertaken in order to discover the views and intentions of medieval legislators
    (E) reviews of the existing scholarly literature concerning women and medieval law undertaken as groundwork for the writing of a comprehensive history of medieval law as it applied to women

34. It can be inferred from the passage that, in the author's view, which one of the following factors is most responsible for the current deficiencies in our knowledge of women's legal history?

    (A) most modern legal historians' relative lack of interest in pursuing the subject
    (B) the linguistic and practical difficulties inherent in pursuing research relevant to such knowledge
    (C) a tendency on the part of most modern legal historians to rely too heavily on sources such as commentaries and treatises
    (D) the mistaken view that the field of women's legal history should be defined as the study of laws that apply only, or especially, to women
    (E) the relative scarcity of studies providing a comprehensive overview of women's legal history

In England before 1660, a husband controlled his wife's property. In the late seventeenth and eighteenth centuries, with the shift from land-based to commercial wealth, marriage began to incorporate certain features
(5) of a contract. Historians have traditionally argued that this trend represented a gain for women, one that reflects changing views about democracy and property following the English Restoration in 1660. Susan Staves contests this view; she argues that whatever
(10) gains marriage contracts may briefly have represented for women were undermined by judicial decisions about women's contractual rights.

Shifting through the tangled details of court cases, Staves demonstrates that, despite surface changes, a
(15) rhetoric of equality, and occasional decisions supporting women's financial power, definitions of men's and women's property remained inconsistent— generally to women's detriment. For example, dower lands (property inherited by wives after their husbands'
(20) deaths) could not be sold, but "curtesy" property (inherited by husbands from their wives) could be sold. Furthermore, comparatively new concepts that developed in conjunction with the marriage contract, such as jointure, pin money, and separate maintenance,
(25) were compromised by peculiar rules. For instance, if a woman spent her pin money (money paid by the husband according to the marriage contract for the wife's personal items) on possessions other than clothes she could not sell them; in effect they belonged
(30) to her husband. In addition, a wife could sue for pin money only up to a year in arrears-which rendered a suit impractical. Similarly, separate maintenance allowances (stated sums of money for the wife's support if husband and wife agreed to live apart) were
(35) complicated by the fact that if a couple tried to agree in a marriage contract on an amount, they were admitting that a supposedly indissoluble bond could be dissolved, an assumption courts could not recognize. Eighteenth-century historians underplayed these inconsistencies,
(40) calling them "little contrarieties" that would soon vanish. Staves shows, however, that as judges gained power over decisions on marriage contracts, they tended to fall back on pre-1660 assumptions about property.

(45) Staves' work on women's property has general implications for other studies about women in eighteenth-century England. Staves revises her previous claim that separate maintenance allowances proved the weakening of patriarchy; she now finds that
(50) an oversimplification. She also challenges the contention by historians Jeanne and Lawrence Stone that in the late eighteenth century wealthy men married widows less often than before because couples began marrying for love rather than for financial reasons.
(55) Staves does not completely undermine their contention, but she does counter their assumption that widows had more money than never-married women. She points out that jointure property (a widow's lifetime use of an amount of money specified in the marriage contract)
(60) was often lost on remarriage.

35. Which one of the following best expresses the main idea of the passage?

(A) As notions of property and democracy changed in late seventeenth- and eighteenth-century England, marriage settlements began to incorporate contractual features designed to protect women's property rights.

(B) Traditional historians have incorrectly identified the contractual features that were incorporated into marriage contracts in late seventeenth- and eighteenth-century England.

(C) The incorporation of contractual features into marriage settlements in late seventeenth- and eighteenth-century England did not represent a significant gain for women.

(D) An examination of late seventeenth- and eighteenth-century English court cases indicates that most marriage settlements did not incorporate contractual features designed to protect women's property rights.

(E) Before marriage settlements incorporated contractual features protecting women's property rights, women were unable to gain any financial power in England.

36. Which one of the following best describes the function of the last paragraph in the context of the passage as a whole?

(A) It suggests that Staves' recent work has caused significant revision of theories about the rights of women in eighteenth-century England.

(B) It discusses research that may qualify Staves' work on women's property in eighteenth-century England.

(C) It provides further support for Staves' argument by describing more recent research on women's property in eighteenth-century England.

(D) It asserts that Staves' recent work has provided support for two other hypotheses developed by historians of eighteenth-century England.

(E) It suggests the implications Staves' recent research has for other theories about women in eighteenth-century England.

Source: PrepTest 26, Section 4, Passage 4, Questions 22–27

37. The primary purpose of the passage is to

    (A) compare two explanations for the same phenomenon
    (B) summarize research that refutes an argument
    (C) resolve a long-standing controversy
    (D) suggest that a recent hypothesis should be reevaluated
    (E) provide support for a traditional theory

38. According to the passage, Staves' research has which one of the following effects on the Stones' contention about marriage in late eighteenth-century England?

    (A) Staves' research undermines one of the Stones' assumptions but does not effectively invalidate their contention.
    (B) Staves' research refutes the Stones' contention by providing additional data overlooked by the Stones.
    (C) Staves' research shows that the Stones' contention cannot be correct, and that a number of their assumptions are mistaken.
    (D) Staves' research indicates that the Stones' contention is incorrect because it is based on contradictory data.
    (E) Staves' research qualifies the Stones' contention by indicating that it is based on accurate but incomplete data.

39. According to the passage, Staves indicates that which one of the following was true of judicial decisions on contractual rights?

    (A) Judges frequently misunderstood and misapplied laws regarding married women's property.
    (B) Judges were aware of inconsistencies in laws concerning women's contractual rights but claimed that such inconsistencies would soon vanish.
    (C) Judges' decisions about marriage contracts tended to reflect assumptions about property that had been common before 1660.
    (D) Judges had little influence on the development and application of laws concerning married women's property.
    (E) Judges recognized the patriarchal assumptions underlying laws concerning married women's property and tried to interpret the laws in ways that would protect women.

40. The passage suggests that the historians mentioned in line 5 would be most likely to agree with which one of the following statements?

    (A) The shift from land-based to commercial wealth changed views about property but did not significantly benefit married women until the late eighteenth century.
    (B) Despite initial judicial resistance to women's contractual rights, marriage contracts represented a significant gain for married women.
    (C) Although marriage contracts incorporated a series of surface changes and a rhetoric of equality, they did not ultimately benefit married women.
    (D) Changing views about property and democracy in post-Restoration England had an effect on property laws that was beneficial to women.
    (E) Although contractual rights protecting women's property represented a small gain for married women, most laws continued to be more beneficial for men than for women.

In recent years, scholars have begun to use social science tools to analyze court opinions. These scholars have justifiably criticized traditional legal research for its focus on a few cases that may not be representative
(5) and its fascination with arcane matters that do not affect real people with real legal problems. Zirkel and Schoenfeld, for example, have championed the application of social science tools to the analysis of case law surrounding discrimination against women in
(10) higher education employment. Their studies have demonstrated how these social science tools may be used to serve the interests of scholars, lawyers, and prospective plaintiffs as well. However, their enthusiasm for the "outcomes analysis" technique
(15) seems misguided.

Of fundamental concern is the outcomes analysts' assumption that simply counting the number of successful and unsuccessful plaintiffs will be useful to prospective plaintiffs. Although the odds are clearly
(20) against the plaintiff in sex discrimination cases, plaintiffs who believe that their cause is just and that they will prevail are not swayed by such evidence. In addition, because lawsuits are so different in the details of the case, in the quality of the evidence the plaintiff
(25) presents, and in the attitude of the judge toward academic plaintiffs, giving prospective plaintiffs statistics about overall outcomes without analyzing the reason for these outcomes is of marginal assistance. Outcomes analysis, for example, ignores the fact that
(30) in certain academic sex discrimination cases—those involving serious procedural violations or incriminating evidence in the form of written admissions of discriminatory practices—plaintiffs are much more likely to prevail.

(35) Two different approaches offer more useful applications of social science tools in analyzing sex discrimination cases. One is a process called "policy capturing," in which the researcher reads each opinion; identifies variables discussed in the opinion, such as
(40) the regularity of employer evaluations of the plaintiff's performance, training of evaluators, and the kind of evaluation instrument used; and then uses multivariate analysis to determine whether these variables predict the outcome of the lawsuit. The advantage of policy-
(45) capturing research is that it attempts to explain the reason for the outcome, rather than simply reporting the outcome, and identifies factors that contribute to a plaintiff's success or failure. Taking a slightly different approach, other scholars have adopted a technique that
(50) requires reading complete transcripts of all sex discrimination cases litigated during a certain time period to identify variables such as the nature of the allegedly illegal conduct, the consequences for employers, and the nature of the remedy, as well as the
(55) factors that contributed to the verdict and the kind of evidence necessary for the plaintiff to prevail. While the findings of these studies are limited to the period covered, they assist potential plaintiffs and defendants in assessing their cases.

41. Which one of the following best expresses the main idea of the passage?

(A)   The analysis of a limited number of atypical discrimination suits is of little value to potential plaintiffs.

(B)   When the number of factors analyzed in a sex discrimination suit is increased, the validity of the conclusions drawn becomes suspect.

(C)   Scholars who are critical of traditional legal research frequently offer alternative approaches that are also seriously flawed.

(D)   Outcomes analysis has less predictive value in sex discrimination cases than do certain other social science techniques.

(E)   Given adequate information, it is possible to predict with considerable certainty whether a plaintiff will be successful in a discrimination suit.

42. It can be inferred from the author's discussion of traditional legal research that the author is

(A)   frustrated because traditional legal research has not achieved its full potential

(B)   critical because traditional legal research has little relevance to those actually involved in cases

(C)   appreciative of the role traditional legal research played in developing later, more efficient approaches

(D)   derisive because traditional legal research has outlasted its previously significant role

(E)   grateful for the ability of traditional legal research to develop unique types of evidence

Source: PrepTest 24, Section 1, Passage 3, Questions 14–20

43. Which one of the following statements about Zirkel and Schoenfeld can be inferred from the passage?

(A) They were the first scholars to use social science tools in analyzing legal cases.

(B) They confined their studies to the outcomes analysis technique.

(C) They saw no value in the analysis provided by traditional legal research.

(D) They rejected policy capturing as being too limited in scope.

(E) They believed that the information generated by outcomes analysis would be relevant for plaintiffs.

44. The author's characterization of traditional legal research in the first paragraph is intended to

(A) provide background information for the subsequent discussion

(B) summarize an opponent's position

(C) argue against the use of social science tools in the analysis of sex discrimination cases

(D) emphasize the fact that legal researchers act to the detriment of potential plaintiffs

(E) reconcile traditional legal researchers to the use of social science tools

45. The information in the passage suggests that plaintiffs who pursue sex discrimination cases despite the statistics provided by outcomes analysis can best be likened to

(A) athletes who continue to employ training techniques despite their knowledge of statistical evidence indicating that these techniques are unlikely to be effective

(B) lawyers who handle lawsuits for a large number of clients in the hope that some percentage will be successful

(C) candidates for public office who are more interested in making a political statement than in winning an election

(D) supporters of a cause who recruit individuals sympathetic to it in the belief that large numbers of supporters will lend the cause legitimacy

(D) purchasers of a charity's raffle tickets who consider the purchase a contribution because the likelihood of winning is remote

46. The policy-capturing approach differs from the approach described in lines 48–59 in that the latter approach

(A) makes use of detailed information on a greater number of cases

(B) focuses more directly on issues of concern to litigants

(C) analyzes information that is more recent and therefore reflects current trends

(D) allows assessment of aspects of a case that are not specifically mentioned in a judge's opinion

(E) eliminates any distortion due to personal bias on the part of the researcher

47. Which one of the following best describes the organization of the passage?

(A) A technique is introduced, its shortcomings are summarized, and alternatives are described.

(B) A debate is introduced, evidence is presented, and a compromise is reached.

(C) A theory is presented, clarification is provided, and a plan of further evaluation is suggested.

(D) Standards are established, hypothetical examples are analyzed, and the criteria are amended.

(E) A position is challenged, its shortcomings are categorized, and the challenge is revised.

In recent years, a growing belief that the way society decides what to treat as true is controlled through largely unrecognized discursive practices has led legal reformers to examine the complex
(5) interconnections between narrative and law. In many legal systems, legal judgments are based on competing stories about events. Without having witnessed these events, judges and juries must validate some stories as true and reject others as false. This procedure is rooted
(10) in objectivism, a philosophical approach that has supported most Western legal and intellectual systems for centuries. Objectivism holds that there is a single neutral description of each event that is unskewed by any particular point of view and that has a privileged
(15) position over all other accounts. The law's quest for truth, therefore, consists of locating this objective description, the one that tells what really happened, as opposed to what those involved thought happened. The serious flaw in objectivism is that there is no such thing
(20) as the neutral, objective observer. As psychologists have demonstrated, all observers bring to a situation a set of expectations, values, and beliefs that determine what the observers are able to see and hear. Two individuals listening to the same story will hear
(25) different things, because they emphasize those aspects that accord with their learned experiences and ignore those aspects that are dissonant with their view of the world. Hence there is never any escape in life or in law from selective perception, or from subjective
(30) judgments based on prior experiences, values, and beliefs.

The societal harm caused by the assumption of objectivist principles in traditional legal discourse is that, historically, the stories judged to be objectively
(35) true are those told by people who are trained in legal discourse, while the stories of those who are not fluent in the language of the law are rejected as false.

Legal scholars such as Patricia Williams, Derrick Bell, and Mari Matsuda have sought empowerment for
(40) the latter group of people through the construction of alternative legal narratives. Objectivist legal discourse systematically disallows the language of emotion and experience by focusing on cognition in its narrowest sense. These legal reformers propose replacing such
(45) abstract discourse with powerful personal stories. They argue that the absorbing, nonthreatening structure and tone of personal stories may convince legal insiders for the first time to listen to those not fluent in legal language. The compelling force of personal narrative
(50) can create a sense of empathy between legal insiders and people traditionally excluded from legal discourse and, hence, from power. Such alternative narratives can shatter the complacency of the legal establishment and disturb its tranquility. Thus, the engaging power of
(55) narrative might play a crucial, positive role in the process of legal reconstruction by overcoming differences in background and training and forming a new collectivity based on emotional empathy.

48. Which one of the following best states the main idea of the passage?

(A) Some legal scholars have sought to empower people historically excluded from traditional legal discourse by instructing them in the forms of discourse favored by legal insiders.

(B) Some legal scholars have begun to realize the social harm caused by the adversarial atmosphere that has pervaded many legal systems for centuries.

(C) Some legal scholars have proposed alleviating the harm caused by the prominence of objectivist principles within legal discourse by replacing that discourse with alternative forms of legal narrative.

(D) Some legal scholars have contended that those who feel excluded from objectivist legal systems would be empowered by the construction of a new legal language that better reflected objectivist principles.

(E) Some legal scholars have argued that the basic flaw inherent in objectivist theory can be remedied by recognizing that it is not possible to obtain a single neutral description of a particular event.

49. According to the passage, which one of the following is true about the intellectual systems mentioned in line 11?

(A) They have long assumed the possibility of a neutral depiction of events.

(B) They have generally remained unskewed by particular points of view.

(C) Their discursive practices have yet to be analyzed by legal scholars.

(D) They accord a privileged position to the language of emotion and experience.

(E) The accuracy of their basic tenets has been confirmed by psychologists.

50. Which one of the following best describes the sense of "cognition" referred to in line 43 of the passage?

(A) logical thinking uninfluenced by passion
(B) the interpretation of visual cues
(C) human thought that encompasses all emotion and experience
(D) the reasoning actually employed by judges to arrive at legal judgments
(E) sudden insights inspired by the power of personal stories

Source: PrepTest 22, Section 1, Passage 2, Questions 9–16

KAPLAN

51. It can be inferred from the passage that Williams' Bell, and Matsuda believe which one of the following to be a central component of legal reform?

E X

(A) incorporating into the law the latest developments in the fields of psychology and philosophy

(B) eradicating from legal judgments discourse with a particular point of view

(C) granting all participants in legal proceedings equal access to training in the forms and manipulation of legal discourse

(D) making the law more responsive to the discursive practices of a wider variety of people

(E) instilling an appreciation of legal history and methodology in all the participants in a legal proceeding

52. Which one of the following most accurately describes the author's attitude toward proposals to introduce personal stories into legal discourse?

E X

(A) strongly opposed
(B) somewhat skeptical
(C) ambivalent
(D) strongly supportive
(E) unreservedly optimistic

53. The passage suggests that Williams, Bell, and Matsuda would most likely agree with which one of the following statements regarding personal stories?

E X

(A) Personal stories are more likely to adhere to the principles of objectivism than are other forms of discourse.

(B) Personal stories are more likely to de-emphasize differences in background and training than are traditional forms of legal discourse.

(C) Personal stories are more likely to restore tranquility to the legal establishment than are more adversarial forms of discourse.

(D) Personal stories are more likely to lead to the accurate reconstruction of facts than are traditional forms of legal narrative.

(E) Personal stories are more likely to be influenced by a person's expectations, values, and beliefs than are other forms of discourse.

54. Which one of the following statements about legal discourse in legal systems based on objectivism can be inferred from the passage?

E X

(A) In most Western societies' the legal establishment controls access to training in legal discourse.

(B) Expertise in legal discourse affords power in most Western societies.

(C) Legal discourse has become progressively more abstract for some centuries.

(D) Legal discourse has traditionally denied the existence of neutral, objective observers.

(E) Traditional legal discourse seeks to reconcile dissonant world views.

55. Those who reject objectivism would regard "the law's quest for truth"(lines 15–16) as most similar to which one of the following?

E X

(A) a hunt for an imaginary animal
(B) the search for a valuable mineral among worthless stones
(C) the painstaking assembly of a jigsaw puzzle
(D) comparing an apple with an orange
(E) the scientific analysis of a chemical compound

What is "law"? By what processes do judges arrive at opinions, those documents that justify their belief that the "law" dictates a conclusion one way or the other? These are among the oldest questions in
(5) jurisprudence, debate about which has traditionally been dominated by representatives of two schools of thought: proponents of natural law, who see law as intertwined with a moral order independent of society's rules and mores, and legal positivists, who see law
(10) solely as embodying the commands of a society's ruling authority.

Since the early 1970s, these familiar questions have received some new and surprising answers in the legal academy. This novelty is in part a consequence of the
(15) increasing influence there of academic disciplines and intellectual traditions previously unconnected with the study of law. Perhaps the most influential have been the answers given by the Law and Economics school. According to these legal economists, law consists and
(20) ought to consist of those rules that maximize a society's material wealth and that abet the efficient operation of markets designed to generate wealth. More controversial have been the various answers provided by members of the Critical Legal Studies movement,
(25) according to whom law is one among several cultural mechanisms by which holders of power seek to legitimate their domination. Drawing on related arguments developed in anthropology, sociology, and history, the critical legal scholars contend that law is an
(30) expression of power, but not, as held by the positivists, the power of the legitimate sovereign government. Rather, it is an expression of the power of elites who may have no legitimate authority, but who are intent on preserving the privileges of their race, class, or gender.
(35) In the mid-1970s, James Boyd White began to articulate yet another interdisciplinary response to the traditional questions, and in so doing spawned what is now known as the Law and Literature movement. White has insisted that law, particularly as it is
(40) interpreted in judicial opinions, should be understood as an essentially literary activity. Judicial opinions should be read and evaluated not primarily as political acts or as attempts to maximize society's wealth through efficient rules, but rather as artistic
(45) performances. And like all such performances, White argues, each judicial opinion attempts in its own way to promote a particular political or ethical value.

In the recent *Justice as Translation*, White argues that opinion-writing should be regarded as an act of
(50) "translation," and judges as "translators." As such, judges find themselves mediating between the authoritative legal text and the pressing legal problem that demands resolution. A judge must essentially "re-constitute" that text by fashioning a new one, which
(55) is faithful to the old text but also responsive to and informed by the conditions, constraints, and aspirations of the world in which the new legal problem has arisen.

56. Which one of the following best states the main idea of the passage?

(A) Within the last few decades, a number of novel approaches to jurisprudence have defined the nature of the law in diverse ways.

(B) Within the last few decades, changes in society and in the number and type of cases brought to court have necessitated new methods of interpreting the law.

(C) Of the many interdisciplinary approaches to jurisprudence that have surfaced in the last two decades, the Law and Literature movement is the most intellectually coherent.

(D) The Law and Literature movement, first articulated by James Boyd White in the mid-1970s, represents a synthesis of the many theories of jurisprudence inspired by the social sciences.

(E) Such traditional legal scholars as legal positivists and natural lawyers are increasingly on the defensive against attacks from younger, more progressive theorists.

57. According to the passage, judicial opinions have been described as each of the following EXCEPT:

(A) political statements
(B) arcane statements
(C) economic statements
(D) artistic performances
(E) acts of translation

Source: PrepTest 21, Section 4, Passage 2, Questions 9–16

58. Which one of the following statements is most compatible with the principles of the Critical Legal Studies movement as that movement is described in the passage?

   (A) Laws governing the succession of power at the death of a head of state represent a synthesis of legal precedents, specific situations, and the values of lawmakers.

   (B) Laws allowing income tax deductions for charitable contributions, though ostensibly passed by lawmakers, were devised by and are perpetuated by the rich.

   (C) Laws governing the tariffs placed on imported goods must favor the continuation of mutually beneficial trade arrangements, even at the expense of long-standing legal precedent.

   (D) Laws governing the treatment of the disadvantaged and powerless members of a given society are an accurate indication of that society's moral state.

   (E) Laws controlling the electoral processes of a representative democracy have been devised by lawmakers to ensure the continuation of that governmental system.

59. Which one of the following does the passage mention as a similarity between the Critical Legal Studies movement and the Law and Literature movement?

   (A) Both offer explanations of how elites maintain their hold on power.

   (B) Both are logical extensions of either natural law or legal positivism.

   (C) Both see economic and political primacy as the basis of all legitimate power.

   (D) Both rely on disciplines not traditionally connected with the study of law.

   (E) Both see the practice of opinion-writing as a mediating activity.

60. Which one of the following can be inferred from the passage about the academic study of jurisprudence before the 1970s?

   (A) It was concerned primarily with codifying and maintaining the privileges of elites.

   (B) It rejected theories that interpreted law as an expression of a group's power.

   (C) It seldom focused on how and by what authority judges arrived at opinions.

   (D) It was concerned primarily with the study of law as an economic and moral agent.

   (E) It was not concerned with such disciplines as anthropology and sociology.

61. Proponents of the Law and Literature movement would most likely agree with which one of the following statements concerning the relationship between the law and judges' written opinions?

   (A) The once-stable relationship between law and opinion-writing has been undermined by new and radical theoretical developments.

   (B) Only the most politically conservative of judges continue to base their opinions on natural law or on legal positivism.

   (C) The occurrence of different legal situations requires a judge to adopt diverse theoretical approaches to opinion-writing.

   (D) Different judges will not necessarily write the same sorts of opinions when confronted with the same legal situation.

   (E) Judges who subscribe to divergent theories of jurisprudence will necessarily render divergent opinions.

62. Which one of the following phrases best describes the meaning of "re-constitute" as that word is used in line 54 of the passage?

   (A) categorize and rephrase
   (B) investigate and summarize
   (C) interpret and refashion
   (D) paraphrase and announce
   (E) negotiate and synthesize

63. The primary purpose of the passage is to

   (A) identify differing approaches
   (B) discount a novel trend
   (C) advocate traditional methods
   (D) correct misinterpretations
   (E) reconcile seeming inconsistencies

Historians of medieval marriage practices ascribe particular significance to Pope Alexander III's twelfth-century synthesis of existing ecclesiastical and legal opinion concerning marriage. Alexander produced a
(5) doctrine that treated marriage as a consensual union rather than as an arrangement made by parents for reasons of economic expediency: under Alexandrine doctrine, a couple could establish marriage by words of mutual consent and without the consent of parents.
(10) These contracts were of two kinds. On the one hand, a binding and immediately effective union was created through the exchange of words of present consent (*per verba de praesenti*). Neither the prior announcement of the intention to wed nor the solemnization conferred by
(15) Church ritual added anything to the validity and permanence of such a contract. On the other hand, a promise to marry was expressed by words of future consent (*per verba de futuro*); such a contract might be terminated by the agreement of the parties or by a
(20) subsequent *de praesenti* contract.

Although Alexandrine doctrine accepted the secular legal validity of those contracts that lacked public announcement and ritual solemnization, it nonetheless attempted to discourage such clandestine
(25) unions and to regulate marriage procedures. According to the doctrine, a marriage was to be preceded by the publication of the marriage announcements, or banns, on three successive Sundays to allow community members to raise any legal objections to the intended
(30) union. Those couples ignoring this requirement were to be excommunicated, and any priest solemnizing an unpublicized union could be suspended for up to three years. However, the essential secular legal validity of the marriage was in no way impaired.
(35) The presence or absence of the banns became the acid test to determine whether a contract was considered clandestine. Consequently, the very term "clandestine" came to cover a multitude of sins. It could apply just as much to the publicly solemnized
(40) marriage that violated Church law with regard to the time and place of the banns as it could to the informal *de praesenti* contract.

Historian Charles Donahue has stressed the controversial nature of Alexander's view that the
(45) consent of the individuals concerned was sufficient to produce a legally binding marriage; so long as they acted in accordance with established bann procedures, a couple could marry without parental consent and still enjoy the blessing of the Church. Furthermore,
(50) Donahue suggests that Alexandrine doctrine can be seen as encouraging marriage as a spiritual union rather than a merely pragmatic arrangement: marriages of love were to be promoted at the expense of those of economic convenience, and the Church was made the
(55) guardian of individual freedom in this area. This interpretation is indeed a radical one, given traditional perceptions of the medieval Church as the most potent authoritarian force in a rigidly hierarchical society.

64. Which one of the following best states the main idea of the message?

(A) The doctrine of marriage by Pope Alexander III represented a synthesis of traditional ecclesiastical and legal opinion and, according to at least one commentator, encouraged clandestine marriages.

(B) The doctrine of marriage promulgated by Pope Alexander III was based on the mutual consent of the persons involved and, according to at least one commentator, encouraged marriages based on love.

(C) Though ostensibly intended to promote marriages based on love rather than on expediency, the doctrine of marriage promulgated by Pope Alexander III in fact represented a tightening of Church authority.

(D) The spoken marriage contracts legitimized by Pope Alexander III were of two kinds: words of present consent and words of future consent.

(E) According to at least one interpretation, the doctrine of marriage promulgated by Pope Alexander III stated that couples who married without ritual solemnization were to be excommunicated from the Church.

65. Which one of the following can be inferred about the role of parents in medieval marriage practices?

(A) Parents were more likely to bow to the dictates of the Church than were their children.

(B) Parents were likely to favor the *de praesenti* rather than the *de futuro* contract.

(C) Parents were more concerned with the ecclesiastical sanction of a marriage than with its legal validity.

(D) Parents did not have the power, under Alexandrine doctrine, to prohibit a marriage based on the mutual consent of the couple rather than an economic expediency.

(E) Parents' concern over the prevalence of clandestine marriages helped bring about the Alexandrine synthesis.

Source: PrepTest A, Section 2, Passage 1, Questions 1–8

66. According to the passage, which one of the following placed couples at risk of being excommunicated under Alexandrine doctrine?

    (A) violation of laws requiring ritual solemnization of vows
    (B) violation of established banns procedures
    (C) marrying without parental consent
    (D) marrying without the blessing of a priest
    (E) replacing a *de futuro* contract with a *de praesenti* contract

67. Which one of the following best defines "clandestine" as that word is used in the second paragraph of the passage?

    (A) legal, but unrecognized by the Church
    (B) legal, but unrecognized by a couple's parents
    (C) recognized by the Church, but legally invalid
    (D) recognized by the Church, but arranged for reasons of economic expediency
    (E) arranged by *de futuro* contract, but subsequently terminated

68. The primary purpose of the passage is to

    (A) question the legitimacy of a scholarly work by examining the facts on which it is based
    (B) trace the influence of an important legal doctrine through several historical periods
    (C) call for a renewed commitment to research into a neglected field
    (D) summarize the history of an era and endorse a new scholarly approach to that era
    (E) explain a historically important doctrine and describe a controversial interpretation of that doctrine

69. Which one of the following can be inferred from the passage concerning the differences between Charles Donahue's interpretation of medieval marriage practices and other interpretations?

    (A) Most other studies have deemphasized the importance of Pope Alexander III.
    (B) Most other studies have seen in Alexandrine doctrine the beginning of modern secular marriage laws.
    (C) Most other studies have not emphasized the medieval Church's promotion of individual choice in marriage.
    (D) Most other studies have misread the complicated legal and ecclesiastical rituals involved in the public announcement and ritual solemnization of marriage.
    (E) Most other studies have concentrated on the ecclesiastical rather than the secular aspects of Alexandrine doctrine.

70. According to the passage, which one of the following distinguished the *de futuro* contract from the *de praesenti* contract?

    (A) One was recognized by Alexandrine doctrine, while the other was considered a secular contract.
    (B) One required the permission of parents, while the other concerned only the couple involved.
    (C) One required the announcement of marriage banns, while the other could be entered into solely through a verbal contract.
    (D) One expressed future intent, while the other established an immediate, binding union.
    (E) One allowed the solemnization of Church ritual, while the other resulted in excommunication.

71. Which one of the following best describes the function of the second paragraph of the passage?

    (A) It presents an interpretation of facts that diverges from the interpretation given in the first paragraph.
    (B) It identifies an exception to a rule explained in the first paragraph.
    (C) It elaborates upon information presented in the first paragraph by presenting additional information.
    (D) It summarizes traditional interpretations of a topic, then introduces a new interpretation.
    (E) It states the objections of the author of the passage to the argument presented in the first paragraph.

Legal cases can be termed "hard" cases if they raise issues that are highly controversial, issues about which people with legal training disagree. The ongoing debate over the completeness of the
(5) law usually concerns the extent to which such hard cases are legally determinate, or decidable according to existing law.

H. L. A. Hart's *The Concept of Law* is still the clearest and most persuasive statement of both the
(10) standard theory of hard cases and the standard theory of law on which it rests. For Hart, the law consists of legal rules formulated in general terms; these terms he calls "open textured," which means that they contain a "core" of settled meaning and a
(15) "penumbra" or "periphery" where their meaning is not determinate. For example, suppose an ordinance prohibits the use of vehicles in a park. "Vehicle" has a core of meaning which includes cars and motorcycles. But, Hart claims, other
(20) vehicles, such as bicycles, fall within the peripheral meaning of "vehicle," so that the law does not establish whether they are prohibited. There will always be cases not covered by the core meaning of legal terms within existing laws; Hart considers
(25) these cases to be legally indeterminate. Since courts cannot decide such cases on legal grounds, they must consider nonlegal (for example, moral and political) grounds, and thereby exercise judicial discretion to make, rather than apply, law.
(30) In Ronald Dworkin's view the law is richer than Hart would grant; he denies that the law consists solely of explicit rules. The law also includes principles that do not depend for their legal status on any prior official recognition or enactment.
(35) Dworkin claims that many cases illustrate the existence of legal principles that are different from legal rules and that Hart's "model of rules" cannot accommodate. For Dworkin, legal rules apply in an all-or-nothing fashion, whereas legal principles do
(40) not: they provide the rationale for applying legal rules. Thus, because Dworkin thinks there is law in addition to legal rules, he thinks that legal indeterminacy and the need for judicial discretion do not follow from the existence of open texture in
(45) legal rules.

It would be a mistake, though, to dispute Hart's theory of hard cases on this basis alone. If Hart's claim about the "open texture" of general terms is true, then we should expect to find legal
(50) indeterminacies even if the law consists of principles in addition to rules. Legal principles, as well as legal rules, contain general terms that have open texture. And it would be absurd to suppose that wherever the meaning of a legal rule is unclear,
(55) there is a legal principle with a clear meaning. Most interesting and controversial cases will occur in the penumbra of both rules and principles.

72. Which one of the following best expresses the main idea of the passage?

A D V

(A) The law will never be complete because new situations will always arise which will require new laws to resolve them.

(B) The most difficult legal cases are those concerning controversial issues about which trained legal minds have differing opinions.

(C) The concept of legal principles does not diminish the usefulness of the concept of the open texture of general terms in deciding whether hard cases are legally determinate.

(D) The concept of legal principles is a deleterious addition to the theory of law since any flaws exhibited by legal rules could also be shared by legal principles.

(E) The inherent inconsistency of terms used in laws provides a continuing opportunity for judges to exercise their discretion to correct defects and gaps in the law.

73. According to the passage, the term "legal principles" as used by Dworkin refers to

A D V

(A) a comprehensive code of ethics that governs the behavior of professionals in the legal system

(B) explicit analyses of the terms used in legal rules, indicating what meanings the terms do and do not cover

(C) legal doctrines that underlie and guide the use of accepted legal rules

(D) legal rules that have not yet passed through the entire legislative procedure necessary for them to become law

(E) the body of legal decisions regarding cases that required judicial discretion for their resolution

Source: PrepTest 17, Section 4, Passage 2, Questions 9–15

74. Which one of the following expresses a view that the author of the passage would most probably hold concerning legal principles and legal rules?

    (A)   Legal rules are applied more often than legal principles when a case involves issues about which legal professionals disagree.

    (B)   Both legal rules and legal principles are officially recognized as valid parts of the law.

    (C)   Hart's "model of rules" has been superseded by a "model of principles" that sheds light on legal determinacy.

    (D)   Legal principles are just as likely as legal rules to have terms that have both core and peripheral meanings.

    (E)   Legal principles eliminate the need for judicial discretion in resolving the problems generated by the open texture of legal rules.

75. In the passage, the author uses the example of the word "vehicle" to

    (A)   illustrate a legal rule that necessarily has exceptions

    (B)   show how legal principles are applied in the construction of legal rules

    (C)   represent the core of settled meaning of a legal term

    (D)   serve as an example of a legal term with both a core and a periphery of meaning

    (E)   provide a counterexample to Hart's concept of the open texture of legal terms

76. It can be inferred that the author of the passage regards Hart's theory of hard cases and the theory of standard law as

    (A)   exhaustive

    (B)   worthy of respect

    (C)   interesting but impractical

    (D)   plausible but unwieldy

    (E)   hopelessly outmoded

77. Which one of the following is true of the term "legally determinate" (line 6) as it is used in the passage?

    (A)   It represents the idea that every crime should have a fixed penalty rather than a range of penalties within which a judge can make an arbitrary choice.

    (B)   It refers to a legal case that can be definitively resolved in favor of one side or the other according to the law in effect at the time.

    (C)   It describes a legal rule that requires judges to limit their actions to applying written law when deciding cases over which people with legal training disagree.

    (D)   It refers to any legal case that involves terms with imprecise meanings and thus relies for its resolution only on the determination of judges.

    (E)   It refers to procedures for determining the legal outcome of complex issues in difficult cases.

78. In the passage, the author is primarily concerned with

    (A)   outlining the problems that might be faced by a legislature attempting to create a complete body of law that would prevent judges from making rather than applying the law

    (B)   justifying the idea that "hard" cases will always exist in the practice of law, no matter what laws are written or how they are applied

    (C)   presenting evidence to support Dworkin's idea that legal rules apply in an all-or-nothing fashion, whereas legal principles apply in more sophisticated ways

    (D)   critiquing the concept of the open texture of legal terms as a conceptual flaw in Hart's otherwise well-regarded book

    (E)   demonstrating that Dworkin's concept of legal principles does not form the basis for a successful attack on Hart's theory of legally indeterminate cases

The English who in the seventeenth and eighteenth centuries inhabited those colonies that would later become the United States shared a common political vocabulary with the English in
(5) England. Steeped as they were in the English political language, these colonials failed to observe that their experience in America had given the words a significance quite different from that accepted by the English with whom they debated;
(10) in fact, they claimed that they were more loyal to the English political tradition than were the English in England.

In many respects the political institutions of England were reproduced in these American
(15) colonies. By the middle of the eighteenth century, all of these colonies except four were headed by Royal Governors appointed by the King and perceived as bearing a relation to the people of the colony similar to that of the King to the English
(20) people. Moreover, each of these colonies enjoyed a representative assembly, which was consciously modeled, in powers and practices, after the English Parliament. In both England and these colonies, only property holders could vote.

(25) Nevertheless, though English and colonial institutions were structurally similar, attitudes toward those institutions differed. For example, English legal development from the early seventeenth century had been moving steadily
(30) toward the absolute power of Parliament. The most unmistakable sign of this tendency was the legal assertion that the King was subject to the law. Together with this resolute denial of the absolute right of kings went the assertion that Parliament
(35) was unlimited in its power: it could change even the Constitution by its ordinary acts of legislation. By the eighteenth century the English had accepted the idea that the parliamentary representatives of the people were omnipotent.

(40) The citizens of these colonies did not look upon the English Parliament with such fond eyes, nor did they concede that their own assemblies possessed such wide powers. There were good historical reasons for this. To the English the word
(45) "constitution" meant the whole body of law and legal custom formulated since the beginning of the kingdom, whereas to these colonials a constitution was a specific written document, enumerating specific powers. This distinction in meaning can be
(50) traced to the fact that the foundations of government in the various colonies were written charters granted by the Crown. These express authorizations to govern were tangible, definite things. Over the years these colonials had often repaired to the charters to
(55) justify themselves in the struggle against tyrannical governors or officials of the Crown. More than a century of government under written constitutions convinced these colonists of the necessity for and efficacy of protecting their liberties against
(60) governmental encroachment by explicitly defining all governmental powers in a document.

79. Which one of the following best expresses the main idea of the passage?

EX ADV

(A) The colonials and the English mistakenly thought that they shared a common political vocabulary.

(B) The colonials and the English shared a variety of institutions.

(C) The colonials and the English had conflicting interpretations of the language and institutional structures that they shared.

(D) Colonial attitudes toward English institutions grew increasingly hostile in the eighteenth century.

(E) Seventeenth-century English legal development accounted for colonial attitudes toward constitutions.

80. The passage supports all of the following statements about the political conditions present by the middle of the eighteenth century in the American colonies discussed in the passage EXCEPT:

EX ADV

(A) Colonials who did not own property could not vote.

(B) All of these colonies had representative assemblies modeled after the British Parliament.

(C) Some of these colonies had Royal Governors.

(D) Royal Governors could be removed from office by colonial assemblies.

(E) In these colonies, Royal Governors were regarded as serving a function like that of a king.

Source: PrepTest 9, Section 1, Passage 4, Questions 21–27

KAPLAN

81. The passage implies which one of the following about English kings prior to the early seventeenth century?

    EX ADV

    (A)   They were the source of all law.
    (B)   They frequently flouted laws made by Parliament.
    (C)   Their power relative to that of Parliament was considerably greater than it was in the eighteenth century.
    (D)   They were more often the sources of legal reform than they were in the eighteenth century.
    (E)   They had to combat those who believed that the power of Parliament was absolute.

82. The author mentions which one of the following as evidence for the eighteenth-century English attitude toward Parliament?

    EX ADV

    (A)   The English had become uncomfortable with institutions that could claim absolute authority.
    (B)   The English realized that their interests were better guarded by Parliament than by the King.
    (C)   The English allowed Parliament to make constitutional changes by legislative enactment.
    (D)   The English felt that the King did not possess the knowledge that would enable him to rule responsibly.
    (E)   The English had decided that it was time to reform their representative government.

83. The passage implies that the colonials discussed in the passage would have considered which one of the following to be a source of their debates with England?

    EX ADV

    (A)   their changed use of the English political vocabulary
    (B)   English commitment to parliamentary representation
    (C)   their uniquely English experience
    (D)   their refusal to adopt any English political institutions
    (E)   their greater loyalty to the English political traditions

84. According to the passage, the English attitude toward the English Constitution differed from the colonial attitude toward constitutions in that the English regarded their Constitution as

    EX ADV

    (A)   the legal foundation of the kingdom
    (B)   a document containing a collection of customs
    (C)   a cumulative corpus of legislation and legal traditions
    (D)   a record alterable by royal authority
    (E)   an unchangeable body of governmental powers

85. The primary purpose of the passage is to

    EX ADV

    (A)   expose the misunderstanding that has characterized descriptions of the relationship between seventeenth- and eighteenth-century England and certain of its American colonies
    (B)   suggest a reason for England's treatment of certain of its American colonies in the seventeenth and eighteenth centuries
    (C)   settle an ongoing debate about the relationship between England and certain of its American colonies in the seventeenth and eighteenth centuries
    (D)   interpret the events leading up to the independence of certain of England's American colonies in the eighteenth century
    (E)   explain an aspect of the relationship between England and certain of its American colonies in the seventeenth and eighteenth centuries

By the time Bentham turned his interest to the subject, late in the eighteenth century, most components of modern evidence law had been assembled. Among common-law doctrines regarding
(5) evidence there were, however, principles that today are regarded as bizarre; thus, a well-established (but now abandoned) rule forbade the parties to a case from testifying. Well into the nineteenth century, even defendants in criminal cases were denied the right to
(10) testify to facts that would prove their innocence.

Although extreme in its irrationality, this proscription was in other respects quite typical of the law of evidence. Much of that law consisted of rules excluding relevant evidence, usually on some rational
(15) grounds. Hearsay evidence was generally excluded because absent persons could not be cross-examined. Yet such evidence was mechanically excluded even where out-of-court statements were both relevant and reliable, but the absent persons could not appear in
(20) court (for example, because they were dead).

The morass of evidentiary technicalities often made it unlikely that the truth would emerge in a judicial contest, no matter how expensive and protracted. Reform was frustrated both by the vested interests of
(25) lawyers and by the profession's reverence for tradition and precedent. Bentham's prescription was revolutionary: virtually all evidence tending to prove or disprove the issue in dispute should be admissible. Narrow exceptions were envisioned: instances in
(30) which the trouble or expense of presenting or considering proof outweighed its value, confessions to a Catholic priest, and a few other instances.

One difficulty with Bentham's nonexclusion principle is that some kinds of evidence are inherently
(35) unreliable or misleading. Such was the argument underlying the exclusions of interested-party testimony and hearsay evidence. Bentham argued that the character of evidence should be weighed by the jury: the alternative was to prefer ignorance to knowledge.
(40) Yet some evidence, although relevant, is actually more likely to produce a false jury verdict than a true one. To use a modern example, evidence of a defendant's past bank robberies is excluded, since the prejudicial character of the evidence substantially outweighs its
(45) value in helping the jury decide correctly. Further, in granting exclusions such as sacramental confessions, Bentham conceded that competing social interests or values might override the desire for relevant evidence. But then, why not protect conversations between social
(50) workers and their clients, or parents and children?

Despite concerns such as these, the approach underlying modern evidence law began to prevail soon after Bentham's death: relevant evidence should be admitted unless there are clear grounds of policy for
(55) excluding it. This clear-grounds proviso allows more exclusions than Bentham would have liked, but the main thrust of the current outlook is Bentham's own nonexclusion principle, demoted from a rule to a presumption.

86. Which one of the following is the main idea of the passage?

(A) Bentham questioned the expediency of modern rules of legal evidence.
(B) Bentham's proposed reform of rules of evidence was imperfect but beneficial.
(C) Bentham's nonexclusion principle should be reexamined in the light of subsequent developments.
(D) Rules of legal evidence inevitably entail imperfect mediations of conflicting values and constraints.
(E) Despite their impairment of judicial efficiency, rules of legal evidence are resistant to change.

87. The author's attitude toward eighteenth-century lawyers can best be described as

(A) sympathetic
(B) critical
(C) respectful
(D) scornful
(E) ambivalent

88. The author mentions "conversations between social workers and their clients" (lines 49–50) most probably in order to

(A) suggest a situation in which application of the nonexclusion principle may be questionable
(B) cite an example of objections that were raised to Bentham's proposed reform
(C) illustrate the conflict between competing social interests
(D) demonstrate the difference between social interests and social values
(E) emphasize that Bentham's exceptions to the nonexclusion principle covered a wide range of situations

Source: PrepTest 33, Section 2, Passage 4, Questions 23–28

89. Which one of the following statements concerning
    the history of the law of evidence is supported by
    information in the passage?

    (A) Common-law rules of evidence have been
         replaced by modern principles.
    (B) Modern evidence law is less rigid than was
         eighteenth-century evidence law.
    (C) Some current laws regarding evidence do not
         derive from common-law doctrines.
    (D) The late eighteenth century marked the beginning
         of evidence law.
    (E) Prior to the eighteenth century, rules of evidence
         were not based on common law.

90. The passage is primarily concerned with which one of
    the following?

    (A) suggesting the advantages and limitations of a
         legal reform
    (B) summarizing certain deficiencies of an outmoded
         legal system
    (C) justifying the apparent inadequacies of current
         evidence law
    (D) detailing objections to the nonexclusion principle
    (E) advocating reexamination of a proposal that has
         been dismissed by the legal profession

91. According to the fourth paragraph of the passage, what
    specifically does Bentham characterize as preference of
    ignorance to knowledge?

    (A) uncritical acceptance of legal conventions
    (B) failure to weigh the advantages of legal reform
    (C) exclusion of sacramental confessions
    (D) refusal to allow the jury to hear and assess
         relevant testimony
    (E) rejection of exceptions to Bentham's
         nonexclusion principle

By the mid-fourteenth century, professional associations of canon lawyers (legal advocates in Christian ecclesiastical courts, which dealt with cases involving marriage, inheritance, and other issues) had
(5) appeared in most of Western Europe, and a body of professional standards had been defined for them. One might expect that the professional associations would play a prominent role in enforcing these standards of conduct, as other guilds often did, and as modern
(10) professional associations do, but that seems not to have happened. Advocates' professional organizations showed little fervor for disciplining their erring members. Some even attempted to hobble efforts at enforcement. The Florentine guild of lawyers, for
(15) example, forbade its members to play any role in disciplinary proceedings against other guild members. In the few recorded episodes of disciplinary enforcement, the initiative for disciplinary action apparently came from a dissatisfied client, not from
(20) fellow lawyers.

At first glance, there seem to be two possible explanations for the rarity of disciplinary proceedings. Medieval canon lawyers may have generally observed the standards of professional conduct scrupulously.
(25) Alternatively, it is possible that deviations from the established standards of behavior were not uncommon, but that canonical disciplinary mechanisms were so inefficient that most delinquents escaped detection and punishment.
(30) Two considerations make it clear that the second of these explanations is more plausible. First, the English civil law courts, whose ethical standards were similar to those of ecclesiastical courts, show many more examples of disciplinary actions against legal
(35) practitioners than do the records of church courts. This discrepancy could well indicate that the disciplinary mechanisms of the civil courts functioned more efficiently than those of the church courts. The alternative inference, namely, that ecclesiastical
(40) advocates were less prone to ethical lapses than their counterparts in the civil courts, seems inherently weak, especially since there was some overlap of personnel between the civil bar and the ecclesiastical bar.

Second, church authorities themselves complained
(45) about the failure of advocates to measure up to ethical standards and deplored the shortcomings of the disciplinary system. Thus the Council of Basel declared that canon lawyers failed to adhere to the ethical prescriptions laid down in numerous papal
(50) constitutions and directed Cardinal Cesarin to address the problem. In England, where medieval church records are extraordinarily rich, similar complaints about the failure of the disciplinary system to reform unethical practices were very common.
(55) Such criticisms seem to have had a paradoxical result, for they apparently reinforced the professional solidarity of lawyers at the expense of the enforcement of ethical standards. Thus the profession's critics may actually have induced advocates to organize
(60) professional associations for self-defense. The critics' attacks may also have persuaded lawyers to assign a

higher priority to defending themselves against attacks by nonprofessionals than to disciplining wayward members within their own ranks.

92. Which one of the following best states the main conclusion of the passage?

(A) Professional organizations of medieval canon lawyers probably only enforced ethical standards among their own members when provoked to do so by outside criticisms.

(B) Professional organizations of medieval civil lawyers seem to have maintained stricter ethical standards for their own members than did professional organizations of medieval canon lawyers.

(C) Professional organizations of medieval canon lawyers apparently served to defend their members against critics' attacks rather than to enforce ethical standards.

(D) The ethical standards maintained by professional associations of medieval canon lawyers were chiefly laid down in papal constitutions.

(E) Ethical standards for medieval canon lawyers were not laid down until professional organizations for these lawyers had been formed.

93. According to the passage, which one of the following statements about law courts in medieval England is true?

(A) Some English lawyers who practiced in civil courts also practiced in church courts, but others served exclusively in one court or the other.

(B) English canon lawyers were more likely to initiate disciplinary proceedings against their colleagues than were English civil lawyers.

(C) English civil lawyers maintained more stringent ethical standards than did civil lawyers in the rest of Europe.

(D) English ecclesiastical courts had originally been modeled upon English civil courts.

(E) English ecclesiastical courts kept richer and more thorough records than did English civil courts.

Source: PrepTest 20, Section 2, Passage 2, Questions 7–14

94. The author refers to the Florentine guild of lawyers in the first paragraph most probably in order to

(A) introduce a theory about to be promoted
(B) illustrate the type of action referred to in the previous sentence
(C) underline the universality of a method discussed throughout the paragraph
(D) point out a flaw in an argument presented earlier in the paragraph
(E) rebut an anticipated objection to a thesis just proposed

95. The author refers to the Council of Basel (line 47) primarily in order to

(A) provide an example of the type of action needed to establish professional standards for canon lawyers
(B) contrast the reactions of English church authorities with the reactions of other bodies to violations of professional standards by canon lawyers
(C) bolster the argument that violations of professional standards by canon lawyers did take place
(D) explain how rules of conduct for canon lawyers were established
(E) describe the development of a disciplinary system to enforce professional standards among canon lawyers

96. According to the information in the passage, for which one of the following ethical violations would documentation of disciplinary action against a canon lawyer be most likely to exist?

(A) betraying a client's secrets to the opposing party
(B) bribing the judge to rule in favor of a client
(C) misrepresenting credentials in order to gain admission to the lawyers' guild
(D) spreading rumors in order to discredit an opposing lawyer
(E) knowingly helping a client to misrepresent the truth

97. Which one of the following is most analogous to the "professional solidarity" referred to in lines 56–57?

(A) Members of a teachers' union go on strike when they believe one of their colleagues to be falsely accused of using an inappropriate textbook.
(B) In order to protect the reputation of the press in the face of a largely hostile public, a journalist conceals distortions in a colleague's news article.
(C) Several dozen recording artists agree to participate in a concert to benefit an endangered environmental habitat.
(D) In order to expedite governmental approval of a drug, a government official is persuaded to look the other way when a pharmaceutical manufacturer conceals evidence that the drug may have minor side effects.
(E) A popular politician agrees to campaign for another, less popular politician belonging to the same political party.

98. The passage suggests that which one of the following is most likely to have been true of medieval guilds?

(A) Few guilds of any importance existed before the mid-fourteenth century.
(B) Many medieval guilds exercised influence over the actions of their members.
(C) Most medieval guilds maintained more exacting ethical standards than did the associations of canon lawyers.
(D) Medieval guilds found it difficult to enforce discipline among their members.
(E) The ethical standards of medieval guilds varied from one city to another.

99. The author would be most likely to agree with which one of the following regarding the hypothesis that medieval canon lawyers observed standards of professional conduct scrupulously?

(A) It is untrue because it is contradicted by documents obtained from the ecclesiastical courts
(B) It is unlikely because it describes behavior markedly different from behavior observed in the same situation in modern society.
(C) It is unlikely because it describes behavior markedly different from behavior observed in a similar area of medieval society.
(D) It is impossible to assess intelligently because of the dearth of civil and ecclesiastical documents.
(E) It is directly supported by documents obtained from civil and ecclesiastical courts.

Natural Sciences Passages

Directions: Each passage in this section is followed by a group of questions to be answered on the basis of what is <u>stated</u> or <u>implied</u> in the passage. For some of the questions, more than one of the choices could conceivably answer the question. However, you are to choose the <u>best</u> answer; that is, the response that most accurately and completely answers the question.

To many developers of technologies that affect public health or the environment, "risk communication" means persuading the public that the potential risks of such technologies are small and (5) should be ignored. Those who communicate risks in this way seem to believe that lay people do not understand the actual nature of technological risk, and they can cite studies asserting that, although people apparently ignore mundane hazards that pose (10) significant danger, they get upset about exotic hazards that pose little chance of death or injury. Because some risk communicators take this persuasive stance, many lay people see "risk communication" as a euphemism for brainwashing done by experts.

(15)   Since, however, the goal of risk communication should be to enable people to make informed decisions about technological risks, a clear understanding about how the public perceives risk is needed. Lay people's definitions of "risk" are more likely to reflect (20) subjective ethical concerns than are experts' definitions. Lay people, for example, tend to perceive a small risk to children as more significant than a larger risk to consenting adults who benefit from the risk-creating technology. However, if asked to rank hazards (25) by the number of annual fatalities, without reference to ethical judgments, lay people provide quite reasonable estimates, demonstrating that they have substantial knowledge about many risks. Although some studies claim to demonstrate that lay people have inappropriate (30) concerns about exotic hazards, these studies often use questionable methods, such as asking lay people to rank risks that are hard to compare. In contrast, a recent study showed that when lay people were given the necessary facts and time, they understood the specific (35) risks of electromagnetic fields produced by high-voltage power transmission well enough to make informed decisions.

Risk communication should therefore be based on the principle that people process new information in (40) the context of their existing beliefs. If people know nothing about a topic, they will find messages about that topic incomprehensible. If they have erroneous beliefs, they are likely to misconstrue the messages. Thus, communicators need to know the nature and (45) extent of recipients' knowledge and beliefs in order to design messages that will not be dismissed or misinterpreted. This need was demonstrated in a research project concerning the public's level of knowledge about risks posed by the presence of radon (50) in the home. Researchers used open-ended interviews and questionnaires to determine what information should be included in their brochure on radon. Subjects who read the researchers' brochure performed

significantly better in understanding radon risks than (55) did a control group who read a brochure that was written using a different approach by a government agency. Thus, careful preparation can help risk communicators to produce balanced material that tells people what they need to know to make decisions (60) about technological risks.

1. Which one of the following best expresses the main point of the passage?

   (A) Risk communicators are effectively addressing the proliferation of complex technologies that have increasing impact on public health and safety.
   (B) Risk communicators should assess lay people's understanding of technologies in order to be able to give them the information they need to make reasonable decisions.
   (C) Experts who want to communicate to the public about the possible risks of complex technologies must simplify their message to ensure that it is understandable.
   (D) Risk communication can be perceived as the task of persuading lay people to accept the impact of a particular technology on their lives.
   (E) Lay people can be unduly influenced by subjective concerns when making decisions about technological risks.

2. The authors of the passage would be most likely to agree that the primary purpose of risk communication should be to

   (A) explain rather than to persuade
   (B) promote rather than to justify
   (C) influence experts rather than to influence lay people
   (D) allay people's fears about mundane hazards rather than about exotic hazards
   (E) foster public acceptance of new technologies rather than to acknowledge people's ethical concerns

Source: PrepTest 24, Section 1, Passage 1, Questions 1–6

KAPLAN

3. According to the passage, it is probable that which one of the following will occur when risk communicators attempt to communicate with lay people who have mistaken ideas about a particular technology?

    (A) The lay people, perceiving that the risk communicators have provided more-reliable information, will discard their mistaken notions.
    (B) The lay people will only partially revise their ideas on the basis of the new information.
    (C) The lay people, fitting the new information into their existing framework, will interpret the communication differently than the risk communicators had intended.
    (D) The lay people, misunderstanding the new information, will further distort the information when they communicate it to other lay people.
    (E) The lay people will ignore any communication about a technology they consider potentially dangerous.

4. Which one of the following is most clearly an example of the kind of risk perception discussed in the "studies" mentioned in line 8?

    (A) A skydiver checks the lines on her parachute several times before a jump because tangled lines often keep the parachutes from opening properly.
    (B) A person decides to quit smoking in order to lessen the probability of lung damage to himself and his family.
    (C) A homemaker who decides to have her house tested for radon also decides not to allow anyone to smoke in her house.
    (D) A person who often weaves in and out of traffic while driving his car at excessive speeds worries about meteorites hitting his house.
    (E) A group of townspeople opposes the building of a nuclear waste dump outside their town and proposes that the dump be placed in another town.

5. It can be inferred that the authors of the passage would be more likely than would the risk communicators discussed in the first paragraph to emphasis which one of the following?

    (A) lay people's tendency to become alarmed about technologies that they find new or strange
    (B) lay people's tendency to compare risks that experts would not consider comparable
    (C) the need for lay people to adopt scientists' advice about technological risk
    (D) the inability of lay people to rank hazards by the number of fatalities caused annually
    (E) the impact of lay people's value systems on their perceptions of risk

6. According to the passage, many lay people believe which one of the following about risk communication?

    (A) It focuses excessively on mundane hazards.
    (B) It is a tool used to manipulate the public.
    (C) It is a major cause of inaccuracies in public knowledge about science.
    (D) It most often functions to help people make informal decisions.
    (E) Its level of effectiveness depends on the level of knowledge its audience already has.

★

Spurred by the discovery that a substance containing uranium emitted radiation, Marie Curie began studying radioactivity in 1897. She first tested gold and copper for radiation but found none. She then
(5) tested pitchblende, a mineral that was known to contain uranium, and discovered that it was more radioactive than uranium. Acting on the hypothesis that pitchblende must contain at least one other radioactive element, Curie was able to isolate a pair of
(10) previously unknown elements, polonium and radium. Turning her attention to the rate of radioactive emission, she discovered that uranium emitted radiation at a consistent rate, even if heated or dissolved. Based on these results, Curie concluded that
(15) the emission rate for a given element was constant. Furthermore, because radiation appeared to be spontaneous, with no discernible difference between radiating and nonradiating elements, she was unable to postulate a mechanism by which to explain radiation.
(20)   It is now known that radiation occurs when certain isotopes (atoms of the same element that differ slightly in their atomic structure) decay, and that emission rates are not constant but decrease very slowly with time. Some critics have recently faulted Curie for not
(25) reaching these conclusions herself, but it would have been impossible for Curie to do so given the evidence available to her. While relatively light elements such as gold and copper occasionally have unstable (i.e., radioactive) isotopes, radioactive isotopes of most of
(30) these elements are not available in nature because they have largely finished decaying and so have become stable. Conversely, heavier elements such as uranium, which decay into lighter elements in a process that takes billions of years, are present in nature exclusively
(35) in radioactive form.
      Furthermore, we must recall that in Curie's time the nature of the atom itself was still being debated. Physicists believed that matter could not be divided indefinitely but instead would eventually be reduced to
(40) its indivisible components. Chemists, on the other hand, observing that chemical reactions took place as if matter was composed of atomlike particles, used the atom as a foundation for conceptualizing and describing such reactions—but they were not
(45) ultimately concerned with the question of whether or not such indivisible atoms actually existed.
      As a physicist, Curie conjectured that radiating substances might lose mass in the form of atoms, but this idea is very different from the explanation
(50) eventually arrived at. It was not until the 1930s that advances in quantum mechanics overthrew the earlier understanding of the atom and showed that radiation occurs because the atoms themselves lose mass—a hypothesis that Curie, committed to the indivisible
(55) atom, could not be expected to have conceived of. Moreover, not only is Curie's inability to identify the mechanism by which radiation occurs understandable, it is also important to recognize that it was Curie's investigation of radiation that paved the way for the
(60) later breakthroughs.

7. Which one of the following most accurately states the central idea of the passage?

   (A) It is unlikely that quantum mechanics would have been developed without the theoretical contributions of Marie Curie toward an understanding of the nature of radioactivity.

   (B) Although later shown to be incomplete and partially inaccurate, Marie Curie's investigations provided a significant step forward on the road to the eventual explanation of radioactivity.

   (C) Though the scientific achievements of Marie Curie were impressive in scope, her career is blemished by her failure to determine the mechanism of radioactivity.

   (D) The commitment of Marie Curie and other physicists of her time to the physicists' model of the atom prevented them from conducting fruitful investigations into radioactivity.

   (E) Although today's theories have shown it to be inconclusive, Marie Curie's research into the sources and nature of radioactivity helped refute the chemists' model of the atom.

Source: PrepTest 37, Section 1, Passage 2, Questions 8–13

8. The passage suggests that the author would be most likely to agree with which one of the following statements about the contemporary critics of Curie's studies of radioactivity?

   (A) The critics fail to take into account the obstacles Curie faced in dealing with the scientific community of her time.

   (B) The critics do not appreciate that the eventual development of quantum mechanics depended on Curie's conjecture that radiating substances can lose atoms.

   (C) The critics are unaware of the differing conceptions of the atom held by physicists and chemists.

   (D) The critics fail to appreciate the importance of the historical context in which Curie's scientific conclusions were reached.

   (E) The critics do not comprehend the intricate reasoning that Curie used in discovering polonium and radium.

9. The passage implies which one of the following with regard to the time at which Curie began studying radioactivity?

   (A) Pitchblende was not known by scientists to contain any radioactive element besides uranium.

   (B) Radioactivity was suspected by scientists to arise from the overall structure of pitchblende rather than from particular elements in it.

   (C) Physicists and chemists had developed rival theories regarding the cause of radiation.

   (D) Research was not being conducted in connection with the question of whether or not matter is composed of atoms.

   (E) The majority of physicists believed uranium to be the sole source or radioactivity.

10. The author's primary purpose in the passage is to

    (A) summarize some aspects of one scientist's work and defend it against recent criticism

    (B) describe a scientific dispute and argue for the correctness of an earlier theory

    (C) outline a currently accepted scientific theory and analyze the evidence that led to its acceptance

    (D) explain the mechanism by which a natural phenomenon occurs and summarize the debate that gave rise to this explanation

    (E) discover the antecedents of a scientific theory and argue that the theory is not a genuine advance over its forerunners

11. The primary function of the first paragraph of the passage is to

    (A) narrate the progress of turn-of-the-century studies of radioactivity

    (B) present a context for the conflict between physicists and chemists

    (C) provide the factual background for an evaluation of Curie's work

    (D) outline the structure of the author's central argument

    (E) identify the error in Curie's work that undermines its usefulness

12. Which one of the following most accurately expresses the meaning of the word "mechanism" as used by the author in the last sentence of the first paragraph?

    (A) the physical process that underlies a phenomenon

    (B) the experimental apparatus in which a phenomenon arises

    (C) the procedure scientists use to bring about the occurrence of a phenomenon

    (D) the isotopes of an element needed to produce a phenomenon

    (E) the scientific theory describing a phenomenon

Experts anticipate that global atmospheric concentrations of carbon dioxide (CO_2) will have doubled by the end of the twenty-first century. It is known that CO_2 can contribute to global warming by
(5) trapping solar energy that is being reradiated as heat from the Earth's surface. However, some research has suggested that elevated CO_2 levels could enhance the photosynthetic rates of plants, resulting in a lush world of agricultural abundance, and that this CO_2
(10) fertilization effect might eventually decrease the rate of global warming. The increased vegetation in such an environment could be counted on to draw more CO_2 from the atmosphere. The level of CO_2 would thus increase at a lower rate than many experts have
(15) predicted.

However, while a number of recent studies confirm that plant growth would be generally enhanced in an atmosphere rich in CO_2, they also suggest that increased CO_2 would differentially increase the growth
(20) rate of different species of plants, which could eventually result in decreased agricultural yields. Certain important crops such as corn and sugarcane that currently have higher photosynthetic efficiencies than other plants may lose that edge in an atmosphere
(25) rich in CO_2. Patterson and Flint have shown that these important crops may experience yield reductions because of the increased performance of certain weeds. Such differences in growth rates between plant species could also alter ecosystem stability. Studies have
(30) shown that within rangeland regions, for example, a weedy grass grows much better with plentiful CO_2 than do three other grasses. Because this weedy grass predisposes land to burning, its potential increase may lead to greater numbers of and more severe wildfires in
(35) future rangeland communities.

It is clear that the CO_2 fertilization effect does not guarantee the lush world of agricultural abundance that once seemed likely, but what about the potential for the increased uptake of CO_2 to decrease the rate of global
(40) warming? Some studies suggest that the changes accompanying global warming will not improve the ability of terrestrial ecosystems to absorb CO_2. Billings' simulation of global warming conditions in wet tundra grasslands showed that the level of CO_2
(45) actually increased. Plant growth did increase under these conditions because of warmer temperatures and increased CO_2 levels. But as the permafrost melted, more peat (accumulated dead plant material) began to decompose. This process in turn liberated more CO_2 to
(50) the atmosphere. Billings estimated that if summer temperatures rose four degrees Celsius, the tundra would liberate 50 percent more CO_2 than it does currently. In a warmer world, increased plant growth, which could absorb CO_2 from the atmosphere, would
(55) not compensate for this rapid increase in decomposition rates. This observation is particularly important because high-latitude habitats such as the tundra are expected to experience the greatest temperature increase.

13. Which one of the following best states the main point of the passage?

(A) Elevated levels of CO_2 would enhance photosynthetic rates, thus increasing plant growth and agricultural yields.
(B) Recent studies have yielded contradictory findings about the benefits of increased levels of CO_2 on agricultural productivity.
(C) The possible beneficial effects of increased levels of CO_2 on plant growth and global warming have been overstated.
(D) Increased levels of CO_2 would enhance the growth rates of certain plants, but would inhibit the growth rates of other plants.
(E) Increased levels of CO_2 would increase plant growth, but the rate of global warming would ultimately increase.

14. The passage suggests that the hypothesis mentioned in the first paragraph is not entirely accurate because it fails to take into account which one of the following in predicting the effects of increased vegetation on the rate of global warming?

(A) Increased levels of CO_2 will increase the photosynthetic rates of many species of plants.
(B) Increased plant growth cannot compensate for increased rates of decomposition caused by warmer temperatures.
(C) Low-latitude habitats will experience the greatest increases in temperature in an atmosphere high in CO_2.
(D) Increased levels of CO_2 will change patterns of plant growth and thus will alter the distribution of peat.
(E) Increases in vegetation can be counted on to draw more CO_2 from the atmosphere.

15. Which one of the following best describes the function of the last paragraph of the passage?

(A) It presents research that may undermine a hypothesis presented in the first paragraph.
(B) It presents solutions for a problem discussed in the first and second paragraphs.
(C) It provides an additional explanation for a phenomenon described in the first paragraph.
(D) It provides experimental data in support of a theory described in the preceding paragraph.
(E) It raises a question that may cast doubt on information presented in the preceding paragraph.

Source: PrepTest 33, Section 2, Passage 3, Questions 15–22

16. The passage suggests that Patterson and Flint would be most likely to agree with which one of the following statements about increased levels of CO_2 in the Earth's atmosphere?

(A) They will not increase the growth rates of most species of plants.

(B) They will inhibit the growth of most crops, thus causing substantial decreases in agricultural yields.

(C) They are unlikely to increase the growth rates of plants with lower photosynthetic efficiencies.

(D) They will increase the growth rates of certain species of plants more than the growth rates of other species of plants.

(E) They will not affect the photosynthetic rates of plants that currently have the highest photosynthetic efficiencies.

17. The author would be most likely to agree with which one of the following statements about the conclusions drawn on the basis of the research on plant growth mentioned in the first paragraph of the passage?

(A) The conclusions are correct in suggesting that increased levels of CO_2 will increase the photosynthetic rates of certain plants.

(B) The conclusions are correct in suggesting that increased levels of CO_2 will guarantee abundances of certain important crops.

(C) The conclusions are correct in suggesting that increased plant growth will reverse the process of global warming.

(D) The conclusions are incorrect in suggesting that enhanced plant growth could lead to abundances of certain species of plants.

(E) The conclusions are incorrect in suggesting that vegetation can draw CO_2 from the atmosphere.

18. The passage supports which one of the following statements about peat in wet tundra grasslands?

(A) More of it would decompose if temperatures rose four degrees Celsius.

(B) It could help absorb CO_2 from the atmosphere if temperatures rose four degrees Celsius.

(C) It will not decompose unless temperatures rise four degrees Celsius.

(D) It decomposes more quickly than peat found in regions at lower latitudes.

(E) More of it accumulates in regions at lower latitudes.

19. Which one of the following, if true, is LEAST consistent with the hypothesis mentioned in lines 22–25 of the passage?

(A) The roots of a certain tree species grow more rapidly when the amount of CO_2 in the atmosphere increases, thus permitting the trees to expand into habitats formerly dominated by grasses with high photosynthetic efficiencies.

(B) When grown in an atmosphere high in CO_2, certain weeds with low photosynthetic efficiencies begin to thrive in cultivated farmlands formerly dominated by agricultural crops.

(C) When trees of a species with a high photosynthetic efficiency and grasses of a species with a low photosynthetic efficiency were placed in an atmosphere high in CO_2, the trees grew more quickly than the grasses.

(D) When two different species of grass with equivalent photosynthetic efficiency were placed in an atmosphere high in CO_2, one species grew much more rapidly and crowded the slower-growing species out the growing area.

(E) The number of leguminous plants decreased in an atmosphere rich in CO_2, thus diminishing soil fertility and limiting the types of plant species that could thrive in certain habitats.

20. According to the passage, Billings' research addresses which one of the following questions?

(A) Which kind of habitat will experience the greatest temperature increase in an atmosphere high in CO_2?

(B) How much will summer temperatures rise if levels of CO_2 double by the end of the twenty-first century?

(C) Will enhanced plant growth necessarily decrease the rate of global warming that has been predicted by experts?

(D) Would plant growth be differentially enhanced if atmospheric concentrations of CO_2 were to double by the end of the twenty-first century?

(E) Does peat decompose more rapidly in wet tundra grasslands than it does in other types of habitats when atmospheric concentrations of CO_2 increase?

Scientists have long known that the soft surface of the bill of the platypus is perforated with openings that contain sensitive nerve endings. Only recently, however, have biologists concluded on the basis of new
(5) evidence that the animal uses its bill to locate its prey while underwater, a conclusion suggested by the fact that the animal's eyes, ears, and nostrils are sealed when it is submerged. The new evidence comes from neurophysiological studies, which have recently
(10) revealed that within the pores on the bill there are two kinds of sensory receptors: mechanoreceptors, which are tiny pushrods that respond to tactile pressure, and electroreceptors, which respond to weak electrical fields. Having discovered that tactile stimulation of the
(15) pushrods sends nerve impulses to the brain, where they evoke an electric potential over an area of the neocortex much larger than the one stimulated by input from the limbs, eyes, and ears, Bohringer concluded that the bill must be the primary sensory organ for the
(20) platypus. Her finding was supported by studies showing that the bill is extraordinarily sensitive to tactile stimulation: stimulation with a fine glass stylus sent a signal by way of the fifth cranial nerve to the neocortex and from there to the motor cortex.
(25) Presumably nerve impulses from the motor cortex then induced a snapping movement of the bill. But Bohringer's investigations did not explain how the animal locates its prey at a distance.

Scheich's neurophysiological studies contribute to
(30) solving this mystery. His initial work showed that when a platypus feeds, it swims along steadily wagging its bill from side to side until prey is encountered. It thereupon switches to searching behavior, characterized by erratic movements of the
(35) bill over a small area at the bottom of a body of water, which is followed by homing in on the object and seizing it. In order to determine how the animal senses prey and then distinguishes it from other objects on the bottom, Scheich hypothesized that a sensory system
(40) based on electroreception similar to that found in sharks might exist in the platypus. In further experiments he found he could trigger the switch from patrolling to searching behavior in the platypus by creating a dipole electric field in the water with the aid
(45) of a small 1.5-volt battery. The platypus, sensitive to the weak electric current that was created, rapidly oriented toward the battery at a distance of 10 centimeters and sometimes as much as 30 centimeters. Once the battery was detected, the
(50) platypus would inevitably attack it as if it were food. Scheich then discovered that the tail flicks of freshwater shrimp, a common prey of the platypus, also produce weak electric fields and elicit an identical response. Scheich and his colleagues believe that it is
(55) reasonable to assume that all the invertebrates on which the platypus feeds must produce electric fields.

21. The primary purpose of the passage is to

(A) explain how the platypus locates prey at a distance

(B) present some recent scientific research on the function of the platypus's bill

(C) assess the results of Bohringer's experimental work about the platypus

(D) present Scheich's contributions to scientific work about the platypus

(E) describe two different kinds of pores on the platypus's bill

22. Which one of the following statements best expresses the main idea of the passage?

(A) Neurophysiological studies have established that the bill of the platypus is one of its primary sensory organs.

(B) Neurophysiological studies have established that the platypus uses its bill to locate its prey underwater.

(C) Bohringer's neurophysiological studies have established that sensory receptors in the bill of the platypus respond to electrical stimulation.

(D) Biologists have concluded that the surface of the bill of the platypus is perforated with openings that contain sensitive nerve endings.

(E) Biologists have concluded that the hunting platypus responds to weak electric fields emitted by freshwater invertebrates.

Source: PrepTest 29, Section 2, Passage 3, Questions 16–21

23. During the studies supporting Bohringer's finding, as they are described in the passage, which one of the following occurred before a nerve impulse reached the motor cortex of the platypus?

    (A) The electroreceptors sent the nerve impulse to the fifth cranial nerve.
    (B) The neocortex induced a snapping movement of the bill.
    (C) The mechanoreceptors sent the nerve impulse via the fifth cranial nerve to the electroreceptors.
    (D) The platypus opened the pores on its bill.
    (E) The fifth cranial nerve carried the nerve impulse to the neocortex.

24. Which one of the following strategies is most similar to Scheich's experimental strategy as it is described in the passage?

    (A) To determine the mating habits of birds, a biologist places decoys near the birds' nests that resemble the birds and emit bird calls.
    (B) To determine whether certain animals find their way by listening for echoes to their cries, a biologist plays a tape of the animals' cries in their vicinity.
    (C) To determine whether an animal uses heat sensitivity to detect prey, a biologist places a heat-generating object near the animal's home.
    (D) A fisherman catches fish by dangling in the water rubber replicas of the fishes' prey that have been scented with fish oil.
    (E) A game warden captures an animal by baiting a cage with a piece of meat that the animal will want to eat.

25. It can be inferred from the passage that during patrolling behavior, the platypus is attempting to

    (A) capture prey that it has detected
    (B) distinguish one kind of prey from another
    (C) detect electric fields produced by potential prey
    (D) stimulate its mechanoreceptors
    (E) pick up the scent of its prey

26. Which one of the following best describes the organization of the passage?

    (A) A hypothesis is presented and defended with supporting examples.
    (B) A conclusion is presented and the information supporting it is provided.
    (C) A thesis is presented and defended with an argument.
    (D) Opposing views are presented, discussed, and then reconciled.
    (E) A theory is proposed, considered, and then amended.

Long after the lava has cooled, the effects of a major volcanic eruption may linger on. In the atmosphere a veil of fine dust and sulfuric acid droplets can spread around the globe and persist for years.
(5) Researchers have generally thought that this veil can block enough sunlight to have a chilling influence on Earth's climate. Many blame the cataclysmic eruption of the Indonesian volcano Tambora in 1815 for the ensuing "year without a summer" of 1816—when parts
(10) of the northeastern United States and southeastern Canada were hit by snowstorms in June and frosts in August.

The volcano-climate connection seems plausible, but, say scientists Clifford Mass and Davit Portman, it
(15) is not as strong as previously believed. Mass and Portman analyzed global temperature data for the years before and after nine volcanic eruptions, from Krakatau in 1883 to El Chichón in 1982. In the process they tried to filter out temperature changes caused by the cyclic
(20) weather phenomenon known as the El Niño-Southern Oscillation, which warms the sea surface in the equatorial Pacific and thereby warms the atmosphere. Such warming can mask the cooling brought about by an eruption, but it can also mimic volcanic cooling if
(25) the volcano happens to erupt just as an El Niño-induced warm period is beginning to fade.

Once El Niño effects had been subtracted from the data, the actual effects of the eruptions came through more clearly. Contrary to what earlier studies had
(30) suggested, Mass and Portman found that minor eruptions have no discernible effect on temperature. And major, dust-spitting explosions, such as Krakatau or El Chichón, cause a smaller drop than expected in the average temperature in the hemisphere (Northern or
(35) Southern) of the eruption—only half a degree centigrade or less—a correspondingly smaller drop in the opposite hemisphere.

Other researchers, however, have argued that even a small temperature drop could result in a significant
(40) regional fluctuation in climate if its effects were amplified by climatic feedback loops. For example, a small temperature drop in the northeastern U.S. and southeastern Canada in early spring might delay the melting of snow, and the unmelted snow would
(45) continue to reflect sunlight away from the surface, amplifying the cooling. The cool air over the region could, in turn, affect the jet stream. The jet stream tends to flow at the boundary between cool northern air and warm southern air, drawing its power from the
(50) sharp temperature contrast and the consequent difference in pressure. An unusual cooling in the region could cause the stream to wander farther south than normal, allowing more polar air to come in behind it and deepen the region's cold snap. Through such a
(55) series of feedbacks a small temperature drop could be blown up into a year without a summer.

27. Which one of the following most accurately expresses the main idea of the passage?

(A) The effect of volcanic eruptions on regional temperature is greater than it was once thought to be.

(B) The effect of volcanic eruptions on regional temperature is smaller than the effect of volcanic eruptions on global temperature.

(C) The effect of volcanic eruptions on global temperature appears to be greater than was previously supposed.

(D) Volcanic eruptions appear not to have the significant effect on global temperature they were once thought to have but might have a significant effect on regional temperature.

(E) Researchers tended to overestimate the influence of volcanic eruptions on global temperature because they exaggerated the effect of cyclical weather phenomena in making their calculations.

28. Not taking the effects of El Niño into account when figuring the effect of volcanic eruptions on Earth's climate is most closely analogous to not taking into account the

(A) weight of a package as a whole when determining the weight of its contents apart from the packing material

(B) monetary value of the coins in a pile when counting the number of coins in the pile

(C) magnification of a lens when determining the shape of an object seen through the lens

(D) number of false crime reports in a city when figuring the average annual number of crimes committed in that city

(E) ages of new immigrants to a country before attributing a change in the average of the country's population to a change in the number of births

29. The passage indicates that each of the following can be an effect of the El Niño phenomenon EXCEPT:

(A) making the cooling effect of a volcanic eruption appear to be more pronounced than it actually is

(B) making the cooling effect of a volcanic eruption appear to be less pronounced than it actually is

(C) increasing atmospheric temperature through cyclic warming of equatorial waters

(D) initiating a feedback loop that masks cooling brought about by an eruption

(E) confounding the evidence for a volcano-climate connection

Source: PrepTest 28, Section 4, Passage 2, Questions 6–13

30. Which one of the following most accurately characterizes what the author of the passage means by a "minor" volcanic eruption (line 30)?

    (A) an eruption that produces less lava than either Krakatau or El Chichón did
    (B) an eruption that has less of an effect on global temperature than either Krakatau or El Chichón did
    (C) an eruption whose effect on regional temperature can be masked by conditions in the hemisphere of the eruption
    (D) an eruption that introduces a relatively small amount of debris into the atmosphere
    (E) an eruption that causes average temperature in the hemisphere of the eruption to drop by less than half a degree centigrade

31. To which one of the following situations would the concept of a feedback loop, as it is employed in the passage, be most accurately applied?

    (A) An increase in the amount of decaying matter in the soil increases the amount of nutrients in the soil, which increases the number of plants, which further increases the amount of decaying matter in the soil.
    (B) An increase in the number of wolves in an area decreases the number of deer, which decreases the grazing of shrubs, which increases the amount of food available for other animals, which increases the number of other animals in the area.
    (C) An increase in the amount of rain in an area increases the deterioration of the forest floor, which makes it harder for wolves to prey on deer, which increases the number of deer, which gives wolves more opportunities to prey upon deer.
    (D) An increase in the amount of sunlight on the ocean increases the ocean temperature, which increases the number of phytoplankton in the ocean, which decreases the ocean temperature by blocking sunlight.
    (E) As increase in the number of outdoor electric lights in an area increases the number of insects in the area, which increases the number of bats in the area, which decreases the number of insects in the area, which decreases the number of bats in the area.

32. The author of the passage would be most likely to agree with which one of the following hypotheses?

    (A) Major volcanic eruptions sometimes cause average temperature in the hemisphere of the eruption to drop by more than a degree centigrade.
    (B) Major volcanic eruptions can induce the El Niño phenomenon when it otherwise might not occur.
    (C) Major volcanic eruptions do not directly cause unusually cold summers.
    (D) The climatic effects of minor volcanic eruptions differ from those of major eruptions only in degree.
    (E) El Niño has no discernible effect on average hemispheric temperature.

33. The information in the passage provides the LEAST support for which one of the following claims?

    (A) Major volcanic eruptions have a discernible effect on global temperature.
    (B) The effect of major volcanic eruptions on global temperature is smaller than was previously thought.
    (C) Major volcanic eruptions have no discernible effect on regional temperature.
    (D) Minor volcanic eruptions have no discernible effect on temperature in the hemisphere in which they occur.
    (E) Minor volcanic eruptions have no discernible effect on temperature in the hemisphere opposite the hemisphere of the eruption.

34. The primary purpose of the last paragraph of the passage is to

    (A) describe how the "year without a summer" differs from other examples of climatic feedback loops
    (B) account for the relatively slight hemispheric cooling effect of a major volcanic eruption
    (C) explain how regional climatic conditions can be significantly affected by a small drop in temperature
    (D) indicate how researchers are sometimes led to overlook the effects of El Niño on regional temperature
    (E) suggest a modification to the current model of how feedback loops produce changes in regional temperature

Between June 1987 and May 1988, the bodies of at least 740 bottlenose dolphins out of a total coastal population of 3,000 to 5,000 washed ashore on the Atlantic coast of the United States. Since some of the
(5) dead animals never washed ashore, the overall disaster was presumably worse; perhaps 50 percent of the population died. A dolphin die-off of this character and magnitude had never before been observed; furthermore, the dolphins exhibited a startling range of
(10) symptoms. The research team that examined the die-off noted the presence of both skin lesions and internal lesions in the liver, lung, pancreas, and heart, which suggested a massive opportunistic bacterial infection of already weakened animals.

(15) Tissues from the stricken dolphins were analyzed for a variety of toxins. Brevetoxin, a toxin produced by the blooming of the alga *Ptychodiscus brevis*, was present in eight out of seventeen dolphins tested. Tests for synthetic pollutants revealed that polychlorinated
(20) biphenyls (PCBs) were present in almost all animals tested.

The research team concluded that brevetoxin poisoning was the most likely cause of the illnesses that killed the dolphins. Although *P. brevis* is
(25) ordinarily not found along the Atlantic coast, an unusual bloom of this organism—such blooms are called "red tides" because of the reddish color imparted by the blooming algae—did occur in the middle of the affected coastline in October 1987. These researchers
(30) believe the toxin accumulated in the tissue of fish and then was ingested by dolphins that preyed on them. The emaciated appearance of many dolphins indicated that they were metabolizing their blubber reserves, thereby reducing their buoyancy and insulation (and
(35) adding to overall stress) as well as releasing stores of previously accumulated synthetic pollutants, such as PCBs, which further exacerbated their condition. The combined impact made the dolphins vulnerable to opportunistic bacterial infection, the ultimate cause of
(40) death.

For several reasons, however, this explanation is not entirely plausible. First, bottlenose dolphins and *P. brevis* red tides are both common in the Gulf of Mexico, yet no dolphin die-off of a similar magnitude
(45) has been noted there. Second, dolphins began dying in June, hundreds of miles north of and some months earlier than the October red tide bloom. Finally, the specific effects of brevetoxin on dolphins are unknown, whereas PCB poisoning is known to impair functioning
(50) of the immune system and liver and to cause skin lesions; all of these problems were observed in the diseased animals. An alternative hypothesis, which accounts for these facts, is that a sudden influx of pollutants, perhaps from offshore dumping, triggered a
(55) cascade of disorders in animals whose systems were already heavily laden with pollutants. Although brevetoxin may have been a contributing factor, the event that actually precipitated the die-off was a sharp increase in the dolphins' exposure to synthetic
(60) pollutants.

35. The passage is primarily concerned with assessing

(A) the effects of a devastating bacterial infection in Atlantic coast bottlenose dolphins
(B) the process by which illnesses in Atlantic coast bottlenose dolphins were correctly diagnosed
(C) the weaknesses in the research methodology used to explore the dolphin die-off
(D) possible alternative explanations for the massive dolphin die-off
(E) relative effects of various marine pollutants on dolphin mortality

36. Which one of the following is mentioned in the passage as evidence for the explanation of the dolphin die-off offered in the final paragraph?

(A) the release of stored brevetoxins from the dolphins' blubber reserves
(B) the date on which offshore dumping was known to have occurred nearby
(C) the presence of dumping sites for PCBs in the area
(D) the synthetic pollutants that were present in the fish eaten by the dolphins
(E) the effects of PCBs on liver function in dolphins

37. Which one of the following is most analogous to the approach taken by the author of the passage with regard to the research described in the third paragraph?

(A) A physics teacher accepts the data from a student's experiment but questions the student's conclusions.
(B) An astronomer provides additional observations to support another astronomer's theory.
(C) A cook revises a traditional recipe by substituting modern ingredients for those used in the original.
(D) A doctor prescribes medication for a patient whose illness was misdiagnosed by another doctor.
(E) A microbiologist sets out to replicate the experiment that yielded a classic theory of cell structure.

Source: PrepTest 26, Section 4, Passage 3, Questions 14–21

38. Which one of the following most accurately describes the organization of the last paragraph?

    (A) One explanation is criticized and a different explanation is proposed.
    (B) An argument is advanced and then refuted by means of an opposing argument.
    (C) Objections against a hypothesis are advanced, the hypothesis is explained more fully, and then the objections are rejected.
    (D) New evidence in favor of a theory is described, and then the theory is reaffirmed.
    (E) Discrepancies between two explanations are noted, and a third explanation is proposed.

39. It can be inferred from the passage that the author would most probably agree with which one of the following statements about brevetoxin?

    (A) It may have been responsible for the dolphins' skin lesions but could not have contributed to the bacterial infection.
    (B) It forms more easily when both *P. brevis* and synthetic pollutants are present in the environment simultaneously.
    (C) It damages liver function and immune system responses in bottlenose dolphins but may not have triggered this particular dolphin die-off.
    (D) It is unlikely to be among the factors that contributed to the dolphin die-off.
    (E) It is unlikely to have caused the die-off because it was not present in the dolphins' environment when the die-off began.

40. The explanation for the dolphin die-off given by the research team most strongly supports which one of the following?

    (A) The biological mechanism by which brevetoxin affects dolphins is probably different from that by which it affects other marine animals.
    (B) When *P. brevis* blooms in an area where it does not usually exist, it is more toxic than it is in its usual habitat.
    (C) Opportunistic bacterial infection is usually associated with brevetoxin poisoning in bottlenose dolphins.
    (D) The dolphins' emaciated state was probably a symptom of PCB poisoning rather than of brevetoxin poisoning.
    (E) When a dolphin metabolizes its blubber, the PCBs released may be more dangerous to the dolphin than they were when stored in the blubber.

41. The author refers to dolphins in the Gulf of Mexico in the last paragraph in order to

    (A) refute the assertion that dolphins tend not to inhabit areas where *P. brevis* is common
    (B) compare the effects of synthetic pollutants on these dolphins and on Atlantic coast dolphins
    (C) cast doubt on the belief that *P. brevis* contributes substantially to dolphin die-offs
    (D) illustrate the fact that dolphins in relatively pollution-free waters are healthier than dolphins in polluted waters.
    (E) provide evidence for the argument that *P. brevis* was probably responsible for the dolphins' deaths

42. Which one of the following factors is explicitly cited as contributing to the dolphins' deaths in both theories discussed in the passage?

    (A) the dolphins diet
    (B) the presence of *P. brevis* in the Gulf of Mexico
    (C) the wide variety of toxins released by the red tide bloom of October 1987
    (D) the presence of synthetic pollutants in the dolphins' bodies
    (E) the bacterial infection caused by a generalized failure of the dolphins' immune systems

The debate over the environmental crisis is not new; anxiety about industry's impact on the environment has existed for over a century. What is new is the extreme polarization of views. Mounting
(5) evidence of humanity's capacity to damage the environment irreversibly coupled with suspicions that government, industry, and even science might be impotent to prevent environmental destruction have provoked accusatory polemics on the part of
(10) environmentalists. In turn, these polemics have elicited a corresponding backlash from industry. The sad effect of this polarization is that it is now even more difficult for industry than it was a hundred years ago to respond appropriately to impact analyses that demand action.

(15) Unlike today's adversaries, earlier ecological reformers shared with advocates of industrial growth a confidence in timely corrective action. George P. Marsh's pioneering conservation tract *Man and Nature* (1864) elicited wide acclaim without embittered
(20) denials. *Man and Nature* castigated Earth's despoilers for heedless greed, declaring that humanity "has brought the face of the Earth to a desolation almost as complete as that of the Moon." But no entrepreneur or industrialist sought to refute Marsh's accusation, to
(25) defend the gutting of forests or the slaughter of wildlife as economically essential, or to dismiss his ecological warnings as hysterical. To the contrary, they generally agreed with him.

Why? Marsh and his followers took environmental
(30) improvement and economic progress as givens; they disputed not the desirability of conquering nature but the bungling way in which the conquest was carried out. Blame was not personalized; Marsh denounced general greed rather than particular entrepreneurs, and
(35) the media did not hound malefactors. Further, corrective measures seemed to entail no sacrifice, to demand no draconian remedies. Self-interest underwrote most prescribed reforms. Marsh's emphasis on future stewardship was then a widely accepted ideal
(40) (if not practice). His ecological admonitions were in keeping with the Enlightenment premise that humanity's mission was to subdue and transform nature.

Not until the 1960s did a gloomier perspective gain
(45) popular ground. Frederic Clements' equilibrium model of ecology, developed in the 1930s seemed consistent with mounting environmental disasters. In this view, nature was most fruitful when least altered. Left undisturbed, flora and fauna gradually attained
(50) maximum diversity and stability. Despoliation thwarted the culmination or shortened the duration of this beneficent climax; technology did not improve nature but destroyed it.

The equilibrium model became an ecological
(55) mystique: environmental interference was now taboo, wilderness adored. Nature as unfinished fabric perfected by human ingenuity gave way to the image of nature debased and endangered by technology. In contrast to the Enlightenment vision of nature,

(60) according to which rational managers construct an ever more improved environment, twentieth-century reformers' vision of nature calls for a reduction of human interference in order to restore environmental stability.

43. Which one of the following most accurately states the main idea of the passage?

E X

(A) Mounting evidence of humanity's capacity to damage the environment should motivate action to prevent further damage.

(B) The ecological mystique identified with Frederic Clements has become a religious conviction among ecological reformers.

(C) George P. Marsh's ideas about conservation and stewardship have heavily influenced the present debate over the environment.

(D) The views of ecologists and industrial growth advocates concerning the environment have only recently become polarized.

(E) General greed, rather than particular individuals or industries should be blamed for the environmental crisis.

Source: PrepTest 23, Section 4, Passage 3, Questions 14–18

44. The author refers to the equilibrium model of ecology as an "ecological mystique" (lines 54–55) most likely in order to do which one of the following?

    EX

    (A) underscore the fervor with which twentieth-century reformers adhere to the equilibrium model

    (B) point out that the equilibrium model of ecology has recently been supported by empirical scientific research

    (C) express appreciation for how plants and animals attain maximum diversity and stability when left alone

    (D) indicate that the ideas of twentieth-century ecological reformers are often so theoretical as to be difficult to understand

    (E) indicate how widespread support is for the equilibrium model of ecology in the scientific community

45. Which one of the following practices is most clearly an application of Frederic Clements' equilibrium model of ecology?

    EX

    (A) introducing a species into an environment to which it is not native to help control the spread of another species that no longer has any natural predators

    (B) developing incentives for industries to take corrective measures to protect the environment

    (C) using scientific methods to increase the stability of plants and animals in areas where species are in danger of becoming extinct

    (D) using technology to develop plant and animal resources but balancing that development with stringent restrictions on technology

    (E) setting areas of land aside to be maintained as wilderness from which the use or extraction of natural resources is prohibited

46. The passage suggests that George P. Marsh and today's ecological reformers would be most likely to agree with which one of the following statements?

    EX

    (A) Regulating industries in order to protect the environment does not conflict with the self-interest of those industries.

    (B) Solving the environmental crisis does not require drastic and costly remedies.

    (C) Human despoliation of the Earth has caused widespread environmental damage.

    (D) Environmental improvement and economic progress are equally important goals.

    (E) Rather than blaming specific industries, general greed should be denounced as the cause of environmental destruction.

47. The passage is primarily concerned with which one of the following?

    EX

    (A) providing examples of possible solutions to a current crisis

    (B) explaining how conflicting viewpoints in a current debate are equally valid

    (C) determining which of two conflicting viewpoints in a current debate is more persuasive

    (D) outlining the background and development of conflicting viewpoints in a current debate

    (E) demonstrating weaknesses in the arguments made by one side in a current debate

Many birds that form flocks compete through aggressive interaction for priority of access to resources such as food and shelter. The result of repeated interactions between flock members is that
(5) each bird gains a particular social status related to its fighting ability, with priority of access to resources increasing with higher status. As the number and intensity of interactions between birds increase, however, so increase the costs to each birds in terms of
(10) energy expenditure, time, and risk of injury. Thus, birds possessing attributes that reduce the number of costly interactions in which they must be involved, without leading to a reduction in status, are at an advantage. An external signal, such as a plumage type,
(15) announcing fighting ability and thereby obviating the actual need to fight, could be one such attribute.

The zoologist Rohwer assented that plumage variations in "Harris sparrows" support the status signaling hypothesis (SSH). He reported that almost
(20) without exception birds with darker throats win conflicts with individuals having lighter plumage. He claimed that even among birds of the same age and sex the amount of dark plumage predicts relative dominance status.

(25) However, Rohwer's data do not support his assertions: in one of his studies darker birds won only 57 out of 75 conflicts; within another, focusing on conflicts between birds of the same age group or sex, darker birds won 63 and lost 62. There are indications
(30) that plumage probably does signal broad age-related differences in status among Harris sparrows: adults, usually dark throated, have higher status than juveniles, who are usually light throated; moreover, juveniles dyed to resemble adults are dominant over undyed
(35) juveniles. However, the Harris sparrows' age-related plumage differences do not signal the status of *individual* birds within an age class, and thus cannot properly be included under the term "status signaling."

The best evidence for status signaling is from the
(40) greater titmouse. Experiments show a strong correlation between the width of the black breast-plumage stripe and status as measured by success in aggressive interactions. An analysis of factors likely to be associated with breast-stripe width (sex, age, wing
(45) length, body weight) has demonstrated social status to be the only variable that correlates with stripe width when the other variables are held constant.

An ingenious experiment provided further evidence for status signaling in the greater titmouse. One of
(50) three stuffed titmouse dummies was mounted on a feeding tray. When a live bird approached, the dummy was turned by radio control to face the bird and present its breast stripe in "display." When presented with a dummy having a narrower breast stripe than their own,
(55) birds approached closely and behaved aggressively. However, when presented with a dummy having a broader breast stripe than their own, live birds acted submissive and did not approach.

48. According to the passage, the status signaling hypothesis holds that the ability to display a recognizable external signal would have the effect on an individual bird of

(A) enabling it to attract a mate of high status
(B) allowing it to avoid costly aggressive interactions
(C) decreasing its access to limited resources
(D) making it less attractive to predatory species
(E) increasing its fighting ability

49. The author refers to the fact that adult Harris sparrows are usually dark throated (lines 31–32), in order to do which one of the following?

(A) support the conclusion that plumage variation among Harris sparrows probably does not signal individual status
(B) argue that plumage variation among Harris sparrows helps to confirm the status signaling hypothesis
(C) indicate that in light of plumage variation patterns among Harris sparrows, the status signaling hypothesis should probably be modified
(D) demonstrate that Harris sparrows are the most appropriate subjects for the study of status signaling among birds
(E) suggest that the signaling of age-related differences in status is widespread among birds that form flocks

Source: PrepTest 20, Section 2, Passage 3, Questions 15–21

50. Which one of the following, if true, would most seriously undermine the validity of the results of the experiment discussed in the last paragraph?

    (A) The live birds all came from different titmouse flocks.
    (B) The physical characteristics of the stuffed dummies varied in ways other than just breast-stripe width.
    (C) No live juvenile birds were included in the experiment.
    (D) The food placed in the feeding tray was not the kind of food normally eaten by titmice in the wild.
    (E) Even the live birds that acted aggressively did not actually physically attack the stuffed dummies.

51. Which one of the following best describes the organization of the passage?

    (A) A hypothesis is introduced and studies relevant to the hypothesis are discussed and evaluated.
    (B) A natural phenomenon is presented and several explanations for the phenomenon are examined in detail.
    (C) Behavior is described, possible underlying causes for the behavior are reported and the likelihood of each cause is assessed.
    (D) A scientific conundrum is explained and the history of the issue is recounted.
    (E) A scientific theory is outlined and opinions for and against its validity as well as experiments supporting each side are compared.

52. According to the passage, which one of the following is true of Rohwer's relationship to the status signaling hypothesis (SSH)?

    (A) Although his research was designed to test the SSH, his data proved to be more relevant to other issues.
    (B) He set out to confirm the SSH, but ended up revising it.
    (C) He set out to disprove the SSH, but ended up accepting it.
    (D) He altered the SSH by expanding it to encompass various types of signals.
    (E) He advocated the SSH, but his research data failed to confirm it.

53. The passage suggests that among birds that form flocks, a bird of high status is most likely to have which one of the following?

    (A) dark throat plumage
    (B) greater-than-average body weight
    (C) offspring of high status
    (D) strong fighting ability
    (E) frequent injuries

54. Which one of the following can be inferred about Harris sparrows from the passage?

    (A) Among Harris sparrows, plumage differences signal individual status only within age groups.
    (B) Among Harris sparrows, adults have priority of access to food over juveniles.
    (C) Among Harris sparrows, juveniles with relatively dark plumage have status equal to that of adults with relatively light plumage.
    (D) Juvenile Harris sparrows engage in aggressive interaction more frequently than do adult Harris sparrows.
    (E) Harris sparrows engage in aggressive interaction less frequently than do greater titmice.

Some meteorologists have insisted that the severity of the drought in sub-Saharan West Africa and its long duration (nearly 40 years to date) must be a sign of a long-term alteration in climate.

(5) Among the theories proposed to explain this change, one hypothesis that has gained widespread attention attributes the drought to a cooling of the Northern Hemisphere. This hypothesis is based on the fact that, between 1945 and the early 1970s, the

(10) average annual air temperatures over the landmasses of the Northern Hemisphere decreased by about half a degree Fahrenheit (approximately one quarter of a degree Celsius—a small but significant amount). Several meteorologists have

(15) suggested that this cooling was caused by an increase in atmospheric dust emanating from volcanic eruptions and from urban and industrial pollution; the dust reflected incoming sunlight, causing the ground to receive less solar radiation

(20) and to transfer less heat to the atmosphere. The cooling seemed to be more pronounced in the middle and high latitudes than in the tropics, an observation that is consistent with the fact that the Sun's rays enter the atmosphere at a greater angle

(25) farther north, and so have to pass through more dust-laden atmosphere on the way to the Earth.

Since winds are set in motion by differences in air pressure caused by unequal heating of the atmosphere, supporters of the cooling hypothesis

(30) have argued that a growing temperature differential between the unusually cool middle and high latitudes and the warm tropical latitudes is causing a southward expansion of the circumpolar vortex—the high-altitude westerly winds that circle

(35) the Northern Hemisphere at middle latitudes. According to this hypothesis, as the circumpolar vortex expands, it forces south other components of large-scale atmospheric circulation and, in effect, displaces the northward-moving monsoon that

(40) ordinarily brings sub-Saharan rain. Proponents have further argued that this change in atmospheric circulation might be long-term since cooling in the Northern Hemisphere could be perpetuated by increases in ice and snow coverage there, which

(45) would lead to reflection of more sunlight away from the Earth, to further cooling, and, indirectly, to further drought in sub-Saharan West Africa.

Despite these dire predictions, and even though the current African drought has lasted longer than

(50) any other in this century, the notion that the drought is caused by cooling of the Northern Hemisphere is, in fact, not well supported. Contrary to the predictions of the cooling hypothesis, during one period of rapid Northern Hemisphere cooling

(55) in the early 1950s, the sub-Sahara was unusually rainy. Moreover, in the early 1980s, when the drought was particularly severe, Northern Hemisphere lands actually warmed slightly. And further doubt has been cast on the hypothesis by

(60) recent analyses suggesting that, when surface temperatures of water as well as land are taken into account, the Northern Hemisphere may not have cooled at all.

55. Which one of the following best expresses the main idea of the passage?

(A) There is strong evidence to support the theory that an increase in atmospheric dust has contributed to the severity of the drought in sub-Saharan West Africa.

(B) The suggestion that Northern Hemisphere cooling is contributing to a decline of rainfall in sub-Saharan West Africa is open to question.

(C) The expansion of the circumpolar vortex has caused a dramatic shift in the atmospheric circulation patterns above sub-Saharan West Africa.

(D) The drought in sub-Saharan West Africa represents a long-term, permanent alteration in global climate patterns.

(E) Meteorologists cannot determine when the drought in sub-Saharan West Africa is likely to end.

56. The author's attitude toward the cooling hypothesis is best described as one of

(A) vehement opposition
(B) cautious skepticism
(C) growing ambivalence
(D) guarded enthusiasm
(E) strong support

57. According to the passage, proponents of the cooling hypothesis suggested that the circumpolar vortex is likely to expand when which one of the following occurs?

(A) The average annual atmospheric temperature of the tropics is significantly higher than normal for an extended period of time.

(B) The average annual snowfall in the Northern Hemisphere is lower than normal for an extended period of time.

(C) The average annual surface temperature of Northern Hemisphere waters is higher than the average annual surface temperature of Northern Hemisphere landmasses.

(D) There is a significant increase in the difference between the average annual atmospheric temperature of the tropics and that of the more northern latitudes.

(E) There is a significant increase in the difference between the average annual atmospheric temperatures of the middle and the high latitudes in the Northern Hemisphere.

Source: PrepTest 17, Section 4, Passage 4, Questions 22–27

58. Which one of the following can be inferred from the passage about the average annual temperature of the air over Northern Hemisphere landmasses before 1945?

    (A) It was higher than it was between 1945 and the early 1970s.
    (B) It was lower than it was during the early 1980s.
    (C) It was the same as it was between 1945 and the early 1970s.
    (D) It was the same as the annual average surface temperature of Northern Hemisphere landmasses and bodies of water between 1945 and the early 1970s.
    (E) It was higher than the annual average surface temperature of Northern Hemisphere landmasses and bodies of water between 1945 and the early 1970s.

59. Which one of the following best describes the organization of the passage?

    (A) Opposing points of view are presented, evidence supporting each point of view is discussed, and then one point of view is developed into a formal hypothesis.
    (B) A theory is discussed, and different points of view about the theory are discussed, supported, and then reconciled.
    (C) A hypothesis is proposed, contradictory evidence is discussed, and then the hypothesis is amended.
    (D) A theory explaining a phenomenon is proposed, supporting evidence is considered, and then the theory is disputed.
    (E) A point of view is presented, a theory supporting the view is proposed, contradictory evidence is presented, and then a different theory is proposed.

60. A proponent of the cooling hypothesis would most likely argue that the return of the monsoon rains to sub-Saharan West Africa would indicate that which one of the following has also occurred?

    (A) The amount of ice and snow coverage over the landmasses of the Northern Hemisphere has increased.
    (B) The average annual temperature of the atmosphere over the middle and high latitudes of the Northern Hemisphere has decreased.
    (C) The average annual temperature of the atmosphere over the tropics in the Northern Hemisphere has increased.
    (D) Other components of large-scale atmospheric circulation, besides the circumpolar vortex, have expanded and moved southward.
    (E) The atmospheric circulation pattern of the high-altitude westerly winds has resumed its normal pattern.

Philosophers of science have long been uneasy with biology, preferring instead to focus on physics. At the heart of this preference is a mistrust of uncertainty. Science is supposed to be the study of what is true
(5) everywhere and for all times, and the phenomena of science are supposed to be repeatable, arising from universal laws, rather than historically contingent. After all, if something pops up only on occasional Tuesdays or Thursdays, it is not classified as science
(10) but as history. Philosophers of science have thus been fascinated with the fact that elephants and mice would fall at the same rate if dropped from the Tower of Pisa, but not much interested in how elephants and mice got to be such different sizes in the first place.

(15) Philosophers of science have not been alone in claiming that science must consist of universal laws. Some evolutionary biologists have also acceded to the general intellectual disdain for the merely particular and tried to emulate physicists, constructing their
(20) science as a set of universal laws. In formulating the notion of a universal "struggle for existence" that is the engine of biological history or in asserting that virtually all DNA evolves at a constant clocklike rate, they have attempted to find their own versions of the
(25) law of gravity. Recently, however, some biologists have questioned whether biological history is really the necessary unfolding of universal laws of life, and they have raised the possibility that historical contingency is an integral factor in biology.

(30) To illustrate the difference between biologists favoring universal, deterministic laws of evolutionary development and those leaving room for historical contingency, consider two favorite statements of philosophers (both of which appear, at first sight, to be
(35) universal assertions): "All planets move in ellipses" and "All swans are white." The former is truly universal because it applies not only to those planets that actually do exist, but also to those that could exist—for the shape of planetary orbits is a necessary
(40) consequence of the laws governing the motion of objects in a gravitational field.

Biological determinists would say that "All swans are white" is universal in the same way, since, if all swans were white, it would be because the laws of
(45) natural selection make it impossible for swans to be otherwise: natural selection favors those characteristics that increase the average rate of offspring production, and so traits that maximize flexibility and the ability to manipulate nature will
(50) eventually appear. Nondeterminist biologists would deny this, saying that "swans" is merely the name of a finite collection of historical objects that may happen all to be white, but not of necessity. The history of evolutionary theory has been the history of the struggle
(55) between these two views of swans.

61. Which one of the following best summarizes the main idea of the passage?

(A) Just as philosophers of science have traditionally been reluctant to deal with scientific phenomena that are not capable of being explained by known physical laws, biologists have tended to shy away from confronting philosophical questions.

(B) While science is often considered to be concerned with universal laws, the degree to which certain biological phenomena can be understood as arising from such laws is currently in dispute.

(C) Although biologists have long believed that the nature of their field called for a theoretical approach different from that taken by physicists, some biologists have recently begun to emulate the methods of physicists.

(D) Whereas physicists have achieved a far greater degree of experimental precision than has been possible in the field of biology, the two fields employ similar theoretical approaches.

(E) Since many biologists are uncomfortable with the emphasis placed by philosophers of science on the need to construct universal laws, there has been little interaction between the two disciplines.

62. The reference to the formulation of the notion of a universal "struggle for existence" (line 21) serves primarily to

(A) identify one of the driving forces of biological history

(B) illustrate one context in which the concept of uncertainty has been applied

(C) highlight the chief cause of controversy among various schools of biological thought

(D) provide an example of the type of approach employed by determinist biologists

(E) provide an example of a biological phenomenon that illustrates historical contingency

Source: PrepTest 35, Section 2, Passage 3, Questions 15–20

63. Which one of the following statements about biology is most consistent with the view held by determinist biologists, as that view is presented in the passage?

    (A) The appearance of a species is the result of a combination of biological necessity and historical chance.
    (B) The rate at which physiological characteristics of a species change fluctuates from generation to generation.
    (C) The causes of a given evolutionary phenomenon can never be understood by biological scientists.
    (D) The qualities that define a species have been developed according to some process that has not yet been identified.
    (E) The chief physical characteristics of a species are inevitable consequences of the laws governing natural selection.

64. It can be inferred from the passage that philosophers of science view the laws of physics as

    (A) analogous to the laws of history
    (B) difficult to apply because of their uncertainty
    (C) applicable to possible as well as actual situations
    (D) interesting because of their particularity
    (E) illustrative of the problem of historical contingency

65. It can be inferred from the passage that determinist biologists have tried to emulate physicists because these biologists believe that

    (A) the methods of physicists are more easily understood by nonscientists
    (B) physicists have been accorded more respect by their fellow scientists than have biologists
    (C) biology can only be considered a true science if universal laws can be constructed to explain its phenomena
    (D) the specific laws that have helped to explain the behavior of planets can be applied to biological phenomena
    (E) all scientific endeavors benefit from intellectual exchange between various scientific disciplines

66. The passage suggests that the preference of many philosophers of science for the field of physics depends primarily upon the

    (A) belief that biological laws are more difficult to discover than physical laws
    (B) popular attention given to recent discoveries in physics as opposed to those in biology
    (C) bias shown toward the physical sciences in the research programs of many scientific institutions
    (D) teaching experiences of most philosophers of science
    (E) nature of the phenomena that physicists study

What it means to "explain" something in science often comes down to the application of mathematics. Some thinkers hold that mathematics is a kind of language—a systematic contrivance of signs, the
(5) criteria for the authority of which are internal coherence, elegance, and depth. The application of such a highly artificial system to the physical world, they claim, results in the creation of a kind of statement about the world. Accordingly, what matters in the
(10) sciences is finding a mathematical concept that attempts, as other language does, to accurately describe the functioning of some aspect of the world.

At the center of the issue of scientific knowledge can thus be found questions about the relationship
(15) between language and what it refers to. A discussion about the role played by language in the pursuit of knowledge has been going on among linguists for several decades. The debate centers around whether language corresponds in some essential way to objects
(20) and behaviors, making knowledge a solid and reliable commodity; or, on the other hand, whether the relationship between language and things is purely a matter of agreed-upon conventions, making knowledge tenuous, relative, and inexact.

(25) Lately the latter theory has been gaining wider acceptance. According to linguists who support this theory, the way language is used varies depending upon changes in accepted practices and theories among those who work in a particular discipline. These
(30) linguists argue that, in the pursuit of knowledge, a statement is true only when there are no promising alternatives that might lead one to question it. Certainly this characterization would seem to be applicable to the sciences. In science, a mathematical statement may be
(35) taken to account for every aspect of a phenomenon it is applied to, but, some would argue, there is nothing inherent in mathematical language that guarantees such a correspondence. Under this view, acceptance of a mathematical statement by the scientific community—
(40) by virtue of the statement's predictive power or methodological efficiency—transforms what is basically an analogy or metaphor into an explanation of the physical process in question, to be held as true until another, more compelling analogy takes its place.

(45) In pursuing the implications of this theory, linguists have reached the point at which they must ask: If words or sentences do not correspond in an essential way to life or to our ideas about life, then just what are they capable of telling us about the world? In science
(50) and mathematics, then, it would seem equally necessary to ask: If models of electrolytes or $E = mc^2$, say, do not correspond essentially to the physical world, then just what functions do they perform in the acquisition of scientific knowledge? But this question
(55) has yet to be significantly addressed in the sciences.

67. Which one of the following statements most accurately expresses the passage's main point?

A D V

(A) Although scientists must rely on both language and mathematics in their pursuit of scientific knowledge, each is an imperfect tool for perceiving and interpreting aspects of the physical world.

(B) The acquisition of scientific knowledge depends on an agreement among scientists to accept some mathematical statements as more precise than others while acknowledging that all mathematics is inexact.

(C) If science is truly to progress, scientists must temporarily abandon the pursuit of new knowledge in favor of a systematic analysis of how the knowledge they already possess came to be accepted as true.

(D) In order to better understand the acquisition of scientific knowledge, scientists must investigate mathematical statements' relationship to the world just as linguists study language's relationship to the world.

(E) Without the debates among linguists that preceded them, it is unlikely that scientists would ever have begun to explore the essential role played by mathematics in the acquisition of scientific knowledge.

68. Which one of the following statements, if true, lends the most support to the view that language has an essential correspondence to the things it describes?

A D V

(A) The categories of physical objects employed by one language correspond remarkably to the categories employed by another language that developed independently of the first.

(B) The categories of physical objects employed by one language correspond remarkably to the categories employed by another language that derives from the first.

(C) The categories of physical objects employed by speakers of a language correspond remarkably to the categories employed by other speakers of the same language.

(D) The sentence structures of languages in scientifically sophisticated societies vary little from language to language.

(E) Native speakers of many languages believe that the categories of physical objects employed by their language correspond to natural categories of objects in the world.

Source: PrepTest 22, Section 1, Passage 4, Questions 22–26

KAPLAN

69. According to the passage, mathematics can be considered a language because it

(A) conveys meaning in the same way that metaphors do

(B) constitutes a systematic collection of signs

(C) corresponds exactly to aspects of physical phenomena

(D) confers explanatory power on scientific theories

(E) relies on previously agreed-upon conventions

70. The primary purpose of the third paragraph is to

(A) offer support for the view of linguists who believe that language has an essential correspondence to things

(B) elaborate the position of linguists who believe that truth is merely a matter of convention

(C) illustrate the differences between the essentialist and conventionalist positions in the linguists' debate

(D) demonstrate the similarity of the linguists' debate to a current debate among scientists about the nature of explanation

(E) explain the theory that mathematical statements are a kind of language

71. Based on the passage, linguists who subscribe to the theory described in lines 21–24 would hold that the statement "The ball is red" is true because

(A) speakers of English have accepted that "The ball is red" applies to the particular physical relationship being described

(B) speakers of English do not accept that synonyms for "ball" and "red" express these concepts as elegantly

(C) "The ball is red" corresponds essentially to every aspect of the particular physical relationship being described

(D) "ball" and "red" actually refer to an entity and a property respectively

(E) "ball" and "red" are mathematical concepts that attempt to accurately describe some particular physical relationship in the world

KAPLAN 77

Like Charles Darwin, Alfred Wegener revolutionized an entire science. Unlike Darwin's ideas, which still stir up much controversy, Wegener's theory of drifting continents is accepted almost without
(5) question, but it did not succeed without a struggle.

In 1912 Wegener suggested that Africa and South America are estranged pieces of a single, ancient supercontinent, Pangaea, that had drifted apart, leaving the Atlantic Ocean between them. However, even
(10) Wegener believed that geological wear and tear over the ages would have damaged the fine detail of ancient coastlines, destroying the best evidence for drift. He never tested the fit between the African and South American coastlines with any exactitude, and for a time
(15) his ideas were virtually ignored. In 1924 Harold Jeffreys, who would become one of the strongest critics of the theory, dismissed it in his landmark book *The Earth*. Apparently after casually observing the shorelines on a globe, Jeffreys concluded that the fit
(20) between Africa and South America was very poor.

Disturbed by Jeffreys' obviously perfunctory observation, S. W. Carey used careful techniques of geometric projection to correct, better than most maps do, for the fact that the continents' margins lie on a
(25) sphere rather than on a flat surface. He found a remarkably close fit. At about the same time, Keith Runcorn found other evidence for drift. When volcanic lava cools and hardens into basalt, it is magnetized by the earth's own magnetic field. The rock's poles
(30) become aligned with the earth's magnetic poles. Though the planet's poles have wandered over the past few hundred million years, the magnetic field of each basalt fragment is still aimed the way the earth's poles were at the time the rock was formed. Although one
(35) would expect that the magnetic fields of rocks of the same age from any continent would all be aligned the way the earth's magnetic field was aligned at that time, the magnetic fields of basalts in North America are now aligned quite differently from rocks formed in the
(40) same epoch in Europe. Thus, the rocks provided clear evidence that the continents had drifted with respect to each other. True to form, Jeffreys brusquely rejected Runcorn's studies. His casual disdain for such observational data led some field geologists to suggest
(45) that his classic should be retitled *An Earth*.

In 1966 compelling proof that the seafloor spreads from the midocean ridges confirmed the hypothesis that molten rock wells up at these ridges from deep within the earth and repaves the seafloor as giant
(50) crustal plates move apart. Thus, seafloor spreading not only explained the long-standing puzzle of why the ocean basins are so much younger than the continents, but also provided evidence that the plates, and so the continents on them, move. Overnight, plate
(55) tectonic theory, with continental drift, became the consensus view.

72. Which one of the following best expresses the main idea of the passage?

(A) Confirmation of Wegener's theory of continental drift came from unexpected sources.
(B) Critics of Wegener's theory of continental drift provided information that contributed to its final acceptance.
(C) The history of the theory of continental drift is similar in a number of ways to the history of Darwin's most important theory.
(D) Though Wegener's theory of continental drift is now generally accepted, Wegener himself was unable to provide any evidence of its accuracy.
(E) Though Wegener's theory of continental drift had significant implications, many years and much effort were required to win its acceptance.

73. Jeffreys' approach to Wegener's theory is most like the approach of which one of the following?

(A) a botanist who concludes that two species are unrelated based on superficial examination of their appearance
(B) a driver who attempts to find a street in an unfamiliar city without a map
(C) a zoologist who studies animal behavior rather than anatomy
(D) a politician who bases the decision to run for office on the findings of a public opinion poll
(E) a psychiatrist who bases treatment decisions on patients' past histories

74. According to the passage, evidence of seafloor spreading helped to explain which one of the following?

(A) the reason for the existence of the giant crustal plates on which the continents are found
(B) the reason basalts retain their magnetic field alignment
(C) the reason the earth's poles have wandered
(D) the composition of the giant crustal plates on which the continents are found
(E) the disparity between the age of the continents and that of the ocean basins

75. Which one of the following phrases, as used in context, most clearly reveals the author's opinion about Jeffreys?

(A) "virtually ignored" (line 15)
(B) "very poor" (line 20)
(C) "obviously perfunctory" (line 21)
(D) "careful techniques" (line 22)
(E) "consensus view" (line 56)

Source: PrepTest A, Section 2, Passage 3, Questions 14–20

76. The author's mention of the fact that some field geologists suggested calling Jeffreys' work *An Earth* (line 45) serves to

    (A)   contrast two of Jeffreys' ideas
    (B)   justify criticisms of Jeffreys' work
    (C)   emphasize an opinion of Jeffreys' work
    (D)   explain the reasons for Jeffreys' conflict with Wegener
    (E)   support an assertion about Jeffreys' critics

77. It can be inferred that Carey believed Jeffreys' 1924 appraisal to be

    (A)   authoritative and supported by indirect evidence
    (B)   obvious but in need of interpretation
    (C)   accurate but in need of validation
    (D)   unquestionably based on insufficient search
    (E)   so deficient as to be unworthy of investigation

78. The information in the passage suggests that which one of the following findings would most clearly undermine evidence for the theory of continental drift?

    (A)   It is discovered that the ocean basins are actually older than the continents.
    (B)   New techniques of geometric projection are discovered that make much more accurate mapping possible.
    (C)   It is determined that the magnetic fields of some basalts magnetized in Europe and North America during the twentieth century have the same magnetic field alignment.
    (D)   It is found that the magnetic fields of some contemporaneous basalts in Africa and South America have different magnetic field alignments.
    (E)   It is determined that Jeffreys had performed careful observational studies of geological phenomena.

It is a fundamental tenet of geophysics that the Earth's magnetic field can exist in either of two polarity states: a "normal" state, in which north-seeking compass needles point to the
(5) geographic north, and a "reverse" state, in which they point to the geographic south. Geological evidence shows that periodically the field's polarity reverses, and that these reversals have been taking place at an increasing rate. Evidence also indicates
(10) that the field does not reverse instantaneously from one polarity state to another; rather, the process involves a transition period that typically spans a few thousand years.

Though this much is known, the underlying
(15) causes of the reversal phenomenon are not well understood. It is generally accepted that the magnetic field itself is generated by the motion of free electrons in the outer core, a slowly churning mass of molten metal sandwiched between the
(20) Earth's mantle (the region of the Earth's interior lying below the crust) and its solid inner core. In some way that is not completely understood, gravity and the Earth's rotation, acting on temperature and density differences within the
(25) outer core fluid, provide the driving forces behind the generation of the field. The reversal phenomenon may be triggered when something disturbs the heat circulation pattern of the outer core fluid, and with it the magnetic field.
(30) Several explanations for this phenomenon have been proposed. One proposal, the "heat-transfer hypothesis," is that the triggering process is intimately related to the way the outer core vents its heat into the mantle. For example, such heat
(35) transfer could create hotter (rising) or cooler (descending) blobs of material from the inner and outer boundaries of the fluid core, thereby perturbing the main heat-circulation pattern. A more controversial alternative proposal is the
(40) "asteroid-impact hypothesis." In this scenario an extended period of cold and darkness results from the impact of an asteroid large enough to send a great cloud of dust into the atmosphere. Following this climatic change, ocean temperatures drop and
(45) the polar ice caps grow, redistributing the Earth's seawater. This redistribution increases the rotational acceleration of the mantle, causing friction and turbulence near the outer core-mantle boundary and initiating a reversal of the magnetic field.
(50) How well do these hypotheses account for such observations as the long-term increase in the frequency of reversal? In support of the asteroid-impact model, it has been argued that the gradual cooling of the average ocean temperature
(55) would enable progressively smaller asteroid impacts (which are known to occur more frequently than larger impacts) to cool the Earth's climate sufficiently to induce ice-cap growth and reversals. But theories that depend on extraterrestrial

(60) intervention seem less convincing than theories like the first, which account for the phenomenon solely by means of the thermodynamic state of the outer core and its effect on the mantle.

79. Which one of the following statements regarding the Earth's outer core is best supported by information presented in the passage?

(A) Heat circulation in the outer core controls the growth and diminution of the polar ice caps.

(B) Impact of asteroids on the Earth's surface alters the way in which the outer core vents its heat into the mantle.

(C) Motion of electrons within the metallic fluid in the outer core produces the Earth's magnetic field.

(D) Friction and turbulence near the boundary between the outer core and the mantle are typically caused by asteroid impacts.

(E) Cessation of heat circulation within the outer core brings on multiple reversals in the Earth's magnetic field.

80. The author's objection to the second hypothesis discussed in the passage is most applicable to which one of the following explanations concerning the extinction of the dinosaurs'?

(A) The extinction of the dinosaurs was the result of gradual changes in the composition of the Earth's atmosphere that occurred over millions of years.

(B) The dinosaurs became extinct when their food supply was disrupted following the emergence of mammals.

(C) The dinosaurs succumbed to the new, colder environment brought about by a buildup of volcanic ash in the atmosphere.

(D) After massively overpopulating the planet, dinosaurs disappeared due to widespread starvation and the rapid spread of disease.

(E) After radical climatic changes resulted from the impact of a comet, dinosaurs disappeared from the Earth.

Source: PrepTest 14, Section 3, Passage 1, Questions 1–6

81. The author mentions the creation of blobs of different temperatures in the Earth's outer core (lines 34–38) primarily in order to

    EX
    ST

    (A) present a way in which the venting of heat from the outer core might disturb the heat-circulation pattern within the outer core

    (B) provide proof for the proposal that ventilation of heat from the outer core into the mantle triggers polarity reversal

    (C) give an example of the way in which heat circulates between the Earth's outer core and the Earth's exterior

    (D) describe how the outer core maintains its temperature by venting its excess heat into the Earth's mantle

    (E) argue in favor of the theory that heat circulation in the Earth's interior produces the magnetic field

82. Which one of the following statements regarding the polarity of the Earth's magnetic field is best supported by information in the passage?

    EX
    ST

    (A) Most, but not all, geophysicists agree that the Earth's magnetic field may exist in two distinct polarity states.

    (B) Changes in the polarity of the Earth's magnetic field have occurred more often in the recent past than in the distant past.

    (C) Heat transfer would cause reversals of the polarity of the Earth's magnetic field to occur more quickly than would asteroid impact.

    (D) Geophysicists' understanding of the reversal of the Earth's magnetic field has increased significantly since the introduction of the heat-transfer hypothesis.

    (E) Friction near the boundary of the inner and outer cores brings on reversal of the polarity of the geomagnetic field.

83. Which one of the following can be inferred regarding the two proposals discussed in the passage?

    EX
    ST

    (A) Since their introduction they have sharply divided the scientific community.

    (B) Both were formulated in order to explain changes in the frequency of polarity reversal.

    (C) Although no firm conclusions regarding them have yet been reached, both have been extensively investigated.

    (D) They are not the only proposals scientists have put forward to explain the phenomenon of polarity reversal.

    (E) Both were introduced some time ago and have since fallen into disfavor among geophysicists.

84. The author mentions each of the following as possible contributing causes to reversals of the Earth's magnetic field EXCEPT

    EX
    ST

    (A) changes in the way heat circulates within the outer core fluid

    (B) extended periods of colder temperatures on the Earth's surface

    (C) the creation of circulating blobs of outer core material of different temperatures

    (D) changes in circulation patterns in the Earth's oceans

    (E) clouding of the Earth's atmosphere by a large amount of dust

Social Sciences Passages

Directions: Each passage in this section is followed by a group of questions to be answered on the basis of what is <u>stated</u> or <u>implied</u> in the passage. For some of the questions, more than one of the choices could conceivably answer the question. However, you are to choose the <u>best</u> answer; that is, the response that most accurately and completely answers the question.

In April 1990 representatives of the Pico Korea Union of electronics workers in Buchon City, South Korea, traveled to the United States in order to demand just settlement of their claims from the parent company
(5) of their employer, who upon the formation of the union had shut down operations without paying the workers. From the beginning, the union cause was championed by an unprecedented coalition of Korean American groups and deeply affected the Korean American
(10) community on several levels.

First, it served as a rallying focus for a diverse community often divided by generation, class, and political ideologies. Most notably, the Pico cause mobilized many young second-generation Korean
(15) Americans, many of whom had never been part of a political campaign before, let alone one involving Korean issues. Members of this generation, unlike first-generation Korean Americans, generally fall within the more privileged sectors of the Korean American
(20) community and often feel alienated from their Korean roots. In addition to raising the political consciousness of young Korean Americans, the Pico struggle sparked among them new interest in their cultural identity. The Pico workers also suggested new roles that can be
(25) played by recent immigrants, particularly working-class immigrants. These immigrants' knowledge of working conditions overseas can help to globalize the perspective of their communities and can help to establish international ties on a more personal level, as
(30) witnessed in the especially warm exchange between the Pico workers and recent working-class immigrants from China. In addition to broadening the political base within the Korean American community, the Pico struggle also led to new alliances between the Korean
(35) American community and progressive labor and social justice groups within the larger society—as evidenced in the support received from the Coalition of Labor Union Women and leading African American unionists.
(40) The reasons for these effects lie in the nature of the cause. The issues raised by the Pico unionists had such a strong human component that differences within the community became secondary to larger concerns for social justice and workers' rights. The workers'
(45) demands for compensation and respect were unencumbered with strong ideological trappings. The economic exploitation faced by the Pico workers underscored the common interests of Korean workers, Korean Americans, the working class more inclusively,
(50) and a broad spectrum of community leaders.

The Pico workers' campaign thus offers an important lesson. It demonstrates that ethnic communities need more than just a knowledge of history and culture as artifacts of the past in order to
(55) strengthen their ethnic identity. It shows that perhaps the most effective means of empowerment for many ethnic communities of immigrant derivation may be an identification with and participation in current struggles for economic and social justice in their
(60) countries of origin.

1. Which one of the following best describes the main topic of the passage?

   (A) the contribution of the Korean American community to improving the working conditions of Koreans employed by United States companies
   (B) the change brought about in the Korean American community by contacts with Koreans visiting the United States
   (C) the contribution of recent immigrants from Korea to strengthening ethnic identity in the Korean American community
   (D) the effects on the Korean American community of a dispute between Korean union workers and a United Stated company
   (E) the effect of the politicization of second-generation Korean Americans on the Korean American community as a whole

2. The passage suggests that which one of the following was a significant factor in the decision to shut down the Pico plant in Buchon City?

   (A) the decreasing profitability of maintaining operations in Korea
   (B) the failure to resolve long-standing disputes between the Pico workers and management
   (C) the creation of a union by the Pico workers
   (D) the withholding of workers' wages by the parent company
   (E) the finding of an alternate site for operations

Source: PrepTest 24, Section 1, Passage 2, Questions 7–13

3. Which one of the following is NOT mentioned in the passage as a recent development in the Korean American community?

 (A) Young second-generation Koran Americans have begun to take an interest in their Korean heritage.
 (B) Recent Korean American immigrants of working-class backgrounds have begun to enter the more privileged sectors of the Korean American community.
 (C) Korean Americans have developed closer ties with activist groups from other sectors of the population.
 (D) Previously nonpolitical members of the Korean American community have become more politically active.
 (E) The Korean American community has been able to set aside political and generational disparities in order to support a common cause.

4. It can be inferred that the author of the passage would most likely agree with which one of the following statements about ethnic communities of immigrant derivation?

 (A) Such communities can derive important benefits from maintaining ties with their countries of origin.
 (B) Such communities should focus primarily on promoting study of the history and culture of their people in order to strengthen their ethnic identity.
 (C) Such communities can most successfully mobilize and politicize their young people by addressing the problems of young people of all backgrounds.
 (D) The more privileged sectors of such communities are most likely to maintain a sense of closeness to their cultural roots.
 (E) The politicization of such a community is unlikely to affect relations with other groups within the larger society.

5. In the second paragraph, the author refers to immigrants from China most probably in order to do which one of the following?

 (A) highlight the contrast between working conditions in the United States and in Korea
 (B) demonstrate the uniqueness of the problem faced by the Pico workers
 (C) offer an example of the type of role that can be played by recent working-class immigrants
 (D) provide an analogy for the type of activism displayed by the Korean American community
 (E) compare the disparate responses of two immigrant communities to similar problems

6. The primary purpose of the passage is to

 (A) describe recent developments in the Korean American community that have strongly affected other ethnic communities of immigrant derivation
 (B) describe a situation in the Korean American community that presents a model for the empowerment of ethnic communities of immigrant derivation
 (C) detail the problems faced by the Korean American community in order to illustrate the need for the empowerment of ethnic communities of immigrant derivation
 (D) argue against economic and social injustice in the countries of origin of ethnic communities of immigrant derivation
 (E) assess the impact of the unionization movement on ethnic communities of immigrant derivation

7. Which one of the following most accurately states the function of the third paragraph?

 (A) It explains why the Pico workers brought their cause to the United States.
 (B) It explains how the Pico cause differed from other causes that had previously mobilized the Korean American community.
 (C) It explains why the Pico workers were accorded such broad support.
 (D) It explains how other ethnic groups of immigrant derivation in the United States have profited from the example of the Pico workers.
 (E) It explains why different generations of Korean Americans reacted in different ways to the Pico cause.

Recently the focus of historical studies of different
ethnic groups in the United States has shifted from the
transformation of ethnic identity to its preservation.
Whereas earlier historians argued that the ethnic
(5) identity of various immigrant groups to the United
States blended to form an American national character,
the new scholarship has focused on the transplantation
of ethnic cultures to the United States. Fugita and
O'Brien's *Japanese American Ethnicity* provides an
(10) example of this recent trend; it also exemplifies a
problem that is common to such scholarship.

In comparing the first three generations of Japanese
Americans (the Issei, Nisei, and Sansei), Fugita and
O'Brien conclude that assimilation to United States
(15) culture increased among Japanese Americans over
three generations, but that a sense of ethnic community
endured. Although the persistence of community is
stressed by the authors, their emphasis in the book
could just as easily have been on the high degree of
(20) assimilation of the Japanese American population in
the late twentieth century, which Fugita and O'Brien
believe is demonstrated by the high levels of education,
income, and occupational mobility achieved by
Japanese Americans. In addition, their data reveal that
(25) the character of the ethnic community itself changed:
the integration of Sanseis into new professional
communities and nonethnic voluntary associations
meant at the very least that ethnic ties had to
accommodate multiple and layered identities. Fugita
(30) and O'Brien themselves acknowledge that there has
been a "weakening of Japanese American ethnic
community life."

Because of the social changes weakening the bonds
of community, Fugita and O'Brien maintain that the
(35) community cohesion of Japanese Americans is notable
not for its initial intensity but because "there remains a
degree of involvement in the ethnic community
surpassing that found in most other ethnic groups at
similar points in their ethnic group life cycle." This
(40) comparative difference is important to Fugita and
O'Brien, and they hypothesize that the Japanese
American community persisted in the face of
assimilation because of a particularly strong
preexisting sense of "peoplehood." They argue that this
(45) sense of peoplehood extended beyond local and family
ties.

Fugita and O'Brien's hypothesis illustrates a
common problem in studies that investigate the history
of ethnic community. Like historians who have studied
(50) European ethnic cultures in the United States, Fugita
and O'Brien have explained persistence of ethnic
community by citing a preexisting sense of national
consciousness that is independent of how a group
adapts to United States culture. However, it is difficult
(55) to prove, as Fugita and O'Brien have attempted to do,
that a sense of peoplehood is a distinct phenomenon.
Historians should instead attempt to identify directly
the factors that sustain community cohesion in
generations that have adapted to United States culture
(60) and been exposed to the pluralism of American life.

8. Which one of the following best summarizes the main
    point of the author of the passage?

    (A) Fugita and O'Brien's study provides a
         comparison of the degree of involvement in
         ethnic community of different groups in the
         United States.

    (B) Fugita and O'Brien's study describes the
         assimilation of three generations of Japanese
         Americans to United States culture.

    (C) Fugita and O'Brien's study illustrates both a
         recent trend in historical studies of ethnic groups
         and a problem typical of that trend.

    (D) Historical studies of ethnic preservation among
         Japanese Americans have done much to define
         the interpretive framework for studies of other
         ethnic groups.

    (E) Historical studies are more concerned with the
         recent development of ethnic communities in the
         United States than with the process of adaptation
         to United States culture.

9. According to the passage, Fugita and O'Brien's data
    indicate which one of the following about the Japanese
    American ethnic community?

    (A) Community bonds have weakened primarily as
         a result of occupational mobility by Japanese
         Americans.

    (B) The community is notable because it has
         accommodated multiple and layered identities
         without losing its traditional intensity.

    (C) Community cohesion is similar in intensity to
         the community cohesion of other ethnic groups
         that have been in the United States for the same
         period of time.

    (D) Community involvement weakened during the
         second generation, but strengthened as the
         third generation regained an interest in cultural
         traditions.

    (E) The nature of the community has been altered
         by Japanese American participation in new
         professional communities and nonethnic
         voluntary associations.

Source: PrepTest 23, Section 4, Passage 4, Questions 19–26

KAPLAN

10. Which one of the following provides an example of a research study that has a conclusion most analogous to that argued for by the historians mentioned in line 4?

(A) a study showing how musical forms brought from other countries have persisted in the United States

(B) a study showing the organization and function of ethnic associations in the United States

(C) a study showing how architectural styles brought from other countries have merged to form an American style

(D) a study showing how cultural traditions have been preserved for generations in American ethnic neighborhoods

(E) a study showing how different religious practices brought from other countries have been sustained in the United States

11. According to the passage, which one of the following is true about the focus of historical studies on ethnic groups in the United States?

(A) Current studies are similar to earlier studies in claiming that a sense of peoplehood helps preserve ethnic community.

(B) Current studies have clearly identified factors that sustain ethnic community in generations that have been exposed to the pluralism of American life.

(C) Current studies examine the cultural practices that make up the American national character.

(D) Earlier studies focused on how ethnic identities became transformed in the United States.

(E) Earlier studies focused on the factors that led people to immigrate to the United States.

12. The author of the passage quotes Fugita and O'Brien in lines 36–39 most probably in order to

(A) point out a weakness in their hypothesis about the strength of community ties among Japanese Americans

(B) show how they support their claim about the notability of community cohesion for Japanese Americans

(C) indicate how they demonstrate the high degree of adaptation of Japanese Americans to United States culture

(D) suggest that they have inaccurately compared Japanese Americans to other ethnic groups in the United States

(E) emphasize their contention that the Japanese American sense of peoplehood extended beyond local and family ties

13. The passage suggests that the author would be most likely to describe the hypothesis mentioned in line 47 as

(A) highly persuasive
(B) original but poorly developed
(C) difficult to substantiate
(D) illogical and uninteresting
(E) too similar to earlier theories

14. The passage suggests which one of the following about the historians mentioned in line 49?

(A) They have been unable to provide satisfactory explanations for the persistence of European ethnic communities in the United States.

(B) They have suggested that European cultural practices have survived although the community ties of European ethnic groups have weakened.

(C) They have hypothesized that European ethnic communities are based on family ties rather than on a sense of national consciousness.

(D) They have argued that European cultural traditions have been transformed in the United States because of the pluralism of American life.

(E) They have claimed that the community ties of European Americans are still as strong as they were when the immigrants first arrived.

15. As their views are discussed in the passage, Fugita and O'Brien would be most likely to agree with which one of the following?

(A) The community cohesion of an ethnic group is not affected by the length of time it has been in the United States.

(B) An ethnic group in the United States can have a high degree of adaptation to United States culture and still sustain strong community ties.

(C) The strength of an ethnic community in the United States is primarily dependent on the strength of local and family ties.

(D) High levels of education and occupational mobility necessarily erode the community cohesion of an ethnic group in the United States.

(E) It has become increasingly difficult for ethnic groups to sustain any sense of ethnic identity in the pluralism of United States life.

Many people complain about corporations, but there are also those whose criticism goes further and who hold corporations morally to blame for many of the problems in Western society. Their criticism is not
(5) reserved solely for fraudulent or illegal business activities, but extends to the basic corporate practice of making decisions based on what will maximize profits without regard to whether such decisions will contribute to the public good. Others, mainly
(10) economists, have responded that this criticism is flawed because it inappropriately applies ethical principles to economic relationships.

It is only by extension that we attribute the quality of morality to corporations, for corporations are not
(15) persons. Corporate responsibility is an aggregation of the responsibilities of those persons employed by the corporation when they act in and on behalf of the corporation. Some corporations are owner operated, but in many corporations and in most larger ones there
(20) is a syndicate of owners to whom the chief executive officer, or CEO, who runs the corporation is said to have a fiduciary obligation.

The economists argue that a CEO's sole responsibility is to the owners, whose primary interest,
(25) except in charitable institutions, is the protection of their profits. CEOs are bound, as a condition of their employment, to seek a profit for the owners. But suppose a noncharitable organization is owner operated, or, for some other reason, its CEO is not
(30) obligated to maximize profits. The economists' view is that even if such a CEO's purpose is to look to the public good and nothing else, the CEO should still work to maximize profits, because that will turn out best for the public anyway.

(35) But the economists' position does not hold up under careful scrutiny. For one thing, although there are, no doubt, strong underlying dynamics in national and international economies that tend to make the pursuit of corporate interest contribute to the public
(40) good, there is no guarantee—either theoretically or in practice—that a given CEO will benefit the public by maximizing corporate profit. It is absurd to deny the possibility, say, of a paper mill legally maximizing its profits over a five-year period by decimating a forest
(45) for its wood or polluting a lake with its industrial waste. Furthermore, while obligations such as those of corporate CEOs to corporate owners are binding in a business or legal sense, they are not morally paramount. The CEO could make a case to the owners
(50) that certain profitable courses of action should not be taken because they are likely to detract from the public good. The economic consequences that may befall the CEO for doing so, such as penalty or dismissal, ultimately do not excuse the individual from the
(55) responsibility for acting morally.

16. Which one of the following most accurately states the main point of the passage?

(A) Although CEOs may be legally obligated to maximize their corporations' profits, this obligation does not free them from the moral responsibility of considering the implications of the corporations' actions for the public good.

(B) Although morality is not easily ascribed to nonhuman entities, corporations can be said to have an obligation to act morally in the sense that they are made up of individuals who must act morally.

(C) Although economists argue that maximizing a corporation's profits is likely to turn out best for the public, a CEO's true obligation is still to seek a profit for the corporation's owners.

(D) Although some people criticize corporations for making unethical decisions, economists argue that such criticisms are unfounded because ethical considerations cannot be applied to economics.

(E) Although critics of corporations argue that CEOs ought to consider the public good when making financial decisions, the results of such decisions in fact always benefit the public.

17. The discussion of the paper mill in lines 42–46 is intended primarily to

(A) offer an actual case of unethical corporate behavior

(B) refute the contention that maximization of profits necessarily benefits the public

(C) illustrate that ethical restrictions on corporations would be difficult to enforce

(D) demonstrate that corporations are responsible for many social ills

(E) deny that corporations are capable of acting morally

Source: PrepTest 22, Section 1, Passage 3, Questions 17–21

18. With which one of the following would the economists mentioned in the passage be most likely to agree?

(A) Even CEOs of charitable organizations are obligated to maximize profits.

(B) CEOs of owner-operated noncharitable corporations should make decisions based primarily on maximizing profits.

(C) Owner-operated noncharitable corporations are less likely to be profitable than other corporations.

(D) It is highly unlikely that the actions of any particular CEO will benefit the public.

(E) CEOs should attempt to maximize profits unless such attempts result in harm to the environment.

19. The conception of morality that underlies the author's argument in the passage is best expressed by which one of the following principles?

(A) What makes actions morally right is their contribution to the public good.

(B) An action is morally right if it carries the risk of personal penalty.

(C) Actions are morally right if they are not fraudulent or illegal.

(D) It is morally wrong to try to maximize one's personal benefit.

(E) Actions are not morally wrong unless they harm others.

20. The primary purpose of the passage is to

(A) illustrate a paradox
(B) argue for legal reform
(C) refute a claim
(D) explain a decision
(E) define a concept

Until recently, few historians were interested in analyzing the similarities and differences between serfdom in Russia and slavery in the United States. Even Alexis de Tocqueville, who recognized the significant
(5) comparability of the two nations, never compared their systems of servitude, despite his interest in United States slavery. Moreover, the almost simultaneous abolition of Russian serfdom and United States slavery in the 1860s—a riveting coincidence that should have
(10) drawn more modern scholars to a comparative study of the two systems of servitude—has failed to arouse the interest of scholars. Though some historians may have been put off by the forbidding political differences between nineteenth-century Russia and the United
(15) States—one an imperial monarchy, the other a federal democracy—a recent study by Peter Kolchin identifies differences that are illuminating, especially with regard to the different kinds of rebellion exhibited by slaves and serfs.

(20) Kolchin points out that nobles owning serfs in Russia constituted only a tiny proportion of the population, while in the southern United States, about a quarter of all White people were members of slave-owning families. And although in the southern
(25) United States only 2 percent of slaves worked on plantations where more than a hundred slaves worked, in Russia almost 80 percent of the serfs worked for nobles who owned more than a hundred serfs. In Russia most serfs rarely saw their owners, who tended
(30) to rely on intermediaries to manage their estates, while most southern planters lived on their land and interacted with slaves on a regular basis.

These differences in demographics partly explain differences in the kinds of resistance that slaves and
(35) serfs practiced in their respective countries. Both serfs and slaves engaged in a wide variety of rebellious activity, from silent sabotage, much of which has escaped the historical record, to organized armed rebellions, which were more common in Russia. The
(40) practice of absentee ownership, combined with the large numbers in which serfs were owned, probably contributed significantly to the four great rebellions that swept across Russia at roughly fifty-year intervals in the seventeenth and eighteenth centuries. The last of
(45) these, occurring between 1773 and 1774, enlisted more than a million serfs in a futile attempt to overthrow the Russian nobility. Russian serfs also participated in smaller acts of collective defiance called the *volnenie*, which typically started with a group of serfs who
(50) complained of grievances by petition and went out on strike. Confrontations between slaves and plantation authorities were also common, but they tended to be much less collective in nature than those that occurred in Russia, probably in part because the number of
(55) workers on each estate was smaller in the United States than was the case in Russia.

21. Which one of the following best states the main idea of the passage?

(A) Differences in the demographics of United States slavery and Russian serfdom can help explain the different kinds of resistance practiced by slaves and serfs in their respective countries.

(B) Historians have yet to undertake an adequate comparison and contrast of Russian serfdom and United States slavery.

(C) Revolts by Russian serfs were commonly characterized by collective action.

(D) A recent study has questioned the value of comparing United States slavery to Russian serfdom, especially in light of the significant demographic and cultural differences between the two countries.

(E) De Tocqueville failed to recognize the fundamental differences between Russian serfdom and United States slavery which more recent historians have identified.

22. According to the author, de Tocqueville was similar to many modern historians in his

(A) interest in the demographic differences between Russia and the United States during the nineteenth century

(B) failure to undertake a comparison of Russian serfdom and United States slavery

(C) inability to explain why United States slavery and Russian serfdom were abolished during the same decade

(D) overestimation of the significance of the political differences between Russia and the United States

(E) recognition of the essential comparability of Russia and the United States

Source: PrepTest 14, Section 3, Passage 4, Questions 21–27

23. Which one of the following assertions, if true, would provide the most support for Kolchin's principal conclusion regarding the relationship of demographics to rebellion among Russian serfs and United States slaves?

   (A) Collective defiance by serfs during the nineteenth century was confined almost exclusively to their participation in the *volnenie*.

   (B) The rebellious activity of United States slaves was more likely to escape the historical record than was the rebellious activity of Russian serfs.

   (C) Organized rebellions by slaves in the Western Hemisphere during the nineteenth century were most common in colonies with large estates that normally employed more than a hundred slaves.

   (D) In the southern United States during the nineteenth century, those estates that were managed by intermediaries rather than by the owner generally relied upon the labor of at least a hundred slaves.

   (E) The intermediaries who managed estates in Russia during the nineteenth century were in general much more competent as managers than the owners of the estates that they managed.

24. The fact that United States slavery and Russian serfdom were abolished during the same decade is cited by the author in the first paragraph primarily in order to

   (A) emphasize that rebellions in both counties eventually led to the demise of the two institutions

   (B) cite a coincidence that de Tocqueville should have been able to foresee

   (C) suggest one reason why more historians should have been drawn to a comparative study of the two institutions

   (D) cite a coincidence that Kolchin's study has failed to explain adequately

   (E) emphasize the underlying similarities between the two institutions

25. The author cites which one of the following as a factor that might have discouraged historians from undertaking a comparative study of Russian serfdom and United States slavery?

   (A) major differences in the political systems of the two counties

   (B) major differences in the demographics of the two counties

   (C) the failure of de Tocqueville to address the subject

   (D) differences in the size of the estates on which slaves and serfs labored

   (E) the comprehensiveness of Kolchin's own work

26. According to the passage, Kolchin's study asserts that which one of the following was true of Russian nobles during the nineteenth century?

   (A) They agreed to the abolition of serfdom in the 1860s largely as a result of their having been influenced by the abolition of slavery in the United States.

   (B) They became more directly involved in the management of their estates as a result of the rebellions that occurred in the previous century.

   (C) They commonly agreed to at least some of the demands that arose out of the *volnenie*.

   (D) They had relatively little direct contact with the serfs who worked on their estates.

   (E) They hastened the abolition of serfdom by failing to devise an effective response to the collective nature of the serfs' rebellious activity.

27. The passage suggests that which one of the following was true of southern planters in the United States?

   (A) They were as prepared for collective protest as were their Russian counterparts.

   (B) Few of them owned plantations on which fewer than a hundred slaves worked.

   (C) They managed their estates more efficiently than did their Russian counterparts.

   (D) Few of them relied on intermediaries to manage their estates.

   (E) The size of their estates was larger on average than the size of Russian estates.

Surviving sources of information about women doctors in ancient Greece and Rome are fragmentary: some passing mentions by classical authors, scattered references in medical works, and about 40

(5) inscriptions on tombs and monuments. Yet even from these fragments we can piece together a picture. The evidence shows that in ancient Greece and Rome there were, in fact, female medical personnel who were the ancient equivalent of what we now call

(10) medical doctors. So the history of women in medicine by no means begins in 1849 with Dr. Elizabeth Blackwell, the first woman to earn an M.D. in modern times, or even in 1321 with Francesca de Romana's licensure to practice general medicine, the

(15) earliest known officially recorded occurrence of this sort.

The very nature of the scant evidence tells us something. There is no list of women doctors in antiquity, no direct comment on the fact that there

(20) were such people. Instead, the scattering of references to them indicates that, although their numbers were probably small, women doctors were an unremarkable part of ancient life. For example, in *The Republic* (421 b.c.), the earliest known source attesting to the

(25) existence of women doctors in Greece, Plato argues that, for the good of the state, jobs should be assigned to people on the basis of natural aptitude, regardless of gender. To support his argument he offers the example that some women, as well as some

(30) men, are skilled in medicine, while others are not. Here, Plato is not trying to convince people that there ought to be women doctors. Rather, he is arguing for an ideal distribution of roles within the state by pointing to something that everyone could already

(35) see—that there were female doctors as well as male.

Moreover, despite evidence that some of these women doctors treated mainly female patients, their practice was clearly not limited to midwifery. Both Greek and Latin have distinct terms for midwife and

(40) doctor, and important texts and inscriptions refer to female practitioners as the latter. Other references provide evidence of a broad scope of practice for women doctors. The epitaph for one named Domnina reads: "You delivered your homeland from disease."

(45) A tribute to another describes her as "savior of all through her knowledge of medicine."

Also pointing to a wider medical practice are the references in various classical medical works to a great number of women's writings on medical

(50) subjects. Here, too, the very nature of the evidence tells us something, for Galen, Pliny the elder, and other ancient writers of encyclopedic medical works quote the opinions and prescriptions of male and female doctors indiscriminately, moving from one to

(55) the other and back again. As with the male doctors they cite, these works usually simply give excerpts from the female authority's writing without biographical information or special comment.

28. Which one of the following most accurately states the main point of the passage?

(A) There is a range of textual evidence indicating that the existence and professional activity of women doctors were an accepted part of everyday life in ancient Greece and Rome.

(B) Some scholars in ancient Greece and Rome made little distinction in their writings between learned women and learned men, as can especially be seen in those scholars' references to medical experts and practitioners.

(C) Although surviving ancient Greek and Roman texts about women doctors contain little biographical or technical data, important inferences can be drawn from the very fact that those texts pointedly comment on the existence of such doctors.

(D) Ancient texts indicate that various women doctors in Greece and Rome were not only practitioners but also researchers who contributed substantially to the development of medical science.

(E) Scholars who have argued that women did not practice medicine until relatively recently are mistaken, insofar as they have misinterpreted textual evidence from ancient Greece and Rome.

29. Which one of the following does the author mention in the passage?

(A) diseases that were not curable in ancient times but are readily cured by modern medicine

(B) a specialized field of medicine that was not practiced by women in ancient Greece and Rome

(C) a scholar who has argued that Francesca de Romana was the first female doctor in any Western society

(D) the extent to which medical doctors in ancient Greece and Rome were trained and educated

(E) ancient writers whose works refer explicitly to the writings of women

Source: PrepTest 49, Section 3, Passage 3, Questions 14–20

30. The primary function of the third paragraph of the passage is to

    (A) provide additional support for the argument presented in the first paragraph
    (B) suggest that the implications of the argument presented in the first paragraph are unnecessarily broad
    (C) acknowledge some exceptions to a conclusion defended in the second paragraph
    (D) emphasize the historical importance of the arguments presented in the first two paragraphs
    (E) describe the sources of evidence that are cited in the first two paragraphs in support of the author's main conclusion

31. Which one of the following could most logically be appended to the end of the final paragraph?

    (A) So it is only by combining the previously mentioned fragments of ancient writings that historians have been able to construct a fairly complete account of some of these women's lives.
    (B) That there were women doctors apparently seemed unremarkable to these writers who cited their works, just as it did to Plato.
    (C) Although the content of each of these excerpts is of limited informative value, the very range of topics that they cover suggests that Plato's claims about women doctors should be reevaluated.
    (D) These texts indicate that during a certain period of ancient Greek and Roman history there were female medical scholars, but it is unclear whether at that time there were also female medical practitioners.
    (E) Nevertheless, these writers' evenhanded treatment of male and female medical researchers must be interpreted partly in light of the conflicting picture of ancient medical practice that emerges from the fragmentary earlier writings.

32. Which one of the following most accurately describes the author's attitude toward the sources of information mentioned in lines 1–5?

    (A) wary that they might be misinterpreted due to their fragmentary nature
    (B) optimistic that with a more complete analysis they will yield answers to some crucial lingering questions
    (C) hopeful that they will come to be accepted generally by historians as authentic documents
    (D) confident that they are accurate enough to allow for reliable factual inferences
    (E) convinced of their appropriateness as test cases for the application of a new historical research methodology

33. The tribute quoted in lines 45–46 is offered primarily as evidence that at least some women doctors in ancient times were

    (A) acknowledged as authorities by other doctors
    (B) highly educated
    (C) very effective at treating illness
    (D) engaged in general medical practice
    (E) praised as highly as male doctors

34. The passage most strongly supports which one of the following inferences about women in ancient Greece and Rome?

    (A) Those who became doctors usually practiced medicine for only a short time.
    (B) Those who were not doctors were typically expected to practice medicine informally within their own families.
    (C) There is no known official record that any of them were licensed to practice general medicine.
    (D) There is no reliable evidence that any of them who practiced general medicine also worked as a midwife.
    (E) Some of those who practiced medicine were posthumously honored for nonmedical civic accomplishments.

Many political economists believe that the soundest indicator of the economic health of a nation is the nation's gross national product (GNP) per capita—a figure reached by dividing the total value of the goods

(5) produced yearly in a nation by its population and taken to be a measure of the welfare of the nation's residents. But there are many factors affecting residents' welfare that are not captured by per capita GNP; human indicators, while sometimes more difficult to calculate

(10) or document, provide sounder measures of a nation's progress than does the indicator championed by these economists. These human indicators include nutrition and life expectancy; birth weight and level of infant mortality; ratio of population level to availability of

(15) resources; employment opportunities; and the ability of governments to provide services such as education, clean water, medicine, public transportation, and mass communication for their residents.

The economists defend their use of per capita GNP

(20) as the sole measure of a nation's economic health by claiming that improvements in per capita GNP eventually stimulate improvements in human indicators. But, in actuality, this often fails to occur. Even in nations where economic stimulation has

(25) brought about substantial improvements in per capita GNP, economic health as measured by human indicators does not always reach a level commensurate with the per capita GNP. Nations that have achieved a relatively high per capita GNP, for example, sometimes

(30) experience levels of infant survival, literacy, nutrition, and life expectancy no greater than levels in nations where per capita GNP is relatively low. In addition, because per capita GNP is an averaged figure, it often presents a distorted picture of the wealth of a nation;

(35) for example, in a relatively sparsely populated nation where a small percentage of residents receives most of the economic benefits of production while the majority receives very little benefit, per capita GNP may nevertheless be high. The welfare of a nation's

(40) residents is a matter not merely of total economic benefit, but also of the distribution of economic benefits across the entire society. Measuring a nation's economic health only by total wealth frequently obscures a lack of distribution of wealth across the

(45) society as a whole.

In light of the potential for such imbalances in distribution of economic benefits, some nations have begun to realize that their domestic economic efforts are better directed away from attempting to raise per

(50) capita GNP and instead toward ensuring that the conditions measured by human indicators are salutary. They recognize that unless a shift in focus away from using material wealth as the sole indicator of economic success is effected, the well-being of the nation may be

(55) endangered, and that nations that do well according to human indicators may thrive even if their per capita GNP remains stable or lags behind that of other nations.

35. Which one of the following titles most accurately expresses the main point of the passage?

E
X
O
T

  (A) "The Shifting Meaning of Per Capita GNP: A Historical Perspective"

  (B) "A Defense of Per Capita GNP: An Economist's Rejoinder"

  (C) "The Preferability of Human Indicators as Measures of National Economic Health"

  (D) "Total Wealth vs. Distribution of Wealth as a Measure of Economic Health"

  (E) "A New Method of Calculating Per Capita GNP to Measure National Economic Health"

36. The term "welfare" is used in the first paragraph to refer most specifically to which one of the following?

E
X
O
T

  (A) the overall quality of life for individuals in a nation

  (B) the services provided to individuals by a government

  (C) the material wealth owned by individuals in a nation

  (D) the extent to which the distribution of wealth among individuals in a nation is balanced

  (E) government efforts to redistribute wealth across society as a whole.

Source: PrepTest 33, Section 2, Passage 1, Questions 1–7

37. The passage provides specific information about each of the following EXCEPT:

    (A) how per capita GNP is calculated
    (B) what many political economists believe to be an accurate measure of a nation's economic health
    (C) how nations with a relatively low per capita GNP can sometimes be economically healthier than nations whose pr capita GNP is higher
    (D) why human indicators may not provide the same picture of a nation's economic health that per capita GNP does
    (E) how nations can adjust their domestic economic efforts to bring about substantial improvements in per capita GNP

38. Which one of the following scenarios, if true, would most clearly be a counterexample to the views expressed in the last paragraph of the passage?

    (A) The decision by a nation with a low level of economic health as measured by human indicators to focus on increasing the levels of human indicators results in slower growth in its per capita GNP.
    (B) The decision by a nation with a low level of economic health as measured by human indicators to focus on increasing domestic production of goods results in significant improvements in the levels of human indicators.
    (C) The decision by a nation with a low level of economic health as measured by human indicators to focus on increasing the levels of human indicators results in increased growth in per capita GNP.
    (D) The decision by a nation with a low per capita GNP to focus on improving its level of economic health as measured by human indicators fails to bring about an increase in per capita GNP.
    (E) The decision by a nation with a low per capita GNP to focus on increasing domestic production of goods fails to improve its economic health as measured by human indicators.

39. The primary function of the last paragraph of the passage is to

    (A) offer a synthesis of the opposing positions outlined in the first two paragraphs
    (B) expose the inadequacies of both positions outlined in the first two paragraphs
    (C) summarize the argument made in the first two paragraphs
    (D) correct a weakness in the political economists' position as outlined in the second paragraph
    (E) suggest policy implications of the argument made in the first two paragraphs

40. Based on the passage, the political economists discussed in the passage would be most likely to agree with which one of the following statements?

    (A) A change in a nation's per capita GNP predicts a similar future change in the state of human indicators in that nation.
    (B) The level of human indicators in a nation is irrelevant to the welfare of the individuals in that nation.
    (C) A high per capita GNP in a nation usually indicates that the wealth in the nation is not distributed across the society as a whole.
    (D) The welfare of a nation's residents is irrelevant to the economic health of the nation.
    (E) The use of indicators other than material wealth to measure economic well-being would benefit a nation.

41. In the passage, the author's primary concern is to

    (A) delineate a new method of directing domestic economic efforts
    (B) point out the weaknesses in one standard for measuring a nation's welfare
    (C) explain the fact that some nations have both a high per capita GNP and a low quality of life for its citizens
    (D) demonstrate that unequal distribution of wealth is an inevitable result of a high per capita GNP
    (E) argue that political economists alone should be responsible for economic policy decisions

Recently, a new school of economics called steady-state economics has seriously challenged neoclassical economics, the reigning school in Western economic decision making. According to the neoclassical model,
(5) an economy is a closed system involving only the circular flow of exchange value between producers and consumers. Therefore, no noneconomic constraints impinge upon the economy and growth has no limits. Indeed, some neoclassical economists argue that
(10) growth itself is crucial, because, they claim, the solutions to problems often associated with growth (income inequities, for example) can be found only in the capital that further growth creates.

Steady-state economists believe the neoclassical
(15) model to be unrealistic and hold that the economy is dependent on nature. Resources, they argue, enter the economy as raw material and exit as consumed products or waste; the greater the resources, the greater the size of the economy. According to these
(20) economists, nature's limited capacity to regenerate raw material and absorb waste suggests that there is an optimal size for the economy, and that growth beyond this ideal point would increase the cost to the environment at a faster rate than the benefit to
(25) producers and consumers, generating cycles that impoverish rather than enrich. Steady-state economists thus believe that the concept of an ever growing economy is dangerous, and that the only alternative is to maintain a state in which the economy remains in
(30) equilibrium with nature. Neoclassical economists, on the other hand, consider nature to be just one element of the economy rather than an outside constraint, believing that natural resources, if depleted, can be replaced with other elements—i.e., human-made
(35) resources—that will allow the economy to continue with its process of unlimited growth.

Some steady-state economists, pointing to the widening disparity between indices of actual growth (which simply count the total monetary value of goods
(40) and services) and the index of environmentally sustainable growth (which is based on personal consumption, factoring in depletion of raw materials and production costs), believe that Western economies have already exceeded their optimal size. In response
(45) to the warnings from neoclassical economists that checking economic growth only leads to economic stagnation, they argue that there are alternatives to growth that still accomplish what is required of any economy: the satisfaction of human wants. One of
(50) the alternatives is conservation. Conservation—for example, increasing the efficiency of resource use through means such as recycling—differs from growth in that it is qualitative, not quantitative, requiring improvement in resource management rather than an
(55) increase in the amount of resources. One measure of the success of a steady-state economy would be the degree to which it could implement alternatives to growth, such as conservation, without sacrificing the ability to satisfy the wants of producers and consumers.

42. Which one of the following most completely and accurately expresses the main point of the passage?

(A) Neoclassical economists, who, unlike steady-state economists, hold that economic growth is not subject to outside constraints, believe that nature is just one element of the economy and that if natural resources in Western economies are depleted they can be replaced with human-made resources.

(B) Some neoclassical economists, who, unlike steady-state economists, hold that growth is crucial to the health of economies, believe that the solutions to certain problems in Western economies can thus be found in the additional capital generated by unlimited growth.

(C) Some steady-state economists, who, unlike neoclassical economists, hold that unlimited growth is neither possible nor desirable, believe that Western economies should limit economic growth by adopting conservation strategies, even if such strategies lead temporarily to economic stagnation.

(D) Some steady-state economists, who, unlike neoclassical economists, hold that the optimal sizes of economies are limited by the availability of natural resources, believe that Western economies should limit economic growth and that, with alternatives like conservation, satisfaction of human wants need not be sacrificed.

(E) Steady-state and neoclassical economists, who both hold that economies involve the circular flow of exchange value between producers and consumers, nevertheless differ over the most effective way of guaranteeing that a steady increase in this exchange value continues unimpeded in Western economies.

43. Based on the passage, neoclassical economists would likely hold that steady-state economists are wrong to believe each of the following EXCEPT:

(A) The environment's ability to yield raw material is limited.

(B) Natural resources are an external constraint on economies.

(C) The concept of unlimited economic growth is dangerous.

(D) Western economies have exceeded their optimal size.

(E) Economies have certain optimal sizes.

Source: PrepTest 28, Section 4, Passage 3, Questions 14–21

44. According to the passage, steady-state economists believe that unlimited economic growth is dangerous because it

    (A) may deplete natural resources faster than other natural resources are discovered to replace them

    (B) may convert natural resources into products faster than more efficient resource use can compensate for

    (C) may proliferate goods and services faster than it generates new markets for them

    (D) may create income inequities faster than it creates the capital needed to redress them

    (E) may increase the cost to the environment faster than it increases benefits to producers and consumers

45. A steady-state economist would be LEAST likely to endorse which one of the following as a means of helping a steady-state economy reduce growth without compromising its ability to satisfy human wants?

    (A) a manufacturer's commitment to recycle its product packaging

    (B) a manufacturer's decision to use a less expensive fuel in its production process

    (C) a manufacturer's implementation of a quality-control process to reduce the output of defective products

    (D) a manufacturer's conversion from one type of production process to another with greater fuel efficiency

    (E) a manufacturer's reduction of output in order to eliminate an overproduction problem

46. Based on the passage, a steady-state economist is most likely to claim that a successful economy is one that satisfies which one of the following principles?

    (A) A successful economy uses human-made resources in addition to natural resources.

    (B) A successful economy satisfies human wants faster than it creates new ones.

    (C) A successful economy maintains an equilibrium with nature while still satisfying human wants.

    (D) A successful economy implements every possible means to prevent growth.

    (E) A successful economy satisfies the wants of producers and consumers by using resources to spur growth.

47. In the view of steady-state economists, which one of the following is a noneconomic constraint as referred to in line 7?

    (A) the total amount of human wants

    (B) the index of environmentally sustainable growth

    (C) the capacity of nature to absorb waste

    (D) the problems associated with economic growth

    (E) the possibility of economic stagnation

48. Which one of the following most accurately describes what the last paragraph does in the passage?

    (A) It contradicts the ways in which the two economic schools interpret certain data and gives a criterion for judging between them based on the basic goals of an economy.

    (B) It gives an example that illustrates the weakness of the new economic school and recommends an economic policy based on the basic goals of the prevailing economic school.

    (C) It introduces an objection to the new economic school and argues that the policies of the new economic school would be less successful than growth-oriented economic policies at achieving the basic goal an economy must meet.

    (D) It notes an objection to implementing the policies of the new economic school and identifies an additional policy that can help avoid that objection and still meet the goal an economy must meet.

    (E) It contrasts the policy of the prevailing economic school with the recommendation mentioned earlier of the new economic school and shows that they are based on differing views on the basic goal an economy must meet.

49. The passage suggests which one of the following about neoclassical economists?

    (A) They assume that natural resources are infinitely available.

    (B) They assume that human-made resources are infinitely available.

    (C) They assume that availability of resources places an upper limit on growth.

    (D) They assume that efficient management of resources is necessary to growth.

    (E) They assume that human-made resources are preferable to natural resources.

Opponents of compulsory national service claim that such a program is not in keeping with the liberal principles upon which Western democracies are founded. This reasoning is reminiscent of the argument
(5) that a tax on one's income is undemocratic because it violates one's right to property. Such conceptions of the liberal state fail to take into account the intricate character of the social agreement that undergirds our liberties. It is only in the context of a community that
(10) the notion of individual rights has any application; individual rights are meant to define the limits of people's actions with respect to other people. Implicit in such a context is the concept of shared sacrifice. Were no taxes paid, there could be no law enforcement,
(15) and the enforcement of law is of benefit to everyone in society. Thus, each of us must bear a share of the burden to ensure that the community is protected.

The responsibility to defend one's nation against outside aggression is surely no less than the
(20) responsibility to help pay for law enforcement within the nation. Therefore, the state is certainly within its rights to compel citizens to perform national service when it is needed for the benefit of society.

It might be objected that the cases of taxation and
(25) national service are not analogous: While taxation must be coerced, the military is quite able to find recruits without resorting to conscription. Furthermore, proponents of national service do not limit its scope to only those duties absolutely necessary to the defense of
(30) the nation. Therefore, it may be contended, compulsory national service oversteps the acceptable boundaries of governmental interference in the lives of its citizens.

By responding thus, the opponent of national service has already allowed that it is a right of
(35) government to demand service when it is needed. But what is the true scope of the term "need"? If it is granted, say, that present tax policies are legitimate intrusions on the right to property, then it must also be granted that need involves more than just what is
(40) necessary for a sound national defense. Even the most conservative of politicians admits that tax money is rightly spent on programs that, while not necessary for the survival of the state, are nevertheless of great benefit to society. Can the opponent of national service
(45) truly claim that activities of the military such as quelling civil disorders, rebuilding dams and bridges, or assisting the victims of natural disasters—all extraneous to the defense of society against outside aggression—do not provide a similar benefit to the
(50) nation? Upon reflection, opponents of national service must concede that such a broadened conception of what is necessary is in keeping with the ideas of shared sacrifice and community benefit that are essential to the functioning of a liberal democratic state.

50. Which one of the following most accurately describes the author's attitude toward the relationship between citizenship and individual rights in a democracy?

(A) confidence that individual rights are citizens' most important guarantees of personal freedom

(B) satisfaction at how individual rights have protected citizens from unwarranted government intrusion

(C) alarm that so many citizens use individual rights as an excuse to take advantage of one another

(D) concern that individual rights represent citizens' only defense against government interference

(E) dissatisfaction at how some citizens cite individual rights as a way of avoiding certain obligations to their government

51. The author indicates that all politicians agree about the

(A) legitimacy of funding certain programs that serve the national good

(B) use of the military to prevent domestic disorders

(C) similarity of conscription and compulsory taxation

(D) importance of broadening the definition of necessity

(E) compatibility of compulsion with democratic principles

Source: PrepTest 26, Section 4, Passage 1, Questions 1–5

52. Which one of the following most accurately characterizes what the author means by the term "social agreement" (line 8)?

    (A) an agreement among members of a community that the scope of their individual liberties is limited somewhat by their obligations to one another

    (B) an agreement among members of a community that they will not act in ways that infringe upon each other's pursuit of individual liberty

    (C) an agreement among members of a community that they will petition the government for redress when government actions limit their rights

    (D) an agreement between citizens and their government detailing which government actions do or do not infringe upon citizens' personal freedoms

    (E) an agreement between citizens and their government stating that the government has the right to suspend individual liberties whenever it sees fit

53. According to the author, national service and taxation are analogous in the sense that both

    (A) do not require that citizens be compelled to help bring them about

    (B) are at odds with the notion of individual rights in a democracy

    (C) require different degrees of sacrifice from different citizens

    (D) allow the government to overstep its boundaries and interfere in the lives of citizens

    (E) serve ends beyond those related to the basic survival of the state

54. Based on the information in the passage, which one of the following would most likely be found objectionable by those who oppose compulsory national service?

    (A) the use of tax revenues to prevent the theft of national secrets by foreign agents

    (B) the use of tax revenues to fund relief efforts for victims of natural disasters in other nations

    (C) the use of tax revenues to support the upkeep of the nation's standing army

    (D) the use of tax revenues to fund programs for the maintenance of domestic dams and bridges

    (E) the use of tax revenues to aid citizens who are victims of natural disasters

Most studies of recent Southeast Asian immigrants to the United States have focused on their adjustment to life in their adopted country and on the effects of leaving their homelands. James Tollefson's *Alien*
(5) *Winds* examines the resettlement process from a different perspective by investigating the educational programs offered in immigrant processing centers. Based on interviews, transcripts from classes, essays by immigrants, personal visits to a teacher-training unit,
(10) and official government documents, Tollefson relies on an impressive amount and variety of documentation in making his arguments about processing centers' educational programs.

Tollefson's main contention is that the emphasis
(15) placed on immediate employment and on teaching the values, attitudes, and behaviors that the training personnel think will help the immigrants adjust more easily to life in the United States is often counterproductive and demoralizing. Because of
(20) concerns that the immigrants be self-supporting as soon as possible, they are trained almost exclusively for low-level jobs that do not require English proficiency. In this respect, Tollefson claims, the processing centers suit the needs of employers more than they suit the
(25) long-term needs of the immigrant community. Tollefson also detects a fundamental flaw in the attempts by program educators to instill in the immigrants the traditionally Western principles of self-sufficiency and individual success. These efforts often
(30) have the effect of undermining the immigrants' sense of community and, in doing so, sometimes isolate them from the moral support and even from business opportunities afforded by the immigrant community. The programs also encourage the immigrants to shed
(35) their cultural traditions and ethnic identity and adopt the lifestyles, beliefs, and characteristics of their adopted country if they wish to enter fully into the national life.

Tollefson notes that the ideological nature of these
(40) educational programs has roots in the turn-of-the-century educational programs designed to assimilate European immigrants into United States society. Tollefson provides a concise history of the assimilationist movement in immigrant education, in
(45) which European immigrants were encouraged to leave behind the ways of the Old World and to adopt instead the principles and practices of the New World.

Tollefson ably shows that the issues demanding real attention in the educational programs for Southeast
(50) Asian immigrants are not merely employment rates and government funding, but also the assumptions underpinning the educational values in the programs. He recommends many improvements for the programs, including giving the immigrants a stronger voice in
(55) determining their needs and how to meet them, redesigning the curricula, and emphasizing long-term language education and job training over immediate employment and the avoiding of public assistance. Unfortunately, though, Tollefson does not offer enough
(60) concrete solutions as to how these reforms could be carried out, despite his own descriptions of the complicated bureaucratic nature of the programs.

55. Which one of the following statements best expresses the main idea of the passage?

(A) Tollefson's focus on the economic and cultural factors involved in adjusting to a new country offers a significant departure from most studies of Southeast Asian immigration.

(B) In his analysis of educational programs for Southeast Asian immigrants, Tollefson fails to acknowledge many of the positive effects the programs have had on immigrants' lives.

(C) Tollefson convincingly blames the philosophy underlying immigrant educational programs for some of the adjustment problems afflicting Southeast Asian immigrants.

(D) Tollefson's most significant contribution is his analysis of how Southeast Asian immigrants overcome the obstacles they encounter in immigrant educational programs.

(E) Tollefson traces a gradual yet significant change in the attitudes held by processing center educators toward Southeast Asian immigrants.

Source: PrepTest 21, Section 4, Passage 4, Questions 22–27

56. With which one of the following statements concerning the educational programs of the immigration centers would Tollefson most probably agree?

    (A) Although the programs offer adequate job training, they offer inadequate English training.
    (B) Some of the programs' attempts to improve the earning power of the immigrants cut them off from potential sources of income.
    (C) Inclusion of the history of immigration in the United States in the programs' curricula facilitates adjustment for the immigrants.
    (D) Immigrants would benefit if instructors in the programs were better prepared to teach the curricula developed in the teacher-training courses.
    (E) The programs' curricula should be redesigned to include greater emphasis on the shared values, beliefs, and practices in the United States.

57. Which one of the following best describes the opinion of the author of the passage with respect to Tollefson's work?

    (A) thorough but misguided
    (B) innovative but incomplete
    (C) novel but contradictory
    (D) illuminating but unappreciated
    (E) well documented but unoriginal

58. The passage suggests that which one of the following is an assumption underlying the educational approach in immigrant processing centers?

    (A) There is a set of values and behaviors that, if adopted by immigrants, facilitate adjustment to United States society.
    (B) When recent immigrants are self-supporting rather than supported by public assistance, they tend to gain English proficiency more quickly.
    (C) Immediate employment tends to undermine the immigrants' sense of community with each other.
    (D) Long-term success for immigrants is best achieved by encouraging the immigrants to maintain a strong sense of community.
    (E) The principles of self-sufficiency and individual success are central to Southeast Asian culture and ethnicity.

59. Which one of the following best describes the function of the first paragraph of the passage?

    (A) It provides the scholarly context for Tollefson's study and a description of his methodology.
    (B) It compares Tollefson's study to other works and presents the main argument of his study.
    (C) It compares the types of documents Tollefson uses to those used in other studies.
    (D) It presents the accepted theory on Tollefson's topic and the method by which Tollefson challenges it.
    (E) It argues for the analytical and technical superiority of Tollefson's study over other works on the topic.

60. The author of the passage refers to Tollefson's descriptions of the bureaucratic nature of the immigrant educational programs in the fourth paragraph most probably in order to

    (A) criticize Tollefson's decision to combine a description of the bureaucracies with suggestions for improvement
    (B) emphasize the author's disappointment in Tollefson's overly general recommendations for improvements to the programs
    (C) point out the irony of Tollefson concluding his study with suggestions for drastic changes in the programs
    (D) support a contention that Tollefson's recommendations for improvements do not focus on the real sources of the programs' problems
    (E) suggest a parallel between the complexity of the bureaucracies and the complexity of Tollefson's arguments

In *The Dynamics of Apocalypse*, John Lowe
attempts to solve the mystery of the collapse of the
Classic Mayan civilization. Lowe bases his study on a
detailed examination of the known archaeological
(5) record. Like previous investigators, Lowe relies on
dated monuments to construct a step-by-step account of
the actual collapse. Using the erection of new
monuments as a means to determine a site's occupation
span, Lowe assumes that once new monuments ceased
(10) to be built, a site had been abandoned. Lowe's analysis
of the evidence suggests that construction of new
monuments continued to increase between A.D. 672
and 751, but that the civilization stopped expanding
geographically; new construction took place almost
(15) exclusively in established settlements. The first signs
of trouble followed. Monument inscriptions indicate
that between 751 and 790, long-standing alliances
started to break down. Evidence also indicates that
between 790 and 830, the death rate in Classic Mayan
(20) cities outstripped the birthrate. After approximately
830, construction stopped throughout the area, and
within a hundred years, the Classic Mayan civilization
all but vanished.

Having established this chronology, Lowe sets
(25) forth a plausible explanation of the collapse that
accommodates the available archaeological evidence.
He theorizes that Classic Mayan civilization was
brought down by the interaction of several factors, set
in motion by population growth. An increase in
(30) population, particularly within the elite segment of
society, necessitated ever more intense farming.
Agricultural intensification exerted stress on the soil
and led to a decline in productivity (the amount of food
produced through each unit of labor invested). At the
(35) same time, the growth of the elite class created
increasing demands for ceremonial monuments and
luxuries, diverting needed labor from the fields. The
theory holds that these stresses were communicated—
and amplified—throughout the area as Mayan states
(40) engaged in warfare to acquire laborers and food, and
refugees fled impoverished areas. The most vulnerable
states thus began to break down, and each downfall
triggered others, until the entire civilization collapsed.

If there is a central flaw in Lowe's explanation, it is
(45) that the entire edifice rests on the assumption that the
available evidence paints a true picture of how the
collapse proceeded. However, it is difficult to know
how accurately the archaeological record reflects
historic activity, especially of a complex civilization
(50) such as the Mayans', and a hypothesis can be tested
only against the best available data. It is quite possible
that our understanding of the collapse might be
radically altered by better data. For example, Lowe's
assumption about monument construction and the
(55) occupation span of a site might well be disproved if
further investigations of Classic Mayan sites
established that some remained heavily settled long
after the custom of carving dynastic monuments had
ceased.

61. Which one of the following best describes the
organization of the passage?

(A) A method used to analyze evidence is described,
an explanation of the evidence is suggested, and
then a conclusion is drawn from the evidence.

(B) A hypothesis is presented, evidence supporting
the hypothesis is provided, and then the
hypothesis is affirmed.

(C) An analysis of a study is presented, contradictory
evidence is examined, and then a direction for
future studies is suggested.

(D) The basis of a study is described, a theory that
explains the available evidence is presented, and
a possible flaw in the study is pointed out.

(E) An observation is made, evidence supporting the
observation is presented, and then contradictions
in the evidence are discussed.

62. Which one of the following best expresses the main idea
of the passage?

(A) In *The Dynamics of Apocalypse*, John Lowe
successfully proves that the collapse of
Classic Mayan civilization was set in motion
by increasing population and decreasing
productivity.

(B) In *The Dynamics of Apocalypse*, John Lowe
breaks new ground in solving the mystery of the
collapse of Classic Mayan civilization through
his use of dated monuments to create a step-by-
step account of the collapse.

(C) In *The Dynamics of Apocalypse*, John Lowe
successfully uses existing data to document the
reduction and then cessation of new construction
throughout Classic Mayan civilization.

(D) Although John Lowe's study is based on a careful
examination of the historical record, it does not
accurately reflect the circumstances surrounding
the collapse of Classic Mayan civilization.

(E) While John Lowe's theory about the collapse of
Classic Mayan civilization appears credible, it is
based on an assumption that cannot be verified
using the archaeological record.

Source: PrepTest 20, Section 2, Passage 4, Questions 22–26

63. Which one of the following is most closely analogous to the assumption Lowe makes about the relationship between monument construction and Classic Mayan cities?

(A) A person assumes that the shortage of fresh produce on the shelves of a grocery store is due to the effects of poor weather conditions during the growing season.

(B) A person assumes that a movie theater only shows foreign films because the titles of the films shown there are not familiar to the person.

(C) A person assumes that a restaurant is under new ownership because the restaurant's menu has changed drastically since the last time the person ate there.

(D) A person assumes that a corporation has been sold because there is a new name for the corporation on the sign outside the building where the company is located.

(E) A person assumes a friend has sold her stamp collection because the friend has stopped purchasing new stamps.

64. It can be inferred from the passage that the author would describe the method Lowe used to construct a step-by-step chronology of the actual collapse of Classic Mayan civilization as

(A) daringly innovative but flawed
(B) generally accepted but questionable
(C) very reliable but outdated
(D) unscientific but effective
(E) unconventional but brilliant

65. The author of the passage would most likely agree with which one of the following statements about the use of the archaeological record to reconstruct historic activity?

(A) With careful analysis, archaeological evidence can be used to reconstruct accurately the historic activity of a past civilization.

(B) Archaeological evidence is more useful for reconstructing the day-to-day activities of a culture than its long-term trends.

(C) The accuracy of the archaeological record for reconstructing historic activity is dependent on the duration of the particular civilization.

(D) The archaeological record is not an appropriate source of data for reconstructing historic activity.

(E) Historic activity can be reconstructed from archaeological evidence, but it is ultimately impossible to confirm the accuracy of the reconstruction.

To some scholars, the European baroque is not merely an aesthetic style characterized by extravagant forms and elaborate ornamentation, but also a political, social, and cultural mentality prevalent in Europe from
(5) approximately 1600 to 1680. This larger view was held by the late Spanish historian José Antonio Maravall, whose writings trace aspects of the modern world—especially the principle of individual liberty in opposition to the state's power—back to the baroque
(10) era as it unfolded in Spain.

Maravall argues that the baroque period was characterized by "monarchical absolutism": monarchs, having suppressed the worst excesses of aristocratic disorder, could now ally themselves with their
(15) nobilities to defend traditional order and values in societies unsettled by the Renaissance's liberating forces of criticism and opposition. These forces appeared especially threatening because deteriorating economic conditions heightened conflict among
(20) different elements of society. For Maravall, baroque culture was the response of the ruling class (including crown, Church, and nobility) to the European social and economic crisis, although that crisis was more acute, and the social structure more frozen, in imperial
(25) Spain than elsewhere. Maravall regards the baroque as a culture of control and containment, or, more dynamically, as a directive culture, designed to reintegrate and unite a society living under the shadow of social and intellectual disruption.

(30) Maravall suggests that even though all the political controls were centralized in the monarchical system, this system of authority was not simply repressive. It was also enticing, promoting a public delight in grandiose artifice by means of devices that ranged from
(35) fireworks displays to theater to religious festivals. Operating upon an urban culture that already possessed characteristics of modern mass culture, these enticements deflected the desire for novelty into areas of life where it represented no challenge to the political
(40) order. Maravall concludes that every aspect of the baroque emerged from the necessity, as public opinion grew increasingly important, of manipulating opinions and feelings on a broad public scale.

Perhaps, however, Maravall's interpretation is
(45) overly influenced by his quest for baroque foreshadowings of "modernity" and by his experience of living under the Spanish dictator Franco. He tends to exaggerate the capacity of those in authority to manipulate a society for their own ideological ends. A
(50) look at the seventeenth-century courts of Charles I in England or Philip IV in Spain suggests that efforts at manipulation were at times wholly counterproductive. In England and Spain during the 1630s, the rulers themselves, not the subjects, succumbed to the illusions
(55) carefully sustained by ceremony, theater, and symbol. The result was that members of the ruling class became dangerously isolated from the outside world, and as the gulf between illusion and reality widened, the monarchy and aristocracy fell headlong into a
(60) credibility gap of their own creation.

66. Which one of the following best expresses the main idea of the passage?

   (A)   Until recently, the baroque has been regarded simply as an aesthetic style; however, Maravall has shown that it was a cultural mentality serving to reinforce monarchical absolutism.

   (B)   Maravall views baroque culture as a strategy for dissipating opposition and managing public opinion; however, he overestimates the strategy's success.

   (C)   Maravall interprets European baroque culture as an expansion of the social and intellectual developments of the Renaissance; however, his view of the seventeenth century is colored by his focus on Spain.

   (D)   Manvall's theory about the intent of the ruling class to control society via baroque culture is refuted by the examples of specific baroque-era monarchies.

   (E)   According to the historian Maravall, baroque culture was a political construct designed essentially to control society and repress dissent.

67. Which one of the following phrases, in the context in which it occurs, most accurately indicates the author's attitude toward Maravall's concept of baroque culture?

   (A)   "This larger view" (line 5)
   (B)   "grandiose artifice" (line 34)
   (C)   "tends to exaggerate" (lines 47–48)
   (D)   "own ideological ends" (line 49)
   (E)   "wholly counterproductive" (line 52)

68. Which one of the following words best expresses the meaning of "directive" as that word is used in line 27 of the passage?

   (A)   straightforward
   (B)   evolving
   (C)   codified
   (D)   guiding
   (E)   compelling

Source: PrepTest A, Section 2, Passage 4, Questions 21–27

69. It can be inferred from the passage that Maravall regarded monarchs of the baroque era as

    (A) increasingly indifferent to unfavorable public opinion
    (B) concerned with the political threat posed by the aristocracy
    (C) captivated by the cultural devices designed to control their subjects
    (D) somewhat successful in countering the disruptive legacy of the Renaissance
    (E) preoccupied with the goal of attaining cultural preeminence for their respective countries

70. In Maravall's view, baroque theater was intended to

    (A) spur economic growth
    (B) echo the consensus of public opinion
    (C) entertain and divert the urban population
    (D) express the emerging principle of individual liberty
    (E) terrify the citizenry with the threat of monarchical repression

71. The main purpose of the passage is to

    (A) contrast two competing theories and offer an evaluation
    (B) challenge a widely accepted viewpoint by means of a counterexample
    (C) explicate an interpretation and introduce a qualification
    (D) articulate opposing arguments and propose a reconciliation
    (E) explain the unprecedented consequences of a political construct

72. Which one of the following pieces of evidence, if it existed, would most weaken Maravall's interpretation of baroque culture?

    (A) confirmation that Maravall himself participated in opposing Franco's authoritarian regime
    (B) the discovery that baroque-era nobility commissioned far more works of art than did the monarchs
    (C) an analysis of baroque art that emphasizes its idealized depiction of the monarchy and aristocracy
    (D) documents indicating that many baroque-era works of art expressed opposition to the monarchy
    (E) documents indicating a conscious attempt on the part of Franco to control Spanish society by cultural means

During the 1940s and 1950s the United States government developed a new policy toward Native Americans, often known as "readjustment." Because the increased awareness of civil rights in these decades
(5) helped reinforce the belief that life on reservations prevented Native Americans from exercising the rights guaranteed to citizens under the United States Constitution, the readjustment movement advocated the end of the federal government's involvement in
(10) Native American affairs and encouraged the assimilation of Native Americans as individuals into mainstream society. However, the same years also saw the emergence of a Native American leadership and efforts to develop tribal institutions and reaffirm tribal
(15) identity. The clash of these two trends may be traced in the attempts on the part of the Bureau of Indian Affairs (BIA) to convince the Oneida tribe of Wisconsin to accept readjustment.

The culmination of BIA efforts to sway the
(20) Oneida occurred at a meeting that took place in the fall of 1956. The BIA suggested that it would be to the Oneida's benefit to own their own property and, like other homeowners, pay real estate taxes on it. The BIA also emphasized that, after readjustment, the
(25) government would not attempt to restrict Native Americans' ability to sell their individually owned lands. The Oneida were then offered a one-time lump-sum payment of $60,000 in lieu of the $0.52 annuity guaranteed in perpetuity to each member of
(30) the tribe under the Canandaigua Treaty.

The efforts of the BIA to "sell" readjustment to the tribe failed because the Oneida realized that they had heard similar offers before. The Oneida delegates reacted negatively to the BIA's first
(35) suggestion because taxation of Native American lands had been one past vehicle for dispossessing the Oneida: after the distribution of some tribal lands to individual Native Americans in the late nineteenth century, Native American lands became
(40) subject to taxation, resulting in new and impossible financial burdens, foreclosures, and subsequent tax sales of property. The Oneida delegates were equally suspicious of the BIA's emphasis on the rights of individual landowners, since in the late
(45) nineteenth century many individual Native Americans had been convinced by unscrupulous speculators to sell their lands. Finally, the offer of a lump-sum payment was unanimously opposed by the Oneida delegates, who saw that changing the
(50) terms of a treaty might jeopardize the many pending land claims based upon the treaty.

As a result of the 1956 meeting, the Oneida rejected readjustment. Instead, they determined to improve tribal life by lobbying for federal monies
(55) for postsecondary education, for the improvement of drainage on tribal lands, and for the building of a convalescent home for tribal members. Thus, by learning the lessons of history, the Oneida were able to survive as a tribe in their homeland.

73. Which one of the following would be most consistent with the policy of readjustment described in the passage?

(A) the establishment among Native Americans of a tribal system of elected government
(B) the creation of a national project to preserve Native American language and oral history
(C) the establishment of programs to encourage Native Americans to move from reservations to urban areas
(D) the development of a large-scale effort to restore Native American lands to their original tribes
(E) the reaffirmation of federal treaty obligations to Native American tribes

74. According to the passage, after the 1956 meeting the Oneida resolved to

(A) obtain improved social services and living conditions for members of the tribe
(B) pursue litigation designed to reclaim tribal lands
(C) secure recognition of their unique status as a self-governing Native American nation within the United States
(D) establish new kinds of tribal institutions
(E) cultivate a life-style similar to that of other United States citizens

75. Which one of the following best describes the function of the first paragraph in the context of the passage as a whole?

(A) It summarizes the basis of a conflict underlying negotiations described elsewhere in the passage.
(B) It presents two positions, one of which is defended by evidence provided in succeeding paragraphs.
(C) It compares competing interpretations of a historical conflict.
(D) It analyzes the causes of a specific historical event and predicts a future development.
(E) It outlines the history of a government agency.

Source: PrepTest 9, Section 1, Passage 2, Questions 7–13

76. The author refers to the increased awareness of civil rights during the 1940s and 1950s most probably in order to

    EX
    ADV

    (A) contrast the readjustment movement with other social phenomena
    (B) account for the stance of the Native American leadership
    (C) help explain the impetus for the readjustment movement
    (D) explain the motives of BIA bureaucrats
    (E) foster support for the policy of readjustment

77. The passage suggests that advocates of readjustment would most likely agree with which one of the following statements regarding the relationship between the federal government and Native Americans?

    EX
    ADV

    (A) The federal government should work with individual Native Americans to improve life on reservations.
    (B) The federal government should be no more involved in the affairs of Native Americans than in the affairs of other citizens.
    (C) The federal government should assume more responsibility for providing social services to Native Americans.
    (D) The federal government should share its responsibility for maintaining Native American territories with tribal leaders.
    (E) The federal government should observe all provisions of treaties made in the past with Native Americans.

78. The passage suggests that the Oneida delegates viewed the Canandaigua Treaty as

    EX
    ADV

    (A) a valuable safeguard of certain Oneida rights and privileges
    (B) the source of many past problems for the Oneida tribe
    (C) a model for the type of agreement they hoped to reach with the federal government
    (D) an important step toward recognition of their status as an independent Native American nation
    (E) an obsolete agreement without relevance for their current condition

79. Which one of the following situations most closely parallels that of the Oneida delegates in refusing to accept a lump-sum payment of $60,000?

    EX
    ADV

    (A) A university offers a student a four-year scholarship with the stipulation that the student not accept any outside employment; the student refuses the offer and attends a different school because the amount of the scholarship would not have covered living expenses.
    (B) A company seeking to reduce its payroll obligations offers an employee a large bonus if he will accept early retirement; the employee refuses because he does not want to compromise an outstanding worker's compensation suit.
    (C) Parents of a teenager offer to pay her at the end of the month for performing weekly chores rather than paying her on a weekly basis; the teenager refuses because she has a number of financial obligations that she must meet early in the month.
    (D) A car dealer offers a customer a $500 cash payment for buying a new car; the customer refuses because she does not want to pay taxes on the amount, and requests instead that her monthly payments be reduced by a proportionate amount.
    (E) A landlord offers a tenant several months rent-free in exchange for the tenant's agreeing not to demand that her apartment be painted every two years, as is required by the lease; the tenant refuses because she would have to spend her own time painting the apartment.

Personal names are generally regarded by European thinkers in two major ways, both of which deny that names have any significant semantic content. In philosophy and linguistics, John Stuart Mill's
(5) formulation that "proper names are meaningless marks set upon...persons to distinguish them from one another" retains currency; in anthropology, Claude Lévi-Strauss's characterization of names as being primarily instruments of social classification has been
(10) very influential. Consequently, interpretation of personal names in societies were names have other functions and meanings has been neglected. Among the Hopi of the southwestern United States, names often refer to historical or ritual events in order both to place
(15) individuals within society and to confer an identity upon them. Furthermore, the images used to evoke these events suggest that Hopi names can be seen as a type of poetic composition.

Throughout life, Hopis receive several names in a
(20) sequence of ritual initiations. Birth, entry into one of the ritual societies during childhood, and puberty are among the name-giving occasions. Names are conferred by an adult member of a clan other than the child's clan, and names refer to that name giver's clan,
(25) sometimes combining characteristics of the clan's totem animal with the child's characteristics. Thus, a name might translate to something as simple as "little rabbit," which reflects both the child's size and the representative animal.

(30) More often, though, the name giver has in mind a specific event that is not apparent in a name's literal translation. One Lizard clan member from the village of Oraibi is named Lomayayva, "beautifully ascended." This translation, however, tells nothing
(35) about either the event referred to—who or what ascended—or the name giver's clan. The name giver in this case is from Badger clan. Badger clan is responsible for an annual ceremony featuring a procession in which masked representations of spirits
(40) climb the mesa on which Oraibi sits. Combining the name giver's clan association with the receiver's home village, "beautifully ascended" refers to the splendid colors and movements of the procession up the mesa. The condensed image this name evokes—a typical
(45) feature of Hopi personal names—displays the same quality of Western Apache place names that led one commentator to call them "tiny imagist poems."

Hopi personal names do several things simultaneously. They indicate social relationships—but
(50) only indirectly—and they individuate persons. Equally important, though, is their poetic quality; in a sense they can be understood as oral texts that produce aesthetic delight. This view of Hopi names is thus opposed not only to Mill's claim that personal names
(55) are without inherent meaning but also to Lévi-Strauss's purely functional characterization. Interpreters must understand Hopi clan structures and linguistic practices in order to discern the beauty and significance of Hopi names.

80. Which one of the following statements most accurately summarizes the passage's main point?

(A) Unlike European names, which are used exclusively for identification or exclusively for social classification, Hopi names perform both these functions simultaneously.

(B) Unlike European names, Hopi names tend to neglect the functions of identification and social classification in favor of a concentration on compression and poetic effects.

(C) Lacking knowledge of the intricacies of Hopi linguistic and tribal structures, European thinkers have so far been unable to discern the deeper significance of Hopi names.

(D) Although some Hopi names may seem difficult to interpret, they all conform to a formula whereby a reference to the name giver's clan is combined with a reference to the person named.

(E) While performing the functions ascribed to names by European thinkers, Hopi names also possess a significant aesthetic quality that these thinkers have not adequately recognized.

81. The author most likely refers to Western Apache place names (line 46) in order to

(A) offer an example of how names can contain references not evident in their literal translations

(B) apply a commentator's characterization of Western Apache place names to Hopi personal names

(C) contrast Western Apache naming practices with Hopi naming practices

(D) demonstrate that other names besides Hopi names may have some semantic content

(E) explain how a specific Hopi name refers subtly to a particular Western Apache site

82. Which one of the following statements describes an example of the function accorded to personal names under Lévi-Strauss's view?

(A) Some parents select their children's names from impersonal sources such as books.

(B) Some parents wait to give a child a name in order to choose one that reflects the child's looks or personality.

(C) Some parents name their children in honor of friends or famous people.

(D) Some family members have no parts of their names in common.

(E) Some family names originated as identifications of their bearers' occupations.

Source: PrepTest 27, Section 3, Passage 2, Questions 8–14

MASTERY PRACTICE

83. The primary function of the second paragraph is to

R E

(A) present reasons why Hopi personal names can be treated as poetic compositions

(B) support the claim that Hopi personal names make reference to events in the recipient's life

(C) argue that the fact that Hopis receive many names throughout life refutes European theories about naming

(D) illustrate ways in which Hopi personal names may have semantic content

(E) demonstrate that the literal translation of Hopi personal names often obscures their true meaning

84. Based on the passage, with which one of the following statements about Mill's view would the author of the passage be most likely to agree?

R E

(A) Its characterization of the function of names is too narrow to be universally applicable.

(B) It would be correct if it recognized the use of names as instruments of social classification.

(C) Its influence single-handedly led scholars to neglect how names are used outside Europe.

(D) It is more accurate than Lévi-Strauss's characterization of the purpose of names.

(E) It is less relevant than Lévi-Strauss's characterization in understanding Hopi naming practices.

85. It can be inferred from the passage that each of the following features of Hopi personal names contributes to their poetic quality EXCEPT:

R E

(A) their ability to be understood as oral texts

(B) their use of condensed imagery to evoke events

(C) their capacity to produce aesthetic delight

(D) their ability to confer identity upon individuals

(E) their ability to subtly convey meaning

86. The author's primary purpose in writing the passage it to

R E

(A) present an anthropological study of Hopi names

(B) propose a new theory about the origin of name

(C) describe several competing theories of names

(D) criticize two influential views of names

(E) explain the cultural origins of names

Although the United States steel industry faces widely publicized economic problems that have eroded its steel production capacity, not all branches of the industry have been equally affected. The steel
(5) industry is not monolithic: it includes integrated producers, minimills, and specialty-steel mills. The integrated producers start with iron ore and coal and produce a wide assortment of shaped steels. The minimills reprocess scrap steel into a limited
(10) range of low-quality products, such as reinforcing rods for concrete. The specialty-steel mills are similar to minimills in that they tend to be smaller than the integrated producers and are based on scrap, but they manufacture much more expensive
(15) products than minimills do and commonly have an active in-house research-and-development effort.

Both minimills and specialty-steel mills have succeeded in avoiding the worst of the economic difficulties that are afflicting integrated steel
(20) producers, and some of the mills are quite profitable. Both take advantage of new technology for refining and casting steel, such as continuous casting, as soon as it becomes available. The minimills concentrate on producing a narrow range
(25) of products for sale in their immediate geographic area, whereas specialty-steel mills preserve flexibility in their operations in order to fulfill a customer's particular specifications.

Among the factors that constrain the
(30) competitiveness of integrated producers are excessive labor, energy, and capital costs, as well as manufacturing inflexibility. Their equipment is old and less automated, and does not incorporate many of the latest refinements in steelmaking technology.
(35) (For example, only about half of the United States integrated producers have continuous casters, which combine pouring and rolling into one operation and thus save the cost of separate rolling equipment.) One might conclude that the older,
(40) labor-intensive machinery still operating in United States integrated plants is at fault for the poor performance of the United States industry, but this cannot explain why Japanese integrated producers, who produce a higher-quality product using less
(45) energy and labor, are also experiencing economic trouble. The fact is that the common technological denominator of integrated producers is an inherently inefficient process that is still rooted in the nineteenth century.
(50) Integrated producers have been unable to compete successfully with minimills because the minimills, like specialty-steel mills, have dispensed almost entirely with the archaic energy- and capital-intensive front end of integrated steelmaking:
(55) the iron-smelting process, including the mining and preparation of the raw materials and the blast-furnace operation. In addition, minimills have found a profitable way to market steel products: as indicated above, they sell their finished products
(60) locally, thereby reducing transportation costs, and concentrate on a limited range of shapes and sizes

within a narrow group of products that can be manufactured economically. For these reasons, minimills have been able to avoid the economic
(65) decline affecting integrated steel producers.

87. Which one of the following best expresses the main idea of the passage?

A D V

(A) United States steel producers face economic problems that are shared by producers in other nations.

(B) Minimills are the most successful steel producers because they best meet market demands for cheap steel.

(C) Minimills and specialty-steel mills are more economically competitive than integrated producers because they use new technology and avoid the costs of the iron-smelting process.

(D) United States steel producers are experiencing an economic decline that can be traced back to the nineteenth century.

(E) New steelmaking technologies such as continuous casting will replace blast-furnace operations to reverse the decline in United States steel production.

88. The author mentions all of the following as features of minimills EXCEPT

A D V

(A) flexibility in their operations

(B) local sale of their products

(C) avoidance of mining operations

(D) use of new steel-refining technology

(E) a limited range of low-quality products

89. The author of the passage refers to "Japanese integrated producers" (line 43) primarily in order to support the view that

A D V

(A) different economic difficulties face the steel industries of different nations

(B) not all integrated producers share a common technological denominator

(C) labor-intensive machinery cannot be blamed for the economic condition of United States integrated steel producers

(D) modern steelmaking technology is generally labor- and energy-efficient

(E) labor-intensive machinery is an economic burden on United States integrated steel producers

Source: PrepTest 6, Section 1, Passage 4, Questions 21–27

90. Which one of the following best describes the
organization of the third paragraph?

ADV

(A) A hypothesis is proposed and supported; then an
opposing view is presented and criticized.

(B) A debate is described and illustrated; then a
contrast is made and the debate is resolved.

(C) A dilemma is described and cited as evidence for
a broader criticism.

(D) A proposition is stated and argued, then rejected
in favor of a more general statement, which is
supported with additional evidence.

(E) General statements are made and details given;
then an explanation is proposed and rejected,
and an alternative is offered.

91. It can be inferred from the passage that United States
specialty-steel mills generally differ from integrated
steel producers in that the specialty-steel mills

ADV

(A) sell products in a restricted geographical area

(B) share the economic troubles of the minimills

(C) resemble specialty-steel mills found in Japan

(D) concentrate on producing a narrow range of
products

(E) do not operate blast furnaces

92. Each of the following describes an industry facing a
problem also experienced by United States integrated
steel producers EXCEPT

ADV

(A) a paper-manufacturing company that experiences
difficulty in obtaining enough timber and other
raw materials to meet its orders

(B) a food-canning plant whose canning machines
must constantly be tended by human operators

(C) a textile firm that spends heavily on capital
equipment and energy to process raw cotton
before it is turned into fabric

(D) a window-glass manufacturer that is unable to
produce quickly different varieties of glass with
special features required by certain customers

(E) a leather-goods company whose hand-operated
cutting and stitching machines were
manufactured in Italy in the 1920s

93. Which one of the following, if true, would best serve as
supporting evidence for the author's explanation of the
economic condition of integrated steel producers?

ADV

(A) Those nations that derive a larger percentage of
their annual steel production from minimills
than the United States does also have a smaller
per capita trade deficit.

(B) Many integrated steel producers are as adept
as the specialty-steel mills at producing
high-quality products to meet customer
specifications.

(C) Integrated steel producers in the United States
are rapidly adopting the production methods of
Japanese integrated producers.

(D) Integrated steel producers in the United States are
now attempting to develop a worldwide market
by advertising heavily.

(E) Those nations in which iron-smelting operations
are carried out independently of steel production
must heavily subsidize those operations in order
to make them profitable.

Mastery Practice

Answers and Explanations

Humanities Passages

Passage 1: Poetry and Fiction
Questions 1–8

Paragraph 1 jumps right into the **Topic**—the division between poetry and fiction in the U.S. The Scope and Purpose won't become clear until later in this Humanities passage, but the first paragraph does narrow the topic for us a bit by focusing in on writers and how they've perpetuated the division between fiction and poetry.

Paragraph 2 suggests a possible reason for the division: U.S. culture doesn't think much of generalists. We also get a good taste for the author's perspective in the last sentence, "…as if ability in one field is diluted or compromised by accomplishment in another." That should clue you in that the author thinks ability is not diminished by involvement in multiple fields, and starts to suggest the Scope of the passage.

Paragraph 3 starts with another strong indication of the author's view, the Keyword "Fortunately." Our author thinks it's a good thing that the boundaries are starting to break down. The rest of the paragraph (and, indeed, the rest of the passage) is devoted to the example of Rita Dove, an author whose work blends elements traditionally associated with poetry and those traditionally associated with fiction. Here, the Scope and Purpose finally come into sharp relief. The **Scope**, or aspect of the poetry/fiction rift our author is most concerned with, is the move toward the breakdown of the barrier between the two, as represented by Rita Dove. The author's **Purpose** is simply to illustrate the trend toward breaking down the poetry/fiction divide that Rita Dove exemplifies. The author's attitude seems to suggest that he advocates for further breakdown of the barrier, but the rest of the passage doesn't quite go that far. Rather than advocating anything, the last paragraph simply explains how Dove bridges the gap between poetry and fiction in her work.

The Big Picture:

Paragraph 1: Rift b/t poetry and fiction; supported by poets & fiction writers

Paragraph 2: Why? U.S. suspicion of generalists

Paragraph 3: Fortunately (author) breaking down; Rita Dove ex.

Paragraph 4: How Dove blends genres/bridges gap

The Questions:

1. (E) Global (Main Point)

Use your Roadmap to predict the answer to a Main Point question up front—never jump into the answer choices blind.

Reviewing T/S/P and our Roadmap, what's the primary thing the author wants us to know? The rift between fiction and poetry is diminishing, as Rita Dove's work illustrates. That's a match for **(E)**, and for the neutral illustration that finishes the passage.

(A) is a distortion: The author makes no claim that the blending of elements is the reason Dove's work has been well received.

(B) The particular elements of Dove's writing are just details. A list of subsidiary details will never be correct when a question asks you for the main point of the entire passage.

(C) Lyrical use of language in narrative fiction is just one illustration of the crossover between genres, not a main point.

(D) is too narrow—there's no mention of the poetry/fiction rift that forms the foundation for the passage.

2. (D) Logic (Parallel Reasoning)

When asked to draw a parallel, generalize the references piece of the passage before examining the answer choices.

The first thing we need to do is go back to the passage and get a nutshell version of what the author says about Dove's literary achievements. Our Roadmap tells us that's probably in Paragraph 4. There, the author tells us that Dove uses techniques typically associated with poetry in her narrative fiction and vice versa. Our correct answer, then, will be about crossing genres, drawing elements from two different ones. That most closely matches **(D)**, in which a choreographer combines elements of two very different types of dance.

(A) The combination element might be tempting, but this ultimately distorts the author's point—Dove's writing doesn't combine 'traditional and nontraditional' methods.

(B) "Theoretical knowledge" is outside the scope of the passage.

(C) There's no true blending here; instead, one medium is consciously used to promote another.

(E) There aren't two genres here, either; guitar solos aren't exactly a departure from rock. **(E)** also introduces the element of work that's not original, something that doesn't come into play at all in the passage.

3. (A) Detail

"According to the passage" is your cue to research the relevant text—don't operate from memory.

The author talked about widely held views in the U.S.in both of the first two paragraphs. There are only two possibilities: from the first paragraph, that poetry should be lyrical and elliptical while fiction is rooted in character and narrative; from the second paragraph, we're suspicious of generalists. Scan the answer choices for either of those things. **(A)** is a match for the last sentence of the first paragraph.

(B) Distortion—the author discusses the differences between the genres, but he never makes a value comparison

(C) Another distortion; the first paragraph says they tend to be operated independently, but says nothing about the balance.

(D) "Most aesthetically effective" is too strong; the author does speak favorably of the outcome when fiction—at least, Dove's fiction—incorporates lyrical elements, but makes no comparison.

(E) Distortion—it's U.S. culture the author says is suspicious of generalists; this is a trap for test takers who skim the answer choices or who try to rely on memory to answer detail questions.

4. (E) Inference (Author's Attitude)

Zero in on the piece of the passage where the author revealed himself.

We could probably answer this question based on just one word of author opinion—that "fortunately" where he talks about the turning tide. From that, we can tell that the author's not a fan, and he's glad to see it changing. We only get author opinion in two other places, and in the final paragraph it's about the appeal of Dove's work, which won't help us answer this question. But in paragraph 2 he let us know that he thought the U.S. culture's suspicion of generalists—which he believes feeds the rift—was unfounded. That's one of those "attitudes and presuppositions underlying the rift" that pop up in **(E)**.

(A) The author isn't perplexed about what caused the rift; he tells us in the second paragraph.

(B) "Astonishment" is a strong word, and we have no reason to believe that the author thinks academics are unaware.

(C) There's no sign of ambivalence; the author makes his position on the division crystal clear.

(D) The final sentence of the passage announces that one writer, at least, bridges the gap.

5. (D) Detail

Use your Roadmap to help you find the answer to Detail questions.

Conveniently enough, we have a paragraph that we labelled "Why?", so we know right where to find the author's view of the cause. Paragraph 2 tells us that the author believes our skepticism about generalists is behind the division, and we find that in **(D)**.

(A) Beware of answer choices that sound true, but don't come from the passage. Our author never makes this claim, so it's outside the scope of the passage.

(B) The author does tell us that the programs for poetry and fiction are usually segregated, but he doesn't say (or imply)

that it's the cause of the rift. In addition, "other literary fields" is outside the scope—this is just about fiction and poetry.

(C) Entirely out of left field: the author doesn't blame publishers, doesn't mention pressure, and "best" doesn't come into play at all.

(E) Maybe it is—or maybe that's the perception—but our author doesn't advance that view.

6. (B) Logic Function

Context is everything in determining the purpose of a particular line, detail, or example.

In order to understand the author's purpose in mentioning a particular experience, we have to understand the purpose of the passage as a whole and of the paragraph in which the reference occurs. This particular experience is mentioned in the midst of the longer example of Dove, and comes on the heels of a description of how she couldn't understand the aversion to blending genres. The Germany reference simply builds on that, providing some background and context for her different perspective on crossing genre lines. That's **(B)**.

(A) The author specifically references U.S. attitudes, but there's no indication that this perspective is common to English speaking societies; in any case, the focus of the paragraph in which this detail falls is on the shift away from the clear division.

(C) Again, the paragraph is about the shift away from a hard poetry/fiction dividing line; it's not about Dove's skills in general.

(D) The focus isn't on Dove (or human interest), but on the trend away from clear fiction/poetry boundaries.

(E) We have no indication in the passage that Dove believes this to be the origin; she references growing up reading both genres.

7. (A) Inference

When an Inference question is wide open, with no direction in the question stem, work from the answer choices.

You should be able to predict an answer for most Reading Comprehension questions, even Inference questions. But when an Inference stem doesn't give you any clues to help you research the passage, that doesn't mean you need to work from memory or guess at the correct answer. Use the Hot Words or other clues in the answer choices to guide your research, like so:

(A) Correct—in paragraph 4, the author refers to each of the works he mentions as either poetry or fiction, even while describing how it incorporates elements of the other. For the record:

(B) is a distortion. The author talks about these elements in paragraph 4, but he's focused on the value of the blend, not comparing one to the other.

(C) is too extreme. "Without precedent" is a tip-off; such strong language is rarely warranted in an Inference question. Here, the passage itself says nothing so categorical; although he doesn't specifically reference another writer who blends elements of the two genres, he indicates that the division overall is breaking down.

(D) is a comparison that's outside the scope; the author doesn't set up any "better than" relationships among the various types of writing and hybrids he discusses.

(E) It seems reasonable that they might, but beware that kind of thinking! The only place the author talked about other forms like drama was in the reference to Dove's experience in Germany, and that isn't tied in specifically to the writers who successfully cross the fiction/poetry boundary—it's just an example of boundary crossing.

8. (A) Inference

Don't let unfamiliar formatting in a question stem throw you off; stay focused on the familiar.

The format of the question is a bit unusual, but take a moment to understand what it's really asking: *What would the author be likely to say about the future of U.S. literature?* That's just a standard Inference question, and one we can answer pretty quickly using our Roadmap. The author says it's "fortunate" that the division is deteriorating; he says Dove is "one example" of writers bridging the gap. What does he expect from the future? Apparently, a continuation of that trend. That's **(A)**.

(B) Markets are outside the scope.

(C) goes too far; the author doesn't talk about the specifics of the relationship between the two or about one or the other as primary—we only know that he thinks the boundaries are coming down.

(D) Contradicts the passage—that's the trend the author says we're finally breaking free of.

(E) Extreme and outside the scope; the focus throughout the passage is on the writers, not the audience.

Passage 2: Harriet Jacobs's Autobiography
Questions 9–15

The **Topic** is Jacobs's book, and the **Scope** is the book's meaning, both for readers at the time and today. In paragraph 1 the author describes what Jacobs did—create an autobiography in the form of, and embodying the values of, a conventional domestic novel—and argues that she demonstrates that those values are shared by free and slave women alike. That's the larger cultural perspective hinted at in lines 5–6 and reinforced in lines 21–22.

In paragraph 2 the author no sooner cites Jacobs's critics, who believe that the domestic-novel underpinnings weaken her book as slave narrative, than he spends the rest of paragraph 2 achieving his **Purpose** of denouncing them. They fail to note that Jacobs may laud the conventional values, but because her protagonist is slave rather than free she falls far short of them: Tragically, and uncharacteristically for the domestic novel, she loses her lover and is separated from her family. To the passage author, then, the tension caused by Jacobs' having both used and undercut domestic novel conventions is part of the book's strength and interest, rather than its weakness. That's the **Main Idea**.

The Questions:

9. (A) Inference (Author's Attitude)

Since the author's entire purpose is to knock down the critics who deplore the very aspect of Jacobs's book that he favors, "complete rejection," **(A)**, can be the only possible answer.

There is no "reluctance" **(B)** in that rejection, no palliative words to the critics who, in our author's eyes, have utterly missed the boat. Since the author does take a stand **(C)**, and it's quite negative **(D)**, **(E)**, the remaining choices can be ignored.

10. (D) Detail

The purview of this Detail question is paragraph 2, for it is there that the tension between the domestic novel genre and what Jacobs made of it is explored. Starting with "Unlike the traditional…" in line 34 down to line 45, we see that Jacobs's protagonist fails to win the ideals of family and domesticity that were a given at the end of the conventional domestic novel, and thus **(D)** is correct.

All four wrong choices are 180s, in that each is manifestly untrue of Jacobs's protagonist. Lines 40–41 make it clear that the protagonist does win her freedom, albeit at a terrible price **(A)**. **(B)** contradicts the entire thrust of lines 8–20, especially lines 18–20. Contrary to **(C)**, clearly the protagonist does encounter obstacles—serious ones; it's just that in most domestic novels, as opposed to Jacobs's text, the obstacles end in marriage. And the stigmas of which **(E)** speaks include the obstacles **(C)** describes, so **(E)** is false as well.

11. (E) Inference

The one and only reference to the critics comes in lines 23–26, so it should be a relatively simple matter to scan those lines and predict something very like **(E)**. It explains, in general terms, how the specific case of Jacobs's "mixture of genres" can compromise the goals or "purposes of the…slave narrative"—in the eyes of the critics, at least.

(A) is a 180 in that it represents our author's view, in stark contrast to that of the critics. **(B)** goes too far; the single sentence in lines 23–26 only asserts that in Jacobs's book "the domestic novel overshadow[s] …the…slave narrative," which is not the same thing as asserting that both genres have been "compromised." **(C)** and **(D)** are bogus, asserting conditions for one genre or the other's being somehow "favored" when genres are mixed, but there's no foundation for either idea in the single cited example of Harriet Jacobs.

12. (A) Logic (Strengthen)

Conveniently, we can move from an expression of the critics' view to a strengthening of same. We should expect to find in the right answer evidence of the watering-down or shortchanging of Jacobs's book, and we find it right away in **(A)**. If Jacobs's contemporary readers saw the book as nothing more than a domestic novel—if, in other words, the domestic aspects "overshadowed" the slave narrative elements—then the critics would be right, and Jacobs's efforts to "perceive [conventional] values within a broader social context" would have come to naught.

(B)'s focus on the issue of abolition dooms it, since the narrative under discussion concerns the freedom of one protagonist, not those of slaves in general. **(C)** would weaken rather than strengthen the critics' position, since it would argue for the mixing of genres that the critics deplore. That Jacobs might have mixed yet another genre into her book **(D)** would have no relevance here unless evidence were provided of the effect of that additional genre on the merits of the book, but **(D)** provides none. And since the critics are concerned with the merits of the book rather than its goals, **(E)** fails as well.

13. (C) Logic Function

The context of the line 49 reference leads squarely to **(C)**. Jacobs's book presents the domestic novel's "hierarchy of values" but shows that a female slave could not achieve them, thus demonstrating the hierarchy's "limitations."

As Jacobs's book is described, it seems inconceivable that the protagonist failed to lament the loss of her family **(A)**. She *shares* the conventional domestic aspirations, so **(C)** is a 180, not to mention a distortion in its rather snide characterization of "conventional values" as "stereotypical." The protagonist's plight **(D)** is caused by her position as a female slave, not by her domestic aspirations, which society dictates she cannot fulfill. **(E)** is a 180 as well; Jacobs's book is the "embodiment of...family and domesticity," not a condemnation of same.

14. (B) Inference

No way to predict an answer here. The author may or may not agree with **(A)**, but certainly Jacobs's book is emphatically not an example of the phenomenon. **(B)**, on the other hand, is justified by line 27–28, where the author explicitly refers to "the domestic novel" and "the typical slave narrative" as "the two genres."

Since Jacobs does just the opposite of **(C)** when she has her protagonist fail to achieve the ideals of the domestic novel, and does so to the author's approbation, **(C)** is the opposite of what we want. **(D)** is a plausible sentiment—who goes out of his or her way to cherish a limp story?—but the author never gets into a detailed comparison of autobiographies and novels, so there's no support for **(D)**. As for **(E)**, the author is throughout far more concerned with the book's literary (and social) merit than any historical accuracy.

15. (C) Logic (Principle)

It is useful to expect an answer that will sum up the author's overall point of view, and **(C)** does just that, picking up on the successes of the book cited in lines 17–22 and again in lines 48–55.

The mood **(A)** of Jacobs's period never enters the author's priorities, nor does historical accuracy **(B)**, as we saw in **(E)** of the previous question. The "perspective...familiar to the majority" in this case would be the domestic novel, but we cannot infer from this passage that the author favors its use by Jacobs because of its familiarity, as **(D)** would have it. **(E)** distorts the terms of the argument; the author is fond of Jacobs' mixing of the domestic and slave-narrative genres, not its mixing of autobiography with some other genre **(E)**.

Passage 3: Rembrandt: Entrepreneur Or Artist? Questions 16–20

Topic and Scope: Rembrandt's approach to art; specifically, how one scholar treats the issue of art vs. commerce in Rembrandt's aesthetic.

Purpose and Main Idea: The author's purpose is to evaluate the persuasiveness of Alpers' argument that Rembrandt's art was largely if not wholly determined by his (Rembrandt's) view of the art marketplace. In the end, the author finds this view too limited, granting some of Alpers' points but arguing that the view of Rembrandt-as-businessman misses some of the importance and validity of Rembrandt-as-artistic-genius. *Both* viewpoints have merit and should be part of the (pardon the pun) picture.

Paragraph Structure: Paragraph 1 begins with two fact-filled sentences that mention the possibly false Rembrandts that Alpers (according to sentence 3) uses as a jumping-off point for her "provocative discussion" of Rembrandt's work.

The alert critical reader will notice that Alpers, or a pronoun referring to her, is mentioned in virtually every sentence in paragraph 2. This fact alone ought to indicate the role of the paragraph: to describe Alpers' interpretation, or more specifically, to provide evidence for Alpers' claim in the first sentence (lines 11–13) that Rembrandt controlled his art to an "unprecedented" degree. The most potent sentence is the fifth one: According to Alpers, everything to Rembrandt was $$$.

Paragraph 3 may have surprised you. Prior to lines 35–37, our author gives every indication that she agrees with Alpers all the way, but suddenly there's a shift: Everything we've just read in paragraph 2, we suddenly realize, puts *too* much emphasis on commerce. In the extended example, the author contrasts Alpers' interpretation of *Claudius Civilis* (i.e. Rembrandt left it undone in order to get more cash) with her own (i.e. the painting isn't undone but simply exemplifies the artist's "meditative style"). Paragraph 3 continues with other non-commercial factors that ought to be considered (lines 51–54), and ends with a clear reference back to the first sentences of paragraph 1: Yes, every painting that's signed "Rembrandt" may not be a Rembrandt, but his art isn't just a matter of dollars and cents (or guilders), either.

The Big Picture:

- Anything the author mentions often is a strong indicator of her interest. Watch for heavy repetition (such as the word "Alpers" in paragraph 2) as a signal of what the author's focus is at any given time.

- The author appears to be 100% in favor of Alpers' interpretation until paragraph 3. Be ready for such shifts, but don't be worried about failing to predict them: They'll usually be announced pretty prominently.

The Questions:

16. (D) Global (Main Point)

The right answer to this "main conclusion" Global question must encompass both the author's interest in Alpers' ideas, and her demurrer that Alpers is all wet in stressing only the commercial aspects of Rembrandt's art. The respectful rhetoric assigned to Rembrandt's art in paragraph 3 makes it clear that to our author, $$$ is far from the whole story. **(D)** gets it right.

(A) The big differences between Rembrandt and other contemporary artists have to do with his "unprecedentedly firm control" (lines 11–13) and his belief in free enterprise over patronage. But these are Alpers' views, and in paragraph 2 only. The scope of the passage is Alpers' treatment of Rembrandt, and because the conclusion about Alpers is missing from **(A)**, this choice won't do.

(B) is Alpers' view, but lacks the corrective element that the passage author stresses and **(D)** picks up on.

(C)'s "one of the first" is meant to evoke "unprecedentedly," (line 12) but that's all that should make **(C)** appealing. What was without precedent was Rembrandt's control, not his view of art as a commodity. **(C)**'s scope is too narrow and lacks the passage's focus on critiquing Alpers.

(E) may be even more narrow than **(C)**, even more lacking in a discussion of Alpers' views and in the comparison of Rembrandt as businessman vs. Rembrandt as genius.

17. (D) Detail

Schwartz appears only once, in paragraph 2, in the context of Alpers' main argument that Rembrandt kept his art under his thumb and resisted the "prevailing patronage system," a view she takes *despite* Schwartz's "brilliant" documentation of the complicated relations between Rembrandt and a wide circle of patrons. So Schwartz and Alpers disagree about the degree of Rembrandt's involvement with patrons. Only **(D)** and **(E)** mention patronage at all, and only **(D)** gets the scope right.

(A), **(B)**, **(C)** All fail to mention or even to refer to patronage, which is the *sole* issue upon which Schwartz can be pinned down.

(E) The Alpers/Schwartz comparison has to do with Rembrandt and the patrons, not with how patronage worked per se. Alpers might readily agree with Schwartz's interpretation of how patronage worked generally, and yet respectfully disagree whether it applied to Rembrandt.

18. (E) Logic Function

This one asks for the purpose of something in paragraph 3, but the whole of paragraph 3 serves one purpose: to correct what the author sees as Alpers' overemphasis on Rembrandt's commercial motivations. Rembrandt, the author argues, was a profound and complex artist influenced by many things other than the demands of the art marketplace, among them the influences mentioned in paragraph 3. **(E)** expresses both the use of the detail in lines 51–54 and the thrust of the paragraph itself, and that's as it should be.

(A) The author is interested in Alpers, not in other critics generally (and is considering Alpers' approach, not others' neglect). **(A)** focuses on the sheer detail, not the use to which it's put.

(B) Though *Claudius Civilis* is discussed just prior to lines 51–54's discussion of the aesthetic influences, that painting isn't explicitly linked to them. *Claudius Civilis* plays a different role.

(C) has it all bollixed up. It's the author who mentions those influences as part of Rembrandt's art. Alpers *ignores* them.

(D) The last sentence of the passage indicates that to the author, commerce is at least part of Rembrandt's art. He approves of Alpers' study; he just thinks it's too limited and incomplete. **(D)** puts way too much emphasis on the aesthetic influences *only* (and puts too much emphasis on one of them, the Haarlem school only).

19. (D) Logic (Strengthen)

Alpers' argument about *Claudius Civilis* really begins with the phrase "For example," which introduces the notion that Rembrandt went out of his way to leave paintings undone so as to make more money. *C.C.* is one such painting. What's the evidence for arguing that Rembrandt wanted the Council to turn it down? It's the author's claim that Rembrandt figured that retouching *C.C.* would bring in more money. That's all well and good, but how would this plan work to Rembrandt's financial benefit? **(D)** explains. If **(D)** is true, and it was customary to charge more for a painting that one had to revise, then Rembrandt's plan as proposed by Alpers sounds more plausible.

(A) actually *weakens* Alpers' argument, by implying that the reason for *C.C.'s* incomplete state was artistic rather than commercial in nature.

(B) That other artists may have used the same broad-stroke, incomplete look in their paintings doesn't speak to why Rembrandt used it in this particular work.

(C) Alpers' argument about *C.C.* mentions nothing about patronage.

(E), if true, would suggest that Rembrandt painted *C.C.* himself, but that sheds no light on why the work was revised.

20. (A) Inference

Alpers and the author are in significant disagreement about the extent to which commerce motivated Rembrandt. But they do *not* disagree that Rembrandt was something of a canny businessman. Check out lines 32–35, which introduce the paragraph criticizing Alpers' overemphasis on commerce by granting Alpers part of her point—the point made by **(A)**, that indeed there's "some truth in the view" that Rembrandt's art was not uninfluenced by commercial considerations. This is of course closely related to the overall purpose of the passage—to assess just how correct Alpers is.

(B) *Au contraire,* lines 3–6 indicate the author's view that a new attribution of so-called "Rembrandt" work would be a very big deal indeed. Alpers probably agrees, since that's the kickoff of her book.

(C) is more or less the key issue on which Alpers and the author *disagree*. Alpers would affirm **(C)**, while the author would differ, saying that both art and commerce should be given some weight. (Hard to see where "historical" shines in, though.)

(D) Since Alpers seems uninterested in Rembrandt's painting techniques, we can't pin her down as to agreement on **(D)**'s point.

(E) goes too far. "Most" of Rembrandt's most famous works were painted by students? Neither Alpers nor the author need accept *that*.

Passage 4: Frida Kahlo
Questions 21–28

Topic and Scope: Frida Kahlo's art; specifically, the political content of an art mostly known and studied on a personal level.

Purpose and Main Idea: The author's purpose is 100% laid out by line 11—to explore the (hitherto under-explored) political aspects of Kahlo's work—and that leads immediately to the main idea that the rest of the passage is there to support: Kahlo's art can be read as a political statement about Mexican freedom, not just as Kahlo's autobiography.

Paragraph Structure: Paragraph 1's first two sentences are decidedly factual in nature, focusing on the personal nature of Kahlo's art: how overt it is, and how deeply studied. The turning point comes at line 7: *"…while X has been less studied. Yet…"* Italics ours. This phrase jumps off the page, providing the key to where the author is sure to go. And indeed, "X" is the political content of Kahlo's art. By ending paragraph 1 with the assertions that Kahlo explored her roots and pushed a political agenda in her art, the author promises to provide evidence to that effect…

… and so he does, in paragraph 2 onward. paragraph 2 is notable in its total concentration on politics, rather than art. We get a lot of facts about Marxism and *Mexicanidad*, a romantic nationalism celebrating the Aztecs. Since we know from paragraph 1 that the passage is about Kahlo and art, we need to see that paragraph 2 is mostly laying out the political influences on this artist, especially highlighting the idealization of "old Mexico," e.g. the Aztec culture. So paragraph 2 is background.

Paragraph 3 picks up on the Aztec influence and brings it (finally) into an artistic context, detailing the Aztec symbolism and imagery that Kahlo used to explore contemporary political issues. (Note the back reference in line 35 to "personal battle"— a reminder that, as we heard in paragraph 1, Kahlo's art is *also* personal, it's not *just* political.) The extended example of a Kahlo work (lines 38–50) has to be read in the context of the previous sentence: Kahlo uses Aztec imagery to explore Mexico's current struggles against the United States. And that's exactly what the details about the 1932 *Self-Portrait*…are telling us.

Paragraph 4 adds little new to the argument: Kahlo used a Mexican folkloric style; she championed Mexican identity; she is seen in popular and mythic terms for those very reasons. This paragraph ends the passage neatly, even eloquently, but the passage's substance and reason for being are pretty much over by the time paragraph 4 comes along.

The Big Picture:
- As you read a passage's opening paragraph, watch for "turning points" such as line 7 here—Keyword phrases that nakedly reveal the author's structure.

- Read for *context*, especially where details are concerned. To understand why, for instance, *Self-Portrait*…is given so much space in paragraph 3, look just before it and understand its context.
- As you get into the body of a passage, don't lose sight of the early hints and ideas that remain part of the author's overall view. Here, for instance, there's so much discussion of Kahlo's politics that one may forget that the (more common) *personal* view of her art still, according to the author, has validity. He is adding to the interpretation of Kahlo, not differing from the old one, but it's easy to forget that as you get deeper into the passage. A good tip: Stop after each paragraph of the passage and recap its key points. That way you're less likely to forget 'em.

The Questions:

21. (C) Global (Main Point)

The phrase "main point" in the question stem indicates a Global question, and here, no Global answer would be complete without including these elements: Kahlo's art, its use of Aztec imagery, and the connection between that imagery and Mexican politics. Only **(C)** conveys all of that.

(A) broadens out the topic too far to Kahlo's *generation*. Also, **(A)**'s doctrines are front and center only in the background paragraph, paragraph 2; **(A)** leaves out all the Aztec symbolism that truly connects Kahlo's politics to her art.

(B) distorts the role of Aztec culture in Kahlo—not merely as a point of reference, but as a whole style, a way of using ancient symbols to spotlight modern concerns.

(D), like **(A)**, focuses on the background paragraph, paragraph 2, and even on just a small part of *that* (lines 14–15).

(E) is wholly culture-based, and explicitly leaves out any political purpose to Kahlo's art. But if a Global question for *this* passage leaves out politics, how can it possibly be right?

22. (B) Inference

We've said several times that the author wants to *add* politics to the list of "Aspects Of Kahlo That Need Studying," not to *replace* the personal/psychoanalytic dimension that has reigned up to now. So the answer must suggest that these two facets can coexist. **(B)** therefore is right on the money. As but one example of the two interpretations' "complementarity," note that the author explicitly shows, in lines 33–38, how Aztec imagery is useful to illuminate both Kahlo's personal concerns and her political agenda.

(A) *Au contraire*. Tempting to those who make a knee-jerk assumption that because the author is pushing a new slant on Kahlo, he must be rejecting the old one. No evidence of that; quite the contrary (see paragraph above).

(C), less blatantly than **(A)** but in the same vein, improperly implies—and with no support—that exploring Kahlo's politics somehow knocks out or invalidates the personal view that has been in effect for years.

(D) What's a "biographical fact"? It's not entirely clear that biography is wholly out of the scope of Kahlo's political art, as **(D)** would have it. In any case, **(D)** implies some sort of disjunction between the personal and political view of Kahlo, reason enough to dismiss it from consideration.

(E) Yet again, a reference to a bogus disjunction between the two interpretations of Kahlo's work, rendered even worse by its focus on the mythic, a side issue brought up only in paragraph 4.

23. (A) Detail

If you were hip to the structure here—if you noted "Political Background" in your head or in the margin of paragraph 2—then re-locating the relevant details shouldn't have been too difficult, and could've helped you to avoid the temptation to move to paragraph 3. Scanning paragraph 2 for the phrase "early 20th century" or "Mexican nationalism" yields lines 12–16, then lines 20–22, which then leads to **(A)**. The labor disputes are one of the "internal Mexican affairs" of which **(A)** speaks.

(B), (C) A staunch nationalist might plausibly want to keep the nation's best workers from emigrating to another country **(B)**, or to make the nation competitive with a major neighbor **(C)**, but the passage never cites either.

(D) One might conceivably take lines 54–56, combine that idea with the U.S. imagery from Kahlo's painting in paragraph 3, and come up with **(D)**. But even with all that stretching (of dubious value), **(D)** would at best be a *Kahlo* view, not in and of itself one held by Mexican nationalists.

(E) uses some of the passage's language, but distorts its ideas. **(E)** takes a brief reference to *Kahlo's* having been "influenced by Marxism," blows that up into a preference for Soviet government, and then ascribes *that* view to Mexican nationalists *in general*.

24. (B) Inference

What's "romantic" (line 24) is Kahlo's "nationalism" (line 25), and the context both above and below that phrase marks *Mexicanidad* as a nationalism that both reveres and makes use of Aztec imagery, linking past Aztec greatness to future Marxist ideals. The sense of looking simultaneously backward to pre-Columbian greatness ("nostalgic") and ahead to true Marxist communality ("idealistic") is what makes **(B)** such a splendid choice.

(A),(C), and **(E)** all share adjectives more appropriately applied to "romantic" in the sense of romantic music like *Clair de lune* or romantic novels like the works of Danielle Steel. Whether

at their worst, **(E)**'s "overwrought," **(A)**'s "escapist," or at their best—**(C)**'s "imaginative," **(A)**'s "dreamy"—these three choices lose sight of the passion for Mexico's Aztec forebears and potential Marxist communal state that characterize Kahlo's thinking, not just in paragraph 3 but throughout the passage.

(D) As reported by the author, *Mexicanidad* does tend to convey a sense of "transcending" earthly cares and struggle, but "impractical" is a far cry from a synonym for "idealistic." We get no sense of Kahlo's feeling that she and the movement are tilting at windmills. In short, **(D)**'s adjectives are problematic while **(B)**'s fit like a glove.

25. (C) Detail EXCEPT

The word "serpent" never appears in the passage, and so **(C)** is the "odd man out." If you missed this question, did you simply skim the choices? Some were tempted to lump the serpent's malevolent image in with the equally grisly "skeleton," "skull," and "bleeding heart," and choose the relatively neutral "sculpture." In any case, we hear about Kahlo adopting Aztec images in lines 30–31, which produce **(A)** and **(E)**, and later in lines 45–49, which generate **(B)** and **(D)**.

26. (E) Logic Function

Reading for structure and summarizing paragraph topics in our *initial* reading of the passage makes questions like this easier. In particular, knowing that paragraph 2 is devoted to an extended discussion of Kahlo's political influences helps place paragraph 3 in context. paragraph 3 begins with "In her paintings," a clear transition to the topic of how her art internalized her political beliefs. Midway through paragraph 3 we get the awesome Keyword phrase "for example," clarifying why the author brings in the 1932 *Self-Portrait* in the first place: to illustrate the point made in lines 30–38, and especially in the second sentence of the paragraph, which is the "generalization" to which **(E)** refers.

All four wrong answers omit something key—i.e., the use of the 1932 work as an extended example. Each commits errors of *commission* as well:

(A), (B) The only "contrast" or "conflict" in paragraph 3 is between the U.S. and Mexican images. And those aren't "ideas" **(A)** or "concepts" **(B)**, and they aren't "reconciled" **(B)**.

(C) Only one theme is present in paragraph 3, that of how Kahlo's art was influenced by politics.

(D) To explicate means to render understandable or intelligible that which is unclear. That's not the function of the *Self-Portrait* details (that's not what an "example" does); and in any case they are not in the service of an abstract "principle," but rather a hard generalization about the effect of Aztec imagery on Kahlo's artwork. One has to work hard to make **(D)** fit, quite the contrary with **(E)**.

27. (C) Inference

The specific phrase "economic development" occurs not
in paragraph 2, but in paragraph 4. We learn there that
Kahlo was not willing to jeopardize Mexican cultural identity
in the construction of a planned economy. This qualified
endorsement for a Marxist economic plan is best summed up
by **(C)**.

(A) is the reaction that one might expect of a dyed-in-the-wool
Marxist. But Kahlo's concerns (lines 54–56) don't justify an
unqualified endorsement.

(B) Too negative in the other direction.

(D) Too neutral, flying in the face of lines 54–55.

(E) Too ambivalent.

28. (D) Global (Main Point)

Relatively easy to pre-phrase IF you have noted the author's
suggestion of the political view as a *supplement* to the already
ubiquitous personal interpretation of Kahlo's art.

(A) Content rather than style is the author's main interest
here—or, rather, the confluence between the two. It's not so
much a "critique" as an examination, anyway.

(B), (C) Two different ways to approach an artist's work cannot
properly be called "theories" or "arguments." One has to be
rigorous with language, even in LSAT answer choices. There is
no "reconciliation" going on in this passage.

(E) Nothing new about Kahlo has been discovered, though it *is*
a new slant, which supports **(D)** rather than **(E)**.

Passage 5: Zora Neale Hurston
Questions 29–36

Topic and Scope: Zora Neale Hurston; specifically, different assessments of her novel, *Their Eyes Were Watching God*.

Purpose and Main Idea: The author's purpose is to explain why Hurston's novel has only recently received widespread praise, her main idea being simply that the development of new strands of literary criticism accounts for this turnaround.

Paragraph Structure: Paragraph 1 introduces the passage's basic question: Why was such an important and eventually influential novel dismissed when it first appeared? Paragraph 2 says that the novel was misunderstood and condemned, especially in the Black literary community, because it was out of step with the Black "protest fiction" of the time. Paragraph 3 explains that the rise of feminist and Afrocentric literary criticism has been behind the new appreciation of Hurston's novel.

The Big Picture:

- Passages like this one—where topic, scope, and purpose become clear early on—are a good place to begin work on the Reading Comprehension section on test day. Passages that begin with a lot of unfocused details are best left for later in the section.

- This passage features a classic structure that you'll surely see on test day. A "problem" is presented up front; and the rest of the passage is devoted to probing and "solving" this problem.

- Book review passages often mention different authors and different works. Keep them straight in your mind—the questions will probably test to see that you're aware of the differences between/among authors and books.

The Questions:

29. (E) Inference

Lines 15–18 say that Wilson's work, "unlike" Hurston's, was totally ignored upon its publication. But, like Hurston's work, it has recently been the object of literary inquiry.

(A) The passage doesn't say when Wilson's book was published, so we can't conclude that it was written at the same time as Hurston's novel. Moreover, Wilson's work didn't receive *any* critical attention.

(B) According to the passage (lines 1–5), it's *Hurston's* novel that has heavily influenced the writing of later Black women.

(C) This passage is mostly concerned with the literary establishment's tardy appreciation of Wilson's novel, not with the public, but even the few references to the public suggest that **(C)** is off. Readers were put off (lines 36–38), "and the novel went quietly out of print" (line 40)—not signs of wide readership.

(D) Lines 15–18 make it clear that Wilson's novel *was* published.

30. (B) Inference

Paragraph 2 mentions that Hurston's book went out of print because it wasn't understood by much of the Black literary establishment and readership. (It was Harriet Wilson's novel, not Hurston's, that was relegated to obscurity because of critical neglect.)

(A) *Au contraire.* Hurston's novel received a lot of flak from reviewers when it appeared.

(C) Afrocentric interpretations of Hurston's novel, paragraph 3 reveals, are a more recent development.

(D) Paragraphs 2 and 3 make it clear that Hurston's work doesn't belong to the genre known as "protest fiction."

(E) The passage says that the book received mixed reviews from White and Black critics. There's not enough information to conclude that "most" reviewers gave it a less than positive reception.

31. (C) Global (Main Point)

This choice captures the author's topic (Hurston's novel); scope (earlier versus later assessments of her novel); and purpose (to explain why Hurston's novel has recently won acclaim).

(A) focuses on a detail in paragraph 2.

(B) According to the author, Afrocentric literary critics have *also* helped to bring Hurston's novel to prominence. Besides, this passage also discusses why Hurston's novel wasn't well-received initially—an aspect of the passage that **(B)** doesn't address.

(D) Hurston's novel was trashed by some early literary critics precisely because it wasn't "protest fiction."

(E) focuses on a detail in paragraph 3.

32. (E) Detail

According to lines 52–56, the recent rise of Afrocentric literary analysis has brought to light Black folklore traditions as represented in literature.

(A) distorts a detail in paragraph 3. Indeed, the only thing we're told about Gates is that he has written perceptively about Hurston's novel.

(B) and **(D)** are beyond the scope of the passage, which is about literary criticism of Hurston's novel. We aren't told much about Black novelists as a group. For all we know, Black novelists writing before or during the 1940s *did* use folklore in their works.

(C) Again, we don't know what other Black authors were doing; so, we can't conclude that Hurston was the first to incorporate Black folklore into a novel.

33. (C) Inference

Paragraph 2 strongly implies that Wright's *Native Son* fell into the genre of "protest fiction," which explored the issue of racism in the United States. In other words, whereas Hurston's novel concentrated on the life of one individual in the Black community (lines 39–40), Wright's novel focused on the entire community.

(A) Since Wright's book fit into the dominant genre of the era, it's highly unlikely that it got a worse reception than Hurston's novel, especially since we're told that Wright's novel was "much acclaimed."

(B) 180. Wright's novel is far *more* typical of mid-century Black writing than Hurston's.

(D) We can't say that Wright's book has got more folklore in it than Hurston's, because the passage doesn't tell us exactly what's *in* his book. Except for the one reference, *Native Son* is outside the scope of the passage.

(E) No comparison is possible between Wright's book and Hurston's on the issue of feminist and Afrocentric attention, because the passage doesn't provide us with feminist and Afrocentric comments on Wright's novel.

34. (B) Inference

Lines 29–33 say that Black writers of the 1940s believed that Black literature should fall into the "protest fiction" genre—that is, they believed that it should tackle the issue of racism against Blacks. The novel outlined in choice **(B)** has just such a focus.

(A), **(C)**, **(D)**, and **(E)** None of the novels in these choices focuses on racial discrimination. **(D)**'s "unjust working conditions" is not the same as racial discrimination.

35. (C) Inference

In paragraph 2, the author notes that some mid-century reviewers dismissed Hurston's book because it doesn't deal with racism, the issue that interested them. In paragraph 3, the author notes that later reviewers, influenced by feminism or Afrocentrism, applauded the book because it deals with issues of concern to feminists and Blacks. Hence, the author is likely to agree with the notion that literary critics' "ideological perspectives and assumptions about the purpose of art" color their analysis of art.

(A) and **(D)** The author would probably disagree with these statements. After all, she largely attributes the early demise, as well as the later revival, of Hurston's novel to the efforts of literary critics.

(B) The author doesn't discuss any "experimental" works of fiction, whatever that term means. Thus, there's no telling what she'd have to say about how literary critics initially view them.

(E) is too strong. True, the author notes that literary critics make much of the ideological premises of a book; but there's nothing in the passage to indicate that she thinks that they hone in on this aspect of a work above all else.

36. (B) Global (Primary Purpose)

The passage is mainly about the reassessment of Hurston's novel that grew out of new forms of literary criticism.

(A) What misconception?

(C) distorts the contents of the passage. True, the author discusses early and more recent critiques of Hurston's novel; but she doesn't attempt to "reconcile" them.

(D) What conventional approach?

(E) What new discovery?

Passage 6: Countee Cullen
Questions 37–43

The **Topic** is Harlem Renaissance poet Countee Cullen, the **Scope** his themes and styles. Those are introduced in paragraph 1, where we learn that he wrote "lofty thoughts, beautifully expressed" and as a result preferred "controlled . . . European . . . and Christian religious" forms and images.

Paragraph 2 introduces critical praise for Cullen's aforementioned skills (lines 18–23) and critical disapproval (lines 23–33), centering on the allegation that Cullen's conventional romantic forms were inappropriate for handling racial themes. Then we get Cullen's rebuttal (lines 33–41) and the author's view (paragraph 3) that confirms his **Purpose** as defending Cullen against said criticism as a poet of both religious and racial themes. Cullen himself saw his work as properly encompassing both types of themes and the author agrees. Indeed, while Cullen became more interested in religion in later years (lines 45–46), his interest in racial issues grew over time as well (lines 56–58).

The Big Picture:

Paragraph 1: Cullen's themes & stylistic preferences (conventional)

Paragraph 2: Praise (18–23), criticism (23–33), and CC's rebuttal (33–41) [Draw brackets in the margin to separate these.]

Paragraph 3: Author's defense of CC: religion & race each had a place

The Questions:

37. (B) Global (Main Point)

The only choice that picks up on the author's purpose—the defense of Cullen against the charge that the poet drifted away from racial issues in his work—is **(B)**.

(A) This assertion directly contradicts lines 54–55.

(C) This choice echoes a claim made by Cullen's critics in lines 23–25. Cullen would hardly agree with it.

(D) If anything in the passage sounds like Cullen's "primary goal" it'd be lines 9–10, certainly nothing so narrow (or so uninvolved with both religious and racial themes) as "the atmosphere" of "the English ballad."

(E) While Cullen explored his religious and racial interests, there's no sense that the latter was somehow dependent on the former.

38. (E) Inference

While no line reference appears in the question to provide guidance, the Hot Worlds "Cullen's conception of poetry" do, and they send us to paragraph 1 in general and lines 9–11

in particular. Only **(E)** reflects "lofty thoughts" expressed in "controlled poetic forms," as described there.

(A) The only reference to Cullen's use of English atmosphere—and it's only the opinion of "some critics," at that—deals with one particular poem and the atmosphere of the *ballad form* only.

(B) "Disregarding" the conventional form is just the opposite of what Cullen would do; a 180 choice.

(C) "Radical innovations" in poetic form wasn't Cullen's thing either; another 180 choice.

(D) Romantic upheaval would certainly be a Cullen topic, but again, "great stylistic freedom" is the exact opposite of his style.

39. (C) Detail EXCEPT

That which is *not* characteristic of Cullen's poetry would be things like gritty realism, ugly expression, or **(C)**, "formal experimentation." Stylistically, as we've discussed in all of the questions so far, Cullen was a notable traditionalist.

(A) Reflected in line 8.

(B) Mentioned explicitly in lines 13–14.

(D) When lines 42–43 say that racial references "decline in Cullen's later work," the implication is that they were more numerous earlier, thus supporting **(D)**.

(E) Lines 51–54, almost verbatim.

40. (A) Inference

Once again we are asked about Cullen's affinity for conventions of style. Once again we get Hot Words ("controlled poetic forms") that send us to paragraph 2. Once again we see a right answer picking up passage text almost word for word: **(A)** is lines 9–11.

(B) Controlled forms may have been appropriate to religious themes, but the latter aren't cited as having led to Cullen's use of those forms; the desire for beautiful expression is.

(C) "Only" signifies a necessary condition, but there's no sense that racial issues couldn't be addressed by Cullen or anyone else using more radical or experimental forms.

(D) What Cullen is spoken of having "rejected" is an alleged dichotomy in his work between artistic and racial concerns (30–34). No such rejection as **(D)** mentions is described here.

(E) The very fact that Cullen used controlled forms to deal with racial issues confirms that **(E)** is not a true statement.

41. (B) Logic Function

The poems in paragraph 2 are all accompanied by critics' views of same. Indeed, critical views of Cullen are part of the overall purpose of paragraph 2, followed by the rebuttal that is our author's primary concern. So **(B)** has it right.

(A) Cullen's specific poetical successes vs. failures are not the author's concern here.

(C) Accusations of vacillation, while hurled at Cullen in the past, are not made by our admiring author.

(D), (E) Racial themes are only explicitly alluded to with regard to two of the three specific poems cited. Both **(D)** and **(E)** ignore the author's broader interest in verse forms in lines 18–30. (Also, how could **(D)** be correct and **(E)** wrong, or vice versa? They're almost identical.)

42. (A) Inference

The critics around line 18 are in favor of Cullen's use of European-style verse, as **(A)** reflects.

(B) Cullen's education and upbringing are part of the discussion that ends paragraph 1, but the critics discussed one line later are off on another topic.

(C) The author is not interested in evaluating where Cullen's work was strong and where it was weak.

(D), (E) The critics in line 18 don't mention racial issues explicitly, so both of these choices can be discarded.

43. (E) Global (Organization of Passage)

Choice **(E)** reflects our Roadmap exceptionally closely, each of its clauses summing up one of the paragraphs. The only real danger would be to allow too much time to be eaten up with the other choices. The first three can be discarded because in all of paragraph 1 there is very little "biographical information," outlined or otherwise. Besides that:

(A) The poems in paragraph 2 aren't offered to "trace" Cullen's development. (Rather, they illustrate both pro and con commentary his work engendered.)

(B) Both criticism and praise of Cullen's use of European forms appear midway, and (as we've said over and over) the author is not interested in Cullen's "success" *per se*, but in what he wrote and how.

(C) Cullen's approach to poetry writing comes at the outset of the passage, not midway as **(C)** would have it. and Cullen's biography occupies little or no space here.

(D) This choice begins satisfactorily, as does the correct answer. But again, the poems in paragraph 2 weren't chosen because they were "most notable"—they were chosen because they illustrate critical reactions of the time. And racial themes get at least equal treatment to religious ones, though **(D)** ignores that fact.

Passage 7: Critics of Invisible Man
Questions 44–51

The **Topic** is introduced quickly as Ralph Ellison's 1952 novel *Invisible Man*, and before paragraph 1 is over we discover that the **Scope** is the two-pronged criticism of the "thematic blend" in which Ellison engaged. He took from European writers as well as from the African American experience to the chagrin of those who believed that he should've been more engaged with the politics and culture of his time, and that his reliance on European themes weakened his impact on African American writing. Why does the author take all this up? His **Purpose** is to rebut the criticism, which he does first by citing Ellison's views in paragraph 2. Then, in paragraphs 3 and 4, he describes characteristics of a different art—jazz music—that successfully blends European and African American culture in a way that is analogous to what Ellison tried to do in his novel. In the end, the author's rebuttal asserts that the very qualities that critics felt weakened *Invisible Man* actually served to strengthen both the book and Ellison's artistry.

The Questions:

44. (A) Inference

Attacking the choices in order results quickly in success here. Lines 32–41 expand on the idea that **(A)** propounds, though more or less in reverse order, with lines 32–37 illustrating how U.S. jazz can absorb European influence and 37–41 asserting that "in like manner" Ellison blended cultural forms.

Since our author shows little or no interest in political action—that's the concern of Ellison's critics, lines 11–13—he can be said to hold no belief as to how a writer can bring about such action **(B)**. **(C)** skews the passage unmercifully: It's not that *Invisible Man* enhanced general appreciation for jazz, but that jazz can help one better appreciate *Invisible Man*. **(D)** is wrong because it mischaracterizes *Invisible Man*'s protagonist (who is mostly defined here by his alienation), and because focusing on the "difficulty" of fusing cultures is inappropriate for a passage that celebrates a writer's ability to do just that. **(E)** can be discarded on the grounds of tone alone: to the author there is nothing "unfortunate" about Ellison's style.

45. (A) Inference

The reference to Ellison's critics sends us squarely to paragraph 1. Since their ire was based on their allegations that Ellison eschewed activism (lines 9–13) and opted out of a contribution to a distinct African American style (lines 13–16), either or both of those would surely have led to a more favorable reception for *Invisible Man*, and **(A)** picks up on the former.

There's no indication that critics wanted Ellison to transform himself from novelist to historian **(B)**—this choice seems based on a distortion of the opening sentence. Moreover, the

critics' beef was that he was disengaged from the political present, not its past **(C)**. **(D)** widens the scope too far, to "American literature" in general; critics were concerned with Ellison's contribution to African American novelistic style, not with an American/European break *per se*. Meanwhile, nowhere are the critics' views of the book dependent on its reception **(E)**…and besides, inferably, reviews come out some time *before* any audience is generated.

46. (E) Inference

The phrase in question is in the context of how Ellison "replied" to the summary in the previous sentence, lines 17–20, so it must be Ellison's way of alluding to the "sacrific[ing of writers'] individuality" that his critics would have literature do, so as to push some kind of socio-political, activist agenda. **(E)** describes the writer's role of which Ellison strongly disapproves.

(A)'s "recurring themes" comes out of nowhere. "Separation" **(B)** and "isolation" **(C)** sound rather like segregationist ideas, but each choice distorts the text. The only artistic separation the author writes of is the separation between the critics and Ellison **(B)**, and the personage in isolation in the passage **(C)** is the protagonist of Ellison's novel, not artists *per se*. **(D)** goes against the grain of Ellison's view that audiences can and do appreciate art; Ellison would deny such "obstacles."

47. (E) Logic Function

Paragraph 3's first sentence announces the purpose of the paragraph: The author seeks to introduce a different model—the jazz model—for appreciating *Invisible Man*'s achievement. That's **(E)** in a nutshell.

No reference is made in paragraph 3 (or anywhere else, really) to Ellison's relationship with other writers "within his discipline" **(A)**. **(B)** is way off—to borrow its wording a bit, the purpose of paragraph 3 is to affirm the *usefulness* of examining one art form to illuminate another. That's far from **(B)** but is darned close to correct choice **(E)**. Choice **(C)**, like many other wrong choices in this passage, misunderstands the references to jazz as some sort of assertion that jazz had a direct influence on *Invisible Man*, when nothing of the sort is implied. Meanwhile, **(D)** seems to assert that the author has some interest in celebrating jazz from the perspective of Ralph Ellison, but if anything that relationship is exactly backward—a 180.

48. (C) Detail

Jazz is discussed in paragraphs 3 and 4, of course, and a quick rereading of the claims made about jazz may help you get through these brief answer choices even more rapidly. As it turns out, four choices are outside the scope, because the author never discusses whether jazz is or is not widely accessible **(A)**, is or is not the most complex form **(B)**, avoids or embraces politics **(D)**, or has influenced much, little, or no modern literature **(E)**. (We can't even be sure that jazz influenced Ellison. Yes, Ellison loved and celebrated jazz, and jazz has parallels that shed light on *Invisible Man* but that doesn't mean that jazz has to have been, any kind of conscious influence on Ellison.) Anyhow, **(C)** is explicitly stated in lines 32–37.

49. (C) Inference

The hot words "Ellison" and "audience" take us squarely to lines 26–28, the only place where Ellison expresses a view about his readers. "Such a view"—the critics' view, the one with which both Ellison and our author take issue—makes an assumption that the audience can only see the world from their own perspective. Since to Ellison that assumption is "narrow," he must believe that the audience is sharp and sensitive enough to react from multiple perspectives, which is what **(C)** is getting at. As we noted, Ellison respects the audience.

(A) echoes rather than counters the "narrow assumption" that audiences are comfortable only with one view of the world. Ellison's view of his critics is that their view is misguided and narrow, not necessarily that it's "groundless" **(B)**; besides, nowhere is any connection made between criticism and subsequent audience reaction. *Audience awareness* and *conscientiousness* are two terms that are featured in **(D)** but nowhere in the text. And **(E)** is perhaps an even more obvious 180 than is **(A)** in its implied contempt for the audience's too-limited perceptions.

50. (D) Global (Primary Purpose)

As noted earlier, paragraph 2 brings in Ellison's views, and paragraphs 3 and 4 mention jazz, in order to counter the criticism expressed in paragraph 1. **(D)**'s "certain novelist" is Ralph Ellison, of course, and **(D)** sums up the main criticism adequately.

Ellison's mere "importance" **(A)** is never in question; certainly, "importance" is both too shallow and too broad to echo the incisive focus on themes that we find in the text. No literary "trend" **(B)** is the focus of the passage, and in any case **(B)** focuses too narrowly on jazz alone. **(C)**'s "relevance" is about as useful as **(A)**'s "importance," and **(C)** is otherwise a 180 in its implication that *Invisible Man* was a socio-politically engaged novel. Besides running counter to the passage's ideas about "thematic blending," **(E)** is the broadest choice of all, utterly ignoring *Invisible Man*, Ellison, and the critics.

51. (B) Detail EXCEPT

When a question asks "which question is NOT answered?," it may be faster to locate the four that are.

Ellison had a "love for…jazz" (line 31) in answer to **(A)**, and the words "He replied" in line 20 confirm that the rest of paragraph 2 answers **(C)**'s question. The answer to **(D)** is "from both European and African American traditions," and that's supplied by lines 39–41 and 47–49. The same lines that confirmed **(C)** as correct in question 18, lines 32–37, address **(E)**'s query. But as we noted in discussing wrong choice **(E)** in that same question, the author uses jazz to illuminate *Invisible Man* but never asserts that jazz consciously influenced its author, so **(B)** is the question that goes unanswered.

Passage 8: James Porter
Questions 52–59

Topic and Scope: The art scholar James Porter; specifically, his pioneering recognition of the influence of Africa on African-American artists.

Purpose and Main Idea: The author's purpose is to express the range and innovativeness of Porter's investigations into the African roots of African-American art. Since this is mainly an act of reportage, the Main Idea turns out to be little more than the announcement in paragraph 1's first sentence that Porter deserves the credit for bringing to light a little-known artistic influence. Everything else in the passage expands on that credit.

Paragraph Structure: Paragraph 1, as noted just above, gives Porter credit for his innovative work, taking us back to his first experience of connecting African cultural artifacts to African-American artists.

Paragraph 2 obligingly begins with the words "An example...occurs," and it turns out to be Porter's early discovery that two major artists were in fact African-American rather than Euro-American. That example ends at line 26; the rest of this unusually lengthy paragraph separates Porter's work from that of Alain LeRoy Locke, always returning to the main idea that Porter was a major innovator. The paragraph ends with a tip of the hat to Porter's own paintings which, unsurprisingly given his scholarly interests, also demonstrate African influence.

Paragraph 3's opening words "In his later years" are almost as helpful as paragraph 2's in terms of alerting us to the structure. As the phrase suggests, paragraph 3 explains Porter's scholarly interests before his death, including revisions and expansions of his 1943 book. We should finally notice that his unfinished final work represented a major shift of scope on Porter's part—from the African influence on African-American artists to its influence on "the art of the Western world generally" (lines 54–55).

The Big Picture:

- Remember that not every Reading Comprehension passage is an extensive argument, one in which the author is assembling 50–60 lines of evidence to support or prove her thesis. *Most* are arguments, but some (like this one) are more reportage in their nature, that is, almost 100% factual with very little author interpretation.

- Keep an eye on the author's scope, and note when and where it shifts. Here, we need to realize that Porter's work (and most of the passage) focus on the African influence on *African-American* art. The scope only broadens to Western art in general in Porter's last years (and in the passage's last sentence).

- Speaking of scope, when a single paragraph goes beyond 15 lines or so, expect the scope of that paragraph to shift before it's through. (As an example, notice how much ground paragraph 2 covers here.) This is a sign of author ambitiousness rather than ineptitude, and it means that when a question comes out of a long paragraph we may not be able to locate its answer quite as fast.

The Questions:

52. (E) Global (Main Point)

The answer choices in this main idea question are lengthy, but all that verbiage is simply there to blind us to the fact that only **(E)** picks up on what Porter's scholarship was all about. **(E)** picks up on the hint in the very first sentence. Notice how far and wide the four wrong choices wander:

(A) gives predecessors way too much credit, and weakens Porter's due standing as "the first" (line 1).

(B) has a big scope problem. The connections that **(B)** dismisses in its phrase "In addition to" are the ones that occupy lines 1–52!

(C) is flatly untrue: Locke beat Porter to the punch in recognizing African-American art. And the brief reference to his unfinished work doesn't, of course, belong in a statement of the main idea.

(D), like the other wrong choices, blows up Porter's last, unfinished work way too far in importance, and dismisses his main work in a subordinate opening clause.

53. (B) Logic Function

Locke is cited (lines 26–31) as the first writer to pen books exclusively dealing with African-American artists, but almost immediately he is saddled with the criticism that he never "[addressed] the critical issue of African precursors." However, "Porter's book addressed this issue..." So Locke is brought in, ultimately, to set Porter's accomplishments apart from his peers—in other words, **(B)**. In studying the African roots of African-American artists, Porter was truly one of a kind.

(A), **(E)** Both of these choices, which explicitly cite Locke as a direct influence on Porter, are unwarranted inferences that seem to be based on the fact that both men taught at the same institution. That could've been sheer coincidence; certainly there's no evidence that Locke had anything to do with influencing Porter. In fact, contrary to **(A)**, Porter didn't build on Locke but took off in a different direction.

(C) Only the assumption that LSAT passages discuss only obscure authors—which isn't always the case—could draw one to **(C)**. No evidence of Porter's obscurity is present.

(D) True, Porter was not the first to acknowledge African-American artists. But he *was* the first to trace their African cultural influences, contrary to **(D)**.

54. (B) Detail

A perfect example of how a knee-jerk response to a question's line reference can get you into trouble. The reference to the 1943 book drives you to paragraph 2, but it is paragraph 3 out of which the right answer comes: lines 44–47, where we learn that Porter subsequently revised and improved his original book. **(B)** has it right. The important thing here was to recall the paragraph 3 reference and relate it back to the discussion one paragraph earlier—or, at least, to see why the other four choices fail:

(A) The 1943 reaction to the book goes unaddressed. For all we know it was a big hit back then.

(C) Since Locke's books failed to "[address] the critical issue of African precursors" and Porter's did, there's little reason to believe that their conclusions would disagree.

(D) 180: A book that the author later "revised and corrected" would hardly be considered "definitive."

(E), once again, involves the issue that Porter was working on at his death in 1970, not the topic of the 1943 work.

55. (D) Inference

Paragraph 2 clearly announces the Duncanson/Johnston investigation (lines 16–25) as "An example of this aspect of Porter's research." And "this aspect" refers to the previous paragraph, specifically to Porter's effort to explore the "cultural territory." So even before we hit lines 16–25, we expect to encounter an example of the linkage that Porter found between Africa and America.

The actual inference for this question is pretty straightforward, a formal syllogism: Duncanson and Johnston were Hudson River School painters (lines 18–21); both men were of African descent (lines 23–24); therefore, at least some Hudson River School painters were of African descent—and that's **(D)**. In a way, the wrong choices are more interesting, as they illustrate the kind of flim-flam that the test writers throw in to distract your attention from a credited choice:

(A) It's certainly true that Duncanson and Johnston were of African ancestry, and that they were part of the Hudson River School. But were they "defining" members of that school? Can we draw inferences from their work about the School as a whole? No—not enough evidence. Moreover, just how did Porter figure out the ancestry of the artists? It *might* have been through their use of African "iconography," but again, we cannot be sure; maybe in this case Porter's evidence was African themes, or painting styles. So two key elements of **(A)** are not supported by the text (and choice **(A)** has a third problem; see the discussion of **(E)**, below.)

(B) Not enough information about the Hudson River School style vs. Duncanson and Johnston's styles is provided to justify **(B)**'s inference. Duncanson and Johnston's work may be *100%*

in line with School style and yet still reveal evidence of the painters' African ancestry.

(C) Here again, as with **(A)**, the specific evidence that Porter used to infer Duncanson and Johnston's African ancestry is never mentioned, so we cannot be sure that their work is reflective of African crafts from the given centuries. Another problem with **(C)**, of course, is that it alludes to Duncanson and Johnston as "Euro-American," a phrase originally applied to them but abandoned after Porter's findings.

(E), like **(A)**, infers that Duncanson and Johnston must have demonstrated West African influences in their art. But West Africa is never mentioned in paragraph 2, on which this question is based, so whatever African influence Porter found in Duncanson and Johnston's work, it need not have been *West* African in origin. Yes, West African craft pieces were part of Porter's original research project (paragraph 1). But did they play a role in the Duncanson/Johnston investigation? No way to tell.

56. (D) Inference

All we know about Porter's unfinished work is that's an area that remains wide open for study (lines 54–56), and that it widened the scope of his earlier interests, from African-American art in particular to "the art of the Western world generally" (lines 54–55). All of the choices, which we must examine in turn, begin with the words "If completed," meaning they're all hypothetical; and since they are hypothetical, it'll be dangerous to depart from the scope of what we discussed above.

(A), **(B)** That Porter later revised his 1943 book does not, in and of itself, imply that his unfinished book would have contradicted **(A)** or amended **(B)** his conclusions in the earlier one. Indeed, why would it have done so, since the new book was to cover a different topic?

(C), like **(A)** and **(B)**, inappropriately relates the unfinished book to the 1943 one, since the former was to have gone beyond African-American art to Western art generally. Even if African-American artwork were to be mentioned in the unfinished work, there's no way to tell whether Porter would have done the kind of specific updating that **(C)** describes.

(D) simply asserts that the new book's scope would have been broadened beyond that of Porter's 1943 volume. Quite so. (Notice that **(D)** uses the word "scope" in exactly the same way that we at Kaplan do!) The earlier work dealt with the influence of African art on African-American artists, and the later work expanded the study to its influence on the Western world in general.

(E) drags in "Porter's contemporaries." If that refers to Locke, he appears in paragraph 2 not paragraph 3, and in a context totally unrelated to Porter's later unfinished work. If that refers to other writers, they go unmentioned in the text.

57. (C) Logic (Parallel Reasoning)

This request for an "analogous observation" is not unlike a Parallel Reasoning question in Logical Reasoning. The test writers are looking for a choice that closely parallels the passage situation in its important particulars. Your approach, therefore, should be to characterize what the author is doing in its broad particulars, and be brutal at tossing out the choices that violate your pre-phrasing.

First, of course, you need to realize that Porter's discovery of African-American artifacts is discussed in paragraph 1, lines 6–15. A quick reread reveals that as Porter studied these household items, he found distinct traces of West African influence, from which he began to build his portrait of African-American art. We should, therefore, demand of the answer choices a situation that relates people's work in one locale (America) to that of their forebears in another locale (West Africa).

(A) gives as much emphasis to the *differences* between Haitian customs and those of other locales as to the similarities. That, and the fact that **(A)** mentions *two* areas of influence, move this choice away from a close analogy.

(B) focuses on the American popular music influence on what is being composed in Africa. This choice would be more analogous if it specifically identified Americans living in Africa *and composing there*. But it does not.

(C) has people from China who are, though writing in Canada, explicitly influenced by Chinese themes. That's the analogy, with China standing in for Africa and Canada for the U.S.

(D)'s emphasis on "popularity" renders this choice faulty. The issue is explicit cultural influences on a group, not the popularity of any of the group's work.

(E) gets all bollixed up between native influences and Spanish influences on Mexican artists. Such elements as "conscious imitation" and "response to influences" are significant in **(E)** but have nothing to do with what Porter was discovering as reported by paragraph 1.

58. (A) Inference

Porter's own artwork only comes up in paragraph 2, lines 38–43. While we should go there to refresh our memory and get ready to spot the correct inference among the choices, the key phrase is line 39's "these ties," which sends us back to the previous sentence: Those ties are "ties to African artisanship," which Porter made a "conscious effort to maintain...in his own paintings." We can infer, then, that like many of the artworks he wrote about, Porter's paintings include examples of African crafts—and that's **(A)**.

(B) We're never told that Porter's painting preceded his scholarly interests, as **(B)** would have it. If anything, its placement late in this chronologically-based passage would suggest that Porter's art was a later pursuit rather than an earlier one.

(C) is made up out of whole cloth. There's not a scintilla of evidence that Porter illustrated his books with his own paintings.

(D) focuses on the motivation for Porter's painting, but for all we know it was a mere pastime. **(D)** doesn't even make much sense: Since Porter's theories posited a profound African influence on many artists, his own personal efforts to follow an African model would hardly "prove" those theories.

(E) is flatly contradicted by paragraph 3's statement that Porter died with considerable academic work left unfinished. In any event, as with **(B)**, the fact that the discussion of Porter's art comes in the middle of this chronological passage would suggest that it was a part of his middle years.

59. (E) Inference

Though Porter's last work was to deal with a broader canvas than his earlier one—he was to examine "the art of the Western world generally" rather than zeroing in on African-American art—he still had the same basic interest in charting African influences. So "relevant evidence" would consist of African influences on some aspect of Western art, and beyond just America.

(A), **(B)**, **(C)** Each of these has it backwards, presenting possible earlier European influence on African-American craftwork **(A)**, North African graphics **(B)**, or African-American quilts **(C)**.

(D) sticks to the same scope as the 1943 work, namely, the influence of African culture on African-American artists. It doesn't explicitly speak to Porter's broadened interests.

(E) does the job: Images of Central African masks in European paintings would certainly be fodder for a discussion of African cultural influences on one aspect of Western art. Porter surely would have found such a linkage to be relevant.

Passage 9: Piano Music
Questions 60–67

Topic and Scope: The London Pianoforte school; specifically, Temperley's contribution to preserving this school's musical heritage.

Purpose and Main Idea: The author's purpose is to describe how Temperley's musical anthology contributes to our knowledge of the London Pianoforte school. Her main idea is that Temperley's anthology is critical to our understanding of this school.

Paragraph Structure: Paragraph 1 presents a number of facts about the London Pianoforte school—chiefly, what it was (a collection of musical types who developed the piano) and why relatively little has been known about its music (much of its music simply hasn't been available to later musicologists). While the passage's topic is made clear in this paragraph, neither its scope, purpose nor main idea is likewise evident.

Paragraph 2 performs two essential functions in the passage: it reveals the passage's scope (Temperley's anthology) and provides us with our first glimpse of the author's opinion (she applauds Temperley's effort to preserve the London school's heritage). According to the author, Temperley's anthology will help us to understand the development of piano music in England and the rest of Europe as well as to trace the historical development of the piano itself.

Paragraphs 3 and 4 delve more deeply into one implication of Temperley's anthology. Contrary to earlier research on the London school, especially that of Alexander Ringer, Temperley's work suggests that the London school's members weren't really unified on the issue of musical style. Rather, the London school was a school only in the sense that its members produced their music during the same era and in the same locale. His modified view of the London school is endorsed by the author.

The Big Picture:

- On Test Day, passages that begin with a lot of descriptive detail—passages whose scope, purpose, and main idea aren't quickly and easily discernible—should generally be done later rather than sooner. They're usually tougher to get a handle on than passages that begin with a strong statement of authorial intent. However, if you're comfortable with a particular topic and you feel that working on this topic would be a good way to ease into the Reading Comp. section, feel free to start your Test Day work with this type of passage.

- Some Paragraphs are more important than others. In this case, paragraphs 2–4 are more important than paragraph 1. Why? These paragraphs reflect the author's opinion; and most Reading Comp. questions deal in some way with the author's opinion. The bottom

line: during a first read through of any passage, focus more of your mental energy on those paragraphs that reflect the author's views.

The Questions:

60. (B) Global (Main Point)

The phrase "main point" in the question stem indicates a Global question; therefore, you've got to look for the answer choice that captures the passage's basic theme. Paragraph 1 introduces us to the London Pianoforte school, while paragraphs 2–4 explain how and why Temperley's anthology contributes greatly to our understanding of this important musical school.

(A) focuses on an issue dealt with only in paragraphs 3 and 4. Hence, this choice isn't broad enough to capture the passage's basic theme. Besides, Temperley's anthology merely *redefines* the essence of the London Pianoforte school, emphasizing historical era rather than musical style; he doesn't ultimately claim that this school is an invention of later musicologists, the contents of lines 37–38 notwithstanding.

(C) distorts the thrust of the passage, which claims that Temperley's anthology should improve scholarship about the London Pianoforte school. The author doesn't make the claim that this school's music itself "has been revived" by his work.

(D) This passage focuses specifically on Temperley's anthology. It doesn't dwell on the broader issue of the utility of primary sources in musicological research.

(E) Quite apart from the fact that this choice never mentions Temperley's anthology, it focuses on an issue dealt with only in paragraphs 2 and 4. True, the development of the piano influenced European musicians (see especially lines 49–55); but its influence on these musicians isn't the passage's main concern.

61. (E) Inference

Reading Comp. Inference questions rarely require you to make new deductions. Usually, correct answers to these questions simply rephrase information that's already in the text. That's the case in this question. Choice **(E)** echoes the idea expressed in lines 5–8: in modern times, even musicians haven't been exposed to the work of the London Pianoforte school.

(A) The only reference to John Field's nocturnes appears in lines 11–12, which state that his work, in contrast to that of most members of the London Pianoforte school, has been accessible to modern musicologists. That's quite different from saying that his work typifies this school's style. Indeed, paragraphs 3 and 4 make the point that this school had no typical musical style.

(B) Lines 10–12 state that Clementi's *Gradus ad Parnassum* has "remained familiar enough" to modern musicologists.

Again, that's quite different from saying that it's the "best-known work" of the London Pianoforte school.

(C) The passage never comments on whether "original scores" of the London Pianoforte school have survived. We only know that the music itself has survived. Hence, we can't conclude that no "original scores" have survived to the present.

(D) The passage claims that Temperley's anthology makes available much music that had previously been unavailable. It doesn't claim that no one had tried to make this music available before him; rather, just that he's the first one to succeed in making it available.

62. (D) Detail

Both Clementi and Field are mentioned only once in the passage (lines 10–12). In these lines, we're explicitly told that their works are examples of those that "have remained familiar" to modern musicologists. Choice **(D)** echoes this idea.

(A) To the contrary. Lines 12–13 indicate that Clementi's and Field's works have been preserved mainly "in editions lacking scholarly rigor."

(B) To the contrary. Lines 10–12 cite Clementi's and Field's works as examples of those that "have remained familiar."

(C) The passage never mentions what "leaders of the London Pianoforte school" thought about Clementi's and Field's works.

(E) While we're told that Temperley's anthology reproduces the works of 49 members of the London Pianoforte school (lines 22–23), we're not told whether reproductions of Clementi's and Field's works are among these 49. Besides, the passage's lone reference to their works is not linked to its discussion of Temperley's anthology.

63. (A) Logic (Weaken)

Ringer's argument is described in paragraph 4, so you've got to look there for clues about what would undermine it. Lines 40–42 tell us that Ringer thought that Beethoven had to look outside of Austria for "creative" music models. This implies that Ringer believed that Austrian musicians weren't creative. Thus, if Austrian musicians actually composed innovative piano music, Ringer's argument about their creativity would certainly be undermined.

(B) According to lines 47–48, Ringer argues that the London Pianoforte school exercised influence on the music world "in the decades just before and after 1800." Hence, the finding that Clementi et al.—who were members of this school—produced most of their compositions from 1790–1810 would, if anything, support Ringer's view. It certainly wouldn't undermine that view.

(C) Ringer asserts that Beethoven's music was influenced by the works of the London Pianoforte school. That Beethoven's

music may also have been influenced by the works of Continental musicians does not undermine this view.

(D) According to lines 44–46, Ringer's argument incorporates the idea that the musicians of the London Pianoforte school adopted similar stylistic principles.

(E) Where the members of the London Pianoforte school were born and why they ended up in London is not relevant to Ringer's argument, which deals only with the music of this school and its influence on other musicians.

64. (B) Inference

Right after the phrase "advances of the Broadwood piano" (lines 49–50), we're given several specific examples of these advances (lines 50–51)—a "reinforced frame, extended compass, triple stringing, and pedals." In other words, the word "advances" refers to improvements in the piano itself. Choice **(B)** reflects this idea, albeit in more general terms.

(A) What enticements? What instrument manufacturers? Neither enticements nor instrument manufacturers are mentioned in the passage.

(C) and **(D)** err in claiming that the word "advances" refers to piano music instead of the piano itself. The context in which this word is used, however, makes it evident that the word refers to the instrument.

(E), like **(A),** is outside the scope of the passage. We're not given any information about musicians' opinions of the piano.

65. (B) Logic Function

Despite the question stem's claim, you don't really need an overview of the entire passage to find the correct answer to this question. Indeed, the first sentence of paragraph 3 lets you know what the paragraph is going to be about: whether the London Pianoforte school rightfully deserves to be called a school. The rest of the paragraph simply grapples with this question.

(A) The first couple of sentences of paragraph 2 make plain the author's positive attitude toward Temperley's anthology, which isn't even mentioned in paragraph 3.

(C) Ringer's argument is summarized in paragraph 4.

(D) In lines 31–38, the author notes that, musically speaking, the London Pianoforte school probably doesn't deserve to be called a school at all. The musical styles of its members were too diverse for it to be labeled a school on this basis.

(E) Like Ringer's argument, the London Pianoforte school's contributions to music are discussed in paragraph 4.

66. (E) Global (Primary Purpose)

This question, like #1, is a global question. But, in contrast to #1, it asks about the author's purpose, not her main point. Paragraph 1 tells us that, historically, not much has been known about the London Pianoforte school. Paragraph 2 tells us that Temperley's anthology has changed this state of affairs, while paragraphs 3 and 4 point out how Temperley's anthology has contributed to our knowledge of this school, helping to correct some past misconceptions about it. Only choice **(E)** is broad enough to capture the contents of all four paragraphs.

(A) The relationship between Beethoven's music and the development of the piano is brought up only in paragraph 4.

(B) While lines 23–27 indicate that Temperley's anthology should lead to new evaluations of the development of piano music in England and on the continent, his particular views on these issues are never described.

(C) Likewise, Temperley's particular views on the matter of how changes in piano design may have affected the London Pianoforte school's music aren't mentioned.

(D) An alternative to Ringer's theory is discussed only in paragraph 4.

67. (B) Inference

Temperley's own views about the London Pianoforte school are mentioned in just two places: at the end of paragraphs 3 and 4. The second reference is the one that's relevant to answering this question. In lines 56–59, we learn that Temperley defines the London Pianoforte school as consisting of those musicians who developed piano music between the years 1766 and 1873. Choice **(B)** reflects this idea.

(A) To the contrary. Lines 37–38 suggest that Temperley felt that the members of the London Pianoforte school *did not* share the same "stylistic principles and artistic creeds." It was Ringer who believed that they shared these things.

(C) According to paragraph 4, Ringer and (perhaps) the author feel that Beethoven was influenced by the London Pianoforte school. We don't know whether Temperley holds this view.

(D) To the contrary. Temperley defines the London Pianoforte school to include musicians who worked on piano music between *1766* and *1863*. This period extends well beyond "the decades just before and just after 1800."

(E) Lines 52–55 suggest that the author believes that the London Pianoforte school's music had an influence on Continental musicians. We aren't told whether Temperley shares this view.

Passage 10: Miles Davis
Questions 68–73

Topic and Scope: Miles Davis; specifically, his contributions to the development of new forms of jazz.

Purpose and Main Idea: The author's purpose is to argue that Davis's contributions to the development of jazz haven't received adequate recognition by music critics. The author's main idea is that jazz critics haven't given Davis his due because they haven't approved of his musical innovations.

Paragraph Structure: Paragraph 1 sets up the rest of the passage. In the very first sentence, the author provides his opinion of Davis's role in the development of jazz: it has been "astonishingly productive." Nevertheless, the author points out in the next sentence, Davis hasn't gotten enough credit for his contributions. Note that the Contrast Keyword "Yet" (line 3) signals a conflict between the author's opinion of Davis and the opinion of others. In the final sentence of this paragraph, the author lays out this conflict in more detail: music critics haven't given Davis his due because they haven't approved of his musical innovations. At this point in the passage, you've already got sufficient information to figure out what the author's going to do in the rest of the text: since he disagrees with the critics, it's predictable that he's going to explain why they're wrong by discussing Davis's contributions to jazz.

Paragraph s 2, 3, and 4 bear out this prediction. Paragraph 2 discusses his contributions to what would become known as "West Coast cool" jazz; paragraph 3 discusses his innovations regarding chord patterns; and paragraph 4 discusses his late 1960s efforts to create jazz in the music studio—a development that has particularly irked critics. Rather than try to memorize all of the many details in these paragraphs, you should simply note where particular details are located in the text; by following this procedure, you'll be able to refer back quickly to any detail in the passage should it be necessary to answer a question.

Paragraph 5 wraps up the passage by discussing *why* music critics haven't given Davis his due—up to this point in the text, you should have noted, the author hasn't really tackled the *why* of it. According to the author, the most likely reason that critics have attacked Davis is that he was an innovator. Ironically, the author notes, despite the fact that jazz is an innovative music form, jazz critics don't always approve of innovation.

The Big Picture:

- On Test Day, a passage like this one is a good place to start work on the Reading Comp. section. The passage's topic, scope, purpose, and main idea are all in evidence by the end of paragraph 1. Moreover, information in this paragraph lets you know where the passage is going to head in subsequent paragraphs, making this passage easy to follow.

- Not all paragraphs are equally important. In this passage, paragraphs 1 and 5 are the most important, because they focus on the author's purpose and main idea. Paragraphs 2, 3, and 4, on the other hand, contain a lot of descriptive detail that merely supports the author's purpose and main idea. On Test Day, focus more closely on those paragraphs where the author's voice comes through—most of the questions will be answered by these paragraphs.

The Questions:

68. (B) Global (Main Point)

In the first sentence of the passage, the author states that Miles Davis has made a major contribution to the development of jazz. In the next sentence, the author notes that Davis has not received just recognition for his efforts, however. (The Contrast Keyword "Yet" (line 3) signals the contrast between the ideas in the first and second sentences.) The author then devotes the rest of the passage to discussing why his opinion of Davis (stated in the first sentence) is right, while the critics' opinion of Davis (revealed in the second sentence) is wrong. Indeed, lines 1–9 and lines 55–58 capture the sentiments expressed in choice **(B)**.

(A) According to the author, Davis has had an "astonishingly productive" (line 2) jazz career. Jazz critics, not the author, take issue with Davis's musical accomplishments.

(C) This choice distorts ideas introduced in lines 53–58. According to the passage, the reason that jazz critics haven't given Davis his due isn't directly linked to his longevity or productivity, but rather to his frequent shifts in musical style. Moreover, lines 53–58 don't say that praise has "generally [been] reserved for artists with more tragic life stories."

(D) is beyond the scope of the passage. Since the text doesn't deal with *all* of the major stylistic changes affecting twentieth-century jazz, but only those that Davis played a part in pioneering, there's no basis for concluding that Davis played a major role in pioneering *most* of the stylistic changes of the twentieth century. It's possible that there are dozens of other major stylistic changes that Davis had no part in pioneering.

(E) To the contrary. According to the passage, jazz critics haven't been kind to Davis.

69. (E) Detail

If you made a mental roadmap of the passage, you would have gone directly to paragraph 2, which discusses "West Coast cool" jazz. Lines 12–17 reveal that this style of jazz was pioneered in New York City by Davis and his collaborators.

(A) While paragraph 2 says that Davis helped to invent "West Coast cool" jazz, it doesn't say that he helped to popularize it. Indeed, the first sentence of paragraph 3 says that Davis moved on to an even newer form of jazz by the late 1950s, suggesting that his role in "West Coast cool" jazz was restricted to that of inventor.

(B) and **(D)** According to paragraph 3, the jazz style pioneered by Davis in the late 1950s—that is, the style he pioneered *after* "West Coast cool" jazz—was "characterized by a unified and integrated sound" (line 26) and "introduced a wide variety of chord change patterns" (lines 20–24).

(C) The passage never provides information about ensemble *size* as it pertains to Davis's music.

70. (A) Inference

Since you're asked about Davis's jazz before 1948, paragraph 2—which discusses the changes he improvised in 1948—is crucial to this question. Lines 13–15 state that Davis invented a new form of jazz in 1948—one that contained slower tempos and more ensemble playing. Thus, it's logical to infer that the jazz played by Davis before 1948 featured quicker tempos and more solo playing.

(B) The fact that the jazz style improvised by Davis in 1948 featured ensemble playing at least "as much as" (line 14) solo playing indicates that the pre-1948 jazz played by Davis must have favored solo playing over ensemble playing.

(C) According to the passage, *Davis* has improvised new forms of jazz since 1948 in order to expand this music's boundaries. But there's nothing in the passage to support the contention that the pre-1948 jazz that he played was a reaction to even more restrictive jazz styles.

(D) Purist jazz critics, according to lines 45–48, have attacked Davis's musical innovations. However, based on this fact alone we can't conclude that they believe that the pre-1948 jazz that he played is the only authentic form of jazz. For instance, jazz purists might regard some post-1948 jazz styles developed by musicians other than Davis as equally authentic.

(E) While we're told in line 12 that Davis improvised a new form of jazz in New York City in 1948, we aren't told anything about where the pre-1948 jazz that he played was performed. It might have been primarily in New York City jazz clubs, but the passage doesn't say so.

71. (E) Inference (Author's Attitude)

When you're asked about an attitude, look for words or phrases that shed light on that attitude. In this passage, the author's attitude toward Davis's music is very evident in the first two sentences of the text. In the first sentence, the author refers to Davis's career as "astonishingly productive." In the second sentence, the author calls Davis a "genius." These words and phrases indicate that author has nothing but praise for Davis's work.

(A)–(D) All of these choices suggest that the author displays less than wholehearted support for Davis. Indeed, choices **(A)** and **(B)** indicate that the author isn't supportive at all.

72. (D) Logic (Parallel Reasoning)

The studio procedure in question is discussed in lines 38–41. The essence of this procedure involved constructing a new whole (a finished piece of music) from different parts (various taped segments of music). Choice **(D)** reflects the same exact relationship: a new whole (the collage) is constructed out of different parts (individual photographs).

(A), (B), (C), (E) None of these choices reflects this fundamental relationship. Choice **(C)**, which is tricky, violates the relationship in the sense that nothing new is created. The orchestra and the piece of music it plays already exist.

73. (B) Logic (Weaken)

To weaken the author's argument, you've first got to be clear about his argument. What he argues—in both paragraphs 1 and 5—is that jazz critics haven't given Davis credit for his contribution to jazz because they disapprove of his repeated changes in style. Thus, if it was true that many of these same critics were fond of other musicians who also engaged in this sort of musical behavior, the author's argument would be weakened.

(A) Lines 42–48 suggest that jazz critics, in the author's opinion, believe that improvisational playing is at the heart of jazz; hence, the fact that they admire this trait in jazz players would not weaken the author's argument.

(C) Although some jazz purists attacked Davis for having Herbie Hancock play an electric rather than an acoustic piano (lines 32–34), the major criticism leveled against Davis by jazz critics has to do with his radical changes in style, not his use of electronic instruments.

(D) As we mentioned in question 1, it's not the span of Davis's career that critics object to; it's what he's done in that career that irks them.

(E) Again, Davis was attacked for his radical approach to jazz, not an alleged lack of "musicality."

Passage 11: Deconstruction
Questions 74–80

Topic and Scope: The literary philosophy of deconstruction; specifically, the connection between its terminology and its methods.

Purpose and Main Idea: The author's Purpose is to demonstrate that links exist between deconstruction's terminology and its methods; the author argues that deconstructionist terminology provides clear insights into deconstruction's methods.

Paragraph Structure: Paragraphs 1 and 2 essentially point out that deconstructionist terminology reflects the philosophy's methods. The words—along with their prior meanings—that deconstructionists have "borrowed or adapted from stock" to define their philosophy imply certain things about that philosophy.

Paragraph 3 is the heart of the text. This paragraph discusses the specific ways in which the term *deconstruction* sheds light on deconstructionist methods. Basically, this term, which is taken from the construction industry, highlights deconstructionist efforts to demolish, rather than simply criticize, literary works.

The Big Picture:

- Many of you may have found this a difficult passage because of its rather abstract nature. Don't worry if you don't understand all of the points made by the author—you're not going to be asked about most of them. The most important thing to pick up on in a passage like this one is the author's critical tone—that's what'll really help you to answer questions.

- Since this passage isn't easy, a savvy test taker might well have left it for last. On Test Day, begin work on the Reading Comprehension section with a more "concrete" passage.

The Questions:

74. (A) Global (Main Point)

This choice nicely captures the Topic, Scope, and Purpose of the passage. The correct answer to global questions must be broad enough to encompass the contents of the entire passage. Avoid choices—like **(B)**, **(C)**, and **(D)** here—that blow up details into Main Ideas.

(B) These literary terms didn't pre-date deconstruction; rather, deconstructionists turned these words into literary terms. Besides, this is a mere detail in paragraph 2; it's certainly not the text's Main Idea.

(C) also plays on a detail in paragraph 2.

(D) focuses on a detail in paragraph 3. Moreover, this choice reflects the author's opinion of deconstruction, which isn't necessarily what deconstructionists think of deconstruction.

(E) This choice contradicts the author's critical attitude toward evaluating literature in light of "borrowed or adapted" terminology.

75. (E) Detail

This choice is a good paraphrase of lines 15–18.

(A) The author never claims that deconstruction would have been impossible without the use of these terms. He refers to them simply to highlight an aspect of deconstructionist philosophy.

(B) is a 180 choice. Lines 12–15 indicate that deconstructionists have chosen neologisms for very specific reasons.

(C) The author never says that deconstruction "contains inherent contradictions." What he says is that deconstructionists are on the lookout for contradictions in the work of others.

(D) is another 180 choice. Deconstructionists are interested enough "in the relationship between words and their referents" that they've developed terminology to illustrate this relationship.

76. (C) Logic (Parallel Reasoning)

The author's belief about innovation in language (lines 1–6) is that it consists of giving new meanings to existing words. **(C)** expresses precisely the same relationship—existing components "are made to function in new ways."

None of the other choices reflects the author's fundamental idea about "borrowing or adapting" something that already exists to serve a new end.

77. (B) Logic Function

In lines 44–46, the author sets up a contrast between *deconstruction* and *criticism*. In lines 46–56, he fleshes out this contrast by defining *criticism* and showing how it differs from *deconstruction*.

(A) Lines 46–56 do contain an example of sorts—the example of the building. This example, however, is in the text because it *supports* the contrast that the author makes.

(C), **(D)**, and **(E)** are beyond the scope of the text. If anything, the author makes an argument in lines 46–56; he doesn't undermine one **(C)**. Nor does he "codify a system" **(D)** or "dismiss an objection" **(E)**: what system? What objection?

78. (C) Logic Function

In paragraph 1, the author argues that the old meaning of words doesn't disappear when people use these words in new ways. In paragraph 2, the author provides an example of this phenomenon by showing that the word "signify" conjures up a certain idea, even though deconstructionists don't have this idea in mind when they use this word.

(A), **(B)** paragraph 2 neither "introduces a hypothesis" **(A)** nor "qualifies a claim" **(B)**. It simply backs up an abstract argument made in paragraph 1 with a concrete example.

(D) distorts a detail in the last sentence of paragraph 2.

(E) paragraph 3 "presents a contrasting view"—a view that takes issue with deconstruction.

79. (B) Inference

In paragraph 3, the author's disapproval of deconstruction, which he thinks "has no overtones of skill or wisdom," is evident. Equally apparent is his approval of criticism, which is based on "skill and insight."

(A) Deconstructionists—not the author—think that it's important to "demonstrate false assumptions and inherent contradictions."

(C) The author has problems with deconstructionist philosophy, not with the number of deconstructionists (or, for that matter, other critics) who may analyze a work.

(D) is a metaphor for an analytic process favored by deconstructionists. The author is critical of this analytic process.

(E) distorts a detail in lines 32–34. The author doesn't make any judgements about text structures; he makes a judgement about differing modes of literary criticism.

80. (D) Inference (Author's Attitude)

This choice both reflects the author's generally negative attitude toward deconstruction, and echoes his comment in lines 28–30.

(A), **(B)**, **(C)** The author isn't "guardedly optimistic" **(A)** or "enthusiastic" **(C)** about deconstruction. Nor does he "endorse" it in any respect **(B)**. Indeed, he's critical of deconstruction's search for authorial bias, as well as the way it uses words and neologisms.

(E) is too strongly negative in tone. Besides, according to the author, deconstructionists don't think of literary criticism as a "creative act." Just the opposite; it's a repetitive, "mechanical" process.

Passage 12: Kelley on Communism in Alabama
Questions 81–85

This is a typical LSAT Humanities "book review" passage. The author of the passage outlines the argument made in the book and shows how it is different than the typical scholarship on the subject. The **Topic** in this passage is Kelley's book on Communism in Alabama. In the first paragraph, we also learn the **Scope**, which is Kelley's explanation of how the Communist party attracted and organized African Americans. The **Purpose** (and remember, this is the author of the passage's purpose, not Kelley's purpose) is simply to outline Kelley's argument—that the Popular Front period lessened African-American support for Communism. The **Main Idea** sums up the Topic, Scope, and Purpose: Kelley's book shows how the Communist party tried to attract and organize African Americans in Alabama.

The first paragraph introduces the Topic (Kelley's book) and the Scope. The key is the second sentence (lines 3–8), which centers around the Keywords "not" and "but." The reason our author finds Kelley's book noteworthy is because it focuses on how Communism came to attract and organize African Americans.

Paragraph 2 contrasts Kelley's book with "most scholarship," which defends the Popular Front period of American Communism. The Keyword "while" (line 16) helps us see the author's point: by focusing on African Americans, Kelley shows problems with the Popular Front.

In the third paragraph, the author takes a step back in time to show how Kelley's book argues that the Third Period, which preceded the Popular Front, was actually better for African Americans. The Keyword "but" (line 28) signals Kelley's evidence: the rhetoric of Third Period offered "deliverance" to African Americans.

The fourth paragraph brings us back to Kelley's thesis that the Popular Front era was less attractive for African Americans. Kelley's reasons are summed up in lines 40–48: as the Communists tried to appeal to a broader audience, they backed down from the "deliverance" of African Americans.

Paragraph 5, which starts off with the Contrast Keywords "even so," is typical of LSAT passages. It is a moderating paragraph, included simply to make sure that the author doesn't seem too extreme. Here, the author makes sure that we know that Kelley included other factors in his discussion of why Communism lost ground with African Americans.

The Big Picture:

Paragraph 1: Kelley's book explores Communism in Alabama, especially how African Americans organized.

Paragraph 2: Most scholars defend Communism in 30s and 40s; Kelley: Popular Front (PF) bad for African Americans.

Paragraph 3: Before PF, Third Period attracted African Americans with extreme "deliverance" rhetoric and anti-lynching stance.

Paragraph 4: PF cautious; decreased "deliverance" message.

Paragraph 5: PF not sole factor in decline

The Questions:

81. (E) Global (Main Point)

At the end of a passage, take a moment to sum up the Main Idea of the passage; this is a ready-made prediction for Global questions.

As soon as we read the words "main point," we know that we are ready for this Global question. We simply use our summary of the author's main point (that Kelley's book shows how the Communist party tried to attract and organize African Americans in Alabama) and find the answer that matches: **(E)**. This language in this answer—that Kelley's book "offers new insights"—matches because we know that our author contrasted *Hammer and Hoe* with "most scholarship."

(A) distorts our author because it states that *Hammer and Hoe* "fails to fully explicate the relationship between Communism and African American[s] ..." Our author does not criticize Kelley's work.

(B) fails to mention Kelley's book—the Topic of the passage—and misses our author's point by concentrating on the necessity of ideological purity, which was the focus of "most scholarship," not Kelley's book.

(C) mentions Kelley's book, but for the wrong reason. Our author said it was interesting because it focused on how Communism attracted African Americans, not as a model for unity between liberals and radicals.

(D) This answer also misses the topic of the passage by failing to mention Kelley's book. It also distorts our author's purpose by focusing on the "true measure of success of the Communist Party."

82. (A) Detail EXCEPT

In Detail EXCEPT questions, choose the answer that contradicts the author and/or eliminate answers that were cited by the author.

Detail EXCEPT questions can be big "time sinks." To avoid hunting and pecking your way through the passage, consider the reference in the question stem and focus your research on the relevant paragraph or section. Here, the question asks us what the passage said about Communism in Alabama *before* the 1930s, that is, before the Popular Front. This information was contained in the third paragraph, where the author introduced Kelley's discussion of the Third Period or in the fourth paragraph, which contrasted the Popular Front with its predecessor. Savvy test takers will pick **(A)** immediately because their Roadmap will have summarized Kelley's point that the Third Period was popular with African Americans precisely because it attacked white chauvinism.

If you didn't immediately see that answer **(A)** was correct, you could still get the correct answer here by eliminating any answer that was mentioned in the third or fourth paragraphs. Answer **(B)** is knocked out by lines 35–37. **(C)** is mentioned in lines 29–32. **(D)** is right in line with lines 25–28. Answer **(E)** comes from paragraph 4, lines 41–43. Because the author says that during the Popular Front, interest in local African-American issues declined, he is stating that before the 1930s, interest in local African-American issues must have been higher.

83. (A) Logic Function

Use your Roadmap to answer "paragraph function" questions.

This question really brings home the importance of circling Keywords and paraphrasing paragraphs as we read and Roadmap passages. A well-trained test taker will answer this question correctly with minimum effort and maximum efficiency by noting that she has already summarized the paragraph (e.g., *¶2: Most scholars defend Communism in 30s and 40s; Kelley: Popular Front (PF) bad for African Americans*) and has the Contrast Keyword "while" circled in line 16. The roadmap thus serves as a powerful prediction leading to the correct answer: **(A)**.

(B) distorts the author, who thinks Kelley's criticism of the Popular Front is valuable.

(C) is out of scope. Remember, our author's Topic is Kelley's book, and this answer prioritizes debate about the usefulness of political approaches.

(D) is a faulty use of detail. The differences between the Popular Front and the Third Period are discussed in paragraphs 3 and 4. Note: always realize when the answer to one question can help you with the answer to another. In this case, Question 17 should definitely alert us that this is a wrong answer choice.

(E) This answer is too extreme. The author says that Kelley's book is valuable, not that it is the *only* way to study Communism in America.

84. (A) Inference

When a question asks what the author "would most likely agree with," consider the opinions expressed in the passage.

This Inference question asks us to understand the author's opinion concerning the Popular Front. The reference to the Popular Front is helpful, but doesn't really take us to one specific paragraph, so we should consider our summary of the author's Topic, Scope, and Purpose. The author's overall Purpose seemed to be to explain how Kelley advanced the idea that the Popular Front reduced Communism's appeal

to African Americans. This accords with answer **(A)**. All four wrong answers are 180s: they directly misstate or contradict something that the passage said.

(B) Kelley's statement (in lines 50–52) that the Popular Front initially appealed to African Americans contradicts this.

(C) The author tells us in paragraph 4 that Kelley believed that the Popular Front's cautiousness decreased communism's appeal for African Americans.

(D) Like **(C)**, this answer directly contradicts Kelley's argument that the Popular Front decreased the appeal of communism for African Americans.

(E) It was the extreme rhetoric of the Third Period that *attracted* African Americans, according to Kelley.

85. (B) Inference

The LSAT may ask you to draw inferences on different people's opinions; always predict an answer in line with the point of view of the party referred to in the question stem.

This is an interesting question because it asks us to infer what a Communist Party organizer would think, rather than what the author or Kelley would agree with. The key reference in the question stem is to the differences between the party's position during the Third Period and the Popular Front. This leads us to paragraphs 3 and 4. According to the passage, the Third Period was more extreme in its rhetoric and the Popular Front more cautious. So, we should expect the correct answer to reflect this difference. Answer **(B)** fits the bill since it contains a sweeping call to revolution.

(A) is a 180. The Third Period organizer would have been more likely than the Popular Front organizer to call for African Americans to resist the majority culture.

(C) This answer distorts what Kelley told us about the Third Period, which is that it was more likely to work on local issues confronting African Americans.

(D) Another 180. It was during the more cautious Popular Front era, not the Third Period, that the Communist organizers sought to build a bridge with liberal causes.

(E) This answer would also be more typical of the Popular Front organizer, who would have been more measured, than of the wilder Third Period organizer.

Passage 13: Fake Art
Questions 86–92

Topic and Scope: Fake art; specifically, Mark Jones's book-length examination of that subject.

Purpose and Main Idea: Our author's purpose is to review what Jones does in his book; in her phrase, she wants to "reveal the study's broader concerns." The Main Idea is simply that, as Jones illustrates, the issue of fake vs. original art is far more complicated than the mere question of "Was something faked?" The motive behind faking proves to be important, and in some cultures, function is key as well.

Paragraph Structure: Paragraph 1 begins by telling us a necessary condition for fake art—that the motive of the copyer be to deceive; the work's merit is a separate thing. The author immediately uses Mark Jones' book *Fake?* to carry further the idea that fakery isn't just a matter of making a copy: There are other relevant issues, motive being one big one. And indeed, the paragraph lists situations that fall "somewhere between the two extremes" of original on the one hand, and fake on the other. One can readily concede that neither copying a master's work, nor deliberately evoking the past, nor copying for teaching purposes, nor making facsimiles to be sold (close paraphrases of the four items in lines 8–11), meets the definition of "intended to deceive." They're not original; but they're not fake either, at least by lines 1–2's definition. So it *is* a knotty issue.

Paragraph 2, as lines 12–17 promise, distills the bulk of *Fake?: The Art Of Deception* into a Cook's tour of how and why art was faked, from ancient Rome (where a big market in ancient Greek stuff inspired much fakery), through the Middle Ages (an era too religious to countenance much artistic funny business), to the Renaissance (where fakery really came into its own, for the reasons laid out in lines 23–27). And all the way through, the alert critical reader—that's you, right?—should be thinking about each era in the light of lines 12–17's promise to focus on "the many different motives" at work in art collection and art fakery. Presumably Jones's book takes one to the present day, but our author has polished off her take on present-day fakery in paragraph 1 and so our chronological summary stops with the often-faked Michelangelo.

Paragraph 3 is really a side trip: The author's still on the topic of fake art, but the scope has shifted to a specific exception that is illustrated by a specific example from Jones's book. African art, we're told, illustrates that in some cultures, functionality is important to whether a copy is fake or not. She offers the two Bambara *chi wara* masks—identical but for the pegs that attach the mask to a cap during a ritual—as an example of an instance in which authenticity hinges on function.

The Big Picture:

- Your understanding of necessary vs. sufficient conditions is tested all over the LSAT—even here in Reading Comp. (see, for example, sentence 1). Always look to differentiate between that which is *required* to bring about a result, and that which is *enough* to bring about a result.

- Not only must you watch for the author's point of view; you must watch for its *absence*. Here, in contrast to other "book-review" passages where authors see both pros and cons in the works under consideration, our author seems to sign on to everything that's in Jones's book; she neither carps nor criticizes. It's important to notice that.

- Finally, watch for paragraphs that are relevant to the broad topic but represent a distinct scope shift. paragraph 3 is one such. You'll be tested on this.

The Questions:

86. (C) Global (Primary Purpose)

The question is simple: "What's the passage doing?" But the given choices are so brief that all five may look appealing. Your best bet is first to come up with your *own* statement of the purpose. As we've seen, the overall passage brings up, and discusses at length, issues about fake art raised by Jones's book. It *is*, therefore, an "exploration." And from paragraph 1, where we learn that much artwork can fall into an ambiguous middle ground between original and fake, to the very last sentence—a hint that even the artistic creators, the Bambara, might disagree with self-styled experts as to what is "fake"—the author never fails to reinforce the idea that the question of what constitutes fake art is a complex one. **(C)** is amply justified.

(A) describes a passage in which different people's points of view are brought together/synthesized. But this is Mark Jones's book as viewed by a very sympathetic author. Nothing to reconcile.

(B) *Jones* takes a chronological approach, says lines 12–13, but the passage author does not.

(D) describes a passage in which the author tries to get us to accept a new—usually her own—vision. But this author is simply articulating aspects of *Jones's* vision.

(E) "Explanation" doesn't apply; "interpretation" would be better. But in any event, our author likes Jones's book very much. No rejection here.

87. (D) Global (Main Point)

Your pre-phrasing of the author's main point should have encompassed the idea—supported by Jones's work and explained approvingly by our author—that "fakery" goes well beyond the mere circumstances of a copy's creation. That's not word for word **(D)**, but it's darned close.

KAPLAN

(A) We don't learn enough about every past culture to know whether "virtually every" one sees art fakery. Certainly medieval Europe did not (lines 20–23). And anyway, that fakery "flourishes whenever art collecting" does (lines 15–16) implies that the degree of art fakery varies from era to era and, therefore, from culture to culture.

(B) Artistic merit and the whole issue of fakery are separate issues, says paragraph 1, but that doesn't imply that one is "less important than" the other.

(C) According to lines 37–38, only in *some* cultures is authenticity something that cannot be proven.

(E) Not only is no such extreme prediction about art fakery supported by the text, but the tone of paragraph 2 implies that fakery will go on whenever art collecting does.

88. (C) Detail

We need go no further than lines 1–2 for this one. The necessary condition for fake art is that it be "an artwork intended to deceive," and **(C)** just provides a straightforward paraphrase of that idea.

(A), (D), and **(E)** are all mentioned in paragraph 1 as examples of "middle ground" situations in which the issue of fake vs. original is mighty blurry. None of them acts as a *definition* of fake art.

(B) Deliberate *fooling* is what characterizes fake art, not deliberate *imitation*. Deliberate imitation need not be fake—as paragraph 1 makes clear. It depends on the creator's motive…which brings us back to **(C)**.

89. (E) Detail EXCEPT

In this "odd man out" question, four of the choices play a role in the passage, which suggests that the right answer is probably outside of its scope. We can review the text, or seek out the wrong choices, or search for the odd man out directly. In any case, your search is aided if you realize that paragraph 2's review of Jones's chronology stops at Michelangelo, and so we never get a chance to hear about **(E)**, names of any contemporary artists whose work has been faked. All of the others appear:

(A) Lines 8–11 list those categories.

(B) Ancient Rome and the Renaissance would be two such cultures.

(C) For example, lines 25–27 detail qualities that were prized during the Renaissance.

(D) African art (lines 37–38) is one culture in which the categories don't apply.

90. (C) Inference

The only reference to artistic merit comes in paragraph 1, specifically lines 2–3, where we learn that "merit" and "fakery" are two wholly separate issues. Search for that sentiment and you find it squarely in **(C)**.

(A), (B) Both try to interrelate the issues of merit and fakery, **(A)** arguing that they're mutually exclusive, **(B)** that they're correlated. Neither: They are separate issues altogether—as **(C)** realizes.

(D), (E) Each mentions an element that the passage never alludes to, or even implies.

91. (E) Inference

The author's definition of authenticity appears not once but twice in paragraph 3: Lines 39–40 and 49–50 both assert that the functionality of an object determines its authenticity. Among the choices, then, we need to find an object "tied to the form's original function," and only **(E)**—a copied item "designed to serve its traditional role"—meets that definition. The other choices mention function not at all; even **(D)**, which describes an object virtually identical to its original, falls short because we never hear that the ceremonial crown is meant to be used.

92. (D) Logic Function

In our analysis of the Paragraph Structure, above, we called paragraph 3 a "side trip," a visit to a different kind of cultural milieu and a very different sense of how the issue of fakery applies there. **(D)** picks up on paragraph 3's shift of scope to "another facet" of the distinction between original and fake.

(A) The opening paragraph poses no question for paragraph 3, or any other, to answer.

(B), (C) What paragraph 3 has to offer, of course, is new to it, having no necessary relation to paragraph 2 except that both discuss an aspect of the general topic of fakery.

(E) paragraph 3 has no real and definite link to paragraph 1, either, much as **(E)** would like to make one.

Law Passages

Passage 1: Jury Unanimity
Questions 1–7

As is often the case, the first sentence clues us into the **Topic** of the passage, jury trials. As paragraph 1 develops, we can see that the **Scope** is the wisdom of the unanimity requirement—the demand that all jurors agree before a decision is reached. Paragraph 1 fully defines the unanimity requirement, and introduces the objections of critics who feel that the unanimity requirement is a "costly relic" (line 13) that too easily creates the possibility of mistrial. Although the author's **Purpose** is not explicitly stated, the fact that this opposition to unanimity is described in the first paragraph may give us a hint that the author is going to rebut this criticism. (If the author agreed with the critics, what else would be left to say in the remainder of the essay?)

The first sentence of paragraph 2 is a nice paraphrase of the **Main Idea** of the passage, and also confirms our suspicion of the author's **Purpose**—to argue that jury unanimity is too important to abandon. The paragraph goes on to state that jury trials are actually relatively rare, and hung juries are even rarer. The author then presents supporting evidence that experienced test-takers should recognize as LSAT question fodder: "[jury] deadlock does not demonstrate a flaw in the criminal justice system" (lines 29–31) as some critics may contend, but in fact demonstrates that juries are doing what they are supposed to. If a jury can't agree, it's because neither case was completely convincing.

Paragraph 3 concludes by noting that innocent people are sometimes convicted, and abolishing the unanimity requirement would probably greatly increase the likelihood of this happening. Finally, the author states that society as a whole cannot have as much confidence in the justness of a verdict if the opinions of any jurors are dismissed.

The Questions:

1. (E) Global (Main Point)

In critically reading the passage, we identified the first sentence of paragraph 2 as a summary of the Main Idea. Choice **(E)** uses most of the same wording, and expresses the same idea—jury unanimity provides benefits which outweigh its cost, so it should remain a requirement in important trials.

(A) focuses too much on the rarity of jury trials, and does not address why they are important. **(B)** introduces "irresponsible" jurors, a concept not contained in the passage. While **(C)** is a point made by the author, it leaves out the important idea that the benefits of jury unanimity outweigh the objections cited by critics. The author seems to believe that jurors are already doing what they are supposed to do (31–33), so **(D)** is also off base.

2. (D) Inference (Author's Attitude)

We've already determined (in reading the passage and in answering question 1) that the author endorses jury unanimity, and "firm support" **(D)** characterizes this attitude nicely. **(A)**, **(B)**, and **(C)** don't express sufficient support and confidence, while "unreasoned reverence" **(E)** goes overboard.

3. (A) Logic (Principle)

We'll need to quickly consult our roadmap to remember what's covered in paragraph 3. The author writes that some innocent people are already convicted, and that eliminating the unanimity requirement would only make this more likely. He further writes that dismissing the opinion of a dissenting reviewer would eliminate an important component in the deliberation process. It's clear, then, that the author believes the requirement is extremely important to prevent unjust verdicts, and that it's worth using strong methods to do so **(A)**.

Although **(B)** discusses fairness, it places responsibility on the judge, rather than the jury. **(C)** is too strong in predicting the complete elimination of unjust verdicts, and **(D)** safeguards against irresponsible jurists, a topic unmentioned in the passage. **(E)** states that the jury system is "inherently flawed," which, although perhaps true, is not an underlying principle of the third paragraph of this passage.

4. (C) Inference

If you tackled question 3 right before this, you'll have the flow of paragraph 3 fresh in your mind—the paragraph lists three reasons why jury unanimity is important for individual trials and society in general. There's no point in trying to prephrase here, so move on to the answer choices. **(C)** sums up the thinking in the paragraph by stressing the importance of each juror, and makes a more general point by comparing the jury system to democracy in general. This emphasizes the importance of jury unanimity and closes the passage with an uplifting rhetorical tone.

(A) discusses a "separate tradition," but there is nothing in the passage that would support this distinction. **(B)** and **(E)** go pretty far off base by introducing the new topics of public debate and scientific prosecution methods. The last sentence of the passage is not a good place to introduce entirely new ideas! Although the author has been arguing against the critics of jury unanimity, there's no indication that he regards such criticism as undermining "the integrity of the entire legal system" **(D)**.

5. (A) Inference

Once you reread the sentence, you can see we are looking for another word that describes someone who won't budge. (You might predict the word *stubborn*.) **(A)**, *obstinate*, means exactly that, and so fits the bill perfectly.

Although the words *suspicious* **(B)**, *careful* **(C)**, *conscientious* **(D)**, and *naive* **(E)** could all be plugged into the sentence and still make some sense, they would all change the meaning of the sentence much more than the correct answer. In the sentence, the author is describing the view of critics, and the language in the rest of the sentence ("costly relic") expresses this negative view of the jury unanimity. The words *careful* and *conscientious* express too positive an opinion of the holdout juror, while *suspicious* and *naive* have connotations that are unwarranted here.

6. (C) Detail

Consult your road map to find the place where the author discusses the cost of dismissing the opinion of a juror. It's at the end of paragraph 3, lines 51–54: "if even one juror has doubts that are dismissed out of hand, society's confidence that a proper verdict has been reached would be undermined." This matches up very well with **(C)**.

Although the author does state that juries are usually hung in only the closest cases, he never *explicitly* states that only the closest cases would be affected by ignoring dissenters **(A)**. **(B)** presents the new and irrelevant topic of juries' respect towards one another. **(D)** and **(E)** both incorrectly imply that the author feels deadlocked juries represent a flaw in the legal system when he actually believes they are a necessary and important component.

7. (D) Inference

We obviously can't prephrase here, so let's dive right into the answer choices. A quick glance tells us that most of the answer choices deal with the author's attitude towards hung juries. Answer choice **(D)** is a nice summation of the author's views on this topic, since he certainly believes that "hung juries are acceptable," and also believes that they usually occur when neither party has made a sufficiently compelling case.

We've already noted that the author feels hung juries occur when neither side has a sufficiently compelling case, so it wouldn't be right to say that "an error in judgment" **(A)** is indicated. Since the passage only addresses the topic of jury unanimity, the justice system in general **(B)**, or even the entire jury system **(C)**, are both too broad for us to infer the author's views. **(E)** is a 180 answer choice, since the author believes doing away with jury unanimity (and therefore having fewer hung juries) would prevent the fair hearing of all jurors' opinions.

Passage 2: Medieval Women
Questions 8–15

Topic and Scope: Medieval women; specifically, the actual level of power and status of women in thirteenth-century England.

Purpose and Main Idea: The author's purpose is to refute a common perception held by medievalists regarding public vs. private law by analyzing the specific case of medieval women. The main idea is that regardless of the fact that women were traditionally excluded from public roles, their acquisition of land conferred legal and economic benefits that allowed them to exercise power in the feudal system.

Paragraph Structure: Paragraph 1 begins with a view that the author finds "simplistic"—the view, held by medievalists, that there is a clear distinction between medieval public and private law. The aggressive critical reader will demand that the author go beyond the simplistic to reveal the more complex view—and that's what happens. Yes, the author agrees that women were legally excluded from public roles, but he goes on to argue that women's control of land, then the main source of wealth, had serious political implications. The paragraph ends with the example of widowed women, who, according to the author, seemed to have many legal and economic rights that normally are grouped in the public domain.

Paragraph 2 tells of the mechanisms by which medieval women might attain land. There are many examples listed, including things such as "partible inheritance," "bridal dowry," "dower," "jointure," and implications of the Magna Carta. No need to obsess over these details now; it's best to simply label this paragraph (on the page or just in your head) "how women got land," and go on to find out what the author plans to do next.

Well, now that we know how they got it, we probably want to know—and can reasonably expect to find out—how medieval women used their land to attain power and influence. (After all, unless we hear about that, the author will have failed to support his contention that women's control "had important political implications.") And we do get precisely what we expect from paragraph 3. Once again, your best bet here is to notice these details while, on a larger scale, you concentrate on this paragraph's overall function in the passage: It's there to tell us how women were able to exert political, legal, and economic influence. It's included, as expected, as evidence for the author's original claim of the "simplistic" distinction made by the medievalists in the first sentence.

The Big Picture:

- Be on the lookout for sentences that scream out authorial opinion or intent. A sentence like "Examination . . . shows this distinction to be overly simplistic" is like gold in an RC passage. A key task in Reading Comp. is separating the important ideas from

the mere details, and any sentence that essentially says "I, the author, think so-and-so . . ." is worthy of much attention. You may wish to underline or circle such statements as they appear; doing so will create a roadmap of the passage's essential themes.

- There are three main things to consider when previewing an RC passage: 1) Is the content manageable? If you have an interest in history or women's studies, or if you don't have any particular *aversion* to these topics, so far so good. 2) Is the passage structure straightforward? You may wish to hold off on passages that seem to go all over the map early on; latch on to passages that have paragraphs with clearly delineated topics. 3) What's the payoff? Some passages have eight questions, others five. If all the other factors look good, go for the passages with the larger payoffs. You should be able to formulate an effective attack on the section if you pay attention to these few considerations when choosing the order in which to tackle the passages.

- Simplify the passage's ideas and paraphrase the paragraph topics so you'll know where to look for various kinds of information. Here, the three paragraphs nicely form one coherent story: We're told first that a general distinction regarding the medieval period may not be correct because it overlooks the fact that medieval women could obtain and use land. How did they get it? That's paragraph 2. How did they use it? That's paragraph 3. End of story. With such a straightforward passage structure, you shouldn't have had much trouble locating the area of the passage relevant to each question.

The Questions:

8. (C) Global (Main Point)

The main idea is referred to early on. It's tied to the notion, which as we've seen runs through the entire passage, that women in medieval England obtained some important forms of power through the ownership of land. This is referred to as early as the sentence beginning in line 6: The laws and customs of the day, as **(C)** has it, enabled some women to control land in such a way as to exert economic and political power despite the official legal restrictions against them. Choice **(C)** is an excellent paraphrase of the long sentence found in lines 6–13—the "important political implications in the feudal system" from the passage is fleshed out along the way and jibes nicely with **(C)**'s "exercise a certain amount of power." The scope of **(C)** is perfect, too: the status and power situation of some women in thirteenth-century England. All in all, a perfect summary of the idea governing the text.

(A) The author doesn't argue that land wealth enabled medieval women to dodge the legal restrictions. Rather, he argues that such wealth enabled women to exercise certain forms of power despite those restrictions. In other words, the author doesn't say that the legally forbidden public roles such as soldier, justice, and jury member became available for rich women of status. The author only indicates that some women were able to procure for themselves power in matters not traditionally considered "private."

(B) We know that marital status was one factor in the economic independence of medieval women—for example, widows had more economic autonomy than married women. Inheritance was a factor, too, but we have no way of knowing which factor primarily influenced medieval women's economic independence. And even if the author made this clear, the issue of this comparison is still too narrow to encapsulate the entire main idea.

(D) No comparison is made between widow's rights and autonomy in the thirteenth century and any previous centuries. Even if we infer such a comparison from the events listed in the second paragraph (the Magna Carta and the "jointure" law in effect after 1272), this issue, like the issue in **(B)**, pales in comparison to the real thrust of the passage.

(E) describes the thrust of the second paragraph nicely, but fails to address the overall issue, which is not merely that medieval women could get land, but rather that they could use it to wield certain kinds of power and influence.

9. (E) Inference

Regarding he views in question, the author overtly states in lines 5–6 that the distinction proposed by the medievalists is "overly simplistic." That's our starting point: the pre-phrased "distinction is bad." **(D)** and **(E)** address the "distinction" directly: The beginnings of both are nearly identical, and both are good up to "fails to address/consider . . ." But only **(E)** stays within the scope. The author states that the distinction is bad/simplistic, and then goes on to elaborate on the political implications of land ownership. It is thus reasonable to infer the connection: The author thinks the distinction posed by the medievalists stinks *because* it fails to consider the political influence medieval women derived from owning land.

(A), (C) As far as we're concerned, the medievalists are on record on exactly one issue: the distinction between medieval public and private law. We know nothing about their views on other subjects such as the role of medieval landowners, or the amount of wealth controlled by medieval women; these are issues only our author takes up. We therefore can't tell whether the medievalists even hold these views, let alone whether the author agrees with them.

(B) The author doesn't address the general issue of which realm of law had weightier political implications. He merely argues that *some women* were able to exert greater influence than their legal status might seem to allow. This is a long way from saying that public medieval law in general had more political implications than private law.

(D), as mentioned above, is promising for a bit, but then veers off the track: The author argues by citing general trends, not by presenting "actual legal cases." We can't infer that the author feels the medievalists' distinction is simplistic because they fail to mention these; he himself makes no mention of actual cases.

10. (B) Inference

The lines leading up to the line cited in the stem speak of women's, especially widows', feudal authority and legal independence resulting from land ownership. The Keyword "Moreover" in line 59 tells us to expect more of the same, and indeed, we're told that "the scope of their *sway* is indicated by the fact that some controlled not merely single estates, but multiple counties." In this context, we can only interpret "sway" to mean "power" or "influence"; this is the only reading of the word that's in line with the preceding context, and either word would make for a fine pre-phrase. The testmakers went with another synonym in **(B)**—dominion.

(A) The definition of vacillate is "to *sway* to and fro in regard to an opinion"—that is, to waver. But this kind of sway is fully out of context here; to this point women are described as strong, autonomous, more powerful than expected. "Vacillation" denotes weakness, wavering, an unsure state of mind, which doesn't fit in this concluding sentence.

(C), (D) The words "predisposition" and "inclination" introduce an element of forethought or desire on the part of women that doesn't fit with the gist of the sentence. The author is not arguing that the women in question were able to control multiple counties rather than single estates merely because they were "predisposed" or "inclined" to do so; they were able to do this because of the power and influence that came from owning land. This is the notion that's developed throughout; to conclude the passage "Moreover, the scope of their *predisposition/inclination . . .*" simply makes no sense.

(E) A "mediation" is an intervention that reconciles competing parties, a concept that sticks out like a sore thumb if placed in the middle of the concluding sentence.

11. (C) Logic Function

As noted in the Paragraph Structure section, the first paragraph introduces the notion that medieval women exerted influence through the acquisition of land. paragraph 2 tells us how this came to be—all the different mechanisms that functioned at that time to place this primary form of wealth in women's hands. **(C)** has it right: The second paragraph explains how the circumstances described in the first came to be.

(A) The historical events mentioned in paragraph 2 (Magna Carta, and the 1272 jointure law) only serve to further the claim made earlier on—that women were able to control land. These events are not directly tied to the points made in the final paragraph regarding the kinds of influence that resulted from such land ownership.

(B) The information in the second paragraph can't be said to truly represent a sequence of events. Even though the years 1215 and 1272 are mentioned, we can't infer that the customs and events described in this paragraph are listed so as to form a sequence that leads to a particular result in the following paragraph. Just because women were able to acquire land doesn't mean that this must inevitably lead to the use of the wealth conferred by the land as discussed in paragraph 3.

(D) If the second paragraph simply described the effects of an event, we would expect a structure implying such a causal relationship: "Because of this, here's what happened." We get nothing of the kind, nor can we even reasonably say that there's any such "event" in the first paragraph to begin with. Rather, the first paragraph describes a set of circumstances, in accordance with correct choice **(C)**.

(E) The only group that puts forth an argument (albeit indirectly) in the first paragraph is the medievalists; the author references their distinction between public and private law. The second paragraph has nothing directly to do with this distinction; the author's evaluation of this theory ("it's simplistic") comes earlier, in paragraph 1. Paragraph 2 presents evidence to back up the author's notion that other factors need to be considered. In paragraph 2, then, the author doesn't evaluate the medievalists' earlier claim; rather he presents facts that lend support to his earlier evaluation.

12. (E) Detail

The amount of a widow's land relative to that of her eldest son is discussed in the beginning of paragraph 3: In lines 45–47, the author states that "the amount of land the widow controlled could exceed that of her son or of other male heirs." This seems to be paradoxical given the reference in lines 22–23 that under primogeniture "the eldest son [inherited] all," but the resolution of the paradox comes at line 42–43: Many widows had inheritances in additions to dowers. Inferably, then, a widow who controlled both could have more land than one son with his legal inheritance—choice **(E)**.

(A) According to lines 29–30, the customary amount of "dower" was 1/3 of the late husband's land. If the widow got this amount and the eldest son got the remaining 2/3, then the son, not the widow, would control more land.

(B) If primogeniture was enforced, then the widow's daughters would be irrelevant as far as land allotment was concerned; they would get land only if there was no surviving son. Even with three daughters, this widow's son stood to receive all of the land. So the information in **(B)** does nothing to ensure that this particular widow would control more land than her son.

(C), (D) "Primogeniture" is defined as the eldest son receiving all the land, and "jointure" is a means by which land can fall

to a widow. Enforcement of the first and the lack of the second work in favor of the son, not the widow, when it comes to amassing land.

13. (D) Detail

"Mentioned in the passage" is another sure sign of an Explicit Text question. All you need to do is find the relevant text. In what situation could a married woman have taken on some of the duties associated with land ownership in thirteenth-century England? Most of the passage deals with widows; the only real references to married women come in lines 16–18 and the last paragraph. The latter is the key to this question, as the long sentence in lines 47–55 details the obligations associated with owning feudal lands. In lines 55–56, we find out that many married women fulfilled "these duties" when their husbands were away at court or at war. "The absence of the woman's husband" in **(D)** is a perfect paraphrase of this.

(A), (B), and **(E)** All contain paragraph 2 terms (Magna Carta, inheritance rights, and jointure) referring to the customs and mechanisms that made it possible for women to get land. None of these things explain why the tasks normally undertaken by a husband would be done instead by his wife.

(C) *Au contraire*, the duties associated with the ownership of feudal lands were customarily satisfied by the husband. We're told of only one circumstance in which the wife would assume these duties, and it's listed in lines 55–56 and paraphrased in correct choice **(D)**.

14. (A) Logic Function

A question about a prepositional phrase? Sounds crazy, no? But everything has a purpose on the LSAT, and for whatever reason it's the purpose of that wee phrase "in England" that is the topic at hand. It appears in paragraph 2, which we recall is about how the medieval woman, especially the widow, was able to get her hands on property through the custom of granting her "dower," equivalent to 1/3 of the deceased husband's land. Now: Consider how the sentence in question would read with the phrase "in England" missing: "Called 'dower,' this grant had greater legal importance . . ." etc. *That* meaning is clear: There was one and only one name for the grant, and it's "dower." Therefore, the only conceivable reason the author could have for inserting "in England" is if the grant existed in countries other than England, but was called something different there. Without that implication, the insertion of "in England" is superfluous. So **(A)** is the purpose that the phrase achieves.

(B) at best describes the purpose of the word "dower" (if in fact dower qualifies as a "code of law," which isn't at all clear). But what's it got to do with England?

(C) That the author confines his discussion of dower to England may imply that dower was more important there than elsewhere. But the mere use of the phrase "in England" doesn't make that implication.

(D)'s comparison of more vs. fewer means of controlling property, in England vs. elsewhere, is not apt, given that the overall context in lines 26–34 has to do with widows' rights generally. The only comparison made, and it's an implicit one, is described by correct choice **(A)**.

(E) would probably be O.K. if the text ran "First called 'dower' in 1178," and the question asked for the purpose of the phrase "in 1178." But as is, **(E)** is irrelevant.

15. (B) Global (Primary Purpose)

At the outset we described the author's primary purpose as "to refute a common perception held by medievalists regarding public vs. private law by analyzing the specific case of medieval women." While the first part would have a place in the correct answer, the testmakers chose to focus exclusively on the second. And indeed, the author *does* spend most of his time concentrating on the legal status and economic situation of women in thirteenth-century England, so this wording—"evaluate" these things in light of "a particular historical group"—fits the bill.

(A), (C) There is no past legal controversy here, nor is the author resolving a debate between different parties. There's only a present theory held by medievalists, one that the author finds lacking.

(D) "*Modern* economic situation" is where this one goes astray. The only economic situation discussed is that relating to 13th-century England.

(E) The author's purpose is to discuss not one event, per se, but rather his take on a situation, a set of circumstances. The enactment of Magna Carta would be considered an "event," but Magna Carta is a mere detail in support of the author's main thesis. There is no "event" at the heart of this passage about which the author presents "new evidence."

Passage 3: Stolen Art
Questions 16–22

Topic and Scope: Stolen art; specifically, legislation intended to protect "good-faith" purchasers of stolen art.

Purpose and Main Idea: The author's Purpose is to argue against such legislation; the author's specific Main Idea is that such legislation is not only unnecessary to protect good-faith purchasers, but is also unfair to those who seek to reclaim stolen art.

Paragraph Structure: Paragraph 1 describes the new legislation designed to protect good-faith purchasers of allegedly stolen art, essentially saying that the burden of proof lies entirely with those who want to recover the art, and restricting the amount of time that they have to do so. Paragraph 2 discusses the rationale behind the legislation, making the point that without such a law any individual or organization that has made a good-faith purchase of art is in jeopardy of losing it.

The Keyword "however" at the beginning of paragraph 3 signals that we're about to get the author's opinion. He argues against the legislation on two grounds: (1) it's unnecessary because there haven't been many "reclamation suits" and (2) it's unfair to those who seek to recover stolen art because its stipulations make it virtually impossible for them to press a claim. In paragraph 4, the author goes on to argue that a different type of legislation is necessary—legislation that makes it easier for the rightful owners of stolen art to find and reclaim their property.

The Big Picture:

- This passage is a pretty good place to begin work on the reading comprehension section. Why? The subject matter is very accessible, and the author's voice is plainly evident from line 25 on. Moreover, even before you get to line 25, it's predictable that the first two paragraphs are simply a set up for an authorial counterargument.

- Don't worry about taking in all of the author's various reasons (in paragraph 3) for arguing that the intended legislation is unfair to those who want to recover stolen property—you can always look them up if the questions demand it.

The Questions:

16. (C) Global (Main Point)

This choice neatly encompasses the author's Topic, Scope, and Purpose.

(A) is a 180 choice. In lines 25–26, the author contends that reclamation suits haven't been a problem; therefore, he argues, legislation to "clarify" the rights of museums isn't necessary. Moreover, this choice is too narrow in focus—the author looks at more than simply "the legal position of museums . . ."

(B) is beyond the scope of the text. According to the text, James Burke, a museum director, supports the new legislation; but that's quite different from saying that museum directors in general urged it on the government. In fact, the passage doesn't say anything about the attitudes of museum directors in general.

(D) is also beyond the scope of the text. First, the passage doesn't refer to "clashes" between "museum professionals" and "members of the academic community." Second, the passage is about a specific piece of legislation concerning stolen art, not about arts-related legislation in general.

(E), too, is beyond the scope. The passage doesn't discuss any alleged "desire of some governments to use legislation and litigation to recover cultural property." Moreover, the author's attitude toward the recovery of stolen art is such that he would be unlikely to speak of legal "abuses" by governments that actually sought to reclaim art.

17. (B) Inference

Lines 3–5 make it abundantly clear that the "uncertainty" referred to in line 2 concerns "the ownership of art," specifically legal challenges to the current owners by those who claim that the art was previously stolen. The rest of the passage takes up this very theme.

(A) is beyond the scope of the text. The passage deals with the legal issue of ownership of allegedly stolen art; it doesn't discuss the moral issues involved in ownership of "great art."

(C) If anyone has got questions about the origins of art works, it's the people who'd like to reclaim them.

(D) is also beyond the scope of the text. The passage doesn't discuss "disputes" between "cultural institutions vying for the opportunity to purchase" a piece of art.

(E) Current art owners aren't worried about damage or theft, but rather legal challenges to their ownership.

18. (C) Inference

In the absence of a statute of limitations on the recovery of art, Burke is afraid that any country might pass a law at any time to the effect that all art works produced within its territory are "cultural property" that rightfully belong to it. Such a legal decision, he goes on to argue, could involve museums that possess art works from such a country in "ruinous" court battles. Choice **(C)** reflects precisely the sort of scenario that Burke fears.

(A) Burke is worried about art works currently held by museums, not those that they might be prevented from buying in the future.

(B), (E) Burke is concerned about possible national, not international, legal developments.

(D) There's nothing in the passage to indicate that Burke thinks that private collectors pose a threat to museums.

19. (C) Detail

In paragraph 2, Burke refers to foreign governments as potential adversaries of his nation's museums.

(A), (D), (E) Burke never even mentions commercial art dealers **(A)**, private art collectors **(D)**, or other countries' museums **(E)**.

(B) If anything, Burke views law enforcement officials in his own country as potential allies. He does, after all, praise his country's new legislation.

20 (A) Inference

This choice is a nice paraphrase of lines 25–26, where the author, on the basis of past history, disputes Burke's fears (expressed in the previous paragraph) that widespread reclamation suits could do serious harm to current art holders.

(B), (E) The author explicitly states that reclamation suits haven't yet become a problem. And certainly not as a result of supportive legislation **(B)**, which isn't on the government's agenda, or a growth in theft **(E)**, which isn't even mentioned in the text.

(C) is a 180 choice. The author says that reclamation suits *haven't* been a problem up to this point in time.

(D) How could the author believe that lawsuits are a sign of frustration, legitimate or otherwise, when he suggests that they've been a very infrequent occurrence?

21. (D) Inference (Author's Attitude)

Paragraphs 3 and 4 clearly demonstrate that the author opposes the proposed legislation with a series of careful arguments. His attitude, in other words, is best described as one of "reasoned opposition."

(A), (B), (E) These choices wrongly suggest that the author supports—with greater or lesser enthusiasm—the proposed legislation. As a matter of fact, in paragraph 4, he proposes counterlegislation.

(C) The author opposes the legislation on the grounds that it is unnecessary to protect good-faith purchasers, as well as unfair to those who are legitimately trying to reclaim stolen art. This type of opposition certainly doesn't qualify as "fearful apprehension."

22. (E) Inference

In paragraph 4, the author advocates legislation that would make it easier for rightful owners of art to recover stolen property. A law that mandated the collection and distribution of information about art thefts would certainly make it easier for rightful owners to recover their property.

(A) In lines 35–37, the author contends that museum publications aren't a solution to publicizing and locating stolen art.

(B) Who should hold onto art that is the subject of litigation isn't an issue that the author delves into.

(C) The author favors those who want to reclaim stolen property, not museums that would like to keep it.

(D) The author's concerned with the reclamation of stolen art, not with museum-to-museum sales of it.

Passage 4: Course Packs and Copyright
Questions 23–28

The **Topic** of this 100% objective passage is "course packs," the **Scope** a court case testing the legality of course packs under copyright law, and the author's **Purpose** is to survey each side's case and report on the outcome; again, no authorial point of view appears. Paragraph 1 outlines the case for the defense after defining what course packs are. The owner of the copy shop believes that his selling excerpts from longer books chosen by professors is justified because it's too difficult to get publishers' permissions (lines 9–12) and because the packs are cheaper for students than the originals (lines 12–16). Paragraph 2 lists four factors involved in copyright protection, and it's the fourth of them—"the effect of [course packs on the original books'] market value"—that is, what the plaintiffs in this case relied upon (lines 27–31). They lost, and lines 31–44 outlines why: the court held that course packs don't affect the books' market value (31–35), that the profit the copy shop owner made is irrelevant (35–39), and that he was protected because he charged by the page irrespective of content (39–44).

Paragraph 3 broadens the discussion of course packs because the court reasoned more broadly as well. It ruled that academic inefficiency makes course packs a normal part of doing business (45–50), and that a third party, like Mr. Copy Shop, is entitled to do for the academic community what they could legally do for themselves—that is, make copies.

The Big Picture:

Paragraph 1: Defendant's case

Paragraph 2: Plaintiff's case, and holding for defendant [lines 21–31, and 31–44, bracketed in margin]

Paragraph 3: Broader holding in favor of photocopying

The Questions:

23. (A) Global (Main Point)

When a passage is largely or wholly objective, the "main point" will summarize the scope and purpose.

(A) directly reflects paragraph 3's summary of the issues that were raised in paragraphs 2 and 3.

(B) Too narrow. The basis of the price of the course packs (lines 40–44) is one of several details relating to the court's holding. Moreover, it's the original book sources, not the course packs themselves, which were under copyright.

(C) Besides ignoring the specific case that the entire passage is based on, **(C)** lists the three copyright factors (21–26) on which the case didn't hinge.

(D) No publishers are enjoined from seeking future suits based on this one holding.

(E) The court held that the copy-shop case was not an "exploitation of . . . copyrighted materials" (49–50) which is wholly different from calling it an "exception to copyright law."

24. (E) Logic Function

Never base your answer on memory. Always research the relevant text.

Lines 23–27 (the list of the four factors involved in copyright protection cases) is simply the backdrop or, as **(E)** puts it, "context," for the specific lawsuit filed in this case.

(A) The specific actions of the defendant don't immediately relate to lines 23–27. In any case, "exempt from copyright law" seems extreme for the particular holding described here.

(B) Lines 23–27 deal with all four factors, but only the last of them was involved in this case, and it led to the case—it doesn't "explain the charges."

(C) Flaw in the publishers' reasoning? That's an odd way to describe the reasons for a perfectly reasonable lawsuit. (They just happened to lose, that's all.) In any case, lines 23–27 are broader in scope than the case itself.

(D) This is a totally objective passage; nothing in it is designed to "defend" anything.

25. (C) Inference

When two differing points of view appear in a passage, expect questions asking about one to have wrong answers that deal with the other.

(A) Why would the copy-shop owner have an opinion as to how to calculate a copyrighted work's market value? He's just making copies.

(B) The owner knows these particular publishers are opposed to course packs, but need not agree that others are.

(C) The first thing we heard from the owner (lines 10–12) was that one rationale for course packs was the lengthy, difficult, and expensive process of getting publishers' permissions. Inferably, as correct choice **(C)** says, there'd probably be less willful duplication of copyrighted material if copy shops could obtain permissions more readily.

(D) The rewriting of copyright law is certainly a view that the plaintiffs would hold, but not the defendant.

(E) Other materials sold at copy shops, if any, are outside the scope of the passage.

26. (D) Inference

Research individual answer choices before making your final selection.

(A) The implied comparison with other areas of the law, in terms of complexity or anything else, is irrelevant to this passage.

(B) Only one court's holding is described here, so there's no basis for an accusation of inconsistency among judges.

(C) The scope is solely course packs, not other types of materials. And it's probably going too far to say that the court's holding renders course packs "protected under copyright law" since the packs themselves aren't copyrighted. Rather, the packs aren't prohibited by the law.

(D) Lines 45–50 describe a "new practice" that made the court in question redefine one application of copyright law, so **(D)** is inferable.

(E) It's highly unlikely that the entire field of copyright law would have as its primary concern the educational use of printed works. In any case, its primary concern is outside the scope of this description of one court case.

27. (B) Logic (Parallel Reasoning)

When you're asked about a minor figure in a passage, be sure to consult all of that figure's passage appearances.

The professors only appear in lines 12–15 and lines 51–54. In the former, we hear that they assign readings to students; in the latter, we hear that they can use a third party to reproduce such readings and sell them to students. That's exactly what's going on in **(B)**, where the choir director stands for the professors, the recording studio for the copy shop, and the choir for the students. (And one can imagine the other choir reacting as happily as the university publishers did.)

(A), (C), (D), (E) None of these choices involves a third party's intervention in the reproduction and sale of an item. And the professors are not the ones selling the course packs.

28. (D) Logic (Strengthen)

Strengthening an argument in Reading Comprehension is just like doing so in Logical Reasoning.

The publisher's argument, in specific, was that course packs diminish the market value of the original books being excerpted. The court thought otherwise (lines 31–35), but if **(D)** were true and sales of the original books on campus decreased markedly, that might cause the court to change its mind.

(A) The defendant's profits weren't relevant to the publishers' argument.

(B) Whether the professors brought their business to the shop on their own or because of the owner's direct solicitation has nothing to do with this case.

(C) Like **(A)**, this choice hinges on the owner's earning ability. Outside the scope.

(E) That permissions were not obtained is a given. No contribution by the original authors would be needed.

Passage 5: Women and Medieval English Law
Questions 29–34

Topic and Scope: The history of medieval English law; specifically, the prevalence of historical scholarship detailing the medieval English legal system's actual effects on women.

Purpose and Main Idea: The author's purpose is to document the lack of scholarship dealing with the ways in which medieval English women were affected in their day-to-day lives by the then-current practices of English law. The Main Idea is that this deficiency, explained simply by historians' lack of interest in women's legal history, has led to an incomplete picture of the legal experience of medieval English women.

Paragraph Structure: There are only two paragraphs here, both of them lengthy. The first sentence lays out the problem—a "dearth," or lack, of books or articles dealing with the relationship between medieval English law and women as that relationship is documented in actual court records. And it doesn't take long to find out how the author feels about this: "This is a serious deficiency, . . ." since such records tell us the real story—that is, how the law *actually affected* women, not simply what it was *intended* to do or what people *thought* it did. These latter things, intentions and interpretations, can be discovered in other sources (don't worry about memorizing them now; underline them if you prefer), but these sources can't get at the specific day-to-day issues like the ones listed next (again, take note that there are examples here, but don't worry about assimilating them all). The paragraph ends by stating a necessary condition (*only* by studying a lot of real cases can light be shed on the types of issues listed)—and by reiterating the problem brought up in the beginning: this work has simply not been done to any significant extent.

A good critical reader can anticipate a number of places this can go in paragraph 2: Some plans for filling in the historical record on this topic, perhaps. Or maybe some other legal subjects that *have* been adequately covered, for example. Or, as our author chooses, a discussion of the *reason* for this particular lack of hard evidence derived from actual court cases. Most of the court records are written in obscure languages and have never been published, not to mention that the quantity is overwhelming. But these things are no excuse: The real reason, according to the author, is that historians simply don't care about women's legal history to begin with. Even when legal historians *do* write about laws relating to women, they do so out of an interest in a particular idea or event, not from any overriding concern for the effect on women *per se*. The result is predictable: not a lot of info out there on the author's area of concern, the actual legal experiences of medieval English women. But the passage does end with a small ray of hope—the situation is slowly improving.

The Big Picture:

- When there are only two paragraphs to a passage, the passage structure shouldn't be too difficult to grasp. This is a good thing. On the other hand, the danger with this kind of passage structure is that you'll get bogged down in details in the middle of either or both paragraphs and lose sight of the big picture. Make sure you concentrate on the overall gist of each paragraph, and come back to pick up specific details later if necessary.

- And speaking of details, lists often contain the kind of details you can gloss over. Get a sense of what the list itself represents, but don't try to memorize every entry. Know what the list is, where it is, and how it fits into the overall context of the paragraph, and then move on.

- Good critical readers always anticipate as they read, asking themselves "why is the author telling me this." If a passage happens to go in a direction you didn't expect, no biggie—roll with the punches, make adjustments, and never stop focusing on purpose and structure.

The Questions:

29. (D) Inference

First up is an Inference question concerning the sources listed in line 12; hopefully you didn't have any trouble tracking the reference down. These are the things (treatises, commentaries and statutes) that the author laments give no solid information on the real legal experience of medieval English women. They do come in handy, however in answering "the latter two questions," which refers to the issues in lines 9–10: how the law was intended to affect women or thought to affect them. Any of this will suffice. **(D)** focuses on the author's lament as repeated throughout the passage, while question 44 later on deals with the flip side, the things these sources are good for.

(A) The author would not agree with **(A)**, believing as he does that these sources do not illuminate what should be considered a major part of medieval law, namely, the real-world influence it had on women's lives.

(B) If anything, the author would prefer the medieval sources, because at least contained therein one could find information on just how the law at that time affected women. On that count, the sources listed in line 12 are of no help.

(C) The relevance of these sources to modern legal institutions and ideas is outside the scope. The author bemoans one fundamental lack on the part of these treatises, commentaries, and statutes—and this isn't it.

(E) If there *are* writers interested specifically in women's legal history—and the author seems skeptical of that—they won't find answers in these sources to the questions that the author thinks they should find interesting. The first three words should have tipped you off: The whole point is that the author *doesn't* find these sources valuable for serious inquiries into women's legal history.

30. (D) Logic Function

Now we're asked how the first paragraph is put together. Perhaps a scan of the beginning of each choice saved you a little time here—the complaint that underlies the entire passage is that of a lack, a dearth, a "deficiency" as it's put in line 7 and in correct choice **(D)**. The deficiency is first described as the dearth of books and articles on the author's chosen subject. The nature of the deficiency is then discussed—that's all that specific stuff regarding the unanswered questions brought up in lines 16–25. Do we then get a remedy that represents the "sole possible means" of correcting the problem? Yup: Doing quantitative case studies is the "only" way to even begin to answer these questions. A perfect paraphrase, completing a perfect choice.

(A) At best, the first sentence implies that the deficient sources are necessary to the study of this topic, but it goes too far to say that the necessary preparations are actively "discussed." Even if we let this slide, there certainly are no excuses made for why such "preparations" weren't begun earlier.

(B) "A problem is described . . ."—fair enough. Uh-oh, it's downhill fast after that. ". . . a taxonomy of . . . questions relevant to its solution is proposed"? No—examples of questions that are unanswerable *due to the problem* are presented. There's no discussion here about what kind of questions might help solve the problem. The author states flat-out that only one remedy is possible, and even that's not guaranteed to clear up the whole picture.

(C) is way too vague. What "discipline" are we talking about here? Legal scholarship in general? And where's the prediction? The final sentence is an assertion, not a prediction. **(C)** just doesn't match up.

(E) begins a little better than **(A)**; at least here we can say that "resources" refers to court records whereas it's hard to tell in **(A)** what "preparations" refers to. But the "list of questions" that follow is meant to demonstrate the kinds of things that can't be determined *without* those resources, not highlight the inherent limitations of the resources themselves. The problem is not the court records, but the fact that no one's consulting them on this matter.

31. (D) Detail

Next we get a Detail question, and the subject matter doesn't stray far from the author's main concern. What would the quantitative studies of all those court cases be good for? Well, for exactly what the author wants—insight into the real legal experience of medieval English women. When the author says in lines 25–28 that these studies are the only hope to answer "these questions," the questions he's referring to are the ones

listed above that deal with, as **(D)** aptly puts it, "how medieval women's lives were really affected by medieval laws."

(A), **(B)** The sources listed in line 12 are the ones that are able to shed light on the intentions of medieval laws. Nowhere are we told that the court records can do this too. And **(B)**'s "unconscious or hidden motives" is even one step removed from "stated intentions," and once again we have no way of knowing that the court records will be of any use exposing those.

(C) The author believes that studying the court records from medieval cases can provide insight into the real legal experience of medieval women. What these records could possibly reveal about modern legal institutions is anyone's guess, and certainly isn't something that's stated in the passage.

(E) Categorizing the legal documents relating to medieval women isn't the issue here—no one seems concerned about that. The author wants to know what's in these records, not how to categorize them.

32. (A) Detail

As we alluded to earlier, question 44 represents the flip side of question 41. In that one, we were asked to recognize that the sources listed in line 12, much to the consternation of our author, provide little insight on the actual legal experience of medieval English women. However, as we've seen, these sources *can* shed light on what the author refers to as the "latter questions"—namely "how the law was *intended* to affect them or *thought* to affect them" (lines 9–10). These topics appear in choice **(A)**: "intent and opinion of commentators" is right on the money.

(B) The sentence beginning "And quite apart from provisions…" in lines 19–21 suggests that these sources may indicate aspects of the law that applied to women only, but nowhere is it stated or implied that these treatises, statutes, and commentaries speak to the "overall effectiveness" of English law.

(C) It seems we would need to consult the court records to obtain this kind of specific information. Insights on intent and legal commentaries wouldn't reveal women's actual probability of success.

(D) seems to be a takeoff on the question of how women's privileges may have been thwarted by intimidation or harassment (lines 16–18), but there are two immediate problems with this: First, this is the type of question that the sources in line 12 *cannot* answer. And second, we're not told who may be thwarting their rights, so "male relatives" is too specific here. If you axed this choice right off the bat by simply considering male relatives outside the scope, good for you.

(E) Again, this is something that's too specific to glean from the sources in line 12. Nothing that goes beyond intentions and interpretations can fit the bill here.

33. (C) Inference

When we pursue the line reference, we see that "the relevant scholarship" is followed by "has not been undertaken . . ." That can only mean one thing: The author's talking here about the kind of scholarship that few have undertaken, the dearth of which forms the basis of his lament—quantitative studies of court records documenting the real effects of medieval English law on women, choice **(C)**.

(A) and **(B)** deal with the kind of factors that the author proposes, and then dismisses, as reasons why "the relevant scholarship" has not been undertaken. The kinds of scholarly pursuits mentioned in these choices cannot therefore represent the relevant scholarship itself, which again is the scrupulous examination of actual court records to determine the real deal for medieval women.

(D) harks back to the sources in line 12, but we've seen time and again how these statutes, treatises and commentaries do not provide the insights the author craves. In light of the author's concerns, the work described in **(D)** would be irrelevant scholarship.

(E) What "existing scholarly literature?" According to the first sentence, one would be hard pressed to *find* such scholarship, due to a "dearth of published books or articles" on the subject. The whole problem, according to the author, is that there aren't enough sources to write such a comprehensive history on the topic. The "relevant scholarship" can't refer to reviews of a bounty of material that (according to the author) doesn't exist.

34. (A) Inference

Last up is an Inference question, and again the topic doesn't stray far at all from the main issue at hand, namely the deficiency that so irks our author. Lines 39–41 clearly state the author's explanation—lack of interest on the part of historians. The sentence that follows clears up which historians the author means here: modern legal historians, most of which don't give a hoot about how laws affect women. And the sentence in lines 46–48 clinches it: "Very few legal historians have started with an interest in women's history . . ." Put it all together and we've got choice **(A)**.

(B) refers to the difficulties the author introduces, but dismisses, as possible reasons for the deficiency in question.

(C) says that the historians are looking in the wrong place, concentrating on the type of sources listed in line 12. This is tricky, because in paragraph 1 the author *does* state that 19th- and 20th-century scholars did concentrate on treatises and commentaries when writing about medieval law. But

it's not as if modern scholars *wanted* to understand how the law affected medieval women and they simply got bogged down in the wrong sources. That makes the deficiency sound more accidental than it is, when the reason is more straightforward—they simply lacked the interest.

(D) No such definition of women's legal history is given. This, therefore, cannot be an obstacle to the type of scholarship the author favors.

(E) gets things backwards. It is the lack of books and articles on this particular topic that makes it difficult, according to the author, to produce such comprehensive studies.

Passage 6: English Marriage Contracts
Questions 35–40

Topic and Scope: English women's property rights; specifically, Susan Staves' research on the effect of post-Restoration contracts on women's rights.

Purpose and Main Idea: Our author's purpose is to assess (using Staves' data and conclusions) the "traditional assumption" of historians that events following the 1660 Restoration "represented a gain for women" (line 6). The Main Idea is largely Staves'. Staves "contests this view" (line 9) and asserts that post-1660 events "generally [worked] to women's detriment" (line 18). Our author cites all of this approvingly.

Paragraph Structure: Paragraph 1 begins with five lines that neatly sum up the marriage situation pre- and post-Restoration. But what did the latter—the growth of marriage contracts—mean for women? Historians have called it an advance, but Staves disagrees sharply.

Paragraph 2, as one might expect, lays out the evidence for paragraph 1's assertions. It's a longish paragraph, 32 lines long, yet it stays remarkably "on topic" throughout by focusing on the specific details of post-1660 marriage contracts and why the phenomenon fell short of being a genuine gain for women. (In passing, we learn the derivation of the common expression "pin money" in lines 26–28. Who says the LSAT can't be educational?) Anyway, the gist of it all is that there were so many subtleties and niceties and "inconsistencies" (line 39) in the contracts that judges tended to rely on pre-1660 reasoning. And thanks to line 1–2, we know what *that* meant for women: nothing good.

Paragraph 3's first sentence announces that the paragraph is going beyond the narrow concerns of paragraph 1 and 2, to discuss the "general implications" of the above-described work. In specific, we learn that Staves herself was moved to reexamine a previous conclusion (lines 47–50), and that she issued a challenge to the thinking of two colleagues. It's a pretty detailed paragraph; you might well have jotted down the word "IMPLICATIONS" next to it, and circled the names of Mr. and Mrs. Stone, but then figured, Hey, I can read this closely when and if the questions demand it. That would be a bold and strategic decision that we'd applaud!

The Big Picture:

- The passage author doesn't always announce his concerns in a subtle or timid way. Sometimes it's blatant, as here: "traditionally argued"; "Staves contests"; "Staves demonstrates"—these three phrases alone signal the author's convictions on the topic. Go after such hints, and hang on to them fiercely. They're the key to quick and easy points.

- Don't work harder than you need to. Once you realize what's going on in paragraph 3, you don't really need to study the paragraph in detail unless and until a

question demands it. The likelihood is that most of these questions (and there are only six, after all) are going to deal with the main line of argument, the first 45 out of 60 lines. *That's* what you need to understand. Deal with the rest when the time comes.

The Questions:

35. (C) Global (Main Point)

By the time paragraph 1 is finished, we know that the author's main idea is simply an echo of Staves' conclusion about the true meaning of post-1660 marriage contracts for women. Nothing in the following 48 lines is cause to alter that analysis, and when you search for that idea among the choices, **(C)** should jump out. It's got topic, scope, purpose, and thrust just right.

(A) simply echoes (at even greater length) the gist of the passage's second sentence, but it echoes nothing of the historians' traditional assumption or Staves' rebuttal. Totally factual, it falls far short of being the main idea.

(B) The historians' error—the passage tells us—is not that they got the details of the contracts wrong, but that they missed the contracts' impact on the rights of women.

(D) blows up paragraph 2's details about court cases—Staves' evidence, after all, not her conclusion—into the main point. **(D)** is actually factually incorrect (many if not most settlements *did* have features designed to protect women), but even if it were right-on, it's still way too narrow to qualify as an answer to this Global question.

(E) is way off: The only references to the pre-Restoration era (choice **(E)**'s focus) are in the first sentence, as background, and in paragraph 2's last sentence, a detail about how judges interpreted marriage contracts to wives' detriment.

36. (E) Logic Function

While discussing paragraph 3 in our analysis above, we said that simply labeling the paragraph with the word "IMPLICATIONS" was adequate in terms of the structure. What we couldn't have known at the time was that it'd be adequate to get a question right as well. A search for a choice that focuses on that concept should yield **(E)**, rapidly and accurately.

(A)'s use of past tense is inappropriate given that we're studying a paragraph that announces its interest in future implications (lines 45–47) and that is otherwise written in present tense. Moreover, nothing in paragraph 3 lives up to **(A)**'s grandiose phrase "caused significant revision of theories." What's described in the paragraph is theory *adjustment*, at most.

(B) Staves qualified one of her *own* claims (lines 47–50). Beyond that, her own research hardly promises to qualify her own work further—kind of an absurd idea, no?

(C) Nothing in paragraph 3 is identified as "more recent" than the Staves research described in paragraph 1 and 2.

Also, paragraph 3 does not for a moment support Staves' work, of course; the paragraph goes beyond it to discuss the work's implications—which brings us back to **(E)**.

(D) *Au contraire,* her recent work has *countered* one of her own past views as well as one proposed by a pair of colleagues.

37. (B) Global (Primary Purpose)

The author's purpose, as we've seen, is to highlight the way in which Staves' research undermines the view of traditional historians about the impact of Restoration thinking on women. This is made clear in paragraph 1 and is reflected in **(B)**.

(A) "Explanation for a phenomenon" is a poor phrase for what's going on here. Staves is not so much explaining a phenomenon as examining the *impact* of one. In any case, hers is the sole view in which the passage takes primary interest; neither the traditional historians nor Mr. and Mrs. Stone is explored in the same depth.

(C) There's no sense that this is a "controversy" at all, let alone one of long standing. The view that women's rights took a step forward after 1660 was long held as consensus; as far as we can tell, it only became controversial when Susan Staves came along.

(D) No, the passage suggests that *Staves* has *already* reevaluated a hypothesis of *long standing*. **(D)** gets almost everything wrong, which is quite a hat-trick for an eight-word answer choice.

(E) *Au contraire,* Staves is out to deep-six the traditional theory.

38. (A) Detail

Any heightened interest was probably replaced by an immediate letdown as you realized that the Stones mentioned in the question are the married scholars of paragraph 3 and not the Rolling Stones. (Too bad; we'd bet that Mick Jagger and Keith Richards have some interesting views on English marriage contracts.) The relationship between Staves' work and that of the Stones has three elements: (1) She challenges a contention of theirs (lines 50–51); (2) she doesn't completely blow that contention out of the water (line 55); (3) she counters an assumption of theirs (lines 56–57). Correct choice **(A)** tosses back (2) and (3) almost verbatim.

(B), (C), (D) Regardless of each one's window dressing, all are flatly *au contraire* in that line 55 clearly indicates that Staves does *not* "refute" the Stones' ideas **(B)**, show that they "cannot be correct" **(C)**; or prove them "incorrect" **(D)**.

(E) Even if the phrase "qualifies [their] contention" applies to paragraph 3, **(E)**'s assessment of the Stones' data as "accurate but incomplete" dooms this choice. Lines 55–60 indicate that the couple inaccurately stated that Restoration-era widows possessed more wealth than women who had never married.

39. (C) Detail

For the first and only time, a question asks us to plunge into the morass of detail in paragraph 2. But we needn't

linger on most of the troublesome stuff, which mostly deals with provisions of marriage contracts and the ways in which women's rights could be compromised anyway. The paragraph only shifts to judges' decisions at the very very end, where we hear that despite the much-trumpeted protections of women's rights, judges tended to interpret contracts in pre-1660, pro-husband ways. **(C)** gives us lines 41–44 pretty much verbatim.

(A) goes way too far; there's no evidence supporting the kind of misconduct that **(A)** accuses the judges of. As far as we can tell, they were forced because of a highly confused situation to fall back on pre-1660 assumptions. That's a very different thing.

(B) Those who claimed that the "inconsistencies . . . would soon vanish" were 18th-century historians (lines 38–40), not judges.

(D) *Au contraire,* it sounds as if judges had quite a bit of influence indeed. After all, it is "the tangled details of court cases" (line 13) that Staves studied; who is mentioned as trying to work out the tangles *but* the judges?

(E) If judges were "[trying] to interpret the laws in ways" favorable to women, we never hear about it. And if they were in fact doing so, why would they "fall back on pre-1660 assumptions" that would support the husbands' possession of property?

40. (D) Inference

After a lot of exploration of the latter parts of the passage, we're back at line 5. The historians, remember, "have traditionally argued that" the trend towards marriage contracts was a big plus for women. And that's *all* we hear about the historians. Scanning the choices, we find, incredibly, **(D)** echoing lines 5–8 about as closely as it possibly could. Dynamite!

(A) is the exact opposite of what those historians have assumed (in terms of when the benefits to women came in); and we can't even be sure that Staves or our author would agree with **(A)**, either, since the choice makes a curious distinction between changed views and later benefits that the passage never brings up.

(B) starts out OK, but the reference to "initial judicial resistance" doesn't tie in to paragraph 1 whatsoever.

(C) is closer to Staves' and the author's view than that of the historians that both are trying to debunk. Also the historians would hardly use the phrase "surface changes" to describe the altered worldview that they perceived to take place after the Restoration.

(E) What's with the "small gain"? The historians assumed that it was a gain; "small" is never mentioned. And the view that men continued to maintain an advantage is closer to the views of Staves and our author than to the historians.

Passage 7: Social Science Tools For Law
Questions 41–47

Topic and Scope: Social science methods as tools for legal analysis; specifically, the use of such tools in the analysis of sex discrimination cases.

Purpose and Main Idea: The author's purpose is to describe the recent use of social science tools in the analysis of legal opinions, and to explain why some social science tools are more helpful than others to prospective plaintiffs in sex discrimination cases. The Main Idea is that the outcomes analysis approach is inferior to more qualitative approaches such as "policy capturing" and a method involving full transcript readings over a limited time.

Paragraph Structure: Paragraph 1 is chock full of juicy (well, at least important) information. The author begins simply enough by citing a recent trend in legal analysis: Social science is now being used to analyze court opinions. The author then cites a pair of scholars (Zirkel and Schoenfeld) who have demonstrated certain successes in the application of social science tools to sex discrimination cases. All well and good, but a curveball awaits in the final sentence, signaled by the Keyword "However"—it seems the author believes their enthusiasm for a particular kind of technique, "outcomes analysis," is off base.

Left with a cliffhanger at the end of paragraph 1, the natural question to ask the author is "*why* is their enthusiasm misguided?"—and paragraph 2 doesn't disappoint. As the name implies, outcomes analysis is concerned with, you guessed it, outcomes; namely, how many plaintiffs won and how many lost. Outcomes analysis assumes that a raw count of winners and losers is useful to future plaintiffs, but the author disagrees. First of all, plaintiffs who fully believe in their cause are unlikely to take such statistics into account when deciding to go forward with a case. Secondly, this approach ignores the crucial qualitative factors involved in legal cases; it doesn't delve into the *reasons* behind the decisions, so it's not all that helpful in predicting what will happen in the future.

Where's the author likely to go with this? It's no surprise that in paragraph 3 the author describes what he considers to be better social science methods for analyzing sex discrimination cases. "Policy capturing" and the method of conducting full readings of case transcripts over a limited time are described, and advantages of each are cited—a fairly standard wrap-up to this tightly-structured passage.

The Big Picture:

- As you read, keep track of what the author favors and disdains, and where the author is likely to go each step of the way. Here, the author *is* in favor of the use of social science tools in legal analysis, but not much in favor of one particular brand: outcomes analysis. That's what we find up through the end of paragraph 2.

But it's rare indeed for an author to simply state "this stinks" and leave it at that. Predictably, in paragraph 3, the author essentially follows up his "I don't really like outcomes analysis" with "here are some methods I do like." Other possible endings are "here's how to fix outcomes analysis," or "here's what other people say might work."

- Paraphrase and condense the passage's ideas as much as possible. There are three ideas, one from each paragraph, that taken together form a thorough summary of the entire passage. 1) Supporters' enthusiasm for outcomes analysis seems misguided. 2) Outcomes analysis is of marginal assistance because it doesn't analyze the *reasons* for outcomes. 3) Two other social science approaches are better for analyzing sex discrimination cases. Boil it down to this, and you're ready for the questions.

The Questions:

41. (D) Global (Main Point)

The three points in the bullet immediately above tell the whole story: Using social science tools can help prospective plaintiffs to analyze sex discrimination cases, but one form, outcomes analysis, is inferior to other forms. Outcomes analysis is introduced and challenged in paragraph 1, and its limitations are discussed at length in paragraph 2. To choose a choice that ignores outcomes analysis is to ignore two-thirds of the passage. Even the two alternatives are discussed in light of their merits relative to the faults of outcomes analysis. That's why they need not even be named in correct choice **(D)**—referring to them as "other social science techniques" is enough. **(D)** is the only choice that mentions outcomes analysis, and it doesn't fail to include the other major elements of the passage: sex discrimination cases, and the reason to employ these techniques in the first place, prediction.

(A) There's nothing to suggest that sex discrimination in the field of higher education is an example of an "atypical" discrimination suit. And even if it were, is this the overall point the author is trying to make? What about outcomes analysis, or the other techniques mentioned at the end? **(A)** is far from being the main idea of the passage.

(B) The number of factors analyzed in a sex discrimination suit relates to the predictive value of the analysis; nothing in the passage suggests what relation it has to the validity of decisions.

(C) makes too much of the notion, found in paragraph 1, that one pair of scholars is bullish on a particular technique that the author isn't crazy about. It's a far stretch from this to say that the whole passage is mainly about scholars' inability to find alternatives to traditional legal research.

(E) is too extreme. The author argues that certain techniques may be valuable in assisting prospective plaintiffs in assessing their cases. That's far from saying that having enough information will allow one to predict the outcome of cases "with considerable certainty."

42. (B) Inference

Traditional legal research appears in line 3. When the author says that proponents of the use of social science methods for legal analysis have "justifiably" criticized the traditional approach, the word "justifiably" tells us that the author *agrees* with such criticisms. Therefore, we can infer that the author himself is critical of such research, and a quick scan of the beginning of each choice brings us to **(B)**. But be careful; remember that "half-right, half-wrong" choices lurk among the wrong choices in Reading Comp. Does the rest of choice **(B)** pan out? Sure. The author's reason for agreeing with critics of traditional research—its focus on cases that "do not affect real people with real legal problems"—is perfectly in line with **(B)**'s "has little relevance to those actually involved in cases."

(A) and **(D)** both blow the author's disdain out of proportion; **(A)** by a little, and **(D)** by a lot. Simply saying "this criticism is justified" is far from being "frustrated" and even further from being "derisive." **(D)** can be eliminated on that first word alone. As for **(A)**, even though "frustrated" doesn't seem to fit, it may be worth checking out the rest of the choice—and that goes astray, too: The notion of the "full potential" of legal research is outside of the scope.

(C) and **(E)** can both be eliminated on the basis of their first words: All we know is that the author agrees with the scholars' criticism of traditional legal research; we certainly cannot infer from this that he feels "appreciative" or "grateful" toward it.

43. (E) Inference

It may be an Inference question, but we know right where to look: Zirkel and Schoenfeld are only mentioned once, and it's right in the beginning of the first paragraph. We know point blank what they think: Like the author, they're in favor of using social science tools to analyze sex discrimination cases. Unlike the author, they're enthusiastic about outcomes analysis. It's hard to form a pre-phrase from this alone, but since this is all we know about these two, surely this will be enough. So with their position in mind, the best bet is to simply test out each choice.

(A) and **(B)** both distort information in the passage. Must Zirkel and Schoenfeld have been the *first* to use such tools in this way, as **(A)** asserts? No; just because they're in favor of it doesn't mean they were the originators. Similarly, must outcomes analysis be the *only* techniques they've studied, choice **(B)**? Again, no. Just because they've studied this technique doesn't mean they haven't studied others as well.

(C) is too extreme. Sure, Zirkel and Schoenfeld criticize traditional legal research and prefer the use of social science tools to analyze court cases involving sex discrimination. But that's not to say, as **(C)** does, that it's good for nothing. We can't infer they saw "no value" in traditional legal research from the fact that they saw some weaknesses in that process and preferred another to it.

(D) "Policy capturing" appears long after our last sighting of Zirkel and Schoenfeld. We have no way of knowing what, if any, opinion they have on this approach.

(E) Zirkel and Schoenfeld are enthusiastic about outcomes analysis, and they feel that their studies demonstrate that plaintiffs would benefit from the use of social science analysis. The author challenges their enthusiasm mostly by proposing reasons why this technique is not of much value to plaintiffs. It all adds up to the reasonable inference in **(E)**—Zirkel and Schoenfeld must believe that the outcomes analysis information *would* be useful to plaintiffs.

44. (A) Logic Function

Again the topic of traditional legal research arises, this time in the form of a logic question. We're asked *why* the author brings this up, and here a pre-phrase is possible. We know that the passage is not overwhelmingly about this topic, but it *is* mentioned for a reason. Again, as in question 10, the phrase "justifiably criticized" helps us to see the author's intent in mentioning this example. The passage is about the use of social science tools in legal research; the specific weaknesses of traditional legal research are cited as the reasons *why* the use of social science tools is preferred in the analysis of certain kinds of cases. After line 6, we never hear about traditional legal research again. Basically, then, traditional research is mentioned to set up the scenario, to introduce the need for the real topic of the passage, social science tools. **(A)** has it right: It provides background information for what is to follow.

(B) There are no real "opponents" here: Regarding the limitations of traditional legal research, the author and the scholars are in perfect agreement.

(C) 180: As discussed above, the weaknesses of traditional legal research are explored so as to impress upon the reader the benefits of using social science tools in the analysis of sex discrimination cases.

(D) is an extreme choice: The fact that one form of legal research may not be helpful to certain kinds of plaintiffs doesn't mean that the author is trying to show that the actions of legal researchers *harm* potential plaintiffs.

(E) There is no indication that the author is trying to convince the traditional researchers themselves to use the social science methods. All we know is that the author agrees with

side, according to the reformers, are privileged *because* they speak the legal jargon. Thus we can infer, as **(B)** has it, that fluency in the form of legal discourse characteristic of most objectivist-based Western societies confers power. But there's even a stronger basis for this inference, one that perhaps clinched it for you, and it comes directly from the sentence in lines 49–52: The author states that personal narratives can foster "a sense of empathy between legal insiders and people traditionally excluded from legal discourse, *and hence, from power*." From this sentence alone we can infer that fluency in legal discourse confers power (see the second bullet point below for a further enunciation of this).

(A) Here's that issue of "training" again, and once again, it's off the mark: We know that people who are trained in legal discourse have an advantage in the current system over people who aren't. However, where they *get* this training is never addressed in the passage.

(C) is a distortion. The passage equates the objectivist-driven form of legal discourse with abstraction (line 45), but nowhere is it implied that the level of this abstraction has progressively increased over time.

(D) Another 180! Traditional legal discourse has been based on the objectivist principle for centuries. Far from denying the existence of neutral, objective observers, this principle is based on the existence of such observers.

(E), if anything, also goes against the grain of the passage. Traditional objectivist legal discourse seeks the one objective truth associated with any event. The proposed personal stories approach, on the other hand, seems to believe in the possibility that many different stories can be true regarding an event, depending on who tells of it, with what emotion, and based on what personal experience. Therefore, the personal stories approach is more likely than traditional legal discourse to promote the reconciliation of dissonant world views—it suggests that many different accounts can be right *in their own way*. The objectivists would never accept that.

55. (A) Logic (Parallel Reasoning)

The final question on this passage is an application question: What would "the law's quest for truth" seem like to someone who rejects objectivism? The first step in such an endeavor is to determine what such a person would believe. Use what you already know: Someone who rejects objectivism would probably agree with the author's objection to this philosophy stated in lines 19–20: "... there is no such thing as the neutral, objective, observer." Since legal "truth" is an objectivist principle, such a person would not believe in the existence of such a truth, in the ability to precisely determine "what really happened." So to such a critic of objectivism, "the law's quest for truth" would amount to a fruitless search for a non-existent entity. This could be your pre-phrase, in some

form or another. The closest analogy among the choices is **(A)**'s "hunt for an imaginary animal."

All of the wrong choices center around things that *exist*, while to the opponent of objectivism "truth" *doesn't* exist.

(B) This mineral may be hard to find, but it exists.

(C) This puzzle may be hard to assemble, but it exists.

(D) Both kinds of fruit, of course, exist, not to mention that such a comparison strays from the notion of a quest or a search.

(E) An "analysis" is off the mark as well, as it doesn't match the "quest" element of the stem. But besides that, the chemical compound, you guessed it, *exists*, and thus an analysis of it cannot be similar to the quest for a *non*-existent truth.

Passage 9: Legal Views
Questions 56–63

Topic and Scope: The nature of law; specifically, various views about the nature of law.

Purpose and Main Idea: The author's purpose is to describe several different views about the nature of law. His main idea is that a number of new approaches to defining the nature of law have emerged since the 1970s.

Paragraph Structure: Paragraph 1 does two things: (1) it reveals the passage's topic—the nature of law—and (2) it tells us that, historically, there have been two views about the nature of law—the Naturalist view, which considers law to be the embodiment of universal moral precepts, and the Positivist view, which considers law to be a set of rules determined by society's legitimate ruling elite. Up to this point, we can't yet conclude anything specific about the passage's scope, purpose, and main idea; all we can say with certainty is that the rest of the passage will explore this general topic in more detail.

Paragraph 2's first sentence reveals the passage's scope: views about the nature of law that have emerged since the 1970s. The rest of this paragraph sketches two of these views. According to the Law and Economics school, the law is a system of rules intended to maximize society's wealth. According to the Critical Legal Studies school, law is a system of rules intended to legitimize the authority of existing holders of power. This school, we're told, differs from the earlier positivist school in that it doesn't necessarily consider the ruling elite to be a legitimate source of authority. While we know the author's topic and scope by the end of this paragraph, we still don't have enough information to conclude anything about his purpose and main idea.

Paragraphs 3 and 4 describe yet another modern view of the nature of law—that of James Boyd White, the founder of the Law and Literature school. According to this view, which takes issue with both the Law and Economics and Critical Legal Studies schools, law should be viewed as a literary process in which judges continually rewrite older laws to solve modern problems, thereby creating new laws. Only after reaching the end of the passage can we conclude that the author's purpose is essentially descriptive and that his main point is simply that a number of novel views about the nature of law have sprung up over the past few decades.

The Big Picture:

- If a passage contains more than one point of view, make certain that you can distinguish between (or among) them. A number of questions will surely test to see that you can make distinctions.

- If a passage contains a lot of details, don't worry about picking them all up during a first read through. Instead, just note where specific details may be found (by paragraph), so that you can quickly relocate them should this become necessary to answer questions.

The Questions:

56. (A) Global (Main Point)

The phrase "main idea" in the question stem signals a Global question. Thus, you're looking for an answer that's broad enough to encompass the contents of the entire passage, yet narrow enough to refer to its specific subject matter. **(A)** is the only choice that fits the bill. The first paragraph describes the two traditional, contrasting approaches to the law—the Naturalist and Positivist schools. The final three paragraphs, on the other hand, describe a number of more recent, disparate approaches to the law—the Law and Economics school, the Critical Legal Studies school, and the Law and Literature school.

(B) What changes in society? What types of cases? What numbers of cases? This passage is confined to describing several *legal theories*. It doesn't deal with changes in society or legal cases.

(C) and **(D)** are too narrow in scope. The Law and Literature school is addressed only in the last two paragraphs of the passage. Besides, the author never favors this school over the others **(C)**. Nor does he claim that it is based on a synthesis of "many theories of jurisprudence" **(D)**.

(E) The author doesn't claim that adherents of the older legal schools are under attack by adherents of more recent legal schools. He simply notes that new interpretations of the nature of law have sprung up over the last few decades.

57. (B) Detail EXCEPT

This is a straightforward but time-consuming Detail question. It's time-consuming because you really have no choice but to look up each choice in the text, searching for the one that *doesn't* appear. None of the legal schools mentioned in the passage refers to judicial opinions as "arcane" (i.e., obscure or incomprehensible).

(A), (D), (E) The Law and Literature school has described judicial opinions as "political statements" **(A)**, "artistic performances" **(D)**, and "acts of translation" **(E)**. See lines 45–47, lines 44–45, and lines 49–50, respectively. Lines 29–34 indicate that the Critical Legal Studies school also considers judicial opinions to be "political statements."

(C) Lines 19–22 indicate that the Law and Economics school considers judicial opinions to be "economic statements."

58. (B) Inference

Lines 32–34 tell us that Critical Legal theorists believe that laws reflect the interests of elites "who may have no legitimate authority." We're further told that these elites use laws to protect "the privileges of their race, class, or gender." The statement in choice **(B)** reflects this mindset. In contrast to lawmakers, the rich aren't a legitimate source of authority. Yet they've "devised and perpetuated" income tax laws—laws that permit them to keep their wealth out of the government's hands.

(A) sounds like something a member of the Law and Literature school would say. These folks, lines 45–57 point out, are the ones that speak of law as an outgrowth of a combination of legal precedent, current events, and judicial values.

(C) sounds like something a member of the Law and Economics school would say. These folks, lines 19–22 reveal, talk about the connection between economic processes and law.

(D) sounds like something a member of the Naturalist school might say. These folks, lines 7–9 tell us, emphasize the connection between morality and law.

(E) sounds like something a member of the Positivist school would say. These folks, lines 9–11 indicate, speak of law being made by society's legitimate ruling authorities.

59. (D) Detail

Lines 14–17 suggest that the modern, post-1970 schools inquiring into the nature of law share one trait in common: they've all been influenced by "academic disciplines and intellectual traditions previously unconnected with the study of law." Lines 27–29 relate the particular academic disciplines and intellectual traditions that have influenced the Critical Legal Studies school, while line 36 points out that the Law and Literature school is also "interdisciplinary."

(A) While the Critical Legal Studies school is concerned with how elites maintain their power through the law (see lines 29–34), the Law and Literature school is concerned only with how *new law* is developed.

(B) It might be argued that the Critical Legal Studies school is an extension of legal positivism since both dwell on the connection between law and authority; however, the Law and Literature school is not a descendent of either natural law or legal positivism, which focus on moral and political issues, respectively. The Law and Literature school dwells primarily on the connection between law and literary activity.

(C) Neither the Critical Legal Studies school nor the Law and Literature school is concerned with the connection between law and economics. Rather, it's the Law and Economics school that deals with this issue. Moreover, the Critical Legal Studies school argues that the power of many political elites

is illegitimate, while the Law and Literature school doesn't explicitly comment on the nature of legitimate political power.

(E) Only the Law and Literature school looks upon judicial opinion-writing as a "mediating activity" (see lines 48–53).

60. (E) Inference

Collectively, lines 12–17 tell us that "academic disciplines and intellectual traditions previously unconnected with the study of law" have had an impact on the study of law since the 1970s. Put differently, these academic disciplines and intellectual traditions, including anthropology and sociology, *didn't* affect the study of law *before* the 1970s.

(A) The study of law before and after 1970 has been concerned with the nature of law itself, not with "codifying and maintaining the privileges of elites."

(B) The pre-1970s Positivist school, lines 9–11 indicate, drew a direct connection between law and the political power of groups.

(C) The fact that the post-1970 Law and Literature school focuses primarily on judicial opinions doesn't mean that this issue was necessarily ignored in the pre-1970 study of law.

(D) Neither the Naturalist nor Positivist schools focused on economic issues. Rather, the post-1970 Law and Economics school concentrates on this issue.

61. (D) Inference

The Law and Literature school's view of how judges render opinions is dealt with in paragraph 4; so, you'll need to go there for the information necessary to answer this question. Individual judges, according to this school, reinterpret established legal texts in order to solve current legal problems. Since members of this school believe that judicial opinions are based on individual decisions, it follows logically that they would also believe that different judges might come to different decisions when faced with the same legal situation.

(A), (C), (E) Judges, according to the Law and Literature school's members, make decisions by adapting established legal texts to current legal problems. There's nothing in the passage to indicate that Law and Literature school members think that "theories" of law have anything to do with judicial decision making.

(B) is inconsistent with the Law and Literature school's emphasis on judicial adaptability. Since members of this school feel that *all* judges reinterpret established legal texts, they wouldn't endorse the view that some judicial opinions are based purely on natural law or legal positivist doctrine.

62. (C) Inference

In lines 48–50, we're told that judges are "translators" and that judicial opinion-writing is "an act of translation." Later, in lines 54–57, we're told that judges essentially reinterpret and rewrite established legal texts in order to deal with present legal problems. In this context, then, the word "re-constitute" means "interpret and refashion" **(C)**.

(A), **(B)**, **(D)**, and **(E)** One word is off in each of these choices. There's nothing in the Law and Literature school's view of judicial decision making to suggest that judges "categorize" **(A)**, "summarize" **(B)**, "announce" **(D)**, or "negotiate" **(E)** anything.

63. (A) Global (Primary Purpose)

The phrase "primary purpose" means that this question, like question 75, is a Global question. Once again, then, you've got to consider the *entire* passage, not just a portion of it. If you recognized that the author restricts himself to describing various notions about the nature of law—he doesn't advocate any of them—**(A)** should have jumped out at you.

(B), **(C)**, **(D)** are all inconsistent with the author's descriptive purpose. "Discount" **(B)**, "advocate" **(C)**, and "correct" **(D)** all incorrectly suggest that the author offers his own point of view in the passage.

(E) What inconsistencies does the author reconcile? He simply describes different views.

Passage 10: Alexandrine Doctrine
Questions 64–71

Like many Law Passages, this one is heavy on the jargon and complex language, with a couple of Latin terms thrown in for good measure. The author's voice doesn't show up until the very end of the passage, when he finally explains the "significance" of Alexandrine doctrine that is alluded to at the beginning of the passage. As is common for difficult passages, however, the question set is relatively easy.

The passage announces its **Topic,** *medieval marriage practices*, in the first line. The **Scope** is set forth in the next few lines. The author is interested in Pope Alexander III's synthesis of religious and legal opinion regarding the formation of marriage contracts. The **Purpose** and **Main Idea** are not obvious at this point, so we forge ahead.

Paragraph 1: Under Alexandrine doctrine, marriage was a consensual union between the partners, rather than an economic arrangement made by the parents. The consent of the parents was unnecessary (lines 4–9). A marriage contract could take immediate effect (*per verba de praesenti)*, or could be a promise to marry in the future (*per verba de futuro)*.

In paragraph 2, the author clarifies the distinction between legal and Church-sanctioned marriage. Marriage contracts made without public announcement and ritual solemnization were legal (lines 21–23), but the Church discouraged such "clandestine" marriages. Punishment included excommunication for the couple, and any priest who participated in that couple's wedding was also punished.

The eventual expansion in meaning of the term "clandestine" is described in paragraph 3. The author's view finally becomes apparent in paragraph 4, when we learn about the historian Charles Donahue, who stressed the controversial (lines 44–49) nature of Alexander's views on marriage. Finally, in the last lines of the passage (lines 55–58), the author explains just what is so "significant" (line 2) and "radical" (line 56) about this interpretation of Alexandrine doctrine: the contrast between the Church as the guardian of individual freedom when it came to marriage, and the traditional view of the Church as "the most potent authoritarian force in a rigidly hierarchical society."

The Big Picture:

Paragraph 1: Marriage contracts—consensual

Paragraph 2: Church regs. for punishment

Paragraph 3: "Clandestine" meaning expanded

Paragraph 4: Donahue: impact of Alexandrine view

The Questions:

64. (B) Global (Main Idea)

Where the author lacks a strong voice, your Roadmap will enable you to identify the Main Idea of the passage.

The author spends most of the passage describing Alexandrine doctrine, but at the end, appears to agree with Donahue's evaluation of the doctrine as "controversial." The Roadmap tells us that the bulk of the passage contains the description of the Alexandrine doctrine under which marriage was a union based on mutual consent and love. Answer choice **(B)** says just that.

(A) is a 180. Alexandrine doctrine *discouraged*, rather than encouraged, clandestine marriage.

(C) Alexandrine doctrine made the Church the "guardian of individual freedom" in the area of marriage—Donahue's interpretation of the doctrine is controversial precisely because of the contrast between the Church's approval of individual control over the decision to marry, and the Church's authoritarian position in other social contexts.

(D) Details, such as the two types of marriage contracts mentioned here, are never the main idea of a passage.

(E) Couples who married without public announcements prior to the marriage were excommunicated. The passage does not state whether those who wed without ritual solemnization were excommunicated. Even if this were not a distortion of the passage, the answer choice would describe a detail rather than the Main Idea of the passage.

65. (D) Inference

The right answer choice for an Inference question must be true, based solely upon the text.

What can be inferred about the role of parents in medieval marriage practices? We are told their consent was unnecessary for a valid marriage. Given that, **(D)** must be true—under Alexandrine doctrine, parents could not prohibit a couple from marrying based on mutual consent of the couple rather than economic expediency.

(A) is outside the scope of the passage. The passage never addresses whether parents were more likely to bow to the dictates of the Church than were their children.

(B) The author never discusses parental preferences as between the two types of marriage contracts.

(C) The author says nothing about parental concerns for Church versus legal recognition of any particular marriage.

(E) The Alexandrine synthesis attempted to discourage clandestine marriages, but there is no mention of whether this approach was due to parental concerns about such unions.

66. (B) Detail

Use your Roadmap to help you research the correct answer for a Detail question.

The penalty of excommunication is discussed in paragraph 2: couples who failed to make public marriage announcements ("banns") for three successive Sundays before their intended wedding were subject to excommunication. That's **(B)**.

(A), (D), and **(E)** Don't fall for this faulty use of detail. Paragraph 3 suggests that violation of requirements for ritual solemnization **(A)** or priestly blessing **(D)** of the marriage contract would make the marriage "clandestine," but the passage says nothing about such violations leading to excommunication. Likewise, Paragraph 1 states that a *de futuro* contract could be replaced by a *de praesenti* contract, but whether the contract indicated a present or future intent to marry was not described as a factor in a couple's risk of excommunication **(E)**.

(C) A 180. Alexandrine doctrine specifically permitted couples to receive the Church's blessing even if they married without the consent of their parents.

67. (A) Detail

Use clues in the question stem, including Hot Words and specific text references, to research Detail questions.

Paragraph 2 makes it clear that the Church would excommunicate couples that chose to have a clandestine marriage, but their marriage would still be legally valid. Answer choice **(A)** best reflects this idea.

(B) A clandestine union would be legal, but the author says nothing about whether the couple's parents would recognize the union.

(C) 180. The Church would not recognize a clandestine marriage as described in the second paragraph, but the marriage *would* be legally valid.

(D) Another 180. The Church would not recognize a clandestine marriage. The passage draws no connection between a clandestine marriage and a marriage arranged for reasons of economic expediency.

(E) *De futuro* contracts are not mentioned in paragraph 2, and a terminated marriage contract is not clandestine.

68. (E) Global (Primary Purpose)

Your Roadmap, as well as your understanding of the passage Topic, Scope, and Main Idea will help clarify the purpose of the passage.

The Main Idea of the passage was to describe the Alexandrine doctrine of marriage, and the author ends the passage by noting Donahue's "radical" interpretation of the doctrine. The correct answer choice should reflect both aspects of the passage, and answer choice **(E)** does just that.

(A) Nothing in the passage suggests the author questions the legitimacy of any of the scholarly work discussed in the passage.

(B) There is no discussion of "several" historical periods—only the medieval period is discussed.

(C) The author makes no call for further research, nor does the author characterize the field of medieval history as "neglected."

(D) The passage is limited to one small aspect of life in the medieval era, not the history of an era *per se*. The author does not recommend a new scholarly approach to that era.

69. (C) Inference

Always research the context of details mentioned in the question stem.

Paragraph 4 tells us that under Donahue's interpretation, the Alexandrine doctrine made the Church the guardian of individual freedom with respect to marriage. By contrast, the author notes the "traditional perception" of the Church as an authoritarian force. **(C)** captures this contrast.

5 The passage begins by telling us that historians of medieval marriage practices in general ascribe particular significance to Alexandrine doctrine.

(B) While it is plausible that certain modern marriage laws can be traced back to Alexandrine doctrine, the author makes no connection between Alexandrine doctrine and modern marriage laws.

(D) is a train wreck. It is almost as if the LSAT writers pulled words from the passage at random to create this answer choice. The author never suggests other studies of medieval marriage have "misread" any aspect of the rituals, and never describes the legal and ecclesiastical rituals as being particularly complicated or susceptible to misunderstanding. The author does not describe "rituals" for public announcement or ritual solemnization of marriage.

(E) offers up an irrelevant comparison. The contrast between Donahue and other scholars has nothing to do with a shift in focus from legal to ecclesiastical views.

70. (D) Detail

Watch for technical terms when you read the passage, as you are likely to be asked about them.

Paragraph 1 explicitly states that a *de praesenti* contract was binding and immediately effective, while a *de futuro* contract expressed a promise to marry in the future. That's answer choice **(D)**.

(A) makes a false distinction. Both types of marriage contracts were recognized under Alexandrine doctrine.

(B) The author makes it quite clear that under Alexandrine doctrine, parental consent was never required.

(C) Both types of contracts were verbal (verbal meaning "expressed by words"—when you get to law school the distinction will be between *oral* and written contracts). Both types of marriage contracts required a formal announcement ("banns") to be recognized by the Church.

(E) According to the passage, marriage without the announcement of marriage banns resulted in excommunication. Either type of marriage contract could permit the solemnization of the marriage through Church ritual.

71. (C) Logic Function

Consider the context of the paragraph at issue to answer a Logic/Function question.

Our Roadmap tells us that the second paragraph is where the author describes how the Church discouraged "clandestine" marriages. A quick scan of the paragraph reveals that it also clarifies the distinction between marriage contracts that are legally valid and those that comply with ecclesiastical requirements. Answer choice **(C)** best captures this idea.

(A) is a 180. The paragraph elaborates on a distinction mentioned in the first paragraph; there are no divergent interpretations.

(B) The rule mentioned in the first paragraph was that couples could get married without obtaining the consent of their parents. The second paragraph contains no exception to this rule.

(D) There is neither a summary of traditional interpretations of a topic nor is there an introduction of a new interpretation in paragraph 2.

(E) The first paragraph did not contain an argument, so the second paragraph could not possibly set forth objections to a prior argument.

Passage 11: "Hard" Cases n Law
Questions 72–78

Topic and Scope: The concept of "hard" (tough; controversial) legal cases; specifically, to what extent such cases are "legally determinate," defined by the author as "decidable under existing law."

Purpose and Main Idea: The author's purpose is to compare two legal thinkers' views of the law as a means of evaluating when and how controversial cases can be decided under existing law. By the end, certainly in the final sentence, we see that the author finds merit in both views but, in the main, finds Hart's conception of the open-endedness of legal terminology to be both persuasive and useful.

Paragraph Structure: Paragraph 1 presents some fundamental terminology and definitions—"hard" cases and "determinate"—as it lays out the passage's fundamental issue: How can hard cases be decided? Paragraph 2 belongs to Hart: his conception of law as legal rules with "open-textured" general terminology; an extended example; and the suggestion that some cases need to be decided on moral or political, rather than strictly legal, grounds because their terminology isn't specific or determinate enough. Dworkin is the focus of paragraph 3: To him the law isn't just Hart's rules, but also includes *principles*, and the two work in tandem to render "legal indeterminacy"—the deciding of cases on other than legal grounds—a non-issue. Paragraph 4, as noted above, is comfortable with both concepts—both rules and principles— as the author forges a middle ground, deciding finally that there do exist difficult cases and a branch of law where things are simply not cut-and-dried, and judges must exercise some discretion.

The Big Picture:

- This passage is a strong candidate for being left until last: It's dense and difficult from the first few lines. Most students find this kind of windy text to be more manageable if it's approached after a lot of easier points are under one's belt.

- Don't be nervous when a passage seems to involve a lot of intricate field-specific jargon, as this passage does. If the jargon important enough, then it will be clearly defined.

- It is quite possible that you successfully attacked all or a majority of this passage's 7 questions without really knowing what the author was talking about. Don't worry, because that is quite common. The beauty of LSAT Reading Comprehension is that if we get the *gist* of what's being discussed in a passage, we get a strong handle on the questions posed.

The Questions:

72. (C) Global (Main Point)

Dworkin's concept is legal principles; Hart's is open-textured legal rules; paragraph 4 indicates the author's level of comfort with both; and **(C)** sums it all up and gets the topic and scope right, to boot.

(A) begs the question of the topic and scope—the determinacy of "hard" cases—and comes down squarely on the side of the need for resolving all cases through law alone, something the author rejects.

(B) is the choice for those who grab paragraph 1 and not much else. The definition of "hard" cases is a jumping-off point for the real issue of how such cases are to be decided, and **(B)** mentions none of that.

(D)'s negative judgment of Dworkin's concept of legal principles is not supported by the author—indeed, the author embraces the concept in paragraph 4.

(E) is a pretty radical distortion of this passage's content and tone. Hart's definition of legal terminology as "open textured" implies (quite sensibly) that language has some inherent flexibility of meaning—even legal language—and that judges need to exercise some judgment as a result; but all of that is a far cry from accusations of "inherent inconsistency" and "defects and gaps in the law."

73. (C) Detail

This choice nicely paraphrases lines 40–41.

(A) sounds like a plausible definition of the term "legal principles" on its face, but it has nothing to do with Dworkin or, indeed, with anything else in the passage.

(B) Legal principles, as defined by Dworkin, don't explain legal rules: They coexist with them, within the body of established law (see lines 35–37).

(D) Dworkin believes that law exists outside of legal rules.

(E) Dworkin seems to be opposed to the notion that some cases need judicial discretion (lines 42–45), so he would not coin the term "legal principles" to mean cases that required same.

74. (D) Inference

The answer comes from the final sentence—as well as the realization that rules are Hart's concept, principles are Dworkin's, and the author is trying to effect a synthesis of the two in the final paragraph. The "penumbra of both rules and principles," of course, is (lines 15–16) the place where things are not cut-and-dried and determinate.

(A) The author never posits which—rules or principles—is appealed to more often in hard cases.

(B) "Official recognition," whatever that means, has nothing to do with this "think piece" on legal determinacy, the author's effort to work out a theory of one part of the law.

(C) Far from arguing that rules have been superseded by principles, the author believes that both exist in the law.

(E) No, the author hints strongly that those cases "in the penumbra of both rules and principles" (lines 56–57) will, in fact, require judges' discretion for their decidability.

75. (D) Logic Function

This choice sums up lines 18–22.

(A) and **(B)** are off because the word "vehicle" is a *term*, not a rule or principle in and of itself.

(C) and **(E)** *Au contraire,* "vehicle" was chosen precisely because it does *not* necessarily have one settled meaning **(C)**, because it's Hart's concept *in action* **(E)**.

76. (B) Inference

This answer comes directly out of lines 8–11, which tie Hart's concept to the standard law and describe Hart's ideas as "clear" and "persuasive."

(A) "Clear" and "persuasive" don't imply that a work or theory covers a topic "exhaustively." No evidence for this one.

(C) and **(D)** are each half-right, half-wrong. Interesting, sure; plausible, o.k.; but "impractical" or "unwieldy"? It's unlikely that a theoretical think piece like this one would traffic much in practicality anyway; but if anything, the author does seem to see practical and workable (as opposed to "unwieldy") value in Hart's concept (see paragraph 4).

(E) Hopelessly wrong. No matter how far back in history Hart's work dates—and of course we get no info to that effect—the author seems to find it relevant and well worth studying.

77. (B) Inference

Some examinees, thrown by all of the heavy-duty terminology in paragraph 1, failed to see that "determinate" is clearly defined by lines 6–7 and paraphrased in **(B)**. Very straightforward. A demonstration of how one's frame of mind can make or break a particular LSAT question.

(A) Penalties—sentences, punishments, etc.—are way beyond the scope of this investigation.

(C) The concept of judicial discretion doesn't come into the passage until much later, and then only in passing. This choice picks up on some terminology from the previous sentence (lines 1–3) but is otherwise incoherent.

(D) defines "*in*determinate" pretty well.

(E) No reference to codified procedures can be found anywhere near line 6.

78. (E) Global (Primary Purpose)

This choice as written basically just sums up two lines, lines 46–47, but that fact shouldn't unduly trouble you: After all, paragraph 4 is where the passage's individual discussions of Hart and Dworkin is heading—it is, therefore, the most important paragraph—and lines 46–47 do encapsulate paragraph 4. So despite **(E)**'s evocation of only two lines, they *are* the most important lines and can stand acceptably as the author's purpose.

(A) Nonsense. The in-practice role of the legislative branch is about as far removed from this passage's concerns as can be.

(B) is an issue that was raised and disposed of in paragraph 1. The topic may be "hard" cases, but the scope moves away from their definition to their determinacy, something that **(B)** ignores but **(E)** exploits.

(C) paraphrases lines 38–41, but these lines aren't nearly as all-encompassing as lines 46–47. And in terms of the author's main purpose, Dworkin certainly doesn't deserve the pride of place that **(C)** assigns him.

(D) If anyone is in the "critiquing Hart" business, it's Dworkin and not our author, who is trying to synthesize the views of the two thinkers.

Passage 12: England and Its Colonies
Questions 79–85

This passage compares the political attitudes and institutions of England's American colonies with those of England itself in the two centuries prior to our independence. *Don't try to understand the two points of view in depth, start by understanding them in a broad sense. You can always go back and analyze in more detail as the questions demand, but why do more work than you need to?*

Notice that the passage gets underway by defining the two groups in question (the English in America and the ones at home) as "sharing a common political vocabulary," and almost immediately announces that one group "had given the words a significance quite different." The gist of the rest is that the colonial government was set up much the same way as that of the Mother Country (paragraph 2), but that attitudes towards that setup differed on either side of the Atlantic; paragraph 3 explains how the English in England felt and the last paragraph sums up the colonials' views.

To tie this all up, basically you should have come away from the passage with the idea that the colonists and the English gave different meanings to the same political terms (such as "constitution") and, as a consequence, perceived similar political institutions very differently. That comparison/contrast is the big idea here.

The Questions:

79. (C) Global (Main Point)

No sooner said than done, we are rewarded with a point for choice **(C)** in this Global question. This question is probably one that you could have answered correctly after reading paragraph 1 and a cursory skim of the rest, but even if you waited till late to answer it, the choice of **(C)** should be pretty much Q.E.D. *Many answers to Global questions go wrong because they're too broad or too narrow in scope—particularly the latter. Some wrong choices will refer to only a small segment of the passage, while others won't seem to refer to the specific content of the passage at all.* Choice **(B)**, for instance, sums up paragraph 2 only, while Colonial attitudes, the subject of **(D)**, come up only in paragraph 4 (not to mention the fact that increasing eighteenth-century hostility is something we carry with us from our outside knowledge of the American Revolution, not from the passage itself). **(A)** and **(E)**, meanwhile, contradict or at least distort the text. Contrary to **(A)**, the colonists and English did too share a common political vocabulary, though they differed over the meanings of the political terms they shared. And contrary to **(E)**, as paragraph 4 suggests, colonial attitudes toward constitutions were influenced by the contents of the charters granted to the colonies by England, not by English legal developments in the seventeenth century.

80. (D) Detail EXCEPT

Eliminate the statements that you know are supported by the passage, and see what's left. As always, of course, *first figure out which paragraph(s) specifically are likely to contribute to the search.* Here it's paragraph 2, even though the topic of the question is colonial politics only, while the paragraph is about what the colonies and England had in common. Anyway, it says there that, at the time, people who didn't own property couldn't vote **(A)**, each of the colonies had a representative assembly that resembled Britain's Parliament **(B)**, and some colonies had Royal Governors **(C)** who were regarded as similar in function to a king **(E)**. That leaves choice **(D)**, and indeed, the passage never states that colonial assemblies could remove Royal Governors from office. What the passage does say, in paragraph 4, is that sometimes the colonists struggled with these governors in order to protect their rights, but that's entirely different from saying that the colonists could remove them from office.

Incidentally, we'd like to point out that choice **(A)**—a wrong answer in that it's inferable from the passage—is in fact the contrapositive of one of the author's statements, namely line 24. "Only property holders could vote" can be translated to "*If one was a voter, then one had to be a property holder,*" and after reversing and negating the terms, you're left with choice **(A)**. *We mention this not because we think it was so difficult to reject* **(A)**, *but because we wanted to reinforce the idea that translating "only if" statements to simple "if/thens," and using the contrapositive, are skills that you should be ready to exercise throughout the exam. You never know when those will be precisely what they're testing for.*

81. (C) Inference

When you want to know about English kings—when you want to know about England period—paragraph 3 is where you search. The kings' power relative to that of Parliament, we are told there, was declining from the early seventeenth century onward. In fact, by the eighteenth century, Parliament was considered all-powerful. In other words, the kings' power relative to that of Parliament was much greater before the early seventeenth century than later on...which makes **(C)** correct.

Wrong choice **(A)** may have been a bit tricky, since sentences 3 and 4 of paragraph 3 imply that English kings pre-1600 were absolute authorities who were not subject to the law. However, that's very different from saying that they were the *source* of the law back then. Just because they weren't subject to the law doesn't mean that they made it. While choice **(B)** contradicts information in the passage (if pre-1600 English kings weren't subject to the law then, by definition, they could not have flouted it), you may have been tempted by it anyway, since some tend to associate contempt for law with absolute, contemptuous rulers. Choice **(D)** is outside the scope of the passage: we're told only about Parliament's role in English legal reform, not the role played by the kings, if any. Likewise, we aren't told whether English kings, before the early seventeenth century, had to struggle against people who thought that Parliament should be the absolute power in the land **(E)**, although starting around 1600, obviously, English kings were forced to battle such people. And lost.

82. (C) Detail

When looking for evidence, listen for signals of same. Those include "because," and "since," and phrases like "The most unmistakable sign of this tendency," lines 30–31. Of course, the "sign" mentioned there (the announcement in law that the King was subject to the law) is not what the testmakers chose for the right answer, though they could have done so. Rather, we are told that "together with" that evidence went another piece—that by the eighteenth century, the English had accepted the notion of Parliament as an all-powerful institution. And as an example of that unlimited power we're given correct choice **(C)**.

Since eighteenth-century Englishmen accepted the absolute power of Parliament, they could not, as **(A)** alleges, have been uncomfortable with institutions that had absolute power. So **(A)** is a contradiction. Regarding **(B)**, the English may very well have thought that their interests would be better taken care of by Parliament than by the king—why else would they accept Parliament's new power? *But you must always remember the question that's being posed. A statement that is consistent with the author's view—that is, a "true" statement—is not enough.* Why the English made Parliament omnipotent goes unmentioned in the passage, so it's clearly not the evidence used by the author to support anything. Much the same can be said about **(D)** and **(E)**. **(D)** certainly gives a reason for popular dissatisfaction with a king—although I'm sure you're aware that royal stupidity has historically not been a disqualification for leadership, and in any case the passage is discussing kings in general, not one dumb monarch—but in any case it's simply not cited by the author. Likewise, that the English didn't object to the expanding power of Parliament may be taken as an indication that they supported governmental reform **(E)**, but it's not explicitly cited here, and so neither **(D)** nor **(E)** can possibly be dubbed "evidence used by the author."

83. (E) Inference

This is one of the tougher questions in the set, because its topic is what the colonists probably viewed as a source of their quarrel with England, while the passage is mostly devoted to the attitudes of colonists and the English about *political institutions*, and is only in passing interested in their views of each other. Also, it's not immediately apparent where in the passage the answer is to be found. *For some questions, there's really no faster and surer technique than to simply skim the five choices and decide which of them seem like something in*

the passage. Employing this technique on this question can pay off quickly. For one thing, you surely don't need to check the passage to see that **(D)** is flat-out wrong—the colonies adopted many institutions from England, of course. One of those shared institutions was a representative Parliament, so **(B)** cannot be the "pressure point"; in fact, so many things are described as having been shared that **(C)**, too, should have jumped out as a major distortion of the text. "Uniquely English?" Not hardly. Unsure about **(A)**, you should probably recall that vocabulary comes up in paragraph 1, and can quickly see there that **(A)** is a 180: since "the colonials failed to observe that" they were using words differently (lines 6–7), that couldn't have been a contemporary source of tension. This leaves **(E)**, the right answer, support for which is found in lines 10–12.

Of course, if you simply saw the word "debates" in the question and found the word "debated" in line 9, the whole thing becomes moot: **(E)** is clearly supported right then and there.

84. (C) Detail

We know that the issue of a constitution comes up in paragraph 4 only, so *you might well want to skim the relevant paragraph before proceeding back to the answer choices.* How did the English attitude toward their Constitution differ from the colonists' attitude toward constitutions in general? Signals like "whereas" (line 47) and "This distinction in meaning" (line 49) pinpoint the location, and probably anyone who's ever taken Civics 101 was not surprised to learn that the English constitution is an unwritten set of precedents and conventions, while the colonists wanted the thing on paper. The former is summed up in **(C)**, of course, and notice once again that *right answers tend to use paraphrase to put a bit of a spin on the passage text*, although you're hardly going out on a limb by deciding that "a cumulative corpus of legislation and legal traditions" is a pretty close equivalent of "the whole body of law and legal custom" (lines 45–46).

That notwithstanding, many students erred and chose **(A)**, because the rhetoric just cited, describing the English Constitution, certainly sounds lofty enough to justify **(A)**. However, noting that that body of laws and customs dates back to the beginning of the kingdom is not to say that it was seen as the "legal foundation" of that kingdom. Indeed, the very fact that the English were willing to allow Parliament to change the Constitution suggests that they did not view it as such. **(B)**, a limp distillation of **(C)**, leaves out the entire legal issue. (As worded, **(B)** describes a copy of Emily Post's *Etiquette* more accurately than any constitution.) Finally, that eighteenth-century Englishmen acknowledged Parliament's right to change the English Constitution indicates that they didn't regard the Constitution as "an unchangeable body of governmental powers" **(E)**, although we can't be sure whether they had ever accepted that the king possessed the same right **(D)**.

85. (E) Global (Primary Purpose)

Sometimes passages will come with two Global questions associated with them. When this is the case, one question will usually be more abstract (and, hence, more difficult) than the other. Use your answer to the easier question to help you answer the more difficult one. Well, we've already seen that the Main Idea of the passage is that the colonists and English gave different meanings to the same political terms, which, in turn, led them to assign very different roles to similar political institutions, causing some political debate and disagreement between them. In more abstract terms, the passage explains a dimension of the relationship between the American colonies and England in the seventeenth and eighteenth centuries. So, choice **(E)** is the correct answer.

(A) sounds like something carried over from poor Goody and his misinterpretation of Athenian democracy in the previous passage. This passage discusses only the author's views, not those of other scholars; therefore, it can't be said to expose a misunderstanding about anything. Nor, for that matter, is there any hint that the author is trying to "settle a debate" about anything, so **(C)** can be just as quickly rejected. **(B)** is too narrow in scope: the brief glimpse we get of England's treatment of the colonies (and the reason for it) in the last paragraph can hardly be called the main focus of the passage. Finally, one wonders if anyone chose **(D)** and, if so, whether that person ever really *read* **(D)**. "Interpret the events leading up to independence"? American independence is maybe, *maybe* hinted at by lines 2–3, but that's it. At best, one might say that this passage explains some of the attitudes that later contributed to the development of the American *Constitution*. But that was 1789, and **(D)** points us to 1776, and the author is interested in neither one.

Passage 13: Bentham's Rules Of Evidence Reform
Questions 86–91

Though written in five paragraphs, this passage neatly breaks down into two halves at lines 26–28. Prior to that, on the **Topic** of evidence law, we've heard about the "extremely irrational" common-law rules of evidence that prevailed until the late 1700s, notably the refusal to allow defendants to testify, and how "unlikely that the truth would emerge" as a result of excluding such obviously (to our eyes) relevant evidence. The **Scope** of the passage is directed toward Bentham's revolutionary reforms in lines 1–2 (though the author knows that we cannot appreciate what Bentham proposed without the context of lines 2–26, which is why Bentham emerges so late in the text).

Lines 26–32 explain Bentham's broadly non-exclusionary prescription for solving the problem. The author spends paragraph 4 explaining some problems with Bentham's prescription—some evidence should be excluded that Bentham would permit—and devotes paragraph 5 to the upshot of it all: With exceptions, the general policy ("presumption" rather than a "rule") is that relevant evidence should be heard.

The Questions:

86. (B) Global (Main Point)

The right idea here must pick up on the topic and scope, and must reflect the author's view that Bentham had more or less the right idea, with reservations. That can only be **(B)**.

Bentham did do what **(A)** is saying, but this encompasses only the first 26 lines, not the nature of Bentham's reforms nor the author's critique of same. The author is content with Bentham's influence on the law today (lines 55–59) and so makes no call for the reexamination that **(C)** suggests. **(D)** hearkens back to the first sentence of paragraph 4 but otherwise fails to so much as mention Bentham, whose proposal to improve the rules of evidence is at the heart of the passage. **(E)** suffers from the same lack of focus on Bentham, who is the passage's principal character, and fails to recognize that thanks to Bentham the rules did change, resistant or not.

87. (B) Inference (Author's Attitude)

18th century law is discussed at length in lines 1–26, but 18th century law*yers* only come up once, in lines 24–26. The reform of the policy that the author has previously called "extreme in its irrationality" was "frustrated" by lawyers' self-interest and excessive reverence for the past. That's all critical **(B)**, but the words chosen aren't nasty enough to justify **(D)**'s "scornful." One wonders how the passage could possibly be written in order to make "sympathetic" **(A)** right and "respectful" **(C)** wrong or vice versa—two choices that are functionally identical must always be incorrect—but nevertheless each is

too positive in tone. "Ambivalent" **(E)** might be tempting if you misread the question as dealing with 18th century legal practice in general, because the author does concede some sanity, or at least modernity, in it. But the question is squarely pointed at lines 24–26, which couldn't be less ambivalent.

88. (A) Logic Function

The line reference appears in the context of the previous sentence which begins with "Further," indicating that it's continuing the previous thought—which was the idea of the entire fourth paragraph, that there were difficulties with Bentham's nonexclusionary principle. That's all you need to see to choose **(A)**.

Since the author is, in paragraph 4, questioning an aspect of a proposal of Bentham's from over 200 years ago, the tone of **(B)** is way off. Lines 49–50 mention examples of how Bentham's policy might contradict itself, not examples of a phrase associated with Bentham one sentence earlier **(C)**. **(D)** creates an unwarranted distinction in that "interests" and "values" are never separated in the way that **(D)** suggests. And contrary to **(E)**, the lines in question are acting as counterevidence to Bentham and not as examples of his views.

89. (B) Inference

The question stem is so broad as to cover the entire text of the passage, so there's no telling where the right answer will emerge. Best to go through them in some order and look for that which must be true. The passage's first sentence makes it clear that contrary to **(A)**, many long-established common-law rules remain. **(B)** emerges as the right answer in that it picks up on the thrust of the passage: Thanks in part to Bentham, modern law has been moved to accept more relevant evidence—hence appear "less rigid"—than did law in the 1700s. **(C)** is tricky. There are some aspects of common-law rules that are not in place today, notably the bizarre rule described in lines 6–8. But we cannot infer than any of the current rules in place do *not* date back to the common law. Remember, nonexclusion of evidence had been "demoted from a rule to a presumption" (lines 58–59). In other respects, as far as we can tell from the text, "most components of modern evidence law had been assembled" (lines 2–4) by the late 1800s—a fact that serves to knock out **(D)** and **(E)** as well, each of which misunderstands what was going on in that era. The 1800s are important in the passage because they saw the work of Bentham, nothing more.

90. (A) Global (Primary Purpose)

Correct choice **(A)** has its priorities straight; this passage exists because the author wants to show the usefulness as well as the limitations of Bentham's principle of nonexclusion of relevant evidence.

Choices **(B)** and **(C)** believe that the passage's purpose is to indict "an outmoded legal system" **(B)** or to paper over "inadequacies." Both choices are far too negative and lose sight of the focus on Bentham and his reforms, many of which remain in place, with the author's approval, today. **(D)** refers only to portions of lines 30–50, and not even all of those 21 lines at that. No contemporary proposal has either been made or dismissed **(E)**; Bentham's reforms date back to the late 1800s, less we forget.

91. (D) Detail

Bentham saw the "prefer[ence of] ignorance to knowledge" (line 39) as the alternative to nonexclusion, that is, the policy of letting in all relevant evidence, personal or hearsay or whatever. Since nonexclusion is the policy he favored, exclusion—or **(D)**—sums up what is meant by line 39's phrase.

Choice **(A)** is a state of affairs Bentham and our author would surely oppose, but it is not explicitly connected to the phrase in question. **(B)**'s "failure to weigh" is O.K., but we expect to read "failure to weigh all relevant evidence." **(B)** dribbles off into the inane and irrelevant "advantages of legal reform," so it qualifies as a 1/2 right-1/2 wrong choice. Bentham granted the exclusion of sacramental confessions **(C)**, so he would not indict those confessions as a preference of ignorance. And the phrase certainly doesn't apply to objections to Bentham's exceptions to his new principle **(E)**; this idea runs far afield of the specific context of lines 37–39.

Passage 14: Medieval Lawyers
Questions 92–99

Topic and Scope: Medieval religious lawyers; specifically, why medieval religious lawyers failed to enforce ethical codes of conduct among themselves.

Purpose and Main Idea: The author's purpose is to explain why medieval religious lawyers failed to enforce ethical codes of conduct. His specific main idea is that they failed to do so because they didn't have either the procedures or the will necessary to do so.

Paragraph Structure: Paragraph 1 reveals the passage's topic and scope. The first sentence of the text tells you that the passage is going to be about medieval religious lawyers, while the next couple of sentences narrow the text's scope to the issue of non-enforcement of ethical codes of conduct. The rest of this paragraph simply supplies some further details about non-enforcement. Up to this point, the author hasn't explicitly stated either his purpose or main idea; however, it's predictable that his purpose will be to explain why codes of conduct weren't enforced. If he isn't going to examine this question, why would he introduce the issue in the first place?

Paragraph 2 confirms this prediction. The author describes two possible reasons why medieval religious lawyers failed to enforce ethical codes: (1) ethical violations were rare and (2) medieval religious lawyers didn't have the necessary tools to police themselves properly. Note that while the author's purpose has now become clear, his specific main idea (i.e., what he believes) still hasn't been stated.

At last, the opening sentence of paragraph 3 introduces the passage's main idea: the author says that the latter explanation is the more compelling of the two. The rest of paragraph 3 and all of paragraph 4 supply more information concerning why the author believes that medieval religious lawyers were delinquent: in a nutshell, evidence from medieval court and church records backs up the claim that they were delinquent.

Paragraph 5 adds that medieval religious lawyers, under attack by the church for their failure to enforce codes of conduct, reacted defensively: instead of rooting out corrupt lawyers, they opted for group solidarity, thereby protecting those who violated legal ethics.

The Big Picture:

- On Test Day, a passage like this one—a passage in which the author's purpose and main idea aren't made explicit early on—should be left for later in the Reading Comp. section, even if its content and prose are as uncomplicated as the content and prose of this passage. In general, passages in which the author's purpose and main idea appear early on are easier to handle.

- Note the classic structure of this passage. The first paragraph introduces a "problem"—the failure of medieval religious lawyers to enforce codes of conduct. The second paragraph provides proposed "solutions" to this problem—the two possible explanations concerning lack of enforcement. The remaining paragraphs "solve" the problem—the author provides his opinion and evidence to support that opinion. On Test Day, you may well run into a passage that proposes a "problem," discusses possible "solutions" to the problem, and then "solves" the problem.

The Questions:

92. (C) Global (Main Point)

The phrase "main conclusion" in the question stem indicates a "global" question; therefore, you've got to look for the answer choice that incorporates the basic theme of the passage. Paragraphs 1–4 tell us that medieval religious lawyers failed to enforce ethical codes of conduct, while paragraph 5 indicates that their professional organizations were more intent on defending their members than in rooting out unethical behavior. Choice **(C)** captures the basic theme of the text.

(A) To the contrary. Paragraph 5 explicitly says that "outside criticisms," if anything, *discouraged* medieval religious lawyers from acting against unethical behavior.

(B) focuses on a detail in paragraph 3. The passage concentrates primarily on a shortcoming of medieval *religious* lawyers; it's not primarily devoted to a comparison of medieval religious and civil lawyers.

(D) focuses on a detail in paragraph 4. Again, this passage concentrates primarily on a shortcoming of medieval religious lawyers; it's only incidentally concerned with the sources of ethical standards for medieval religious lawyers.

(E) The passage doesn't say which came first: the professional legal organizations or the ethical standards that they were to uphold. Besides, this issue isn't at the heart of the passage.

93. (A) Detail

Since this question asks about medieval English courts, your mental roadmap of the passage should have guided you straight to paragraph 3, where those courts are discussed. Lines 42–43 say that "there was *some* overlap of personnel between the civil bar and the ecclesiastical bar." In other words, *some* lawyers served in both court systems. This suggests, in turn, that *other* lawyers served exclusively in either the religious or the civil court system.

(B) To the contrary. Lines 31–35 indicate that civil lawyers were more likely to initiate disciplinary measures against colleagues.

(C) and (D) are outside the scope of the text. The passage never refers to the disciplinary standards of civil lawyers in other parts of Europe (C). Nor does it say whether one English court system was modeled on the other one (D).

(E) Although lines 51–52 do mention that medieval church records in England are "extraordinarily rich," the author doesn't claim that these records are richer than those kept by the civil court system.

94. (B) Logic Function

Whenever a question asks about why the author has included a particular detail in the passage, the answer lies in understanding the context in which that detail appears. In this case, lines 14–16 tell us that the Florentine legal guild wouldn't permit its members to participate in disciplinary actions against fellow members. The lines just before these lines—that is, lines 13–14—state that some religious legal organizations tried to impede efforts to discipline members. The author mentions the Florentine guild, then, in order to illustrate (through a specific example) a type of behavior that he discusses in the previous sentence.

(A) What theory? The author never introduces or promotes any theory. He simply explains a phenomenon —the failure of medieval religious lawyers to enforce ethical codes.

(C) Line 13 indicates that *some* legal organizations tried to impede efforts to discipline wayward lawyers. Thus, the author doesn't mention the Florentine guild in order to highlight a *universal* phenomenon.

(D) To the contrary. The example of the Florentine guild *supports* the author's contention that some medieval legal organizations tried to impede efforts to discipline their members.

(E) What objection? The only perspective presented in the passage is that of the author.

95. (C) Logic Function

This question should be approached in exactly the same way as question 106: context is key. In lines 44–47, the author cites the medieval church as an organization that supports his argument that religious lawyers failed to deal with unethical behavior in their ranks. The example of the Council of Basel (lines 47–51) simply provides concrete evidence to show that the stance of the medieval church does indeed support his view.

(A) The Council of Basel, according to lines 47–51, instructed Cardinal Cesarini to find a way to get religious lawyers to adhere to ethical standards already in existence; this council had no role in establishing such standards.

(B) is outside the scope of the passage. The text never explicitly compares the reaction of the English church to that of other bodies regarding unethical behavior by medieval religious lawyers.

(D) is outside the scope of the passage, too. Lines 49–50 simply mention that ethical standards were set down by the Pope; they never *explain how* these rules of conduct were actually established.

(E) is also outside the scope of the passage. The text never describes *the development* of a disciplinary system to enforce ethical behavior. It just discusses why the system didn't work.

96. (A) Inference

The single reference to documented "disciplinary enforcement" against wayward lawyers occurs in lines 17–20. In these lines, we're told that all of the recorded instances of disciplinary enforcement involve cases brought by *dissatisfied clients* against their lawyers. Thus, choice (A) constitutes the ethical violation most likely to be documented.

(B) and (E) are instances of unethical behavior that would assist clients. In other words, clients wouldn't have protested these sorts of ethical lapses.

(C) and (D) are instances of unethical behavior that don't even concern clients. Thus, clients wouldn't have been likely to protest these sorts of ethical lapses.

97. (B) Logic (Parallel Reasoning)

In the context of paragraph 5, the phrase "professional solidarity" refers to the concept of protecting the profession (i.e., the legal profession) from the attacks of non-professionals (i.e., non-lawyers) at the expense of tackling an internal problem (i.e., unethical behavior by lawyers). Choice (B) reflects precisely the same notion of professional solidarity: journalism (a profession) is protected from the attacks of non-journalists (the public) at the expense of tackling an internal problem (bad journalism).

(A), (C), (D), (E) None of these choices reflects the ideal of protecting the "group" from "outsiders" at the price of condoning a "problem" with the group. Choices (A) and (D) might have been a bit tricky, though. (A) is wrong because it lacks the element of a cover-up: the teachers believe one of their own has been *falsely accused*. (D) is wrong because it involves members of *two different groups*: the government and the pharmaceutical industry.

98. (B) Inference

Medieval guilds in general, as opposed to medieval lawyers' guilds in particular, are mentioned only in paragraph 1; so, the answer to this question lies there. Lines 6–10 suggest that medieval guilds in general, contrary to the behavior of religious lawyers' guilds, enforced ethical codes of conduct. Put another way, they "exercised influence over the actions of their members."

(A), **(C)**, **(E)** are outside the scope of the passage. This text doesn't discuss matters prior to the mid-fourteenth century **(A)**. It also doesn't compare the ethical standards of guilds in general to the ethical standards of religious lawyers' guilds **(C)**. Nor does it discuss ethical codes on a city-by-city basis **(E)**.

(D) appears to be contradicted by the passage. If, as lines 6–10 suggest, medieval guilds regularly enforced standards, it's unlikely that they found it difficult to do so. In any case, there's no information in the text to suggest that they had trouble enforcing standards.

99. (C) Inference

This choice reflects the author's reasoning in lines 31–38, where he contrasts unfavorably the behavior of medieval religious lawyers with their contemporary civil counterparts.

(A) is too strongly worded. In line 10, the author says that it doesn't "seem" as if medieval lawyers upheld ethical codes. In short, the author isn't quite as certain about his conclusion as the word "untrue" would imply.

(B) The author bases his case for the poor behavior of medieval religious lawyers entirely on medieval evidence. He doesn't resort to comparisons with modern society.

(D) and **(E)** The author makes it clear throughout the text that he believes that medieval religious lawyers *weren't* scrupulous in their observance of ethical codes of conduct; and he bases his conclusion in part on documentary evidence.

Natural Sciences Passages

Passage 1: Risk Communication
Questions 1–6

Topic and Scope: Risk communication; specifically, the goal of risk communication and how it can be most effectively applied to meet this goal.

Purpose and Main Idea: The authors' purpose is to define and explain the concept and the goal of "risk communication," and then to propose a way in which this goal can best be met. The authors note the distinction between the "experts" and "lay people," (non-experts), and in the end support a people-centered approach: Since the goal of risk communication is to provide a basis for the public to make informed decisions about technological risk, risk communicators should take the knowledge and beliefs of recipients into account when developing their communications in order to ensure the successful transmission of their message.

Paragraph Structure: In paragraph 1, the authors describe what risk communication means to many producers of potentially harmful technologies: convincing an ignorant public that the new technologies are in fact *not* very harmful. Because some risk communicators operate under this principle, it's no wonder that lay people equate this notion of risk communication with "brainwashing."

The Keywords "Since, however" in the beginning of paragraph 2 suggest that a shift is about to take place. Indeed, the authors proceed to define the goal of risk communication, and suggest that the method of the communicators described in paragraph 1 falls short because they don't truly understand the public's perception of risk. Sure, lay people think differently about the subject than experts, but under some circumstances people demonstrate substantial knowledge about risks. Sure, some studies suggest that common people worry disproportionately about certain fears compared to others, but the authors go on to question the validity of those studies. The authors firmly establish themselves in paragraph 2 as "pro lay people"—given the right time and materials, the average person can understand enough about technological risk to make an informed decision.

Not surprisingly, the authors proceed to offer a recommendation in paragraph 3, indicated strongly by an assertion in the first sentence of the paragraph regarding what risk communication *should* entail: It should be formulated with people's pre-existing beliefs in mind. This will prevent miscommunication and make it less likely that the public will ignore the message because it is too difficult to understand. The radon example is offered as support for this notion, and the final sentence, featuring the always helpful Keyword "thus," provides a nice summary of the authors' overall point.

The Big Picture:

- The first sentence of each paragraph is often a "topic sentence"—pay careful attention to how each paragraph begins: Here, paragraph 1 offers a common start: "**To many** developers..." This kind of beginning often means that a theory or practice will be cited, one that the author or another party described by the author will evaluate or challenge. The first few words of paragraph 2 strongly suggest that the authors here are taking the challenge route: "**Since, however**..." And the first few words of the final paragraph, predictably, finish the story: "Risk communication **should**, therefore..." These topic sentences are very useful in nailing down the passage's scope and structure.

- Don't get bogged down on seemingly complicated concepts like "electromagnetic fields" or "radon in the home." You don't need to know *what* these are, but rather what they *represent* in the context of the passage. Here, these are simply examples of risks that the public may not sufficiently understand, and that may, according to the authors, require some explanation before effective risk communication can take place. Good critical readers understand the limits of what they're expected to know.

- The authors' main point doesn't always appear in the beginning of the passage, so don't tune out after paragraph 1. If you hang in until the end, there will always be clear signs as to why the passage was written, and that is, first and foremost, what you're trying to ascertain in your first reading of the passage.

The Questions:

1. (B) Global (Main Point)

The sentiment in **(B)** echoes throughout the second and third paragraphs. Line 16: "enable people to make informed decisions"; lines 45–47: know about the public's knowledge and beliefs "in order to design messages that will not be dismissed or misinterpreted"; lines 57–60: "produce balanced material that tells people what they need to know to make decisions." The authors repeatedly assert their belief in lay people's ability to make informed decisions regarding technological risk as long as they are prepped in the right way. **(B)** has all the elements of the authors' main idea.

(A) If anything, the authors would disagree with **(A)**, insofar as they recommend a different orientation for risk communication.

(C) distorts the authors' recommendation in the third paragraph: The authors believe that risk communicators should custom-design their messages to ensure that they're not misinterpreted, but this doesn't necessarily imply that the messages need to be *simplified*.

(D) expresses the belief of certain risk communicators mentioned in paragraph 1 (the "brainwashing angle"), but it is this very perception of risk communication that the authors challenge in the rest of the passage.

(E) is a small detail that is admitted by the authors in paragraph 2, but the authors go on to challenge its importance in the grand scheme of things. In any case, this is way too minor a point to represent the authors' overall main idea.

2. (A) Inference

The same concept discussed in the bullet point above leads us to the point here: Give the people the information necessary to make decisions. Present the relevant background of technological issues so that non-experts, the lay people, don't tune out or misunderstand. The "brainwashing" model of risk communication is faulty, according to the authors. All of this points to choice **(A)**: Explaining, not persuading, should be the primary purpose of risk communication.

(B) and **(E)** both smack of the mentality of the risk communicators mentioned in paragraph 1, those interested in persuading the public that risks should be ignored. The authors don't see risk communication's role as trying to promote or justify anything, **(B)**, but rather to get the facts on the table so that the people themselves can reasonably decide. And **(E)**'s "foster public acceptance" is even closer to the persuasive "brainwashing" approach that we know the authors disdain.

(C)'s "influence" is perhaps too strong a word for the authors' opinion regarding the role of risk communication, but **(C)** also has another huge problem: It gets the target audience backwards. Risk communication is not geared toward experts—it's created *by* experts for the sake of lay people.

(D) It is those risk communicators who aim to be persuasive who mention the distinction between the public's perception of exotic and mundane hazards, and the authors basically dismiss such studies as unreliable. Besides, according to the experts, lay people aren't much afraid of mundane hazards, so why would the authors see the alleviation of the *lesser* fear to be the purpose of risk communication?

3. (C) Detail

This answer comes right out of lines 42–43: "If they have erroneous beliefs, they are likely to *misconstrue* the messages." That is to say, the beliefs will remain intact and cause a misinterpretation, or as **(C)** has it, they will interpret the communication differently than it was intended.

(A) *Au contraire*: In this confrontation, it is the intended message that will undergo change, not the previous beliefs of the people.

(B) isn't as extreme as **(A)**, but it's wrong for essentially the same reason: There is no indication here that the people's prior mistaken beliefs will be affected at all by the introduction of new information; in fact, the opposite is suggested. The fact that lay people will bungle any message that conflicts with their beliefs strongly implies that their beliefs remain firm.

(D) begins on the right track—the people *will* misconstrue, that is, misunderstand the new information—but what's to say that they will *further* distort it when telling other people? There is no support for this next step, so **(D)**, promising at first, is out.

(E) It is inferable that the authors believe that messages that are *incomprehensible* may be dismissed, but we're interested in what happens when people have mistaken beliefs about the topic. Those people, as explained above, aren't likely to ignore the new info. Rather, they are likely to misinterpret it.

4. (D) Inference

The studies mentioned in line 8 are described fully in lines 8–11. While people pay little attention to "mundane," that is, everyday hazards that are in fact dangerous, they worry too much about "exotic" dangers that in reality are not as dangerous as the everyday hazards. We need to look through the choices for the example that seems to match this type of risk perception. It's doubtful that we can pre-phrase the exact examples that the correct choice will contain, but we can at least pre-phrase the *kind* of examples we're looking for: We want people to be all uptight about something that's interesting (exotic) yet fairly safe, and carefree about something routine yet dangerous. In general, then, we're looking for a somewhat irrational perception of risks.

(A) Nothing crazy about this: Skydiving is clearly exotic *and* dangerous, and it's perfectly reasonable to double- and triple-check the mechanisms.

(B) Smoking is surely dangerous, but it's hard to tell whether smoking can be characterized as exotic or mundane (maybe it depends on what movies we watch). In any case, like the skydiver in **(A)**, this person is making a rational decision based on a reasonable perception of risk, so this doesn't accord well with the studies cited.

(C) Cautious, maybe. But not crazy.

(D) Here's the loon we're looking for: Swerving in and out of traffic at high speeds is a dangerous way to engage in an otherwise mundane activity, yet despite the real danger involved the driver seems fairly unconcerned. Maybe that's because his psychic energy is spent on worrying about meteors hitting his house, an event that's, well, *very* unlikely. This is certainly a strange, perhaps inverted perception of risk, and it matches the kind of mentality described in the study.

(E) Ah, the old NIMBY defense—"Not In My Back Yard." This attitude may not be very socially appropriate, but there's nothing unusual about this perception of risk; it's another reasonable concern about a real danger.

5. (E) Inference

Next we're looking for a view likely to be held by the authors rather than the risk communicators of paragraph 1, and by now we know a lot about the positions of each. The risk communicators mentioned early on are those who favor the persuasive approach—convince the people there is no harm—and we know how the authors feel about that. Nonsense, they say: The people are not stupid; just give them the facts and they'll decide for themselves how to perceive the risks involved with new technologies. And in order to create effective risk communication in this mode, it's necessary to know what people believe, because they "process new information in the context of their existing beliefs." Another way of saying this is that lay people's values impact on how they perceive risk and on how risk communication should be implemented. Choice **(E)** is nicely in line with this point of view, and clearly in conflict with the attitude of the "persuaders."

(A) Possible reactions to "new or strange" technologies are not discussed by either group.

(B) distorts the authors' challenge to the study mentioned in the middle of the second paragraph: It is the experts who rig such studies such that lay people are forced to compare risks that aren't comparable, not the lay people themselves who have a "tendency" to do so.

(C) If "scientist" is synonymous with "expert" in this case, then this is an *au-contraire* choice: The risk communicators in paragraph 1, not the authors, think that people should simply take the advice of experts.

(D) The authors claim just the opposite—that under the right circumstances, lay people *are* able to rank hazards by annual fatalities with some accuracy. It would go against their argument to emphasize the public's *inability* to do this.

6. (B) Detail

There are a few places where we find out what lay people think, but there's only one place where we find out what some lay people think *about risk communication*, and that's paragraph 1. Again, the answer for this Explicit Text question is virtually given on the page; all we have to do is a little translating. The relevant lines are 12–14: "…many lay people see 'risk communication' as a euphemism for brainwashing done by experts." **(B)** says the same thing, only substituting "manipulate the public" for "brainwashing."

(A) Some experts believe that lay people focus too heavily on exotic, not mundane hazards. Lay people themselves don't express any view on this distinction in regard to their beliefs about risk communication.

(C) In this passage, lay people don't express any beliefs about the issue of accuracy in regard to risk communication. The only blame they seem to place on the practice is in relation to those who take the overly persuasive stance.

(D) and **(E)** remind us more of the authors' ideas than any notions we can attribute to lay people. The authors believe that risk communication *should* function to help people make informed decisions **(D)**, but there is no indication that lay people feel that it does in fact accomplish this. The same goes for **(E)**: The authors certainly seem to believe that the effectiveness of risk communication is impacted by the knowledge level of the public, but we have no way of knowing that the public itself feels this way.

Passage 2: Marie Curie
Questions 7–12

We can see right away that Marie Curie is the **Topic** of the passage and the **Scope** is Curie's ideas about radiation, but the **Main Idea** and **Purpose** aren't apparent in the first paragraph. Instead, the first paragraph describes Curie's efforts to understand the nature of radiation. She first uncovered the radioactive elements polonium and radium, and then attempted to explain the mechanism of radiation, but wasn't able to explain why or how radiation occurs because the rate of radiation seemed constant and spontaneous.

With paragraph 2, we get a better idea about the author's **Purpose**: to argue that critics are wrong to criticize Curie for not discovering the true nature of radiation. The paragraph goes on to explain one of the reasons that it was "impossible" (line 26) for Curie to do so: the radiation of lighter elements can't be observed in nature, since these elements finish decaying so rapidly, while other heavier radioactive elements decay so slowly that they are *only* present in radioactive form. The radiation of heavy elements thus incorrectly appears to be a different kind of process, rather than a different degree of a more common process. (The LSAT often tests your understanding of this kind of subtle distinction.)

Paragraphs 3 and 4 give another reason Curie could not have deduced the subatomic nature of radiation: physicists like Curie believed matter to be ultimately made up of irreducible units. This led Curie to the erroneous assumption that radiation occurred through the loss of atoms. It was not until the 1930s that radiation was discovered to be the loss of mass from the atoms themselves. We now have a good fix on the **Main Idea**: the entire philosophy of matter in Curie's time prevented her from discovering the true nature of radiation, but her contributions were central to later discoveries.

The Questions:

7. (B) Global (Main Point)

As usual, we identified the Main Idea as part of our critical reading of the passage: current scientific ideas prevented Curie from discovering the true nature of radiation, but her contributions helped lead to later discoveries. Although **(B)** doesn't address why Curie didn't find the nature of radiation, it acknowledges that her theory was "incomplete and partially inaccurate" and also that it was instrumental to later discoveries. This doesn't exactly match our prediction, but it still sums up the passage nicely.

Although the passage mentions quantum mechanics in passing, it can hardly be said to be part of the central idea of the passage **(A)**. The language of **(C)** is too strong—the author would never describe Curie's career as "blemished by her failure." Although Curie's view of the atom did prevent her from discovering the true nature of radiation, the author

would disagree with the statement that her research wasn't fruitful **(D)**, since it led to many other important discoveries. Curie's research led to discoveries about radiation, but it was quantum mechanics that allowed a more accurate understanding of the atom, so **(E)** is also wrong.

8. (D) Inference

Paragraphs 2, 3, and 4 all argue that Curie could not have made certain discoveries because of some very basic assumptions about matter made by the scientific community in Curie's time. Criticisms about Curie's understanding of radiation are thus unreasonable. **(D)** says exactly this.

(A) goes outside the scope of the passage, since we never see mention of obstacles in dealing with the scientific community. **(B)** again confuses why quantum mechanics is referenced in the passage—quantum mechanics led to a better understanding of the atom, which in turn led to a better understanding of radiation. The author never implies that quantum mechanics followed from the work of Curie. The author mentions the differing conceptions of the atom held by chemists and physicists **(C)** and implies that critics fail to appreciate why this was important to Curie's understanding, but he never intimates that critics were entirely unaware that these differing conceptions existed in the first place. The author is debating the criticism of Curie's understanding of the mechanism of radiation. We have no reason to believe these critics addressed Curie's discovery of the two elements mentioned in the first paragraph **(E)**.

9. (A) Inference

This question could be rather time consuming, since we have no way to research or predict an answer and the choices deal with several different areas of the passage. Luckily, we can find support for the very first answer choice—since polonium and radium are referred to as "previously unknown" (line 10), we can safely infer that scientists before Curie were not aware of the presence of these elements in pitchblende.

We know that even Curie was "unable to postulate a mechanism by which to explain radiation" (lines 18–19), so it makes no sense that the scientists before her would have specific ideas about how radiation arises **(B)**. **(C)** is one of many answer choices for this passage based on an incorrect understanding of why the author discusses the theories of physicists versus chemists in Curie's time. The author mentions the understanding of atomic structure held by each group, but never makes a distinction about concepts of radiation, so we can eliminate **(C)**. Though scientists did not fully understand the atomic nature of matter, we can't conclude that no research was being done in this area **(D)**, nor can we conclude that scientists felt uranium was the only radioactive element **(E)**.

10. (A) Global (Primary Purpose)

During reading, we already decided the author's purpose was to argue that critics are wrong to criticize Curie for not discovering the true nature of radiation. **(A)** describes this as a more general principle, and fits our prediction nicely.

Although the author declares Curie could not have known the true nature of radiation, he certainly doesn't argue that her conception was actually more correct than the present understanding, so we can dismiss **(B)**. The author spends very little time outlining currently accepted theories **(C)**, so this can't be the primary purpose. **(D)** might be seen to address some areas of the passage, but it introduces the idea of a debate, which doesn't really appear in the passage. More importantly, **(D)** makes no mention of the work of a particular scientist (Curie). The author never investigates the antecedents of Curie's work **(E)**. If you were tempted by this answer because you thought of Curie's work as the antecedent of present theories, you should notice that the author would never agree that the modern understanding of radiation is not an advance over Curie's work.

11. (C) Logic Function

Remember that we weren't able to identify the Main Idea in the first paragraph because it was so expository—it was a big information download that set up the playing field for the remainder of the passage. **(C)**, "the factual background for an evaluation of Curie's work," sums this up nicely.

(A) uses the word *narrate*, which doesn't quite fit, and also is too broad. The passage deals only with Curie's investigations. **(B)** is yet another wrong answer choice about physicists vs. chemists. There's no "conflict" between the groups, and the first paragraph certainly doesn't bear on the discussion, anyway. We can dismiss **(D)** since we weren't even sure of the author's Main Idea in the first paragraph, so we can't say that it outlines the central argument. **(E)** can be dismissed quickly, since the author of this passage would never dismiss the usefulness of Curie's work.

12. (A) Inference

Of course, your first move should be to reread the sentence: "...she was unable to postulate a mechanism by which to explain radiation." What was Curie trying to postulate? An explanation for how radiation works. In other words, "the physical process that underlies a phenomenon," choice **(A)**.

Nothing in the passage discusses an "experimental apparatus," so we can rule out **(B)**. We also know that scientists are not responsible for bringing about radiation (unless they're setting off bombs), so **(C)** doesn't fit here. We can also eliminate **(D)** as too specific, since Curie didn't know that isotopes' decay is the cause of radiation. **(E)** is a surprisingly tricky answer choice, since we often associate

theories with postulating. Note, however, that this is a very strange way to use the word *mechanism*. Although statement **(E)** might work in the passage, it's not an acceptable definition of the word *mechanism*.

Passage 3: Benefits Of CO_2?
Questions 13–20

As the title that we have applied to this passage indicates, the **Topic** is CO_2, and the **Scope** is the allegation, described in paragraph 1, that the expected global increase in CO_2 may in time both enhance the world's agricultural output, and even retard or reverse the very real threat to global warming, as all that new plant life sucks up more CO_2.

The **Purpose** is gradually revealed in paragraph 2 as the author lists all sorts of possible negative consequences of an increase in CO_2, and as you read you might have noted them in passing—lower crop yields (lines 20–25), encouragement of weeds (lines 25–27); changes in "ecosystem stability" (lines 29–35), the last illustrated by an extended example regarding weed growth and brushfires. The key realization is that all of these depressing prospects are meant to rebut the first of the two optimistic suggestions (lines 6–9). We should expect paragraph 3 to rebut the second, and it does: The question of whether increased CO_2 can slow or reduce global warming is posed in lines 36–40, and the rest of the paragraph answers it. Contrary to paragraph 1's rosy scenario, evidence exists that CO_2 would just keep increasing.

The Questions:

13. (C) Global (Main Point)

The right answer must address both paragraph 1's optimism and paragraph 2 and 3's pessimism regarding the benefits of increased global CO_2, and **(C)** does so, even alluding (in its last nine words) to the structure that differentiates paragraph 2 and paragraph 3.

(A) is a 180, as it represents the point of view in paragraph 1 that the author seeks to debunk. **(B)** is a distortion. Studies of plant growth have not been contradictory. Rather, studies agree that plant growth in general would be enhanced, albeit to the detriment of certain types of plants (lines 16–21). **(D)** is true, but a detail, and one that leaves out the key global warming issue. **(E)** is too pat and categorical, and loses sight of the author's purpose—to rebut the optimism detailed in paragraph 1 about increased CO_2.

14. (B) Inference

There's a lot of verbiage in the question stem, but the last two words are the key because they direct us to the proper paragraph. Yes, the hypothesis appears in paragraph 1, but its weakness in terms of global warming comes in paragraph 3. The "particularly important" (lines 56–57) observation that sums up the ultimate effect of CO_2 appears in lines 53–56 and is echoed almost verbatim by **(B)**.

(A) is a benefit of increased CO_2, not a drawback per se. **(C)** reflects the last sentence, which merely presents an illustrative example, and distorts it: Lines 56–60 assert that the *high-*

level latitudes will experience the greatest temperature increase. **(D)** assigns peat far too much importance, since as it appears in the passage it's merely part of the illustrative tundra example, and **(D)**'s phrases "change patterns" and "alter the distribution" are too fuzzy to reflect the passage as written. **(E)** is a detail used in paragraph 1 to support rather than undercut the hypothesis.

15. (A) Logic Function

This one is a slam-dunk to those who constructed a Roadmap. Indeed, both paragraph 2 and 3 share the same purpose, the one articulated in **(A)**.

The passage isn't about a problem **(B)** so much as a proposed bright scenario that the author wants to undermine. What paragraph 3 "explains" **(C)** is why the benefits of CO_2 won't extend to decreasing global warming. **(D)**'s word "support" makes it a definite 180. **(E)** is half-right, half-wrong. Paragraph 3 "raises a question that may cast doubt," all right, but not on paragraph 2's data. As noted above, paragraph 2 and 3 work hand-in-hand to achieve **(A)**'s purpose.

16. (D) Inference

(D) is a straightforward inference from lines 22–27, where Patterson & Flint come in. Certain crops (corn, sugarcane) "may experience yield reductions...because of the increased performance of certain weeds." That's what **(D)** is asserting.

No information as to Patterson and Flint's prediction about "most plants" can be found, so **(A)** and **(B)** are too broad (and **(B)** too apocalyptic) for this passage. That some crops with high photosynthetic efficiency may lose their growth edge doesn't imply that low-efficiency crops won't see their growth enhanced **(C)**. In fact, if weeds are low-efficiency, then **(C)** is 180 off, just as **(E)** is in its contradiction, more or less, of lines 22–25.

17. (A) Inference

The major element of paragraph 1's rosy hypothesis that the author believes to be correct, as confirmed by lines 16–18, is that through increased CO_2 plants' rate of photosynthesis could be "enhanced," or increased, and thus enhance plant growth "generally." That's what **(A)** asserts (and what wrong choice **(D)** contradicts, as a matter of fact). But **(B)** is wrong because based on paragraph 2 it looks as if "important crops" like corn and sugarcane will be negatively impacted, while weeds will be enhanced. **(C)** gets the author's main idea 180 degrees wrong: That's the position he believes to be *incorrect*. **(E)**, finally, refers to an element of paragraph 1 (lines 11–13) that the author seems to agree with, not dispute.

18. (A) Inference

Paragraph 3 is where tundra comes in, and the inference comes right out of lines 46–53 in particular. We're told that upon the melting of the permafrost, the decomposition of peat "liberated more CO_2," and that another 4°C increase in temperature "would liberate 50% more." The missing link in that equation is **(A)**: The author must believe that more peat would decompose. Where else, in the context of these eight lines, would the increased CO_2 come from?

(B) has it backwards—the peat decomposition *frees* CO_2 rather than absorbing it. The peat is already decomposing, so **(C)**'s suggestion that decomposition won't begin until a 4°C temperature increase makes no sense. And no comparisons to peat deposits elsewhere—their rate of decomposition **(D)** or their accumulation **(E)**—play any role in the passage.

19. (C) Inference EXCEPT

The four lines in question speculate that key, high-photosynthetic-efficiency crops may "lose that edge" after a major increase in CO_2. On that basis alone, **(A)** and **(B)** can both be quickly dismissed because they are explicit examples of low-efficiency plants crushing higher-efficiency ones. **(E)** doesn't mention efficiency explicitly, but its description of soil rendered less fertile and plants rendered fewer in number and weaker, all in the presence of high CO_2, certainly is consistent with lines 22–25. And so is **(D)**, in a different way. "Consistent," remember, means "non-contradictory," and for one of two grass species of equal efficiency to crowd out the other in a high CO_2 environment doesn't contradict anything the author says. But **(C)** explicitly does. In **(C)**, contrary to lines 22–25, high-efficiency trees in the presence of high CO_2 are outstripping the low-efficiency grasses.

20. (C) Detail

Not only is **(C)** the issue directly addressed by Billings' tundra research, but it's the question answered by the whole of paragraph 3, and indeed by the passage overall. Billings is the major test case presented by the author of the hypothesis that increased CO_2 could in the end help to reverse global warming.

(A) and **(E)** are both wrong for the same reason: The author never compares the conditions in specific earth habitats in order to make his case. **(B)** creates a serious distortion when it attaches the concept of "doubling" of CO_2 levels, way back in lines 1–3, to Billings' research, which in any case provides no precision as to rising temperature levels. (The 4°C figure is merely hypothetical, and merely deals with the tundra example.) **(D)**'s question, is answered—and in the affirmative—by paragraph 2, but not by Billings' research specifically

Passage 4: The Platypus's Bill
Questions 21–26

Topic and Scope: The platypus; specifically, recent research illuminating how its bill enables it to locate and catch prey.

Purpose and Main Idea: The author's purpose is to present the "new evidence" (lines 4–5) as to how the platypus uses its bill to find underwater prey, the Main Idea essentially being the combination of the reported findings of Bohringer and Scheich: One sensory receptor present in the bill acts as the main sensory organ, while the other picks up electrical impulses to sense prey at a distance.

Paragraph Structure: Two long paragraph's—but not to worry, structure is everything when it comes to science passages, and *everything* in this passage comes in twos: two paragraph's, two researchers, two types of sensory receptors found on the platypus's bill, two separate but related processes described. Everything, we can infer, is being presented in response to a mystery: How can the platypus—blind, deaf, and smell-less underwater—detect prey?

Paragraph 1 concentrates on the work of Bohringer, who examined the mechanoreceptors, the "pushrod" receptors found on the bill. Her finding—"supported by studies" (line 20)—is that the mechs are the main sensory organ of the platypus, more so than the limbs, eyes, or ears. But the paragraph ends with a question: How can the platypus detect prey at a distance?

Paragraph 2 reports, at length, Scheich's rather certain answer to that question. The platypus's motions are described, a hypothesis drawn (lines 39–41), and experiments done to test same. Presumably all prey emit electrical impulses, and the electroreceptors on the platypus's bill pick up on them.

The Big Picture:

- Don't be freaked out by scientific detail. What's more important than understanding it chapter-and-verse is having a strong sense of structure—of what's happening where. What's going on in each paragraph? What are the most important ideas? As long as you have a firm handle on the passage Roadmap, you should be able to go back and locate answers for individual questions with little effort.

- Many science passages begin as this one does: "Such & such is known. What is [or has been] *not* known, is...."

The Questions:

21. (B) Global (Primary Purpose)

The passage lives up to the promise of lines 3–8, and that's just what **(B)** summarizes.

(A), **(D)** Both refer only to paragraph 2—to Scheich and the question left open (lines 26–28) at the end of paragraph 1.

(C), meanwhile, refers only to paragraph 1. Bohringer no more deserves pride of place in a Global right answer than Scheich does.

(E) is a purpose taken up and achieved in lines 10–14 alone. The rest of the passage concerns the *function* of those pores, the key issue that **(E)** ignores but that **(B)** celebrates.

22. (B) Global (Main Point)

This question piggybacks right onto the previous one. The recent research mentioned in question 20 **(B)** reveals that the bill is the part of the platypus that locates prey.

(A) is the conclusion drawn by Bohringer in lines 18–20 and supported through line 26. If that's the Main Idea, then what are lines 26–56 there for?

(C) The electrical stimulation of the bill comes up in paragraph 2 only—again, too limited a focus for the Main Idea. We must keep in mind that it's the *use* of the bill that concerns both neurophysiologists and our author.

(D) is something that, according to sentence 1, has been "long known."

(E) is the "conclusion" only in the sense that it's the point at which the passage ends. But **(E)**'s claim about the platypus's response to electric fields is but one detail in an elaborate process that takes up the entire passage and that is summed up by **(B)**.

23. (E) Detail

"Which...occurred *before*"—this question implies that we are to keep an eye on chronology, and on the chronology of paragraph 1 because that's the domain of Bohringer. The language of the question stem appears in lines 25–26, and one awesome Sequence Keyword is there to help us: "[N]erve impulses from the motor cortex *then*" (emphasis Kaplan's). That "then" means that whatever precedes those nerve impulses has to have been described immediately prior to line 25; and that's where we find the substance of **(E)**. A signal is "sent by way of the fifth cranial nerve to the neocortex and from there to the motor cortex."

(A), by evoking the fifth cranial nerve, sounds a lot like **(E)**, and perhaps if you chose **(A)** it was because you neglected to read **(E)** altogether. That's a pity, because **(A)** includes a glaring error. Remember, in paragraph 1 Bohringer is studying the effect of the *mechano*receptors, the "pushrods," on the platypus's activity. It is *tactile*, not electrical, stimulation that paragraph 1 and, implicitly, question 18 are concerned with. The role of the *electro*receptors is the domain of Scheich in paragraph 2.

(B) See lines 25–26. The bill's snapping occurs *after*—really as a result of—the nerve impulse's reaching the motor cortex.

(C) There are those electroreceptors again. They play no role in the Bohringer research in paragraph 1, as far as we know.

(D) Nothing in the passage indicates that the pores ever "open" at all, whether by design or accident.

24. (C) Logic (Parallel Reasoning)

This question has a kind of Parallel Reasoning feel to it. We are looking for an experiment analogous with that of Scheich in paragraph 2, which means we need to re-read lines 41–50. Placing a small battery in the water triggered a switch in the platypus behavior from "patrolling" to "searching," which led Scheich to believe that those bill electroreceptors are sensitive to the electrical charges of prey. Well, if you use electricity to confirm whether an entity senses electricity, what's the best way to confirm whether an entity senses heat? Use heat. **(C)** has the right analogy.

(A) goes wrong because of the decoy element: Scheich didn't put out fake shrimp to lure the platypus.

(B) errs in its evocation of "echoes." What Scheich is trying to prove is that the platypus senses the electrical impulses of its prey, not that it's somehow picking up its *own* electricity by indirection.

(D), like **(A)**, goes wrong in establishing the idea of a decoy or replica.

(E) would be analogous if Scheich had placed bait in the water to lure the platypus. But he didn't. He placed a battery— an artificial generator of the same kind of force that, he hypothesized, the prey generates. That's a far cry from **(E)**, but it is **(C)** in a nutshell.

25. (C) Inference

"Patrolling behavior" is mentioned but once, at line 43; but "searching behavior" is mentioned twice, and it's that phrase that proves to be the key to the question, as the former behavior is shown to precede the latter. According to lines 42+, Scheich realized that "he could trigger the switch from patrolling to searching behavior" by setting up his battery charges. This parallels the earlier assertion (lines 31–34) that the platypus "swims along... *until prey is discovered. It thereupon switches to searching behavior*" (emphasis Kaplan's). Inferably, then, when it patrols the platypus swims until potential prey is detected, which means when the prey sets off its electrical charge. That's **(C)**.

(A) According to lines 33–37, "searching behavior... is followed by homing in on the object and seizing it." So **(A)** is a later, not earlier, step in the process.

(B) The differences between prey never come into play.

(D) Scope shift! The mechanoreceptors are part of Bohringer's experiments in paragraph 1, and in any case those are tactile (rather than electrical) receptors that, as the author says, "[do] not explain how the animal locates its prey at a distance," which is what it's doing when it's patrolling.

(E) Plausible-sounding, perhaps, but it's established (lines 7–8) that the platypus doesn't smell when it's underwater.

26. (B) (Global (Organization of Passage)

As abstract-structure questions go this one is far from the toughest, and that's because this passage's structure is close to the simplest: We find out what's been learned about the platypus's bill and its hunt for prey (lines 3–8), and then find out how scientists arrived at their conclusion. **(B)** has it exactly right.

(A)'s language about "supporting examples" would be more appropriate to a passage about, say, how various sea creatures use their bills to survive. We would hear about the platypus, yes, but also about other creatures and how their behavior bolsters a theory. "Supporting examples" carries a different connotation from "supporting evidence," and the latter is what occupies our author's attention.

(C) "An argument" is not evidence. This author presents the evidence for a conclusion, as **(B)** says. In any event he has no interest in "defending" anything. He is reporting on the work of others.

(D) No opposing views are laid out and no reconciliation is made. This choice seems to refer to the distinction between Bohringer's work and Scheich's, but while we know that their findings may be separate, they are nonetheless complementary rather than in opposition.

(E) No amendment takes place, at the end of the passage or anywhere else.

Passage 5: Volcanoes and Climate
Questions 27–34

Topic and Scope: Volcanic eruption; specifically, the relationship between world climatic conditions and the spreading of a volcano's dust and sulfuric acid that can persist for years.

Purpose and Main Idea: The author's purpose is to use the Mass and Portman data to combat the idea that there is, as has been generally believed, a strong connection between volcanic eruptions and climate. The Main Idea turns out to be that eruptions seem to have little or no effect on *global* climate but may well have a significant if indirect effect on the climate of a particular *region*.

Paragraph Structure: Paragraph 1 recounts the long-held belief that the dust veil and sulfuric acid thrown up by a massive volcanic event can muck up Earth's climate. Anecdotal facts are recounted. But no sooner has paragraph 2 acknowledged the "plausibility" of the volcano-climate connection than the author conjures up Mass and Portman to shoot it down. The problem is the El Niño phenomenon, and you don't have to follow all the details in paragraph 2 (or live in Southern California, for that matter) to get the idea that El Niño is a weather event whose effects can both "mask" (hide) and "mimic" (duplicate) the kind of cooling trend traditionally associated with the aftermath of a volcanic erruption.

Then, paragraph 3 explains what Mass and Portman found when they separated the effects of El Niño from contemporary temperature data: Small volcanic eruptions didn't disturb temperature at all, and big ones lowered hemispheric temperature only a tiny amount.

So, is the whole volcano-climate connection idea wrong? Not according to the "other researchers" cited in paragraph 4, who bring up the distinction between global climate change and *regional* change. The latter, they seem to believe, can certainly be affected by an eruption, and the paragraph goes on to speculate how, to wit, the process by which the slight temperature drop that an eruption might precipitate could essentially remove summer from parts of the U.S. and Canada. This process is called a "feedback loop," and even if that term seems depressingly technical, the idea of a "loop" or circle can readily be seen in the way in which lines 41–42 begin the example of "a small temperature drop" and end at line 56 with a mighty cold "year without a summer."

The Questions:

27. (D) Global (Main Point)

If you try to prephrase the author's main point—as you always should—you have to figure that it's got to encompass two ideas: the fallacy of the widely held belief that volcanic eruption can significantly impact world climatic conditions and the possibility (in paragraph 4) that volcanoes can affect *regional* climate. Only **(D)** touches both bases. Regional temperature is paragraph 4 only, so **(A)** leaves out two-thirds of the passage. Because the passage details that volcanoes' influence on global temperature is minimal whereas their possible influence on a region is large, **(B)** qualifies as a 180 choice—getting the passage emphasis exactly backward. **(C)**, too, is a 180. The author couldn't do more to diminish the effect **(C)** describes. Finally, **(E)** has an element of a 180 in its distortion of a key detail. The "researchers" of line 5 tended to overestimate the effects of volcanic eruption not because they "exaggerated" the effect of such phenomena as El Niño, but because they overlooked or discounted it. Besides, **(E)** *is* focused on detail and not on the big picture.

28. (E) Logic (Parallel Reasoning)

El Niño's warming effect, lines 23–26 point out, can either mask the cooling of a volcanic eruption or mimic it. After its effect is subtracted, the eruption's climatic impact is seen as minimal. Because subtracting El Niño leads to a logical distortion, ignoring a huge alternative explanation for certain climatic conditions, we want this in our analogous situation. We find it in **(E)**. Before you decide that a population's average age has changed because of a higher birth rate, you'd better check out other plausible explanations such as the one **(E)** suggests. Maybe many of **(E)**'s immigrants are old enough to cause the higher average age all by themselves; maybe the birth rate is in fact stable. Ignoring those immigrants would be like ignoring El Niño.

(A) is not a case of misleading data. Actually, it would be physically impossible to not take into account a package's entire weight when trying to weigh the contents, unless you were to remove the contents and weigh them separately, in which case the package's overall weight would be of no interest to you. If you wanted to count the number of coins in a pile, **(B)**, it would be entirely appropriate to ignore their monetary value. It's difficult to imagine, without technical expertise alien to the LSAT, how not taking into account lens magnification, **(C)**, would affect determining an object's shape. Size, maybe, but the shape is what it is. **(D)** is trying to make a straightforward computation and not, as in the stimulus and **(E)**, trying to figure out the effect of some phenomenon.

29. (D) Detail EXCEPT

The important thing here is that you restrict your analysis to paragraph 2 and the early part of paragraph 3, the only places in which El Niño comes into play. From lines 18–29, we basically get four facts about El Niño, and not coincidentally, those four facts have been turned into the four wrong choices. Lines 18–22 say that El Niño warms the surface of the Pacific and hence—choice **(C)**—"warms the atmosphere." Paragraph 2 continues by noting that an El Niño can "mask the cooling brought about by" a volcanic eruption—that's **(B)**; and then it

Passage 6: Dolphin Deaths
Questions 35–42

Topic and Scope: Dolphins; specifically, the massive death of a whole bunch of bottlenose dolphins over a one-year period.

Purpose and Main Idea: The author's purpose is to evaluate two distinct hypotheses for the great dolphin die-off of 1987–88, and the Main Idea turns out to be that the second of the two described is more plausible, largely because a set of facts that supports the second theory is at odds with the first one.

Paragraph Structure: Paragraph 1 is utterly factual in nature, telling us about an unprecedented one-year die-off of Atlantic bottlenose dolphins that took the lives of between 1/4 and 1/2 of all of the creatures at that time. Paragraph 2 is factual too, informing us about brevetoxin that was present in only 8 out of 17 dolphins tested, and synthetic pollutants that were present in almost all 17.

Given that very discrepancy, we may be surprised to note, in paragraph 3, that the research team ended up citing brevetoxin as the major cause of the die-off, but so they did. The paragraph goes on to outline the team's hypothesis that the *P. brevis* alga led to a brevetoxin buildup, and lines 32–40 outline the resulting, sad series of greater and greater medical problems that, to the research team, solves the mystery.

Then, whammo: Promptly (if politely), paragraph 4 attacks the researchers' conclusion just described, in a series of rebuttal arguments helpfully labeled "First," "Second," and "Finally." The last of those three—the comparison of the unknown effects of brevetoxin with the known effects of PCBs, lines 47–52—does double duty, both closing the door on the team's hypothesis and opening the door to the author's; and the rest of the passage lays out his contention that synthetic pollutants were to blame, a hypothesis that the facts favor.

The Big Picture:

- As you read, always take note of the difference between the facts the author reports and the conclusions that he or she draws from them. The latter, of course, will always be more important. Don't get discouraged if the author's point of view doesn't come up until late (here, line 41!). Hang in there. Sooner or later, *why* the author is taking up all of this factual material will be revealed.

- As always, resist the temptation to get bogged down in detail. Understand the broad lines of argument (here, the basic situation; the team's hypothesis; and the author's hypothesis), and don't worry about mastering all of the stats and biochemical terminology. Instead, wait for the questions to tell you how deeply you have to get into the supporting material.

The Questions:

35. (D) Global (Primary Purpose)

The author's desire to explore why the dolphins died in such unprecedented numbers in 1987–88 should be clear by line 24. To be sure, the author's desire to assess *two different* hypotheses isn't totally revealed until the very end, and hence we cannot be 100% comfortable with **(D)** until, say, line 52. But even before paragraph 4, **(D)** is the only one that gets the scope right. Look what we get in the wrong choices:

(A) describes, at best, the purpose of paragraph 1 only. By line 15 the author is already going beyond **(A)** to assessing *why* the creatures got infected and died.

(B) is too broad—it fails to focus on the 1987–88 die-off—and is inaccurate to boot: The research team *incorrectly* diagnosed the illnesses.

(C) If the team's "research methodology" were at fault, the author would reject its data. Yet he not only accepts the data, but uses them to support the hypothesis he favors. What he finds fault with is the team's *conclusion*, which is a very different thing from **(C)**.

(E) is, like **(B)**, too broad in ignoring the specific 1987–88 die-off. And the reference to "various" pollutants suggests a passage in which each pollutant's effect is listed and evaluated, which is far from what we get here.

36 (E) Detail

The final paragraph explanation of which the question speaks is the "alternative hypothesis" in lines 52–60, the idea that somehow a huge amount of synthetic pollutants "triggered a cascade of disorders" in the poor dolphins. The principal evidence for this hypothesis, as noted above, is provided simultaneously with the rebuttal of the research team's explanation, especially in lines 47–52's suggestion that brevetoxin may have less to do, and PCBs more, with the dolphin die-off. In those lines we hear about the deleterious effects of PCBs on various organs, all of which amount to that "cascade of disorders." As it happens, correct choice **(E)** singles out liver function among that group, though it could just have validly mentioned immune deficiency or skin lesions.

(A) Paragraph 3 says (lines 32–37) that the metabolizing blubber reserves released *pollutants*, not brevetoxin. And even if **(A)** were accurate, it wouldn't support the explanation in paragraph 4, because in paragraph 4 our author is downplaying brevetoxin's role in the disaster.

(B) The calendar is used (lines 45–47) to rebut the research team's hypothesis, not to beef up the author's. No date on which offshore dumping took place is mentioned—indeed, the fact that the author doesn't cite a specific date might be seen as a weakness in his explanation.

(C) Similar to **(B)** and the date: Location is used (lines 42–45) solely to cast doubt on the research team's explanation. While almost all the dead dolphins contained PCBs in their system, their source is unclear; no such dumping sites as **(C)** mentions are identified.

(D) might on quick appraisal seem plausible, since it mentions synthetic pollutants. But lines 52–56 explicitly indict "a sudden influx of pollutants" as the likely principal culprit, not any PCBs that may or may not have been ingested in the dolphins' diet. Back in paragraph 3, remember, it was *brevetoxin* present in the diet that was thought to cause the die-off—in the discredited hypothesis, at any rate.

37. (A) Logic (Parallel Reasoning)

In paragraph 3 the author relates the evidence that the research team found for its brevetoxin hypothesis, but it's not until paragraph 4 that he reveals his point of view on the team's reasoning, which is of course that their rather sound evidence does not lead to their conclusion; rather, it supports a very different hypothesis from the one the team came up with. This is almost exactly repeated in **(A)**.

(B) Unlike the astronomer in **(B)**, the author seeks to undercut someone else's theory, by coming up with a better one of his own.

(C) The passage features no revision of evidence that would be necessary for **(C)** to be an appropriate analogy.

(D)'s emphasis on action—the doctor prescribing medication—has no parallel in the passage. **(D)** would be a better choice if it read, "A doctor makes a correct diagnosis using a patient's chart from which a colleague made an earlier misdiagnosis."

(E) totally loses sight of the author's disagreement with the conclusion that the team drew from the evidence compiled in paragraph 3.

38. (A) Logic Function

Most "organization of a paragraph" questions are relatively easy to pre-phrase, and this one may be easier than most, given the paragraph's opening sentence (lines 41–42), the Keywords "First," "Second," and "Finally," and line 52's "An alternative hypothesis." All of that suggests that the author is simply moving from a detailed critique of one explanation, to the presentation of another and better one. And that's choice **(A)** all the way.

(B) The argument that paragraph 4 refutes is summed up in paragraph 3, and it's refuted primarily through counterevidence. **(B)** mucks all of that up.

(C) would make for an interesting and elaborate paragraph, but it's not this one. Once the author finishes his objections to the research team's hypothesis, it's dropped in favor of the new one.

(D) gets it all wrong. The paragraph begins with evidence that weakens a theory, not one in its favor, and the theory is subsequently tossed out.

(E) Where does this "third explanation" come from?

39. (E) Inference

What would the author agree about brevetoxin? The very wording of the question strongly suggests that we are looking for an opinion, rather than a statement of fact, about the toxin formed by *P. brevis*, and the most obvious opinion the author holds is the unlikelihood that brevetoxin was the primary cause of the dolphin die-off. And darned if they didn't choose that as the right answer. Contrary to the research team's findings, the author concedes only that the toxin "may have been a contributing factor" (line 57), but the toxin cannot have been Cause #1 because the "unusual bloom of" *P. brevis* only occurred months after the die-off. This is what we get in **(E)**.

(A) creates an unwarranted distinction between the animals' skin lesions and bacterial infections. They're not separated in the author's discussion, so we cannot make any inferences about a comparison between them. Also, nowhere does the author say that brevetoxin "could not have contributed" to the dolphins' poor health. Quite the contrary; see line 57.

(B) Even if the ease of formation of brevetoxin were within the author's scope—which it is not—there is nothing to link the formation of the toxin with the presence of pollutants. As far as we can tell, *P. brevis* blooms and creates brevetoxin, and that's all she wrote.

(C) is a half-right, half-wrong choice: The latter portion of **(C)** is on the money—this particular die-off is not the direct result of brevetoxin poisoning—but nowhere is brevetoxin directly linked with liver function and damaged immune system. The author specifically goes out of his way to say that "the specific effects of brevetoxin on dolphins are unknown..." (lines 47–48). This choice just grabs a bunch of terms from the text and hopes that you'll find all the familiar words tempting. We hope you didn't.

(D) Their common phrase "It is unlikely" may have made both **(D)** and **(E)** stand out, initially. But in conrast to **(D)**, line 57 comments that "brevetoxin may have been a contributing factor."

40. (E) Inference

The question stem directs us squarely to paragraph 3, where the research team's conclusion and evidence are discussed. From here, it's best to attack the choices:

(A) Other marine animals are outside the scope here.

(B) distorts the reference (lines 24–25) to the normal absence of *P. brevis* on the Atlantic coast. *P. brevis's* presence is cited by the research team as evidence for the brevetoxin hypothesis, but there's no sense that the brevetoxin was deadlier simply *because* the alga is rarely found there.

(C) "Usually" kills this choice handily. The evidence here deals with *one* (and atypically massive) dolphin die-off; no inference can be made about bottlenose dolphin disease in general.

(D) is closer to a statement of the author's preferred explanation for the die-off, than an inference suggested by paragraph 3. Remember, the team's explanation in paragraph 3 is that brevetoxin was, in fact, the source of the creatures' initial emaciation.

(E) refers to blubber, and so do lines 32–37, where we read that among other effects, the dolphins' metabolizing of their blubber reserves released "stores of…accumulated…PCB's, which further exacerbated their condition." This directly supports **(E)**'s inference that PCB's stored in the blubber may be less dangerous than when released, especially since (lines 37–40) the "combined impact" led to the dolphins' death. So **(E)** is correct here.

41. (C) Logic Function

Dolphins and the Gulf of Mexico are dragged in as part of the first piece of counterevidence (labeled "First") to the research team's brevetoxin hypothesis. Dolphins and *P. brevis* share the Gulf, but no such massive die-off as occurred on the Atlantic coast in '87–'88 has ever been noted there, which to the author works against the team's conclusions. **(C)** spells this out pretty explicitly.

(A) Who has asserted that dolphins avoid *P. brevis* areas? Maybe they should, if they knew what was good for them, but no one has made this assertion so why would our author seek to "refute" it?

(B) No such comparison is raised, and indeed, the presence of PCBs and other synthetic pollutants may or may not be a factor in the Gulf of Mexico; it's never mentioned.

(D)'s implication that the Gulf of Mexico is "relatively pollution-free" is utterly unsupported by the text. What the Gulf has been free of is massive dolphin die-offs. It could be polluted as can be, for all we know.

(E) The author is out to show that *P. brevis* was most likely *not* the primary cause of the die-off. **(E)** misunderstands the author's purpose at that point (lines 42–45) in the paragraph, which (again) is to cast doubt on the team's hypothesis.

42. (D) Detail

We need a piece of evidence that is explicitly supportive of both the (discredited) brevetoxin explanation and the (author's) PCB explanation. Where better to seek such a thing than lines 47 and beyond, where the latter is described and the former polished off (and where we've located the answers to at least 3 questions thus far)? One more time: The author sees synthetic pollutants as the major cause of death (lines 57–60), brevetoxin as *perhaps* a contributor. The research team, on the other hand, while crediting brevetoxin as the first domino in the chain, goes on to point to "synthetic pollutants…which further exacerbated" [the dolphins'] condition [and]…made the dolphins vulnerable to [their]…ultimate cause of death" (lines 36–40). Since the "combined impact" of brevetoxin and PCBs gets the nod from the research team, while the author credits PCBs mostly, **(D)** meets the question's demands.

(A) As noted earlier, in the discussion of question 35 **(D)**, the author's hypothesis makes no mention of a dietary contributor to the dolphin die-off.

(B) As noted in our discussion of question 40, the Gulf of Mexico makes a brief appearance solely to provide counterevidence to the team's explanation.

(C) The red tide bloom of October, 1987 may well have contributed to the problem from the research team's point of view (though the fact that the die-off began maybe 5 months earlier is cited as a weakness of that hypothesis). But nowhere does the author cite that bloom as relevant to *his* explanation.

(E) is tricky, because it's both explicitly cited as part of the team's conclusions (lines 37–40) and generally consistent with those of the author. But you cannot run away from the stem's demand for a factor "*explicitly cited…in both theories.*" Mere consistency is not enough. **(E)**'s massive immune failure is simply not present in lines 52–60, and it would have to be so for **(E)** to be correct.

Passage 7: Environmental Crisis Perspectives
Questions 43–47

Topic and Scope: Environmental crisis; specifically, the way the debate over of the environmental crisis has changed over the last 100 years.

Purpose and Main Idea: The author's purpose is to describe the change that has taken place from 100 years ago to the present, in the debate over industry's impact on the environment. The main idea is that the "extreme polarization of views" characteristic of today's environmental debate is a relatively new thing, and is bound to make dealing with the environmental crisis even more difficult.

Paragraph Structure: Paragraph 1 offers some history on the environmental debate; the author notes that awareness of the crisis *itself* is not new and goes back at least 100 years. In response to growing environmental harm and growing pessimism about the ability for society to deal with such harm, environmentalists have lashed out at industry. These "accusatory polemics" have provoked a backlash by industry. The author then adds her own opinion: This "polarization," that is, the extreme hard line taken by each group today, is only going to make it harder to deal with the environmental crisis than was the case 100 years ago.

Paragraph 2 sets up a contrast between the relationship between reformers and industrial supporters 100 years ago and their relationship today: Back then, the reformers and industrialists were pretty much on the same page in that they both recognized the problem, and shared in the confidence that solutions were at hand. The author cites the example of Marsh, who decried environmental hazards posed by industry yet didn't receive any backlash from industrialists; in fact, they mostly agreed with him.

Paragraph 3 goes on to explain *why* the industrialists and entrepreneurs of the later 1800's agreed with Marsh and didn't fight him: Inherent in Marsh's critique was the notion that improvement of the situation was inevitable. He never fought the idea that harnessing the power of nature was desirable; he only railed against the bumbling techniques employed. The industrialists agreed with his general message—that what they were doing was fine and good, but they must learn to do it better, with less damage to the environment. Marsh didn't point fingers, and the corrective actions he suggested didn't entail much sacrifice on the part of industry. This all explains why there was little or no conflict 100 years ago between reformers and industrialists.

Not surprisingly, the final two paragraphs tell the other side of the story: how the relationship between the reformers and industrialists turned adversarial. According to paragraph 4, it happened around the 1960's when Clements' equilibrium model began to hold sway. This posed an entirely new philosophy: Leave nature alone; it's at its best when man

doesn't interfere; technology can only destroy nature. No wonder the industrialists turned reactionary: This philosophy runs directly counter to their aims, and we now understand better the evolving rift between the two groups.

Paragraph 5 simply fleshes out the equilibrium model, and notes its influence on the environmentalist movement. It reinforces the difference between twentieth-century reformers' vision of nature and the earlier Enlightenment vision of nature.

The Big Picture:

- We might expect the author to follow up on her opinion expressed at the end of the first paragraph, but essentially she doesn't. The rest of the passage deals mostly with the history of the debate, and is not directly about how solving the problem is harder now than in the past. So while this passage promises at one point to take on an opinionated tone, it is for the most part descriptive.

- When a debate is introduced, strive to determine where the author stands on the issue, if he or she even takes a stand. Here, the author doesn't explicitly take sides, but does state that the extreme nature of the debate itself, the "polarization" she refers to, will make it harder for industry to respond to a situation that "demands action." Although we may expect a stronger opinion on the debate itself, her main concern is how and when this polarization evolved.

- Learn to recognize time clues and to understand what they tell us regarding the author's concerns. In the first sentence, the author says that a current debate is not new. She then goes on to speak about the nature of the debate in the 1860's, and then jumps to the debate in the 1960's. All of this strongly suggests that the author's purpose is to describe an historical development, a notion that helps bag a few questions directly.

- Think ahead as you read, and always pay careful attention to structural signals. The word "Why?" as the first word of paragraph 3 can only mean one thing: The author in this paragraph is going to explain the phenomenon of the previous paragraph, namely, *why* there was no apparent conflict in the late nineteenth century between environmental reformers like Marsh and the leaders of industry. Anticipating the author's next move and using structural signals can help you to incorporate each paragraph into the gist of the unfolding story.

The Questions:

43. (D) Global (Main Point)

We begin the set with a standard Main Idea question, and the Idea was discussed above. In the first two sentences, the author presents the notion that while the debate over the environmental crisis is not new, the extreme polarization of views characteristic of the crisis today *is* new. The rest of the passage supports this point: She tells us about how the debate used to be, and how it has since changed to the type of debate we may be familiar with today. **(D)** captures the notion of this "recent polarization" in the environmental crisis, which is the primary notion the passage was written to express.

(A) Never does the author put forth a recommendation of what should be done. The passage is mainly descriptive; it describes the evolving nature of a debate. The closest the author herself comes to stepping away from pure description is when she laments, in paragraph 1, that the "sad effect" of the polarization of views will be to make it more difficult to deal with the crisis. But even this is not a full-fledged call to action as **(A)** would have it.

(B) is certainly suggested in the passage, but tells only half, or even less, of the full story here. **(B)** might be correct if the passage were entirely about Clements, his theory, and his followers. But Clements and the convictions of recent ecological reformers are presented to highlight the new nature of the environmental crisis as a whole.

(C) seems to mix things up: Marsh heavily influenced the debate in the 19th century, not today. In paragraph 3, the author states that "Marsh's emphasis on future stewardship was *then* a widely accepted ideal," and we hear no more of Marsh as the debate shifts to the present.

(E) is also in line with Marsh's critique as discussed in paragraph 3, but falls way short of representing the overall main idea of the passage. This choice could only fly if the author were setting out an indictment—but she isn't.

44. (A) Logic Function

The elements of the "mystique" of Clements' model are given immediately after the lines cited in the stem: Interference was taboo, the wilderness adored, technology vilified. Calling the model a "mystique" is meant to reinforce just how strongly the ecological reformers accepted and clung to this model, almost as if in worship. The somewhat exotic phrase "ecological mystique," then, is meant to convey this great devotion to Clements' model, or, as **(A)** puts it, to "underscore the fervor" with which reformers have taken to this model.

(B), (E) There's no such connection stated between the equilibrium model and scientific research or the scientific community. The model seems to contrast with the rational worldview of the Enlightenment, and it would therefore not be likely that the model would need support from "empirical

scientific research" or gain acceptance in the scientific community.

(C) deals with the specifics of the model itself, while the phrase "ecological mystique" speaks to the reception the model received from adherents and their strong devotion to it.

(D) deciphers the word "mystique" as "mystery," as in "the theory is so mysterious, we don't know what it means." No such misunderstanding is implied at all, as the strong and direct impact of the theory on reformers discussed in the remainder of the final paragraph shows. The equilibrium model is understood fine by reformers; the word "mystique" is meant to suggest the influence it attained among them.

45. (E) Inference

Continuing with Clements' equilibrium model, we're asked to locate the case among the choices that accords best with this model. Well, we're familiar with its tenets as laid out in paragraph's 3 and 4—leave the environment alone; technology is bad—so it's simply a matter of seeing which choice reflects these principles. **(E)** is perfectly in line with this "hands off" approach: *set aside* land, *maintain* it as wilderness, *prohibit* extraction or use of the land's natural resources. Clements and his followers would surely approve.

(A), (C), and **(D)** All three clearly violate the spirit of the equilibrium model, which is against tinkering with the environment and certainly against technological interference. Each of these choices proposes just the sort of tinkering and interfering that adherents to the Clements model seek to avoid.

(B) The equilibrium model is founded on the notion that the best thing to do is to leave nature alone, and that on its own, nature itself will bring about a favorable state of affairs regarding stability and diversity of organisms. Presumably, adherents to the model wouldn't want any interference from industry. While they may not be averse to "corrective measures," such measures wouldn't necessarily constitute an application of the model.

46. (C) Inference

What would Marsh and today's reformers agree on? Well, remember, although Marsh had a different overall philosophy than current reformers, he did consider the environmental damage caused by industry to be a serious problem, and one worthy of attention. Even though he essentially supported the philosophy of industry, he did believe that industry was doing a bad job of harnessing the resources of the earth, and was thus "despoiling" the planet in the name of greed. The same concept is used to describe the current reformers' position in paragraph 4: "*Despoliation* thwarted the culmination or shortened the duration of this beneficent climax . . ." Both Marsh and the current reformers, then, feel that human despoliation has caused damage to the environment—choice **(C)**.

(A) Marsh probably agrees with **(A)**, as he believed that reforms would spring from industry's natural self-interests. But we have no way of knowing how today's reformers would feel about how regulation would impact on industry's self-interest; this topic is never discussed in light of the current reformers.

(B), like **(A)**, this is an explicit notion of Marsh's as detailed in the third paragraph. But as for current reformers, we don't even know if they believe that a solution is possible; in fact, a more pessimistic outlook is hinted at in the 1st and 4th paragraphs. We know that they think a "hands off" approach is best; but to say that they believe that *solving* the environmental crisis won't be difficult and costly is going a bit too far given the information presented.

(D) is a little extreme for either side. While we may reasonably infer that Marsh, in his pro-industry stance, may have placed economic priorities on equal footing with environmental concerns, we have no actual evidence that he believed these concerns to be equal. The current reformers would seem even less likely to consider economic growth to be as important as environmental improvement, but again, we're given no hard data on this comparison. All in all, then, there's no way we can say that the two groups would agree on this issue.

(E), like **(A)** and **(B)**, comes right out of the philosophy of Marsh, but it concerns an issue that we can only guess about as to the reformers' opinion (and if we did propose to guess, our guess would be that the reformers would *not* agree with Marsh on this point anyway).

47. (D) Global (Primary Purpose)

We leave this passage with one last Global question, this one concerning the author's purpose. Nothing new here; we've seen early on that the author set out to describe a debate, or rather, to detail how the nature of a debate has changed over the course of roughly 100 years. She starts out by saying the current debate, i.e. the conflict of viewpoints, is not new. She then proceeds to discuss the history of the debate, and how the issue came to stand as it does now. **(D)** hits every angle of this: The author does sets out to provide background on the current debate, and to chart its progress to the present. The tone is right on target as well; the author is mostly content to tell us about the debate without jumping into the fray herself.

Many of the wrong choices go astray by attempting to attribute too much to the author's intentions:

(A) While we may look on the equilibrium model as one possible solution to the environmental crisis, it's not even presented as such; it's presented only as the current reformers' view of the best course of action. But is this their overall "solution" to the problem? Do they even have a full "solution"? We don't know. But even if we deem this model a "solution," this is only a small part of the passage, ignoring the historical and evolving relationship between the environmentalists and reformers that occupies the lion's share of the author's attention. If **(A)** *were* intended to represent the author's purpose, how differently the passage would read: "Here's one possible solution advocated by so and so. Now here's another . . ." and so on. This is not what we get.

(B) The author doesn't set out to reconcile the two "polarized" viewpoints; she merely tries to show how and when the viewpoints *became* polarized, and that it wasn't always that way.

(C), **(E)** As we've noted over and over, the author doesn't take sides here. She never attempts to determine which side of the debate is more *persuasive*, nor does she attempt to expose weaknesses of one of the parties to the debate.

Passage 8: Status Signaling Among Birds
Questions 48–54

Topic and Scope: The status signaling hypothesis; specifically, the extent to which this hypothesis is supported by observable evidence.

Purpose and Main Idea: The author's purpose is to describe the extent to which the status signaling hypothesis is supported by observable evidence. Since this passage is descriptive rather than argumentative, the author presents no specific main idea of her own.

Paragraph Structure: Paragraph 1 provides a lot of background information on the relationship between the fighting prowess of birds and their access to resources, like food and shelter. Essentially, this paragraph notes that there's a positive relationship between the two—the better a bird is at fighting, the greater its access to resources. However, as the paragraph also notes, actual fighting is potentially costly to birds, so they've developed external indicators of fighting ability, such as plumage type, which allow them to gain access to the amount of resources their fighting prowess commands without having to engage in actual violence in order to acquire those resources. Up to this point, you can't really make any firm predictions about where the passage is headed, except to note that it's likely to continue to probe the relationship between indicators of fighting prowess and access to resources.

At the beginning of paragraph 2, we're told that this relationship is known as the "status signaling hypothesis" (SSH). The remainder of paragraph 2 and all of paragraph 3 are devoted to a discussion of whether Rohwer's experiments with Harris sparrows support the SSH. Rohwer, we're told, believes that his experiments support the notion that a direct relationship exists between indicators of fighting ability and access to resources. The author, on the other hand, contends that Rohwer's experiments don't support the SSH.

In paragraphs 4 and 5, the author contends that experiments with the greater titmouse provide much greater support for the SSH. In this case, unlike that of the Harris sparrow, she asserts, there is a strong correlation between plumage type and access to resources.

The Big Picture:

- Like most LSAT science passages, this one contains a lot of details. On Test Day, when you tackle the science passage, don't focus on the details. Instead, try to grasp the basic process or relationship—in this case, the SSH—that all science passages are built around. Most of the questions will focus on this process or relationship.

- It's especially important to make a mental roadmap of a science passage. Since the passage will most likely involve rather complex ideas and details, you'll need to refer back to it regularly; and you don't want to waste a lot of time by repeatedly scanning the entire passage for specific ideas or details.

The Questions:

48. (B) Detail

Your roadmap of the passage should have led you back to paragraph 1, where the SSH is explained. An "external signal," according to lines 14–16, permits a bird to communicate its status to others of its species, thus gaining access to the resources commanded by its status, without having to engage in actual fighting with others of its species.

(A) and **(D)** are outside the scope of the passage. The SSH concerns the relationship between fighting ability—as indicated by external markers—and access to resources. It isn't concerned with mating behavior **(A)**. Nor is it concerned with the relationship between *different* species **(D)**.

(C) An external signal could just as well increase a bird's access to resources—if the signal it displays indicates to other birds that it occupies a high (as opposed to a low) status within the flock.

(E) An external signal is simply an *indicator* of a bird's fighting ability. It doesn't increase or decrease that fighting ability.

49. (A) Logic Function

In the first sentence of paragraph 3, the author claims that Rohwer is wrong to conclude that plumage variations in Harris sparrows support the SSH. In the rest of this paragraph, which includes her own discussion of the plumage variations in adult and juvenile Harris sparrows, the author simply supports her conclusion with factual evidence.

(B) To the contrary. The author claims that plumage variations in Harris sparrow's *do not* support the SSH.

(C) The author takes issue with Rohwer's conclusions, not with the SSH.

(D) In paragraph 4, the author suggests that the greater titmouse is a more appropriate species for studying the SSH than the Harris sparrow.

(E) is outside the scope of the passage. The text focuses on the validity of the SSH, which has nothing to do with "age-related differences" among birds. Lines 35–38, in fact, explicitly say that age-related differences have no relation to the SSH.

50. (B) Logic (Weaken)

The experiment in question was intended to test the effect of breast-stripe width on titmouse behavior. In order for this experiment's results to be valid, all variables other than breast-stripe width must be held constant across all of the dummies. If the dummies varied, say, in size as well as in breast-stripe width, there'd have been no way to tell whether the titmice were responding to the dummies' breast-stripe or their size.

(A) There's nothing in the passage to suggest that titmice from different flocks would respond differently to the dummies.

(C) There's also nothing in the passage to suggest that juveniles are inherently more aggressive or submissive than adult titmice.

(D) The issue isn't whether the food in the tray was authentic, but how badly the titmice in the experiment wanted the food in the tray and what they were willing to do to get it.

(E) The issue isn't physical violence per se, but aggressive vs. passive behavior in response to breast-stripe width.

51. (A) Global (Organization of Passage)

Paragraph 1 presents the Status Signaling Hypothesis itself. Paragraphs 2–3 discuss and evaluate Rohwer's study, which tested the SSH, while paragraphs 4–5 discuss and evaluate the titmice study, which also tested the SSH.

(B) The SSH is an *explanation of* a natural phenomenon; it isn't a natural phenomenon. Moreover, the rest of the passage is devoted to discussions of tests of this *single hypothesis*, not to different explanations of a natural phenomenon.

(C) The passage discusses tests of the SSH, not the *underlying causes* of the behavior it purports to explain.

(D) What scientific conundrum (i.e., problem)? And where's the history of this conundrum?

(E) What opinions *against the validity of the SSH* are presented? And where are the experiments that support these opinions? Rohwer's experiments, although they don't support the SSH, weren't necessarily intended to undermine this hypothesis.

52. (E) Detail

This question deals with Rohwer's study, so your mental roadmap should have sent you back to paragraphs 2–3, where his study is discussed. Lines 17–19 indicate that Rohwer himself believes that his experimental results support the SSH. In lines 25–26, however, the author contends that his results don't support this hypothesis; the rest of paragraph 3 explains why she believes this to be so.

(A) What other issues? The author never mentions that Rohwer's results have relevance for issues other than the SSH.

(B) The author doesn't claim that Rohwer revised the SSH. She simply claims that his experimental results don't support the *existing* hypothesis.

(C) We're not told anything about what Rohwer set out to do. Again, the author says only that his experimental results failed to support the *existing* hypothesis.

(D) According to the author, Rohwer tested the *existing* hypothesis.

53. (D) Inference

This question probes the logic behind the SSH, so your roadmap should have sent you back to paragraph 1, where the SSH is explained. Indeed, lines 1–7 assert that there's a relationship between fighting ability and social status: birds that are able to fight effectively have high social status within the flock.

(A) Throat plumage, according to the passage, is an issue only among one species of bird: the Harris sparrow. Besides, according to the passage, dark throat plumage isn't a mark of high status per se among members of this species, but rather is a mark of age.

(B) and (C) are outside the scope of the passage. The text never probes either the connection between social status and body weight (B) or the connection between social status of parents and offspring (C).

(E) The passage never says that high status birds are likely to suffer *frequent* injuries. Indeed, high status birds should be able to *avoid* frequent injuries by avoiding fights (by communicating their status to other birds through external signals).

54. (B) Inference

Lines 31–32 state that adult Harris sparrows have higher status than juveniles. We already know, from previous questions, that the higher a bird's status, the greater its access to resources. Hence, it's inferable that adult sparrows are favored over juveniles with respect to access to food supplies.

(A) Lines 35–37 say that plumage differences *don't* signal status within age groups.

(C) According to paragraph 3, adults have higher status than juveniles. The text doesn't qualify this conclusion by saying that darker-throated juveniles have equal status to lighter-throated adults.

(D) and (E) are outside the scope of the passage. The text never compares the aggressiveness of adult and juvenile Harris sparrows (D). Hence, there's no basis for concluding that juveniles are more aggressive. Likewise, the passage never compares the aggressiveness of Harris sparrows and greater titmice (E). Hence, there's no basis for concluding that greater titmice are more aggressive.

Passage 9: African Drought
Questions 55–60

Topic and Scope: Sub-Saharan West Africa's drought; specifically, a hypothesis that explains why sub-Saharan West Africa has been caught up in a long and severe drought.

Purpose and Main Idea: The author's purpose is to describe and assess a widespread hypothesis (the "cooling" theory) about the cause of sub-Saharan West Africa's drought; the author's main idea is that this hypothesis is unconvincing.

Paragraph Structure: Paragraph 1 sets out the basic hypothesis: A cooling of the Northern Hemisphere has caused the drought. Paragraphs 1 and 2 explain the reasoning behind this hypothesis. Essentially, atmospheric dust has reflected sunlight away from the ground, lowering the Northern Hemisphere's air temperature, which, in turn, has affected wind patterns, ultimately leading to less rainfall in sub-Saharan West Africa. Moreover, this detrimental development, proponents of the hypothesis believe, might be long term.

Paragraph 3 shifts gears from description to opinion. In this paragraph, the author basically says that the hypothesis is refuted by the meteorological facts.

The Big Picture:

- This passage contains a mass of details. Don't worry about assimilating all of them during a first read through. Instead, get a sense of each paragraph's purpose. This way you'll know instantly where to find the details that you may need.

- It's sometimes easier to grasp a complicated scientific process if you create a picture of it in your mind. Passages like this one that have long descriptions of a process are very susceptible to this strategy. Even non-meteorologists and non-geographers can get an adequate sense of the cooling hypothesis if s/he pictures the process mentally.

- Tough passages often have easy questions. Don't blow off a tough passage because you think that you won't be able to answer any of the questions. You'll be sacrificing some easy points if you do.

The Questions:

55. (B) Global (Main Point)

This choice encompasses the passage's topic (African drought); scope (a widespread hypothesis about the cause of the drought); and purpose (to describe and take issue with this hypothesis).

(A) *Au contraire.* The author says that the "cooling hypothesis," which is based on the role of atmospheric dust, is "not well supported" by the meteorological facts.

(C) focuses on a detail in paragraph 2, not the passage as a whole.

(D) Like **(C)**, this choice focuses on a detail in paragraph 2. Besides, this view is held by proponents of the "cooling hypothesis." It's not the author's view.

(E) is beyond the scope of the passage, which offers no information about when the African drought is likely to end.

56. (B) Inference (Author's Attitude)

In paragraph 3, the author says that the "cooling hypothesis" is "not well supported"; and he offers a number of meteorological facts that appear to undermine it. But he knocks the hypothesis in a very restrained tone. That's why "cautious skepticism" is a better description of his attitude than "vehement opposition" **(A)**.

(C) The author's not "ambivalent" about the hypothesis. Lines 48–50 suggest that he gave it some credence at some point, but that's only the slightest of suggestions.

(D) and **(E)** suggest that the author's a proponent of the hypothesis. That clearly isn't the case.

57. (D) Detail

Lines 33–34 is where this "circumpolar vortex," so called, is first mentioned; and what "is causing" (line 32) it? Lines 30–32 tell us. Expansion of the circumpolar vortex, according to those who endorse the "cooling hypothesis," occurs when there's a growth in the temperature differential between the tropical latitudes and more northerly latitudes.

(A) focuses on the tropics exclusively—no can do.

(B) distorts a detail in paragraph 2. If anything, the circumpolar vortex might expand if there's *heavier* than normal snowfall for an extended period.

(C) is beyond the scope of the passage, which doesn't mention temperature differentials between water and land.

(E) The significant difference is between the tropical latitudes, on the one hand, and the middle and high latitudes, on the other.

58. (A) Inference

Note that the question asks specifically about Northern Hemisphere *landmasses*, not about the Northern Hemisphere in general. That makes the information in lines 8–12 relevant here, and clearly those temperatures declined after 1945. **(A)** just describes that the other way round: Temps were *higher, before.* Incidentally, information in lines 58–63 isn't relevant because it refers to the Northern Hemisphere in general.

(B) Since we're not given actual figures, we have no way to compare the pre-1945 period to the 1980s. All we know is that temperatures were warmer in both eras than they were between 1945 and the early 1970s.

(C) Lines 8–12 state otherwise.

(D) and **(E)** We aren't given the actual data that would permit either comparison.

59. (D) Global (Organization of Passage)

Paragraph 1 sets out the "cooling hypothesis," which addresses the cause of the African drought; the rest of paragraph 1—as well as all of paragraph 2—describes the hypothesis and its supporting evidence; and paragraph 3 disputes the hypothesis.

(A) An opposing point of view—the author's—isn't presented until the end of the passage. The formal hypothesis comes first.

(B) The author's view and that of proponents of the "cooling hypothesis" aren't reconciled; they're simply discussed.

(C) The author questions the "cooling hypothesis," but he never "amends" it. As far as we know, he simply rejects it.

(E) What second theory? The author doesn't offer one of his own.

60. (E) Inference

Lines 36–40 indicate that those who endorse the "cooling hypothesis" believe that the sub-Saharan drought has been caused by a shift in normal wind patterns. This shift, they contend, has kept monsoon rains from reaching the sub-Saharan region. Thus, they would probably say that the return of such rains means that wind patterns have returned to normal.

(A) *Au contraire.* According to supporters of the "cooling hypothesis," an increase in ice and snow coverage would be likely to keep the rains at bay.

(B) *Au contraire aussi.* Again, according to hypothesis advocates, such a development would likely perpetuate the sub-Saharan drought.

(C) Hypothesis advocates never directly link conditions in the tropics with sub-Saharan rain.

(D) Another *au contraire* choice. Lines 36–40 identify this development as part of the causal chain of sub-Saharan drought.

Passage 11: Mathematics As Language
Questions 67–71

Topic and Scope: Math as language; specifically, whether language is fixed or changing, and the implications of that for using math to convey scientific knowledge.

Purpose and Main Idea: Well, this is about as dense a passage as has ever come down the LSAT pike—the kind of passage for which the concept of *gist* was invented. The gist of the author's purpose is to describe the debate over the nature of language, and then to touch upon the impact of that debate on how mathematics (the basis of scientific explanation) can be used and understood.

Paragraph Structure: The passage gets dense right away, but let's keep our heads and *transform* it into something manageable. Paragraph 1 is all about how mathematics is used as the "language" in which science is explained. Math meets the common definition of language, after all (lines 4–6), and thus "tells" scientists things when applied to "some aspect of the world" (line 12). The phrase "Some thinkers hold..." is the problem here, because those with LSAT experience are used to anticipating "But *other* thinkers believe otherwise," a contrast that never comes; lines 3–6 turn out to be a sentiment that the author flatly agrees with and uses as evidence. But that's a trap that should cause only momentary aggravation at worst. By the end of paragraph 1 we simply need to have gleaned the idea that "math is the language of science."

Paragraph 2 begins with a helpful sentence, helpful in that it cements for us the topic ("the issue of scientific knowledge") and scope ("At the center of the issue...[are] questions about the relationship between language and what it refers to.") Then we *do* get a "Some argue X/Other argue Y" construct, and it hinges on the issue of whether the meaning of language is fixed, solid, and essential, or whether it's fluid and dependent upon common agreement. (Even on a superficial level one can begin to see the implications of this debate in terms of paragraph 1. If language is fluid, and if math is a language, then how can math be used with precision?)

Paragraph 3 also begins helpfully, in that the author announces himself squarely in the second, "fluid" camp. Language in *most* disciplines, we're told, depends on what's going on in the disciplines themselves and will vary over time. Why should scientific "language" be any different?, asks sentence 4, and the rest of the paragraph goes on to reply "It shouldn't and it isn't." The sense of the rest—and it *is* difficult, no doubt about it—is that math isn't so much a precise statement, as an imprecise metaphor or analogy that will work until a better one comes along. Unsure about exactly what he's talking about? Doesn't matter; we have the gist of it. Let's plug on.

Paragraph 4 announces the change of scope right away: "the implications of this theory" (line 45). The author implies that in non-science fields, such as literature and history perhaps, a dilemma exists: If words have no fixed meaning, then what can we truly learn from spoken or written language? And by the same token, in science—where math, lest we forget, IS the "language"—what can we really learn from $E = mc^2$, a seemingly precise "equation" which, according to the author's theory, isn't precise at all, but a bunch of vague metaphors that may change over time? (This is more or less what we speculated at the end of paragraph 2. See above.) Anyhow, the author concludes by intoning that science hasn't begun to explore those questions. Fortunately, we don't have to explore *any* of it any further. We just want the payoff (in points) of having mastered this thing.

The Big Picture:

- "Transformation." That's what we need to do with every passage, especially the ones that employ difficult concepts in difficult language. Boil it down to simple terms—transform it into something you can mull over—and don't worry if you can't make sense out of every single point. Trust that the passage wouldn't be on the LSAT if it weren't, on some level, do-able. Hang in there, THINK about the basic ideas, and the rewards will be waiting for you.

- Always be on the lookout for phrases like "Some thinkers hold..." (line 3). Recognize that they *usually* indicate that a contrary view is coming up, but also keep in mind that (as in this passage) the author can surprise you.

- Often when a passage is of greater than average reading difficulty, the editors will see to it that the opening of each paragraph gives special help. So it is here. Keep that in mind when you encounter a tough passage; expect the 1st sentence of each paragraph to provide real assistance. Let that be an anchor for your technique and your confidence.

- Check out, in advance, how many questions a passage carries with it, and let that guide you in your strategic attack on the section. This one only comes with 5 points attached, and certainly one or two of those have to be low-to mid-difficulty, answerable on a pretty superficial level. So attack such a passage with a sense of breezy fun. It's just not worth getting all bent out of shape over. Even if you absorbed it all—unlikely, given the time constraints—there'd be no real payoff for all that exhausting work. So chill. Concentrate on topic, scope, and purpose, and on paraphrasing the sentences that most communicate the author's views. And that will be enough for the lion's share of points. To wit:

The Questions:

67. (D) Global (Main Point)

(D) has it all. It gets the topic and scope right (the difficulty of using math to acquire and describe scientific knowledge), brings in the author's often-discussed parallel to the use of language in other disciplines, and even hints at the issue raised in paragraph 4's last sentence—the issue in which scientific inquiry has been deficient.

As usual, each of the wrong choices includes serious errors of omission and commission that should allow us to settle on **(D)** even if we are unsure about **(D)**'s strengths:

(A) According to the author, mathematics *is* a language, but **(A)**'s claim that science must rely on both language and mathematics seems to imply that they are different. Moreover, from paragraph 1 on the author is scrupulous to restrict his main focus to math and science. "Language" is used to illuminate certain problems in scientific awareness.

(B)'s reference to some math being more precise than other math has no relationship to the passage's ideas. The contrast set up in paragraph 3 is clearly precision vs. imprecision.

(C) The future "progress" of science, as a concept, never appears in the text, nor is there any reference to "abandon[ing] the pursuit of new knowledge." And what "scientists must [do]" is deftly spelled out in **(D)**; it has nothing to do with **(C)**'s talk of going back to *past* knowledge to decide how we figured it out originally—whatever that means.

(E) According to the last sentence of the passage, the question of the function of mathematics in the acquisition of knowledge "has yet to be significantly addressed." The author wouldn't congratulate linguists for beginning a discussion that hasn't happened.

68. (A) Logic (Strengthen)

This is one of the tougher ones, partly because the choices are all long and dense and remarkably similar, and partly just because it's a logic question ("support the view that"). The key is recognizing that the view we need to support— "that language has an essential correspondence to . . . things"— is the *first* of the two theories described (lines 18–21) in paragraph 2. In this view, language is fixed and precise. This means that you need to search for a choice indicating language to be "solid and reliable," and you don't have to search for long, because **(A)** does the job. That two *independently*-developed languages categorize objects in the very same way supports the notion that there's something unchanging and definite about the relationship between words and objects; even two totally independent languages both pick up on the same things.

(B) Close but no cigar. Close to **(A)**, in fact; darned close. But if one of the two similar languages derived from the other, as **(B)** suggests, then we can't infer from them that language

has a *universal* dimension. The linguistic categories common to both of **(B)**'s languages could be unique to them, with no relationship to those in other languages, in which case the *second* hypothesis wins support.

(C), even more so than **(B)**, connects the linguistic categories within *one* unique language and leaves out its correspondence with other languages.

(D) Highlighting "sentence structure" seems a little narrow for a passage about general theories of language. But worse than that is the way in which **(D)** narrows its attention to societies that have scientific sophistication, because that starts to smack of the *second* theory's concept of "agreed-upon conventions." Maybe those very sharp societies have linguistic agreement that differs totally from that which is found in the more backward ones—thus weakening, rather than supporting, the idea in question. To put it another way, theory 1 would gain more credence if the sentence structure in *all* societies, regardless of how advanced they were, was similar or identical. But that brings us back to **(A)**, doesn't it?

(E) is outside of the scope. What speakers of a language *believe* their language to do or be is irrelevant to whether language does, in fact, have a universal dimension.

69. (B) Detail

Even students driven daffy by the middle of the text will hopefully recall that the passage begins with the very definition for which this question asks, lines 3–4. **(B)** substitutes "collection" for "contrivance" but is otherwise verbatim.

(A), **(E)** In theory 2, language *is* metaphor (lines 38–44), relying on agreed-upon conventions (line 23). But does it *define* language? No one's agreed on that, even less on whether mathematics meets that criterion.

(C) is a concept from theory 1, not necessarily relevant to math and *certainly* not presented as a sheer definition of language.

(D) refers to the way mathematics is used in science, not to what makes math a language. The power to explain is the function and beauty of language but not, insofar as the passage is concerned anyway, its definition.

70. (B) Logic Function

The first sentence of paragraph 3 makes it clear that the paragraph's topic is theory 2, the one described in lines 21–24, and if you're wondering whether the author strays from it, take note of the signposts: "According to linguists who support this view," (lines 26–27); "These linguists argue that" (lines 29–30); and "Under this view," (line 38). These Keyword phrases alone tell us that all along, paragraph 3 is embroidering the theory that language is fluid and a matter of convention—of course, **(B)**'s "elaborate" is more of an LSAT word than "embroider."

(A) *Au contraire*, **(A)** evokes theory 1 not 2.

(C) is wrong in asserting that paragraph 3 is a compare/contrast vehicle between the two theories. In fact, theory 1 is left behind by the time we get to paragraph 3, and it's no wonder: Inferably theory 1 poses fewer problems for the idea of math as language (if it's precise, it's precise, right?). The author's real interest is in whether language is in fact vague and changing, and that's why he devotes all of paragraph 3 (and paragraph 4) to that issue.

(D) According to the last sentence (lines 54–55) the debate in science has barely begun, so it's hard to see what **(D)** is talking about, let alone define paragraph 3 in **(D)**'s terms. What paragraph 3 *does* do is show that the same linguistic issues may apply in science as elsewhere, but that's the "elaboration" to which correct choice **(B)** refers.

(E) hearkens back to paragraph 1. By paragraph 3 we're exploring just what *kind* of language mathematics is.

71. (A) Inference

An extrapolation question. There's nothing about balls, red or otherwise, in the passage; instead we have to apply the passage's ideas to this concrete example. But which ideas? The key is to check out lines 21–24 and recognize that we're talking theory 2 here—the one that believes language to be un-fixed, a matter of common agreement. To those holding this view, the English sentence "The ball is red" is true simply because all English speakers agree upon what "ball" and "red" mean. That's **(A)**.

(B) The issue is why "The ball is red" is true, not whether there might or might not be better ways of saying it, e.g. "The sphere is scarlet."

(C) *Au contraire.* "Essential correspondence" is part of theory 1, not 2.

(D)'s entity vs. property distinction isn't a key element of *either* theory.

(E) "The ball is red" is a conventional-language sentence that is true for different reasons, depending on which theory one supports. That has nothing to do with mathematics, which is a parallel but totally different aspect of the passage.

Passage 12: Wegener's Theory of Continental Drift
Questions 72–78

This Natural Science's passage is an attractive candidate for the first passage to attack in this section. The author's voice is strong and clear right from the very beginning. Add in the organization of the passage into four paragraphs, as well as a payoff of seven questions, and this is a passage to jump on.

In paragraph 1 (only five lines long!), the author announces the **Topic** (Wegener's theory of continental drift), **Scope** (the theory's struggle for acceptance), **Purpose** (to describe the controversy surrounding the eventual acceptance of Wegener's theory), and **Main Idea** (Wegener's theory revolutionized science and is well-accepted today, but that acceptance came following significant struggle and controversy).

Paragraph 2 brings us information about the controversy, specifically Jeffreys's rejection of Wegener's theory that Africa and South America were pieces of a single, ancient supercontinent, which had drifted apart. Note the author's disdain for Jeffreys's opinion, which was based on "casual" observation of shorelines on a globe.

Because we know that Wegener's theory is currently well-accepted and we know that the author has no respect for Jeffreys's opinions against the validity of the theory, we are looking forward to evidence supporting the theory. The author does not disappoint us.

In paragraph 3, the author discusses Carey and Runcorn's "careful" research that supported continental drift. Not missing an opportunity to note how wrong Jeffreys was in his criticism of Wegener's theory, the author ends the paragraph by relating the stinging insult directed toward Jeffreys by some field geologists in response to Jeffreys's "brusque rejection" of and "casual disdain" for Runcorn's research.

Paragraph 4 delivers the coup de grace, the "compelling" evidence relating to seafloor spreading, which put the controversy to rest and made continental drift the consensus view.

The Big Picture:

Paragraph 1: Continental drift—controversial at first

Paragraph 2: Jeffreys's critique

Paragraph 3: Carey and Runcorn's research supports theory

Paragraph 4: Seafloor spreading supports theory

The Questions:

72. (E) Global (Main Idea)

The correct answer choice for a Main Idea question will justify the inclusion of just about everything in the passage.

As we noted in the initial review of the passage, the main idea of this passage is that Wegener's theory of continental drift revolutionized science and is well-accepted today, but that broad acceptance was preceded by much struggle and controversy. That's answer choice **(E)**.

(A) The author never indicates whether Carey or Runcorn's research, or evidence of seafloor spreading, was unexpected. If anything, the seafloor spreading evidence was expected because the author states that the evidence "confirmed the hypothesis" that molten rock welled up on the seafloor and pushed apart the tectonic plates and the continents on them.

(B) The only critic identified by the author is Jeffreys, and Jeffreys did nothing to facilitate the acceptance of Wegener's theory.

(C) Darwin's theory is mentioned in the first paragraph, as contrast to Wegener's theory. According to the author, the two scientists' theories are alike in that they revolutionized science, but they are dissimilar in that while Darwin's ideas remain controversial, Wegener's theories currently are accepted almost without question. Darwin's ideas are never mentioned again after line 5 of the passage, so any comparison between Wegener's and Darwin's theories cannot be the Main Idea of the passage.

(D) In paragraph 2 the author notes that Wegener felt that the best evidence for continental drift had likely eroded away, but there is no suggestion in the passage that Wegener himself provided no evidence whatsoever to support his theory. Moreover, the point of the sections of the passage detailing work by other researchers that ultimately proved Wegener's theory was not to show that Wegener himself didn't come up with the evidence, but to show that Wegener's theory was correct.

73. (A) Logic (Parallel Reasoning)

Doing a careful analysis of the argument or situation to be matched *before* attacking the answer choices will make a Parallel Reasoning question much easier to answer.

This question asks us to find the answer choice describing a situation most parallel to Jeffreys's approach to Wegener's theory. Looking back to the author's descriptions of Jeffreys's approach in paragraph 2 and at the end of paragraph 3, we recall that Jeffreys's approach was "casual," "brusque," and not thoughtful or well-reasoned. We'll need to test each answer choice to find a similar approach:

(A) The botanist draws a conclusion about two species based on "superficial" examination of their appearance. This one looks good, but we'll check the others to be sure we haven't missed anything.

(B) According to the passage, Jeffreys was not wandering aimlessly, like a driver in an unfamiliar city, trying to find a street without a map. Rather, Jeffreys knew the city (Earth), but was unwilling to consider that the city might not have always been configured the way it appeared to him.

(C) Jeffreys's problem wasn't that he chose an inappropriate or disfavored field of study within his discipline.

(D) Jeffreys did not base his opinions on the consensus of either the public or those within his field. He simply dismissed Wegener's theory without giving adequate consideration to the evidence that Wegener might be correct.

(E) For a psychiatrist to base his treatment decisions on his patients' past histories might actually be sound medical practice. However, Jeffreys based his opinions on superficial and unreasoned reactions to the theory and to the evidence supporting Wegener's theory.

(A) is the only answer choice that captures the lack of intellectual rigor in Jeffreys's approach, and it is our correct answer choice.

74. (E) Detail

Never rely on your memory to answer a Detail question.

The keywords "seafloor spreading" give us an easy hook to scan for, and we find information about seafloor spreading in paragraph 4. Lines 50–54 tell us that evidence of seafloor spreading explained the puzzle of why the ocean basins are so much younger than the continents. Answer choice **(E)** speaks to that very point.

(A) The author indicates that seafloor spreading occurs as the earth's giant crustal plates move apart, but seafloor spreading is not posited as the "reason for the existence" of those giant crustal plates.

(B) The author states that basalts retain a magnetic field in alignment with the earth's magnetic field at the time the basalts were formed, but never suggests any reason *why* basalts retain their magnetic field alignment. The fact that basalts and seafloor spreading are not discussed in the same paragraph is another clue that this is not the correct answer.

(C) The author notes that the earth's poles have wandered over the past few hundred million years, but the reasons why remain a mystery to the reader of this passage.

(D) The passage says nothing about the composition of the earth's giant crustal plates.

75. (C) Inference (Author's Attitude)

When more than one viewpoint is discussed in a passage, watch for clues about the author's attitude toward the proponents of each view.

This passage is scattered with evidence of the author's lack of respect for Jeffreys's "scholarship" on which Jeffreys based his rejection of Wegener's theory. In paragraph 2, the author notes that Jeffreys dismissed Wegener's theory "[a]pparently after casually observing the shorelines on a globe...." Paragraph 3 describes the thoughtful research that supported the theory of continental drift, done by researchers who were "[d]isturbed by Jeffreys's obviously perfunctory observation." After describing this new evidence that the continents had moved with respect to one another, the author states, "True to form, Jeffreys brusquely rejected" the studies. The author then relates how Jeffreys's "casual disdain" for the observational data that supported Wegener's theory led some field geologists so suggest that Jeffreys's classic book, *The Earth*, should be retitled, *An Earth*. (Those geologists can really come up with cutting insults.) **(C)** captures this sense of Jeffrey's arrogant and feckless dismissal of Wegener's theory.

(A) According to the author, Jeffreys did not ignore Wegener's theory. We are told that Jeffreys considered Wegener's theory and dismissed it without any real consideration. Moreover, the context of the reference shows that the author was not using these words to describe Jeffreys.

(B) While the author might agree that Jeffreys's response to Wegener's theory was "very poor," the context of that quote shows that the phrase referred not to Jeffreys but to the apparent fit between the shorelines of Africa and South America.

(D) The author describes S.W. Carey and not Jeffreys, as using "careful techniques." The careful reader could have eliminated this answer choice immediately upon noting how positive the phrase is—this author clearly considers Jeffreys's research techniques to be slipshod and lackadaisical, not "careful."

(E) Jeffreys's opinion never became the consensus view. Rather, the observational data that Jeffreys scorned, along with the evidence of seafloor spreading, turned *Wegener's* theory (along with plate tectonics) into the consensus view.

76. (C) Logic Function

Context is the key to understanding the function of anything mentioned in the passage.

Mention of the field geologists' insulting renaming of Jeffreys's classic book comes at the end of a paragraph describing careful research by scholars who were "disturbed" by Jeffreys's approach. The insult shows that not only was the author unimpressed by Jeffreys's brusque dismissal of the evidence supporting Wegener's theory, but also Jeffreys's colleagues thought little of Jeffreys's scholarship in this regard. That's answer choice **(C)**.

(A) The author describes only one of Jeffreys's ideas: his belief that Wegener was wrong.

(B) The insult by the field geologists is itself criticism of Jeffreys's work. The author justifies criticism of Jeffreys's work due to its lack of substance.

(D) The insult explains nothing. It is simply evidence that Jeffreys's colleagues found his objections to Wegener's theory to be insubstantial.

(E) Other than identifying the field geologists as critics of Jeffreys, the author makes (and thus supports) no assertions about those critics.

77. (D) Inference

When a passage contains multiple viewpoints, stop and be sure that you are clear on which of those viewpoints are at issue for the question at hand.

Paragraph 3 begins with the author describing Carey as "disturbed" by Jeffreys's "obviously perfunctory" observations. Carey not only discounted Jeffreys's opinions because of Jeffreys's inadequate research, but also performed his own "careful" research to counter Jeffreys's critique. **(D)** best matches that evaluation of Carey's opinion about Jeffreys's work.

We can quickly eliminate **(A)**, **(B)**, and **(C)** because all of them imply that Carey agreed with Jeffreys's conclusions.

(E) captures the idea that Carey found Jeffreys's appraisal of Wegener's theory to be deficient, but Carey did not decline to investigate Jeffreys's critique. To the contrary, he applied "careful techniques" to the problem, and found evidence contrary to Jeffreys's opinions.

78. (A) Logic (Weaken)

One way to weaken an argument is to falsify some of the evidence used to support the conclusion.

The author cites three key pieces of evidence to support Wegener's theory of continental drift: the match between the continental margins of Africa and South America, the varying alignment of magnetic fields in basalts of the same age in North America and Europe, and the evidence of seafloor spreading due to new rock being formed at the midocean ridges, which explains how the ocean basins can be younger than the continents (paragraphs 3 and 4). Answer choice **(A)** undermines this evidence by offering the possibility that the ocean basins are older than the continents.

(B) The possibility that new techniques could allow for more accurate mapping could go either way with respect to the theory of continental drift. Better mapping would not necessarily render the theory less likely to be valid.

(C) According to the passage, the planet's magnetic poles have wandered over the course of a "few hundred million years" (line 32). Evidence that basalts formed (and magnetized) in North America and Europe during the past 100 years are magnetically aligned in the same direction says nothing about whether the continents on which those rocks are found have moved relative to one another over the eons.

(D) is completely consistent with the theory of continental drift, since the author tells us that basalts become magnetically aligned at the time they are formed. This is a restatement of one of the pieces of evidence supporting the theory, not a weakener.

(E) This answer choice is too broad and vague to constitute a weakener of the argument. Were the geological phenomena that Jeffreys "carefully" studied at all related to the evidence supporting continental drift? If not, then those studies could not possibly undermine the theory of continental drift. Even if Jeffreys had made "careful observational studies" of geologic phenomena relevant to the theory of continental drift, were those studies made before or after he criticized Wegener's theory? If they were completed afterward, for all we know, Jeffreys changed his mind and became a continental drift supporter.

Passage 13: Earth's Magnetic Field
Questions 79–84

Topic and Scope: Earth's magnetic field; specifically, reversals in the magnetic field's polarity.

Purpose and Main Idea: The author's Purpose is to discuss the process that results in reversals of the magnetic field's polarity, as well as two distinct hypotheses that try to explain these reversals; since this text is essentially descriptive, there really isn't a specific Main Idea, though the author does say (in the last paragraph) that the "heat-transfer hypothesis" offers a better explanation than the "asteroid-impact hypothesis."

Paragraph Structure: Paragraph 1 introduces the Topic and Scope of the passage. The rest of this paragraph and all of paragraph 2 provide a lot of scientific facts about the Earth's magnetic field, particularly facts about what is known (not much) about the process of polarity reversal.

Paragraph 3 outlines both the "heat-transfer hypothesis" and the "asteroid-impact hypothesis" of polarity reversal. In paragraph 4, on the other hand, the author asserts that the "heat-transfer hypothesis" is a more compelling explanation of polarity reversal.

The Big Picture:

- A good grasp of the passage doesn't mean assimilating all of the details (they can be looked up should this become necessary). Rather, it means comprehending what the author's doing in the text—in this case, describing a scientific process and two hypotheses that purport to explain it.

- Although this isn't a very difficult Science passage, it's still not a good place to begin work on the section. Why? Because the author's Purpose isn't entirely clear until late in the passage. Passages that begin with a mass of facts—instead of a clear statement of authorial intent—are generally best left for later in the section. Moreover, a brief scan of the question set suggests that it's not going to be an especially easy one.

- Note, however, that this passage conforms to a structure that's common in Science passages: a scientific process is described and competing explanations of it are then evaluated.

The Questions:

79. (C) Inference

This choice is a nice paraphrase of lines 16–21, which state that the Earth's magnetic field is generated by the movement of free electrons in the hot metallic fluid that constitutes the Earth's outer core.

(A) distorts the "asteroid-impact hypothesis." According to this hypothesis, "heat circulation in the outer core" is affected by changes in the polar ice caps, not the other way around.

(B) combines elements of both the "heat-transfer hypothesis" and the "asteroid-impact hypothesis" into a statement that has no support in the text.

(D) is part of the "asteroid-impact hypothesis"—a hypothesis that may or may not turn out to be correct.

(E) also distorts information in the text, which says that reversals in magnetic field polarity may be related to *changes* in "the heat circulation pattern of the outer core fluid..." (lines 27–28).

80. (E) Inference

In lines 59–63, the author's objection to the "asteroid-impact hypothesis" is that it depends on an "extraterrestrial intervention," which he finds less compelling than explanations that rest on terrestrial (or earthly) events. Of the choices, only **(E)** presents an extraterrestrial explanation—cometary impact—for the extinction of the dinosaurs.

Choices **(A)**–**(D)** each present an "earthly" reason for the disappearance of the dinosaurs—the type of reason that the author favors when it comes to explaining earthly events, whether magnetic field reversals or species extinction.

81. (A) Logic Function

The author mentions hotter and cooler blobs in the context of describing the "heat-transfer hypothesis." This hypothesis suggests that heat circulation patterns in the outer core are affected by the way in which heat is vented from the outer core.

(B) distorts information in the text, which makes it clear that magnetic field reversal is thought to be caused by a disturbance in heat circulation patterns in the outer core (lines 26–28).

(C) is too vague. The author mentions the blobs only in the context of laying out a *specific* hypothesis about magnetic field reversal. **(C)** is also beyond the passage's scope: the text dwells on the Earth's interior, not its exterior.

(D) focuses on the substance of the detail, rather than why the author included it in the text.

(E) also distorts information in the text. According to lines 16–18, it is an accepted fact that the magnetic field itself is produced by the movement of free electrons in the outer core's fluid.

82. (B) Inference

Lines 8–9 say that geological evidence demonstrates that magnetic field reversals have been occurring with greater frequency in the recent past.

(A) Lines 1–3 state that "[i]t is a fundamental tenet of geophysics that the Earth's magnetic field can exist in either of two polarity states..." A fundamental tenet is something that is agreed upon by everyone in the discipline. Besides, there's no sense in the text that any geophysicists contest this fact.

(C) is beyond the scope of the text. This passage is about the "underlying causes" (lines 14–15) of magnetic field reversals, not about how fast they occur. The only point made about the speed of these reversals is that they occur over a period of thousands of years.

(D) The "heat-transfer hypothesis" is simply one possible explanation that geophysicists have come up with to account for a process that they don't fully understand. To say that it has enhanced their knowledge of magnetic field reversal is an overstatement.

(E) Magnetic field reversal is thought to result from changes in heat circulation patterns in the outer core, not from friction along the boundary of inner and outer cores.

83. (D) Inference

Although this passage discusses just two hypotheses about magnetic field reversal, we're told that others exist. The last sentence of the text explicitly refers to "*theories* that depend on extraterrestrial intervention" and "*theories* like the first" (i.e., "earthly" theories).

(A) is beyond the scope of the text. We're not told what geophysicists *in general* think about these hypotheses, let alone whether "they have sharply divided the scientific community." All we can infer from the text is that there is some support for both hypotheses.

(B) These two hypotheses were formulated to address the "underlying causes" of magnetic field reversal. That they might also address the issue of reversal frequency is simply a by-product of their primary function.

(C) is a "half-right, half-wrong" choice. True, no firm conclusions about either hypothesis have yet been reached; but there's no information about the *extent* to which the two have been explored.

(E) is beyond the scope of the text. We aren't told precisely when either hypothesis was formulated. Moreover, both hypotheses have at least some support among geophysicists.

84. (D) Detail EXCEPT

Changes in oceanic circulation patterns aren't mentioned anywhere in the text as possible contributors to magnetic field reversals. The "asteroid-impact hypothesis" does speak of temperature drops in and redistribution of seawater, but these events are different from changes in oceanic circulation patterns.

(A) Geophysicists think that change in heat circulation in outer core fluid is the basic cause of magnetic field reversals. They part company, however, over what causes the change in heat circulation.

(B) and **(E)** are components of the "asteroid-impact hypothesis."

(C) is part of the "heat-transfer hypothesis."

Social Sciences Passages

Passage 1: Korean Americans and Ethnic Identity
Questions 1–7

Topic and Scope: Korean Americans; specifically, the effect on the Korean American community of a specific Korean labor struggle.

Purpose and Main Idea: The author's purpose is to explore how the Pico Korea Union struggle impacted Korean Americans in a variety of ways. The Main Idea takes that a step further, in that the author moves from that specific example to the implications for other ethnic communities whose forebears were immigrants. They, like Korean Americans, would do well to get involved with similar campaigns in their countries of origin.

Paragraph Structure: Paragraph 1 provides the factual background—the formation of the union, the subsequent plant closing, and the 1990 visit of some of the workers that galvanized the Korean American community. Then the author announces his purpose, to demonstrate the "[deep effects]...on several levels" (lines 9–10) that the whole situation had on Korean Americans.

Paragraph 2 amply lives up to its promise to detail those "several levels." The plethora of Continuation Keywords— "First...In addition...also... In addition...also"—nicely highlights the function of the paragraph: to describe the effects of the Pico Korea Union visit. No matter how you slice up paragraph 2, the author sees a wide range of positive things coming out of the Pico workers' story. You didn't need to memorize all the details here; you just needed to know where to look for them.

Paragraph 3 announces its scope early: *reasons* for the effects mentioned in paragraph 2. You might have summarized them in your head as "The Pico struggle was non-political and economically based, and spoke to Korean Americans' hearts." That's more or less why the Pico struggle was able to engage them so profoundly, as the author sees it.

Paragraph 4 is, of course, the "important lesson" (line 52) offered by lines 1–50. The author never mentions Koreans, but broadens out his interest to the implications for *all* ethnic communities. This is how we know that paragraph 4 holds the Main Idea, as described above.

The Big Picture:

- The passage will always live up to its early promises. Here, when the author says that the Pico situation "affected...on several levels," you *know* you will hear about those effects. Be aggressive and seek all of this out: *Find* those effects; don't just passively wait for the author to "tell you stuff."

- Circle or underline important Keywords, and use them to help you establish the author's main interests and organize the passage. Be especially watchful for Emphasis Keywords, such as "an unprecedented...deeply affected" (lines 7–9), or "Most notably" (line 13), or "an important lesson" (lines 51–52).

- A passage need not end (as this one does) with an appeal to broader ideas, but when it does, you will usually find there an expression of the author's main concerns. Keep such a paragraph in mind when attacking Global questions.

The Questions:

1. (D) Global (Main Point)

The subject matter announced in paragraph 1 never varies, namely: how the Pico Korea Union dispute "deeply affected the Korean American community on several levels" (lines 9–10). It's carried through, from the list of effects in paragraph 2 to the *reason* for those effects in paragraph 3. True, the "important lesson" in paragraph 4 does broaden out from the Korean American example to other ethnicities, but that doesn't change the fundamental topic of the passage overall.

(A) describes an admirable endeavor but not one found in this passage, which essentially explores the raising of Korean American *consciousness* about Korean issues rather than what Korean Americans subsequently did, or do, about them.

(B) "Contacts with Koreans" is much too broad, given the passage's focus on the one inciting incident of the visiting delegation.

(C), (E) Each of these choices mentions one of paragraph 2's "effects." **(C)** evokes Effect #2's "new interest in...cultural identity" (line 23), and **(E)** smacks of Effect #1 (lines 21–22). So each is too narrow. Also, both choices, like **(B)**, lose sight of the author's specific focus on the fallout from the Pico workers' struggle and visit. **(E)** has one additional problem in that lines 13–15 and others make it clear that politicization has occurred, but the passage ends before the *effect* of that politicization is spelled out.

2. (C) Inference

Any question about the specific details of the Pico plant shutdown must come out of paragraph 1, since from line 9 on, the author is wholly interested in Korean American *reactions* to that shutdown following the workers' visit. And paragraph 1 is rather terse, lines 6–7 merely asserting—in line with **(C)**—that Pico closed the plant "upon the formation of the union."

(A), (E) Each of these is a plausible reason why one might close down a plant, but neither is mentioned in paragraph 1 or anywhere else.

(B), (D) Both of these relate to the issue of "economic exploitation faced by the Pico workers" (line 47). Yes, disputes seem to have raged for some time **(B)**, and wages were withheld, **(D)**, but both are more effects of the closing rather than its cause.

3. (B) Detail EXCEPT

The stem phrase "recent development" is surely code for "recent effect of the labor struggle and workers' visit"—in other words, a hint that paragraph 2 should be our focus. Since this is an all-of-the-following-EXCEPT question, each of us can choose among three plausible approaches: Review the paragraph and then consult the choices; scan the choices for obvious wrong answers and *then* go back to paragraph 2; or search for the "odd man out" directly.

In this case, the right answer is likely to be outside the scope of the text, and so it turns out: **(B)**'s assertion (that working class Korean immigrants have entered the Korean American community's "more privileged sectors") is a distortion, formed by combining line 19's reference to privileged, alienated Korean Americans, with lines 23–32's reference to Korean immigrant workers hitting it off with their Chinese counterparts.

The other four choices show up in paragraph 2 and some are supported elsewhere as well: Youngsters' interest in their Korean heritage **(A)** is mentioned in lines 17–21. Closer activist ties **(C)** is how the paragraph ends, lines 33–36. Greater political activity **(D)** comes in at lines 13–17. And setting aside differences **(E)** is alluded to at lines 11–13 and again at lines 46–50.

4. (A) Inference

Immigrants per se are first mentioned at line 26, but the phrase "ethnic communities of immigrant derivation" (line 57) comes right out of paragraph 4, and it's there we should look for the right answer. The whole point of paragraph 4 is that such a community can find "empowerment" by staying tapped into struggles in its country of origin—and there you have **(A)**.

(B) *Au contraire*, the author thinks ethnic communities "need more than just" (line 53) a sense of history and culture.

(C) The passage never mentions any appeal to the youth "of all backgrounds," but if anything, the passage would suggest that the best means of getting youth fired up is keeping in touch with the country of origin—which, again, is **(A)**.

(D) *Au contraire*, according to lines 17–21 the privileged tend to feel alienation, not closeness.

(E) The Korean American experience would seem to contradict **(E)**'s idea that a politicized community cannot use that new energy to change relations with other groups.

5. (C) Logic Function

The Chinese immigrants appear once only, at the end of the long sentence in lines 26–32. And that whole sentence is solely there in the context of the *previous* sentence—lines 23–26, the third major effect: "new roles that can be played by recent immigrants," especially such working-class ones as the Koreans who had such a warm meeting with their Chinese counterparts. **(C)** sums up those lines.

(A), (B) The Chinese workers' problems, if any, are never mentioned, let alone **(A)** compared to or **(B)** set apart from those of the Pico workers.

(D) No activism on the part of the Chinese is mentioned.

(E), like **(A)** and **(B)**, hinges on your not noticing that the author makes no explicit or implicit comparison between Chinese workers and Koreans; their meeting is evidence of what can happen when immigrants' perspectives and experience are put to use. And that's that.

6. (B) Global (Primary Purpose)

In advance of scanning the choices, we should be seeking a statement that reflects the author's interest, from line 9 to the end, in the effects of the Pico workers' struggle and their visit on the Korean American community. Only **(B)** meets that definition. And **(B)** is even more satisfactory in that it ties the specific Korean American example to the broader implications for other former-immigrant ethnic communities. Sure, they're mentioned only in paragraph 4, but from the tone of that paragraph they're obviously part of the author's keen interest in the Pico story in the first place (remember the reference to "an *important* lesson"?).

(A) distorts what **(B)** makes clear. At best, the author's point (see paragraph 4) is that "recent developments in the Korean American community" have *implications* for other communities, not a direct strong effect.

(C) The "problems faced" that the author describes are largely those of the Korean workers in Buchon City, not those of Korean Americans. And it's the positive effects of the Korean American reaction to the overseas struggle—not the community's own "problems"—that hold a lesson for other ethnic communities.

(D) The author's purpose, as we've seen, is to describe a series of effects on one community and propose a broader application of those effects on others. **(D)**'s phrase "argue against" is inappropriate here. This passage is not a call to arms "against…injustice."

(E) is too broad in its phrase "unionization movement" (we're considering one union here); is inaccurate (what had an "impact" is the plant closing and workers' visit, not the union itself); and is distorted (the lesson for ethnic communities is to be found in the Korean American experience, not in unions).

7. (C) Logic Function

Paragraph 3's purpose, as we've seen, is clear from its first seven words (line 40): "The reasons for these effects lie in...." Detailing those reasons is what the paragraph is about and what **(C)** is getting at.

(A), **(E)** Both begin promisingly with "explain why," but each departs from the question's scope. It's paragraph 1 that explains the Pico workers' trip east **(A)**. Meanwhile, any intergenerational reactions **(E)** come out in paragraph 2. If anything, paragraph 3 highlights a *blurring* of differences, lines 42–44, in contrast to **(E)**'s focus on them.

(B) There's no explicit back-reference to *previous* Korean American causes.

(D) Paragraph 3 centers on the reasons why the Pico cause received such broad support, not how other ethnic groups benefited from the Pico experience. If anything, paragraph 4 suggests how other ethnic groups *may* benefit from the example of the Pico workers, but **(D)**, stating that the ethnic groups "have profited" already, is still too strong.

Passage 2: Japanese American Ethnicity
Questions 8–15

Topic and Scope: Studies of ethnic identity; specifically, Fugita & O'Brien's study of the ethnic history of Japanese Americans.

Purpose and Main Idea: The author's purpose is to show why Fugita & O'Brien exemplify both a new trend in ethnic studies (the new focus on the preservation of ethnic identity) and a problem *within* that trend (the hard-to-prove assumption that some sort of ethnic consciousness preexists within a people).

Paragraph Structure: Paragraph 1 is sweet, providing in one fell swoop all of the following: the *scope* of the passage; a *conflict* between new and old methods; and a strong indication of *what must follow*. *Scope*: We see the author clearly and rapidly narrow the scope from ethnic studies in general, to an interest in "preservation" of ethnicity in the United States in particular, to this one particular study by Fugita & O'Brien. *Conflict* is present between the earlier historians—who have focused on assimilation or "transformation"—and the new ones, of whom Fugita & O'Brien are the exemplars. *What must follow?* The last sentence articulates, about as clearly as any one sentence could, the overall structure of what we're about to read: how Fugita & O'Brien's work is a good example of the new trend, and how it reveals "a common problem." We know the passage won't end until both issues are raised.

Paragraph 2 is interesting. No sooner has the author presented the main thesis of Fugita & O'Brien's book—that Japanese ethnic identity sustained itself among the first three generations in the United States—than he announces that their very data could just as easily be used to support the notion that Japanese Americans were highly assimilated! (Remember, that would be the thrust of the "earlier historians" mentioned in paragraph 2. We don't expect to see recent-trenders Fugita & O'Brien support that old-fashioned idea. But there it is.) The rest of paragraph 2 keeps piling on the assimilation ideas, ending with that which we are surprised to hear Fugita & O'Brien "themselves acknowledge": that indeed, the Japanese American ethnic community has been weakened as the later generations have become part of the overall American fabric.

Are they backtracking? Betraying the new trend? Not really. In paragraph 3 we learn that Fugita & O'Brien stay in step by arguing how remarkable it is that, *despite* all the assimilation movement and pressure, so much Japanese American ethnic identity has survived, and we learn that they ascribe this to the sense of "peoplehood" that, Fugita & O'Brien posit, has kept the community cohesive. And the promised "problem" surfaces around just this peoplehood issue in paragraph 4. The author doesn't see the sense in positing a sense of peoplehood separate from a group's assimilation, because it can't be proved; one can't put one's finger on it. Don't give an arguable and imprecise term like "peoplehood" the credit for keeping ethnic communality alive, our author advises; instead (lines 57–60), enumerate the specific and concrete factors that "sustain community cohesion" simultaneously as that ethnic group is adapting to the pluralistic culture.

The Big Picture:

- Always watch how an author narrows his scope in the course of the first paragraph or two. Not all authors do so quite as blatantly as this one, but "scoping out the scope" is always a necessary task. Unless and until you perceive precisely where the author's interest lies, you cannot have a handle on the overall passage or its parts.

- Many Reading Comprehension passages (and many questions on those passages) depend on *contrasts*. In your initial reading, look to identify contrasts and keep them under control. Here, we have the basic difference between the two trends in ethnic studies (the different interests in assimilation vs. preservation), and also between the avowed aim of Fugita & O'Brien and the points that the author claims their book actually raises. Both broad contrasts are central to the questions and answers that follow.

- In Reading Comprehension, promises made are promises kept. When the author promises to return to an issue (as he does here, with the line 11 reference to "common problem"), you can be sure that he will. However, *you* have a responsibility too: You must keep the promise in mind. Throughout this passage you should've been saying to yourself, "OK, I see the 'trend' (line 10); where's the 'problem' (line 11)?" That way you would instantly have seen how lines 47–56 live up to the promise of lines 10–11.

The Questions:

8. (C) Global (Main Point)

We said in our discussion of paragraph 1 above that that last sentence (lines 8–11) deftly defines where the passage will go thereafter. **(C)** falls right in line.

(A), (D) From the title of Fugita & O'Brien's book alone, we should see that their interest, and hence the author's, is primarily on the one ethnic group. The implications for studies of other groups are faintly expressed at best.

(B) Paragraph 2 makes it clear that Fugita & O'Brien *do* describe Japanese American assimilation, or at least that their data support same. But Fugita & O'Brien's interest is in being part of the *new* trend.

(E) is a distortion of paragraph 1's idea that the trend in ethnic studies has shifted from assimilation to preservation. **(E)** doesn't even *mention* preservation, and ignores both Japanese Americans and Fugita & O'Brien to boot.

9. (E) Detail

Fugita & O'Brien's ideas are described throughout their passage, but their *data* per se—the focus of the question—are only cited in paragraph 2, starting at line 24. There we're told that Fugita & O'Brien's data support the idea that the involvement of Japanese Americans (particularly the Sansei generation) in other organizations and communities changed the nature of the ethnic community overall. **(E)** says "altered" instead of "changed"—big deal—but is otherwise right in line with lines 24–29.

(A) "Occupational mobility" is part of a trio of elements (lines 22–23) that attest to the relative assimilation of Japanese Americans. The single focus on one member of the trio is an unwarranted distinction.

(B) Yes, the Japanese American community has had to accomodate multiple and layered identities (lines 28–29), but has it done so without losing any intensity? No, lines 29–32 say there has been a weakening of Japanese American community life.

(C) has three problems. 1: Cohesion is *greater* among Japanese Americans than among other groups (lines 36–39). 2: The comparison made there is not between groups over the same time period, but between similar points in each group's separate "group life cycle." 3: This discussion of cohesion has to do not with Fugita & O'Brien's data but with the interpretations they make in their book. Other than all that, **(C)** is fine.

(D) The passage reports a deepening of assimilation from the 1st generation to the 3rd; the "regained interest" among the Sansei is bogus as far as the passage is concerned.

10. (C) Logic (Parallel Reasoning)

The historians arguing around line 4 predate the new trend; they're the guardians of the old approach, the one that examines how ethnic groups have assimilated. "Transformed" and "blended into" are the author's operative words. If you set off in search of a choice that highlights blending and assimilation, **(C)** should pretty much jump out at you. Disparate styles forming an "American" style—that's what lines 4–6 are all about.

(A), **(D)**, **(E)** *Au contraire*, all three mention influences that begin outside the U.S. and *stay* separate or disparate.

(B) Paragraph 2 is not explicit enough as to whether ethnic associations' makeup and purpose do or do not foster assimilation and blending.

11. (D) Detail

More or less a follow-up to the previous question, which again brings us back to paragraph 1: Earlier studies emphasized the assimilation of ethnic groups into the overall American fabric, while current ones emphasize preservation of group identities. **(D)** reflects the former.

(A) "Peoplehood" is defined for us as a current-studies idea, not at all a point of similarity with earlier scholars.

(B) represents what the author is, in paragraph 4, asking scholars to do (lines 57–60) in contrast to their current practice.

(C) *Au contraire*, any reference to an "American national character" is an early-studies concern.

(E) The question of why immigration occurred is outside the scope of both studies.

12. (B) Logic Function

The Fugita & O'Brien quote in lines 36–39 is in the context of paragraph 3's overall purpose: to explain how, in the face of so much evidence that three generations of Japanese Americans have assimilated into American life, they can still (as representatives of the current trend in ethnic studies) emphasize the persistent "community cohesion" among that particular ethnic group. In other words, the quote is evidence— it *is* preceded by the evidence Keyword "because," after all—of Fugita & O'Brien's belief, stated first in lines 16–17 and reiterated in paragraph 3, that Japanese American community cohesion endured.

(A) The author attacks Fugita & O'Brien's hypothesis one paragraph later, and the basis for the criticism is different from the topic of the quote in question.

(C) The author shows how Fugita & O'Brien demonstrate Japanese American adaptation in the *second* paragraph .

(D), like **(A)**, misunderstands paragraph 3 as the one in which the author takes issue with Fugita & O'Brien; and even in paragraph 4 he doesn't chastise them for a faulty comparison between this ethnic group and others.

(E) The author's presentation of Fugita & O'Brien's "peoplehood" idea *follows* the quote in question. The quote explains *that* Japanese American community endured; peoplehood explains *why*. Two different issues.

13. (C) Inference

The line 47 hypothesis—described in paragraph 3—is that a Japanese American sense of "peoplehood" kept the community cohesive. That notion is subsequently attacked in paragraph 4; **(C)** is lines 54–56 in simpler terms. Note how the first sentence of paragraph 4 links the peoplehood hypothesis described in paragraph 3 to the attack made 10 lines later.

(A) Way too positive.

(B) Lines 49–50 state that the peoplehood idea isn't especially original to Fugita & O'Brien, and so it wouldn't be any better or worse "developed" than any similar hypothesis made by their contemporary colleagues.

(D) "Illogical"? Maybe; the author does question a central assumption that Fugita & O'Brien are making. But it's "interesting" enough that the author devotes an entire passage to it!

(E) The problem with the hypothesis lies not in its similarity to other ideas in ethnic studies, whether early or current, but in its inherent weakness.

14. (A) Inference

The historians in line 49 are tarred with the same brush that the author applies to Fugita & O'Brien. All are taken to task for hanging their theory of enduring community cohesion on a vague and hard-to-prove notion of group consciousness, and all are urged instead, in lines 57–60, to start identifying the concrete factors that keep ethnic group identity strong once it's transplanted to America. The author's expressed need for *all* historians to follow that methodology makes **(A)** inferable: Those studying European ethnicities have been no more successful than Fugita & O'Brien have.

(B) draws a weird (and unsupported) contrast between surviving elements and weakened elements; it's not present in Fugita & O'Brien so it can't be ascribed to the scholars of Europe.

(C) *Au contraire,* lines 49–54 clearly state that Fugita & O'Brien and the scholars of Europe both cite "a sense of national consciousness" as the basis of persistent ethnic identity.

(D) plays off a detail from the last line of the passage. The author believes that historians *should* explain how the pluralism of American life has affected cultural traditions, but there's no indication that they do so.

(E) Given everything we've heard about the assimilation pressures operating on one ethnic group, **(E)** would be an odd position indeed for a scholar to hold about another one. In any case, the sole reference to scholars of European Americans is in the context of the *reason* for the persistence of community, not its *extent.*

15. (B) Inference

Note that we must extrapolate Fugita & O'Brien's views about Japanese Americans to a more general view, because no group is mentioned by name in the choices. There's no way to predict which of their ideas will be highlighted in the right answer, so your best bet is to quickly review the main ones; and lines 13–17, their main thesis, is probably the best place to start. Fugita & O'Brien clearly believe that Japanese Americans have managed to sustain their "sense of ethnic community" while adapting to American culture generally, so they must believe **(B)** to be true.

(A) *Au contraire*, paragraph 2 (and especially lines 13–16 and 29–32) makes it clear that Fugita & O'Brien concede that time has been a weakener of Japanese American cultural cohesion. Certainly the 3rd, Sansei generation is cited as more assimilated than the others.

(C) No, to Fugita & O'Brien a community's strength is primarily dependent on "peoplehood," which (lines 45–46) "extended beyond family ties."

(D) Education and job mobility are two of the factors that *demonstrate* how strongly Japanese Americans have assimilated (lines 19–24), not the factors that have *caused* a weakening of ethnic community. (Note that the third member of the trio, income, is left out—a hint that the choice is wrong.)

(E) Fugita & O'Brien would likely agree that if a group's "peoplehood" is strong, it could help to sustain community cohesion even in the face of U.S. pluralism. No reference is made anywhere to things being especially tough these days.

Passage 3: CEO Moral Responsibility
Questions 16–20

Topic and Scope: The morality of corporate behavior; specifically, CEO's moral responsibility to uphold and enhance the public good.

Purpose and Main Idea: The author's purpose is to describe two groups' (critics of corporations and economists) view on the moral responsibility of corporations, and then to side with one of the groups. The main idea is that the critics of corporations are right in believing that corporations and their CEOs have a moral responsibility above and beyond simply maximizing profit; they must also consider the public good when making decisions that affect the community at large.

Paragraph Structure: Paragraph 1 sets up the debate: Critics blame corporations for many of the ills of Western society, and their criticism isn't limited to illegal practices; it also includes the overarching mentality that informs corporate behavior: maximizing profit. Economists say phooey—business isn't about ethics, it's about money, so keep your morality to yourself.

Surprisingly, paragraph 2 doesn't help much in advancing the argument or shedding light on the debate. We want to know the author's take on this debate, but we'll have to wait for a clear expression of this. Paragraph 2 offers, at best, a slight hint that the author believes that corporations should have the moral responsibility of individuals since a corporation is simply an aggregate of individuals acting in the corporation's behalf. But even this is hazy; we're not really sure where the author stands yet, or how the discussion of owner-operated corporations in the last sentence of the paragraph relates to the debate at hand.

Luckily, the final two paragraphs resolve the debate for us in strikingly clear fashion. First, paragraph 3 presents the economists' seemingly "airtight" argument: Except in charitable organizations, maximizing profits for owners is built into the CEO's job. If the CEO doesn't like this, he or she shouldn't have taken the job. But even when the CEO *isn't* obligated to maximize profits and *is* concerned with the public good, the best approach is to *maximize profits anyway*, because that's the surest route to enhancing the public good. Thus, the "airtight" argument: Any way you look at it, maximizing corporate profit is both good and necessary.

We need not wait long for the author's rebuttal of this position and the presentation of his own opinion: The first sentence of paragraph 4 says the economists' argument is a pile of nonsense. The author attacks the economists' assumption that maximization of profit *necessarily* benefits the public, and presents a hypothetical example intended to demonstrate just the opposite. The author concludes with the hard line position that the potential personal drawbacks of acting morally (which

in the case of CEOs, includes penalty or dismissal) do not excuse CEOs from the responsibility to act morally.

The Big Picture:

- When a debate is introduced, our main concern is to find out where the author stands on the issue. Does he take a side? Reject both sides? Introduce his own view? As mentioned above, paragraph 2 is a bit of a letdown because it doesn't help us fully nail down the author's opinion. There could be a detail question based on paragraph 2 (in fact, there's not even that), but as for the main point, we have to look further. And if you hang in there, the author's main point explodes out of the first sentence of paragraph 4, and is then elaborated on further. All of which is to say . . .

- Don't always expect the main idea to jump out of the first paragraph—in some passages, the main idea doesn't fully emerge until somewhere near the end. Always keep your eye out for the author's main idea, no matter where in the passage it may appear.

- Strive to nail down each passage's structure, and then keep this structure in mind while answering the questions. If you need to refer back to the passage, this mental roadmap will be your guide. Not every passage is blocked out as nicely as this one: paragraph 1 defines the debate, paragraph 2 fills the picture in a bit, paragraph 3 presents the economists' view, paragraph 4 gives us the author's rebuttal and main idea. But every passage has *some* structure, and the better you understand that structure, the easier it will be to refer back to the passage when necessary.

The Questions:

16. (A) Global (Main Point)

We begin, predictably, with a Global question looking for the author's main point. As we discussed above, the main idea becomes evident at the beginning of the final paragraph: The economists are wrong, and CEOs *do* have a moral obligation to public welfare above and beyond their legal responsibility to maximize profit. The rest of paragraph 4 supports this opinion; the author believes CEOs must act morally even at the risk of losing their jobs. A pretty strong opinion, and **(A)** captures it nicely.

(B) harps on that corporation/individual relationship discussed in the second paragraph, but as mentioned above, paragraph 2 is the least informative paragraph in regards to the author's opinion. **(B)** may be hinted at in that second paragraph, but this relationship between individual and corporate morality is far from the main point of the passage; much greater authorial opinion is conveyed in the last paragraph in which the author actually takes a side in the debate and defends that position.

(C) places the profit motive above the public good, and thus goes against the grain of the author's argument; in the final paragraph, the author argues for just the reverse.

(D) would be closer to being correct if the entire last paragraph didn't exist. **(D)** merely restates one of the economists' arguments, but entirely ignores the author's stance in the matter, the espousal of which is the reason the passage was written.

(E) accords nicely with the economists' position that public good results even from economically-oriented decisions. But again, as in **(D)**, this ignores the author's position, which states just the opposite.

17. (B) Logic Function

There's only one true concrete example given by the author, and this question asks about it: Why does the author mention the paper mill in lines 42–46? This example comes right on the heels of the author's dismissal of one aspect of the economists' position: It immediately follows the statement "there is no guarantee that a CEO will benefit the public by maximizing corporate profit." The example therefore backs up this claim: The author implies that decimating a forest or polluting a lake to generate profit for paper mill owners is obviously not in the public's interest, and yet it's "absurd" to believe that this *won't* happen if the money is there to be made. Thus, as **(B)** correctly states, the paper mill example is used to argue against the economists' view that all economically-oriented decisions by CEOs will *necessarily* benefit the public.

(A), (D) The author offers the paper mill as an example of a likely possibility; it is a hypothetical situation that the author conjures up to make a point. It is absurd, according to the author, to deny the *possibility* of such a mill that destroys the environment in the name of profits. The author is not pointing to an *actual* existing paper mill, which is why **(A)** and **(D)** are both off the mark.

(C) is tempting, but approaches the issue from the wrong angle. The paper mill example is used to demonstrate that profit-seeking doesn't always have beneficial effects, so the discussion of the paper mill is *related* to the issue of harmful corporate behavior. However, the discussion is confined to the potential *existence* of harmful effects related to profit-seeking. The question of whether ethical restrictions would *curtail* harmful corporate behavior is another issue.

(E) is too extreme. Even if the paper mill *was* an actual mill, our author would be mighty desperate to use this one example to prove that corporate morality is impossible. Besides, as we've seen from **(C)**, this approach is off the mark—the author is using this example to argue not against corporate morality, per se, but against the notion that profit-seeking is *always* beneficial to the public.

18. (B) Inference

What do the economists think? By now, you should be pretty clear on that issue; the economists weigh in at the end of paragraph 1 in their objection to the corporation bashers, and their position is presented at length in paragraph 3. Their message boils down to profit profit profit—in any situation. According to the economists, every CEO except those heading charitable organizations should seek to maximize profits. In that case, CEOs of owner-operated *noncharitable* corporations should go for the green, choice **(B)**.

(A) *Au contraire*: The one exception the economists make regarding the principle of maximizing profit is found in line 25's "except in charitable institutions."

(C) The whole debate revolves around the act of seeking maximum profit; what type of corporations are more successful in this mission, that is, are *more profitable* than others, is one step removed from this scope.

(D) contradicts the economists, who argue that maximizing profits, a commonplace goal of corporate CEOs, can't help but benefit the public; maximizing profits "will turn out best for the public anyway" (lines 33–34).

(E) The economists avoid the environment issue like the plague, possibly because their "maximum profit all the time" principle is more questionable when it leads to serious environmental consequences. So there's no way we can infer they would place the environment above corporate profits. It is the *author* who raises the point of the environment (forests and lakes) in the context of his paper mill example.

19. (A) Logic (Principle)

We now shift to the author's viewpoint. The stem may be a little wordy, but all it's asking for is the principle that accords best with the author's view of morality, and that issue isn't far from the author's main point. CEOs have a moral obligation to pursue the public good; this idea of the "public good" is littered throughout the passage. It's no surprise, then, that the principle of morality that underlies the author's opinion is related to the public good, which brings us directly to choice **(A)**.

(B) goes too far. The notion of "penalty" surfaces in the last sentence, which states that even if a CEO faces penalty or dismissal, he or she must still act morally. That's a long way from saying that the risk of penalty *guarantees* the morality of an action. For example, the author would ostensibly feel that a CEO who decimates a forest for profit may incur the risk of penalty, but wouldn't argue that because of this risk the destruction of the forest is a morally good act.

(C) No, the author condemns those perfectly *legal* activities that CEOs sanction that work against the public good. In the first paragraph, the author mentions that there *is* criticism of corporate fraudulent and illegal acts, but then turns the focus of the argument away from these blatant corporate abuses to the more subtle abuses—the *legal* activities carried out to ensure maximum profit that do harm to the public at large.

(D) A classic distortion of the text: **(D)** combines the notion of maximizing profit with the notion of the public good to produce the hybrid concept of "maximizing one's personal benefit." Nowhere does this concept appear in the passage. Even if we assume that "personal benefit" means the same thing as "maximizing profits," **(D)** still doesn't fit because the author isn't against profits per se, the author merely believes that there are ethical restrictions on profit-seeking.

(E), like **(B)**, goes too far: The author may believe that actions that detract from the public good are morally wrong, but that doesn't mean that actions that do no harm to people *cannot* be morally wrong.

20. (C) Global (Primary Purpose)

No use wasting a lot of time here: As we know, the author thinks that the economists' position is wrong, and offers an alternative view on the issue. Once again, the first sentence of the last paragraph (lines 35–36) tells the story— "the economists' position does not hold up under careful scrutiny." The rest of the paragraph tells why. To refute the economists' claim, choice **(C)**, is the reason this passage was written.

(A) There is no paradoxical situation presented here, just one position countered by another.

(B) The passage is about the morality, not the legality of corporate behavior. In fact, it is implied that the kind of actions to which the author takes exception are legal; he opposes them because they don't accord with his conception of morality.

(D) and **(E)** are both too weak to represent the author's purpose here; they both ignore the fact that the author argues against a position and presents a case for his own view.

Passage 4: Russian Serfdom, U.S. Slavery
Questions 21–27

Topic and Scope: Kolchin's comparative study of serfdom in Russia and slavery in the United States; specifically, Kolchin's identification of important differences between the two systems.

Purpose and Main Idea: Author wants to outline Kochin's findings, "especially with regard to the different kinds of rebellion exhibited by slaves and serfs."

Paragraph Structure: Paragraph 1 explains that very few historians have compared slavery and serfdom, with the final sentence introducing Kolchin's book. Paragraph 2 notes key differences in the number and population size of slave-or serf-owning estates in Russia and the United States. Paragraph 3 explains that these demographic differences "partly explain differences in the kinds of resistance that slaves and serfs practiced in their respective countries." Resistance was common in both countries, but large, organized, armed rebellions were more common in Russia. Conflicts between U.S. owners and slaves were frequent but less collective, mostly because there were fewer workers on each estate in the United States.

The Big Picture:

- This History passage focuses on a book. That's common. What's unusual is that the author gives no direct *critical assessment* of Kolchin's ideas. The author just lays out Kolchin's findings, implying that his work is satisfactory.
- The academic lingo is long-winded, but the paragraphs organize things nicely—certainly a dividend for the pressured test taker. Paragraph 1: a long intro to Kolchin; paragraph 2: the key demographics; paragraph 3: differences in forms of rebellion.

The Questions:

21. (A) Global (Main Point)

(A) captures the gist of the key final sentence of paragraph 1, and it echoes the thrust of paragraph 3. Plus it echoes the content of paragraph 2, which supplies the demographic facts that explain the differences in forms of slave and serf resistance.

(B) contradicts the passage. Kolchin has now written such a study—and the implication is that it's at least "adequate."

(C) refers to a detail in paragraph 3. It entirely leaves out the companion issue of slave resistance in the United States.

(D) distorts the passage, which never suggests that Kolchin is skeptical of comparative studies. On the contrary—he's written one!

(E) De Toqueville is a passing detail in paragraph 1.

22. (B) Detail

(B) paraphrases the first 2–3 sentences. It's as simple as that.

(A) contradicts the opening sentence: "Until recently, *few historians were interested* in analyzing the similarities and differences between" serfdom and slavery.

(C) distorts the passage, which never suggests any "inability" on de Toqueville's part—he simply never addressed the issue of abolition in the two countries.

(D) Like **(A)**, **(D)** contradicts the first sentence.

(E) is half-right, half-wrong. De Toqueville "recognized the significant comparability of the two nations…" but his commonality with other historians was that he never compared slavery and serfdom.

23. (C) Logic (Strengthen)

(C) is consistent with key info in paragraphs 2–3. Organized rebellions were common in Russia because most serfs lived on large estates, which encouraged collective forms of resistance. A parallel idea would be that any organized rebellions occurring in the United States would, like those in Russia, have occurred on large estates.

(A) would weaken Kolchin's theme. His idea is that Russian conditions tended to encourage *hugely explosive revolts*, not merely "smaller collective acts of defiance"—the *volnenie*.

(B) picks up on info in the second sentence of paragraph 3: much of the rebelliousness in both countries—which took the form of silent sabotage—escaped the historical record. Kolchin's major point, however, is that demographics accounted for differences in the occurrence of *overt armed rebellion*, not silent sabotage. Plus, if there were armed revolts in the United States that escaped the historical record, then that would raise questions about, not strengthen, Kolchin's findings.

(D) goes on at length without saying anything especially relevant.

(E) would undercut Kolchin, who points to a revealing correlation between the likelihood of serf revolt and the fact that most Russian estates were managed by intermediaries.

24. (C) Logic Function

(C) paraphrases the passage. The author's surprised that the coincidence of abolition in Russia and the United States "failed to arouse the interest of scholars." As **(C)** says, that coincidence should have prompted comparative study of the two institutions.

(A) The passage never explains what led to abolition in either country.

(B) The passage never suggests that de Toqueville missed something he should have noticed.

(D) No criticism of Kolchin's book is ever made.

(E) is inconsistent with the passage, which stresses key differences between slavery and serfdom.

25. (A) Detail

This choice repeats info in the last sentence of paragraph 1: "...historians might have been put off by the forbidding political differences between nineteenth-century Russia and the United States."

None of the other choices are suggested.

26. (D) Detail

(D) is a simple paraphrase of the point made in the last sentence of paragraph 2: "In Russia most serfs rarely saw their owners...." Cut quickly through ultra-long wrong choices. Every one of these sounds suspicious in its opening words: the passage says zilch about nobles *agreeing to the abolition of serfdom*...**(A)**, *becoming more directly involved in estate management*...**(B)**, *commonly agreeing to any demands*...**(C)**, or *hastening the abolition of serfdom*...**(E)**.

(A) Never suggested. The only action attributed to the nobles was their *relying on intermediaries* to manage their estates.

(B) Ditto. Never suggested.

(C) Never suggested.

(E) Never suggested.

27. (D) Inference

(D) is pretty directly stated in the last sentence of paragraph 2, the same material that provided the answer to question 26.

(A) The passage never says that any estate owner—Russian or U.S.—was "prepared for collective protest."

(B) 180: most southern planters—98% of them, implies paragraph 2—owned fewer than 100 slaves.

(C) Tempting, since most Russian estates were managed by intermediaries, but not clearly implied. **(D)** is far better.

(E) 180, according to paragraph 2.

Passage 5: Ancient female doctors
Questions 28–34

As usual, the **Topic** of this passage, surviving sources of information about women doctors in ancient Greece and Rome, is introduced immediately. We learn in line 2 that these sources are "fragmentary," but it is not until lines 5–6 that the **Scope** of the passage becomes clear. We'll spend the rest of the passage learning what the author thinks these surviving bits of evidence tell us about the female doctors in ancient times. In another twist, the author tells us immediately what she believes the surviving evidence proves: that female medical professionals who were on a par with male medical doctors existed in ancient times, which pushes back the start date for the history of women in medicine. This sounds a lot like her **Main Idea**. While it is rare that the **Main Idea** would show up in the first paragraph of an LSAT passage, it is not unheard of, and it is clear from the Conclusion Keywords in lines 6–7 ("the evidence shows that…") and 10 ("So…") that the author is putting forward her opinion.

The next paragraphs support the idea that the author's conclusion appears early. Paragraph 2, paragraph 3, and paragraph 4 all discuss the evidence that, according to the author, shows that there were female medical doctors in ancient Greece and Rome. Paragraph 2 discusses the nature of the evidence, and the fact that women doctors were apparently common enough that they did not merit special notice. Paragraph 3 and paragraph 4 bring up two other aspects of medical practice by women in ancient times: female doctors' practice was not limited to midwifery, and female doctors were apparently considered with male doctors indiscriminately. All three of these paragraphs merely provide evidence for the conclusion expressed in paragraph 1. The **Purpose** of the passage will take this into account—it is to prove that women were medical doctors in ancient times.

The Big Picture:

Paragraph 1: surviving info on women in medicine in ancient times shows they were full doctors

Paragraph 2: nature of surviving evidence, what that shows

Paragraph 3: female doctors, not just midwives

Paragraph 4: similarity between male & female doctors

The Questions:

28. (A) Global (Main Idea)

Even when the author's Main Idea appears before the end of the passage, it must take the scope of the entire passage into account.

While the author might have been generous enough to give us her conclusion early on, that doesn't mean we can slack off for the rest of the passage. We've still got to be sure we know how the remainder of the passage figures into her argument, and we've got to make sure that the correct answer includes the scope of those later paragraphs. The only choice that accurately sums up the scope of the entire passage while still providing a paraphrase of the author's conclusion is **(A)**—the "range of textual evidence" in this choice is a crucial component of the author's main idea.

(B) focuses on the details about the writings of Pliny the Elder from the final paragraph, making this a classic Faulty Use of Detail wrong answer choice.

(C) distorts the evidence as cited by the author. She emphasized the fact that ancient writings make no special comment on the existence of female doctors, showing that female doctors were not so rare as to warrant such notice.

(D) distorts the text. The author definitely argues that female medical practitioners rose to the level of doctor, but not necessarily that they were also researchers.

(E) Scholars arguing that women did not practice medicine in ancient times do not appear in the passage—if they exist at all, perhaps the author will deal with them in her next article.

29. (E) Detail

Never answer a Detail question on a hunch.

The answer to this question must be contained in the passage. After all, we're asked for something that the author mentions. We should take the time to skim through the text to make sure we've found the correct answer to this Detail question. This research probably won't take too long, and it will pay off when we can be certain we've got the correct answer before moving on. Our research will lead us to **(E)**; the author mentions in paragraph 4 that Pliny the Elder and other ancient writers "quote the opinions and prescriptions of male and female doctors indiscriminately. (53–54)"

(A) Most people reading this passage can probably think of a few diseases that have become curable only with the advent of modern medicine, but that doesn't mean that the author of the passage mentions them.

(B) Paragraph 3 mentions evidence that some female doctors treated mainly female patients, but does so in the course of showing "evidence of a broad scope of practice for women doctors (42–43)" in ancient times.

(C) Francesca de Romana is mentioned in paragraph 1 as a candidate for the first female doctor, but a specific scholar advancing her candidacy is nowhere to be found.

(D) The training of medical doctors in ancient Greece and Rome is outside the scope of the passage.

30. (A) Logic Function

Your Roadmap will help you answer questions on the purpose of a paragraph.

According to our Roadmap, the third paragraph tells us that female doctors in ancient times were more than just midwives; this information is additional evidence for the Main Idea expressed in paragraph 1. This provides us with a powerful pre-phrase of the answer, which is matched by **(A)**.

(B) runs contrary to the author's argument in paragraph 1. The argument in the first paragraph is the author's own; why would she later argue that her own conclusion is too broad?

(C) is too detailed. Paragraph 3 does mention in passing some exceptions to the earlier conclusion—the female doctors who treated mainly female patients—but acknowledging their existence is not the primary focus of the paragraph.

(D) and **(E)** paragraph 3 advances its own argument—that women docs weren't just midwives—as evidence for the conclusion formed in paragraph 1. It does not include anything that relates to both of the prior paragraphs.

31. (B) Inference

Anything added to the passage must conform to the author's opinion.

You could be forgiven for assuming that this was somehow a Global question. After all, it does ask us to continue the final paragraph of the passage, and most of us are in the habit of placing the conclusion of our arguments somewhere near the end of the passage. But the looser language ("could most logically be appended") suggests that our task is Inference. We'll do our research in the final paragraph and look for an answer choice that logically continues its argument. We will, however, be careful to make sure that our correct answer stays within the scope of the passage.

Paragraph 4 is focuses on "references in various classical works to . . . women's writings on medical subjects (47–50)." The important fact about these references, according to the author, is that they are made in the same manner as references to the work of male doctors, without any special distinction on the basis of the gender of the writer. Any continuation of this paragraph should further the author's argument in the paragraph. Only **(B)** does so, and even takes the extra step of connecting the argument in paragraph 4 to the similar argument made in paragraph 2.

(A)'s strong phrase "only by" should make us skeptical, and that skepticism pays off: it contradicts some information in the final paragraph, which says that the references to women's writing were made "without biographical information (57–58)."

(C) and **(D)** are also 180s, but they go further than **(A)** did and contradict the author's earlier arguments.

(E) adds an element to the final paragraph that undermines the argument already made, suggesting that there is a "conflicting picture of ancient medical practice" rather than evidence for the uniform acceptance of women doctors.

32. (D) Inference (Author's Attitude)

In Author's Attitude questions, ask whether the attitude in question is positive or negative, and to what degree. Each answer choice in this question begins with an adjective, and—much like scanning the verbs in a **Purpose** question—we can scan the adjectives in an Attitude question. The "sources of information" mentioned in lines 1–5 are "fragmentary (2)," but the author argues that "even from these fragments we can piece together a picture." In fact, the information contained in these fragments, and the deductions made based on that information, is the focus of the entire passage. It sounds like the author is assuming that the information we can glean from these bits and pieces is accurate, and that assumption is found in **(D)**.

(A) The author is not "wary" of misinterpretation. There is nothing to suggest that the author believes that the fragmentary nature of the information makes it prone to misinterpretation.

(B) The author is not "optimistic" about lingering questions. It is hard to imagine a more complete analysis than the author gives in her work, and the passage doesn't suggest that there are any "lingering questions" left unanswered.

(C) The author is not "hopeful" about the sources' acceptance. This choice applies more to the author's attitude towards her own conclusion than to the information she used to arrive at it.

(E) The author is not "convinced" of the sources' "appropriateness as test cases." Additionally, a "new historical research methodology" is well outside the scope of the passage.

33. (D) Logic Function

Look out for different ways that the LSAT can phrase classic question types.

While question 19 is not phrased like most of the Logic Function questions that we've come across in our practice, it still asks us how a particular detail figures into the passage as a whole. Thankfully, once we've figured out what type of question we're dealing with, we can still use Kaplan's tried-and-true strategies—in this case, digging into the context of a detail to determine how it is used. The tribute in question is part of paragraph 3, which focuses on the breadth of women doctors' practice in ancient times, and the fact that it was not simply midwifery. This quote must have been used to support the claim of the paragraph as a whole, which we find in **(D)**.

(A) The only reference to "other doctors" comes in paragraph 4's discussion of references to doctors' opinions in ancient medical works. These doctors are never said to acknowledge each other.

(B) While the tribute quoted does mention one woman doctor's "knowledge of medicine," there is no evidence that her knowledge was acquired through education.

(C) could be correct in a Detail question, but not in a Logic Function question. The epitaphs certainly suggest that the women mentioned were effective, but that implication is not the purpose of the statements' inclusion in the paragraph.

(E) makes an irrelevant comparison. The only tributes mentioned in this paragraph are for a female doctor—we have no tributes to male doctors for comparison.

34. (C) Inference

Scan the passage carefully to find support for the correct answer to an Inference question.

An Inference is something that must be true based on the information in the passage. The support for it will not necessarily be a lengthy citation of evidence or the conclusion of a paragraph. In fact, it is often the case that an Inference is supported by only a single, easily missed reference in the passage. When that is the case, we must carefully research the passage to find the correct answer, using the passage's scope and Roadmap to guide our research.

(A) Our research turns up no references to how long women doctors practiced. Eliminate.

(B) The focus of the passage is squarely on women who were medical doctors—those who were not doctors, and any informal medicine they may have practiced, are outside the scope of the passage. Eliminate.

(C) Lines 13–16 refer to "Francesca de Romana's licensure to practice general medicine." According to the passage, this took place in 1321, and was "the earliest known officially recorded occurrence of this sort." This means that there must not be any known official records of a licensed female doctor before 1321—so no such records existed for women in ancient Greece and Rome, which is stated almost directly in paragraph 2's "There is no list of women doctors in antiquity." **(C)** must be true, and is correct. For the record:

(D) If anything, paragraph 3's discussion of the distinction between doctors and midwives suggests that there were some female doctors who acted as midwives, although their practice was not limited to midwifery. Eliminate.

(E) The only posthumous honors in the passage are the epitaphs in paragraph 3, both of which are for medical—not civic—accomplishments. Eliminate.

Passage 6: Measuring Economic Health
Questions 35–41

The **Topic** is raised in the very first sentence: the economic health of a nation. The **Scope** is confirmed, as usual, in the first few lines, and it can be expressed as a question: What should be used to measure that health? The answer to that question comes in lines 9–12 and turns out to be the **Main Idea**, that "human indicators"—hard to pinpoint as they are—are more helpful ("sounder measures") than the traditional yardstick of per capita GNP (a concept the author takes pains to define for those unfamiliar with it). So the author has a persuasive **Purpose**; he wants us to get away from the standard that traditional political economists have employed.

Paragraph 1 lays all of that out, and ends by clarifying what the author means by the aforementioned human indicators, which turn out to refer to the facts of people's everyday existence rather than some average dollar amount. Paragraph 2's scope is defined in 19–23, since the author cannot claim that improving per capita "often fails to" stimulate human indicators without providing supporting evidence. Lines 24–45 represent that evidence. The gist of it is twofold: There exist examples of high per capita GNP nations that suffer on a human level (lines 28–32); and while per capita GNP may be high *on the average*, that economic health may not be trickling down to the vast majority of a nation's citizens (lines 32–45). Paragraph 3 discusses nations—unnamed—that evidently have already been persuaded by the author's argument; they already have moved toward a policy of improving human indicators rather than improving per capita GNP.

The Questions:

35. (C) Global (Main Point)

The right answer here, as in any Global question, must encompass the passage's topic, scope, and purpose, and only **(C)** does so. "Preferability" alludes to the author's persuasive purpose and strong point of view, and the rest of **(C)** is equally on target.

Per capita GNP's meaning **(A)** is established in lines 3–6, never shifts, and never gets an "historical" treatment. **(B)** sounds like the title for an interesting passage-length article, but insofar as this passage is concerned **(B)** only encompasses lines 19–23. Even if you take **(D)**'s "vs." phrases to stand for per capita GNP and human indicators respectively—and doing so is a huge distortion of both terms—**(D)** wrongly casts the whole passage as a balanced debate, failing to signal the author's decided preference. **(E)**, like **(A)**, implies that the definition of per capita GNP has changed, and wholly ignores the human indicators that are at the heart of the Scope.

Kudos, incidentally, if you chose to move right from question 1 to the other Global question at the end of the set.

36. (A) Detail

The categorical language ("is used," "refer most specifically") suggests that we can go right to the passage reference to pick up the meaning of "welfare," first introduced in lines 6 and 7. The thrust of it has to do with the topic, that of measuring economic health, and that's **(A)**.

(B) alludes to a few of the human indicators of economic welfare (lines 15–18), but not to the broader concept of welfare itself. **(C)** is a component of per capital GNP but like **(B)**, it alludes to a gauge of economic welfare rather than to what welfare means. **(D)** and **(E)**, meanwhile, cannot possibly be correct because they bring up concepts—distribution and redistribution of wealth, and balance—that don't emerge until late in paragraph 2 and 3, far removed from this question's realm.

37. (E) Detail EXCEPT

Pinpointing the information mentioned in the four wrong choices may be the fastest way to identify the choice that goes undescribed. **(A)** is clearly lines 3–6, and the full sentence in lines 1–6 addresses **(B)**. **(C)** is explained in lines 55–58, while those same lines, not to mention lines 28–39, go into detail as to **(D)**'s issue (as well they might; **(D)**'s issue is at the heart of the entire argument). But **(E)** is never discussed, and no wonder: Why would the author include information as to how to improve the very measuring factor—per capita GNP—that he wants nations to eschew?

38. (B) Logic (Weaken)

Predicting the right answer helps you wade through the morass of the lengthy answer choices. Since the last paragraph lauds nations that are trying to improve human indicators of economic health rather than per capita GNP, a counterexample would naturally describe the opposite, and so **(B)** does. A nation that improves domestic production (a function of GNP, "the goods produced yearly in a nation") and thereby sees improvement on a daily human level is behaving not in line with paragraph 3 but rather just as the author's opponents, the economists in lines 19–23, would advocate.

(A), **(C)**, and **(E)** all mention nations that are following paragraph 3's lead by shifting focus away from material-wealth indicators to human indicators. That each sees a different result in terms of its per capita GNP—slower growth in **(A)**, increased growth in **(C)**, and flatness in **(D)**—doesn't obscure the fact that these three nations are going about the improvement process in the right way, paragraph 3's way. And **(E)** exemplifies exactly the unhappy result predicted by lines 52–55.

39. (E) Logic Function

If your Roadmap more or less paralleled the one we describe above you probably had little problem choosing **(E)**. ¶ 3 takes the author's argument about measuring economic health into the real world of nations' economic policy decisions.

The debate is wholly tilted toward human indicators—we've known that since lines 8–12—so no such "synthesis" as **(A)** proposes is ever made and the dual debunking described by **(B)** is just that: de-bunk. If any summary **(C)** of the argument occurs, it's back in lines 8–12. And since the author is out to demolish the political economists **(D)**, not correct them, **(D)** goes way off.

40. (A) Inference

As long as you remember that the political economists in question are the author's opponents, the ones who insist that per capita GNP is the way to measure economic health, you should be able to stride or stumble toward **(A)**, in which a nation's economy is responding exactly how lines 21–23 predict.

(B) is far too harsh. By arguing that improved per capita GNP will improve a nation's human indicators, the political economists are implicitly investing those human elements with relevance. **(D)** is a somewhat daffy position for anyone to hold since, in the context of the passage, "welfare" and "economic health" are more or less synonymous (see question 2). And **(C)** and **(E)** are the 180 choices, direct opposites to that which the question desires. Each represents a position with which the author would be far more comfortable than would his political-economist foes.

41. (B) Global (Primary Purpose)

The entire thrust of the passage is to turn nations away from per capita GNP as a measurement of economic health and toward a more human set of factors, and that's the gist of **(B)**.

(A) blows up paragraph 3 into the primary concern. Overall the author is trying to lay out the philosophical underpinnings, as it were, for the real-world economic behavior that the passage stops short of outlining. **(C)** and **(D)** concern themselves with paragraph 2 details rather than the overall purpose, and **(E)** goes way outside the scope with the utterly irrelevant question of who is to make the decisions.

Passage 7: Steady-State Economics
Questions 42–49

Topic and Scope: Steady-state economics: Specifically, the position of this new school, a serious challenger to the reigning school, on the issue of diminishing natural resources.

Purpose and Main Idea: The author's Purpose is to describe some fundamental principles of a new school of economic thought by drawing contrasts with the tenets of the reigning model, neoclassicism. His main point—it's difficult to call it a Main Idea as the author allows little or no personal opinion to come through—is that the steady-state economists take issue with the idea that economic growth can be unlimited. They want to effect a balance with nature and limitations on growth, confident that humanity's ability to satisfy wants won't be compromised.

Paragraph Structure: Paragraph 1 lays out the battle lines right away: A new economic school is challenging the reigning one. The rest of the paragraph details the neoclassical definition of economy (a closed loop) and its fundamental (as far as the passage is concerned) principle, namely that "growth has no limits" (line 8). Growth should not be checked; growth indeed is necessary for solving economic problems.

Paragraph 2 offers the steady-staters' reply to that position. To them, economics is not a closed loop because the outside forces of nature intervene. Nature, whose resources run out and whose ability to process waste is limited also. In sharp contrast to the "Growth: Yes" tenet of neoclassicism, the central steady-state belief is that unlimited growth tends to "impoverish rather than enrich," and so steady-staters want to see a balance made with nature. The author brings in the neoclassicists one more time, in lines 30–36, where we hear their answer to the above: Nature is not a separate outside force but part of the entire picture, and new resources can be created should natural ones run out.

Paragraph 3 shifts from the broad lines of steady-stater argument to a specific, though related, concern: Some believe, probably to the fury of the neoclassicists, that optimum growth has already been reached. In other words, an "equilibrium with nature" had better be made pretty darned quick. Their proposal for doing so includes conservation, the focus of the final 10 lines. Growth is quantitative, whereas conservation is qualitative—the latter is but one "alternative to growth" that, say the steady-staters, can satisfy human wants and still keep nature and economics balanced.

The Questions:

42. (D) Global (Main Point)

Notwithstanding the unconscionable length of the choices, what we need in the answer to a Main Point question is a focus on the steady-state school, and an emphasis on the key issue of growth. Only **(D)** provides both of those things while still managing to characterize the passage's ideas acceptably. It properly alludes to the steady-stater view (as outlined in paragraph 2) that growth must be limited, and sums up the notion (presented in paragraph 3) that alternative means to growth exist that can keep satisfying humanity. Let's see where the others go wrong:

(A) sums up the neoclassical position pretty well, but in speaking of steady-staters merely in passing, it fails utterly as the main point. It is, after all, steady-state ideas that are explored in the greatest detail (and rightly so: They are the new kids on the block, the ones with the new ideas); steady-staters begin and end the passage. On top of all that, **(A)** reflects almost nothing of paragraph 3. These are all key reasons for rejecting **(A)** decisively.

(B) All, not some, neoclassicists believe in unlimited growth. Anyway, the substance of **(B)** ends at passage line 13. Fully 47 lines of text go unreflected by **(B)**.

(C) All, not some, steady-staters argue against unlimited growth. And they never concede the potential of such qualitative strategies as conservation to lead, even temporarily, to "stagnation" (a term used only by the neoclassicists in opposition to the steady-state view, lines 44–47).

(E) spends half of its length on similarities between the two economic schools, when the entire passage is devoted to separating them. And **(E)** never mentions the key issue of the passage—that of economic growth.

43. (A) Inference EXCEPT

This question is the LSAT equivalent of a tongue-twister. Unpack it before proceeding further. "The neoclassicists would believe that steady-staters are wrong to believe..." The question is talking about sentiments that the steady-staters hold but that neoclassicists would oppose. And there are four of them; this is an "all of the following EXCEPT." Four of the choices are both consistent with steady-stater philosophy and contradictory to neoclassicism.

What do steady-staters believe? In limits to growth. In the dangers of growth. In our dependence on nature. And in the need for alternatives to growth, such as conservation, to ensure that though growth is limited, we can still satisfy human wants and needs. We can expect to see such ideas reflected in the wrong choices.

(A) Surely the steady-staters believe that natural resources—what **(A)** calls "the environment's ability to yield raw material"—are going to run out sometime. And the neoclassicists don't disagree. Oh, sure, the neoclassicists are optimistic about humanity's ability to replenish whatever is lost, so they aren't worried about nature's resources running out. But they do acknowledge that it may happen. That makes **(A)** what we want for this question. All of the other choices, as expected, reflect steady-state ideas that are anathema to the old guard:

(B) Lines 30–32 vs. lines 19–22.

(C) Line 8 vs. lines 26–28.

(D), (E) Lines 7–8 vs. lines 37–44.

44. (E) Detail

Ask yourself: Where in the passage does the idea of "danger" come in? If you don't recall that this particular Keyword is mentioned about halfway, you can simply skim through the passage in search of the word, and there it is at line 28. The Conclusion Keyword "thus" ("Steady-state economists thus believe that . . .") sends us backward to find the evidence for that conclusion in the previous sentence. Once the economy hits optimal growth, further growth "would increase the cost to the environment at a faster rate than the benefit . . ." (lines 23–24). This quote is virtually **(E)** word for word. The other four choices' "faster rates" are utterly distinct from line 28 and its preceding context. So none of them can be correct.

45. (B) Inference EXCEPT

If the right answer is *least* likely to be endorsed by a steady-stater, it follows that the four wrong choices are *more* likely to get his endorsement, meaning that four of the choices would help to reduce growth while satisfying human wants. All of that must send us to paragraph 3 and specifically to lines 47 and beyond, where the steady-staters' proposals, so to speak, are described. Conservation is named as one of the alternatives to growth "that still . . . [satisfy] human wants" (lines 48–49), and the author describes conservation as "qualitative, not quantitative": It involves better management of resources "rather than an increase in the amount of resources" (i.e., rather than more growth).

Four of the choices will match that qualitative ideal.

(A) Recycling is smart resource management. This statement would please the steady-stater.

(B) Cheaper fuel has nothing to do with better management of resources, though it's likely to save the manufacturer money. So it's probably the odd-man-out correct answer.

(C) Quality control, to reduce the number of defective products, is smart resource management.

(D) So is a switch to greater fuel efficiency. [Note the sharp contrast to **(B)**, which saves money only.]

(E) Reducing output to avoid overproduction couldn't be smarter. As anticipated, **(B)** is the odd man out.

46. (C) Logic (Principle)

The word "success" appears towards the end of paragraph 3, line 56, but even if you didn't recall it you still could have inferred an answer to this question by appealing to the passage's broadest ideas. We know that the steady-staters want to limit growth; we know they want to see a balance with nature; and we know that they don't want to inconvenience or deprive mankind in the process. All of that leads us to **(C)**, which of course is directly echoed in the final sentence: "One measure of . . . success" will be a balance between helping nature by checking growth and the satisfying of wants.

(A) is a principle that sounds more in line with the neoclassical argument, dealing as it does with the prospect of utilizing man-made resources. The steady-staters seem to believe that if measures like conservation are successful, the resources provided by nature can go a long way.

(B) Want *creation* isn't part of the passage's scope. Want *satisfaction* is.

(D) The steady-staters want to limit growth because, if unchecked, it would threaten the Earth's balance. That doesn't mean they oppose all growth. **(D)** is just too extreme, even radical, for the views here, and distorts those views to boot.

(E) The words "spur growth" should be a tip-off that this is a neoclassical idea and, hence, just the opposite of the way in which a steady-stater would define success.

47. (C) Detail

In Detail questions, signaled by the kind of categorical language we see here, we need to stay very close to the passage's text and should expect to pull the answer right out of it. In Inference questions, we often have to paraphrase one passage reference or (more likely) combine two or three passage references in order to come up with the right answer. The work on this Detail question is trickier than most in that, although it sends us to line 7, the information is to be found nowhere near that line. Indeed, the question is getting at much broader issues. Paragraph 2 more or less acts as a direct answer to the neoclassical definition of economy outlined in paragraph 1, and it's early in paragraph 2 that we learn a chief difference between the two schools: To the neoclassicist, nothing outside of the economy acts as a check on growth, whereas to the steady-stater, nature is a huge outside check on which the economy is dependent. The limited ability of nature to "regenerate new material and absorb waste" (lines 20–21) is the basis of the steady-stater's denial that growth is unlimited, and is the basis of correct choice **(C)** to boot. Further support for **(C)**—in the admittedly unlikely event that you kept reading down to the end of paragraph 2 for a question that began at line 7—is offered in lines 30–32: Neoclassicists "consider nature to be just one element of the economy rather than an outside constraint," implying that to the steady-stater, nature is such a constraint. **(C)** is the only choice that alludes to a facet of nature. The four wrong choices all mention elements of economic reality, either **(A)** and **(B)**'s major factors worth considering, or **(D)** and **(E)**'s potential dangers to economic health worth avoiding. But none of the four checks economic behavior, and that's what this question is looking for.

48. (D) Logic Function

Building a Roadmap will always involve thinking about a paragraph's purpose, so one should always have a leg up on questions like this one. Paragraph 3, you'll recall, describes the rather apocalyptic opinion of some steady-staters that optimum growth has already been reached; the reaction of neoclassicists; and the proposal from steady-staters that the switch be made from the quantitative (growth) to the qualitative (conservation). This analysis matches up with the abstract language of **(D)**: The "objective" comes in lines 44–47; the "additional policy" is conservation; and the "goal an economy must meet" is the satisfaction of human wants. **(A)**'s wording is weird. "[C]ontradicts" the ways of interpreting data? Don't they mean "contrasts"? Also, the author shows no interest in "judging" between them. **(B)** can't possibly be right because the author takes no stand on either school's position and makes no recommendation. **(C)**, like **(B)**, implies author bias that is absent here. **(E)** seems to think that paragraph 3 is mostly about neoclassicism, the "prevailing . . . school," when that school is only mentioned in passing; and **(E)** is also off because both schools agree on "the basic goal" of an economy: satisfying human needs.

49. (B) Inference

By now we have pinpointed the few locations in which neoclassical economists' views are expressed, and we need only refresh our memory of them before searching for the one answer choice that is reflected somewhere in those locations. Correct choice **(B)** comes out of paragraph 2 and lines 30–36, the assertion that the "process of unlimited growth" can go on by replacing depleted natural resources "with other elements—i.e., human-made resources." Unlimited growth would be possible only if man-made resources were equally unlimited.

(A) The very fact that the neoclassicists have a remedy in mind (outlined in lines 30–36) for the depletion of natural resources indicates that they do not believe **(A)** to be true.

(C) "Growth has no limits" (line 8), remember?

(D) And because growth has no limits, neoclassicists are granting no necessary condition for growth such as **(D)** describes. In any case, as far as the passage goes, management inefficiency is a steady-state concern (line 54).

(E) No such preference is even hinted at. The neoclassicists will just roll with the punches: If natural resources run out, we'll simply replace them with the man-made kind.

Passage 8: National Service
Questions 50–54

Topic and Scope: Compulsory national service; specifically, whether or not it is within the rights of a liberal democratic state to compel compulsory service.

Purpose and Main Idea: The author's main idea is clearly stated in the last sentence of paragraph 2, signaled by the Keyword "Therefore": A democratic state can legitimately compel its citizens to perform national service when that service is necessary for the benefit of society. The author's purpose in the passage is to show why this is so and to refute actual and anticipated arguments of the opponents of this notion.

Paragraph Structure: Paragraph 1 begins by describing an argument made by opponents of compulsory national service: Compulsory service contradicts the principles of Western democracy. The second sentence draws an analogy between this argument and another argument—that income taxes are undemocratic because they violate the right to property. The author then criticizes the tax argument as failing to consider that the social contract imposes obligations on citizens even as it extends individual rights. The author declares that income taxes are justified by the need for law enforcement, which benefits everyone in society.

Paragraph 2 presents the author's argument in a nutshell: Since the responsibility to defend a nation is at least as important as the responsibility to pay for law enforcement, it is therefore within the rights of a state to compel compulsory service when such service is needed for the benefit of society.

Paragraph 3 lays out a possible objection to the author's argument—we know this is a hypothetical argument the author is anticipating in advance from the phrase "it might be objected..." Taxes and compulsory service are not really analogous, opponents might claim, for two reasons. First, government cannot collect taxes without coercion, but it can find volunteers for the military. Second, a compulsory national service might not limit its scope only to duties that are absolutely necessary to defense.

Paragraph 4 answers that objection by assigning a broad definition to the word "need": If one agrees that tax money should be spent on more than just the survival of the state, then one must also agree that a nation's needs rightly include more than just national defense. Thus, compulsory national service can include duties beyond national defense and still be considered democratic.

The Big Picture:

- For many, this passage was a good place to start the section. Even though the passage has only five questions, the subject matter is accessible (maybe even interesting), and the author's point of view comes across early.

- Just as you should read the first sentence of each paragraph carefully, so should you pay extra attention to the last sentence of an entire passage. The last sentence often summarizes the author's main idea in a clear and helpful way.

The Questions:

50. (E) Inference (Author's Attitude)

A careful consideration of purpose and main idea can help us describe an author's attitude or tone. Here, the author argues that a democratic state can legitimately compel its citizens to perform national service when that service is necessary for the benefit of society. This argument is directed in response to a claim that compulsory service amounts to a squelching of individual rights. The author rejects that claim by concluding that each of us must share the burdens imposed by community (lines 16–17). In other words, the author argues that rights do not override obligations, an attitude captured nicely by **(E)**.

(A), (B) These are too positive and nearly contradict the author's attitude. Each might accurately express the attitude of an opponent of compulsory service, but the author sees individual rights as of little importance in the absence of sacrifice and shared responsibilities **(A)**, and sees individual rights as defining the limits of people's actions with respect to other people (line 12) rather than as limiting government interference **(B)**.

(C), (D) These are too negative and are beyond the scope of the passage. The author does not discuss whether citizens are taking advantage of each other **(C)** or how many defenses there might be to government interference **(D)**.

51. (A) Detail

The passage mentions politicians only once (line 41). If we compare that entire sentence with the stem and choice **(A)**, it should be clear that "even the most conservative of politicians admits" reasonably translates to "all politicians agree" and that "great benefit to society" translates to "the national good."

(B) The notion of using the military to quell civil disorders appears in line 46 as a challenge to the opponents of national service; can they deny, asks the author, that such a thing benefits the country? But the author is no longer speaking of politicians at this point, so the author does *not* directly indicate that all politicians would agree to this kind of use of the military.

(C), (D) The author argues that conscription and compulsory taxation are similar, and that the definition of necessity should be broadened. But a politician who is opposed to compulsory service might disagree on both counts.

(E) Again, it is the *author* who argues that compulsion is compatible with democratic principles. Opponents of compulsion argue otherwise—and it is quite possible that that group includes some politicians.

52. (A) Inference

What does "social agreement" mean in the context of the rest of Paragraph 1? In the sentence before the reference in question, the author mentions the argument that income taxes are undemocratic. We are told that "Such conceptions...fail to take into account" the social agreement. Thus, the social agreement must contradict the argument that a law is undemocratic simply because it violates an individual right. The next sentence explains how we arrive at this contradiction: The social agreement involves community and the deliberate limitation of rights, the same idea summarized in **(A)**.

(B) is an *au-contraire* choice. It is the position of the opponents to compulsory service, not of the author. The words "fail to take into account" (line 7) tell us the author wants to contradict those opponents.

(C) and **(D)** go beyond the scope of the passage. The author does not write about petitioning the government for redress, nor does he write about how limits on government actions are codified.

(E) greatly distorts the author's argument. The author argues that liberties must be balanced against responsibilities and shared sacrifice, not that the government can legitimately suspend liberties at whim.

53. (E) Detail

If you grasp the main idea of the passage, this question is a snap. The author's main point is that compulsory service, like taxation, does not violate the principles of democracy if we expand the definition of "need" to include more than just activities necessary for national survival. **(E)** summarizes that idea concisely.

(A) *Au contraire*. The military may be able to find recruits without compulsion, but the author writes that taxation must be coerced (lines 24–7).

(B) The author's point is that they are *not* at odds with individual rights, that individual rights have application only in the context of the needs of the larger community (lines 9–17).

(C) The author writes about "shared sacrifice" in the first and last paragraphs but mentions nothing about relative levels of sacrifice, either for taxation or national service.

(D) *Au contraire*. According to the author, both national service and taxation are within the legitimate boundaries of democratic government.

54. (B) Inference

In lines 46–47, the author lists several military activities that are not necessary for defense in a "survival of the nation" sense, yet must be viewed even by opponents of compulsory service as legitimate reasons for taxation. These activities all have one thing in common—they directly provide a "needed" benefit to the society paying the taxes. Only **(B)** does not confer a direct benefit back onto the taxpayers, and thus might be found objectionable.

(A), **(C)** These expenditures fall into the category of defending the nation from outside aggression, which the author writes is "certainly" within a state's rights (paragraph 2) and is admitted to by opponents of national service (lines 33–35).

(D) and **(E)** are both listed as expenditures that are of great benefit to society—and thus fall within the author's widened definition of "need."

Passage 9: Southeast Asian Immigrants
Questions 55–60

Topic and Scope: Southeast Asian immigrants; specifically, educational programs in immigrant processing centers.

Purpose and Main Idea: The author's purpose is to describe and critique Tollefson's views about educational programs in immigrant processing centers. Her main idea is that Tollefson is correct to argue that the philosophy of these centers has caused adjustment problems for immigrants.

Paragraph Structure: Paragraph 1 introduces Tollefson's *Alien Winds*, describing how it's different from earlier works that look at Southeast Asian immigrants. Instead of focusing on immigrants themselves, it focuses on immigrant processing centers. Predictably, paragraph 2 takes up where paragraph 1 leaves off: it goes into further detail about Tollefson's views. Essentially, Tollefson argues that these centers do immigrants a long-term disservice by encouraging immediate employment and rapid adoption of Western ideals. Paragraph 3 notes that Tollefson traces the philosophy of today's immigrant processing centers to programs initiated at the beginning of this century—programs that were intended to assimilate European immigrants into the American mainstream.

Up to this point, we've been given an extended discussion of Tollefson's ideas. The author's views of Tollefson's work have yet to be made clear. Paragraph 4 provides the author's views. While she *approves* of his critique of immigrant processing centers as well as his recommendations for changing their focus, she's *critical* of his failure to furnish concrete proposals for implementing reform.

The Big Picture:

- You're likely to see a book review passage on Test Day. If it appears, this passage will be highly predictable. It will contain two basic elements: a description of a particular book and a critique of that book. In most cases, the description will precede the critique.

- Because this type of passage is so predictable, it's often a good place to begin work on the Reading Comp. section, especially if no other passage jumps out at you as extremely manageable.

- In a book review passage, it's crucial to be clear on the difference between the book's views and the author's views. Many of the questions will test to see that you can distinguish between them.

The Questions:

55. (C) Global (Main Point)

In paragraphs 1–3, the author discusses Tollefson's critique of immigrant processing centers—their educational programs, he claims, make it difficult for immigrants to achieve success in American society. In line 48, the author describes this critique

as "able"—that is, on target. Only choice **(C)** accurately reflects the author's attitude toward Tollefson's critique.

(A) While the author notes that Tollefson's work constitutes "a significant departure from most studies of Southeast Asian immigration," she also notes that his study focuses exclusively on immigrant processing centers, not on broader economic or cultural issues.

(B) The author's only criticism of Tollefson's critique is that it doesn't offer enough concrete proposals for reforming immigrant processing centers. She never claims either that current center programs have positive effects on immigrant lives or that Tollefson has overlooked this reality.

(D) Neither Tollefson nor the author claims that immigrants succeed in spite of the educational programs in immigrant processing centers. Quite the contrary. Both argue that these programs have caused harm to immigrants.

(E) What change? Neither Tollefson nor the author traces any change in the harmful attitudes held by immigrant processing center educators.

56. (B) Inference

Tollefson's ideas about educational programs offered at immigrant processing centers are dealt with in paragraph 2; so, look there for the information necessary to answer this question. At the beginning of this paragraph, we're told that Tollefson believes that these programs emphasize immediate employment (line 15) and economic self-sufficiency (line 20). Later in this paragraph, we're told that he thinks that these characteristics of the educational programs sometimes cause immigrants to lose business opportunities (lines 32–33) within their own communities. Choice **(B)**, then, echoes his ideas.

(A) To the contrary. Tollefson thinks that these programs provide *inadequate* job training to immigrants—training that doesn't address their long-term needs (see lines 19–25).

(C) Tollefson's problem with the educational programs of immigrant processing centers is with the *underlying assumptions* of these programs. Thus, he wouldn't argue that these programs would better serve immigrants simply by teaching the history of immigration to the United States.

(D) While Tollefson apparently visited a teacher-training unit (line 9) as part of his research, he doesn't discuss "teacher-training courses." Nor does he comment on the competence of the teachers themselves. Besides, his real problem is with the *underlying assumptions* of the educational programs.

(E) To the contrary. Lines 26–38 tell us that Tollefson believes that the existing emphasis placed on Western values, beliefs, and practices in these programs has been harmful to immigrants. Hence, he wouldn't want an even greater emphasis on these things.

57. (B) Inference (Author's Attitude)

This question asks about the *author's* opinion, which is revealed in paragraph 4. Essentially, the author argues that Tollefson's critique of immigrant processing centers offers new insights into problems with these centers, but few genuine solutions to these problems. Choice (B) acknowledges the author's sense that Tollefson's study is on the right track, but isn't the final word on the topic.

(A) Since the author doesn't think Tollefson provides solutions to the problems he points out, she wouldn't argue that his work is "thorough." Moreover, she wouldn't consider it "misguided" either. Indeed, she acknowledges the study's importance, even while she's critical of it.

(C) What contradictions in Tollefson's work does the author speak of?

(D) "Illuminating" fits, but "unappreciated" doesn't. After all, the author never comments on what others think of Tollefson's work. She provides only her own opinion of it.

(E) Since she says that Tollefson's study "relies on an impressive amount and variety of documentation," the author would agree that it's "well documented." But she wouldn't argue that it's "unoriginal." In fact, she makes a point (in paragraph 1) of saying that his work takes a different approach to studying Southeast Asian immigrants than earlier works. In other words, she'd probably claim that his work is original.

58. (A) Logic (Assumption)

In lines 27–29, we're told that the educational programs offered at immigrant processing centers have tried to "instill in the immigrants the traditionally Western principles of self-sufficiency and individual success." Why would the centers try to instill these principles unless the people who run their educational programs believe that these principles could help immigrants adjust to life in America? Indeed, that choice (A) is an assumption made by such people is confirmed by the first sentence of paragraph 2.

(B) The only point made about language proficiency occurs in lines 19–22, where we're told that educational programs at processing centers prepare immigrants for jobs that don't require English proficiency. Based on this information, we can't conclude that those in charge of educational programs at processing centers think that English is best learned on the job.

(C) That immediate employment tends to undermine a sense of community among immigrants is a view held by Tollefson (see lines 29–31). Whether those in charge of education at the processing centers believe that immediate employment breaks down communal bonds is an entirely different matter—one that the passage doesn't comment on.

(D) Lines 34–38 tell us that the people in charge of educational programs at processing centers encourage immigrants to shed their "cultural traditions and ethnic

identity" in order to make it in America—a stance that's not consistent with a belief in the importance of maintaining communal solidarity.

(E) If the people in charge of educational programs at the processing centers think that self-sufficiency and individual success are principles "central to Southeast Asian culture and ethnicity," why would their programs strive to instill these values in Southeast Asian immigrants?

59. (A) Logic Function

Paragraph 1 does two things: (1) it differentiates Tollefson's work from earlier works about Southeast Asian immigrants and (2) it tells us something about how Tollefson gathered data for his work. In other words, this paragraph sets Tollefson's work in the larger context of Southeast Asian immigrant studies and describes its methodology.

(B) The first part of this choice is accurate enough—paragraph 1 does compare Tollefson's work to other works. The second part of this choice, however, is off target—Tollefson's main argument appears in paragraph 2.

(C) While paragraph 1 compares Tollefson's work to other works, it doesn't compare his *methodology* to those employed in these other works.

(D) What theory?

(E) The author's opinion about Tollefson's work isn't revealed until paragraph 4. Moreover, she never rates his work as "superior" or "inferior" to other works in the field of Southeast Asian immigrant studies.

60. (B) Logic Function

The Keyword "despite" (line 61) is crucial. It signals that what follows is intended to reinforce the sentence's earlier conclusion (lines 59-61). The author, in other words, is particularly disappointed with Tollefson's "overly general recommendations" for improving immigrant educational programs because she recognizes that implementing reforms will be such a difficult task.

(A) What the author's critical of is not Tollefson's decision to talk about bureaucracy and reform in the same breath, but rather his inability to prescribe specific measures for overcoming bureaucratic obstacles.

(C) What irony? The author's has no problem with Tollefson offering solutions to existing problems; she just doesn't like the particular solutions that he proposes.

(D) The author never contends that Tollefson fails to identify the real problems with the educational programs. What she says is that he fails to offer workable *solutions* to these problems.

(E) What parallel? The author never suggests that Tollefson's arguments are as complicated as the bureaucracy that he examines.

Passage 10: Mayan Civilization
Questions 61–65

Topic and Scope: Lowe's book about Mayan civilization; specifically, a description and analysis of Lowe's theory concerning the collapse of Mayan civilization.

Purpose and Main Idea: The author's purpose is to describe and analyze Lowe's theory about the collapse of Mayan civilization. The author's specific main idea is that Lowe's theory, though plausible, could be undermined by the discovery of new evidence about the downfall of Mayan civilization.

Paragraph Structure: In paragraph 1, the author describes Lowe's theory about the collapse of Mayan civilization. Essentially, that theory is based on archaeological evidence. According to Lowe, the decline of Mayan civilization can be traced by looking at where monuments were built and what was inscribed on them. To this point in the passage, the author is content to summarize Lowe's views; she doesn't advance any of her own views about Lowe's theory. Nevertheless, it's predictable that she's going to do so in subsequent paragraphs. Most non-science passages, after all, go beyond mere description, to make some sort of argument.

Paragraph 2 delivers on the prediction. In the first sentence, the author argues that Lowe's theory is "plausible" because it fits the available archaeological evidence. The author then goes on to discuss additional details of Lowe's theory, which is based on the notion that population growth set off a chain reaction of events that eventually culminated in the downfall of Mayan civilization.

In paragraph 3, the author offers a criticism of Lowe's theory. She doesn't take issue with his view per se. Rather, she notes that his explanation *could* turn out to be bogus. Archaeological evidence, she goes on, isn't definitive; and new evidence about Mayan civilization—evidence that could undermine Lowe's theory—*might* one day come along.

The Big Picture:

- This passage is a classic *book review* passage. On Test Day, you will most likely see a book review passage. If you do, keep in mind that book review passages tend to have a very particular structure: the author first summarizes the book's contents and then offers praise/criticism of the book.

- In book review passages, it's very important to distinguish between the author's view and that contained in the book. Many of the questions will test to see that you can distinguish between the two.

The Questions:

61. (D) Global (Organization of Passage)

This choice hits the nail on the head. In paragraph 1, the author describes the basis of Lowe's theory—the archaeological evidence relating to the decline of Mayan civilization. In paragraph 2, she describes the "guts" of the theory—how population growth set off a series of events that ended with the destruction of Mayan civilization. And, in paragraph 3, the author refers to a potential problem with the theory—because archaeological evidence isn't definitive, the theory could be undermined by the discovery of new evidence.

(A) and **(B)** mistakenly suggest that the author presents an opinion of her own concerning the collapse of Mayan civilization. Rather, she simply states that Lowe's theory, while plausible given the available evidence, could be undermined by new evidence.

(C) and **(E)** What evidence that contradicts Lowe's study is presented (C and E)? And where does the author suggest a specific direction for future studies about the collapse of Mayan civilization **(C)**?

62. (E) Global (Main Point)

In line 25, the author refers to Lowe's theory as "plausible," or credible. But, in lines 44–53, she notes that his evidence isn't definitive and that his theory, therefore, could be overturned by the discovery of better evidence.

(A) and **(D)** mistakenly suggest that the author takes a stand on the correctness of Lowe's theory. Her opinion is actually more circumspect. She notes that, while the theory is *plausible* based on what is currently known about Mayan civilization, it could be undermined if better evidence about the Mayans eventually comes to light. In other words, she believes that the theory has yet to be proven right or wrong.

(B) The author never claims that Lowe's theory "breaks new ground." Indeed, in lines 5–7, she notes that previous investigators also examined the collapse of Mayan civilization by looking at Mayan monuments. Furthermore, she doesn't claim that Lowe has come up with a definitive explanation of this civilization's collapse.

(C) misrepresents the focus of the author's comments. She's interested in Lowe's theory about the *collapse of Mayan civilization*, which does involve the examination of Mayan construction. However, she's not interested in Lowe's discussion of Mayan construction per se.

63. (E) Logic (Parallel Reasoning)

According to lines 9–10, Lowe assumes that the Mayans left a place soon after they stopped building new monuments there. In other words, he assumes no additions indicates abandonment. Similarly, the person in choice **(E)** assumes no additions to the stamp collection indicates abandonment of the stamp collection.

(A)–(D) None of these choices reflects the "no additions = abandonment" relationship.

64. (B) Inference

In lines 5–7, the author mentions that "investigators" before Lowe used the same archaeological method as he did to examine the collapse of Mayan civilization. So, she'd characterize this method as "generally accepted." In lines 47–49, however, she suggests that this method may not reflect historical reality. In other words, she'd also characterize it as "questionable."

(A) and **(E)** The author wouldn't characterize a method that she acknowledges has been used by a number of investigators as either "daringly innovative" **(A)** or "unconventional" **(E)**.

(C) and **(D)** Nor would the author characterize a method that she acknowledges is problematic as either "very reliable" **(C)** or "effective" **(D)**.

65. (E) Inference

Since the author says that Lowe's theory—which is based on archaeological evidence—is "plausible," she would probably agree with the generalization that archaeological evidence can be used to reconstruct history. However, in lines 47–49, she also makes the point that it's impossible to know the extent to which archaeological evidence reflects historical reality.

(A) Lines 47–49 indicate that the author is considerably more skeptical of the value of archaeological evidence than this choice would suggest.

(B) is outside the scope of the passage. The author never brings up any comparison between the "day-to-day activities" of a culture and "its long-term trends."

(C) In line 49, the author suggests that archaeological evidence is particularly problematic when it's used to mine the history of a "complex" civilization. In any case, the complexity of a civilization has nothing to do with its duration.

(D) While the author is skeptical about whether archaeological evidence actually reflects historical reality, she's not against using it to reconstruct the past. If she felt that the use of archaeological evidence was bogus, she wouldn't have called Lowe's theory "plausible."

Passage 11: Maravall and the European Baroque
Questions 66–72

The section ends with a Social Sciences passage detailing Maravall's theory that the European baroque period was not just an aesthetic style, but also a discrete historical period with political, social, and cultural phenomena that foreshadowed certain aspects of the modern world.

Paragraph 1 announces the **Topic:** the European baroque. The **Scope** is Maravall's theory about the baroque being more than an aesthetic style. The author's **Purpose** and **Main Idea** are not completely clear until the last paragraph, where the author, after describing Maravall's interpretation, offers mild criticism of Maravall's theory.

In paragraph 2, the author discusses Maravall's argument that the baroque was a period when the ruling classes asserted control over a society that had become unsettled by the Renaissance's "liberating forces of criticism and opposition."

Paragraph 3 is where the author explains Maravall's view of how the monarchy and aristocracy controlled the masses, using "grandiose artifice" such as fireworks displays, theater, and religious festivals as tools of manipulation.

In paragraph 4, however, the author argues that Maravall's interpretation goes too far, and that he tends to exaggerate the capacity of rulers and aristocrats to manipulate society for their own ideological ends. Moreover, according to the author, the theatrics and symbolism of the baroque negatively affected members of the ruling class, "dangerously isolating" them from the outside world and leading the monarchy and aristocracy into a credibility gap that made them less effective in controlling their societies.

The Big Picture:

Paragraph 1: Maravall—baroque as political, social, cultural phenomenon, pre-modern

Paragraph 2: Baroque culture: control and containment

Paragraph 3: Political controls: repressive but enticing

Paragraph 4: Author: M. overstates rulers' powers to control society

The Questions:

66. (B) Global (Main Idea)

Watch out for answer choices that employ a faulty use of details.

Our Roadmap tells us that this passage is all about Maravall's view of baroque culture as a tool used by the ruling classes to manipulate and control society at large, and that the author believes that Maravall overstates the success of this strategy for social control. That's answer choice **(B).**

(A) This answer choice is tempting, as it talks about the concept of the baroque being more than an aesthetic style, and notes Maravall's concept of baroque culture as a way that rulers manipulated and controlled the general public. However, the passage never indicates that Maravall's interpretation of the European baroque is a "recent" development in historical analysis.

(C) This is another tempting wrong answer choice, because the passage does tie the European baroque to the Renaissance, but *not* as an "expansion" of the social and intellectual developments of the Renaissance. Rather, the baroque is seen as a reaction to the unsettling effect of the Renaissance on society at large. Further, the author suggests that Maravall was overly influenced by his experience of living under the Spanish dictator Franco, as opposed to any suggestion that Maravall's ideas were colored by his "focus" on Spain.

(D) starts off in a promising way, talking about Maravall's theory of the ruling class using culture as a means of social control, but the term "refuted" is much too strong for the mild criticism offered by the author in the final paragraph.

(E) This answer choice is good as far as it goes, but it leaves out the whole last paragraph, where the author suggests that Maravall might have been overly influenced by his desire to see a foreshadowing of modern society in the baroque era, and by his experience of living under the dictatorship of Franco in Spain. This answer choice also fails to capture the author's point that the strategy of using baroque culture to control a society was not necessarily effective, and may even have been counterproductive at times. This failure to account for a significant portion of the passage makes this an incorrect answer choice for a Global question.

67. (C) Inference (Author's Attitude)

Your Roadmap should clue you in to places within the passage where the author's attitude is apparent.

Our Roadmap indicates that the author's criticism of Maravall's theory comes in paragraph 4, beginning with line 44. Since we are looking for an answer choice that reflects the author's attitude "in context," we can quickly eliminate answer choices **(A)** and **(B)**, which point to earlier sections of the passage.

(C) Lines 47–48 and the phrase "tends to exaggerate" precisely describe the author's attitude toward Maravall. That's our right answer.

(D) The phrase "own ideological ends" at line 49 is in the right paragraph, but in context, refers to the motives of rulers in promoting the baroque culture, not the author's attitude toward Maravall's concept of baroque culture.

(E) Likewise, the phrase "wholly counterproductive," in context, refers to the attempts by the ruling class to use baroque culture as a means of social control. Not a good answer choice when placed into context.

68. (D) Inference

It is especially important to check for context when the question involves the meaning of a word used in the passage.

We see the word "directive" used most frequently as a noun meaning "order," but in this passage the author uses the word as an adjective, describing Maravall's concept of the baroque as a culture of control and containment, designed to "reintegrate and unite" a society that had been disrupted. This sense of baroque culture as being a tool of manipulation gives the use of the word "directive" a meaning along the lines of "guiding," answer choice **(D)**.

(A) "Direct" may mean "straightforward," but Maravall's view of the Baroque as a "directive" culture reflected a sense of manipulation of the public. Not at all "straightforward."

(B) Maravall viewed the "directive" Baroque culture as a way of changing society (for the benefit of the ruling classes), but the word "evolving" does not capture Maravall's point. "Evolving" suggests a process that is not necessarily directed by outside forces, whereas Maravall viewed the changes in society during the Baroque era as the result of the conscious effort of the ruling classes to reestablish their authority and control over society.

(C) While a "directive" may be a codification of rules or instructions, Maravall's view of baroque culture was that it served to *entice* the interest of the masses, and *redirect* their desire for novelty into areas where that desire would pose no threat to the political order. There is no sense that baroque culture was somehow bound by some type of code.

(E) The author uses Maravall's concept of a "directive" culture as the springboard for a discussion of how the baroque culture served to entice the general public into submitting to the authority of the ruling classes. "Compelling" is too strong of a term to describe this enticement.

69. (D) Inference

Your understanding of the scope of the passage can help you eliminate wrong answer choices on an Inference question.

The author tells us that Maravall believed that during the baroque era, monarchs used the enticements of baroque culture to defend traditional order and values that had been disrupted during the tumult of the Renaissance. That's answer choice **(D)**.

(A) The passage never suggests that Maravall regarded the monarchs as increasingly indifferent to unfavorable public opinion. To the contrary, Maravall argued that every aspect of baroque culture was related to the importance of manipulating public opinion.

(B) According to the passage, the aristocracy was aligned with the monarchs, part of the ruling classes who used baroque culture to achieve ideological ends.

(C) The author, and not Maravall, suggests that the monarchs were themselves captivated by baroque culture, which caused the ruling class to become "dangerously isolated" from the outside world.

(E) The passage never suggests that Maravall saw the monarchs of Spain and England (or any other monarchs) as striving for cultural preeminence among the countries of Europe.

70. (C) Inference

Research, then pre-phrase your answer choice.

Baroque theater is mentioned in paragraph 3, as one of the means by which the ruling class delighted and redirected the general populace, so as to avoid challenge to the political order. Answer choice **(C)** says just that.

(A) While Maravall saw baroque culture as a response to the European social and economic crisis after the Renaissance, the passage never suggests that Maravall saw baroque theater as a way to spur economic growth.

(B) In Maravall's view, baroque theater, along with other diverting spectacles, was intended to channel and manipulate public opinion, not reflect any consensus of public opinion.

(D) The emerging principle of individual liberty was precisely what baroque culture was intended to suppress.

(E) Baroque theater was intended to entice, not terrify, the citizenry. It was intended to deflect their attention away from the repressive nature of the monarchy.

71. (C) Global (Purpose of the Passage)

Be ruthless in eliminating answer choices that do not match your Roadmap.

Our Roadmap reminds us that the first three paragraphs of the passage are spent explaining Maravall's theory of baroque culture, and the last paragraph briefly sets forth the author's mild criticism of Maravall's theory. Answer choice **(C)** follows that Roadmap quite nicely.

(A) While the author does not entirely agree with Maravall's theory, she does not set forth any competing theory to contrast with Maravall's theory.

(B) The author challenges Maravall's viewpoint, but offers no indication as to whether the view of Maravall and "some" other scholars about the European baroque is widespread.

(D) Given the tentative and mild nature of the author's critique of Maravall's theory, that critique cannot fairly be called an "opposing" argument. Further, the author makes no attempt to reconcile that critique with Maravall's views.

(E) "Explain" is a good verb for beginning the answer choice, but it's all downhill from there. The author never describes any "consequences" following from Maravall's view of the baroque as a political construct.

72. (D) Logic (Weaken)

One way to weaken an argument is to break down the relationship between the evidence and the conclusion.

Maravall argues that the extravagant and elaborate art that characterized the baroque period served to distract the populace from the repressive nature of the monarchy. If many baroque era works of art in fact expressed opposition to the monarchy, as in **(D)**, that would undercut Maravall's theory about baroque culture.

(A) The author notes that Maravall lived under the Franco dictatorship, and suggests that Maravall's life experiences colored his view of baroque art. The precise nature of Maravall's life experiences, however, says nothing about whether or not baroque art and culture was a way of controlling the population for the benefit of the ruling classes.

(B) Both the nobility and the monarchs are described by Maravall as being part of the "ruling class" that used baroque art to manipulate public opinion. Any purported difference in the number of artworks commissioned by the nobility versus the monarchs would not affect the validity of the argument that both groups used art to achieve their ideological ends.

(C) If we were to learn that baroque art provided an idealized depiction of the monarchy and aristocracy, that would fit right in with Maravall's view that baroque art was used to strengthen the position of nobility and royalty within that society.

(E) Evidence that the dictator Franco sought to control Spanish society by cultural means would, if anything, strengthen Maravall's argument, as another example of those in power using art and culture to manipulate and control society at large.

Passage 12: Native American Readjustment
Questions 73–79

This passage outlines the post-World War II conflict between the federal government's policy of Native American "readjustment," outlined in paragraph 1, and an alternative view held by some Native Americans themselves. *When you see that a passage is based on a contrast, don't endeavor to understand all of its nuances. It's usually enough to work out the broad outlines.* Here, we see that basically the government called for greater assimilation of Native Americans into mainstream society, on the grounds that reservation life may have limited the Constitutional rights of the people. In contrast, and at about the same time, Native Americans wanted to strengthen tribal unity and identity instead of assimilating.

Paragraph 1 ends by promising that the Wisconsin Oneida tribe's experience with BIA will act as evidence for the clash, and that promise is fulfilled by the rest of the passage. In paragraph 2 we get the details of the BIA's readjustment offer to the Oneida— essentially, inducements to convert the tribe from collective to private land ownership (including the taxes that, no surprise, accompany it). We find out in paragraph 3 why the Oneida rejected the deal. *Structural signals really help you sort out any kind of list, particularly a list of "reasons why" something happened:* you might have wanted to seek out and highlight "first suggestion" (lines 36–37), "equally suspicious of" (line 45), and "Finally" (line 49), as a way of sorting out which reason in paragraph 3 links up to which offer in paragraph 2. But of course, as lines 33–35 announce, all three reasons basically boil down to the same thing: the tribe had heard it all before. Paragraph 4 hints at the consequences of that rejection, linking up "the lessons of history" (line 60) with line 35.

The Questions:

73. (C) Inference

As paragraph 1 mentions, a central tenet of readjustment was the belief that Native Americans should be assimilated into mainstream America. A program designed to encourage Native Americans to move from reservations (whose residents consist solely of members of the same tribe) to urban areas (where they would be certain to mix with individuals of different backgrounds) would go a long way toward accomplishing readjustment's goal of assimilating Native Americans into mainstream society. That makes choice **(C)** the scenario most consistent with the policy of readjustment.

The scenarios presented in each of the wrong choices would have the opposite effect of that intended by readjustment. Rather than promote assimilation, each of these developments would tend to strengthen Native American institutions and identity, an outcome favored by Native Americans themselves, not by those who advocated readjustment. *A common wrong-*

answer choice on the LSAT is the choice that contradicts information in the passage, so be aware of it.

74. (A) Detail

The outcome of the '56 meeting is the topic of paragraph 4, so look there. After rejecting readjustment in the wake of the meeting, the Oneida asked instead for federal funds for such things as better education and housing. Put another way, they wanted to improve the quality of life for members of the tribe, as correct choice **(A)** says. *Remember, correct answers often put a little spin on the passage text—a bit of paraphrase.*

Wrong choices **(B)** and **(E)** contradict information in the passage. In contrast to what **(B)** says, the Oneida were already pursuing land claims before the 1956 meeting (claims mentioned in paragraph 3, in fact). And **(E)** is a readjustment idea: in rejecting readjustment, the Oneida were attempting to maintain their distinct lifestyle, not to pursue one similar to that of other Americans. **(C)** is outside the scope of the passage: we're never told what position the Oneida took on their political status, before or after the 1956 meeting. Finally, while we're told that Native Americans in general wanted to develop tribal institutions in order to preserve their traditional way of life, the passage never specifically says that the Oneida sought new tribal institutions after the 1956 meeting, eliminating **(E)**.

75. (A) Logic Function

As we've already mentioned, the role of paragraph 1 is to describe two policies toward Native Americans that were in conflict during the 1940s and 1950s, setting the stage for the description of how this conflict played itself out in the specific instance of the Wisconsin Oneida vs. the BIA. In more abstract terms, which is what the question demands, paragraph 1 explains the cause of a specific conflict discussed later in the passage. That makes choice **(A)** the correct answer.

Of the wrong choices, **(B)** is perhaps the most difficult to eliminate. Paragraph 1 does present two positions, those of the federal government and Native Americans on readjustment. But so does the rest of the passage, which presents both sides of the story in the description of the BIA-Oneida negotiations over readjustment. True, the author sides with the Oneida, but it's an exaggeration for **(B)** to say that he "defends" their case to the exclusion of that made by the BIA. Moreover, this choice is inferior to choice **(A)** because it doesn't allude to the 1956 meeting that is the topic of the remaining paragraphs. Far from comparing interpretations of a historical conflict **(C)**, paragraph 1 provides background information necessary to *comprehend* a historical conflict. By the same token, paragraph 1 explains why a historical event unfolded the way it did; it includes no "analysis" of causes and certainly includes no future predictions **(D)**. Finally, **(E)** is completely off base. Paragraph 1 a history of the BIA? The agency isn't even mentioned until line 18.

76. (C) Logic Function

Pick up the phrase "increased awareness" in line 6, recognize through the "because" that the phrase is providing evidence for a conclusion, read a few more lines, and you're home free. This awareness led to a feeling that reservation life might limit the Constitutional rights of Native Americans and, in turn, to the "readjustment movement" (lines 8–9). **(C)** sums that up pithily.

The author does contrast the readjustment movement with another social phenomenon **(A)**, namely the Native American effort to assert unity and identity, but doesn't begin to do so until line 13, which is too far removed from the civil rights reference. *Watch out for choices that are true (according to the passage), but irrelevant to the question at hand.* Regarding **(B)**, increased awareness of civil rights played a part in determining government policy, not that of Native Americans. In fact, we're never told why Native Americans were so concerned to protect their unity and identity, just that they were concerned with these things. The text doesn't tell us anything about the specific motives of BIA bureaucrats **(D)**; we know only that they supported the policy of readjustment. *In Reading Comp., as in Logical Reasoning, choices that question people's motives tend to be incorrect.* As for **(E)**, if anything the author sides with Native Americans against readjustment, and certainly has no advocative purpose in paragraph 1 or anywhere else. Why the heck would he be fostering support for a policy dating back more than a quarter of a century, anyway?

77. (B) Inference

We already know that readjustment advocates believed that the federal government should end its special involvement in Native American affairs. **(B)** makes this point, though in a slightly different way. Saying that Native Americans should be treated by the government in precisely the same way as others are treated is more or less equivalent to saying that the government should butt out.

Advocates of readjustment would disagree with all four wrong choices for the simple reason that they all endorse the notion that it's the government's role to help maintain Native Americans as a community apart or, at least, to provide them with significant support. Indeed, it is opponents of readjustment who would be likely to agree with the sentiments expressed in **(A)**, **(C)**, **(D)**, and **(E)**. After all, according to the passage, opponents of readjustment wanted the federal government to improve the quality of life for Native Americans while maintaining the special status of Native American land.

78. (A) Inference

The treaty in question is mentioned only once, in the last sentence of paragraph 2, but it is implicitly alluded to at the end of paragraph 3 and it's there that the answer is to be found. How come? Because (as you'll recall), each of the offers made by the BIA in paragraph 2 got an Oneida reaction, and each reaction is described in turn in paragraph 3. This is an excellent example of how *some questions require you to relate two or more references from different parts of the passage.* The "lump-sum payment" (line 29 and again at line 50) was of course "in lieu of" (lines 29–30) the Canandaigua Treaty provisions, which the Oneida were clearly loath to change because doing so might put at risk certain ongoing land claims. **(A)** is a bit vague but on target. At least it gets the positive tone right.

Of the wrong choices, **(B)** and **(E)** can be eliminated on the basis of their negative tone. It's not the Treaty that was a source of problems **(B)** but the readjustment policy, and **(E)** is a genuine *180 choice—one which gives us the exact opposite of what the question is asking for.* **(C)** and **(D)** are positive statements but poor choices. Since the tribe and the government were already bound together by the Canandaigua Treaty, the delegates would have no reason to view the treaty as a model for a potential future agreement with the federal government **(C)**. And as for **(D)**, it's really reaching to describe the Oneidas' desire to affirm tribal identity as an aspiration to become "an independent…nation"; and even if that were a fair characterization, the passage never links it up with the Canandaigua Treaty.

79. (B) Logic (Parallel Reasoning)

Treat a Reading Comp. parallel reasoning question like any other; there should be no difference in your approach. We're fortunate in that this one picks up on the issues we were just exploring in the previous question. Lines 29–32 describe the payment and lines 49–53 describe the refusal. Remember, the rejection was not based on financial grounds, but on the fact that the $60,000 would alter the terms of the Canandaigua Treaty and jeopardize certain pending land claims. So a parallel situation would involve someone turning down an offer not on financial grounds, but because it would have dire legal consequences. That's **(B)**, of course—and notice that the gesture of the Oneidas and that of the employee share a certain selflessness that makes the parallel even tighter.

None of the other choices reflects this logic. In choices **(A)**, **(C)**, and **(D)**, the student, the teenager, and the customer, respectively, refuse the deals offered to them by the university, the parents, and the car dealer, respectively, purely on financial grounds. In none of these scenarios is a deal refused for a legal reason (or, for that matter, a selfless one). Finally, although the scenario in choice **(E)** involves a legal issue, the tenant really refuses the landlord's offer because it would inconvenience her, not because accepting it might jeopardize a legal position.

Passage 13: Functions of Names
Questions 80–86

Topic and Scope: Personal names; specifically the function personal names serve in different cultures.

Purpose and Main Idea: The author's purpose is to take issue with the popular opinion that personal names have only a limited function. Mill and Levi-Strauss have only a limited conception of the role of personal names, but their theories don't mesh with the functions of names in certain Native American cultures. The main idea is closely related to this point. Native American names go far beyond merely distinguishing one person from another or indicating social class; they can also reflect the character and experiences of the name-bearer, and they can be poems in and of themselves.

Paragraph Structure: Paragraph 1 begins by setting up the views with which the author will disagree. Mill thinks names just distinguish one person from another. Under this view, we could all exchange our names for serial numbers without losing anything important. Levi-Strauss, whose work never seems to go out of style, says that the primary purpose of names is to indicate one's social class. (Hmm . . . then why are so many people called "King?") As usual, the generally-accepted views are set up so that our author can knock them down. The vehicle for doing so is the Hopi tradition. The Hopis use names for other purposes besides those described by Mill and Levi-Strauss. Hopi names have a broader role in placing individuals within society. Moreover, Hopi names can be poems in and of themselves.

Paragraph 2 answers the question: "how so?" How do Hopi names go above and beyond the limits suggested by Mill and Levi-Strauss? For starters, we learn that Hopis receive different names as they complete rites of passage. Also, names are sometimes given to recognize the name-bearers characteristics or a connection with another clan.

Paragraph 3 begins with the emphasis Keyword phrase "More often, though," which indicates that an even more important distinction will be made. We learn that Hopi names sometimes refer to people and events that are not apparent from the literal translations of the names. Put into the proper context, Hopi names can be poems in and of themselves.

Paragraph 4 brings it all together, arguing that while Hopi names can serve the functions Mill and Levi-Strauss stress, they can do much more. Only with a proper understanding of the full cultural context can Hopi names be appreciated, so Mill and Levi-Strauss have missed something important.

The Big Picture:

- **Conventional wisdom tends to take a beating on the LSAT. Whenever an author says that most people believe something, you can bet that the author is going to argue that the opposite is the case. So when we learn in paragraph 1 that personal names are "generally regarded" in a certain way, we can bet the author will say something different.**

- **Whenever a passage contains multiple views, make sure you keep them straight. You can bet that the questions will test whether you've picked up on how they compare and contrast.**

- **On the LSAT, a promise made is a promise kept. When we see the author's claim in paragraph 1 that Hopi names can be seen as poems, we can bet that the author will try to back up that point somewhere along the way.**

- **Many LSAT passages include examples to illustrate the larger point being made. If you already understand that larger point, go ahead and skim the example. But if the general point has escaped you thus far, latch on to the example to help you make the larger point more concrete.**

The Questions:

80. (E) Global (Main Point)

The author's main point must encompass the scope of the entire passage. This passage explains how Hopi names go beyond the functions described by Mill and Levi-Strauss, and only **(E)** reflects this sentiment.

(A) starts off OK, but Hopi names do *more* than identify individuals and classify them.

(B) draws an unwarranted comparison. Yes, Hopi names have a poetic effect, but they also perform perfectly well distinguishing people and indicating social relationships. This isn't an "either/or" situation. Hopi names can do it all (lines 48–53).

(C) goes beyond the scope. We know from the last paragraph that interpreters that don't understand the full context of Hopi names won't understand their full significance, but we don't know whether any European thinkers have acquired that knowledge.

(D)'s reference to a precise formula goes too far. We get some examples of naming practices, but not enough to make the generalization in **(D)**. Even if we could, **(D)** is too narrow to be the author's main point.

- **Always read the entire choice. A number of these choices start off OK, but then go astray.**

81. (B) Logic Function

The stem takes us to the end of the third paragraph. Reading a few lines back for context, we find that the reference to Western Apache place names followed the long discussion of the Hopi name Lomayayva, a name that referred to a complicated image in a condensed way. The author then indicates that the full meaning of this name is like a Western Apache place name in that they are both compact poetic compositions. So the description of Western Apache place names is applied to Hopi names, and the description fits. **(B)** describes this relationship.

(A) No such example is provided. We learn that Western Apache place names are tiny poems, but we never learn anything about how their literal translations compare to their true meaning. In fact, we aren't given any specific place names at all.

(C) While there is a similarity between the two in the images they evoke, the actual naming practices are never compared, no less contrasted.

(D) The author is trying to prove something about *Hopi* names. While the quote does support the notion that Western Apache names also may have some deeper meaning, that isn't why they are mentioned.

(E) is a distortion. The Hopi name is similar to Western Apache place names simply because they both are like tiny imagist poems. No particular place name is mentioned in the passage.

- **Focus on the why, and not the what. By constantly asking why the author is writing, you put yourself in a good position to answer Logic questions like this one.**
- **When you get a line reference, make sure you start re-reading a few lines *above* the reference. Often, those lines are the key to the question.**

82. (E) Inference

Levi-Strauss was mentioned in the first paragraph. His view is described in lines 7–10. Basically, he thought that names indicate one's place in society. With that in mind, let's look at the choices:

(A) and **(C)** have nothing to do with the social characteristics of the parents or the child, so they can't be correct here.

(B) sounds like the "little rabbit" example cited in paragraph 2, but that was a Hopi example that demonstrated that the Levi-Strauss view was *too limited*. A name that refers to the child's looks or personality doesn't establish that person's place in society, so **(B)** doesn't work.

(D), if anything, goes against the grain of Levi-Strauss's theory. If denoting social status is the primary function of names, one would expect there to be at least some similarity in the names of family members.

(E), however, does the job, so to speak. One's occupation is directly connected to one's place in society, so being named after one's job is an example of names indicating one's social classification.

- **Always keep the different views straight. If you do, you can zero in on the relevant text and find the correct answer quickly.**

83. (D) Logic Function

The second paragraph backs up the author's claim in paragraph 1 that Hopi names can signify more than Mill and Levi-Strauss thought. The rites of passage example and the "little rabbit" example both indicate that names can have meaning. In other words, they can have semantic content, as **(D)** indicates.

(A) and **(E)** come from the wrong paragraph. The "poetic composition" stuff referred to in **(A)** comes in paragraph 3. As for **(E)**, the only literal translation we get is "little rabbit," which doesn't obscure any meaning. The name giver just thinks the kid looks like a little rabbit. Nothing mysterious there. The name with a misleading literal translation was "Lomayayva," but that comes from the third paragraph.

(B) is too limited. The paragraph does claim that Hopis receive names that refer to events in the recipient's life, but this claim is made to support the larger claim in **(D)**. It isn't the paragraph's main point.

(C) goes too far. Yes, they receive many names throughout their lives, but this doesn't by itself refute the European theories. The author's argument is much more complex than that.

- **Many Reading Comp. wrong answer choices refer to something in the text but don't answer the question asked. That's why it's so important to focus on the paragraph structure as you read. Knowing what is said where will help you avoid choices that come from the wrong paragraph.**

84. (A) Inference

Mill was one of the theorists mentioned in paragraph 1. They were the ones whose ideas didn't capture the aesthetic delight of Hopi names, so we should look for a choice that reflects the author's dissatisfaction. **(A)** fits the bill: Mill's view is too narrow to apply to Hopi names, since those names have a variety of functions distinct from mere identification.

(B) says that Mill's view would be correct if it were combined with the views of Levi-Strauss, but the author takes issue with *both* views.

(C) goes too far. Sure, Mill's narrow view didn't help matters, but that doesn't mean that nothing else was a factor as well.

88. (A) Detail EXCEPT

Since four of the choices are true of minimills, it is likely that the right answer will instead be true of one of the other branches. Two effective tactics here: (1) using the passage (or your homemade lists) to locate minimill details, and throwing out choices that reflect them, or (2) seeking out a choice clearly associated with another branch but not with minimills (or, of course, one that has nothing to do with any branch). A clear contrast comes in lines 23–28, and that generates the correct answer: It's the specialty mills that "preserve flexibility in their operations" (A), in contrast to the minimills' "narrow range."

(B), (E) Lines 23–28 and 59–61 indicate the minimills' focus on local sales (B) and limited product range (E).

(C) Minimills work only with scrap (lines 11–14), and have dispensed of the iron-smelting process, "including the mining…of raw materials" (lines 52–56).

(D) Like specialty mills, minimills "take advantage of new steel-refining technology" (lines 21–22).

89. (C) Logic Function

The reference to Japanese integrated producers at line 43 is preceded by "…but this cannot explain why," signaling that the purpose of the reference must be to rebut some assertion or explanation. Indeed, lines 39–42 mention a conclusion that "one might" make, that old labor-intensive machinery is the reason for the financial weakness of the U.S. steel industry, but that conclusion won't fly. If it were so, how come the Japanese companies, whose machinery is new and less labor-intensive, are also having financial woes? The Japanese situation shows, according to the author, that the weakness of the U.S. industry must not be due to the labor-intensive machinery. (C) explains that use to which the detail is put.

(A) *Au contraire*, the Japanese and U.S. integrated producers have economic woes in common.

(B) *Au contraire*, lines 46–49 confirm that ALL integrated producers share the same "common technological denominator": inefficiency.

(D) Hardly. See lines 46–49, "an inherently inefficient process" since the 19th century.

(E) may be a true statement, but not one that the Japanese counterexample sheds any light on.

90. (E) Logic Function

As we've seen, paragraph 3 outlines the problems plaguing integrated producers, after which one possible reason for poor performance (labor-intensive machinery) is rejected and another (inherent inefficiency) is proposed in its place. All of that is (E) in a nutshell.

(A) ignores lines 29–39's detailing of the troubles of integrated producers, and then mixes up what follows: If anything, first we get a hypothesis (i.e. a working theory) that's criticized, followed by an opposing view that's supported.

(B) is just words. The author's blaming the industry's problems on inefficiency rather than machinery does not constitute the "resolution" of a "debate."

(C) A dilemma is an inherent contradiction. Paragraph 3 points to no such paradox.

(D) More words, ignoring lines 29–39 altogether. And there is no move from the specific to the general in paragraph 3.

91. (E) Inference

Your lists of details can be exceptionally useful in questions like this one. (So can a reminder that paragraphs 1 and 4 are the main paragraphs comparing the three branches of the steel industry; almost certainly one or both of those paragraphs will yield question 25's answer.) The fundamental difference between integrated producers on the one hand, and specialty-steel mills (ditto minimills) on the other hand, is that the former smelt iron ore and coal while the latter just work with scrap. Lines 50–57 spell out that both of the smaller branches "have dispensed almost entirely with" such "front-end" elements as (E)'s blast furnaces.

(A), (D) Both are minimill details (lines 23–28). Specialty-steel mills retain flexibility.

(B) *Au contraire*, lines 17–20 tell us that specialty-steel mills share relative economic health with the minimills.

(C) distorts the example of the Japanese steel industry: The only Japanese counterparts mentioned in the passage are the integrated producers, discussed in paragraph 3.

92. (A) Logic (Parallel Reasoning) EXCEPT

An interesting question of the "analogy" or "parallel reasoning" type. Four of the choices face similar problems as integrated producers; we must find the odd man out. Your best tactic is to refresh your memory as to the problems of integrated producers, i.e. to reread paragraph 3, and then skim the choices for parallels. One way or another you should be left with (A). It seems as if the only problem that integrated producers are *not* faced with is a shortage of raw iron ore and coal. While everything else seems to be going wrong for the integrated mills, a lack of raw materials is never mentioned as a problem.

(B) shares the problem of "excessive labor" costs (line 31).

(C) describes the problem of heavy capital expenditures cited in line 31, and again in lines 50–54.

(D) speaks to "manufacturing inflexibility" (line 32).

(E) Old and "less automated" equipment is the problem here, as it is for the integrated producers in lines 32–34.

93. (E) Logic (Strengthen)

By this time, your familiarity with the problems facing integrated producers is probably keen enough that you can study each choice, in whatever order, and discern fairly readily which one best matches up with the author's explanation for the condition of this segment of the steel industry:

(A) has to do with a nation's economic health, not that of one of its industries.

(B) If integrated producers share a characteristic with the small and profitable specialty-steel mills, then that *weakens* any explanation about why the former are doing badly.

(C) The Japanese integrated producers are also in trouble. If the ones in the U.S. mimicked their quality, reduced energy, and reduced labor, then matters might improve, but that's not what we're looking for here. The fact that they're adopting the Japanese style doesn't tie in with why they are currently in the condition the author describes.

(D) speaks to efforts on the part of integrated producers to improve their lot; again, as with **(C)**, that is outside the scope of the question of why they are down on their luck in the first place.

(E) suggests that the "front-end" task of iron-smelting—in which we know integrated producers are engaged—is capital-intensive and unprofitable (lines 50–57), so much so that in other countries it requires government subsidy. This is solid evidence that, as the author alleges, iron smelting is indeed a drag on the integrated producers' economic performance.

Timing
Practice

Reading Comprehension 1

PrepTest 47, Section II
October 2005

SECTION II

Time—35 minutes

26 Questions

<u>Directions:</u> Each passage in this section is followed by a group of questions to be answered on the basis of what is <u>stated</u> or <u>implied</u> in the passage. For some of the questions, more than one of the choices could conceivably answer the question. However, you are to choose the <u>best</u> answer; that is, the response that most accurately and completely answers the question, and blacken the corresponding space on your answer sheet.

In 1963, a three-week-long demonstration for jobs at the construction site of the Downstate Medical Center in Brooklyn, New York, became one of the most significant and widely publicized campaigns of
(5) the civil rights movement in the United States. An interdenominational group made up mostly of locally based African American ministers, who had remained politically moderate until then, organized and led hundreds of people in an aggressive protest. Their
(10) efforts relied mainly on the participation and direct financial support of the ministers' own congregations and other congregations throughout Brooklyn. The goal of this campaign was to build a mass movement that would force changes in government policies as
(15) well as in trade union hiring practices, both of which they believed excluded African Americans from construction jobs.

Inspired by the emergence of African American religious leaders as key figures elsewhere in the civil
(20) rights movement, and reasoning that the ministers would be able to mobilize large numbers of people from their congregations and network effectively with other religious leaders throughout the city, the Congress of Racial Equality (CORE), a national civil
(25) rights organization, had decided to ask the ministers to lead the Downstate campaign. However, by organizing a civil disobedience campaign, the ministers were jeopardizing one of the very factors that had led CORE to seek their involvement: their
(30) positions as politically moderate community leaders. Urban African American ministers and churches had been working for decades with community and government organizations to address the social, political, and economic concerns of their
(35) communities, and ministers of African American congregations in Brooklyn had often acted as mediators between their communities and the government. Many of them also worked for major political parties and ran for political office themselves.
(40) By endorsing and leading the Downstate protest, the ministers were risking their political careers and their reputations within their communities for effecting change through established political channels.

The Downstate campaign ended with an
(45) agreement between the ministers and both government and union officials. This agreement did not include new legislation or a commitment to a specific numerical increase in jobs for African Americans, as the protestors had demanded. But even
(50) though some civil rights activists therefore considered the agreement incomplete, government officials did

pledge to enforce existing antidiscrimination legislation. Moreover, the Downstate campaign effectively aroused public concern for the previously
(55) neglected problem of discrimination in the construction industry. It also drew public attention, which had hitherto focused on the progress of the civil rights movement primarily in the southern United States, to the additional need to alleviate
(60) discrimination in the North. Finally, throughout the campaign, the ministers managed to maintain their moderate political ties. The dual role played by the ministers—activists who nonetheless continued to work through established political channels—served
(65) as a model for future ministers who sought to initiate protest actions on behalf of their communities.

1. It can be reasonably inferred from the passage that the author's attitude is most favorable toward which one of the following?

    (A) the ways in which the Downstate campaign altered the opinions of union leaders

    (B) the impact that the Downstate campaign had on the implementation of new antidiscrimination legislation

    (C) CORE's relationship to the demonstrators in the Downstate campaign

    (D) the effects that the Downstate campaign had on public awareness

    (E) the way in which the leaders of the Downstate campaign negotiated the agreement that ended the campaign

GO ON TO THE NEXT PAGE.

2. Which one of the following assertions about the results of the Downstate campaign does the author affirm in the passage?

    (A) It achieved all of its participants' goals for changes in union policy but not all of its participants' goals for government action.

    (B) It directly achieved neither all of its participants' goals for government action nor all of its participants' goals for changes in union hiring policies.

    (C) It achieved all of its participants' goals for changes in government policies, but did not achieve all of its participants' goals for union commitment to hiring policies.

    (D) It achieved all of its particular goals for government action immediately, but only gradually achieved some of its participants' desired effects on public opinion.

    (E) It eventually achieved all of its participants' particular goals for both government action and establishment of union hiring policies, but only after extended effort and significant risk.

3. The primary function of the reference to past activities of ministers and churches (lines 31–38) is to

    (A) demonstrate that the tactics used by the leaders of the Downstate campaign evolved naturally out of their previous political activities

    (B) explain why the leaders of the Downstate campaign decided to conduct the protest in the way they did

    (C) provide examples of the sorts of civil rights activities that the leaders of CORE had promoted

    (D) indicate how the Downstate campaign could have accomplished its goals by means other than those used

    (E) underscore the extent to which the Downstate campaign represented a change in approach for its leaders

4. Which one of the following does the author affirm in the passage?

    (A) CORE was one of several civil rights organizations that challenged the hiring practices of the construction industry.

    (B) The Downstate campaign relied primarily on CORE and other national civil rights organizations for most of its support.

    (C) After the Downstate campaign, concern for discrimination in the construction industry was directed primarily toward the northern United States.

    (D) Many ministers of African American congregations in Brooklyn had sought election to political office.

    (E) In response to the Downstate campaign, union officials pledged to adopt specific numerical goals for the hiring of African Americans.

5. The passage most clearly suggests that which one of the following is true of the group of ministers who led the Downstate campaign?

    (A) The Downstate campaign did not signal a significant change in their general political and social goals.

    (B) After the Downstate campaign, they went on to organize various other similar campaigns.

    (C) They had come together for the purpose of addressing problems in the construction industry well before CORE's involvement in the Downstate campaign.

    (D) They were criticized both by CORE and by other concerned organizations for their incomplete success in the Downstate campaign.

    (E) Prior to the Downstate campaign, many of them had not been directly involved in civil rights activities.

GO ON TO THE NEXT PAGE.

The Cultural Revolution of 1966 to 1976, initiated by Communist Party Chairman Mao Zedong in an attempt to reduce the influence of China's intellectual elite on the country's institutions, has had
(5) lasting repercussions on Chinese art. It intensified the absolutist mind-set of Maoist Revolutionary Realism, which had dictated the content and style of Chinese art even before 1966 by requiring that artists "truthfully" depict the realities of socialist life in
(10) China. Interest in nonsocial, nonpolitical subjects was strictly forbidden, and, during the Cultural Revolution, what constituted truth was entirely for revolutionary forces to decide—the only reality artists could portray was one that had been thoroughly
(15) colored and distorted by political ideology.

Ironically, the same set of requirements that constricted artistic expression during the Cultural Revolution has had the opposite effect since; many artistic movements have flourished in reaction to the
(20) monotony of Revolutionary Realism. One of these, the Scar Art movement of the 1980s, was spearheaded by a group of intellectual painter who had been trained in Maoist art schools and then exiled to rural areas during the Cultural Revolution.
(25) In exile, these painters were for perhaps the first time confronted with the harsh realities of rural poverty and misery—aspects of life in China that their Maoist mentors would probably have preferred they ignore. As a result of these experiences, they developed a
(30) radically new approach to realism. Instead of depicting the version of reality sanctioned by the government, the Scar Art painters chose to represent the "scarred reality" they had seen during their exile. Their version of realist painting emphasized the day-
(35) to-day hardships of rural life. While the principles of Revolutionary Realism had insisted that artists choose public, monumental, and universal subjects, the Scar artists chose instead to focus on the private, the mundane, and the particular; where the principles of
(40) Revolutionary Realism had demanded that they depict contemporary Chinese society as outstanding or perfect, the Scar artists chose instead to portray the bleak realities of modernization.

As the 1980s progressed, the Scar artists' radical
(45) approach to realism became increasingly co-opted for political purposes, and as this political cast became stronger and more obvious, many artists abandoned the movement. Yet a preoccupation with rural life persisted, giving rise to a related development known
(50) as the Native Soil movement, which focused on the native landscape and embodied a growing nostalgia for the charms of peasant society in the face of modernization. Where the Scar artists had reacted to the ideological rigidity of the Cultural Revolution by
(55) emphasizing the damage inflicted by modernization, the Native Soil painters reacted instead by idealizing traditional peasant life. Unfortunately, in the end Native Soil painting was trivialized by a tendency to romanticize certain qualities of rural Chinese society
(60) in order to appeal to Western galleries and collectors.

6. Which one of the following titles most accurately captures the main point of the passage?

(A) "Painting and Politics: A Survey of Political Influences on Contemporary Chinese Art"
(B) "How Two Movements in Chinese Painting Transformed the Cultural Revolution"
(C) "Scarred Reality: A Look into Chinese Rural Life in the Late Twentieth Century"
(D) "The Rise of Realism in Post-Maoist Art in China"
(E) "The Unforeseen Artistic Legacy of China's Cultural Revolution"

7. Which one of the following works of art would be most compatible with the goals and interests of Scar Art as described in the passage?

(A) a painting of a village scene in which peasants commemorate a triumph over cruel political officials
(B) a painting symbolically representing the destruction caused by a large fire
(C) a painting depicting the weary face of a poorly clothed peasant toiling in a grain mill
(D) a painting caricaturing Mao Zedong as an overseer of farm workers
(E) a painting of two traditionally dressed peasant children walking in a summer wheat field

8. Which one of the following statements about realism in Chinese art can most reasonably be inferred from the passage?

(A) The artists who became leaders of the Native Soil movement practiced a modified form of realism in reaction against the styles and techniques of Scar Art.
(B) Chinese art has encompassed conflicting conceptions of realism derived from contrasting political and artistic purposes.
(C) The goals of realism in Chinese art have been effectively furthered by both the Scar Art movement and the Native Soil movement.
(D) Until the development of the Scar Art movement, interest in rural life had been absent from the types of art that prevailed among Chinese realist painters.
(E) Unlike the art that was predominant during the Cultural Revolution, Scar Art was not a type of realist art.

GO ON TO THE NEXT PAGE.

9. It can be inferred from the passage that the author would be LEAST likely to agree with which one of the following statements regarding the Cultural Revolution?

    (A) It had the ironic effect of catalyzing art movements at odds with its policies.

    (B) The art that was endorsed by its policies was less varied and interesting than Chinese art since the Cultural Revolution.

    (C) Much of the art that it endorsed did not accurately depict the realities of life in China but rather a politically motivated idealization.

    (D) Its effects demonstrate that restrictive policies generally foster artistic growth more than liberal policies do.

    (E) Its impact has continued to be felt in the Chinese art world years after it ended.

10. The primary function of the first paragraph is to

    (A) introduce the set of political and artistic ideas that spurred the development of two artistic movements described in the subsequent paragraphs

    (B) acknowledge the inescapable melding of political ideas and artistic styles in China

    (C) explain the transformation of Chinese society that came about as a result of the Cultural Revolution

    (D) present a hypothesis about realism in Chinese art that is refuted by the ensuing discussion of two artistic movements

    (E) show that the political realism practiced by the movements discussed in the ensuing paragraphs originated during the Cultural Revolution

11. It can be inferred from the passage that the author would be most likely to agree with which one of the following views of the Native Soil movement?

    (A) Its development was the inevitable consequence of the Scar Art movement's increasing politicization.

    (B) It failed to earn the wide recognition that Scar Art had achieved.

    (C) The rural scenes it depicted were appealing to most people in China.

    (D) Ironically, it had several key elements in common with Revolutionary Realism, in opposition to which it originally developed.

    (E) Its nostalgic representation of rural life was the means by which it stood in opposition to Revolutionary Realism.

GO ON TO THE NEXT PAGE.

Until recently, biologists were unable to explain the fact that pathogens—disease-causing parasites—have evolved to incapacitate, and often overwhelm, their hosts. Such behavior is at odds with the
(5) prevailing view of host-parasite relations—that, in general, host and parasite ultimately develop a benign coexistence. This view is based on the idea that parasites that do not harm their hosts have the best chance for long-term survival: they thrive because
(10) their hosts thrive. Some biologists, however, recently have suggested that if a pathogen reproduced so extensively as to cause its host to become gravely sick, it could still achieve evolutionary success if its replication led to a level of transmission into new
(15) hosts that exceeded the loss of pathogens resulting from the host's incapacitation. This scenario suggests that even death-causing pathogens can achieve evolutionary success.

One implication of this perspective is that a
(20) pathogen's virulence—its capacity to overcome a host's defenses and incapacitate it—is a function of its mode of transmission. For example, rhinoviruses, which cause the common cold, require physical proximity for transmission to occur. If a rhinovirus
(25) reproduces so extensively in a solitary host that the host is too unwell to leave home for a day, the thousands of new rhinoviruses produced that day will die before they can be transmitted. So, because it is transmitted directly, the common cold is unlikely to
(30) disable its victims.

The opposite can occur when pathogens are transported by a vector—an organism that can carry and transmit an infectious agent. If, for example, a pathogen capable of being transported by a mosquito
(35) reproduces so extensively that its human host is immobilized, it can still pass along its genes if a mosquito bites the host and transmits this dose to the next human it bites. In such circumstances the virulence is likely to be more severe, because the
(40) pathogen has reproduced to such concentration in the host that the mosquito obtains a high dose of the pathogen, increasing the level of transmission to new hosts.

While medical literature generally supports the
(45) hypothesis that vector-borne pathogens tend to be more virulent than directly transmitted pathogens—witness the lethal nature of malaria, yellow fever, typhus, and sleeping sickness, all carried by biting insects—a few directly transmitted pathogens such as
(50) diphtheria and tuberculosis bacteria can be just as lethal. Scientists call these "sit and wait" pathogens, because they are able to remain alive outside their hosts until a new host comes along, without relying on a vector. Indeed, the endurance of these pathogens,
(55) many of which can survive externally for weeks or months before transmission into a new host—compared, for instance, to an average rhinovirus life span of hours—makes them among the most dangerous of all pathogens.

19. Which one of the following most accurately summarizes the main idea of the passage?

(A) A new hypothesis about the host-incapacitating behavior of some pathogens suggests that directly transmitted pathogens are just as virulent as vector-borne pathogens, due to the former's ability to survive outside a host for long periods of time.

(B) A new hypothesis about the host-incapacitating behavior of some pathogens suggests that, while most pathogens reproduce so extensively as to cause their hosts to become gravely sick or even to die, some eventually develop a benign coexistence with their hosts.

(C) A new hypothesis about the host-incapacitating behavior of some pathogens suggests that they are able to achieve reproductive success because they reproduce to a high level of concentration in their incapacitated hosts.

(D) A new hypothesis about the host-incapacitating behavior of some pathogens suggests that they are generally able to achieve reproductive success unless their reproduction causes the death of the host.

(E) A new hypothesis about the host-incapacitating behavior of some pathogens suggests that pathogen virulence is generally a function of their mode of transmission, with vector-borne pathogens usually more virulent than directly transmitted pathogens, except for those directly transmitted pathogens able to endure outside their hosts.

20. According to the passage, the prevailing view of the host-parasite relationship is that, in general,

(A) the host is ultimately harmed enough to prevent the parasite from thriving

(B) a thriving parasite will eventually incapacitate its host

(C) a parasite must eventually be transmitted to a new host in order to survive

(D) the parasite eventually thrives with no harm to its host

(E) ultimately the host thrives only if the parasite thrives

21. With which one of the following statements about the prevailing view of host-parasite relations would the biologists mentioned in line 10 be most likely to agree?

(A) The view contradicts most evidence of actual host-parasite relations.

(B) The view suggests that even death-causing pathogens can achieve evolutionary success.

(C) The view presumes the existence of a type of parasite behavior that does not exist.

(D) The view ignores the possibility that there is more than one way to achieve evolutionary success.

(E) The view erroneously assumes that hosts never harm the parasites that feed off them.

GO ON TO THE NEXT PAGE.

22. The examples of diphtheria and tuberculosis bacteria provide the most support for which one of the following conclusions about the dangerousness of pathogens?

    (A) The most dangerous pathogens are those with the shortest life spans outside a host.

    (B) Those pathogens with the greatest endurance outside a host are among the most dangerous.

    (C) Those pathogens transported by vectors are always the most dangerous.

    (D) The least dangerous pathogens are among those with the longest life spans outside a host.

    (E) Those pathogens transmitted directly are always the least dangerous.

23. Which one of the following, if true, would most seriously challenge the position of the biologists mentioned in line 10?

    (A) Most pathogens capable of causing their hosts' deaths are able to achieve reproductive success.

    (B) Most pathogens transmitted from incapacitated hosts into new hosts are unable to overwhelm the new hosts.

    (C) Most pathogens that do not incapacitate their hosts are unable to achieve reproductive success.

    (D) Most hosts that become gravely sick are infected by pathogens that reproduce to relatively high concentrations.

    (E) Most pathogens transmitted from incapacitated hosts are unable to reproduce in their new hosts.

24. Which one of the following most accurately describes the organization of the passage?

    (A) introduction of a scientific anomaly; presentation of an explanation for the anomaly; mention of an implication of the explanation; discussion of two examples illustrating the implication; discussion of exceptions to the implication

    (B) introduction of a scientific anomaly; presentation of an explanation for the anomaly; discussion of two examples illustrating the explanation; discussion of exceptions to the explanation; mention of an implication of the explanation

    (C) introduction of a scientific anomaly; presentation of an explanation for the anomaly; discussion of two examples illustrating the explanation; mention of an implication of the explanation; discussion of examples illustrating the implication

    (D) introduction of a scientific anomaly; presentation of an implication of the anomaly; discussion of two examples illustrating the implication; discussion of exceptions to the implication

    (E) introduction of a scientific anomaly; discussion of two examples illustrating the anomaly; presentation of an explanation for the anomaly; discussion of examples illustrating the explanation

25. The passage implies that which one of the following is a reason that rhinoviruses are unlikely to be especially virulent?

    (A) They immobilize their hosts before they have a chance to reproduce extensively enough to pass directly to new hosts.

    (B) They cannot survive outside their hosts long enough to be transmitted from incapacitated hosts to new hosts.

    (C) They cannot reproduce in numbers sufficient to allow vectors to obtain high enough doses to pass to new hosts.

    (D) They cannot survive long enough in an incapacitated host to be picked up by vectors.

    (E) They produce thousands of new rhinoviruses each day.

26. The primary purpose of the passage is to

    (A) compare examples challenging the prevailing view of host-parasite relations with examples supporting it

    (B) argue that the prevailing view of host-parasite relations is correct but is based on a mistaken rationale

    (C) offer a modification to the prevailing view of host-parasite relations

    (D) attack evidence that supports the prevailing view of host-parasite relations

    (E) examine the origins of the prevailing view of host-parasite relations

S T O P

IF YOU FINISH BEFORE TIME IS CALLED, YOU MAY CHECK YOUR WORK ON THIS SECTION ONLY.
DO NOT WORK ON ANY OTHER SECTION IN THE TEST.

Answer Key

1. D
2. B
3. E
4. D
5. A
6. E
7. C
8. B
9. D
10. A
11. E
12. D
13. A
14. A
15. E
16. B
17. C
18. C
19. E
20. D
21. D
22. B
23. E
24. A
25. B
26. C

Reading Comprehension 2

PrepTest 45, Section II
December 2004

Reading Comprehension 2

SECTION III
Time—35 minutes
27 Questions

Directions: Each passage in this section is followed by a group of questions to be answered on the basis of what is <u>stated</u> or <u>implied</u> in the passage. For some of the questions, more than one of the choices could conceivably answer the question. However, you are to choose the <u>best</u> answer; that is, the response that most accurately and completely answers the question, and blacken the corresponding space on your answer sheet.

A number of natural disasters in recent years—such as earthquakes, major storms, and floods—that have affected large populations of people have forced relief agencies, communities, and entire nations to

(5) reevaluate the ways in which they respond in the aftermaths of such disasters. They believe that traditional ways of dealing with disasters have proved ineffective on several occasions and, in some cases, have been destructive rather than helpful to the

(10) communities hit by these sudden and unexpected crises. Traditionally, relief has been based on the premise that aid in postdisaster situations is most effective if given in the immediate aftermath of an event. A high priority also has been placed on the

(15) quantity of aid materials, programs, and personnel, in the belief that the negative impact of a disaster can be counteracted by a large and rapid infusion of aid.

Critics claim that such an approach often creates a new set of difficulties for already hard-hit

(20) communities. Teams of uninvited experts and personnel—all of whom need food and shelter—as well as uncoordinated shipments of goods and the establishment of programs inappropriate to local needs can quickly lead to a secondary "disaster" as

(25) already strained local infrastructures break down under the pressure of this large influx of resources. In some instances, tons of food have disappeared into local markets for resale, and, with inadequate accounting procedures, billions of dollars in aid

(30) money have gone unaccounted for.

To develop a more effective approach, experts recommend shifting the focus to the long term. A response that produces lasting benefit, these experts claim, requires that community members define the

(35) form and method of aid that are most appropriate to their needs. Grassroots dialogue designed to facilitate preparedness should be encouraged in disaster-prone communities long before the onset of a crisis, so that in a disaster's immediate aftermath, relief agencies

(40) can rely on members of affected communities to take the lead. The practical effect of this approach is that aid takes the form of a response to the stated desires of those affected rather than an immediate, though less informed, action on their behalf.

(45) Though this proposal appears sound, its success depends on how an important constituency, namely donors, will respond. Historically, donors—individuals, corporations, foundations, and governmental bodies—have been most likely to

(50) respond only in the immediate aftermath of a crisis.

However, communities affected by disasters typically have several long-term needs such as the rebuilding of houses and roads, and thus the months and years after a disaster are also crucial. Donors that

(55) incorporate dialogue with members of affected communities into their relief plans could foster strategies that more efficiently utilize immediate aid as well as provide for the difficulties facing communities in the years after a disaster.

1. Which one of the following most accurately expresses the main point of the passage?

(A) The most useful response to a natural disaster is one in which relief agencies allow victims to dictate the type of aid they receive, which will most likely result in the allocation of long-term rather than immediate aid.

(B) The quantity of aid given after a natural disaster reflects the desires of donors more than the needs of recipients, and in some cases great quantities of aid are destructive rather than helpful.

(C) Aid that focuses on long-term needs is difficult to organize because, by its very definition, it requires that relief agencies focus on constructing an adequate dialogue among recipients, providers, and donors.

(D) Disaster relief efforts have been marked by inefficiencies that attest to the need for donors and relief agencies to communicate with affected communities concerning how best to meet not only their short-term but also their long-term needs.

(E) Though the years after a disaster are crucial for communities affected by disasters, the days and weeks immediately after a disaster are what capture the attention of donors, thus forcing relief agencies into the role of mediators between the two extremes.

GO ON TO THE NEXT PAGE.

KAPLAN

LSAT EXTREME STUDENTS: THIS SECTION IS ADMINISTERED AT AN IN-CLASS WORKSHOP. DO NOT USE THIS SECTION FOR PRACTICE.

Reading Comprehension 2

2. Which one of the following examples best illustrates the type of disaster response recommended by the experts mentioned in the third paragraph?

   (A) After a flood, local officials reject three more expensive proposals before finally accepting a contractor's plan to control a local river with a dam.

   (B) Following a plan developed several years ago by a relief agency in consultation with donors and community members, the relief agency provides temporary shelter immediately after a flood and later helps rebuild houses destroyed by the flood.

   (C) Immediately after a flood, several different relief agencies, each acting independently, send large shipments of goods to the affected community along with teams of highly motivated but untrained volunteers to coordinate the distribution of these goods.

   (D) At the request of its donors, a private relief agency delays providing any assistance to victims of a flood until after the agency conducts a thorough study of the types of aid most likely to help the affected community in the long run.

   (E) After a flood, government officials persuade local companies to increase their corporate giving levels and to direct more aid to the surrounding community.

3. The author of the passage would be most likely to agree with which one of the following statements?

   (A) Disaster relief plans are appropriate only for disaster-prone communities.

   (B) When communities affected by disasters have articulated their long-term needs, donors typically have been responsive to those needs.

   (C) Donors would likely provide more disaster relief aid if they had confidence that it would be used more effectively than aid currently is.

   (D) It is not the amount of aid but rather the way this aid is managed that is the source of current problems in disaster relief.

   (E) Few communities affected by disasters experience a crucial need for short-term aid.

4. The author discusses donors in the final paragraph primarily in order to

   (A) point to an influential group of people who have resisted changes to traditional disaster response efforts

   (B) demonstrate that the needs of donors and aid recipients contrast profoundly on the issue of disaster response

   (C) show that implementing an effective disaster relief program requires a new approach on the part of donors as well as relief agencies

   (D) illustrate that relief agencies and donors share similar views on the goals of disaster response but disagree on the proper response methods

   (E) concede that the reformation of disaster relief programs, while necessary, is unlikely to take place because of the disagreements among donors

5. It can be inferred from the passage that the author would be most likely to view a shift toward a more long-term perspective in disaster relief efforts as which one of the following?

   (A) a development that would benefit affected communities as well as aid providers who have a shared interest in relief efforts that are effective and well managed

   (B) a change that would help communities meet their future needs more effectively but would inevitably result in a detrimental reduction of short-term aid like food and medicine

   (C) an approach that would enable aid recipients to meet their long-term needs but which would not address the mismanagement that hampers short-term relief efforts

   (D) a movement that, while well intentioned, will likely be undermined by the unwillingness of donors to accept new methods of delivering aid

   (E) the beginning of a trend in which aid recipients play a major role after a disaster and donors play a minor role, reversing the structure of traditional aid programs

6. Which one of the following inferences about natural disasters and relief efforts is most strongly supported by the passage?

   (A) Although inefficiencies have long been present in international disaster relief programs, they have been aggravated in recent years by increased demands on relief agencies' limited resources.

   (B) Local communities had expressed little interest in taking responsibility for their own preparedness prior to the most recent years, thus leaving donors and relief agencies unaware of potential problems.

   (C) Numerous relief efforts in the years prior to the most recent provided such vast quantities of aid that most needs were met despite evidence of inefficiency and mismanagement, and few recipient communities questioned traditional disaster response methods.

   (D) Members of communities affected by disasters have long argued that they should set the agenda for relief efforts, but relief agencies have only recently come to recognize the validity of their arguments.

   (E) A number of wasteful relief efforts in the most recent years provided dramatic illustrations of aid programs that were implemented by donors and agencies with little accountability to populations affected by disasters.

GO ON TO THE NEXT PAGE.

Reading Comprehension 2

The moral precepts embodied in the Hippocratic oath, which physicians standardly affirm upon beginning medical practice, have long been considered the immutable bedrock of medical ethics,
(5) binding physicians in a moral community that reaches across temporal, cultural, and national barriers. Until very recently the promises expressed in that oath—for example to act primarily for the benefit and not the harm of patients and to conform to various standards
(10) of professional conduct including the preservation of patients' confidences—even seemed impervious to the powerful scientific and societal forces challenging it. Critics argue that the oath is outdated; its fixed moral rules, they say, are incompatible with more flexible
(15) modern ideas about ethics. It also encourages doctors to adopt an authoritarian stance that depreciates the privacy and autonomy of the patient. Furthermore, its emphasis on the individual patient without regard for the wider social context frustrates the physician's
(20) emerging role as gatekeeper in managed care plans and impedes competitive market forces, which, some critics believe, should determine the quality, price, and distribution of health care as they do those of other commodities. The oath is also faulted for its
(25) omissions: its failure to mention such vital contemporary issues as human experimentation and the relationships of physicians to other health professionals. Some respected opponents even cite historical doubts about the oath's origin and
(30) authorship, presenting evidence that it was formulated by a small group of reformist physicians in ancient Greece and that for centuries it was not uniformly accepted by medical practitioners.

This historical issue may be dismissed at the
(35) outset as irrelevant to the oath's current appropriateness. Regardless of the specific origin of its text—which, admittedly, is at best uncertain—those in each generation who critically appraise its content and judge it to express valid
(40) principles of medical ethics become, in a more meaningful sense, its authors. More importantly, even the more substantive, morally based arguments concerning contemporary values and newly relevant issues cannot negate the patients' need for assurance
(45) that physicians will pursue appropriate goals in treatment in accordance with generally acceptable standards of professionalism. To fulfill that need, the core value of beneficence—which does not actually conflict with most reformers' purposes—should be
(50) retained, with adaptations at the oath's periphery by some combination of revision, supplementation, and modern interpretation. In fact, there is already a tradition of peripheral reinterpretation of traditional wording; for example, the oath's vaguely and
(55) archaically worded proscription against "cutting for the stone" may once have served to forbid surgery, but with today's safer and more effective surgical techniques it is understood to function as a promise to practice within the confines of one's expertise,
(60) which remains a necessary safeguard for patients' safety and well-being.

7. Which one of the following most accurately states the main point of the passage?

(A) The Hippocratic oath ought to be reevaluated carefully, with special regard to the role of the physician, to make certain that its fundamental moral rules still apply today.

(B) Despite recent criticisms of the Hippocratic oath, some version of it that will continue to assure patients of physicians' professionalism and beneficent treatment ought to be retained.

(C) Codes of ethics developed for one society at a particular point in history may lose some specific application in later societies but can retain a useful fundamental moral purpose.

(D) Even the criticisms of the Hippocratic oath based on contemporary values and newly relevant medical issues cannot negate patients' need for assurance.

(E) Modern ideas about ethics, especially medical ethics, obviate the need for and appropriateness of a single code of medical ethics like the Hippocratic oath.

8. Which one of the following most accurately describes the organization of the material presented in the passage?

(A) A general principle is described, criticisms of the principle are made, and modifications of the principle are made in light of these criticisms.

(B) A set of criticisms is put forward, and possible replies to those criticisms are considered and dismissed.

(C) The history of a certain code of conduct is discussed, criticisms of the code are mentioned and partially endorsed, and the code is modified as a response.

(D) A general principle is formulated, a partial defense of that principle is presented, and criticisms of the principle are discussed and rejected.

(E) The tradition surrounding a certain code of conduct is discussed, criticisms of that code are mentioned, and a general defense of the code is presented.

GO ON TO THE NEXT PAGE

LSAT EXTREME STUDENTS: THIS SECTION IS ADMINISTERED AT AN IN-CLASS WORKSHOP. DO NOT USE THIS SECTION FOR PRACTICE.

Reading Comprehension 2

9. The passage cites which one of the following as a value at the heart of the Hippocratic oath that should present no difficulty to most reformers?

   (A) creation of a community of physicians from all eras, nations, and cultures

   (B) constant improvement and advancement of medical science

   (C) provision of medical care to all individuals regardless of ability to pay

   (D) physician action for the benefit of patients

   (E) observance of established moral rules even in the face of challenging societal forces

10. The author's primary purpose in the passage is to

    (A) affirm society's continuing need for a code embodying certain principles

    (B) chastise critics within the medical community who support reinterpretation of a code embodying certain principles

    (C) argue that historical doubts about the origin of a certain code are irrelevant to its interpretation

    (D) outline the pros and cons of revising a code embodying certain principles

    (E) propose a revision of a code embodying certain principles that will increase the code's applicability to modern times

11. Based on information in the passage, it can be inferred that which one of the following sentences could most logically be added to the passage as a concluding sentence?

    (A) The fact that such reinterpretations are so easy, however, suggests that our rejection of the historical issue was perhaps premature.

    (B) Yet, where such piecemeal reinterpretation is not possible, revisions to even the core value of the oath may be necessary.

    (C) It is thus simply a failure of the imagination, and not any changes in the medical profession or society in general, that has motivated critics of the Hippocratic oath.

    (D) Because of this tradition of reinterpretation of the Hippocratic oath, therefore, modern ideas about medical ethics must be much more flexible than they have been in the past.

    (E) Despite many new challenges facing the medical profession, therefore, there is no real need for wholesale revision of the Hippocratic oath.

12. Each of the following is mentioned in the passage as a criticism of the Hippocratic oath EXCEPT:

    (A) The oath encourages authoritarianism on the part of physicians.

    (B) The version of the oath in use today is not identical to the oath formulated in ancient Greece.

    (C) The oath fails to address modern medical dilemmas that could not have been foreseen in ancient Greece.

    (D) The oath's absolutism is incompatible with contemporary views of morality.

    (E) The oath's emphasis on the individual patient is often not compatible with a market-driven medical industry.

13. Which one of the following can most accurately be used to describe the author's attitude toward critics of the Hippocratic oath?

    (A) enthusiastic support

    (B) bemused dismissal

    (C) reasoned disagreement

    (D) strict neutrality

    (E) guarded agreement

14. Which one of the following would be most suitable as a title for this passage if it were to appear as an editorial piece?

    (A) "The Ancients versus the Moderns: Conflicting Ideas About Medical Ethics"

    (B) "Hypocritical Oafs: Why 'Managed Care' Proponents are Seeking to Repeal an Ancient Code"

    (C) "Genetic Fallacy in the Age of Gene-Splicing: Why the Origins of the Hippocratic Oath Don't Matter"

    (D) "The Dead Hand of Hippocrates: Breaking the Hold of Ancient Ideas on Modern Medicine"

    (E) "Prescription for the Hippocratic Oath: Facelift or Major Surgery?"

GO ON TO THE NEXT PAGE.

Reading Comprehension 2

A lichen consists of a fungus living in symbiosis (i.e., a mutually beneficial relationship) with an alga. Although most branches of the complex evolutionary family tree of fungi have been well established, the
(5) evolutionary origins of lichen-forming fungi have been a mystery. But a new DNA study has revealed the relationship of lichen-forming fungi to several previously known branches of the fungus family tree. The study reveals that, far from being oddities,
(10) lichen-forming fungi are close relatives of such common fungi as brewer's yeast, morel mushrooms, and the fungus that causes Dutch elm disease. This accounts for the visible similarity of certain lichens to more recognizable fungi such as mushrooms.

(15)   In general, fungi present complications for the researcher. Fungi are usually parasitic or symbiotic, and researchers are often unsure whether they are examining fungal DNA or that of the associated organism. But lichen-forming fungi are especially
(20) difficult to study. They have few distinguishing characteristics of shape or structure, and they are unusually difficult to isolate from their partner algae, with which they have a particularly delicate symbiosis. In some cases the alga is wedged between
(25) layers of fungal tissue; in others, the fungus grows through the alga's cell walls in order to take nourishment, and the tissues of the two organisms are entirely enmeshed and inseparable. As a result, lichen-forming fungi have long been difficult to
(30) classify definitively within the fungus family. By default they were thus considered a separate grouping of fungi with an unknown evolutionary origin. But, using new analytical tools that allow them to isolate the DNA of fungi in parasitic or symbiotic
(35) relationships, researchers were able to establish the DNA sequence in a certain gene found in 75 species of fungi, including 10 species of lichen-forming fungi. Based on these analyses, the researchers found 5 branches on the fungus family tree to which
(40) varieties of lichen-forming fungi belong. Furthermore, the researchers stress that it is likely that as more types of lichen-forming fungi are analyzed, they will be found to belong to still more branches of the fungus family tree.

(45)   One implication of the new research is that it provides evidence to help overturn the long-standing evolutionary assumption that parasitic interactions inevitably evolve over time to a greater benignity and eventually to symbiosis so that the parasites will not
(50) destroy their hosts. The addition of lichen-forming fungi to positions along branches of the fungus family tree indicates that this assumption does not hold for fungi. Fungi both harmful and benign can now be found both early and late in fungus
(55) evolutionary history. Given the new layout of the fungus family tree resulting from the lichen study, it appears that fungi can evolve toward mutualism and then just as easily turn back again toward parasitism.

15. Which one of the following most accurately states the main point of the passage?

(A) New research suggests that fungi are not only parasitic but also symbiotic organisms.

(B) New research has revealed that lichen-forming fungi constitute a distinct species of fungus.

(C) New research into the evolutionary origins of lichen-forming fungi reveals them to be closely related to various species of algae.

(D) New research has isolated the DNA of lichen-forming fungi and uncovered their relationship to the fungus family tree.

(E) New research into the fungal component of lichens explains the visible similarities between lichens and fungi by means of their common evolutionary origins.

16. Which one of the following most accurately describes the author's purpose in the last paragraph of the passage?

(A) to suggest that new research overturns the assumption that lichen-forming fungi are primarily symbiotic, rather than parasitic, organisms

(B) to show that findings based on new research regarding fungus classification have implications that affect a long-standing assumption of evolutionary science

(C) to explain the fundamental purposes of fungus classification in order to position this classification within the broader field of evolutionary science

(D) to demonstrate that a fundamental assumption of evolutionary science is verified by new research regarding fungus classification

(E) to explain how symbiotic relationships can evolve into purely parasitic ones

GO ON TO THE NEXT PAGE.

LSAT EXTREME STUDENTS: THIS SECTION IS ADMINISTERED AT AN IN-CLASS WORKSHOP. DO NOT USE THIS SECTION FOR PRACTICE.

Reading Comprehension 2

17. Which one of the following most accurately describes the organization of the passage?

    (A) explanation of the difficulty of classifying lichens; description of the DNA sequence of lichen-forming fungi; summary of the implications of this description

    (B) definition of lichens; discussion of new discoveries concerning lichens' evolutionary history; application of these findings in support of an evolutionary theory

    (C) definition of lichens; discussion of the difficulty in classifying their fungal components; resolution of this difficulty and implications of the resulting research

    (D) discussion of the symbiotic relationship that constitutes lichens; discussion of how new research can distinguish parasitic from symbiotic fungi; implications of this research

    (E) explanation of the symbiotic nature of lichens; discussion of the problems this poses for genetic researchers; delineation of the implications these problems have for evolutionary theory

18. According to the passage, the elimination of which one of the following obstacles enabled scientists to identify the evolutionary origins of lichen-forming fungi?

    (A) The DNA of lichen-forming fungi was not easy to separate from that of their associated algae.

    (B) Lichen-forming fungi are difficult to distinguish from several common fungi with which they are closely related.

    (C) Lichen-forming fungi were grouped separately from other fungi on the fungus family tree.

    (D) Lichen-forming fungi are far less common than more recognizable fungi such as mushrooms.

    (E) The DNA of lichen-forming fungi is significantly more complex than that of other fungi.

19. Which one of the following, if true, most weakens the author's criticism of the assumption that parasitic interactions generally evolve toward symbiosis?

    (A) Evolutionary theorists now postulate that symbiotic interactions generally evolve toward greater parasitism, rather than vice versa.

    (B) The evolutionary tree of fungi is somewhat more complex than that of similarly parasitic or symbiotic organisms.

    (C) The DNA of fungi involved in symbiotic interactions is far more difficult to isolate than that of fungi involved in parasitic interactions.

    (D) The placement of lichen-forming fungi as a separate group on the fungus family tree masked the fact that parasitic fungi sometimes evolved much later than symbiotic ones.

    (E) Branches of the fungus family tree that have evolved from symbiosis to parasitism usually die out shortly thereafter.

GO ON TO THE NEXT PAGE.

Reading Comprehension 2

The following passage was written in the late 1980s.

The struggle to obtain legal recognition of aboriginal rights is a difficult one, and even if a right is written into the law there is no guarantee that the future will not bring changes to the law that
(5) undermine the right. For this reason, the federal government of Canada in 1982 extended constitutional protection to those aboriginal rights already recognized under the law. This protection was extended to the Indian, Inuit, and Métis peoples, the
(10) three groups generally thought to comprise the aboriginal population in Canada. But this decision has placed on provincial courts the enormous burden of interpreting and translating the necessarily general constitutional language into specific rulings. The
(15) result has been inconsistent recognition and establishment of aboriginal rights, despite the continued efforts of aboriginal peoples to raise issues concerning their rights.

Aboriginal rights in Canada are defined by the
(20) constitution as aboriginal peoples' rights to ownership of land and its resources, the inherent right of aboriginal societies to self-government, and the right to legal recognition of indigenous customs. But difficulties arise in applying these broadly conceived
(25) rights. For example, while it might appear straightforward to affirm legal recognition of indigenous customs, the exact legal meaning of "indigenous" is extremely difficult to interpret. The intent of the constitutional protection is to recognize
(30) only long-standing traditional customs, not those of recent origin; provincial courts therefore require aboriginal peoples to provide legal documentation that any customs they seek to protect were practiced sufficiently long ago—a criterion defined in practice
(35) to mean prior to the establishment of British sovereignty over the specific territory. However, this requirement makes it difficult for aboriginal societies, which often relied on oral tradition rather than written records, to support their claims.
(40) Furthermore, even if aboriginal peoples are successful in convincing the courts that specific rights should be recognized, it is frequently difficult to determine exactly what these rights amount to. Consider aboriginal land claims. Even when
(45) aboriginal ownership of specific lands is fully established, there remains the problem of interpreting the meaning of that "ownership." In a 1984 case in Ontario, an aboriginal group claimed that its property rights should be interpreted as full ownership in the
(50) contemporary sense of private property, which allows for the sale of the land or its resources. But the provincial court instead ruled that the law had previously recognized only the aboriginal right to use the land and therefore granted property rights so
(55) minimal as to allow only the bare survival of the

community. Here, the provincial court's ruling was excessively conservative in its assessment of the current law. Regrettably, it appears that this group will not be successful unless it is able to move its
(60) case from the provincial courts into the Supreme Court of Canada, which will be, one hopes, more insistent upon a satisfactory application of the constitutional reforms.

20. Which one of the following most accurately states the main point of the passage?

   (A) The overly conservative rulings of Canada's provincial courts have been a barrier to constitutional reforms intended to protect aboriginal rights.

   (B) The overwhelming burden placed on provincial courts of interpreting constitutional language in Canada has halted efforts by aboriginal peoples to gain full ownership of land.

   (C) Constitutional language aimed at protecting aboriginal rights in Canada has so far left the protection of these rights uncertain due to the difficult task of interpreting this language.

   (D) Constitutional reforms meant to protect aboriginal rights in Canada have in fact been used by some provincial courts to limit these rights.

   (E) Efforts by aboriginal rights advocates to uphold constitutional reforms in Canada may be more successful if heard by the Supreme Court rather than by the provincial courts.

21. Which one of the following most accurately describes the author's main purpose in lines 11–14 of the passage?

   (A) to demonstrate that the decisions of the provincial courts rarely conform to the goals of the constitutional reforms

   (B) to locate the source of a systemic problem in protecting aboriginal rights in Canada

   (C) to identify the specific source of problems in enacting constitutional reforms in Canada

   (D) to describe one aspect of the process by which constitutional reforms are enacted in Canada

   (E) to criticize the use of general language in the Canadian constitution

GO ON TO THE NEXT PAGE.

Reading Comprehension 3

PrepTest 44, Section I
October 2004

Reading Comprehension 3

SECTION I

Time—35 minutes

27 Questions

<u>Directions:</u> Each passage in this section is followed by a group of questions to be answered on the basis of what is <u>stated</u> or <u>implied</u> in the passage. For some of the questions, more than one of the choices could conceivably answer the question. However, you are to choose the <u>best</u> answer; that is, the response that most accurately and completely answers the question, and blacken the corresponding space on your answer sheet.

The Canadian Auto Workers' (CAW) Legal Services Plan, designed to give active and retired autoworkers and their families access to totally prepaid or partially reimbursed legal services, has
(5) been in operation since late 1985. Plan members have the option of using either the plan's staff lawyers, whose services are fully covered by the cost of membership in the plan, or an outside lawyer. Outside lawyers, in turn, can either sign up with the plan as a
(10) "cooperating lawyer" and accept the CAW's fee schedule as payment in full, or they can charge a higher fee and collect the balance from the client. Autoworkers appear to have embraced the notion of prepaid legal services: 45 percent of eligible union
(15) members were enrolled in the plan by 1988. Moreover, the idea of prepaid legal services has been spreading in Canada. A department store is even offering a plan to holders of its credit card.
While many plan members seem to be happy to
(20) get reduced-cost legal help, many lawyers are concerned about the plan's effect on their profession, especially its impact on prices for legal services. Some point out that even though most lawyers have not joined the plan as cooperating lawyers, legal fees
(25) in the cities in which the CAW plan operates have been depressed, in some cases to an unprofitable level. The directors of the plan, however, claim that both clients and lawyers benefit from their arrangement. For while the clients get ready access to
(30) reduced-price services, lawyers get professional contact with people who would not otherwise be using legal services, which helps generate even more business for their firms. Experience shows, the directors say, that if people are referred to a firm and
(35) receive excellent service, the firm will get three to four other referrals who are not plan subscribers and who would therefore pay the firm's standard rate.
But it is unlikely that increased use of such plans will result in long-term client satisfaction or in a
(40) substantial increase in profits for law firms. Since lawyers with established reputations and client bases can benefit little, if at all, from participation, the plans function largely as marketing devices for lawyers who have yet to establish themselves. While
(45) many of these lawyers are no doubt very able and conscientious, they will tend to have less expertise and to provide less satisfaction to clients. At the same time, the downward pressure on fees will mean that the full-fee referrals that proponents say will come
(50) through plan participation may not make up for a firm's investment in providing services at low plan

rates. And since lowered fees provide little incentive for lawyers to devote more than minimal effort to cases, a "volume discount" approach toward the
(55) practice of law will mean less time devoted to complex cases and a general lowering of quality for clients.

1. Which one of the following most accurately expresses the main point of the passage?

   (A) In the short term, prepaid legal plans such as the CAW Legal Services Plan appear to be beneficial to both lawyers and clients, but in the long run lawyers will profit at the expense of clients.

   (B) The CAW Legal Services Plan and other similar plans represent a controversial, but probably effective, way of bringing down the cost of legal services to clients and increasing lawyers' clientele.

   (C) The use of prepaid legal plans such as that of the CAW should be rejected in favor of a more equitable means of making legal services more generally affordable.

   (D) In spite of widespread consumer support for legal plans such as that offered by the CAW, lawyers generally criticize such plans, mainly because of their potential financial impact on the legal profession.

   (E) Although they have so far attracted many subscribers, it is doubtful whether the CAW Legal Services Plan and other similar prepaid plans will benefit lawyers and clients in the long run.

2. The primary purpose of the passage is to

   (A) compare and contrast legal plans with the traditional way of paying for legal services

   (B) explain the growing popularity of legal plans

   (C) trace the effect of legal plans on prices of legal services

   (D) caution that increased use of legal plans is potentially harmful to the legal profession and to clients

   (E) advocate reforms to legal plans as presently constituted

GO ON TO THE NEXT PAGE.

KAPLAN

LSAT EXTREME STUDENTS: THIS SECTION IS ADMINISTERED AT AN IN-CLASS WORKSHOP. DO NOT USE THIS SECTION FOR PRACTICE.

Reading Comprehension 3

3. Which one of the following does the author predict will be a consequence of increased use of legal plans?

   (A) results that are largely at odds with those predicted by lawyers who criticize the plans

   (B) a lowering of the rates such plans charge their members

   (C) forced participation of lawyers who can benefit little from association with the plans

   (D) an eventual increase in profits for lawyers from client usage of the plans

   (E) a reduction in the time lawyers devote to complex cases

4. Which one of the following sequences most accurately and completely corresponds to the presentation of the material in the passage?

   (A) a description of a recently implemented set of procedures and policies; a summary of the results of that implementation; a proposal of refinements in those policies and procedures

   (B) an evaluation of a recent phenomenon; a comparison of that phenomenon with related past phenomena; an expression of the author's approval of that phenomenon

   (C) a presentation of a proposal; a discussion of the prospects for implementing that proposal; a recommendation by the author that the proposal be rejected

   (D) a description of an innovation; a report of reasoning against and reasoning favoring that innovation; argumentation by the author concerning that innovation

   (E) an explanation of a recent occurrence; an evaluation of the practical value of that occurrence; a presentation of further data regarding that occurrence

5. The passage most strongly suggests that, according to proponents of prepaid legal plans, cooperating lawyers benefit from taking clients at lower fees in which one of the following ways?

   (A) Lawyers can expect to gain expertise in a wide variety of legal services by availing themselves of the access to diverse clientele that plan participation affords.

   (B) Experienced cooperating lawyers are likely to enjoy the higher profits of long-term, complex cases, for which new lawyers are not suited.

   (C) Lower rates of profit will be offset by a higher volume of clients and new business through word-of-mouth recommendations.

   (D) Lower fees tend to attract clients away from established, nonparticipating law firms.

   (E) With all legal fees moving downward to match the plans' schedules, the profession will respond to market forces.

6. According to the passage, which one of the following is true of CAW Legal Services Plan members?

   (A) They can enjoy benefits beyond the use of the services of the plan's staff lawyers.

   (B) So far, they generally believe the quality of services they receive from the plan's staff lawyers is as high as that provided by other lawyers.

   (C) Most of them consult lawyers only for relatively simple and routine matters.

   (D) They must pay a fee above the cost of membership for the services of an outside lawyer.

   (E) They do not include only active and retired autoworkers and their families.

7. Which one of the following most accurately represents the primary function of the author's mention of marketing devices (line 43)?

   (A) It points to an aspect of legal plans that the author believes will be detrimental to the quality of legal services.

   (B) It is identified by the author as one of the primary ways in which plan administrators believe themselves to be contributing materially to the legal profession in return for lawyers' participation.

   (C) It identifies what the author considers to be one of the few unequivocal benefits that legal plans can provide.

   (D) It is reported as part of several arguments that the author attributes to established lawyers who oppose plan participation.

   (E) It describes one of the chief burdens of lawyers who have yet to establish themselves and offers an explanation of their advocacy of legal plans.

GO ON TO THE NEXT PAGE.

Reading Comprehension 3

In the field of historiography—the writing of history based on a critical examination of authentic primary information sources—one area that has recently attracted attention focuses on the responses
(5) of explorers and settlers to new landscapes in order to provide insights into the transformations the landscape itself has undergone as a result of settlement. In this endeavor historiographers examining the history of the Pacific Coast of the
(10) United States have traditionally depended on the records left by European American explorers of the nineteenth century who, as commissioned agents of the U.S. government, were instructed to report thoroughly their findings in writing.

(15) But in furthering this investigation some historiographers have recently recognized the need to expand their definition of what a source is. They maintain that the sources traditionally accepted as documenting the history of the Pacific Coast have too
(20) often omitted the response of Asian settlers to this territory. In part this is due to the dearth of written records left by Asian settlers; in contrast to the commissioned agents, most of the people who first came to western North America from Asia during this
(25) same period did not focus on developing a self-conscious written record of their involvement with the landscape. But because a full study of a culture's historical relationship to its land cannot confine itself to a narrow record of experience, these
(30) historiographers have begun to recognize the value of other kinds of evidence, such as the actions of Asian settlers.

As a case in point, the role of Chinese settlers in expanding agriculture throughout the Pacific Coast
(35) territory is integral to the history of the region. Without access to the better land, Chinese settlers looked for agricultural potential in this generally arid region where other settlers did not. For example, where settlers of European descent looked at willows
(40) and saw only useless, untillable swamp, Chinese settlers saw fresh water, fertile soil, and the potential for bringing water to more arid areas via irrigation. Where other settlers who looked at certain weeds, such as wild mustard, generally saw a nuisance,
(45) Chinese settlers saw abundant raw material for valuable spices from a plant naturally suited to the local soil and climate.

Given their role in the labor force shaping this territory in the nineteenth century, the Chinese settlers
(50) offered more than just a new view of the land. Their vision was reinforced by specialized skills involving swamp reclamation and irrigation systems, which helped lay the foundation for the now well-known and prosperous agribusiness of the region. That
(55) 80 percent of the area's cropland is now irrigated and that the region is currently the top producer of many specialty crops cannot be fully understood by historiographers without attention to the input of Chinese settlers as reconstructed from their
(60) interactions with that landscape.

8. Which one of the following most accurately states the main point of the passage?

(A) The history of settlement along the Pacific Coast of the U.S., as understood by most historiographers, is confirmed by evidence reconstructed from the actions of Asian settlers.

(B) Asian settlers on the Pacific Coast of the U.S. left a record of their experiences that traditional historiographers believed to be irrelevant.

(C) To understand Asian settlers' impact on the history of the Pacific Coast of the U.S., historiographers have had to recognize the value of nontraditional kinds of historiographic evidence.

(D) Spurred by new findings regarding Asian settlement on the Pacific Coast of the U.S., historiographers have begun to debate the methodological foundations of historiography.

(E) By examining only written information, historiography as it is traditionally practiced has produced inaccurate historical accounts.

9. Which one of the following most accurately describes the author's primary purpose in discussing Chinese settlers in the third paragraph?

(A) to suggest that Chinese settlers followed typical settlement patterns in this region during the nineteenth century

(B) to argue that little written evidence of Chinese settlers' practices survives

(C) to provide examples illustrating the unique view Asian settlers had of the land

(D) to demonstrate that the history of settlement in the region has become a point of contention among historiographers

(E) to claim that the historical record provided by the actions of Asian settlers is inconsistent with history as derived from traditional sources

10. The passage states that the primary traditional historiographic sources of information about the history of the Pacific Coast of the U.S. have which one of the following characteristics?

(A) They were written both before and after Asian settlers arrived in the area.

(B) They include accounts by Native Americans in the area.

(C) They are primarily concerned with potential agricultural uses of the land.

(D) They focus primarily on the presence of water sources in the region.

(E) They are accounts left by European American explorers.

GO ON TO THE NEXT PAGE.

LSAT EXTREME STUDENTS: THIS SECTION IS ADMINISTERED AT AN IN-CLASS WORKSHOP. DO NOT USE THIS SECTION FOR PRACTICE.

Reading Comprehension 3

11. The author would most likely disagree with which one of the following statements?

    (A) Examining the actions not only of Asian settlers but of other cultural groups of the Pacific Coast of the U.S. is necessary to a full understanding of the impact of settlement on the landscape there.

    (B) The significance of certain actions to the writing of history may be recognized by one group of historiographers but not another.

    (C) Recognizing the actions of Asian settlers adds to but does not complete the writing of the history of the Pacific Coast of the U.S.

    (D) By recognizing as evidence the actions of people, historiographers expand the definition of what a source is.

    (E) The expanded definition of a source will probably not be relevant to studies of regions that have no significant immigration of non-Europeans.

12. According to the passage, each of the following was an aspect of Chinese settlers' initial interactions with the landscape of the Pacific Coast of the U.S. EXCEPT:

    (A) new ideas for utilizing local plants
    (B) a new view of the land
    (C) specialized agricultural skills
    (D) knowledge of agribusiness practices
    (E) knowledge of irrigation systems

13. Which one of the following can most reasonably be inferred from the passage?

    (A) Most Chinese settlers came to the fic Coast of the U.S. because the climate w milar to that with which they were familiar

    (B) Chinese agricultural methods in the teenth century included knowledge of swa reclamation.

    (C) Settlers of European descent used wil ustard seed as a spice.

    (D) Because of the abundance of written s es available, it is not worthwhile to exam the actions of European settlers.

    (E) What written records were left by Asian lers were neglected and consequently lost t scholarly research.

14. Which one of the following, if true, would most to strengthen the author's main claim in the last sen e of the passage?

    (A) Market research of agribusinesses owned b descendants of Chinese settlers shows that the market for the region's specialty crops grown substantially faster than the market f any other crops in the last decade.

    (B) Nineteenth-century surveying records indicat that the lands now cultivated by specialty cro businesses owned by descendants of Chinese settlers were formerly swamp lands.

    (C) Research by university agricultural science departments proves that the formerly arid land now cultivated by large agribusinesses contain extremely fertile soil when they are sufficiently irrigated.

    (D) A technological history tracing the development of irrigation systems in the region reveals that their efficiency has increased steadily since the nineteenth century.

    (E) Weather records compiled over the previous century demonstrate that the weather patterns in the region are well-suited to growing certain specialty crops as long as they are irrigated.

GO ON TO THE NEXT PAGE.

Reading Comprehension 3

The survival of nerve cells, as well as their performance of some specialized functions, is regulated by chemicals known as neurotrophic factors, which are produced in the bodies of animals,
(5) including humans. Rita Levi-Montalcini's discovery in the 1950s of the first of these agents, a hormonelike substance now known as NGF, was a crucial development in the history of biochemistry, which led to Levi-Montalcini sharing the Nobel Prize
(10) for medicine in 1986.

In the mid-1940s, Levi-Montalcini had begun by hypothesizing that many of the immature nerve cells produced in the development of an organism are normally programmed to die. In order to confirm this
(15) theory, she conducted research that in 1949 found that, when embryos are in the process of forming their nervous systems, they produce many more nerve cells than are finally required, the number that survives eventually adjusting itself to the volume of
(20) tissue to be supplied with nerves. A further phase of the experimentation, which led to Levi-Montalcini's identification of the substance that controls this process, began with her observation that the development of nerves in chick embryos could be
(25) stimulated by implanting a certain variety of mouse tumor in the embryos. She theorized that a chemical produced by the tumors was responsible for the observed nerve growth. To investigate this hypothesis, she used the then new technique of tissue culture, by
(30) which specific types of body cells can be made to grow outside the organism from which they are derived. Within twenty-four hours, her tissue cultures of chick embryo extracts developed dense halos of nerve tissue near the places in the culture where she
(35) had added the mouse tumor. Further research identified a specific substance contributed by the mouse tumors that was responsible for the effects Levi-Montalcini had observed: a protein that she named "nerve growth factor" (NGF).
(40) NGF was the first of many cell-growth factors to be found in the bodies of animals. Through Levi-Montalcini's work and other subsequent research, it has been determined that this substance is present in many tissues and biological fluids, and that it is
(45) especially concentrated in some organs. In developing organisms, nerve cells apparently receive this growth factor locally from the cells of muscles or other organs to which they will form connections for transmission of nerve impulses, and sometimes from
(50) supporting cells intermingled with the nerve tissue. NGF seems to play two roles, serving initially to direct the developing nerve processes toward the correct, specific "target" cells with which they must connect, and later being necessary for the continued
(55) survival of those nerve cells. During some periods of their development, the types of nerve cells that are affected by NGF—primarily cells outside the brain and spinal cord—die if the factor is not present or if they encounter anti-NGF antibodies.

15. Which one of the following most accurately expresses the main point of the passage?

(A) Levi-Montalcini's discovery of neurotrophic factors as a result of research carried out in the 1940s was a major contribution to our understanding of the role of naturally occurring chemicals, especially NGF, in the development of chick embryos.

(B) Levi-Montalcini's discovery of NGF, a neurotrophic factor that stimulates the development of some types of nerve tissue and whose presence or absence in surrounding cells helps determine whether particular nerve cells will survive, was a pivotal development in biochemistry.

(C) NGF, which is necessary for the survival and proper functioning of nerve cells, was discovered by Levi-Montalcini in a series of experiments using the technique of tissue culture, which she devised in the 1940s.

(D) Partly as a result of Levi-Montalcini's research, it has been found that NGF and other neurotrophic factors are produced only by tissues to which nerves are already connected and that the presence of these factors is necessary for the health and proper functioning of nervous systems.

(E) NGF, a chemical that was discovered by Levi-Montalcini, directs the growth of nerve cells toward the cells with which they must connect and ensures the survival of those nerve cells throughout the life of the organism except when the organism produces anti-NGF antibodies.

16. Based on the passage, the author would be most likely to believe that Levi-Montalcini's discovery of NGF is noteworthy primarily because it

(A) paved the way for more specific knowledge of the processes governing the development of the nervous system

(B) demonstrated that a then new laboratory technique could yield important and unanticipated experimental results

(C) confirmed the hypothesis that many of a developing organism's immature nerve cells are normally programmed to die

(D) indicated that this substance stimulates observable biochemical reactions in the tissues of different species

(E) identified a specific substance, produced by mouse tumors, that can be used to stimulate nerve cell growth

GO ON TO THE NEXT PAGE.

LSAT EXTREME STUDENTS: THIS SECTION IS ADMINISTERED AT AN IN-CLASS WORKSHOP. DO NOT USE THIS SECTION FOR PRACTICE.

Reading Comprehension 3

17. The primary function of the third paragraph of the passage in relation to the second paragraph is to

   (A) indicate that conclusions referred to in the second paragraph, though essentially correct, require further verification

   (B) indicate that conclusions referred to in the second paragraph have been undermined by subsequently obtained evidence

   (C) indicate ways in which conclusions referred to in the second paragraph have been further corroborated and refined

   (D) describe subsequent discoveries of substances analogous to the substance discussed in the second paragraph

   (E) indicate that experimental procedures discussed in the second paragraph have been supplanted by more precise techniques described in the third paragraph

18. Information in the passage most strongly supports which one of the following?

   (A) Nerve cells in excess of those that are needed by the organism in which they develop eventually produce anti-NGF antibodies to suppress the effects of NGF.

   (B) Nerve cells that grow in the absence of NGF are less numerous than, but qualitatively identical to, those that grow in the presence of NGF.

   (C) Few of the nerve cells that connect with target cells toward which NGF directs them are needed by the organism in which they develop.

   (D) Some of the nerve cells that grow in the presence of NGF are eventually converted to other types of living tissue by neurotrophic factors.

   (E) Some of the nerve cells that grow in an embryo do not connect with any particular target cells.

19. The passage describes a specific experiment that tested which one of the following hypotheses?

   (A) A certain kind of mouse tumor produces a chemical that stimulates the growth of nerve cells.

   (B) Developing embryos initially grow many more nerve cells than they will eventually require.

   (C) In addition to NGF, there are several other important neurotrophic factors regulating cell survival and function.

   (D) Certain organs contain NGF in concentrations much higher than in the surrounding tissue.

   (E) Certain nerve cells are supplied with NGF by the muscle cells to which they are connected.

20. Which one of the following is most strongly supported by the information in the passage?

   (A) Some of the effects that the author describes as occurring in Levi-Montalcini's culture of chick embryo extract were due to neurotrophic factors other than NGF.

   (B) Although NGF was the first neurotrophic factor to be identified, some other such factors are now more thoroughly understood.

   (C) In her research in the 1940s and 1950s, Levi-Montalcini identified other neurotrophic factors in addition to NGF.

   (D) Some neurotrophic factors other than NGF perform functions that are not specifically identified in the passage.

   (E) The effects of NGF that Levi-Montalcini noted in her chick embryo experiment are also caused by other neurotrophic factors not discussed in the passage.

GO ON TO THE NEXT PAGE.

Reading Comprehension 3

The proponents of the Modern Movement in architecture considered that, compared with the historical styles that it replaced, Modernist architecture more accurately reflected the functional
(5) spirit of twentieth-century technology and was better suited to the newest building methods. It is ironic, then, that the Movement fostered an ideology of design that proved to be at odds with the way buildings were really built.
(10) The tenacious adherence of Modernist architects and critics to this ideology was in part responsible for the Movement's decline. Originating in the 1920s as a marginal, almost bohemian art movement, the Modern Movement was never very popular with the public,
(15) but this very lack of popular support produced in Modernist architects a high-minded sense of mission—not content merely to interpret the needs of the client, these architects now sought to persuade, to educate, and, if necessary, to dictate. By 1945 the
(20) tenets of the Movement had come to dominate mainstream architecture, and by the early 1950s, to dominate architectural criticism—architects whose work seemed not to advance the evolution of the Modern Movement tended to be dismissed by
(25) proponents of Modernism. On the other hand, when architects were identified as innovators—as was the case with Otto Wagner, or the young Frank Lloyd Wright—attention was drawn to only those features of their work that were "Modern"; other aspects were
(30) conveniently ignored.

The decline of the Modern Movement later in the twentieth century occurred partly as a result of Modernist architects' ignorance of building methods, and partly because Modernist architects were
(35) reluctant to admit that their concerns were chiefly aesthetic. Moreover, the building industry was evolving in a direction Modernists had not anticipated: it was more specialized and the process of construction was much more fragmented than in
(40) the past. Up until the twentieth century, construction had been carried out by a relatively small number of tradespeople, but as the building industry evolved, buildings came to be built by many specialized subcontractors working independently. The architect's
(45) design not only had to accommodate a sequence of independent operations, but now had to reflect the allowable degree of inaccuracy of the different trades. However, one of the chief construction ideals of the Modern Movement was to "honestly" expose
(50) structural materials such as steel and concrete. To do this and still produce a visually acceptable interior called for an unrealistically high level of craftmanship. Exposure of a building's internal structural elements, if it could be achieved at all,
(55) could only be accomplished at considerable cost— hence the well-founded reputation of Modern architecture as prohibitively expensive.

As Postmodern architects recognized, the need to expose structural elements imposed unnecessary
(60) limitations on building design. The unwillingness of

architects of the Modern Movement to abandon their ideals contributed to the decline of interest in the Modern Movement.

21. Which one of the following most accurately summarizes the main idea of the passage?

(A) The Modern Movement declined because its proponents were overly ideological and did not take into account the facts of building construction.

(B) Rationality was the theoretical basis for the development of the Modern Movement in architecture.

(C) Changes in architectural design introduced by the Modern Movement inspired the development of modern construction methods.

(D) The theoretical bases of the Modern Movement in architecture originated in changes in building construction methods.

(E) Proponents of the Modern Movement in architecture rejected earlier architectural styles because such styles were not functional.

22. Which one of the following is most similar to the relationship described in the passage between the new methods of the building industry and pre-twentieth-century construction?

(A) Clothing produced on an assembly line is less precisely tailored than clothing produced by a single garment maker.

(B) Handwoven fabric is more beautiful than fabric produced by machine.

(C) Lenses ground on a machine are less useful than lenses ground by hand.

(D) Form letters produced by a word processor elicit fewer responses than letters typed individually on a typewriter.

(E) Furniture produced in a factory is less fashionable than handcrafted furniture.

GO ON TO THE NEXT PAGE.

LSAT EXTREME STUDENTS: THIS SECTION IS ADMINISTERED AT AN IN-CLASS WORKSHOP. DO NOT USE THIS SECTION FOR PRACTICE.

Reading Comprehension 3

23. With respect to the proponents of the Modern Movement, the author of the passage can best be described as

    (A) forbearing
    (B) defensive
    (C) unimpressed
    (D) exasperated
    (E) indifferent

24. It can be inferred that the author of the passage believes which one of the following about Modern Movement architects' ideal of exposing structural materials?

    (A) The repudiation of the ideal by some of these architects undermined its validity.
    (B) The ideal was rarely achieved because of its lack of popular appeal.
    (C) The ideal was unrealistic because most builders were unwilling to attempt it.
    (D) The ideal originated in the work of Otto Wagner and Frank Lloyd Wright.
    (E) The ideal arose from aesthetic rather than practical concerns.

25. Which one of the following, in its context in the passage, most clearly reveals the attitude of the author toward the proponents of the Modern Movement?

    (A) "functional spirit" (lines 4–5)
    (B) "tended" (line 24)
    (C) "innovators" (line 26)
    (D) "conveniently" (line 30)
    (E) "degree of inaccuracy" (line 47)

26. The author of the passage mentions Otto Wagner and the young Frank Lloyd Wright (lines 27–28) primarily as examples of

    (A) innovative ___itects whose work was not immediate___ ___preciated by the public
    (B) architects w___ proponents of the Modern Movement c___ed represented the moveme___
    (C) architects who___ ___ork helped to popularize t___ Modern Move___ ___
    (D) architects who g___ ___lly attempted to interpre___ the needs of thei___ ___nts, rather than dictating them
    (E) architects whose ea___ ___ork seemed to archite___ of the Modern Mov___ ___t to be at odds with t___ principles of Modern___

27. The author of the passage is pr___ ___ily concerned with

    (A) analyzing the failure of a___ ___ement
    (B) predicting the future cours___ ___ a movement
    (C) correcting a misunderstandi___ ___bout a movement
    (D) anticipating possible criticis___ ___ a movement
    (E) contrasting incompatible view___ ___ts about a movement

S T O P

IF YOU FINISH BEFORE TIME IS CALLED, YOU MAY CHECK YOUR WORK ON THIS SECTION ONLY. DO NOT WORK ON ANY OTHER SECTION IN THE TEST.

Answer Key

1. E
2. D
3. E
4. D
5. C
6. A
7. A
8. C
9. C
10. E
11. E
12. D
13. B
14. B
15. B
16. A
17. C
18. E
19. A
20. D
21. A
22. A
23. C
24. E
25. D
26. B
27. A

KAPLAN

Reading Comprehension 4

PrepTest 43, Section I
June 2004

SECTION I

Time—35 minutes

28 Questions

<u>Directions:</u> Each passage in this section is followed by a group of questions to be answered on the basis of what is <u>stated</u> or imp___ l in the passage. For some of the questions, more than one of the choices could conceivably answer the question. However, you are to ___ ___se the <u>best</u> answer; that is, the response that most accurately and completely answers the question, and blacken the corresponding sp___ ___ on your answer sheet.

The accumulation of scientific knowledge regarding the environmental impact of oil well drilling in North America has tended to lag behind the actual drilling of oil wells. Most attempts to
(5) regulate the industry have relied on hindsight: the need for regulation becomes apparent only after undesirable events occur. The problems associated with oil wells' potential contamination of groundwater—fresh water within the earth that
(10) supplies wells and springs—provide a case in point.

When commercial drilling for oil began in North America in the mid-nineteenth century, regulations reflected the industry's concern for the purity of the wells' oil. In 1893, for example, regulations were
(15) enacted specifying well construction requirements to protect oil and gas reserves from contamination by fresh water. Thousands of wells were drilled in such a way as to protect the oil, but no thought was given to the possibility that the groundwater itself might need
(20) protection until many drinking-water wells near the oil well sites began to produce unpotable, oil-contaminated water.

The reason for this contamination was that groundwater is usually found in porous and
(25) permeable geologic formations near the earth's surface, whereas petroleum and unpotable saline water reservoirs are generally found in similar formations but at greater depths. Drilling a well creates a conduit connecting all the formations that it
(30) has penetrated. Consequently, without appropriate safeguards, wells that penetrate both groundwater and oil or saline water formations inevitably contaminate the groundwater. Initial attempts to prevent this contamination consisted of sealing off the
(35) groundwater formations with some form of protective barrier to prevent the oil flowing up the well from entering or mixing with the natural groundwater reservoir. This method, which is still in use today, initially involved using hollow trees to seal off the
(40) groundwater formations; now, however, large metal pipe casings, set in place with cement, are used.

Regulations currently govern the kinds of casing and cement that can be used in these practices; however, the hazards of insufficient knowledge
(45) persist. For example, the long-term stability of this way of protecting groundwater is unknown. The protective barrier may fail due to corrosion of the casing by certain fluids flowing up the well, or because of dissolution of the cement by these fluids.
(50) The effects of groundwater bacteria, traffic vibrations,

and changing groundwater chemistry are likewise unassessed. Further, there is no guarantee that well___ drilled in compliance with existing regulations will not expose a need for research in additional areas: ___
(55) the west coast of North America, a major disaster recently occurred because a well's location was bas___ on a poor understanding of the area's subsurface geology. Because the well was drilled in a channel accessing the ocean, not only was the area's
(60) groundwater completely contaminated, but widespre___ coastal contamination also occurred, prompting international concern over oil exploration and initiating further attempts to refine regulations.

1. Which one of the following most accurately states th___ main point of the passage?

    (A) Although now recognized as undesirable, occasional groundwater contamination by oil and unpotable saline water is considered to b___ inevitable wherever drilling for oil occurs.

    (B) Widespread coastal contamination caused by o___ well drilling in North America has prompted international concern over oil exploration.

    (C) Hindsight has been the only reliable means available to regulation writers responsible for devising adequate safeguard regulations to prevent environmental contamination associate___ with oil well drilling.

    (D) The risk of environmental contamination associated with oil well drilling continues to exist because safeguard regulations are often based on hindsight and less-than-sufficient scientific information.

    (E) Groundwater contamination associated with oil well drilling is due in part to regulations designed to protect the oil from contamination by groundwater and not the groundwater from contamination by oil.

GO ON TO THE NEXT PAGE.

2. The passage states which one of the following about underground oil reservoirs?

(A) They are usually located in areas whose subsurface geology is poorly understood.

(B) They are generally less common in coastal regions.

(C) They are usually located in geologic formations similar to those in which gas is found.

(D) They are often contaminated by fresh or saline water.

(E) They are generally found at greater depths than groundwater formations.

3. The author's attitude regarding oil well drilling regulations can most accurately be described as

(A) cynical that future regulatory reform will occur without international concern

(B) satisfied that existing regulations are adequate to prevent unwarranted tradeoffs between resource collection and environmental protection

(C) concerned that regulatory reform will not progress until significant undesirable events occur

(D) optimistic that current scientific research will spur regulatory reform

(E) confident that regulations will eventually be based on accurate geologic understandings

4. The author uses the phrase "the hazards of insufficient knowledge" (line 44) primarily in order to refer to the risks resulting from

(A) a lack of understanding regarding the dangers to human health posed by groundwater contamination

(B) a failure to comprehend the possible consequences of drilling in complex geologic systems

(C) poorly tested methods for verifying the safety of newly developed technologies

(D) an inadequate appreciation for the difficulties of enacting and enforcing environmental regulations

(E) a rudimentary understanding of the materials used in manufacturing metal pipe casings

5. Based on the information in the passage, if a prospective oil well drilled near a large city encounters a large groundwater formation and a small saline water formation, but no oil, which one of the following statements is most likely to be true?

(A) Groundwater contamination is unlikely because the well did not strike oil and hence will not be put in operation.

(B) Danger to human health due to groundwater contamination is unlikely because large cities generally have more than one source of drinking water.

(C) Groundwater contamination is likely unless the well is plugged and abandoned.

(D) Groundwater contamination is unlikely because the groundwater formation's large size will safely dilute any saline water that enters it.

(E) The risk of groundwater contamination can be reduced if casing is set properly and monitored routinely for breakdown.

GO ON TO THE NEXT PAGE.

In many bilingual communities of Puerto Rican Americans living in the mainland United States, people use both English and Spanish in a single conversation, alternating between them smoothly and
(5) frequently even within the same sentence. This practice—called code-switching—is common in bilingual populations. While there are some cases that cannot currently be explained, in the vast majority of cases subtle factors, either situational or rhetorical,
(10) explain the use of code-switching.

Linguists say that most code-switching among Puerto Rican Americans is sensitive to the social contexts, which researchers refer to as domains, in which conversations take place. The main
(15) conversational factors influencing the occurrence of code-switching are setting, participants, and topic. When these go together naturally they are said to be congruent; a set of three such congruent factors constitutes a conversational situation. Linguists
(20) studying the choice between Spanish and English among a group of Puerto Rican American high school students classified their conversational situations into five domains: family, friendship, religion, education, and employment. To test the effects of these domains
(25) on code-switching, researchers developed a list of hypothetical situations made up of two of the three congruent factors, or of two incongruent factors, approximating an interaction in one of the five domains. The researchers asked the students to
(30) determine the third factor and to choose which mix of language—on a continuum from all English to all Spanish—they would use in that situation. When given two congruent factors, the students easily supplied the third congruent factor and strongly
(35) agreed among themselves about which mix they would use. For instance, for the factors of participants "parent and child" and the topic "how to be a good son or daughter," the congruent setting chosen was "home" and the language mix chosen was Spanish
(40) only. In contrast, incongruent factors such as the participants "priest and parishioner" and the setting "beach" yielded less agreement on the third factor of topic and on language choice.

But situational factors do not account for all
(45) code-switching; it occurs even when the domain would lead one not to expect it. In these cases, one language tends to be the primary one, while the other is used only sparingly to achieve certain rhetorical effects. Often the switches are so subtle that the
(50) speakers themselves are not aware of them. This was the case with a study of a family of Puerto Rican Americans in another community. Family members believed they used only English at home, but their taped conversations occasionally contained some
(55) Spanish, with no change in situational factors. When asked what the presence of Spanish signified, they commented that it was used to express certain attitudes such as intimacy or humor more emphatically.

6. Which one of the following most accurately expresses the main point of the passage?

(A) The lives of Puerto Rican Americans are affected in various ways by code-switching.

(B) It is not always possible to explain why code-switching occurs in conversations among Puerto Rican Americans.

(C) Rhetorical factors can explain more instances of code-switching among Puerto Rican Americans than can situational factors.

(D) Studies of bilingual communities of Puerto Rican Americans have caused linguists to revise many of their beliefs about code-switching.

(E) Most code-switching among Puerto Rican Americans can be explained by subtle situational and rhetorical factors.

7. In lines 56–59, the author mentions the family members' explanation of their use of Spanish primarily in order to

(A) report evidence supporting the conclusion that the family's code-switching had a rhetorical basis

(B) show that reasons for code-switching differ from one community to another

(C) supply evidence that seems to conflict with the researchers' conclusions about why the family engaged in code-switching

(D) refute the argument that situational factors explain most code-switching

(E) explain how it could be that the family members failed to notice their use of Spanish

8. Which one of the following questions is NOT characterized by the passage as a question to which linguists sought answers in their code-switching studies involving high school students?

(A) Where do the students involved in the study think that a parent and child are likely to be when they are talking about how to be a good son or daughter?

(B) What language or mix of languages do the students involved in the study think that a parent and child would be likely to use when they are talking at home about how to be a good son or daughter?

(C) What language or mix of languages do the students involved in the study think that a priest and a parishioner would be likely to use if they were conversing on a beach?

(D) What topic do the students involved in the study think that a parent and child would be most likely to discuss when they are speaking Spanish?

(E) What topic do the students involved in the study think that a priest and parishioner would be likely to discuss on a beach?

GO ON TO THE NEXT PAGE.

9. The primary function of the third paragraph of the passage is to

    (A) consider a general explanation for the phenomenon of code-switching that is different from the one discussed in the preceding paragraphs

    (B) resolve an apparent conflict between two explanations for code-switching that were discussed in the preceding paragraphs

    (C) show that there are instances of code-switching that are not explained by the factors discussed in the previous paragraph

    (D) report some of the patterns of code-switching observed among a family of Puerto Rican Americans in another community

    (E) show that some instances of code-switching are unconscious

10. Based on the passage, which one of the following is best explained as rhetorically determined code-switching?

    (A) A speaker who does not know certain words in the primary language of a conversation occasionally has recourse to familiar words in another language.

    (B) A person translating a text from one language into another leaves certain words in the original language because the author of the text invented those words.

    (C) For the purpose of improved selling strategies, a businessperson who primarily uses one language sometimes conducts business in a second language that is preferred by some people in the community.

    (D) A speaker who primarily uses one language switches to another language because it sounds more expressive.

    (E) A speaker who primarily uses one language occasionally switches to another language in order to maintain fluency in the secondary language.

11. It can be inferred from the passage that the author would most likely agree with which one of the following statements?

    (A) Research revealing that speakers are sometimes unaware of code-switching casts doubt on the results of a prior study involving high school students.

    (B) Relevant research conducted prior to the linguists' work with high school students would lead one to expect different answers from those the students actually gave.

    (C) Research conducted prior to the study of a family of Puerto Rican Americans was thought by most researchers to explain code-switching in all except the most unusual or nonstandard contexts.

    (D) Research suggests that people engaged in code-switching are usually unaware of which situational factors might influence their choice of language or languages.

    (E) Research suggests that the family of Puerto Rican Americans does not use code-switching in conversations held at home except for occasional rhetorical effect.

12. Which one of the following does the passage offer as evidence that code-switching cannot be entirely explained by situational factors?

    (A) Linguists have observed that bilingual high school students do not agree among themselves as to what mix of languages they would use in the presence of incongruent situational factors.

    (B) Code-switching sometimes occurs in conversations whose situational factors would be expected to involve the use of a single language.

    (C) Bilingual people often switch smoothly between two languages even when there is no change in the situational context in which the conversation takes place.

    (D) Puerto Rican Americans sometimes use Spanish only sparingly and for rhetorical effect in the presence of situational factors that would lead one to expect Spanish to be the primary language.

    (E) Speakers who engage in code-switching are often unaware of the situational factors influencing their choices of which language or mix of languages to speak.

13. Which one of the following, if true, would most cast doubt on the author's interpretation of the study involving the family discussed in the third paragraph?

    (A) In a previous twelve-month study involving the same family in their home, their conversations were entirely in English except when situational factors changed significantly.

    (B) In a subsequent twelve-month study involving the same family, a particular set of situational factors occurred repeatedly without any accompanying instances of code-switching.

    (C) In a subsequent twelve-month study involving the same family, it was noted that intimacy and humor were occasionally expressed through the use of English expressions.

    (D) When asked about the significance of their use of Spanish, the family members replied in English rather than Spanish.

    (E) Prior to their discussions with the researchers, the family members did not describe their occasional use of Spanish as serving to emphasize humor or intimacy.

GO ON TO THE NEXT PAGE.

Reader-response theory, a type of literary
theory that arose in reaction to formalist literary criticism,
has endeavored to shift the emphasis in the
interpretation of literature from the text itself to the
(5) contributions of readers to the meaning of a text.
According to literary critics who endorse reader-
response theory, the literary text alone renders no
meaning; it acquires meaning only when encountered
by individual readers, who always bring varying
(10) presuppositions and ways of reading to bear on the
text, giving rise to the possibility—even probability—
of varying interpretations. This brand of criticism has
met opposition from the formalists, who study the
text alone and argue that reader-response theory can
(15) encourage and even validate fragmented views of a
work, rather than the unified view acquired by
examining only the content of the text. However,
since no theory has a monopoly on divining meaning
from a text, the formalists' view appears
(20) unnecessarily narrow.

The proponents of formalism argue that their
approach is firmly grounded in rational, objective
principles, while reader-response theory lacks
standards and verges on absolute subjectivity. After
(25) all, these proponents argue, no author can create a
work that is packed with countless meanings. The
meaning of a work of literature, the formalists would
argue, may be obscure and somewhat arcane; yet,
however hidden it may be, the author's intended
(30) meaning is legible within the work, and it is the
critic's responsibility to search closely for this
meaning. However, while a literary work is indeed
encoded in various signs and symbols that must be
translated for the work to be understood and
(35) appreciated, it is not a map. Any complicated literary
work will invariably raise more questions than it
answers. What is needed is a method that enables the
critic to discern and make use of the rich stock of
meanings created in encounters between texts and
(40) readers.

Emphasizing the varied presuppositions and
perceptions that readers bring to the interpretations of
a text can uncover hitherto unnoticed dimensions of
the text. In fact, many important works have received
(45) varying interpretations throughout their existence,
suggesting that reader-based interpretations similar to
those described by reader-response theory had been
operating long before the theory's principles were
articulated. And while in some cases critics' textual
(50) interpretations based on reader-response theory have
unfairly burdened literature of the past with
contemporary ideologies, legitimate additional
insights and understandings continue to emerge years
after an ostensibly definitive interpretation of a major
(55) work has been articulated. By regarding a reader's
personal interpretation of literary works as not only
valid but also useful in understanding the works,
reader-response theory legitimizes a wide range of
perspectives on these works and thereby reinforces
(60) the notion of them as fluid and lively forms of
discourse that can continue to support new
interpretations long after their original composition.

14. Which one of the following most accurately describes
the author's attitude toward formalism as expressed in
the passage?

(A) scholarly neutrality
(B) grudging respect
(C) thoughtless disregard
(D) cautious ambivalence
(E) reasoned dismissal

15. Which one of the following persons displays an
approach that most strongly suggests sympathy with the
principles of reader-response theory?

(A) a translator who translates a poem from Spanish
to English word for word so that its original
meaning is not distorted
(B) a music critic who insists that early music can
be truly appreciated only when it is played on
original instruments of the period
(C) a reviewer who finds in the works of a novelist
certain unifying themes that reveal the novelist's
personal concerns and preoccupations
(D) a folk artist who uses conventional cultural
symbols and motifs as a way of conveying
commonly understood meanings
(E) a director who sets a play by Shakespeare
in nineteenth-century Japan to give a new
perspective on the work

16. With which one of the following statements would the
author of the passage be most likely to agree?

(A) Any literary theory should be seen ultimately as
limiting, since contradictory interpretations of
texts are inevitable.
(B) A purpose of a literary theory is to broaden and
enhance the understanding that can be gained
from a work.
(C) A literary theory should provide valid and strictly
objective methods for interpreting texts.
(D) The purpose of a literary theory is to make clear
the intended meaning of the author of a work.
(E) Since no literary theory has a monopoly on
meaning, a reader should avoid using theories to
interpret literature.

GO ON TO THE NEXT PAGE.

17. The passage states that reader-response theory legitimizes which one of the following?

    (A) a wide range of perspectives on works of literature
    (B) contemporary ideology as a basis for criticism
    (C) encoding the meaning of a literary work in signs and symbols
    (D) finding the meaning of a work in its text alone
    (E) belief that an author's intended meaning in a work is discoverable

18. Which one of the following most accurately describes the author's purpose in referring to literature of the past as being "unfairly burdened" (line 51) in some cases?

    (A) to reinforce the notion that reader-based interpretations of texts invariably raise more questions than they can answer
    (B) to confirm the longevity of interpretations similar to reader-based interpretations of texts
    (C) to point out a fundamental flaw that the author believes makes reader-response theory untenable
    (D) to concede a minor weakness in reader-response theory that the author believes is outweighed by its benefits
    (E) to suggest that reader-response theory can occasionally encourage fragmented views of a work

19. Which one of the following, if true, most weakens the author's argument concerning reader-response theory?

    (A) Reader-response theory is reflected in interpretations that have been given throughout history and that bring additional insight to literary study.
    (B) Reader-response theory legitimizes conflicting interpretations that collectively diminish the understanding of a work.
    (C) Reader-response theory fails to provide a unified view of the meaning of a literary work.
    (D) Reader-response theory claims that a text cannot have meaning without a reader.
    (E) Reader-response theory recognizes meanings in a text that were never intended by the author.

20. The author's reference to "various signs and symbols" (line 33) functions primarily to

    (A) stress the intricacy and complexity of good literature
    (B) grant that a reader must be guided by the text to some degree
    (C) imply that no theory alone can fully explain a work of literature
    (D) illustrate how a literary work differs from a map
    (E) show that an inflexible standard of interpretation provides constant accuracy

21. Which one of the following can most reasonably be inferred from the information in the passage?

    (A) Formalists believe that responsible critics who focus on the text alone will tend to find the same or similar meanings in a literary work.
    (B) Critical approaches similar to those described by formalism had been used to interpret texts long before the theory was articulated as such.
    (C) Formalists would not find any meaning in a text whose author did not intend it to have any one particular meaning.
    (D) A literary work from the past can rarely be read properly using reader-response theory when the subtleties of the work's social-historical context are not available.
    (E) Formalism is much older and has more adherents than reader-response theory.

GO ON TO THE NEXT PAGE.

Faculty researchers, particularly in scientific, engineering, and medical programs, often produce scientific discoveries and invent products or processes that have potential commercial value. Many
(5) institutions have invested heavily in the administrative infrastructure to develop and exploit these discoveries, and they expect to prosper both by an increased level of research support and by the royalties from licensing those discoveries having
(10) patentable commercial applications. However, although faculty themselves are unlikely to become entrepreneurs, an increasing number of highly valued researchers will be sought and sponsored by research corporations or have consulting contracts with
(15) commercial firms. One study of such entrepreneurship concluded that "if universities do not provide the flexibility needed to venture into business, faculty will be tempted to go to those institutions that are responsive to their commercialized desires." There is
(20) therefore a need to consider the different intellectual property policies that govern the commercial exploitation of faculty inventions in order to determine which would provide the appropriate level of flexibility.
(25)   In a recent study of faculty rights, Patricia Chew has suggested a fourfold classification of institutional policies. A supramaximalist institution stakes out the broadest claim possible, asserting ownership not only of all intellectual property produced by faculty in the
(30) course of their employment while using university resources, but also for any inventions or patent rights from faculty activities, even those involving research sponsored by nonuniversity funders. A maximalist institution allows faculty ownership of inventions that
(35) do not arise either "in the course of the faculty's employment [or] from the faculty's use of university resources." This approach, although not as all-encompassing as that of the supramaximalist university, can affect virtually all of a faculty
(40) member's intellectual production. A resource-provider institution asserts a claim to faculty's intellectual product in those cases where "significant use" of university time and facilities is employed. Of course, what constitutes significant use of resources is a
(45) matter of institutional judgment.
    As Chew notes, in these policies "faculty rights, including the sharing of royalties, are the result of university benevolence and generosity. [However, this] presumption is contrary to the common law,
(50) which provides that faculty own their inventions." Others have pointed to this anomaly and, indeed, to the uncertain legal and historical basis upon which the ownership of intellectual property rests. Although these issues remain unsettled, and though universities
(55) may be overreaching due to faculty's limited knowledge of their rights, most major institutions behave in the ways that maximize university ownership and profit participation.
    But there is a fourth way, one that seems to be
(60) free from these particular issues. Faculty-oriented

institutions assume that researchers own their own intellectual products and the rights to exploit them commercially, except in the development of public health inventions or if there is previously specified
(65) "substantial university involvement." At these institutions industry practice is effectively reversed, with the university benefiting in far fewer circumstances.

22. Which one of the following most accurately summarizes the main point of the passage?

(A) While institutions expect to prosper from increased research support and royalties from patentable products resulting from faculty inventions, if they do not establish clear-cut policies governing ownership of these inventions, they run the risk of losing faculty to research corporations or commercial consulting contracts.

(B) The fourfold classification of institutional policies governing exploitation of faculty inventions is sufficient to categorize the variety of steps institutions are taking to ensure that faculty inventors will not be lured away by commercial firms or research corporations.

(C) To prevent the loss of faculty to commercial firms or research corporations, institutions will have to abandon their insistence on retaining maximum ownership of and profit from faculty inventions and adopt the common-law presumption that faculty alone own their inventions.

(D) While the policies of most institutions governing exploitation of faculty inventions seek to maximize university ownership of and profit from these inventions, another policy offers faculty greater flexibility to pursue their commercial interests by regarding faculty as the owners of their intellectual products.

(E) Most institutional policies governing exploitation of faculty inventions are indefensible because they run counter to common-law notions of ownership and copyright, but they usually go unchallenged because few faculty members are aware of what other options might be available to them.

GO ON TO THE NEXT PAGE.

23. Which one of the following most accurately characterizes the author's view regarding the institutional intellectual property policies of most universities?

    (A) The policies are in keeping with the institution's financial interests.
    (B) The policies are antithetical to the mission of a university.
    (C) The policies do not have a significant impact on the research of faculty.
    (D) The policies are invariably harmful to the motivation of faculty attempting to pursue research projects.
    (E) The policies are illegal and possibly immoral

24. Which one of the following institutions would N be covered by the fourfold classification propo   y Chew?

    (A) an institution in which faculty own th   ht to some inventions they create outs'   he institution
    (B) an institution in which faculty ow   their inventions, regardless of any cir   stances, but grant the institution the right t   lect a portion of their royalties
    (C) an institution in which all inv   ns developed by faculty with institutiona' ources become the property of the institu'
    (D) an institution in which all   lty inventions related to public health me the property of the institution
    (E) an institution in which   e faculty inventions created with institut' resources remain the property of the fac   member

25. The passage suggests th   e type of institution in which employees are l   to have the most uncertainty about who owns their   llectual products is the

    (A) commercial f
    (B) supramaxim   university
    (C) maximalis' versity
    (D) resource-provider university
    (E) faculty-oriented university

26. According to the passage, what distinguishes a resource-provider institution from the other types of institutions identified by Chew is its

    (A) vagueness on the issue of what constitutes university as opposed to nonuniversity resources
    (B) insistence on reaping substantial financial benefit from faculty inventions while still providing faculty with unlimited flexibility
    (C) inversion of the usual practices regarding exploitation of faculty inventions in order to give faculty greater flexibility
    (D) insistence on ownership of faculty inventions developed outside the institution in order to maximize financial benefit to the university
    (E) reliance on the extent of use of institutional resources as the sole criterion in determining ownership of faculty inventions

27. The author of the passage most likely quotes one study of entrepreneurship in lines 16–19 primarily in order to

    (A) explain why institutions may wish to develop intellectual property policies that are responsive to certain faculty needs
    (B) draw a contrast between the worlds of academia and business that will be explored in detail later in the passage
    (C) defend the intellectual property rights of faculty inventors against encroachment by the institutions that employ them
    (D) describe the previous research that led Chew to study institutional policies governing ownership of faculty inventions
    (E) demonstrate that some faculty inventors would be better off working for commercial firms

28. The passage suggests each of the following EXCEPT:

    (A) Supramaximalist institutions run the greatest risk of losing faculty to jobs in institutions more responsive to the inventor's financial interests.
    (B) A faculty-oriented institution will make no claim of ownership to a faculty invention that is unrelated to public health and created without university involvement.
    (C) Faculty at maximalist institutions rarely produce inventions outside the institution without using the institution's resources.
    (D) There is little practical difference between the policies of supramaximalist and maximalist institutions.
    (E) The degree of ownership claimed by a resource-provider institution of the work of its faculty will not vary from case to case.

S T O P

IF YOU FINISH BEFORE TIME IS CALLED, YOU MAY CHECK YOUR WORK ON THIS SECTION ONLY.
DO NOT WORK ON ANY OTHER SECTION IN THE TEST.

Answer Key

1. D
2. E
3. C
4. B
5. E
6. E
7. A
8. D
9. C
10. D
11. E
12. B
13. A
14. E
15. E
16. B
17. A
18. D
19. B
20. B
21. A
22. D
23. A
24. B
25. D
26. E
27. A
28. E

Reading Comprehension 5

PrepTest 39, Section III
December 2002

Reading Comprehension 5

SECTION III

Time—35 minutes

28 Questions

Directions: Each passage in this section is followed by a group of questions to be answered on the basis of what is <u>stated</u> or <u>implied</u> in the passage. For some of the questions, more than one of the choices could conceivably answer the question. However, you are to choose the <u>best</u> answer; that is, the response that most accurately and completely answers the question, and blacken the corresponding space on your answer sheet.

The contemporary Mexican artistic movement known as muralism, a movement of public art that began with images painted on walls in an effort to represent Mexican national culture, is closely linked
(5) ideologically with its main sponsor, the new Mexican government elected in 1920 following the Mexican Revolution. This government promoted an ambitious cultural program, and the young revolutionary state called on artists to display Mexico's richness and
(10) possibility. But the theoretical foundation of the movement was formulated by the artists themselves. The major figures in the muralist movement, David Alfaro Siqueiros, Diego Rivera, and José Clemente Orozco, all based their work on a common premise:
(15) that art should incorporate images and familiar ideas as it commented upon the historic period in which it was created. In the process, they assimilated into their work the customs, myths, geography, and history of the local communities that constitute the basis of Mexican
(20) national culture.

But while many muralist works express populist or nationalist ideas, it is a mistake to attempt to reduce Mexican mural painting to formulaic, official government art. It is more than merely the result of the
(25) changes in political and social awareness that the Mexican Revolution represented; it also reflected important innovations in the art world. In creating a wide panorama of Mexico's history on the walls of public buildings throughout the country, muralists
(30) often used a realist style. But awareness of these innovations enabled them to be freer in expression than were more traditional practitioners of this style.

Moreover, while they shared a common interest in rediscovering their Mexican national identity, they
(35) developed their own distinct styles. Rivera, for example, incorporated elements from pre-Columbian sculpture and the Italian Renaissance fresco into his murals and used a strange combination of mechanical shapes to depict the faces and bodies of people.
(40) Orozco, on the other hand, showed a more expressionist approach, with loose brushwork and an openly emotional treatment of form. He relied on a strong diagonal line to give a sense of heightened movement and drama to his work. Siqueiros developed
(45) in a somewhat similar direction as Orozco, but incorporated asymmetric compositions, a high degree of action, and brilliant color.

This stylistic experimentation can be seen as resulting from the demands of a new medium. In
(50) stretching their concepts from small easel paintings with a centralized subject to vast compositions with

mural dimensions, muralists learned to think big and to respect the sweeping gesture of the arm—the brush stroke required to achieve the desired bold effect of
(55) mural art. Furthermore, because they were painting murals, they thought in terms of a continuum; their works were designed to be viewable from many different vantage points, to have an equally strong impact in all parts, and to continue to be viewable as
(60) people moved across in front of them.

1. Which one of the following most accurately expresses the main point of the passage?

(A) Muralism developed its political goals in Mexico in service to the revolutionary government, while its aesthetic aspects were borrowed from other countries.

(B) Inspired by political developments in Mexico and trends in modern art, muralist painters devised an innovative style of large-scale painting to reflect Mexican culture.

(C) The stylistic features of muralism represent a consistent working out of the implications of its revolutionary ideology.

(D) Though the Mexican government supported muralism as a means of promoting nationalist ideology, muralists such as Siqueiros, Rivera, and Orozco developed the movement in contradictory, more controversial directions.

(E) Because of its large scale and stylistic innovations, the type of contemporary Mexican art known as muralism is capable of expressing a much wider and more complex view of Mexico's culture and history than previous artistic movements could express.

2. The author mentions Rivera's use of "pre-Columbian sculpture and the Italian Renaissance fresco" (lines 36–37) primarily in order to provide an example of Rivera's

(A) assimilation of elements of Mexican customs and myth

(B) movement beyond single, centralized subjects

(C) experimentation with expressionist techniques

(D) distinctive manner of artistic expression

(E) underlying resistance to change

GO ON TO THE NEXT PAGE.

LSAT EXTREME STUDENTS: THIS SECTION IS ADMINISTERED AT AN IN-CLASS WORKSHOP. DO NOT USE THIS SECTION FOR PRACTICE.

Reading Comprehension 5

3. Which one of the following aspects of muralist painting does the author appear to value most highly?

   (A) its revolutionary ideology
   (B) its use of brilliant color
   (C) its tailoring of style to its medium
   (D) its use of elements from everyday life
   (E) its expression of populist ideas

4. Based on the passage, with which one of the following statements about art would the muralists be most likely to agree?

   (A) Art should be evaluated on the basis of its style and form rather than on its content.
   (B) Government sponsorship is essential to the flourishing of art.
   (C) Realism is unsuited to large-scale public art.
   (D) The use of techniques borrowed from other cultures can contribute to the rediscovery of one's national identity.
   (E) Traditional easel painting is an elitist art form.

5. According to the passage, the Mexican government elected in 1920 took which one of the following approaches to art following the Mexican Revolution?

   (A) It encouraged the adoption of modern innovations from abroad.
   (B) It encouraged artists to pursue the realist tradition in art.
   (C) It called on artists to portray Mexico's heritage and future promise.
   (D) It developed the theoretical base of the muralist movement.
   (E) It favored artists who introduced stylistic innovations over those who worked in the realist tradition.

6. Which one of the following, if true, most supports the author's claim about the relationship between muralism and the Mexican Revolution (lines 24–27)?

   (A) The major figures in muralism also created important works in that style that were deliberately not political in content.
   (B) Not all muralist painters were familiar with the innovations being made at that time in the art world.
   (C) The changes taking place at that time in the art world were revivals of earlier movements.
   (D) Officials in the Mexican government were not familiar with the innovations being made at that time in the art world.
   (E) Only those muralist works that reflected nationalist sentiments were permitted to be viewed by the public.

7. Which one of the following does the author explicitly identify as a characteristic of Mexican mural art?

   (A) Its subject matter consisted primarily of current events.
   (B) It could be viewed outdoors only.
   (C) It used the same techniques as are used in easel painting.
   (D) It exhibited remarkable stylistic uniformity.
   (E) It was intended to be viewed from more than one angle.

8. The primary purpose of the second paragraph is to

   (A) describe the unifying features of muralism
   (B) provide support for the argument that the muralists often did not support government causes
   (C) support the claim that muralists always used their work to comment on their own historical period
   (D) illustrate how the muralists appropriated elements of Mexican tradition
   (E) argue that muralism cannot be understood by focusing solely on its political dimension

GO ON TO THE NEXT PAGE.

Reading Comprehension 5

Fairy tales address themselves to two communities, each with its own interests and each in periodic conflict with the other: parents and children. Nearly every study of fairy tales has taken the perspective of the
(5) parent, constructing the meaning of the tales by using the reading strategies of an adult bent on identifying universally valid tenets of moral instruction for children.

For example, the plot of "Hansel and Gretel" is set
(10) in motion by hard-hearted parents who abandon their children in the woods, but for psychologist Bruno Bettelheim the tale is really about children who learn to give up their unhealthy dependency on their parents. According to Bettelheim, this story—in which the
(15) children ultimately overpower a witch who has taken them prisoner for the crime of attempting to eat the witch's gingerbread house—forces its young audience to recognize the dangers of unrestrained greed. As dependent children, Bettelheim argues, Hansel and
(20) Gretel had been a burden to their parents, but on their return home with the witch's jewels, they become the family's support. Thus, says Bettelheim, does the story train its young listeners to become "mature children."

There are two ways of interpreting a story: one is a
(25) "superficial" reading that focuses on the tale's manifest content, and the other is a "deeper" reading that looks for latent meanings. Many adults who read fairy tales are drawn to this second kind of interpretation in order to avoid facing the unpleasant truths that can emerge
(30) from the tales when adults—even parents—are portrayed as capable of acting out of selfish motives themselves. What makes fairy tales attractive to Bettelheim and other psychologists is that they can be used as scenarios that position the child as a
(35) transgressor whose deserved punishment provides a lesson for unruly children. Stories that run counter to such orthodoxies about child-rearing are, to a large extent, suppressed by Bettelheim or "rewritten" through reinterpretation. Once we examine his
(40) interpretations closely, we see that his readings produce meanings that are very different from those constructed by readers with different cultural assumptions and expectations, who, unlike Bettelheim, do not find inflexible tenets of moral instruction in the
(45) tales.

Bettelheim interprets all fairy tales as driven by children's fantasies of desire and revenge, and in doing so suppresses the true nature of parental behavior ranging from abuse to indulgence. Fortunately, these
(50) characterizations of selfish children and innocent adults have been discredited to some extent by recent psychoanalytic literature. The need to deny adult evil has been a pervasive feature of our society, leading us to position children not only as the sole agents of evil
(55) but also as the objects of unending moral instruction, hence the idea that a literature targeted for them must stand in the service of pragmatic instrumentality rather than foster an unproductive form of playful pleasure.

9. Which one of the following most accurately states the main idea of the passage?

(A) While originally written for children, fairy tales also contain a deeper significance for adults that psychologists such as Bettelheim have shown to be their true meaning.

(B) The "superficial" reading of a fairy tale, which deals only with the tale's content, is actually more enlightening for children than the "deeper" reading preferred by psychologists such as Bettelheim.

(C) Because the content of fairy tales has historically run counter to prevailing orthodoxies about child-rearing, psychologists such as Bettelheim sometimes reinterpret them to suit their own pedagogical needs.

(D) The pervasive need to deny adult evil has led psychologists such as Bettelheim to erroneously view fairy tales solely as instruments of moral instruction for children.

(E) Although dismissed as unproductive by psychologists such as Bettelheim, fairy tales offer children imaginative experiences that help them grow into morally responsible adults.

10. Based on the passage, which one of the following elements of "Hansel and Gretel" would most likely be de-emphasized in Bettelheim's interpretation of the tale?

(A) Hansel and Gretel are abandoned by their hard-hearted parents.
(B) Hansel and Gretel are imprisoned by the witch.
(C) Hansel and Gretel overpower the witch.
(D) Hansel and Gretel take the witch's jewels.
(E) Hansel and Gretel bring the witch's jewels home to their parents.

11. Which one of the following is the most accurate description of the author's attitude toward Bettelheim's view of fairy tales?

(A) concern that the view will undermine the ability of fairy tales to provide moral instruction
(B) scorn toward the view's supposition that moral tenets can be universally valid
(C) disapproval of the view's depiction of children as selfish and adults as innocent
(D) anger toward the view's claim that children often improve as a result of deserved punishment
(E) disappointment with the view's emphasis on the manifest content of a tale

GO ON TO THE NEXT PAGE.

LSAT EXTREME STUDENTS: THIS SECTION IS ADMINISTERED AT AN IN-CLASS WORKSHOP. DO NOT USE THIS SECTION FOR PRACTICE.

Reading Comprehensi͏

12. The author of the passage would be most likely to agree with which one of the following statements?

   (A) Children who never attempt to look for the deeper meanings in fairy tales will miss out on one of the principal pleasures of reading such tales.

   (B) It is better if children discover fairy tales on their own than for an adult to suggest that they read the tales.

   (C) A child who is unruly will behave better after reading a fairy tale if the tale is suggested to them by another child.

   (D) Most children are too young to comprehend the deeper meanings contained in fairy tales.

   (E) Children should be allowed to enjoy literature that has no instructive purpose.

13. Which one of the following principles most likely underlies the author's characterization of literary interpretation?

   (A) Only those trained in literary interpretation can detect the latent meanings in stories.

   (B) Only adults are psychologically mature enough to find the latent meanings in stories.

   (C) Only one of the various meanings readers may find in a story is truly correct.

   (D) The meanings we see in stories are influenced by the assumptions and expectations we bring to the story.

   (E) The latent meanings a story contains are deliberately placed there by the author.

14. According to the author, recent psychoanalytic literature suggests that

   (A) the moral instruction children receive from fairy tales is detrimental to their emotional development

   (B) fewer adults are guilty of improper child-rearing than had once been thought

   (C) the need to deny adult evil is a pervasive feature of all modern societies

   (D) the plots of many fairy tales are similar to children's revenge fantasies

   (E) the idea that children are typically selfish and adults innocent is of questionable validity

15. It can be inferred from the passage that Bettelheim believes that children are

   (A) uninterested in inflexible tenets of moral instruction

   (B) unfairly subjected to the moral beliefs of their parents

   (C) often aware of inappropriate parental behavior

   (D) capable of shedding undesirable personal qualities

   (E) basically playful and carefree

16. Which one of the following statements is least compatible with Bettelheim's views, as those views are described in the passage?

   (A) The imaginations of children do not draw clear distinctions between inanimate objects and living things.

   (B) Children must learn that their own needs and feelings are to be valued, even when these differ from those of their parents.

   (C) As their minds mature, children tend to experience the world in terms of the dynamics of the family into which they were born.

   (D) The more secure that children feel within the world, the less they need to hold onto infantile notions.

   (E) Children's ability to distinguish between stories and reality is not fully developed until puberty.

GO ON TO THE NEXT PAGE.

Reading Comprehension 5

With the approach of the twentieth century, the classical wave theory of radiation—a widely accepted theory in physics—began to encounter obstacles. This theory held that all electromagnetic radiation—the
(5) entire spectrum from gamma and X rays to radio frequencies, including heat and light—exists in the form of waves. One fundamental assumption of wave theory was that as the length of a wave of radiation shortens, its energy increases smoothly—like a volume
(10) dial on a radio that adjusts smoothly to any setting— and that any conceivable energy value could thus occur in nature.

The major challenge to wave theory was the behavior of thermal radiation, the radiation emitted by
(15) an object due to the object's temperature, commonly called "blackbody" radiation because experiments aimed at measuring it require objects, such as black velvet or soot, with little or no reflective capability. Physicists can monitor the radiation coming from a
(20) blackbody object and be confident that they are observing its thermal radiation and not simply reflected radiation that has originated elsewhere. Employing the principles of wave theory, physicists originally predicted that blackbody objects radiated much more at
(25) short wavelengths, such as ultraviolet, than at long wavelengths. However, physicists using advanced experimental techniques near the turn of the century did not find the predicted amount of radiation at short wavelengths—in fact, they found almost none, a result
(30) that became known among wave theorists as the "ultraviolet catastrophe."

Max Planck, a classical physicist who had made important contributions to wave theory, developed a hypothesis about atomic processes taking place in a
(35) blackbody object that broke with wave theory and accounted for the observed patterns of blackbody radiation. Planck discarded the assumption of radiation's smooth energy continuum and took the then bizarre position that these atomic processes could only
(40) involve discrete energies that jump between certain units of value—like a volume dial that "clicks" between incremental settings—and he thereby obtained numbers that perfectly fit the earlier experimental result. This directly opposed wave theory's picture of
(45) atomic processes, and the physics community was at first quite critical of Planck's hypothesis, in part because he presented it without physical explanation.

Soon thereafter, however, Albert Einstein and other physicists provided theoretical justification for
(50) Planck's hypothesis. They found that upon being hit with part of the radiation spectrum, metal surfaces give off energy at values that are discontinuous. Further, they noted a threshold along the spectrum beyond which no energy is emitted by the metal. Einstein
(55) theorized, and later found evidence to confirm, that radiation is composed of particles, now called photons, which can be emitted only in discrete units and at certain wavelengths, in accordance with Planck's speculations. So in just a few years, what was
(60) considered a catastrophe generated a new vision in physics that led to theories still in place today.

17. Which one of the following most accurately states the main point of the passage?

(A) If classical wave theorists had never focused on blackbody radiation, Planck's insights would not have developed and the stage would not have been set for Einstein.

(B) Classical wave theory, an incorrect formulation of the nature of radiation, was corrected by Planck and other physicists after Planck performed experiments that demonstrated that radiation exists as particles.

(C) Planck's new model of radiation, though numerically consistent with observed data, was slow to win the support of the scientific community, which was critical of his ideas.

(D) Prompted by new experimental findings, Planck discarded an assumption of classical wave theory and proposed a picture of radiation that matched experimental results and was further supported by theoretical justification.

(E) At the turn of the century, Planck and Einstein revolutionized studies in radiation by modifying classical wave theory in response to experimental results that suggested the energy of radiation is less at short wavelengths than at long ones.

18. Which one of the following does the author use to illustrate the difference between continuous energies and discrete energies?

(A) radio waves
(B) black velvet or soot
(C) microscopic particles
(D) metal surfaces
(E) radio volume dials

19. Which one of the following can most clearly be inferred from the description of blackbody objects in the second paragraph?

(A) Radiation reflected by and radiation emitted by an object are difficult to distinguish from one another.

(B) Any object in a dark room is a nearly ideal blackbody object.

(C) All blackbody objects of comparable size give off radiation at approximately the same wavelengths regardless of the objects' temperatures.

(D) Any blackbody object whose temperature is difficult to manipulate would be of little use in an experiment.

(E) Thermal radiation cannot originate from a blackbody object.

GO ON TO THE NEXT PAGE.

LSAT EXTREME STUDENTS: THIS SECTION IS ADMINISTERED AT AN IN-CLASS WORKSHOP. DO NOT USE THIS SECTION FOR PRACTICE.

Reading Comprehension 5

20. The author's attitude toward Planck's development of a new hypothesis about atomic processes can most aptly be described as

    (A) strong admiration for the intuitive leap that led to a restored confidence in wave theory's picture of atomic processes

    (B) mild surprise at the bizarre position Planck took regarding atomic processes

    (C) reasoned skepticism of Planck's lack of scientific justification for his hypothesis

    (D) legitimate concern that the hypothesis would have been abandoned without the further studies of Einstein and others

    (E) scholarly interest in a step that led to a more accurate picture of atomic processes

21. The passage provides information that answers each of the following questions EXCEPT:

    (A) What did Planck's hypothesis about atomic processes try to account for?

    (B) What led to the scientific community's acceptance of Planck's ideas?

    (C) Roughly when did the blackbody radiation experiments take place?

    (D) What contributions did Planck make to classical wave theory?

    (E) What type of experiment led Einstein to formulate a theory regarding the composition of radiation?

22. The primary function of the first two paragraphs of the passage is to

    (A) describe the process by which one theory's assumption was dismantled by a competing theory

    (B) introduce a central assumption of a scientific theory and the experimental evidence that led to the overthrowing of that theory

    (C) explain two competing theories that are based on the same experimental evidence

    (D) describe the process of retesting a theory in light of ambiguous experimental results

    (E) provide the basis for an argument intended to dismiss a new theory

23. The passage is primarily concerned with

    (A) discussing the value of speculation in a scientific discipline

    (B) summarizing the reasons for the rejection of an established theory by the scientific community

    (C) describing the role that experimental research plays in a scientific discipline

    (D) examining a critical stage in the evolution of theories concerning the nature of a physical phenomenon

    (E) comparing the various assumptions that lie at the foundation of a scientific discipline

GO ON TO THE NEXT PAGE.

Reading Comprehension 5

The following passage was written in the mid-1990s.

Users of the Internet—the worldwide network of interconnected computer systems—envision it as a way for people to have free access to information via their personal computers. Most Internet communication
(5) consists of sending electronic mail or exchanging ideas on electronic bulletin boards; however, a growing number of transmissions are of copyrighted works— books, photographs, videos and films, and sound recordings. In Canada, as elsewhere, the goals of
(10) Internet users have begun to conflict with reality as copyright holders look for ways to protect their material from unauthorized and uncompensated distribution.

Copyright experts say that Canadian copyright law,
(15) which was revised in 1987 to cover works such as choreography and photography, has not kept pace with technology—specifically with digitalization, the conversion of data into a series of digits that are transmitted as electronic signals over computer
(20) networks. Digitalization makes it possible to create an unlimited number of copies of a book, recording, or movie and distribute them to millions of people around the world. Current law prohibits unauthorized parties from reproducing a work or any substantial part of it in
(25) any material form (e.g., photocopies of books or pirated audiotapes), but because digitalization merely transforms the work into electronic signals in a computer's memory, it is not clear whether digitalization constitutes a material reproduction—and
(30) so unauthorized digitalization is not yet technically a crime.

Some experts propose simply adding unauthorized digitalization to the list of activities proscribed under current law, to make it clear that copyright holders own
(35) electronic reproduction rights just as they own rights to other types of reproduction. But criminalizing digitalization raises a host of questions. For example, given that digitalization allows the multiple recipients of a transmission to re-create copies of a work, would
(40) only the act of digitalization itself be criminal, or should each copy made from the transmission be considered a separate instance of piracy—even though those who made the copies never had access to the original? In addition, laws against digitalization might
(45) be virtually unenforceable given that an estimated 20 million people around the world have access to the Internet, and that copying and distributing material is a relatively simple process. Furthermore, even an expanded law might not cover the majority of
(50) transmissions, given the vast numbers of users who are academics and the fact that current copyright law allows generous exemptions for those engaged in private study or research. But even if the law is revised to contain a more sophisticated treatment of
(55) digitalization, most experts think it will be hard to resolve the clash between the Internet community, which is accustomed to treating information as raw material available for everyone to use, and the publishing community, which is accustomed to treating
(60) it as a commodity owned by its creator.

24. Which one of the following most accurately expresses the main point of the passage?

(A) Despite the widely recognized need to revise Canadian copyright law to protect works from unauthorized reproduction and distribution over the Internet, users of the Internet have mounted many legal challenges to the criminalizing of digitalization.

(B) Although the necessity of revising Canadian copyright law to protect works from unauthorized reproduction and distribution over the Internet is widely recognized, effective criminalizing of digitalization is likely to prove highly complicated.

(C) While the unauthorized reproduction and distribution of copyrighted works over the Internet is not yet a crime, legal experts believe it is only a matter of time before Canadian copyright law is amended to prohibit unauthorized digitalization.

(D) Despite the fact that current Canadian copyright law does not cover digitalization, the unauthorized reproduction and distribution of copyrighted works over the Internet clearly ought to be considered a crime.

(E) Although legal experts in Canada disagree about the most effective way to punish the unauthorized reproduction and distribution of copyrighted works over the Internet, they nonetheless agree that such digitalization should clearly be a punishable crime.

25. Given the author's argument, which one of the following additions to current Canadian copyright law would most likely be an agreeable compromise to both the Internet community and the publishing community?

(A) Digitalization of copyrighted works is permitted to Internet users who pay a small fee to copyright holders.

(B) Digitalization of copyrighted works is prohibited to Internet users who are not academics.

(C) Digitalization of copyrighted works is permitted to all Internet users without restriction.

(D) Digitalization of copyrighted works is prohibited to all Internet users without exception.

(E) Digitalization of copyrighted works is permitted to Internet users engaged in research.

GO ON TO THE NEXT PAGE.

LSAT EXTREME STUDENTS: THIS SECTION IS ADMINISTERED AT AN IN-CLASS WORKSHOP. DO NOT USE THIS SECTION FOR PRACTICE.

Reading Comprehension

26. The discussion in the second paragraph is intended primarily to explain which one of the following?

    (A) how copyright infringement of protected works is punished under current Canadian copyright law
    (B) why current Canadian copyright law is not easily applicable to digitalization
    (C) how the Internet has caused copyright holders to look for new forms of legal protection
    (D) why copyright experts propose protecting copyrighted works from unauthorized digitalization
    (E) how unauthorized reproductions of copyrighted works are transmitted over the Internet

27. The passage supports each of the following inferences EXCEPT:

    (A) It is unlikely that every instance of digitalization could be detected under a copyright law revised to criminalize digitalization.
    (B) Criminalizing unauthorized digitalization appears to be consistent with the publishing community's treatment of information as an owned commodity.
    (C) When copyright law is revised to cover digitalization, the revised law will include a prohibition on making copies from an unauthorized digitalization of a copyrighted work.
    (D) The number of instances of unauthorized digitalization would likely rise if digitalization technology were made even easier to use.
    (E) Under current law, many academics are allowed to make copies of copyrighted works as long as they are used only for private research.

28. Which one of the following views can most reasonably be attributed to the experts cited in line 32?

    (A) Unauthorized digitalization of a copyrighted work should be considered a crime except when it is done for purposes of private study or research.
    (B) Unauthorized digitalization of a copyrighted work should be considered a crime even when it is done for purposes of private study or research.
    (C) Making a copy of a copyrighted work from an unauthorized digitalization of the work should not be considered a crime.
    (D) Making a copy of a copyrighted work from an unauthorized digitalization of the work should be punished, but not as severely as making an original digitalization.
    (E) Making a copy of a copyrighted work from an unauthorized digitalization of the work should be punished just as severely as making the original digitalization.

S T O P

IF YOU FINISH BEFORE TIME IS CALLED, YOU MAY CHECK YOUR WORK ON THIS SECTION ONLY. DO NOT WORK ON ANY OTHER SECTION IN THE TEST.

Answer Key

1. B
2. D
3. C
4. D
5. C
6. A
7. E
8. E
9. D
10. A
11. C
12. E
13. D
14. E
15. D
16. B
17. D
18. E
19. A
20. E
21. D
22. B
23. D
24. B
25. A
26. B
27. C
28. A

Reading Comprehension 6

PrepTest 38, Section III
October 2002

SECTION III
Time—35 minutes
27 Questions

<u>Directions</u>: Each passage in this section is followed by a group of questions to be answered on the basis of what is <u>stated</u> or <u>implied</u> in the passage. For some of the questions, more than one of the choices could conceivably answer the question. However, you are to choose the <u>best</u> answer; that is, the response that most accurately and completely answers the question, and blacken the corresponding space on your answer sheet.

The myth persists that in 1492 the Western Hemisphere was an untamed wilderness and that it was European settlers who harnessed and transformed its ecosystems. But scholarship shows that forests, in
(5) particular, had been altered to varying degrees well before the arrival of Europeans. Native populations had converted much of the forests to successfully cultivated stands, especially by means of burning. Nevertheless, some researchers have maintained that the extent,
(10) frequency, and impact of such burning was minimal. One geographer claims that climatic change could have accounted for some of the changes in forest composition; another argues that burning by native populations was done only sporadically, to augment the
(15) effects of natural fires.

However, a large body of evidence for the routine practice of burning exists in the geographical record. One group of researchers found, for example, that sedimentary charcoal accumulations in what is now the
(20) northeastern United States are greatest where known native American settlements were greatest. Other evidence shows that, while the characteristics and impact of fires set by native populations varied regionally according to population size, extent of
(25) resource management techniques, and environment, all such fires had markedly different effects on vegetation patterns than did natural fires. Controlled burning created grassy openings such as meadows and glades. Burning also promoted a mosaic quality to North and
(30) South American ecosystems, creating forests in many different stages of ecological development. Much of the mature forestland was characterized by open, herbaceous undergrowth, another result of the clearing brought about by burning.

(35) In North America, controlled burning created conditions favorable to berries and other fire-tolerant and sun-loving foods. Burning also converted mixed stands of trees to homogeneous forest, for example the longleaf, slash pine, and scrub oak forests of the
(40) southeastern U.S. Natural fires do account for some of this vegetation, but regular burning clearly extended and maintained it. Burning also influenced forest composition in the tropics, where natural fires are rare. An example is the pine-dominant forests of Nicaragua,
(45) where warm temperatures and heavy rainfall naturally favor mixed tropical or rain forests. While there are extensive pine forests in Guatemala and Mexico, these primarily grow in cooler, drier, higher elevations, regions where such vegetation is in large part natural
(50) and even prehuman. Today, the Nicaraguan pines occur where there has been clearing followed by

regular burning, and the same is likely to have occurred in the past: such forests were present when Europeans arrived and were found only in areas where native
(55) settlements were substantial; when these settlements were abandoned, the land returned to mixed hardwoods. This succession is also evident elsewhere in similar low tropical elevations in the Caribbean and Mexico.

1. Which one of the following most accurately expresses the main idea of the passage?

    (A)   Despite extensive evidence that native populations had been burning North and South American forests extensively before 1492, some scholars persist in claiming that such burning was either infrequent or the result of natural causes.

    (B)   In opposition to the widespread belief that in 1492 the Western Hemisphere was uncultivated, scholars unanimously agree that native populations were substantially altering North and South American forests well before the arrival of Europeans.

    (C)   Although some scholars minimize the scope and importance of the burning of forests engaged in by native populations of North and South America before 1492, evidence of the frequency and impact of such burning is actually quite extensive.

    (D)   Where scholars had once believed that North and South American forests remained uncultivated until the arrival of Europeans, there is now general agreement that native populations had been cultivating the forests since well before 1492.

    (E)   While scholars have acknowledged that North and South American forests were being burned well before 1492, there is still disagreement over whether such burning was the result of natural causes or of the deliberate actions of native populations.

GO ON TO THE NEXT PAGE.

2. It can be inferred that a forest burned as described in the passage would have been LEAST likely to display

   (A) numerous types of hardwood trees
   (B) extensive herbaceous undergrowth
   (C) a variety of fire-tolerant plants
   (D) various stages of ecological maturity
   (E) grassy openings such as meadows or glades

3. Which one of the following is a type of forest identified by the author as a product of controlled burning in recent times?

   (A) scrub oak forests in the southeastern U.S.
   (B) slash pine forests in the southeastern U.S.
   (C) pine forests in Guatemala at high elevations
   (D) pine forests in Mexico at high elevations
   (E) pine forests in Nicaragua at low elevations

4. Which one of the following is presented by the author as evidence of controlled burning in the tropics before the arrival of Europeans?

   (A) extensive homogeneous forests at high elevation
   (B) extensive homogeneous forests at low elevation
   (C) extensive heterogeneous forests at high elevation
   (D) extensive heterogeneous forests at low elevation
   (E) extensive sedimentary charcoal accumulations at high elevation

5. With which one of the following would the author be most likely to agree?

   (A) The long-term effects of controlled burning could just as easily have been caused by natural fires.
   (B) Herbaceous undergrowth prevents many forests from reaching full maturity.
   (C) European settlers had little impact on the composition of the ecosystems in North and South America.
   (D) Certain species of plants may not have been as widespread in North America without controlled burning.
   (E) Nicaraguan pine forests could have been created either by natural fires or by controlled burning.

6. As evidence for the routine practice of forest burning by native populations before the arrival of Europeans, the author cites all of the following EXCEPT:

   (A) the similar characteristics of fires in different regions
   (B) the simultaneous presence of forests at varying stages of maturity
   (C) the existence of herbaceous undergrowth in certain forests
   (D) the heavy accumulation of charcoal near populous settlements
   (E) the presence of meadows and glades in certain forests

7. The "succession" mentioned in line 57 refers to

   (A) forest clearing followed by controlled burning of forests
   (B) tropical rain forest followed by pine forest
   (C) European settlement followed by abandonment of land
   (D) homogeneous pine forest followed by mixed hardwoods
   (E) pine forests followed by established settlements

8. The primary purpose of the passage is to

   (A) refute certain researchers' views
   (B) support a common belief
   (C) counter certain evidence
   (D) synthesize two viewpoints
   (E) correct the geographical record

GO ON TO THE NEXT PAGE.

Intellectual authority is defined as the authority of arguments that prevail by virtue of good reasoning and do not depend on coercion or convention. A contrasting notion, institutional authority, refers to the power of social institutions to enforce acceptance of arguments that may or may not possess intellectual authority. The authority wielded by legal systems is especially interesting because such systems are institutions that nonetheless aspire to a purely intellectual authority. One judge goes so far as to claim that courts are merely passive vehicles for applying the intellectual authority of the law and possess no coercive powers of their own.

(15) In contrast, some critics maintain that whatever authority judicial pronouncements have is exclusively institutional. Some of these critics go further, claiming that intellectual authority does not really exist—i.e., it reduces to institutional authority. But it can be (20) countered that these claims break down when a sufficiently broad historical perspective is taken: Not all arguments accepted by institutions withstand the test of time, and some well-reasoned arguments never receive institutional imprimatur. The reasonable argument that goes unrecognized in its own time (25) because it challenges institutional beliefs is common in intellectual history; intellectual authority and institutional consensus are not the same thing.

But, the critics might respond, intellectual authority is only recognized as such because of institutional (30) consensus. For example, if a musicologist were to claim that an alleged musical genius who, after several decades, had not gained respect and recognition for his or her compositions is probably not a genius, the critics might say that basing a judgment on a unit of time— (35) "several decades"—is an institutional rather than an intellectual construct. What, the critics might ask, makes a particular number of decades reasonable evidence by which to judge genius? The answer, of course, is nothing, except for the fact that such (40) institutional procedures have proved useful to musicologists in making such distinctions in the past.

The analogous legal concept is the doctrine of precedent, i.e., a judge's merely deciding a case a certain way becoming a basis for deciding later cases (45) the same way—a pure example of institutional authority. But the critics miss the crucial distinction that when a judicial decision is badly reasoned, or simply no longer applies in the face of evolving social standards or practices, the notion of intellectual (50) authority is introduced: judges reconsider, revise, or in some cases throw out the decision. The conflict between intellectual and institutional authority in legal systems is thus played out in the reconsideration of decisions, leading one to draw the conclusion that legal (55) systems contain a significant degree of intellectual authority even if the thrust of their power is predominantly institutional.

9. Which one of the following most accurately states the main idea of the passage?

(A) Although some argue that the authority of legal systems is purely intellectual, these systems possess a degree of institutional authority due to their ability to enforce acceptance of badly reasoned or socially inappropriate judicial decisions.

(B) Although some argue that the authority of legal systems is purely institutional, these systems are more correctly seen as vehicles for applying the intellectual authority of the law while possessing no coercive power of their own.

(C) Although some argue that the authority of legal systems is purely intellectual, these systems in fact wield institutional authority by virtue of the fact that intellectual authority reduces to institutional authority.

(D) Although some argue that the authority of legal systems is purely institutional, these systems possess a degree of intellectual authority due to their ability to reconsider badly reasoned or socially inappropriate judicial decisions.

(E) Although some argue that the authority of legal systems is purely intellectual, these systems in fact wield exclusively institutional authority in that they possess the power to enforce acceptance of badly reasoned or socially inappropriate judicial decisions.

10. That some arguments "never receive institutional imprimatur" (lines 22–23) most likely means that these arguments

(A) fail to gain institutional consensus
(B) fail to challenge institutional beliefs
(C) fail to conform to the example of precedent
(D) fail to convince by virtue of good reasoning
(E) fail to gain acceptance except by coercion

GO ON TO THE NEXT PAGE.

11. Which one of the following, if true, most challenges the author's contention that legal systems contain a significant degree of intellectual authority?

    (A) Judges often act under time constraints and occasionally render a badly reasoned or socially inappropriate decision.

    (B) In some legal systems, the percentage of judicial decisions that contain faulty reasoning is far higher than it is in other legal systems.

    (C) Many socially inappropriate legal decisions are thrown out by judges only after citizens begin to voice opposition to them.

    (D) In some legal systems, the percentage of judicial decisions that are reconsidered and revised is far higher than it is in other legal systems.

    (E) Judges are rarely willing to rectify the examples of faulty reasoning they discover when reviewing previous legal decisions.

12. Given the information in the passage, the author is LEAST likely to believe which one of the following?

    (A) Institutional authority may depend on coercion; intellectual authority never does.

    (B) Intellectual authority may accept well-reasoned arguments; institutional authority never does.

    (C) Institutional authority may depend on convention; intellectual authority never does.

    (D) Intellectual authority sometimes challenges institutional beliefs; institutional authority never does.

    (E) Intellectual authority sometimes conflicts with precedent; institutional authority never does.

13. The author discusses the example from musico primarily in order to

    (A) distinguish the notion of institutional auth from that of intellectual authority

    (B) give an example of an argument possessin intellectual authority that did not prevail own time

    (C) identify an example in which the ascription musical genius did not withstand the test

    (D) illustrate the claim that assessing intellectua authority requires an appeal to institutional authority

    (E) demonstrate that the authority wielded by th arbiters of musical genius is entirely institut

14. Based on the passage, the author would be most like to hold which one of the following views about the doctrine of precedent?

    (A) It is the only tool judges should use if they wis to achieve a purely intellectual authority.

    (B) It is a useful tool in theory but in practice it invariably conflicts with the demands of intellectual authority.

    (C) It is a useful tool but lacks intellectual authority unless it is combined with the reconsidering of decisions.

    (D) It is often an unreliable tool because it prevents judges from reconsidering the intellectual authority of past decisions.

    (E) It is an unreliable tool that should be abandoned because it lacks intellectual authority.

GO ON TO THE NEXT PAGE.

In explaining the foundations of the discipline known as historical sociology—the examination of history using the methods of sociology—historical sociologist Philip Abrams argues that, while people are
(5) made by society as much as society is made by people, sociologists' approach to the subject is usually to focus on only one of these forms of influence to the exclusion of the other. Abrams insists on the necessity for sociologists to move beyond these one-sided
(10) approaches to understand society as an entity constructed by individuals who are at the same time constructed by their society. Abrams refers to this continuous process as "structuring."

Abrams also sees history as the result of
(15) structuring. People, both individually and as members of collectives, make history. But our making of history is itself formed and informed not only by the historical conditions we inherit from the past, but also by the prior formation of our own identities and capacities,
(20) which are shaped by what Abrams calls "contingencies"—social phenomena over which we have varying degrees of control. Contingencies include such things as the social conditions under which we come of age, the condition of our household's
(25) economy, the ideologies available to help us make sense of our situation, and accidental circumstances. The ways in which contingencies affect our individual or group identities create a structure of forces within which we are able to act, and that partially determines
(30) the sorts of actions we are able to perform.

In Abrams's analysis, historical structuring, like social structuring, is manifold and unremitting. To understand it, historical sociologists must extract from it certain significant episodes, or events, that their
(35) methodology can then analyze and interpret. According to Abrams, these events are points at which action and contingency meet, points that represent a cross section of the specific social and individual forces in play at a given time. At such moments, individuals stand forth
(40) as agents of history not simply because they possess a unique ability to act, but also because in them we see the force of the specific social conditions that allowed their actions to come forth. Individuals can "make their mark" on history, yet in individuals one also finds the
(45) convergence of wider social forces. In order to capture the various facets of this mutual interaction, Abrams recommends a fourfold structure to which he believes the investigations of historical sociologists should conform: first, description of the event itself; second,
(50) discussion of the social context that helped bring the event about and gave it significance; third, summary of the life history of the individual agent in the event; and fourth, analysis of the consequences of the event both for history and for the individual.

15. Which one of the following most accurately states the central idea of the passage?

(A) Abrams argues that historical sociology rejects the claims of sociologists who assert that the sociological concept of structuring cannot be applied to the interactions between individuals and history.

(B) Abrams argues that historical sociology assumes that, despite the views of sociologists to the contrary, history influences the social contingencies that affect individuals.

(C) Abrams argues that historical sociology demonstrates that, despite the views of sociologists to the contrary, social structures both influence and are influenced by the events of history.

(D) Abrams describes historical sociology as a discipline that unites two approaches taken by sociologists to studying the formation of societies and applies the resulting combined approach to the study of history.

(E) Abrams describes historical sociology as an attempt to compensate for the shortcomings of traditional historical methods by applying the methods established in sociology.

16. Given the passage's argument, which one of the following sentences most logically completes the last paragraph?

(A) Only if they adhere to this structure, Abrams believes, can historical sociologists conclude with any certainty that the events that constitute the historical record are influenced by the actions of individuals.

(B) Only if they adhere to this structure, Abrams believes, will historical sociologists be able to counter the standard sociological assumption that there is very little connection between history and individual agency.

(C) Unless they can agree to adhere to this structure, Abrams believes, historical sociologists risk having their discipline treated as little more than an interesting but ultimately indefensible adjunct to history and sociology.

(D) By adhering to this structure, Abrams believes, historical sociologists can shed light on issues that traditional sociologists have chosen to ignore in their one-sided approaches to the formation of societies.

(E) By adhering to this structure, Abrams believes, historical sociologists will be able to better portray the complex connections between human agency and history.

GO ON TO THE NEXT PAGE.

17. The passage states that a contingency could be each of the following EXCEPT:

    (A) a social phenomenon
    (B) a form of historical structuring
    (C) an accidental circumstance
    (D) a condition controllable to some extent by an individual
    (E) a partial determinant of an individual's actions

18. Which one of the following is most analogous to the ideal work of a historical sociologist as outlined by Abrams?

    (A) In a report on the enactment of a bill into law, a journalist explains why the need for the bill arose, sketches the biography of the principal legislator who wrote the bill, and ponders the effect that the bill's enactment will have both on society and on the legislator's career.
    (B) In a consultation with a patient, a doctor reviews the patient's medical history, suggests possible reasons for the patient's current condition, and recommends steps that the patient should take in the future to ensure that the condition improves or at least does not get any worse.
    (C) In an analysis of a historical novel, a critic provides information to support the claim that details of the work's setting are accurate, explains why the subject of the novel was of particular interest to the author, and compares the novel with some of the author's other books set in the same period.
    (D) In a presentation to stockholders, a corporation's chief executive officer describes the corporation's most profitable activities during the past year, introduces the vice president largely responsible for those activities, and discusses new projects the vice president will initiate in the coming year.
    (E) In developing a film based on a historical event, a filmmaker conducts interviews with participants in the event, bases part of the film's screenplay on the interviews, and concludes the screenplay with a sequence of scenes speculating on the outcome of the event had certain details been different.

19. The primary function of the first paragraph of the passage is to

    (A) outline the merits of Abrams's conception of historical sociology
    (B) convey the details of Abrams's conception of historical sociology
    (C) anticipate challenges to Abrams's conception of historical sociology
    (D) examine the roles of key terms used in Abrams's conception of historical sociology
    (E) identify the basis of Abrams's conception of historical sociology

20. Based on the passage, which one of the following is the LEAST illustrative example of the effect of a contingency upon an individual?

    (A) the effect of the fact that a person experienced political injustice on that person's decision to work for political reform
    (B) the effect of the fact that a person was raised in an agricultural region on that person's decision to pursue a career in agriculture
    (C) the effect of the fact that a person lives in a particular community on that person's decision to visit friends in another community
    (D) the effect of the fact that a person's parents practiced a particular religion on that person's decision to practice that religion
    (E) the effect of the fact that a person grew up in financial hardship on that person's decision to help others in financial hardship

GO ON TO THE NEXT PAGE.

One of the greatest challenges facing medical
students today, apart from absorbing volumes of
technical information and learning habits of scientific
thought, is that of remaining empathetic to the needs of
(5) patients in the face of all this rigorous training.
Requiring students to immerse themselves completely
in medical coursework risks disconnecting them from
the personal and ethical aspects of doctoring, and such
strictly scientific thinking is insufficient for grappling
(10) with modern ethical dilemmas. For these reasons,
aspiring physicians need to develop new ways of
thinking about and interacting with patients. Training
in ethics that takes narrative literature as its primary
subject is one method of accomplishing this.

(15)   Although training in ethics is currently provided by
medical schools, this training relies heavily on an
abstract, philosophical view of ethics. Although the
conceptual clarity provided by a traditional ethics
course can be valuable, theorizing about ethics
(20) contributes little to the understanding of everyday
human experience or to preparing medical students for
the multifarious ethical dilemmas they will face as
physicians. A true foundation in ethics must be
predicated on an understanding of human behavior that
(25) reflects a wide array of relationships and readily adapts
to various perspectives, for this is what is required to
develop empathy. Ethics courses drawing on narrative
literature can better help students prepare for ethical
dilemmas precisely because such literature attaches its
(30) readers so forcefully to the concrete and varied world
of human events.

The act of reading narrative literature is uniquely
suited to the development of what might be called
flexible ethical thinking. To grasp the development of
(35) characters, to tangle with heightening moral crises, and
to engage oneself with the story not as one's own but
nevertheless as something recognizable and worthy of
attention, readers must use their moral imagination.
Giving oneself over to the ethical conflicts in a story
(40) requires the abandonment of strictly absolute, inviolate
sets of moral principles. Reading literature also
demands that the reader adopt another person's point of
view—that of the narrator or a character in a story—
and thus requires the ability to depart from one's
(45) personal ethical stance and examine moral issues from
new perspectives.

It does not follow that readers, including medical
professionals, must relinquish all moral principles, as is
the case with situational ethics, in which decisions
(50) about ethical choices are made on the basis of intuition
and are entirely relative to the circumstances in which
they arise. Such an extremely relativistic stance would
have as little benefit for the patient or physician as
would a dogmatically absolutist one. Fortunately, the
(55) incorporation of narrative literature into the study of
ethics, while serving as a corrective to the latter stance,
need not lead to the former. But it can give us
something that is lacking in the traditional
philosophical study of ethics—namely, a deeper
(60) understanding of human nature that can serve as a
foundation for ethical reasoning and allow greater
flexibility in the application of moral principles.

21. Which one of the following most accurately states the
main point of the passage?

(A)   Training in ethics that incorporates narrative
literature would better cultivate flexible ethical
thinking and increase medical students' capacity
for empathetic patient care as compared with the
traditional approach of medical schools to such
training.

(B)   Traditional abstract ethical training, because it
is too heavily focused on theoretical reasoning,
tends to decrease or impair the medical student's
sensitivity to modern ethical dilemmas.

(C)   Only a properly designed curriculum that
balances situational, abstract, and narrative
approaches to ethics will adequately prepare
the medical student for complex ethical
confrontations involving actual patients.

(D)   Narrative-based instruction in ethics is becoming
increasingly popular in medical schools because
it requires students to develop a capacity for
empathy by examining complex moral issues
from a variety of perspectives.

(E)   The study of narrative literature in medical
schools would nurture moral intuition, enabling
the future doctor to make ethical decisions
without appeal to general principles.

22. Which one of the following most accurately represents
the author's use of the term "moral imagination" in
line 38?

(A)   a sense of curiosity, aroused by reading, that
leads one to follow actively the development of
problems involving the characters depicted in
narratives

(B)   a faculty of seeking out and recognizing the
ethical controversies involved in human
relationships and identifying oneself with one
side or another in such controversies

(C)   a capacity to understand the complexities of
various ethical dilemmas and to fashion creative
and innovative solutions to them

(D)   an ability to understand personal aspects of
ethically significant situations even if one is not
a direct participant and to empathize with those
involved in them

(E)   an ability to act upon ethical principles different
from one's own for the sake of variety

GO ON TO THE NEXT PAGE.

23. It can be inferred from the passage that the author would most likely agree with which one of the following statements?

    (A) The heavy load of technical coursework in today's medical schools often keeps them from giving adequate emphasis to courses in medical ethics.
    (B) Students learn more about ethics through the use of fiction than through the use of nonfictional readings.
    (C) The traditional method of ethical training in medical schools should be supplemented or replaced by more direct practical experience with real-life patients in ethically difficult situations.
    (D) The failings of an abstract, philosophical training in ethics can be remedied only by replacing it with a purely narrative-based approach.
    (E) Neither scientific training nor traditional philosophical ethics adequately prepares doctors to deal with the emotional dimension of patients' needs.

24. Which one of the following is most likely the author's overall purpose in the passage?

    (A) to advise medical schools on how to implement a narrative-based approach to ethics in their curricula
    (B) to argue that the current methods of ethics education are counterproductive to the formation of empathetic doctor-patient relationships
    (C) to argue that the ethical content of narrative literature foreshadows the pitfalls of situational ethics
    (D) to propose an approach to ethical training in medical school that will preserve the human dimension of medicine
    (E) to demonstrate the value of a well-designed ethics education for medical students

25. The passage ascribes each of the following characteristics to the use of narrative literature in ethical education EXCEPT:

    (A) It tends to avoid the extreme relativism of situational ethics.
    (B) It connects students to varied types of human events.
    (C) It can help lead medical students to develop new ways of dealing with patients.
    (D) It requires students to examine moral issues from new perspectives.
    (E) It can help insulate future doctors from the shock of the ethical dilemmas they will confront.

26. With regard to ethical dilemmas, the passage explicitly states each of the following EXCEPT:

    (A) Doctors face a variety of such dilemmas.
    (B) Purely scientific thinking is inadequate for dealing with modern ethical dilemmas.
    (C) Such dilemmas are more prevalent today as a result of scientific and technological advances in medicine.
    (D) Theorizing about ethics does little to prepare students to face such dilemmas.
    (E) Narrative literature can help make medical students ready to face such dilemmas.

27. The author's attitude regarding the traditional method of teaching ethics in medical school can most accurately be described as

    (A) unqualified disapproval of the method and disapproval of all of its effects
    (B) reserved judgment regarding the method and disapproval of all of its effects
    (C) partial disapproval of the method and clinical indifference toward its effects
    (D) partial approval of the method and disapproval of all of its effects
    (E) partial disapproval of the method and approval of some of its effects

S T O P

IF YOU FINISH BEFORE TIME IS CALLED, YOU MAY CHECK YOUR WORK ON THIS SECTION ONLY.
DO NOT WORK ON ANY OTHER SECTION IN THE TEST.

Answer Key

1. C
2. A
3. E
4. B
5. D
6. A
7. D
8. A
9. D
10. A
11. E
12. B
13. D
14. C
15. D
16. E
17. B
18. A
19. E
20. C
21. A
22. D
23. E
24. D
25. E
26. C
27. E

Reading Comprehension 7

PrepTest 36, Section II
December 2001

SECTION II

Time—35 minutes

26 Questions

Directions: Each passage in this section is followed by a group of questions to be answered on the basis of what is <u>stated</u> or <u>implied</u> in the passage. For some of the questions, more than one of the choices could conceivably answer the question. However, you are to choose the <u>best</u> answer; that is, the response that most accurately and completely answers the question, and blacken the corresponding space on your answer sheet.

Traditionally, members of a community such as a town or neighborhood share a common location and a sense of necessary interdependence that includes, for example, mutual respect and emotional support. But as
(5) modern societies grow more technological and sometimes more alienating, people tend to spend less time in the kinds of interactions that their communities require in order to thrive. Meanwhile, technology has made it possible for individuals to interact via personal
(10) computer with others who are geographically distant. Advocates claim that these computer conferences, in which large numbers of participants communicate by typing comments that are immediately read by other participants and responding immediately to those
(15) comments they read, function as communities that can substitute for traditional interactions with neighbors.

What are the characteristics that advocates claim allow computer conferences to function as communities? For one, participants often share
(20) common interests or concerns; conferences are frequently organized around specific topics such as music or parenting. Second, because these conferences are conversations, participants have adopted certain conventions in recognition of the importance of
(25) respecting each others' sensibilities. Abbreviations are used to convey commonly expressed sentiments of courtesy such as "pardon me for cutting in" ("pmfci") or "in my humble opinion" ("imho"). Because a humorous tone can be difficult to communicate in
(30) writing, participants will often end an intentionally humorous comment with a set of characters that, when looked at sideways, resembles a smiling or winking face. Typing messages entirely in capital letters is avoided, because its tendency to demand the attention
(35) of a reader's eye is considered the computer equivalent of shouting. These conventions, advocates claim, constitute a form of etiquette, and with this etiquette as a foundation, people often form genuine, trusting relationships, even offering advice and support during
(40) personal crises such as illness or the loss of a loved one.

But while it is true that conferences can be both respectful and supportive, they nonetheless fall short of communities. For example, conferences discriminate
(45) along educational and economic lines because participation requires a basic knowledge of computers and the ability to afford access to conferences. Further, while advocates claim that a shared interest makes computer conferences similar to traditional
(50) communities—insofar as the shared interest is analogous to a traditional community's shared

location—this analogy simply does not work. Conference participants are a self-selecting group; they are drawn together by their shared interest in the topic
(55) of the conference. Actual communities, on the other hand, are "nonintentional": the people who inhabit towns or neighborhoods are thus more likely to exhibit genuine diversity—of age, career, or personal interests—than are conference participants. It might be
(60) easier to find common ground in a computer conference than in today's communities, but in so doing it would be unfortunate if conference participants cut themselves off further from valuable interactions in their own towns or neighborhoods.

1. Which one of the following most accurately expresses the central idea of the passage?

(A) Because computer conferences attract participants who share common interests and rely on a number of mutually acceptable conventions for communicating with one another, such conferences can substitute effectively for certain interactions that have become rarer within actual communities.

(B) Since increased participation in computer conferences threatens to replace actual communities, members of actual communities are returning to the traditional interactions that distinguish towns or neighborhoods.

(C) Because participants in computer conferences are geographically separated and communicate only by typing, their interactions cannot be as mutually respectful and supportive as are the kinds of interactions that have become rarer within actual communities.

(D) Although computer conferences offer some of the same benefits that actual communities do, the significant lack of diversity among conference participants makes such conferences unlike actual communities.

(E) Even if access to computer technology is broad enough to attract a more diverse group of people to participate in computer conferences, such conferences will not be acceptable substitutes for actual communities.

GO ON TO THE NEXT PAGE.

2. Based on the passage, the author would be LEAST likely to consider which one of the following a community?

    (A)   a group of soldiers who serve together in the same battalion and who come from a variety of geographic regions
    (B)   a group of university students who belong to the same campus political organization and who come from several different socioeconomic backgrounds
    (C)   a group of doctors who work at a number of different hospitals and who meet at a convention to discuss issues relevant to their profession
    (D)   a group of teachers who work interdependently in the same school with the same students and who live in a variety of cities and neighborhoods
    (E)   a group of worshipers who attend and support the same religious institution and who represent a high degree of economic and cultural diversity

3. The author's statement that "conferences can be both respectful and supportive" (lines 42–43) serves primarily to

    (A)   counter the claim that computer conferences may discriminate along educational or economic lines
    (B)   introduce the argument that the conventions of computer conferences constitute a form of social etiquette
    (C)   counter the claim that computer conferences cannot be thought of as communities
    (D)   suggest that not all participants in computer conferences may be equally respectful of one another
    (E)   acknowledge that computer conferences can involve interactions that are similar to those in an actual community

4. Given the information in the passage, the author can most reasonably be said to use which one of the following principles to refute the advocates' claim that computer conferences can function as communities (line 15)?

    (A)   A group is a community only if its members are mutually respectful and supportive of one another.
    (B)   A group is a community only if its members adopt conventions intended to help them respect each other's sensibilities.
    (C)   A group is a community only if its members inhabit the same geographic location.
    (D)   A group is a community only if its members come from the same educational or economic background.
    (E)   A group is a community only if its members feel a sense of interdependence despite different economic and educational backgrounds.

5. What is the primary function of the second paragraph of the passage?

    (A)   to add detail to the discussion in the first paragraph of why computer conferences originated
    (B)   to give evidence challenging the argument of the advocates discussed in the first paragraph
    (C)   to develop the claim of the advocates discussed in the first paragraph
    (D)   to introduce an objection that will be answered in the third paragraph
    (E)   to anticipate the characterization of computer conferences given in the third paragraph

6. Which one of the following, if true, would most weaken one of the author's arguments in the last paragraph?

    (A)   Participants in computer conferences are generally more accepting of diversity than is the population at large.
    (B)   Computer technology is rapidly becoming more affordable and accessible to people from a variety of backgrounds.
    (C)   Participants in computer conferences often apply the same degree of respect and support they receive from one another to interactions in their own actual communities.
    (D)   Participants in computer conferences often feel more comfortable interacting on the computer because they are free to interact without revealing their identities.
    (E)   The conventions used to facilitate communication in computer conferences are generally more successful than those used in actual communities.

GO ON TO THE NEXT PAGE.

In *Intellectual Culture in Elizabethan and Jacobean England*, J. W. Binns asserts that the drama of Shakespeare, the verse of Marlowe, and the prose of Sidney—all of whom wrote in English—do not alone
(5) represent the high culture of Renaissance (roughly sixteenth- and seventeenth-century) England. Latin, the language of ancient Rome, continued during this period to be the dominant form of expression for English intellectuals, and works of law, theology, and science
(10) written in Latin were, according to Binns, among the highest achievements of the Renaissance. However, because many academic specializations do not overlap, many texts central to an interpretation of early modern English culture have gone unexamined. Even the most
(15) learned students of Renaissance Latin generally confine themselves to humanistic and literary writings in Latin. According to Binns, these language specialists edit and analyze poems and orations, but leave works of theology and science, law and medicine—the very
(20) works that revolutionized Western thought—to "specialists" in those fields, historians of science, for example, who lack philological training. The intellectual historian can find ample guidance when reading the Latin poetry of Milton, but little or none
(25) when confronting the more alien and difficult terminology, syntax, and content of the scientist Newton.

Intellectual historians of Renaissance England, by contrast with Latin language specialists, have surveyed
(30) in great detail the historical, cosmological, and theological battles of the day, but too often they have done so on the basis of texts written in or translated into English. Binns argues that these scholars treat the English-language writings of Renaissance England as
(35) an autonomous and coherent whole, underestimating the influence on English writers of their counterparts on the European Continent. In so doing they ignore the fact that English intellectuals were educated in schools and universities where they spoke and wrote Latin, and
(40) inhabited as adults an intellectual world in which what happened abroad and was recorded in Latin was of great importance. Writers traditionally considered characteristically English and modern were steeped in Latin literature and in the esoteric concerns of late
(45) Renaissance humanism (the rediscovery and study of ancient Latin and Greek texts), and many Latin works by Continental humanists that were not translated at the time into any modern language became the bases of classic English works of literature and scholarship.
(50)   These limitations are understandable. No modern classicist is trained to deal with the range of problems posed by a difficult piece of late Renaissance science; few students of English intellectual history are trained to read the sort of Latin in which such works were
(55) written. Yet the result of each side's inability to cross boundaries has been that each presents a distorted reading of the intellectual culture of Renaissance England.

7. Which one of the following best states the main idea of the passage?

(A) Analyses of the scientific, theological, and legal writings of the Renaissance have proved to be more important to an understanding of the period than have studies of humanistic and literary works.

(B) The English works of such Renaissance writers as Shakespeare, Marlowe, and Sidney have been overemphasized at the expense of these writers' more intellectually challenging Latin works.

(C) Though traditionally recognized as the language of the educated classes of the Renaissance, Latin has until recently been studied primarily in connection with ancient Roman texts.

(D) Many Latin texts by English Renaissance writers, though analyzed in depth by literary critics and philologists, have been all but ignored by historians of science and theology.

(E) Many Latin texts by English Renaissance writers, though important to an analysis of the period, have been insufficiently understood for reasons related to academic specialization.

8. The passage contains support for which one of the following statements concerning those scholars who analyze works written in Latin during the Renaissance?

(A) These scholars tend to lack training both in language and in intellectual history, and thus base their interpretations of Renaissance culture on works translated into English.

(B) These scholars tend to lack the combination of training in both language and intellectual history that is necessary for a proper study of important and neglected Latin texts.

(C) Specialists in such literary forms as poems and orations too frequently lack training in the Latin language that was written and studied during the Renaissance.

(D) Language specialists have surveyed in too great detail important works of law and medicine, and thus have not provided a coherent interpretation of early modern English culture.

(E) Scholars who analyze important Latin works by such writers as Marlowe, Shakespeare, and Sidney too often lack the historical knowledge of Latin necessary for a proper interpretation of early modern English culture.

GO ON TO THE NEXT PAGE.

9. Which one of the following statements concerning the relationship between English and Continental writers of the Renaissance era can be inferred from the passage?

   (A) Continental writers wrote in Latin more frequently than did English writers, and thus rendered some of the most important Continental works inaccessible to English readers.

   (B) Continental writers, more intellectually advanced than their English counterparts, were on the whole responsible for familiarizing English audiences with Latin language and literature.

   (C) English and Continental writers communicated their intellectual concerns, which were for the most part different, by way of works written in Latin.

   (D) The intellectual ties between English and Continental writers were stronger than has been acknowledged by many scholars and were founded on a mutual knowledge of Latin.

   (E) The intellectual ties between English and Continental writers have been overemphasized in modern scholarship due to a lack of dialogue between language specialists and intellectual historians.

10. The author of the passage most likely cites Shakespeare, Marlowe, and Sidney in the first paragraph as examples of writers whose

   (A) nonfiction works are less well known than their imaginative works

   (B) works have unfairly been credited with revolutionizing Western thought

   (C) works have been treated as an autonomous and coherent whole

   (D) works have traditionally been seen as representing the high culture of Renaissance England

   (E) Latin writings have, according to Binns, been overlooked

11. Binns would be most likely to agree with which one of the following statements concerning the English language writings of Renaissance England traditionally studied by intellectual historians?

   (A) These writings have unfortunately been undervalued by Latin-language specialists because of their nonliterary subject matter.

   (B) These writings, according to Latin-language specialists, had very little influence on the intellectual upheavals associated with the Renaissance.

   (C) These writings, as analyzed by intellectual historians, have formed the basis of a superficially coherent reading of the intellectual culture that produced them.

   (D) These writings have been compared unfavorably by intellectual historians with Continental works of the same period.

   (E) These writings need to be studied separately, according to intellectual historians, from Latin-language writings of the same period.

12. The information in the passage suggests wh   ne of the following concerning late-Renaissance s   fic works written in Latin?

   (A) These works are easier for modern sch   o analyze than are theological works   e same era.

   (B) These works have seldom been translat   to English and thus remain inscrutable to   ern scholars, despite the availability of illu   ting commentaries.

   (C) These works are difficult for modern sc   to analyze both because of the concept develop and the language in which they written.

   (D) These works constituted the core of an E   university education during the Renaissa

   (E) These works were written mostly by Con   al writers and reached English intellectuals   in English translation.

13. The author of the passage mentions the poet Milt   d the scientist Newton primarily in order to

   (A) illustrate the range of difficulty in Renaissa Latin writing, from relatively straightforwa very difficult

   (B) illustrate the differing scholarly attitudes tov Renaissance writers who wrote in Latin an those who wrote in English

   (C) illustrate the fact that the concerns of Englis writers of the Renaissance differed from the concerns of their Continental counterparts

   (D) contrast a writer of the Renaissance whose m has long been recognized with one whose literary worth has only recently begun to be appreciated

   (E) contrast a writer whose Latin writings have be the subject of illuminating scholarship with o whose Latin writings have been neglected by philologists

14. The author of the passage is primarily concerned with presenting which one of the following?

   (A) an enumeration of new approaches
   (B) contrasting views of disparate theories
   (C) a summary of intellectual disputes
   (D) a discussion of a significant deficiency
   (E) a correction of an author's misconceptions

GO ON TO THE NEXT PAGE.

Discussions of how hormones influence behavior have generally been limited to the effects of gonadal hormones on reproductive behavior and have emphasized the parsimonious arrangement whereby the
(5) same hormones involved in the biology of reproduction also influence sexual behavior. It has now become clear, however, that other hormones, in addition to their recognized influence on biological functions, can affect behavior. Specifically, peptide and steroid hormones
(10) involved in maintaining the physiological balance, or homeostasis, of body fluids also appear to play an important role in the control of water and salt consumption. The phenomenon of homeostasis in animals depends on various mechanisms that promote
(15) stability within the organism despite an inconstant external environment; the homeostasis of body fluids, whereby the osmolality (the concentration of solutes) of blood plasma is closely regulated, is achieved primarily through alterations in the intake and
(20) excretion of water and sodium, the two principal components of the fluid matrix that surrounds body cells. Appropriate compensatory responses are initiated when deviations from normal are quite small, thereby maintaining plasma osmolality within relatively narrow
(25) ranges.

In the osmoregulation of body fluids, the movement of water across cell membranes permits minor fluctuations in the concentration of solutes in extracellular fluid to be buffered by corresponding
(30) changes in the relatively larger volume of cellular water. Nevertheless, the concentration of solutes in extracellular fluid may at times become elevated or reduced by more than the allowed tolerances of one or two percent. It is then that complementary
(35) physiological and behavioral responses come into play to restore plasma osmolality to normal. Thus, for example, a decrease in plasma osmolality, such as that which occurs after the consumption of water in excess of need, leads to the excretion of surplus body water in
(40) the urine by inhibiting secretion from the pituitary gland of vasopressin, a peptide hormone that promotes water conservation in the kidneys. As might be expected, thirst also is inhibited then, to prevent further dilution of body fluids. Conversely, an increase in
(45) plasma osmolality, such as that which occurs after one eats salty foods or after body water evaporates without being replaced, stimulates the release of vasopressin, increasing the conservation of water and the excretion of solutes in urine. This process is accompanied by
(50) increased thirst, with the result of making plasma osmolality more dilute through the consumption of water. The threshold for thirst appears to be slightly higher than for vasopressin secretion, so that thirst is stimulated only after vasopressin has been released in
(55) amounts sufficient to produce maximal water retention by the kidneys—that is, only after osmotic dehydration exceeds the capacity of the animal to deal with it physiologically.

15. Which one of the following best states the main idea of the passage?

(A) Both the solute concentration and the volume of an animal's blood plasma must be kept within relatively narrow ranges.

(B) Behavioral responses to changes in an animal's blood plasma can compensate for physiological malfunction, allowing the body to avoid dehydration.

(C) The effect of hormones on animal behavior and physiology has only recently been discovered.

(D) Behavioral and physiological responses to major changes in osmolality of an animal's blood plasma are hormonally influenced and complement one another.

(E) The mechanisms regulating reproduction are similar to those that regulate thirst and sodium appetite.

16. The author of the passage cites the relationship between gonadal hormones and reproductive behavior in order to

(A) review briefly the history of research into the relationships between gonadal and peptide hormones that has led to the present discussion

(B) decry the fact that previous research has concentrated on the relatively minor issue of the relationships between hormones and behavior

(C) establish the emphasis of earlier research into the connections between hormones and behavior before elaborating on the results described in the passage

(D) introduce a commonly held misconception about the relationships between hormones and behavior before refuting it with the results described in the passage

(E) summarize the main findings of recent research described in the passage before detailing the various procedures that led to those findings

GO ON TO THE NEXT PAGE.

17. It can be inferred from the passage that which one of the following is true of vasopressin?

   (A) The amount secreted depends on the level of steroid hormones in the blood.
   (B) The amount secreted is important for maintaining homeostasis in cases of both increased and decreased osmolality.
   (C) It works in conjunction with steroid hormones in increasing plasma volume.
   (D) It works in conjunction with steroid hormones in regulating sodium appetite.
   (E) It is secreted after an animal becomes thirsty, as a mechanism for diluting plasma osmolality.

18. The primary function of the passage as a whole is to

   (A) present new information
   (B) question standard assumptions
   (C) reinterpret earlier findings
   (D) advocate a novel theory
   (E) outline a new approach

19. According to the passage, all of the following typically occur in the homeostasis of blood-plasma osmolality EXCEPT:

   (A) Hunger is diminished.
   (B) Thirst is initiated.
   (C) Vasopressin is secreted.
   (D) Water is excreted.
   (E) Sodium is consumed.

20. According to the passage, the withholding of vasopressin fulfills which one of the following functions in the restoration of plasma osmolality to normal levels?

   (A) It increases thirst and stimulates sodium appetite.
   (B) It helps prevent further dilution of body fluids.
   (C) It increases the conservation of water in the kidneys.
   (D) It causes minor changes in plasma volume.
   (E) It helps stimulate the secretion of steroid hormones.

GO ON TO THE NEXT PAGE.

With the elimination of the apartheid system, South
Africa now confronts the transition to a rights-based
legal system in a constitutional democracy. Among
lawyers and judges, exhilaration over the legal tools
(5) soon to be available is tempered by uncertainty about
how to use them. The changes in the legal system are
significant, not just for human rights lawyers, but for
all lawyers—as they will have to learn a less rule-
bound and more interpretative way of looking at the
(10) law. That is to say, in the past, the parliament was the
supreme maker and arbiter of laws; when judges made
rulings with which the parliament disagreed, the
parliament simply passed new laws to counteract their
rulings. Under the new system, however, a
(15) constitutional court will hear arguments on all
constitutional matters, including questions of whether
the laws passed by the parliament are valid in light of
the individual liberties set out in the constitution's bill
of rights. This shift will lead to extraordinary changes,
(20) for South Africa has never before had a legal system
based on individual rights—one in which citizens can
challenge any law or administrative decision on the
basis of their constitutional rights.
      South African lawyers are concerned about the
(25) difficulty of fostering a rights-based culture in a
multiracial society containing a wide range of political
and personal beliefs simply by including a bill of rights
in the constitution and establishing the means for its
defense. Because the bill of rights has been drawn in
(30) very general terms, the lack of precedents will make
the task of determining its precise meaning a
bewildering one. With this in mind, the new
constitution acknowledges the need to look to other
countries for guidance. But some scholars warn that
(35) judges, in their rush to fill the constitutional void, may
misuse foreign law—they may blindly follow the
interpretations given bills of rights in other countries,
not taking into account the circumstances in those
countries that led to certain decisions. Nonetheless,
(40) these scholars are hopeful that, with patience and
judicious decisions, South Africa can use international
experience in developing a body of precedent that will
address the particular needs of its citizens.
      South Africa must also contend with the image of
(45) the law held by many of its citizens. Because the law in
South Africa has long been a tool of racial oppression,
many of its citizens have come to view obeying the law
as implicitly sanctioning an illegitimate, brutal
government. Among these South Africans the political
(50) climate has thus been one of opposition, and many see
it as their duty to cheat the government as much as
possible, whether by not paying taxes or by disobeying
parking laws. If a rights-based culture is to succeed, the
government will need to show its citizens that the legal
(55) system is no longer a tool of oppression but instead a
way to bring about change and help further the cause of
justice.

21. Which one of the following most completely and
     accurately states the main point of the passage?

     (A) Following the elimination of the apartheid system
          in South Africa, lawyers, judges, and citizens
          will need to abandon their posture of opposition
          to law and design a new and fairer legal system.
     (B) If the new legal system in South Africa is to
          succeed, lawyers, judges, and citizens must
          learn to challenge parliamentary decisions based
          on their individual rights as set out in the new
          constitution.
     (C) Whereas in the past the parliament was both the
          initiator and arbiter of laws in South Africa,
          under the new constitution these powers will be
          assumed by a constitutional court.
     (D) Despite the lack of relevant legal precedents and
          the public's antagonistic relation to the law,
          South Africa is moving from a legal system
          where the parliament is the final authority to one
          where the rights of citizens are protected by a
          constitution.
     (E) While South Africa's judges will have to
          look initially to other countries to provide
          interpretations for its new bill of rights,
          eventually it must develop a body of precedent
          sensitive to the needs of its own citizens.

22. Which one of the following most accurately describes
     the author's primary purpose in lines 10–19?

     (A) to describe the role of the parliament under South
          Africa's new constitution
     (B) to argue for returning final legal authority to the
          parliament
     (C) to contrast the character of legal practice
          under the apartheid system with that to be
          implemented under the new constitution
     (D) to criticize the creation of a court with final
          authority on constitutional matters
     (E) to explain why a bill of rights was included in the
          new constitution

23. The passage suggests that the author's attitude toward
     the possibility of success for a rights-based legal system
     in South Africa is most likely one of

     (A) deep skepticism
     (B) open pessimism
     (C) total indifference
     (D) guarded optimism
     (E) complete confidence

GO ON TO THE NEXT PAGE.

24. According to the passage, under the apartheid system the rulings of judges were sometimes counteracted by

    (A) decisions rendered in constitutional court
    (B) challenges from concerned citizens
    (C) new laws passed in the parliament
    (D) provisions in the constitution's bill of rights
    (E) other judges with a more rule-bound approach to the law

25. Which one of the following most accurately describes the organization of the last paragraph of the passage?

    (A) A solution to a problem is identified, several methods of implementing the solution are discussed, and one of the methods is argued for.
    (B) The background to a problem is presented, past methods of solving the problem are criticized, and a new solution is proposed.
    (C) An analysis of a problem is presented, possible solutions to the problem are given, and one of the possible solutions is argued for.
    (D) Reasons are given why a problem has existed, the current state of affairs is described, and the problem is shown to exist no longer.
    (E) A problem is identified, specific manifestations of the problem are given, and an essential element in its solution is presented.

26. Based on the passage, the scholars mentioned in the second paragraph would be most likely to agree with which one of the following statements?

    (A) Reliance of judges on the interpretations given bills of rights in other countries must be tempered by the recognition that such interpretations may be based on circumstances not necessarily applicable to South Africa.
    (B) Basing interpretations of the South African bill of rights on interpretations given bills of rights in other countries will reinforce the climate of mistrust for authority in South Africa.
    (C) The lack of precedents in South African law for interpreting a bill of rights will likely make it impossible to interpret correctly the bill of rights in the South African constitution.
    (D) Reliance by judges on the interpretations given bills of rights in other countries offers an unacceptable means of attempting to interpret the South African constitution in a way that will meet the particular needs of South African citizens.
    (E) Because bills of rights in other countries are written in much less general terms than the South African bill of rights, interpretations of them are unlikely to prove helpful in interpreting the South African bill of rights.

S T O P

IF YOU FINISH BEFORE TIME IS CALLED, YOU MAY CHECK YOUR WORK ON THIS SECTION ONLY.
DO NOT WORK ON ANY OTHER SECTION IN THE TEST.

Answer Key

1. D
2. C
3. E
4. E
5. C
6. B
7. E
8. B
9. D
10. D
11. C
12. C
13. E
14. D
15. D
16. C
17. B
18. A
19. A
20. B
21. D
22. C
23. D
24. C
25. E
26. A

KAPLAN

Reading Comprehension 8

PrepTest 34, Section I
June 2001

SECTION I

Time—35 minutes

26 Questions

Directions: Each passage in this section is followed by a group of questions to be answered on the basis of what is <u>stated</u> or <u>implied</u> in the passage. For some of the questions, more than one of the choices could conceivably answer the question. However, you are to choose the <u>best</u> answer; that is, the response that most accurately and completely answers the question, and blacken the corresponding space on your answer sheet.

Most authoritarian rulers who undertake democratic reforms do so not out of any intrinsic commitment or conversion to democratic ideals, but rather because they foresee or recognize that certain
(5) changes and mobilizations in civil society make it impossible for them to hold on indefinitely to absolute power.

Three major types of changes can contribute to a society's no longer condoning the continuation of
(10) authoritarian rule. First, the values and norms in the society alter over time, reducing citizens' tolerance for repression and concentration of power and thus stimulating their demands for freedom. In some Latin American countries during the 1970s and 1980s, for
(15) example, this change in values came about partly as a result of the experience of repression, which brought in its wake a resurgence of democratic values. As people come to place more value on political freedom and civil liberties they also become more inclined to speak
(20) out, protest, and organize for democracy, frequently beginning with the denunciation of human rights abuses.

In addition to changing norms and values, the alignment of economic interests in a society can shift.
(25) As one scholar notes, an important turning point in the transition to democracy comes when privileged people in society—landowners, industrialists, merchants, bankers—who had been part of a regime's support base come to the conclusion that the authoritarian regime is
(30) dispensable and that its continuation might damage their long-term interests. Such a large-scale shift in the economic interests of these elites was crucial in bringing about the transition to democracy in the Philippines and has also begun occurring incrementally
(35) in other authoritarian nations.

A third change derives from the expanding resources, autonomy, and self-confidence of various segments of society and of newly formed organizations both formal and informal. Students march in the streets
(40) demanding change; workers paralyze key industries; lawyers refuse to cooperate any longer in legal charades; alternative sources of information pierce and then shatter the veil of secrecy and disinformation; informal networks of production and exchange emerge
(45) that circumvent the state's resources and control. This profound development can radically alter the balance of power in a country, as an authoritarian regime that could once easily dominate and control its citizens is placed on the defensive.

(50)   Authoritarian rule tends in the long run to generate all three types of changes. Ironically, all three types can be accelerated by the authoritarian regime's initial success at producing economic growth and maintaining social order—success that, by creating a period of
(55) stability, gives citizens the opportunity to reflect on the circumstances in which they live. The more astute or calculating of authoritarian rulers will recognize this and realize that their only hope of retaining some power in the future is to match these democratic social
(60) changes with democratic political changes.

1. Which one of the following most accurately expresses the main point of the passage?

(A) Authoritarian rulers tend to undertake democratic reforms only after it becomes clear that the nation's economic and social power bases will slow economic growth and disrupt social order until such reforms are instituted.

(B) Authoritarian regimes tend to ensure their own destruction by allowing opposition groups to build support among the wealthy whose economic interests are easily led away from support for the regime.

(C) Authoritarian policies tend in the long run to alienate the economic power base in a nation once it becomes clear that the regime's initial success at generating economic growth and stability will be short lived.

(D) Authoritarian principles tend in the long run to be untenable because they demand from the nation a degree of economic and social stability that is impossible to maintain in the absence of democratic institutions.

(E) Authoritarian rulers who institute democratic reforms are compelled to do so because authoritarian rule tends to bring about various changes in society that eventually necessitate corresponding political changes.

GO ON TO THE NEXT PAGE.

2. The author's attitude toward authoritarian regimes is most accurately described as which one of the following?

   (A) uncertainty whether the changes in authoritarian regimes represent genuine progress or merely superficial changes

   (B) puzzlement about the motives of authoritarian rulers given their tendency to bring about their own demise

   (C) confidence that most authoritarian regimes will eventually be replaced by a more democratic form of government

   (D) insistence that authoritarian rule constitutes an intrinsically unjust form of government

   (E) concern that authoritarian rulers will discover ways to retain power without instituting democratic reforms

3. Which one of the following titles most completely summarizes the content of the passage?

   (A) "Avenues for Change: The Case for Dissent in Authoritarian Regimes"

   (B) "Human Rights Abuses under Authoritarian Regimes: A Case Study"

   (C) "Democratic Coalitions under Authoritarian Regimes: Strategies and Solutions"

   (D) "Why Authoritarian Regimes Compromise: An Examination of Societal Forces"

   (E) "Growing Pains: Economic Instability in Countries on the Brink of Democracy"

4. Which one of the following most accurately describes the organization of the passage?

   (A) A political phenomenon is linked to a general set of causes; this set is divided into categories and the relative importance of each category is assessed; the possibility of alternate causes is considered and rejected.

   (B) A political phenomenon is linked to a general set of causes; this set is divided into categories and an explication of each category is presented; the causal relationship is elaborated upon and reaffirmed.

   (C) A political phenomenon is identified; the possible causes of the phenomenon are described and placed into categories; one possible cause is preferred over the others and reasons are given for the preference.

   (D) A political phenomenon is identified; similarities between this phenomenon and three similar phenomena are presented; the similarities among the phenomena are restated in general terms and argued for.

   (E) A political phenomenon is identified; differences between this phenomenon and three similar phenomena are presented; the differences among the phenomena are restated in general terms and argued for.

5. It can most reasonably be inferred from the passage

   (A) many authoritarian rulers would eventually institute democratic reform even if not pressu to do so

   (B) citizen dissatisfaction in authoritarian regimes highest when authoritarian rule is first imposed

   (C) popular support for authoritarian regimes is lowest when economic conditions are weak

   (D) absolute power in an authoritarian society cannot be maintained indefinitely if the society does no condone the regime

   (E) citizens view human rights abuses as the only objectionable aspect of authoritarian regimes

6. Given the information in the passage, authoritarian rulers who institute democratic reforms decide to do so on the basis of which one of the following principles?

   (A) Rulers should act in ways that allow occasional curbs on their power if the health of the nation requires it.

   (B) Rulers should act in ways that offer the greatest amount of personal freedoms to citizens.

   (C) Rulers should act in ways that speed the transition from authoritarian rule to democracy.

   (D) Rulers should act in ways that ensure the long-term health of the nation's economy.

   (E) Rulers should act in ways that maximize their long-term political power.

GO ON TO THE NEXT PAGE.

The term "blues" is conventionally used to refer to a state of sadness or melancholy, but to conclude from this that the musical genre of the same name is merely an expression of unrelieved sorrow is to miss its deeper
(5)   meaning. Despite its frequent focus on such themes as suffering and self-pity, and despite the censure that it has sometimes received from church communities, the blues, understood more fully, actually has much in common with the traditional religious music known as
(10) spirituals. Each genre, in its own way, aims to bring about what could be called a spiritual transformation: spirituals produce a religious experience and the blues elicits an analogous response. In fact the blues has even been characterized as a form of "secular spiritual." The
(15) implication of this apparently contradictory terminology is clear: the blues shares an essential aspect of spirituals. Indeed, the blues and spirituals may well arise from a common reservoir of experience, tapping into an aesthetic that underlies many aspects of
(20) African American culture.

Critics have noted that African American folk tradition, in its earliest manifestations, does not sharply differentiate reality into sacred and secular strains or into irreconcilable dichotomies between good and evil,
(25) misery and joy. This is consistent with the apparently dual aspect of the blues and spirituals. Spirituals, like the blues, often express longing or sorrow, but these plaintive tones are indicative of neither genre's full scope: both aim at transforming their participants'
(30) spirits to elation and exaltation. In this regard, both musical forms may be linked to traditional African American culture in North America and to its ancestral cultures in West Africa, in whose traditional religions worshippers play an active role in invoking the
(35) divine—in creating the psychological conditions that are conducive to religious experience. These conditions are often referred to as "ecstasy," which is to be understood here with its etymological connotation of standing out from oneself, or rather from one's
(40) background psychological state and from one's centered concept of self.

Working in this tradition, blues songs serve to transcend negative experiences by invoking the negative so that it can be transformed through the
(45) virtuosity and ecstatic mastery of the performer. This process produces a double-edged irony that is often evident in blues lyrics themselves; consider, for example the lines "If the blues was money, I'd be a millionaire," in which the singer reconfigures the
(50) experience of sorrow into a paradoxical asset through a kind of boasting bravado. One critic has observed that the impulse behind the blues is the desire to keep painful experiences alive in the performer and audience not just for their own sake, but also in order to coax
(55) from these experiences a lyricism that is both tragic and comic.

7.   Based on the passage, with which one of the following statements would the author be most likely to agree?

(A)   The emphasis on spiritual transcendence takes the blues out of the realm of folk art and into the realm of organized religion.
(B)   Little of the transcendent aspect of the blues is retained in its more modern, electronically amplified, urban forms.
(C)   Other forms of African American folk art rely heavily on uses of irony similar to those observed in the blues.
(D)   The distinctive musical structure of blues songs is the primary means of producing tensions between sadness and transcendence.
(E)   The blues may be of psychological benefit to its listeners.

8.   Each of the following is indicated by the passage as a shared aspect of the blues and spirituals EXCEPT:

(A)   expressions of sorrow or longing
(B)   a striving to bring about a kind of spiritual transformation
(C)   a possible link to ancestral West African cultures
(D)   the goal of producing exalted emotions
(E)   the use of traditional religious terminology in their lyrics

GO ON TO THE NEXT PAGE.

9. Which one of the following most accurately expresses what the author intends "a common reservoir of experience" (line 18) to refer to?

   (A) a set of experiences that members of differing cultures frequently undergo and that similarly affects the music of those cultures

   (B) set of ordinary experiences that underlies the development of all musical forms

   (C) a set of experiences that contributed to the development of both the blues and spirituals

   (D) a set of musically relevant experiences that serves to differentiate reality into irreconcilable dichotomies

   (E) a set of experiences arising from the folk music of a community and belonging to the community at large

10. The primary purpose of the second paragraph is to

   (A) uncover the shared origin of both the blues and spirituals

   (B) examine the process by which ecstasy is produced

   (C) identify the musical precursors of the blues

   (D) explore the sacred and secular strains of the blues

   (E) trace the early development of African American folk tradition

11. The reference to "standing out from oneself" in line 39 primarily serves to

   (A) distinguish the standard from the nonstandard, and thus incorrect, use of a word

   (B) specify a particular sense of a word that the author intends the word to convey

   (C) point out a word that incorrectly characterizes experiences arising from blues performance

   (D) identify a way in which religious participation differs from blues performance

   (E) indicate the intensity that a good blues artist brings to a performance

12. Which one of the following is most closely analogous to the author's account of the connections among the blues, spirituals, and certain West African religious practices?

   (A) Two species of cacti, which are largely dissimilar, have very similar flowers; this has been proven to be due to the one's evolution from a third species, whose flowers are nonetheless quite different from theirs.

   (B) Two species of ferns, which are closely similar in most respects, have a subtly different arrangement of stem structures; nevertheless, they may well be related to a third, older species, which has yet a different arrangement of stem structures.

   (C) Two types of trees, which botanists have long believed to be unrelated, should be reclassified in light of the essential similarities of their flower structures and their recently discovered relationship to another species, from which they both evolved.

   (D) Two species of grass, which may have some subtle similarities, are both very similar to a third species, and thus it can be inferred that the third species evolved from one of the two species.

   (E) Two species of shrubs, which seem superficially unalike, have a significantly similar leaf structure; this may be due to their relation to a third, older species, which is similar to both of them.

GO ON TO THE NEXT PAGE.

In the eighteenth century the French naturalist Jean Baptiste de Lamarck believed that an animal's use or disuse of an organ affected that organ's development in the animal's offspring. Lamarck claimed that the
(5) giraffe's long neck, for example, resulted from its ancestors stretching to reach distant leaves. But because biologists could find no genetic mechanism to make the transmission of environmentally induced adaptations seem plausible, they have long held that
(10) inheritance of acquired characteristics never occurs. Yet new research has uncovered numerous examples of the phenomenon.

In bacteria, for instance, enzymes synthesize and break down rigid cell walls as necessary to
(15) accommodate the bacteria's growth. But if an experimenter completely removes the cell wall from a bacterium, the process of wall synthesis and breakdown is disrupted, and the bacterium continues to grow—and multiply indefinitely—without walls. This
(20) inherited absence of cell walls in bacteria results from changes in the interactions among genes, without any attendant changes in the genes themselves.

A fundamentally different kind of environmentally induced heritable characteristic occurs when specific
(25) genes are added to or eliminated from an organism. For example, a certain virus introduces a gene into fruit flies that causes the flies to be vulnerable to carbon dioxide poisoning, and fruit flies infected with the virus will pass the gene to their offspring. But if infected
(30) flies are kept warm while they are producing eggs, the virus is eliminated from the eggs and the offspring are resistant to carbon dioxide. Similarly, if an *Escherichia coli* bacterium carrying a certain plasmid—a small ring of genetic material—comes into contact with an *E. coli*
(35) bacterium lacking the plasmid, the plasmid will enter the second bacterium and become part of its genetic makeup, which it then passes to its offspring. The case of the *E. coli* is especially noteworthy for its suggestion that inheritance of acquired characteristics may have
(40) helped to speed up evolution: for example, many complex cells may have first acquired the ability to carry out photosynthesis by coming into contact with a bacterium possessing the gene for that trait, an ability that normally would have taken eons to develop
(45) through random mutation and natural selection.

The new evidence suggests that genes can be divided into two groups. Most are inherited "vertically," from ancestors. Some however, seem to have been acquired "horizontally," from viruses,
(50) plasmids, bacteria, or other environmental agents. The evidence even appears to show that genes can be transmitted horizontally between organisms that are considered to be unrelated: from bacteria to plants, for example, or from bacteria to yeast. Some horizontal
(55) transmission may well be the mechanism for inheritance of acquired characteristics that has long eluded biologists, and that may eventually prove Lamarck's hypothesis to be correct.

13. The passage suggests that many biologists no longer believe which one of the following?

(A) An organ's use or disuse can affect that organ's development.
(B) Some but not all genes are inherited horizontally.
(C) All genes are inherited horizontally.
(D) Some but not all genes are inherited vertically.
(E) All genes are inherited vertically.

14. According to the passage, which one of the following is an acquired characteristic transmitted by altering the interaction among genes rather than be adding or eliminating a gene?

(A) invulnerability to carbon dioxide poisoning
(B) susceptibility to carbon dioxide poisoning
(C) lack of cell walls
(D) presence of cell walls
(E) possession of certain plasmids

15. The primary purpose of the last paragraph it to

(A) suggest a modification to Lamarck's hypothesis
(B) demonstrate the correctness of Lamarck's hypothesis
(C) illustrate the significance of Lamarck's hypothesis
(D) criticize scientists' rejection of Lamarck's hypothesis
(E) explain how recent discoveries may support Lamarck's hypothesis

GO ON TO THE NEXT PAGE.

16. Which one of the following, if true, offers the most support for Lamarck's hypothesis?

    (A) Deer have antlers because antlers make deer more likely to survive and reproduce.
    (B) Anteaters developed long snouts because the anteater stretches its snout in order to reach ants hidden well below ground.
    (C) Potatoes produced from synthetic genes tend to be more resistant to disease than are potatoes produced from natural genes.
    (D) Lions raised in captivity tend to have a weaker sense of direction than do lions raised in the wild.
    (E) Pups born to wild dogs tend to be more aggressive than are pups born to dogs bred for hunting.

17. According to the passage, the inheritance of acquired characteristics is particularly significant because this phenomenon

    (A) may affect the speed at which photosynthesis occurs
    (B) may help to explain the process of natural selection
    (C) may occur without affecting the composition of genes
    (D) may influence the rate at which evolution progresses
    (E) may be changed or stopped under experimental conditions

18. Which one of the following can be inferred from the passage about the absence of cell walls in some bacteria?

    (A) It can be reversed by introducing the appropriate gene.
    (B) It can be brought about by a virally introduced gene.
    (C) It can be caused by the loss of a cell wall in a single bacterium.
    (D) It can be halted, but not reversed, by restoring cell walls to a group of bacteria.
    (E) It can be transmitted horizontally to other bacteria.

GO ON TO THE NEXT PAGE.

When women are persecuted on account of their gender, they are likely to be eligible for asylum. Persecution is the linchpin of the definition of a refugee set out in the *United Nations Convention Relating to*
(5) *the Status of Refugees.* In this document, a refugee is defined as any person facing persecution "for reasons of race, religion, nationality, membership of a particular social group, or political opinion." While persecution on the basis of gender is not explicitly
(10) listed, this omission does not preclude victims of gender-based persecution from qualifying as refugees, nor does it reflect an intention that such persons be excluded from international protection. Rather, women persecuted on account of gender are eligible for asylum
(15) under the category of "social group." The history of the inclusion of the social-group category in the definition of a refugee indicates that this category was intended to cover groups, such as women facing gender-based persecution, who are otherwise not covered by the
(20) definition's specific categories.

The original definition of refugee, which came from the constitution of the International Refugee Organization, did not include social group. However, the above-mentioned *United Nations Convention* added
(25) the category in order to provide a "safety net" for asylum-seekers who should qualify for refugee status but who fail to fall neatly into one of the enumerated categories. The drafters of the *Convention* intentionally left the precise boundaries of the social-group category
(30) undefined to ensure that the category would retain the flexibility necessary to address unanticipated situations.

A broad interpretation of social group is supported by the *Handbook on Procedures and Criteria for*
(35) *Determining Refugee Status* (1979) published by the office of the United Nations High Commissioner for Refugees (UNHCR). The *Handbook* describes a social group as persons of similar background, habits, or social status. This expansive interpretation of the
(40) category is resonant with the intentions of the *Convention* drafters—a malleable category created for future asylum determinations. Since many women fleeing gender-based persecution share a common background and social status, they should fall within
(45) the *Handbook's* definition of a social group. Furthermore, a 1985 UNHCR Executive Committee report counseled member states to use the social-group category to classify women asylum-seekers "who face harsh or inhuman treatment due to their having
(50) transgressed the social mores of the society in which they live."

Such a pronouncement is particularly significant. A position taken by an organization such as the UNHCR is likely to exert a strong influence on the international
(55) community. In particular, the UNHCR's position is likely to have an impact on the interpretation of national asylum laws, since the terms and definitions used in many national laws have been developed under the international consensus that UNHCR represents.

19. According to the passage, which one of the following is true about both the *United Nations Convention* and the UNHCR *Handbook*?

(A) Both documents are likely to exert a strong influence on improving the status of women in countries that are members of the United Nations.

(B) Both documents explicitly support granting refugee status to women fleeing gender-based persecution.

(C) Both documents recommend using the social-group category to classify women refugees seeking asylum from persecution.

(D) Both documents suggest that the social-group category can be applied to a wide variety of asylum-seekers.

(E) Both documents describe a social group as persons who share a similar background and hold a similar status in society.

20. The passage suggests that which one of the following is true about the drafters of the *United Nations Convention*?

(A) They wanted to ensure that the United Nations would be consulted as new reasons for seeking refugee status arose.

(B) They followed the precedent set by the International Refugee Organization concerning the status of refugees seeking asylum from gender-based persecution.

(C) They recognized that it would be difficult to list every possible reason why a person might seek refuge from persecution in the *Convention's* definition of a refugee.

(D) They did not consider persecution on the basis of gender to be as valid a reason for seeking asylum as persecution on the basis of race, nationality, or religion.

(E) They did not list gender as a category in the *Convention's* definition of a refugee because gender-based persecution was not a significant problem at the time the *Convention* was drafted.

GO ON TO THE NEXT PAGE.

21. Which one of the following asylum-seekers would be most likely to qualify for refugee status under the social-group category as it is described in the passage?

    (A) a woman who is unable to earn enough money to support her family because she comes from a poor country
    (B) a woman who has limited opportunities to improve her socioeconomic status because of racial discrimination in her country
    (C) a woman who is unable to obtain an education because she is a member of a particular religious group
    (D) a woman who faces persecution because she rejects the accepted norm in her country concerning arranged marriages
    (E) a woman who faces persecution because she opposes her government's harsh treatment of political prisoners

22. The author describes the definition of social group in the UNHCR Handbook as

    (A) specific but flexible
    (B) obscure but substantive
    (C) exhaustive and impartial
    (D) general and adaptable
    (E) comprehensive and exemplary

23. The author of the passage would most likely agree with which one of the following statements about the definition of a refugee in the constitution of the International Refugee Organization?

    (A) It failed to include some asylum-seekers who should have been considered eligible for refugee status.
    (B) It provided a strong basis to support the claim that women seeking asylum from gender-based persecution should be eligible for asylum.
    (C) It reflected an awareness that some groups of refugees seeking asylum do not easily fall into specific categories.
    (D) It established that a person's social-group membership may be as significant a cause of persecution as a person's race, religion, or nationality.
    (E) It prevented individual nations from refusing asylum to persons who were clearly eligible for such status on the basis of the definition.

24. The author describes persecution as the "linchpin of the definition of a refugee" (line 3) in order to indicate that

    (A) international acceptance of the definition was dependent on reaching consensus about what constituted persecution
    (B) international concern about the number of people fleeing persecution was the primary force behind the creation of the definition
    (C) persecution is a controversial term and it was difficult to reach international agreement about its exact meaning
    (D) persecution is the primary reason why people are forced to leave their home countries and seek asylum elsewhere
    (E) persecution is the central factor in determining whether a person is eligible for refugee status

25. The passage suggests that which one of the following is most likely to be true of the relationship between UNHCR documents concerning refugees and many nations' asylum laws?

    (A) The terms and definitions in the United Nations documents are frequently interpreted more narrowly than are similar terms and definitions in many national asylum laws.
    (B) Many of the specific terms and definitions in the United Nations documents represent a compilation of terms and definitions that were first used in national asylum laws.
    (C) A new interpretation of a term or definition in one of the United Nations documents is likely to influence the interpretation of a similar term or definition in a national asylum law.
    (D) A change in the wording of a specific definition in one of the United Nations documents must also be reflected in any similar terms or definitions contained in national asylum laws.
    (E) The terms and definitions used in many national asylum laws are in direct opposition to the terms and definitions used in the United Nations documents.

26. The primary purpose of the passage is to

    (A) trace the development of the definition of an important term
    (B) interpret the historical circumstances leading to the development of two documents
    (C) resolve two apparently contradictory interpretations of a legal document
    (D) suggest an alternative solution to a much-disputed problem
    (E) argue against the current definition of a specific term

S T O P

IF YOU FINISH BEFORE TIME IS CALLED, YOU MAY CHECK YOUR WORK ON THIS SECTION ONLY.
DO NOT WORK ON ANY OTHER SECTION IN THE TEST.

Answer Key

1. E
2. C
3. D
4. B
5. D
6. E
7. E
8. E
9. C
10. A
11. B
12. E
13. E
14. C
15. E
16. B
17. D
18. C
19. D
20. C
21. D
22. D
23. A
24. E
25. C
26. A

Reading Comprehension 9

PrepTest 30, Section III
December 1999

SECTION III
Time—35 minutes
27 Questions

<u>Directions:</u> Each passage in this section is followed by a group of questions to be answered on the basis of what is <u>stated</u> or <u>implied</u> in the passage. For some of the questions, more than one of the choices could conceivably answer the question. However, you are to choose the <u>best</u> answer; that is, the response that most accurately and completely answers the question, and blacken the corresponding space on your answer sheet.

The okapi, a forest mammal of central Africa, has presented zoologists with a number of difficult questions since they first learned of its existence in 1900. The first was how to classify it. Because it was
(5) horselike in dimension, and bore patches of striped hide similar to a zebra's (a relative of the horse), zoologists first classified it as a member of the horse family. But further studies showed that, despite okapis' coloration and short necks, their closest relatives were
(10) giraffes. The okapi's rightful place within the giraffe family is confirmed by its skin-covered horns (in males), two-lobed canine teeth, and long prehensile tongue.
    The next question was the size of the okapi
(15) population. Because okapis were infrequently captured by hunters, some zoologists believed that they were rare; however, others theorized that their habits simply kept them out of sight. It was not until 1985, when zoologists started tracking okapis by affixing collars
(20) equipped with radio transmitters to briefly captured specimens, that reliable information about okapi numbers and habits began to be collected. It turns out that while okapis are not as rare as some zoologists suspected, their population is concentrated in an
(25) extremely limited chain of forestland in northeastern central Africa, surrounded by savanna.
    One reason for their seeming scarcity is that their coloration allows okapis to camouflage themselves even at close range. Another is that okapis do not travel
(30) in groups or with other large forest mammals, and neither frequent open riverbanks nor forage at the borders of clearings, choosing instead to keep to the forest interior. This is because okapis, unlike any other animal in the central African forest, subsist entirely on
(35) leaves: more than one hundred species of plants have been identified as part of their diet, and about twenty of these are preferred. Okapis never eat one plant to the exclusion of others; even where preferred foliage is abundant, okapis will leave much of it uneaten,
(40) choosing to move on and sample other leaves. Because of this, and because of the distribution of their food, okapis engage in individual rather than congregated foraging.
    But other questions about okapi behavior arise.
(45) Why for example, do they prefer to remain within forested areas when many of their favorite plants are found in the open border between forest and savanna? One possibility is that this is a defense against predators; another is that the okapi was pushed into the
(50) forest by competition with other large, hoofed animals, such as the bushbuck and bongo, that specialize on the

forest edges and graze them more efficiently. Another question is why okapis are absent from other nearby forest regions that would seem hospitable to them.
(55) Zoologists theorize that okapis are relicts of an era when forestland was scarce and that they continue to respect those borders even though available forestland has long since expanded.

1. Which one of the following most completely and accurately expresses the main idea of the passage?

(A) Information gathered by means of radio-tracking collars has finally provided answers to the questions about okapis that zoologists have been attempting to answer since they first learned of the mammal's existence.

(B) Because of their physical characteristics and their infrequent capture by hunters, okapis presented zoologists with many difficult questions at the start of the twentieth century.

(C) Research concerning okapis has answered some of the questions that have puzzled zoologists since their discovery, but has also raised other questions regarding their geographic concentration and feeding habits.

(D) A new way of tracking okapis using radio-tracking collars reveals that their apparent scarcity is actually a result of their coloration, their feeding habits, and their geographic concentration.

(E) Despite new research involving radio tracking, the questions that have puzzled zoologists about okapis since their discovery at the start of the twentieth century remain mostly unanswered.

GO ON TO THE NEXT PAGE.

2. The function of the third paragraph is to

    (A) pose a question about okapi behavior
    (B) rebut a theory about okapi behavior
    (C) counter the assertion that okapis are rare
    (D) explain why okapis appeared to be rare
    (E) support the belief that okapis are rare

3. Based on the passage, in its eating behavior the okapi is most analogous to

    (A) a child who eats one kind of food at a time, consuming all of it before going on to the next kind
    (B) a professor who strictly follows the outline in the syllabus, never digressing to follow up on student questions
    (C) a student who delays working on homework until the last minute, then rushes to complete it
    (D) a newspaper reader who skips from story to story, just reading headlines and eye-catching paragraphs
    (E) a deer that ventures out of the woods only at dusk and dawn, remaining hidden during the rest of the day

4. Suppose that numerous okapis are discovered living in a remote forest region in northeastern central Africa that zoologists had not previously explored. Based on their current views, which one of the following would the zoologists be most likely to conclude about this discovery?

    (A) Okapis were pushed into this forest region by competition with mammals in neighboring forests.
    (B) Okapis in this forest region forage in the border between forest and savanna.
    (C) Okapis in this forest region are not threatened by the usual predators of okapis.
    (D) Okapis moved into this forest region because their preferred foliage is more abundant there than in other forests.
    (E) Okapis lived in this forest region when forestland in the area was scarce.

5. The passage provides information intended to help explain each of the following EXCEPT:

    (A) why zoologists once believed that okapis were rare
    (B) why zoologists classified the okapi as a member of the giraffe family
    (C) why okapis choose to limit themselves to the interiors of forests
    (D) why okapis engage in individual rather than congregated foraging
    (E) why okapis leave much preferred foliage uneaten

6. Based on the passage, the author would be most likely to agree with which one of the following statements?

    (A) The number of okapis is many times larger than zoologists had previously believed it to be.
    (B) Radio-tracking collars have enabled scientists to finally answer all the questions about the okapi.
    (C) Okapis are captured infrequently because their habits and coloration make it difficult for hunters to find them.
    (D) Okapis are concentrated in a limited geographic area because they prefer to eat one plant species to the exclusion of others.
    (E) The number of okapis would steadily increase if okapis began to forage in the open border between forest and savanna.

GO ON TO THE NEXT PAGE.

Tragic dramas written in Greece during the fifth
century B.C. engender considerable scholarly debate
over the relative influence of individual autonomy and
the power of the gods on the drama's action. One early
(5) scholar, B. Snell, argues that Aeschylus, for example,
develops in his tragedies a concept of the autonomy of
the individual. In these dramas, the protagonists
invariably confront a situation that paralyzes them, so
that their prior notions about how to behave or think
(10) are dissolved. Faced with a decision on which their fate
depends, they must reexamine their deepest motives,
and then act with determination. They are given only
two alternatives, each with grave consequences, and
they make their decision only after a tortured internal
(15) debate. According to Snell, this decision is "free" and
"personal" and such personal autonomy constitutes the
central theme in Aeschylean drama, as if the plays
were devised to isolate an abstract model of human
action. Drawing psychological conclusions from this
(20) interpretation, another scholar, Z. Barbu, suggests that
"[Aeschylean] drama is proof of the emergence within
ancient Greek civilization of the individual as a free
agent."
To A. Rivier, Snell's emphasis on the decision
(25) made by the protagonist, with its implicit notions of
autonomy and responsibility, misrepresents the role of
the superhuman forces at work, forces that give the
dramas their truly tragic dimension. These forces are
not only external to the protagonist; they are also
(30) experienced by the protagonist as an internal
compulsion, subjecting him or her to constraint even in
what are claimed to be his or her "choices." Hence all
that the deliberation does is to make the protagonist
aware of the impasse, rather than motivating one
(35) choice over another. It is finally a necessity imposed by
the deities that generates the decision, so that at a
particular moment in the drama necessity dictates a
path. Thus, the protagonist does not so much "choose"
between two possibilities as "recognize" that there is
(40) only one real option.
A. Lesky, in his discussion of Aeschylus' play
Agamemnon, disputes both views. Agamemnon, ruler
of Argos, must decide whether to brutally sacrifice his
own daughter. A message from the deity Artemis has
(45) told him that only the sacrifice will bring a wind to
blow his ships to an important battle. Agamemnon is
indeed constrained by a divine necessity. But he also
deeply desires a victorious battle: "If this sacrifice will
loose the winds, it is permitted to desire it fervently,"
(50) he says. The violence of his passion suggests that
Agamemnon chooses a path—chosen by the gods for
their own reasons—on the basis of desires that must be
condemned by us, because they are his own. In Lesky's
view, tragic action is bound by the constant tension
(55) between a self and superhuman forces.

7. Based on the information presented in the passage,
which one of the following statements best represents
Lesky's view of Agamemnon?

(A) Agamemnon's motivations are identical to those
of the gods.
(B) The nature of Agamemnon's character solely
determines the course of the tragedy.
(C) Agamemnon's decision-making is influenced by
his military ambitions.
(D) Agamemnon is concerned only with pleasing the
deity Artemis.
(E) Agamemnon is especially tragic because of his
political position.

8. Which one of the following paraphrases most accurately
restates the quotation from *Agamemnon* found in lines
48–49 of the passage?

(A) If the goddess has ordained that the only way I
can evade battle is by performing this sacrifice,
then it is perfectly appropriate for me to deeply
desire this sacrifice.
(B) If the goddess has ordained that the only way
I can get a wind to move my ships to battle is
by performing this sacrifice, then it is perfectly
appropriate for me to deeply desire victory in
battle.
(C) If the goddess has ordained that the only way
I can get a wind to move my ships to battle is
by performing this sacrifice, then it is perfectly
appropriate for me to deeply desire this sacrifice.
(D) As I alone have determined that only this
sacrifice will give me victory in battle, I will
perform it, without reservations.
(E) As I have determined that only deeply desiring
victory in battle will guarantee the success of
the sacrifice, I will perform it as ordained by the
goddess.

9. Which one of the following statements best expresses
Rivier's view, as presented in the passage, of what
makes a drama tragic?

(A) The tragic protagonist is deluded by the gods into
thinking he or she is free.
(B) The tragic protagonist struggles for a heroism that
belongs to the gods.
(C) The tragic protagonist wrongly seeks to take
responsibility for his or her actions.
(D) The tragic protagonist cannot make a decision
that is free of divine compulsion.
(E) The tragic protagonist is punished for evading his
or her responsibilities.

GO ON TO THE NEXT PAGE.

10. It can be inferred from the passage that the central difference between the interpretations of Lesky and Rivier is over which one of the following points?

    (A) whether or not the tragic protagonist is aware of the consequences of his or her actions

    (B) whether or not the tragic protagonist acknowledges the role of the deities in his or her life

    (C) whether or not the tragic protagonist's own desires have relevance to the outcome of the drama

    (D) whether or not the actions of the deities are relevant to the moral evaluation of the character's action

    (E) whether or not the desires of the tragic protagonist are more ethical than those of the deities

11. Which one of the following summaries of the plot of a Greek tragedy best illustrates the view attributed to Rivier in the passage?

    (A) Although she knows that she will be punished for violating the law of her city, a tragic figure bravely decides to bury her dead brother over the objections of local authorities.

    (B) Because of her love for her dead brother, a tragic figure, although aware that she will be punished for violating the law of her city, accedes to the gods' request that she bury his body.

    (C) After much careful thought, a tragic figure decides to disobey the dictates of the gods and murder her unfaithful husband.

    (D) A tragic figure, defying a curse placed on his family by the gods, leads his city into a battle that he realizes will prove futile.

    (E) After much careful thought, a tragic figure realizes that he has no alternative but to follow the course chosen by the gods and murder his father.

12. The quotation in lines 21–23 suggests that Barbu assumes which one of the following about Aeschylean drama?

    (A) Aeschylean drama helped to initiate a new understanding of the person in ancient Greek society.

    (B) Aeschylean drama introduced new ways of understanding the role of the individual in ancient Greek society.

    (C) Aeschylean drama is the original source of the understanding of human motivation most familiar to the modern Western world.

    (D) Aeschylean drama accurately reflects the way personal autonomy was perceived in ancient Greek society.

    (E) Aeschylean drama embodies the notion of freedom most familiar to the modern Western world.

13. All of the following statements describe Snell's view of Aeschylus' tragic protagonists, as it is presented in the passage, EXCEPT:

    (A) They are required to choose a course of action with grave consequences.

    (B) Their final choices restore harmony with supernatural forces.

    (C) They cannot rely on their customary notions of appropriate behavior.

    (D) They are compelled to confront their true motives.

    (E) They are aware of the available choices.

14. The primary purpose of the passage is to

    (A) argue against one particular interpretation of Greek tragedy

    (B) establish that there are a variety of themes in Greek tragedy

    (C) present aspects of an ongoing scholarly debate about Greek tragedy

    (D) point out the relative merits of different scholarly interpretations of Greek tragedy

    (E) suggest the relevance of Greek tragedy to the philosophical debate over human motivation

GO ON TO THE NEXT PAGE.

Philosopher Denise Meyerson views the Critical
Legal Studies (CLS) movement as seeking to debunk
orthodox legal theory by exposing its contradictions.
However, Meyerson argues that CLS proponents tend
(5) to see contradictions where none exist, and that CLS
overrates the threat that conflict poses to orthodox legal
theory.

According to Meyerson, CLS proponents hold that
the existence of conflicting values in the law implies
(10) the absence of any uniquely right solution to legal
cases. CLS argues that these conflicting values
generate equally plausible but opposing answers to any
given legal question, and, consequently, that the choice
between the conflicting answers must necessarily be
(15) arbitrary or irrational. Meyerson denies that the
existence of conflicting values makes a case
irresolvable, and asserts that at least some such cases
can be resolved by ranking the conflicting values. For
example, a lawyer's obligation to preserve a client's
(20) confidences may entail harming other parties, thus
violating moral principle. This conflict can be resolved
if it can be shown that in certain cases the professional
obligation overrides ordinary moral obligations.

In addition, says Meyerson, even when the two
(25) solutions are equally compelling, it does not follow that
the choice between them must be irrational. On the
contrary, a solution that is not rationally required need
not be unreasonable. Meyerson concurs with another
critic that instead of concentrating on the choice
(30) between two compelling alternatives, we should rather
reflect on the difference between both of these answers
on the one hand, and some utterly unreasonable answer
on the other—such as deciding a property dispute on
the basis of which claimant is louder. The
(35) acknowledgment that conflicting values can exist, then,
does not have the far-reaching implications imputed by
CLS; even if some answer to a problem is not the only
answer, opting for it can still be reasonable.

Last, Meyerson takes issue with the CLS charge
(40) that legal formalism, the belief that there is a quasi-
deductive method capable of giving solutions to
problems of legal choice, requires objectivism, the
belief that the legal process has moral authority.
Meyerson claims that showing the law to be
(45) unambiguous does not demonstrate its legitimacy:
consider a game in which participants compete to steal
the item of highest value from a shop; while a person
may easily identify the winner in terms of the rules, it
does not follow that the person endorses the rules of
(50) the game. A CLS scholar might object that legal cases
are unlike games, in that one cannot merely apply the
rules without appealing to, and therefore endorsing,
external considerations of purpose, policy, and value.
But Meyerson replies that such considerations may be
(55) viewed as part of, not separate from, the rules of the
game.

15. Which one of the following best expresses the main idea
of the passage?

(A) The arguments of the Critical Legal Studies
movement are under attack not only by legal
theorists, but also by thinkers in related areas
such as philosophy.

(B) In critiquing the Critical Legal Studies movement,
Meyerson charges that the positions articulated
by the movement's proponents overlook the
complexity of actual legal dilemmas.

(C) Meyerson objects to the propositions of the
Critical Legal Studies movement because she
views them as being self-contradictory.

(D) Meyerson poses several objections to the tenets
of the Critical Legal Studies movement, but her
most important argument involves constructing a
hierarchy of conflicting values.

(E) Meyerson seeks to counter the claims that are
made by proponents of the Critical Legal
Studies movement in their effort to challenge
conventional legal theory.

16. The primary purpose of the reference to a game in the
last paragraph is to

(A) provide an example of how a principle has
previously been applied

(B) demonstrate a point by means of an analogy

(C) emphasize the relative unimportance of an
activity

(D) contrast two situations by exaggerating their
differences

(E) dismiss an idea by portraying it as reprehensible

GO ON TO THE NEXT PAGE.

17. The author's primary purpose in the passage is to

    (A) evaluate divergent legal doctrines
    (B) explain how a controversy arose
    (C) advocate a new interpretation of legal tradition
    (D) describe a challenge to a school of thought
    (E) refute claims made by various scholars

18. It can be inferred from the passage that Meyerson would be most likely to agree with which one of the following statements about "external considerations" (line 53)?

    (A) How one determines the extent to which these considerations are relevant depends on one's degree of belief in the legal process.
    (B) The extent to which these considerations are part of the legal process depends on the extent to which the policies and values can be endorsed.
    (C) When these considerations have more moral authority than the law, the former should outweigh the latter.
    (D) If one uses these considerations in determining a legal solution, one is assuming that the policies and values are desirable.
    (E) Whether these considerations are separate from or integral to the legal process is a matter of debate.

19. The phrase "far-reaching implications" (line 36) refers to the idea that

    (A) any choice made between conflicting solutions to a legal question will be arbitrary
    (B) every legal question will involve the consideration of a set of values
    (C) two or more alternative solutions to a legal question may carry equal moral weight
    (D) no legal question will have a single correct answer
    (E) the most relevant criterion for judging solutions is the degree of rationality they possess

20. Which one of the following most accurately describes the organization of the final paragraph in the passage?

    (A) A criticism is identified and its plausibility is investigated.
    (B) The different arguments made by two opponents of a certain viewpoint are advanced.
    (C) The arguments for and against a certain position are outlined, then a new position is offered to reconcile them.
    (D) A belief is presented and its worth is debated on the basis of its practical consequences.
    (E) Two different solutions are imagined in order to summarize a controversy.

21. It can be inferred from the passage that proponents of the Critical Legal Studies movement would be most likely to hold which one of the following views about the law?

    (A) It incorporates moral principles in order to yield definitive solutions to legal problems.
    (B) It does not necessarily imply approval of any policies or values.
    (C) It is insufficient in itself to determine the answer to a legal question.
    (D) It is comparable to the application of rules in a game.
    (E) It can be used to determine the best choice between conflicting values.

GO ON TO THE NEXT PAGE.

While historians once propagated the myth that
Africans who were brought to the New World as slaves
contributed little of value but their labor, a recent study
by Amelia Wallace Vernon helps to dispel this notion
(5) by showing that Africans introduced rice and the
methods of cultivating it into what is now the United
States in the early eighteenth century. She uncovered,
for example, an 1876 document that details that in
1718 starving French settlers instructed the captain of a
(10) slave ship bound for Africa to trade for 400 Africans
including some "who know how to cultivate rice." This
discovery is especially compelling because the
introduction of rice into what is now the United States
had previously been attributed to French Acadians,
(15) who did not arrive until the 1760s.

Vernon interviewed elderly African Americans
who helped her discover the locations where until
about 1920 their forebears had cultivated rice. At the
heart of Vernon's research is the question of why, in an
(20) economy dedicated to maximizing cotton production,
African Americans grew rice. She proposes two
intriguing answers, depending on whether the time is
before of after the end of slavery. During the period of
slavery, plantation owners also ate rice and therefore
(25) tolerated or demanded its "after-hours" cultivation on
patches of land not suited to cotton. In addition,
growing the rice gave the slaves some relief from a
system of regimented labor under a field supervisor, in
that they were left alone to work independently.

(30) After the abolition of slavery, however, rice
cultivation is more difficult to explain: African
Americans had acquired a preference for eating corn,
there was no market for the small amounts of rice they
produced, and under the tenant system—in which
(35) farmers surrendered a portion of their crops to the
owners of the land they farmed—owners wanted only
cotton as payment. The labor required to transform
unused land to productive ground would thus seem
completely out of proportion to the reward—except
(40) that, according to Vernon, the transforming of the land
itself was the point.

Vernon suggests that these African Americans did
not transform the land as a means to an end, but rather
as an end in itself. In other words, they did not
(45) transform the land in order to grow rice—for the
resulting rice was scarcely worth the effort required to
clear the land—but instead transformed the land
because they viewed land as an extension of self and
home and so wished to nurture it and make it their
(50) own. In addition to this cultural explanation, Vernon
speculates that rice cultivation might also have been a
political act, a next step after the emancipation of the
slaves: the symbolic claiming of plantation land that
the U.S. government had promised but failed to parcel
(55) off and deed to newly freed African Americans.

22. Which one of the following titles most completely and
accurately summarizes the contents of the passage?

(A) "The Introduction of Rice Cultivation into what
is now the United States by Africans and Its
Continued Practice in the Years During and After
Slavery"

(B) "The Origin of Rice Cultivation in what is now
the United States and Its Impact on the Economy
from 1760 to 1920"

(C) "Widespread Rice Cultivation by African
Americans under the Tenant System in the Years
After the Abolition of Slavery"

(D) "Cultural and Political Contributions of Africans
who were Brought to what is now the United
States in the Eighteenth Century"

(E) "African American Tenant Farmers and their
Cultivation of Rice in an Economy Committed
to the Mass Production of Cotton"

23. Which one of the following most completely and
accurately describes the author's attitude toward
Vernon's study?

(A) respectful of its author and skeptical toward its
theories

(B) admiring of its accomplishments and generally
receptive to its theories

(C) appreciative of the effort it required and neutral
toward its theories

(D) enthusiastic about its goals but skeptical of its
theories

(E) accepting of its author's motives but overtly
dismissive of its theories

GO ON TO THE NEXT PAGE.

24. As described in the last paragraph of the passage, rice cultivation after slavery is most analogous to which one of the following?

    (A) A group of neighbors plants flower gardens on common land adjoining their properties in order to beautify their neighborhood and to create more of a natural boundary between properties.

    (B) A group of neighbors plants a vegetable garden for their common use and to compete with the local market's high-priced produce by selling vegetables to other citizens who live outside the neighborhood.

    (C) A group of neighbors initiates an effort to neuter all the domestic animals in their neighborhood out of a sense of civic duty and to forestall the city taking action of its own to remedy the overpopulation.

    (D) A group of neighbors regularly cleans up the litter on a vacant lot in their neighborhood out of a sense of ownership over the lot and to protest the city's neglect of their neighborhood.

    (E) A group of neighbors renovates an abandoned building so they can start a program to watch each other's children out of a sense of communal responsibility and to offset the closing of a day care center in their neighborhood.

25. Which one of the following most completely and accurately describes the organization of the passage?

    (A) A historical phenomenon is presented, several competing theories about the phenomenon are described, and one theory having the most support is settled upon.

    (B) A historical discovery is presented, the method leading to the discovery is provided, and two questions left unanswered by the discovery are identified.

    (C) A historical fact is presented, a question raised by the fact is described, and two answers to the question are given.

    (D) A historical question is raised, possible answers to the question are speculated upon, and two reasons for difficulty in answering the question are given.

    (E) A historical question is raised, a study is described that answers the question, and a number of issues surrounding the study are discussed.

26. The passage cites which one of the following as a reason that rice cultivation in the context of the tenant system was difficult to explain?

    (A) Landowners did not eat rice and thus would not tolerate its cultivation on tenant lands.

    (B) Rice was not considered acceptable payment to landowners for the use of tenant lands.

    (C) Tenant farmers did not have enough time "after hours" to cultivate the rice properly.

    (D) The labor required to cultivate rice was more strenuous than that required for cotton.

    (E) Tenant lands used primarily to grow cotton were not suited to rice.

27. The author's primary purpose in the passage is to

    (A) describe the efforts of a historian to uncover evidence for a puzzling phenomenon

    (B) illustrate the historical background of a puzzling phenomenon

    (C) present a historian's theories about a puzzling phenomenon

    (D) criticize the work of previous historians regarding a puzzling phenomenon

    (E) analyze the effects of a puzzling phenomenon on an economic system

S T O P

IF YOU FINISH BEFORE TIME IS CALLED, YOU MAY CHECK YOUR WORK ON THIS SECTION ONLY. DO NOT WORK ON ANY OTHER SECTION IN THE TEST.

Answer Key

1. C
2. D
3. D
4. E
5. E
6. C
7. C
8. C
9. D
10. C
11. E
12. D
13. B
14. C
15. E
16. B
17. D
18. E
19. A
20. A
21. C
22. A
23. B
24. D
25. C
26. B
27. C

KAPLAN

Reading Comprehension 10

PrepTest B, Section III
February 1999

SECTION III
Time—35 minutes
26 Questions

Directions: Each passage in this section is followed by a group of questions to be answered on the basis of what is <u>stated</u> or <u>implied</u> in the passage. For some of the questions, more than one of the choices could conceivably answer the question. However, you are to choose the <u>best</u> answer; that is, the response that most accurately and completely answers the question, and blacken the corresponding space on your answer sheet.

Until recently, many biologists believed that invertebrate "schools" were actually transient assemblages, brought together by wind, currents, waves, or common food sources. Jellyfish groupings,
(5) for example, cannot be described as schools—cohesive social units whose members are evenly spaced and face the same way. However, recent research has found numerous cases in which crustaceans and other invertebrates form schools as fish do. Schooling
(10) crustaceans such as krill regularly collect in such massive numbers that they provide abundant food for fish, seabirds, and whales.

Like schooling fish, invertebrates with sufficient mobility to school will swim in positions that are
(15) consistent relative to fellow school members, and are neither directly above nor directly below a neighbor. The internal structure of such a school changes little with external physical disruption but dramatically with the advent of a predator.
(20) Since schooling is an active behavior, researchers assume that it must bring important benefits. True, schooling would appear to make animals more visible and attractive to predators. However, schooling leaves vast tracts of empty water, thereby reducing a
(25) predator's chances of picking up the school's trail. A large group maintains surveillance better then an individual can, and may discourage predation by appearing to be one massive animal. And although an attacking predator may eat some of the invertebrates,
(30) any individual school member has a good probability of escaping.

In addition to conferring passive advantages, schooling permits the use of more active defense mechanisms. When a predator is sighted, the school
(35) compacts, so that a predator's senses may be unable to resolve individuals, or so that the school can execute escape maneuvers, such as freezing to foil predators that hunt by detecting turbulence. If the predator attacks, the school may split, or may employ "flash
(40) expansion"—an explosive acceleration of animals away from the school's center. When large predators threaten the entire school, the school may attempt to avoid detection altogether or to reduce the density of the school at the point of attack; when small predators
(45) threaten the margin, school members may put on dazzling and confusing displays of synchronized swimming.

Schooling may also enable invertebrates to locate food—when one group member finds food, other
(50) members observe its behavior and flock to the food

source. On the other hand, competition within the school for food may be intense: some mysids circle around to the back of the school in order to eat food particles surreptitiously. Schooling can facilitate the
(55) search for mates, but as a school's numbers rise, food may become locally scarce and females may produce smaller clutches of eggs, or adults may start to feed on the young. Thus, circumstances apparently dictate the optimal size of a school; if that size is exceeded, some
(60) of the animals will join another school.

1. Which one of the following best expresses the main idea of the passage?

(A) The optimal size of a school of invertebrates is determined by many different circumstances, but primarily by issues of competition.

(B) The internal structure of a group of invertebrates determines what defensive maneuvers that group can perform.

(C) Although in many respects invertebrate schools behave in the same way that fish schools do, in some respects the two types of schools differ.

(D) Certain invertebrates have been discovered to engage in schooling, a behavior that confers a number of benefits.

(E) Invertebrate schooling is more directed toward avoiding or reducing predation than toward finding food sources.

2. According to the passage, each of the following is characteristic of an invertebrate school EXCEPT:

(A) The number of members in a school is influenced by external circumstances.

(B) A school's members are arranged directly above and below one another.

(C) A school's members arrange themselves so that they all face in the same direction.

(D) The individual members of a school maintain regular spacing from member to member.

(E) Population increase in a school can diminish reproduction by individual school members.

GO ON TO THE NEXT PAGE.

3. If substituted for the word "resolve" in line 36, which one of the following words would convey the same meaning in the context of the passage?

    (A) control
    (B) answer
    (C) reconcile
    (D) distinguish
    (E) pacify

4. Which line of the following best describes the final paragraph of the passage?

    (A) Arguments for opposing points of view are presented and then reconciled.
    (B) The disadvantages of certain types of choices are outlined and alternative choices are proposed.
    (C) Two different interpretations of a phenomenon are evaluated and one is endorsed as the more plausible.
    (D) The disadvantages of an action are enumerated and the validity of that action is called into question.
    (E) Advantages and disadvantages of a behavior are discussed and some actions for avoiding the adverse consequences are mentioned.

5. According to the passage, jellyfish are an example of invertebrates that

    (A) do not engage in schooling behavior
    (B) form groups with evenly spaced members
    (C) assemble together only to feed
    (D) form schools only when circumstances are advantageous
    (E) collect in such large numbers as to provide abundant food

6. It can be inferred from the passage that if cannibalism were occurring in a large school of crustaceans, an individual crustacean encountering the school would

    (A) try to stay at the edge of the school in order to obtain food
    (B) be more likely to be eaten if it were fully grown
    (C) be unlikely to join that particular school
    (D) try to follow at the back of the school in order to escape predators
    (E) try to confuse school members by executing complex swimming maneuvers

7. Which one of the following, if true, would most clearly undermine the assumption about schooling mentioned in the first sentence of the third paragraph?

    (A) Observation reveals that many groups of invertebrates are unable to execute any defensive maneuvers.
    (B) Biologists find that some predators can always tell the difference between a school and a single large animal.
    (C) Research demonstrates that the less an invertebrate associates with others of its species, the better its chance of survival.
    (D) Biologists confirm that predators are more likely to notice a nearby school of invertebrates than to notice a single invertebrate.
    (E) Researchers determine that the optimal school sizes for numerous species have each declined in previous years.

GO ON TO THE NEXT PAGE.

Many of us can conceive of penalties that seem disproportionate to the crimes they are intended to punish. A sentence of probation for a person convicted of a brutal murder is one example of such an
(5) imbalance. At the other extreme is a sentence of twenty years in prison for shoplifting. But what is the source of these commonsense intuitions about the appropriateness of punishments?

There are two main rationales for punishing
(10) criminals. The first rationale justifies a punishment in terms of its benefit to society. Society is said to benefit whenever the fear of punishment deters a person from committing a crime, or when a convicted criminal is removed from contact with society at large. The second
(15) rationale is that a punishment is justified by the severity of the crime, independent of any benefit to society. This rationale is controversial because some find it difficult to see how a punishment can be justified if it brings no societal benefit; without such
(20) benefit, punishment would appear to be little more than retribution. But from the retributivist point of view, the question to be asked about punishment is not whether it is beneficial, but whether it is just—that is, appropriate.

One problem with the social-benefit rationale is
(25) that it is possible that very harsh penalties even for minor offenses may have great benefit to society. For example, if shoplifters faced twenty-year jail sentences, shoplifting might be deterred. Yet something leads us to say that in such cases the penalty far outweighs the
(30) crime. That is, there appears to be something intuitively wrong, or unjust, about these punishments. And it would seem that this intuition can only find support in a retributive conception of punishment, under which certain types of punishments are
(35) inherently more appropriate than others. The notion of appropriateness is absent from the first rationale, which could conceivably allow for any sort of punishment as long as it benefits society. Retributive considerations, on the other hand, allow for proportionality between
(40) punishments and crimes. This is what fuels our notion of just (as opposed to beneficial) punishment.

However, it can be argued that our intuition of the injustice of an overly harsh punishment is based on our sense that such a punishment is more harmful to the
(45) criminal than beneficial to society; and, similarly, that our intuition that a punishment is just is based on our sense that this punishment fairly balances societal benefit against harm to the criminal. In this way the second rationale can be seen as grounded in the first
(50) and its retributive nature disappears. Thus it seems that even our so-called intuitive notions of the appropriateness of punishments have their basis in the concept of benefit.

8. Which one of the following most accurately states the main point of the passage?

(A) Of the two main rationales for justifying punishing criminals, the retributivist rationale can be shown to be more fundamental, since our sense of the social benefit of punishments can be explained by our intuitions about justice and injustice.

(B) Although social benefit appears to be a reasonable rationale for punishing criminals, the fact that it can justify very harsh penalties for even minor offenses shows its inadequacy and argues for the alternative retributivist rationale.

(C) Because the retributivist rationale for punishing criminals allows for proportionality between punishments and crimes, it is able to support our intuitions that certain penalties are disproportionate to their crimes in a way that the social-benefit rationale cannot.

(D) Because the rationale that punishment is justified by the severity of the crime amounts to no more than retribution, punishment of a criminal can be justified only if it produces a social benefit that outweighs the harm it brings to the criminal.

(E) Although it appears better able to support our intuitions about just and unjust punishment than the social-benefit rationale, the rationale that punishments ought to fit crimes may, in the end, be itself grounded in the concept of benefit.

GO ON TO THE NEXT PAGE.

9. According to the passage, the second rationale for punishing criminals is controversial because it

    (A)   does not employ the notion of social benefit
    (B)   allows for disproportionately severe punishments
    (C)   conflicts with our intuitions about justice
    (D)   implies that punishment does not deter criminals
    (E)   arises from intuition rather than logic

10. Based on the passage, the "retributive nature" of the second rationale for punishing criminals (line 50) consists in that rationale's

    (A)   equating social benefit with harm to criminals
    (B)   regarding punishment as justified by the severity of the crime
    (C)   support for sentences disproportionate to the crimes they punish
    (D)   belief that any punishment that benefits society is just
    (E)   favoring harsher sentences over more lenient ones

11. The author states that our intuition of the injustice of an overly harsh punishment may be based on which one of the following notions?

    (A)   Such punishment brings no benefit to society at large.
    (B)   Such punishment is potentially harmful to the criminal.
    (C)   Such punishment benefits society less than it harms the criminal.
    (D)   Such punishment harms the criminal less than it benefits society.
    (E)   Such punishment attempts to reconcile social benefit with harm to the criminal.

12. It can be inferred from the passage that the author would be most likely to agree with which one of the following characterizations of the second rationale for punishing criminals?

    (A)   It is more widely accepted than the first rationale.
    (B)   It does not have the same potential unfairness as the first rationale.
    (C)   It justifies more kinds of punishments than the first rationale.
    (D)   It is used just in those cases where the first rationale violates our intuitions.
    (E)   It inherently allows more lenient punishment than the first rationale.

13. As expressed in the passage, the author's attitude toward very harsh penalties for minor offenses is most accurately described as

    (A)   reluctant approval of the deterrence they offer against crime
    (B)   mild skepticism that they ultimately benefit society
    (C)   detached indifference toward their effects on criminals
    (D)   scholarly neutrality on whether they are justified
    (E)   implicit disapproval of their moral injustice

14. As described in the second paragraph, the second rationale for punishing criminals is most consistent with which one of the following principles?

    (A)   The correctness of an action depends not on its consequences but on its inherent fairness.
    (B)   The correctness of an action depends not on its consequences but on what society deems correct.
    (C)   The correctness of an action depends partly on its consequences and partly on its inherent fairness.
    (D)   The correctness of an action depends partly on its consequences and partly on its intuitive rightness.
    (E)   The correctness of an action depends entirely on its consequences.

GO ON TO THE NEXT PAGE.

Despite the great differences among the cultures from which we spring, there is a trait shared by many Hispanic-American writers: the use of a European language, Spanish, transplanted to the Western
(5) hemisphere. This fact has marked our literature profoundly and radically. We Hispanic Americans who write in Spanish have attempted from the beginning to break the ties of dependency that linked us with the literature of Spain. We have pursued this goal of ever-
(10) increasing independence through a twofold movement, seeking to adopt the literary forms and styles in vogue in other European and North American literatures, and endeavoring to describe the nature of the United States and give voice to the Hispanic peoples who live there.
(15) These often conflicting tactics can be described as cosmopolitanism and nativism, respectively.

The opposition between cosmopolitanism and nativism has divided the Hispanic-American literary consciousness for generations. For example, the work
(20) of one Mexican-American novelist was praised by some Hispanic-American critics for its skillful adaptation of European literary techniques but criticized for its paucity of specifically Mexican-American settings or characters. On the other hand, a
(25) Cuban-American novel was admired by other Hispanic-American critics for the vivid portrayal of its characters' daily lives but faulted for its "roughness" of form and language.

Cosmopolitanism is the venturing forth into the
(30) public or mainstream culture; nativism, the return to the private or original culture. There are periods in which the outward-oriented sensibility predominates, and others in which tendencies toward self-absorption and introspection prevail. An example of the former
(35) was the rich period of the avant-garde between 1918 and 1930. This was a time of searching and experimentation, when successive European movements from expressionism to surrealism— movements that were also inspiring other North
(40) American writers—had profound influence on many Hispanic-American poets and novelists. This phase, which produced a number of outstanding works of exceptional boldness of expression, was followed by another characterized by a return to our peoples and
(45) our colloquial dialects, by the creation of works less indebted to current trends in the mainstream culture. Throughout our history, a concern for novelty and experimentation has been followed by a return to origins.
(50) We contemporary Hispanic-American writers who write in Spanish live somewhere between the European tradition and the reality of the Americas. Our roots may be European, but our horizon is the land and history of the Americas. This is the challenge that we confront
(55) each day: in order to appreciate the value of one's own culture, one must first venture forth into the public sphere; in order not to disappear into the mainstream, one must return to one's origins. In this way, we attempt to reconcile the opposing tendencies of
(60) cosmopolitanism and nativism.

15. Which one of the following statements most accurately expresses the passage's main point?

(A) Although differing in culture, style, and content, the various branches of Hispanic-American literature are linked by their shared use of the Spanish language, a condition that gives them a strong connection to their European heritage.

(B) Many Hispanic-American writers have attempted to separate their literature from that of Spain through a mixture of cosmopolitanism and nativism, conflicting tendencies that alternately dominate Hispanic-American literature.

(C) Many Hispanic-American writers attempt to reconcile the opposing tendencies of cosmopolitanism and nativism by beginning their careers writing European-influenced novels and later switching to works that utilize specifically Hispanic-American settings.

(D) Despite statements by literary critics to the contrary, the cosmopolitanist and nativist tendencies in Hispanic-American literature do not compete with one another for dominance even though they occur concurrently.

(E) If Hispanic-American literature is to achieve its full potential, it must reconcile the conflicting tendencies of cosmopolitanism and nativism that have isolated writers of differing cultures from one another.

16. According to the passage, many of the Hispanic-American literary works produced between 1918 and 1930 were especially notable for their

(A) unusual expressiveness
(B) use of colloquial language
(C) unprecedented reliance on Spanish literary forms
(D) introspective quality
(E) reduced emphasis on current trends in mainstream North American culture

GO ON TO THE NEXT PAGE.

Reading
Comprehension 10
Answer Grid

NAME
(Please Print)

Glenn

Last Name   Suffix

Jeremy

First Name

Middle Name

1. Ⓐ Ⓑ Ⓒ **Ⓓ** Ⓔ
2. Ⓐ **Ⓑ** Ⓒ Ⓓ Ⓔ
3. Ⓐ Ⓑ Ⓒ **Ⓓ** Ⓔ
4. Ⓐ Ⓑ Ⓒ Ⓓ **Ⓔ**
5. **Ⓐ** Ⓑ Ⓒ Ⓓ Ⓔ
6. Ⓐ Ⓑ **Ⓒ** Ⓓ Ⓔ
7. Ⓐ Ⓑ **Ⓒ** Ⓓ Ⓔ
8. Ⓐ **Ⓑ** Ⓒ Ⓓ **Ⓔ**
9. **Ⓐ** Ⓑ Ⓒ Ⓓ Ⓔ
10. Ⓐ Ⓑ **Ⓒ** Ⓓ Ⓔ
11. Ⓐ Ⓑ **Ⓒ** Ⓓ Ⓔ
12. Ⓐ **Ⓑ** Ⓒ Ⓓ Ⓔ
13. Ⓐ **Ⓑ** Ⓒ Ⓓ **Ⓔ**
14. **Ⓐ** Ⓑ Ⓒ Ⓓ Ⓔ
15. Ⓐ **Ⓑ** Ⓒ Ⓓ **Ⓔ**
16. **Ⓐ** Ⓑ Ⓒ Ⓓ Ⓔ
17. **Ⓐ** Ⓑ Ⓒ Ⓓ **Ⓔ**
18. Ⓐ Ⓑ Ⓒ **Ⓓ** Ⓔ
19. **Ⓐ** Ⓑ Ⓒ Ⓓ Ⓔ
20. Ⓐ **Ⓑ** Ⓒ Ⓓ Ⓔ
21. Ⓐ **Ⓑ** Ⓒ Ⓓ Ⓔ
22. **Ⓐ** Ⓑ Ⓒ Ⓓ Ⓔ
23. Ⓐ Ⓑ **Ⓒ** Ⓓ Ⓔ
24. Ⓐ Ⓑ Ⓒ **Ⓓ** **Ⓔ**
25. Ⓐ Ⓑ Ⓒ **Ⓓ** Ⓔ
26. Ⓐ **Ⓑ** **Ⓒ** Ⓓ Ⓔ
27. Ⓐ Ⓑ Ⓒ Ⓓ Ⓔ
28. Ⓐ Ⓑ Ⓒ Ⓓ Ⓔ
29. Ⓐ Ⓑ Ⓒ Ⓓ Ⓔ
30. Ⓐ Ⓑ Ⓒ Ⓓ Ⓔ

felt the strongest

Tough law passage. should've skipped it

Took a lot of notes. Did it help??

Most confused about them. v. Remm. G

7/7

6/7 ← Great on law passage! "

5/7

0/5 ⟩ Wan dude.

11/28/11

18/26 = 69%   almost there

– ran out of time, so the last reading passage suffered (0/5)

17. According to the passage, the nativist tendency represents an attempt to

    (A) experiment with form and style to illustrate the range of Hispanic-American literary achievement

    (B) adapt the forms and styles of other literatures to the exploration of Hispanic-American themes

    (C) transform the Spanish language into an apt vehicle for any theme

    (D) align Hispanic-American literature with other North American literary movements

    (E) depict the experience of various Hispanic peoples in U.S. settings

18. It can be inferred from the passage that the Hispanic-American literature written in Spanish in the period immediately following 1930 was most likely characterized by

    (A) narrative experimentation

    (B) expressionistic tendencies

    (C) surreal imagery

    (D) use of mainstream literary forms

    (E) greater naturalness of expression

19. The author of the passage suggests that contemporary Hispanic-American writers who write in Spanish are

    (A) continually confronted by cosmopolitanist and nativist influences

    (B) writing more works in the nativist mode than in the cosmopolitanist mode

    (C) unaffected by the debate between cosmopolitanism and nativism that previous generations experienced

    (D) uncertain whether cosmopolitanism and nativism will help achieve their literary goals

    (E) cleanly and strongly divided into cosmopolitanist and nativist camps

20. Based on the passage, the author's attitude toward nativism in Hispanic-American literature is most likely

    (A) enthusiastic support

    (B) general approval

    (C) reluctant acceptance

    (D) strong skepticism

    (E) clear disapproval

21. The primary purpose of the passage is to

    (A) illustrate a general problem of literature by focusing on a particular culture's literature

    (B) illuminate a point of tension in a particular culture's literature

    (C) summarize the achievements of a particular culture's literature

    (D) provoke a discussion of the political aspect of literature by focusing on a particular culture's literature

    (E) refute a prevailing assumption about the development of a particular culture's literature

GO ON TO THE NEXT PAGE.

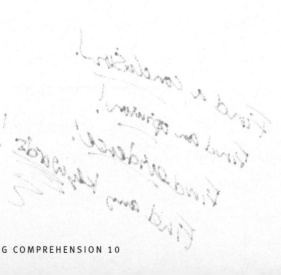

In the past, students of Renaissance women's education extolled the unprecedented intellectual liberty and equality available to these women, but recently scholars have presented a different view of
(5) Renaissance education and opportunity for women. Joan Gibson argues that despite more widespread education for privileged classes of women, Renaissance educational reforms also increased restrictions on women. Humanist education in the
(10) Renaissance was based on the classical division of the liberal arts into seven categories, including the three language arts: grammar, dialectic, and rhetoric. Although medieval monastic education, also based on the classical division, had stressed grammar and
(15) languages in preparation for a life devoted to meditation on religious literature, humanist education revived the classical emphasis on rhetoric—the art of persuasive and declamatory speech—in the context of training for public service in legal and political debate.
(20) All students began with elementary study of grammar and progressed to stylistics and literary criticism. But rhetorical training, which was increasingly undertaken only at the university level, could lead in different directions—to study of composition and oral
(25) expression or to study of persuasion, in conjunction with a dialectic concerned with broad principles of logic and argumentation. Male students routinely learned material through rhetorical, argumentative role-playing, and although many Renaissance authors
(30) expressed horror at their aggressive wrangling, such combativeness was thought still less appropriate for women, who were not supposed to need such preparation for public life.
Thus, humanist education for women encompassed
(35) literary grammatical studies in both classical and vernacular languages, while dialectic and rhetoric, the disciplines required for philosophy, politics, and the professions, were prohibited to women. Even princesses lacked instruction in political philosophy or
(40) the exercise of such public virtues as philanthropy. The prevailing attitude was that girls needed only a generalist education conducted in a family setting and directed toward private enjoyment and the eventual teaching of very young children. Unlike either dialectic
(45) or rhetoric, grammar training cast students in the role of an audience, striving to understand authors and teachers. Women were to form an audience, not seek one; for them, instruction in speaking was confined to books of courtesy.
(50) The coupling of expanded linguistic and literary education for women with the lack of available social roles for educated women led to uneasy resolutions; exceptionally learned women were labeled as preternatural or essentially masculine, or were praised
(55) as virtuous only if they were too modest to make their accomplishments public. Some Italian humanist women gave fashionable oratorical performances, but these were ceremonial in nature rather than designed to influence public affairs. Renaissance women educated
(60) along humanist lines did not tend to write works of

philosophy; instead they became most notable for literary achievements, particularly translations, poetry and tales in the vernacular or correspondence and orations in Latin.

22. Which one of the following best expresses the main idea of the passage?

(A) Although previous scholarship portrayed the Renaissance as a time of expanded education for women, recent scholarship has shown that fewer women received an education during the Renaissance than in medieval times.

(B) The differences in the Renaissance educational curricula for males and females reflected expectations about how the members of each gender would apply their education.

(C) The education of women during the Renaissance did not prepare them for careers in literature, but many of these women managed to contribute noteworthy literary works.

(D) The division of language arts from other liberal arts in the Renaissance reinforced gender-based differences in terms of curriculum.

(E) Even though their respective curricula eventually diverged, males and females in the Renaissance engaged in the same studies during first stages of their educations.

23. Each of the following aspects of Renaissance humanist education is mentioned in the passage EXCEPT:

(A) a method used for rhetorical training
(B) an educational goal
(C) a sequence of subjects that were studied
(D) types of schools for grammar studies
(E) prerequisites for certain careers

GO ON TO THE NEXT PAGE.

24. Which one of the following statements about women's roles during the Renaissance can be inferred from information given in the passage?

    (A) Women played an important role in providing advanced grammar training despite their lack of access to universities.

    (B) Women became increasingly acceptable as orators due to the humanists' interest in classical rhetoric.

    (C) The accepted roles of female students diverged from those of male students at the point when study of stylistics and literary criticism began.

    (D) The women who were acclaimed as authors were those who managed to study subjects omitted from the usual curriculum for female students.

    (E) Women who demonstrated intellectual attainment tended to be regarded as anomalies rather than as models for other women.

25. Which one of the following, if true, would most weaken the distinction between training in grammar and training in dialectic and rhetoric that is drawn in lines 44–47 of the passage?

    (A) Grammar students were encouraged to emulate the compositional techniques used by certain authors and to avoid those of other authors.

    (B) Students of dialectic and rhetoric were encouraged to debate on set subjects rather than on subjects they themselves proposed.

    (C) Grammar training had a different place in the sequence of studies followed by male students than in that followed by female students.

    (D) Grammar training included exercises designed to improve a student's skill at articulating his or her own ideas.

    (E) Training in dialectic and rhetoric focused more on oral expression than on written expression.

26. Which one of the following situations is most analogous to the one introduced in the second sentence of the passage?

    (A) As a new segment of the population is registered to vote, the entire election process is undermined by a government that manipulates the results.

    (B) At the same time that more people become able to afford a certain product, supplies dwindle and the product becomes harder to obtain.

    (C) Although additional workers are employed in an industry, they are prevented from rising above a certain level.

    (D) When a new group of players joins in a game, the original participants become more aggressive in response to the increased competition.

    (E) Even though an increasing number of people are becoming familiar with a new technology, that technology is growing more complicated to master.

S T O P

IF YOU FINISH BEFORE TIME IS CALLED, YOU MAY CHECK YOUR WORK ON THIS SECTION ONLY. DO NOT WORK ON ANY OTHER SECTION IN THE TEST.

0/5

Ran out of time. !!

1/4 (25%) on Main Idea / Main Point questions

Answer Key

1. D
2. B
3. D
4. E
5. A
6. C
7. C
8. E
9. A
10. B
11. C
12. B
13. E
14. A
15. B
16. A
17. E
18. E
19. A
20. B
21. B
22. B
23. D
24. E
25. D
26. C

Reading Comprehension 11

PrepTest 25, Section I
June 1998

SECTION I

Time—35 minutes

26 Questions

<u>Directions:</u> Each passage in this section is followed by a group of questions to be answered on the basis of what is <u>stated</u> or <u>implied</u> in the passage. For some of the questions, more than one of the choices could conceivably answer the question. However, you are to choose the <u>best</u> answer; that is, the response that most accurately and completely answers the question, and blacken the corresponding space on your answer sheet.

Most office workers assume that the messages they send to each other via electronic mail are as private as a telephone call or a face-to-face meeting. That assumption is wrong. Although it is illegal in many

(5) areas for an employer to eavesdrop on private conversations or telephone calls—even if they take place on a company-owned telephone—there are no clear rules governing electronic mail. In fact, the question of how private electronic mail transmissions

(10) should be has emerged as one of the more complicated legal issues of the electronic age.

People's opinions about the degree of privacy that electronic mail should have vary depending on whose electronic mail system is being used and who is reading

(15) the messages. Does a government office, for example, have the right to destroy electronic messages created in the course of running the government, thereby denying public access to such documents? Some hold that government offices should issue guidelines that allow

(20) their staff to delete such electronic records, and defend this practice by claiming that the messages thus deleted already exist in paper versions whose destruction is forbidden. Opponents of such practices argue that the paper versions often omit such information as who

(25) received the messages and when they received them, information commonly carried on electronic mail systems. Government officials, opponents maintain, are civil servants; the public should thus have the right to review any documents created during the conducting of

(30) government business.

Questions about electronic mail privacy have also arisen in the private sector. Recently, two employees of an automotive company were discovered to have been communicating disparaging information about their

(35) supervisor via electronic mail. The supervisor, who had been monitoring the communication, threatened to fire the employees. When the employees filed a grievance complaining that their privacy had been violated, they were let go. Later, their court case for unlawful

(40) termination was dismissed; the company's lawyers successfully argued that because the company owned the computer system, its supervisors had the right to read anything created on it.

In some areas, laws prohibit outside interception of

(45) electronic mail by a third party without proper authorization such as a search warrant. However, these laws to not cover "inside" interception such as occurred at the automotive company. In the past, courts have ruled that interoffice communications may be

(50) considered private only if employees have a

"reasonable expectation" of privacy when they send the messages. The fact is that no absolute guarantee of privacy exists in any computer system. The only solution may be for users to scramble their own

(55) messages with encryption codes; unfortunately, such complex codes are likely to undermine the principal virtue of electronic mail: its convenience.

1. Which one of the following statements most accurately summarizes the main point of the passage?

(A) Until the legal questions surrounding the privacy of electronic mail in both the public and private sectors have been resolved, office workers will need to scramble their electronic mail messages with encryption codes.

(B) The legal questions surrounding the privacy of electronic mail in the workplace can best be resolved by treating such communications as if they were as private as telephone conversations or face-to-face meetings.

(C) Any attempt to resolve the legal questions surrounding the privacy of electronic mail in the workplace must take into account the essential difference between public-sector and private-sector business.

(D) At present, in both the public and private sectors, there seem to be no clear general answers to the legal questions surrounding the privacy of electronic mail in the workplace.

(E) The legal questions surrounding the privacy of electronic mail in the workplace can best be resolved by allowing supervisors in public-sector but not private-sector offices to monitor their employees' communications.

GO ON TO THE NEXT PAGE.

2. According to the passage, which one of the following best expresses the reason some people use to oppose the deletion of electronic mail records at government offices?

   (A) Such deletion reveals the extent of government's unhealthy obsession with secrecy.
   (B) Such deletion runs counter to the notion of government's accountability to its constituency.
   (C) Such deletion clearly violates the legal requirement that government offices keep duplicate copies of all their transactions.
   (D) Such deletion violates the government's own guidelines against destruction of electronic records.
   (E) Such deletion harms relations between government employees and their supervisors.

3. Which one of the following most accurately states the organization of the passage?

   (A) A problem is introduced, followed by specific examples illustrating the problem; a possible solution is suggested, followed by an acknowledgment of its shortcomings.
   (B) A problem is introduced, followed by explications of two possible solutions to the problem; the first solution is preferred to the second, and reasons are given for why it is the better alternative.
   (C) A problem is introduced, followed by analysis of the historical circumstances that helped bring the problem about; a possible solution is offered and rejected as being only a partial remedy.
   (D) A problem is introduced, followed by enumeration of various questions that need to be answered before a solution can be found; one possible solution is proposed and argued for.
   (E) A problem is introduced, followed by descriptions of two contrasting approaches to thinking about the problem; the second approach is preferred to the first, and reasons are given for why it is more likely to yield a successful solution.

4. Based on the passage, the author's attitude toward interception of electronic mail can most accurately be described as

   (A) outright disapproval of the practice
   (B) support for employers who engage in it
   (C) support for employees who lose their jobs because of it
   (D) intellectual interest in its legal issues
   (E) cynicism about the motives behind the practice

5. It can be inferred from the passage that the author would most likely hold which one of the following opinions about an encryption system that could encode and decode electronic mail messages with a single keystroke?

   (A) It would be an unreasonable burden on a company's ability to monitor electronic mail created by its employees.
   (B) It would significantly reduce the difficulty of attempting to safeguard the privacy of electronic mail.
   (C) It would create substantial legal complications for companies trying to prevent employees from revealing trade secrets to competitors.
   (D) It would guarantee only a minimal level of employee privacy, and so would not be worth the cost involved in installing such a system.
   (E) It would require a change in the legal definition of "reasonable expectation of privacy" as it applies to employer-employee relations.

6. Given the information in the passage, which one of the following hypothetical events is LEAST likely to occur?

   (A) A court rules that a government office's practice of deleting its electronic mail is not in the public's best interests.
   (B) A private-sector employer is found liable for wiretapping an office telephone conversation in which two employees exchanged disparaging information about their supervisor.
   (C) A court upholds the right of a government office to destroy both paper and electronic versions of its in-house documents.
   (D) A court upholds a private-sector employer's right to monitor messages sent between employees over the company's in-house electronic mail system.
   (E) A court rules in favor of a private-sector employee whose supervisor stated that in-house electronic mail would not be monitored but later fired the employee for communicating disparaging information via electronic mail.

7. The author's primary purpose in writing the passage is to

   (A) demonstrate that the individual right to privacy has been eroded by advances in computer technology
   (B) compare the legal status of electronic mail in the public and private sectors
   (C) draw an extended analogy between the privacy of electronic mail and the privacy of telephone conversations or face-to-face meetings
   (D) illustrate the complexities of the privacy issues surrounding electronic mail in the workplace
   (E) explain why the courts have not been able to rule definitively on the issue of the privacy of electronic mail

GO ON TO THE NEXT PAGE.

While a new surge of critical interest in the ancient Greek poems conventionally ascribed to Homer has taken place in the last twenty years or so, it was nonspecialists rather than professional scholars who
(5) studied the poetic aspects of the *Iliad* and the *Odyssey* between, roughly, 1935 and 1970. During these years, while such nonacademic intellectuals as Simone Weil and Erich Auerbach were trying to define the qualities that made these epic accounts of the Trojan War and its
(10) aftermath great poetry, the questions that occupied the specialists were directed elsewhere: "Did the Trojan War really happen?" "Does the bard preserve Indo-European folk memories?" "How did the poems get written down?" Something was driving scholars away
(15) from the actual works to peripheral issues. Scholars produced books about archaeology, and gift-exchange in ancient societies, about the development of oral poetry, about virtually anything except the *Iliad* and the *Odyssey* themselves as unique reflections or
(20) distillations of life itself—as, in short, great poetry. The observations of the English poet Alexander Pope seemed as applicable in 1970 as they had been when he wrote them in 1715: according to Pope, the remarks of critics "are rather Philosophical, Historical,
(25) Geographical . . . or rather anything than Critical and Poetical."

Ironically, the modern manifestation of this "nonpoetical" emphasis can be traced to the profoundly influential work of Milman Parry, who attempted to
(30) demonstrate in detail how the Homeric poems, believed to have been recorded nearly three thousand years ago, were the products of a long and highly developed tradition of oral poetry about the Trojan War. Parry proposed that this tradition built up its
(35) diction and its content by a process of constant accumulation and refinement over many generations of storytellers. But after Parry's death in 1935, his legacy was taken up by scholars who, unlike Parry, forsook intensive analysis of the poetry itself and focused
(40) instead on only one element of Parry's work: the creative limitations and possibilities of oral composition, concentrating on fixed elements and inflexibilities, focusing on the things that oral poetry allegedly can and cannot do. The dryness of this kind
(45) of study drove many of the more inventive scholars away from the poems into the rapidly developing field of Homer's archaeological and historical background.

Appropriately, Milman Parry's son Adam was among those scholars responsible for a renewed
(50) interest in Homer's poetry as literary art. Building on his father's work, the younger Parry argued that the Homeric poems exist both within and against a tradition. The *Iliad* and the *Odyssey* were, Adam Parry thought, the beneficiaries of an inherited store of
(55) diction, scenes, and concepts, and at the same time highly individual works that surpassed these conventions. Adam Parry helped prepare the ground for the recent Homeric revival by affirming his father's belief in a strong inherited tradition, but also by
(60) emphasizing Homer's unique contributions within that tradition.

8. Which one of the following best states the main idea of the passage?

    (A) The Homeric poems are most fruitfully studied as records of the time and place in which they were written.

    (B) The Homeric poems are the products of a highly developed and complicated tradition of oral poetry.

    (C) The Homeric poems are currently enjoying a resurgence of critical interest after an age of scholarship largely devoted to the poems' nonpoetic elements.

    (D) The Homeric poems are currently enjoying a resurgence of scholarly interest after an age during which most studies were authored by nonacademic writers.

    (E) Before Milman Parry published his pioneering work in the early twentieth century, it was difficult to assign a date or an author to the Homeric poems.

9. According to the passage, the work of Simone Weil and Erich Auerbach on Homer was primarily concerned with which one of the following?

    (A) considerations of why criticism of Homer had moved to peripheral issues

    (B) analyses of the poetry itself in terms of its literary qualities

    (C) studies in the history and nature of oral poetry

    (D) analyses of the already ancient epic tradition inherited by Homer

    (E) critiques of the highly technical analyses of academic critics

GO ON TO THE NEXT PAGE.

10. The passage suggests which one of the following about scholarship on Homer that has appeared since 1970?

   (A) It has dealt extensively with the Homeric poems as literary art.
   (B) It is more incisive than the work of the Parrys.
   (C) It has rejected as irrelevant the scholarship produced by specialists between 1935 and 1970.
   (D) It has ignored the work of Simone Weil and Erich Auerbach.
   (E) It has attempted to confirm that the *Iliad* and the *Odyssey* were written by Homer.

11. The author of the passage most probably quotes Alexander Pope (lines 24–26) in order to

   (A) indicate that the Homeric poems have generally received poor treatment at the hands of English critics
   (B) prove that poets as well as critics have emphasized elements peripheral to the poems
   (C) illustrate that the nonpoetical emphasis also existed in an earlier century
   (D) emphasize the problems inherent in rendering classical Greek poetry into modern English
   (E) argue that poets and literary critics have seldom agreed about the interpretation of poetry

12. According to the passage, which one of the following is true of Milman Parry's immediate successors in the field of Homeric studies?

   (A) They reconciled Homer's poetry with archaeological and historical concerns.
   (B) They acknowledged the tradition of oral poetry, but focused on the uniqueness of Homer's poetry within the tradition.
   (C) They occupied themselves with the question of what qualities made for great poetry.
   (D) They emphasized the boundaries of oral poetry.
   (E) They called for a revival of Homer's popularity.

13. Which one of the following best describes the organization of the passage?

   (A) A situation is identified and its origins are examined.
   (B) A series of hypotheses is reviewed and one is advocated.
   (C) The works of two influential scholars are summarized.
   (D) Several issues contributing to a current debate are summarized.
   (E) Three possible solutions to a long-standing problem are posed.

GO ON TO THE NEXT PAGE.

Even in the midst of its resurgence as a vital tradition, many sociologists have viewed the current form of the powwow, a ceremonial gathering of native Americans, as a sign that tribal culture is in decline.
(5) Focusing on the dances and rituals that have recently come to be shared by most tribes, they suggest that an intertribal movement is now in ascension and claim the inevitable outcome of this tendency is the eventual dissolution of tribes and the complete assimilation of
(10) native Americans into Euroamerican society. Proponents of this "Pan-Indian" theory point to the greater frequency of travel and communication between reservations, the greater urbanization of native Americans, and, most recently, their increasing
(15) politicization in response to common grievances as the chief causes of the shift toward intertribalism.

Indeed, the rapid diffusion of dance styles, outfits, and songs from one reservation to another offers compelling evidence that intertribalism has been
(20) increasing. However, these sociologists have failed to note the concurrent revitalization of many traditions unique to individual tribes. Among the Lakota, for instance, the Sun Dance was revived, after a forty-year hiatus, during the 1950's. Similarly, the Black Legging
(25) Society of the Kiowa and the Hethuska Society of the Ponca—both traditional groups within their respective tribes—have gained new popularity. Obviously, a more complex societal shift is taking place than the theory of Pan-Indianism can account for.

(30) An examination of the theory's underpinnings may be critical at this point, especially given that native Americans themselves chafe most against the Pan-Indian classification. Like other assimilationist theories with which it is associated, the Pan-Indian view is
(35) predicated upon an a priori assumption about the nature of cultural contact: that upon contact minority societies immediately begin to succumb in every respect—biologically, linguistically, and culturally—to the majority society. However, there is no evidence
(40) that this is happening to native American groups.

Yet the fact remains that intertribal activities are a major facet of native American culture today. Certain dances at powwows, for instance, are announced as intertribal, other as traditional. Likewise, speeches
(45) given at the beginnings of powwows are often delivered in English, while the prayer that follows is usually spoken in a native language. Cultural borrowing is, of course, old news. What is important to note is the conscious distinction native Americans
(50) make between tribal and intertribal tendencies.

Tribalism, although greatly altered by modern history, remains a potent force among native Americans: It forms a basis for tribal identity, and aligns music and dance with other social and cultural
(55) activities important to individual tribes. Intertribal activities, on the other hand, reinforce native American identity along a broader front, where this identity is directly threatened by outside influences.

14. Which one of the following best summarizes the main idea of the passage?

(A) Despite the fact that sociologists have only recently begun to understand its importance, intertribalism has always been an influential factor in native American culture.

(B) Native Americans are currently struggling with an identity crisis caused primarily by the two competing forces of tribalism and intertribalism.

(C) The recent growth of intertribalism is unlikely to eliminate tribalism because the two forces do not oppose one another but instead reinforce distinct elements of native American identity.

(D) The tendency toward intertribalism, although prevalent within native American culture, has had a minimal effect on the way native Americans interact with the broader community around them.

(E) Despite the recent revival of many native American tribal traditions, the recent trend toward intertribalism is likely to erode cultural differences among the various native American tribes.

15. The author most likely states that "cultural borrowing is, of course, old news" (lines 47–48) primarily to

(A) acknowledge that in itself the existence of intertribal tendencies at powwows is unsurprising

(B) suggest that native Americans' use of English in powwows should be accepted as unavoidable

(C) argue that the deliberate distinction of intertribal and traditional dances is not a recent development

(D) suggest that the recent increase in intertribal activity is the result of native Americans borrowing from non-native American cultures

(E) indicate that the powwow itself could have originated by combining practices drawn from both native and non-native American cultures

16. The author of the passage would most likely agree with which one of the following assertions?

(A) Though some believe the current form of the powwow signals the decline of tribal culture, the powwow contains elements that indicate the continuing strength of tribalism.

(B) The logical outcome of the recent increase in intertribal activity is the eventual disappearance of tribal culture.

(C) Native Americans who participate in both tribal and intertribal activities usually base their identities on intertribal rather than tribal affiliations.

(D) The conclusions of some sociologists about the health of native American cultures show that these sociologists are in fact biased against such cultures.

(E) Until it is balanced by revitalization of tribal customs, intertribalism will continue to weaken the native American sense of identity.

GO ON TO THE NEXT PAGE.

17. The primary function of the third paragraph is to

    (A) search for evidence to corroborate the basic assumption of the theory of Pan-Indianism

    (B) demonstrate the incorrectness of the theory of Pan-Indianism by pointing out that native American groups themselves disagree with the theory

    (C) explain the origin of the theory of Pan-Indianism by showing how it evolved from other assimilationist theories

    (D) examine several assimilationist theories in order to demonstrate that they rest on a common assumption

    (E) criticize the theory of Pan-Indianism by pointing out that it rests upon an assumption for which there is no supporting evidence

18. Which one of the following most accurately describes the author's attitude toward the theory of Pan-Indianism?

    (A) critical of its tendency to attribute political motives to cultural practices

    (B) discomfort at its negative characterization of cultural borrowing by native Americans

    (C) hopeful about its chances for preserving tribal culture

    (D) offended by its claim that assimilation is a desirable consequence of cultural contact

    (E) skeptical that it is a complete explanation of recent changes in native American society

19. With which one of the following statements would the author of the passage be most likely to agree?

    (A) The resurgence of the powwow is a sign that native American customs are beginning to have an important influence on Euroamerican society.

    (B) Although native Americans draw conscious distinctions between tribal and intertribal activities, there is no difference in how the two types of activity actually function within the context of native American society.

    (C) Without intertribal activities, it would be more difficult for native Americans to maintain the cultural differences between native American and Euroamerican society.

    (D) The powwow was recently revived, after an extended hiatus, in order to strengthen native Americans' sense of ethnic identity.

    (E) The degree of urbanization, intertribal communication, and politicization among native Americans has been exaggerated by proponents of the theory of Pan-Indianism.

20. Which one of the following situations most clearly illustrates the phenomenon of intertribalism, as that phenomenon is described in the passage?

    (A) a native American tribe in which a number of powerful societies attempt to prevent the revival of a traditional dance

    (B) a native American tribe whose members attempt to learn the native languages of several other tribes

    (C) a native American tribe whose members attempt to form a political organization in order to redress several grievances important to that tribe

    (D) a native American tribe in which a significant percentage of the members have forsaken their tribal identity and become assimilated into Euroamerican society

    (E) a native American tribe whose members often travel to other parts of the reservation in order to visit friends and relatives

21. In the passage, the author is primarily concerned with doing which one of the following?

    (A) identifying an assumption common to various assimilationist theories and then criticizing these theories by showing this assumption to be false

    (B) arguing that the recent revival of a number of tribal practices shows sociologists are mistaken in believing intertribalism to be a potent force among native American societies

    (C) questioning the belief that native American societies will eventually be assimilated into Euroamerican society by arguing that intertribalism helps strengthen native American identity

    (D) showing how the recent resurgence of tribal activities is a deliberate attempt to counteract the growing influence of intertribalism

    (E) proposing an explanation of why the ascension of intertribalism could result in the eventual dissolution of tribes and complete assimilation of native American into Euroamerican society

GO ON TO THE NEXT PAGE.

Scientists typically advocate the analytic method of studying complex systems: systems are divided into component parts that are investigated separately. But nineteenth-century critics of this method claimed that

(5) when a system's parts are isolated its complexity tends to be lost. To address the perceived weaknesses of the analytic method these critics put forward a concept called organicism, which posited that the whole determines the nature of its parts and that the parts of a

(10) whole are interdependent.

Organicism depended upon the theory of internal relations, which states that relations between entities are possible only within some whole that embraces them, and that entities are altered by the relationships

(15) into which they enter. If an entity stands in a relationship with another entity, it has some property as a consequence. Without this relationship, and hence without the property, the entity would be different— and so would be another entity. Thus, the property is

(20) one of the entity's defining characteristics. Each of an entity's relationships likewise determines a defining characteristic of the entity.

One problem with the theory of internal relations is that not all properties of an entity are defining

(25) characteristics: numerous properties are accompanying characteristics—even if they are always present, their presence does not influence the entity's identity. Thus, even if it is admitted that every relationship into which an entity enters determines some characteristic of the

(30) entity, it is not necessarily true that such characteristics will define the entity; it is possible for the entity to enter into a relationship yet remain essentially unchanged.

The ultimate difficulty with the theory of internal

(35) relations is that it renders the acquisition of knowledge impossible. To truly know an entity, we must know all of its relationships; but because the entity is related to everything in each whole of which it is a part, these wholes must be known completely before the entity

(40) can be known. This seems to be a prerequisite impossible to satisfy.

Organicists' criticism of the analytic method arose from their failure to fully comprehend the method. In rejecting the analytic method, organicists overlooked

(45) the fact that before the proponents of the method analyzed the component parts of a system, they first determined both the laws applicable to the whole system and the initial conditions of the system; proponents of the method thus did not study parts of a

(50) system in full isolation from the system as a whole. Since organicists failed to recognize this, they never advanced any argument to show that laws and initial conditions of complex systems cannot be discovered. Hence, organicists offered no valid reason for rejecting

(55) the analytic method or for adopting organicism as a replacement for it.

22. Which one of the following most completely and accurately summarizes the argument of the passage?

(A) By calling into question the possibility that complex systems can be studied in their entirety, organicists offered an alternative to the analytic method favored by nineteenth-century scientists.

(B) Organicists did not offer a useful method of studying complex systems because they did not acknowledge that there are relationships into which an entity may enter that do not alter the entity's identity.

(C) Organicism is flawed because it relies on a theory that both ignores the fact that not all characteristics of entities are defining and ultimately makes the acquisition of knowledge impossible.

(D) Organicism does not offer a valid challenge to the analytic method both because it relies on faulty theory and because it is based on a misrepresentation of the analytic method.

(E) In criticizing the analytic method, organicists neglected to disprove that scientists who employ the method are able to discover the laws and initial conditions of the systems they study.

23. According to the passage, organicists' chief objection to the analytic method was that the method

(A) oversimplified systems by isolating their components

(B) assumed that a system can be divided into component parts

(C) ignored the laws applicable to the system as a whole

(D) claimed that the parts of a system are more important than the system as a whole

(E) denied the claim that entities enter into relationships

GO ON TO THE NEXT PAGE.

24. The passage offers information to help answer each of the following questions EXCEPT:

    (A) Why does the theory of internal relations appear to make the acquisition of knowledge impossible?

    (B) Why did the organicists propose replacing the analytic method?

    (C) What is the difference between a defining characteristic and an accompanying characteristic?

    (D) What did organicists claim are the effects of an entity's entering into a relationship with another entity?

    (E) What are some of the advantages of separating out the parts of a system for study?

25. The passage most strongly supports the ascription of which one of the following views to scientists who use the analytic method?

    (A) A complex system is best understood by studying its component parts in full isolation from the system as a whole.

    (B) The parts of a system should be studied with an awareness of the laws and initial conditions that govern the system.

    (C) It is not possible to determine the laws governing a system until the system's parts are separated from one another.

    (D) Because the parts of a system are interdependent, they cannot be studied separately without destroying the system's complexity.

    (E) Studying the parts of a system individually eliminates the need to determine which characteristics of the parts are defining characteristics.

26. Which one of the following is a principle upon which the author bases an argument against the theory of internal relations?

    (A) An adequate theory of complex systems must define the entities of which the system is composed.

    (B) An acceptable theory cannot have consequences that contradict its basic purpose.

    (C) An adequate method of study of complex systems should reveal the actual complexity of the systems it studies.

    (D) An acceptable theory must describe the laws and initial conditions of a complex system.

    (E) An acceptable method of studying complex systems should not study parts of the system in isolation from the system as a whole.

S T O P

IF YOU FINISH BEFORE TIME IS CALLED, YOU MAY CHECK YOUR WORK ON THIS SECTION ONLY.
DO NOT WORK ON ANY OTHER SECTION IN THE TEST.

Answer Key

1. D
2. B
3. A
4. D
5. B
6. C
7. D
8. C
9. B
10. A
11. C
12. D
13. A
14. C
15. A
16. A
17. E
18. E
19. C
20. B
21. C
22. D
23. A
24. E
25. B
26. B

KAPLAN

Reading Comprehension 12

PrepTest February 1997, Section II

SECTION II

Time—35 minutes

27 Questions

Directions: Each passage in this section is followed by a group of questions to be answered on the basis of what is <u>stated</u> or <u>implied</u> in the passage. For some of the questions, more than one of the choices could conceivably answer the question. However, you are to choose the <u>best</u> answer; that is, the response that most accurately and completely answers the question, and blacken the corresponding space on your answer sheet.

Historian Philippe Ariès claimed that in medieval Europe childhood was not viewed as a distinct period in human development, with a special character and needs. His argument for this
(5) thesis relied heavily on medieval text illustrations, which distinguish children from adults principally by their stature, rather than by a distinctively childlike appearance: the children look like miniature adults. Ariès also suggested that high
(10) infant mortality rates in the Middle Ages induced indifference toward offspring as a defense mechanism against establishing close ties with infants unlikely to survive. Shulamith Shahar's recent research challenges this established
(15) conception of the medieval view of childhood.

Shahar has had to work hard to find evidence to support her interpretation of the medieval conception of childhood, since works that reveal parents' personal attitudes, such as Giovanni
(20) Morelli's journal, are exceptional. Shahar makes intelligent use of medical writing and theological works. Particularly illuminating are medieval accounts of saints' lives, which despite their emphasis on personal piety reveal much concerning
(25) their subjects' childhoods and which provide evidence of parental concern for children. Even more significant are accounts of saints' miracles involving the healing of sick infants and the blessing of young couples with children.
(30) Shahar also discusses the period in childhood from ages 7 to 11 when boys of the wealthier classes were placed in monasteries or as apprentices in the household of a "master" of a trade. To some this custom might imply a perception of childhood
(35) insufficiently distinguished from adulthood, or even indifference to children, evidenced by the willingness to send young children away from home. Shahar points out, however, that training was in stages, and children were not expected to live as
(40) adults or to assume all the tasks of maturity at once. Furthermore, Shahar quotes a telling number of instances in which parents of apprentices sued masters for maltreatment of their children. Shahar concludes that parents placed their children in
(45) monasteries or as apprentices not to be rid of them, but because it was a social norm to ensure one's children a future niche in society.

Shahar's work is highly persuasive, but as a rebuttal to Ariès, it is uncomfortably incomplete.
(50) Shahar succeeds in demonstrating that people in

the Middle Ages did view childhood as a definite stage in human development and that they were not indifferent toward their children. But central to Ariès' position was the contention that the family as
(55) a powerful and private institution organized around children is a relatively modern ideal, whose origins Ariès related to the growing influence of the middle classes in the postmedieval period. Ariès felt that this implied something novel about the
(60) development of perceptions of childhood and of the family. Shahar does not comment on these larger issues.

1. The passage is primarily concerned with

   (A) criticizing and dismissing a traditional theory
   (B) describing and evaluating recent research
   (C) reconciling two explanations for the same phenomenon
   (D) refuting a recent hypothesis
   (E) summarizing information about an unusual phenomenon

2. The passage supports which one of the following statements about the treatment of childhood in medieval documents?

   (A) Medieval accounts of childhood tend to emphasize the piety of their subjects.
   (B) Medieval accounts of saints' lives focus on stories of miracles rather than on the childhood of their subjects.
   (C) Medical and theological writings provide scant evidence of parental concern for children.
   (D) In medieval text illustrations, children were distinguished from adults by their appearance rather than by their stature.
   (E) In medieval text illustrations, children were not depicted with childlike features.

GO ON TO THE NEXT PAGE.

3. Which one of the following best describes the function of the first paragraph of the passage?

   (A) It presents important evidence that a traditional theory has failed to take into account.

   (B) It describes the historical sources that have been the focus of a recent debate.

   (C) It describes an argument that will be challenged by evidence provided in the passage.

   (D) It describes a puzzling historical phenomenon that will be accounted for in the passage.

   (E) It summarizes important information about the historical period that is discussed in the passage.

4. In the third paragraph, the author mentions the period in childhood from ages 7 to 11 most likely in order to

   (A) compare perceptions of childhood in the Middle Ages with perceptions of childhood in the postmedieval period

   (B) suggest that Shahar was unaware of important social norms in medieval communities

   (C) show how Shahar supports her argument about the conception of childhood in the Middle Ages

   (D) suggest that class and gender had important effects on the way in which children were treated in the Middle Ages

   (E) point out the differences between medieval and modern conceptions of children's role in the family

5. Which one of the following, if true, would provide the LEAST support for Shahar's arguments as they are described in the passage?

   (A) Medieval documents contain stories of children, seemingly stillborn, who were miraculously restored to life by the intercession of saints.

   (B) The children of peasants remained at home in the later stages of childhood, gradually taking on more serious tasks until the time came for marriage.

   (C) Impoverished parents left their children at foundling hospitals because they were confident that their children would be better cared for there than they would have been at home.

   (D) The details of the saints' childhoods in the accounts of saints' lives were invented by medieval writers and did not reflect the attitudes of parents in the Middle Ages.

   (E) Parents in the wealthier classes who did not place their children as apprentices were criticized for not providing their children with a secure future.

6. It can be inferred from the passage that Ariès would be likely to agree with all of the following statements EXCEPT:

   (A) Parents in the Middle Ages felt indifferent toward their children.

   (B) Conceptions of childhood and the family changed in the postmedieval period as a result of the growing influence of the middle classes.

   (C) The ideal of the family as a powerful and private institution developed in the Middle Ages.

   (D) People in the Middle Ages viewed their children as miniature adults.

   (E) The family in the Middle Ages was not organized around the children.

7. Shahar's work as it is described in the passage does NOT provide an answer to which one of the following questions?

   (A) Did parents feel affection for their children in spite of the fact that many infants were unlikely to survive?

   (B) How did social norms influence parents' decisions about their children's futures?

   (C) How did the changing perception of the family in the Middle Ages affect the perception of childhood?

   (D) Were parents concerned about their children when they reached the ages of 7 to 11?

   (E) Did parents in the Middle Ages view childhood as a distinct stage in human development?

8. The author would most likely agree with which one of the following statements about Shahar's research in relation to Ariès' theories about childhood in the Middle Ages?

   (A) Shahar's research challenges some of Ariès' arguments, but it does not refute his central position.

   (B) Shahar's research is provocative, but it does not add anything to Ariès' arguments.

   (C) Shahar's research effectively refutes Ariès' central position and presents a new interpretation of childhood and the family in the Middle Ages.

   (D) Shahar's research confirms some of Ariès' arguments but casts doubt on other of Ariès' arguments.

   (E) Shahar's research is highly informative and provides more information about infant mortality rates during the Middle Ages than did Ariès' work.

GO ON TO THE NEXT PAGE.

Increases in the amount of carbon dioxide (CO_2) and other trace gases in the Earth's atmosphere can contribute to what has been called greenhouse warming, because those compounds allow the Sun's
(5) energy to reach the surface of the Earth, thereby warming it, but prevent much of that energy from being reradiated to outer space. Measuring devices set up at several locations around the world have revealed a 20 percent increase in atmospheric CO_2
(10) over the course of the past century—from 290 parts per million in 1880 to 352 parts per million in 1989. Several studies agree that it is plausible that the CO_2 content of the atmosphere may well double from its 1880 level by around the middle of the
(15) twenty-first century.

To project how much the global temperature will increase in response to a doubling of atmospheric CO_2 should be simple: since the CO_2 content has increased by about 20 percent over the past century,
(20) we should be able to observe the increases in global temperature during the same period and base future projections on that data. The prevailing view is that the climatic record over the past century for the entire globe reveals a net increase in
(25) temperature ranging from 0.5 to 1.0 degree Fahrenheit (approximately 0.25 to 0.5 degrees Celsius). But set against this conclusion is the fact that data gathered over the past century in North America, where observations are numerous and
(30) accurate, does not confirm such an increase. And even if the temperature rise is real, another puzzle remains: is the rise in global temperatures a natural fluctuation or a result of the increase in greenhouse gases?
(35) Because of inconclusive data and the complexity of the problem, some scientists predict an increase as small as two degrees Fahrenheit (one degree Celsius) in the average global temperature over the next half century, whereas others predict increases
(40) of up to nine degrees Fahrenheit (five degrees Celsius). It makes a great difference whether the actual increase is at the low or high end of this range. Although human beings are probably resilient enough to adapt to the effects of an
(45) increase of approximately two degrees Fahrenheit (one degree Celsius), an increase of nine degrees Fahrenheit (five degrees Celsius) is believed to be the difference in temperature that separates the end of the last great ice age, 12,000 years ago, from
(50) the present.

In light of such uncertainty, the wisest policy is not to forestall action. Steps that make sense for economic or environmental reasons besides greenhouse warming, such as replacing fossil-fuel
(55) energy with solar energy, could be taken first, whether or not climate warming is taking place. Then, as scientific knowledge grows and uncertainties are reduced, more costly measures could be taken, if warranted, hence closely tying
(60) policy decisions to the latest information available. Scientists and others have aptly called this type of action a "no regrets" policy.

9. Which one of the following statements best expresses the main idea of the passage?

(A) Approaching the problem of greenhouse warming with a "no regrets" policy encourages government agencies to implement affordable but most likely ineffective measures.

(B) Inconclusive data concerning the rise in global temperature over the next half century suggests that politicians should wait until all uncertainties are resolved before taking action.

(C) Costly measures must be taken soon to prevent further increases in greenhouse gases and thus a dangerous rise in global temperatures.

(D) Given the lack of agreement about the effects of greenhouse gases on global temperature, the best policy is to implement sensible measures now and respond to new scientific knowledge as it appears.

(E) Scientists would be able to provide a more accurate estimate of the probable effects of greenhouse warming over the next half century if politicians took steps now to eliminate other environmental problems that contribute to global warming.

10. The passage suggests that a rise in global temperature over the next half century, if it occurs, could result from

(A) a natural climatic variation
(B) an increase in solar reradiation
(C) a 20 percent decrease in atmospheric CO_2 from current levels
(D) a decrease in trace gases in the atmosphere
(E) the replacement of fossil-fuel energy with solar energy

11. Which one of the following best describes the organization of the passage?

(A) A scientific problem is described, discrepancies among proposed solutions to it are evaluated, and a course of action is recommended.

(B) A scientific dispute is discussed and the case for one side is made, taking into account its political repercussions.

(C) A phenomenon is described, different views of its effects are presented, and a policy taking into account these differences is proposed.

(D) A solution to a scientific puzzle is advanced and its implications for action are discussed.

(E) A generally accepted scientific formula is explained in order to introduce a detailed examination of a case that violates the principle.

GO ON TO THE NEXT PAGE.

12. The author refers to the meteorological data gathered in North America over the past century in order to

    (A) show how differing views on the extent of the rise in global temperature can be resolved

    (B) argue that any warming detected over the past century has most likely been the result of a natural climatic fluctuation

    (C) argue against the prevailing view that the amount of atmospheric CO_2 has increased by about 20 percent over the past century

    (D) suggest that there should be more numerous and accurate observation points outside of North America

    (E) present evidence that casts doubt on the view that global temperature has increased over the past century

13. It can be inferred that the author of the passage would most likely agree with which one of the following statements about a response to global warming?

    (A) The most effective measures that could be undertaken to reverse greenhouse warming are not necessarily the most costly.

    (B) Costly measures necessary to combat greenhouse warming should be undertaken only when the rise in temperature begins to exceed human beings' capacity to adapt to such an increase.

    (C) Given the current state of knowledge about greenhouse warming, less costly measures should be implemented before expensive measures are tried.

    (D) Scientists' uncertainty about the effect of greenhouse warming on global temperature might be resolved more quickly if a "no regrets" policy were embraced.

    (E) Any measure intended to reduce greenhouse warming should be implemented only if it also addresses other environmental problems.

14. Which one of the following is most analogous to the course of action recommended in the last paragraph?

    (A) In response to uncertain predictions regarding the likelihood that an asteroid will collide with Earth, the government has decided to fund an inexpensive but scientifically valuable program to track asteroids and to determine whether more costly measures are warranted.

    (B) Although scientists have not pinpointed how a newly discovered disease is spread, the government has implemented a preventive health program to combat the disease by preventing any likely means by which the disease might be communicated.

    (C) In light of uncertain estimates about the remaining amount of fossil-fuel energy on the Earth, the government has set up a costly program to convert all industrial machinery to run on less expensive alternative fuels.

    (D) Faced with many discrepant predictions about the depletion of the Earth's ozone layer, the government has decided to adapt the preventive measures suggested by the scientific group that predicted the most rapid depletion.

    (E) In response to scientific predictions that a disastrous earthquake is highly probable in a certain region, the government has added new requirements to building codes that require relatively inexpensive modifications of existing structures.

GO ON TO THE NEXT PAGE.

There are two especially influential interpretations of nineteenth-century British feminists' opposition to efforts to restrict women's hours of work: that of liberal legal historians on the

(5) one hand and that of labor historians on the other. For legal historians, the nineteenth century was an "age of collectivism," in which an emphasis on welfare replaced the emphasis on individual rights, and the state came to be seen as a protector of its

(10) inhabitants rather than as a "referee" among citizens. Women and children were the first beneficiaries of maximum-hours restrictions that would eventually spread to men as well. British feminists, according to these scholars, could not

(15) afford to seem to favor these "special" laws for women because their single-minded campaign for women's suffrage relied so heavily on arguments derived from eighteenth-century theories of individual rights and equality. Most labor historians,

(20) on the other hand, explain the feminist opposition to protective laws as coming from middle-class women who blindly ignored the injustices against which such laws' supporters struggled continuously. Labor historians attack the feminists for having a

(25) selfish ideology, one that asked that privileged women be allowed to enjoy equal treatment with privileged men, but not that the economic bases of social relations be rethought.

Recently, however, feminist historians have

(30) begun to uncover plentiful reasons for feminist mistrust of government and trade-union efforts to protect women. Their studies of women's trade unions reveal, as the earlier histories did not, the tensions between women and men within the

(35) trade-union movement. They document that male-dominated trade unions often supported, and sometimes even sponsored, protective labor legislation aimed at forcibly excluding women from wage labor, either in order to maintain a husband's

(40) right to his wife's unpaid labor in the home or to preserve jobs for men. Such gender conflicts were complicated, as other feminist scholars have demonstrated, by self-interested government policies that alternately enticed women into jobs in

(45) order to end labor shortages or pushed them out to provide jobs for men. Finally, the studies show that state labor policy toward women was always deeply influenced by a desire to control female morality and to influence child-bearing decisions.

(50) Whether protective labor legislation for women is just or expedient is still in dispute today, and legal scholars disagree on what criteria to use to evaluate such laws. The labor historians' class-based analyses are no more fully adequate than the liberal legal

(55) historians' benign evolutionary depictions. Feminist historians have a major contribution to make to both the reconstruction of the historical record dealing with women and labor legislation and to broader theories of law as an instrument of social

(60) control and of social change.

15. It can be inferred from the passage that by "age of collectivism" (line 7) the author means a period in which

(A) coalitions among various social classes began to be established in order to promote common legislative goals

(B) legislators began to treat workers as members of a social class rather than as individuals when drafting labor legislation

(C) the competing interests of the various social classes were commonly harmonized by subordinating them to the needs of the state

(D) only needs and goals common to all classes in society became part of society's legislative agenda

(E) the state's role as active promoter of social welfare took precedence over its role as guarantor of individual liberties

16. The passage suggests that histories of nineteenth-century British protective labor laws written by liberal legal historians would be most likely to differ from those written by labor historians in which one of the following ways?

(A) The former would represent such laws as the gradual outgrowth of a general shift in societal ideas; the latter would represent such laws as hard-won reforms that were resisted by powerful elites.

(B) The former would analyze the philosophical underpinnings of arguments in favor of such laws; the latter would dismiss the practical consequences of such laws for those who espoused them.

(C) The former would approve of the motives of feminists who opposed such laws; the latter would refuse to consider seriously the ideology of such feminists.

(D) The former would dispute the existence of inequities in nineteenth-century British society; the latter would examine the historical record carefully in order to highlight such injustices.

(E) The former would portray the effects of such laws as overwhelmingly beneficial; the latter would treat such laws somewhat unsympathetically because of the laws' negative impact on many workers.

GO ON TO THE NEXT PAGE.

17. It can be inferred from the passage that feminist historians believe that one inadequacy of most labor historians' studies of nineteenth-century feminist opposition to protective labor legislation for women was that the studies

   (A) minimized the contribution of enlightened members of the middle class to the passage of such laws

   (B) ignored the philosophical shift in women's perceptions of the state's role that preceded these laws

   (C) overlooked the disadvantages such laws may have presented for nineteenth-century working-class women

   (D) misread the degree to which nineteenth-century feminists focused exclusively on obtaining the vote

   (E) underestimated the potential benefits working-class women would have derived from political equality with men

18. The author implies that liberal legal historians believe that British feminists withheld support from laws restricting women's working hours for which one of the following reasons?

   (A) The feminists felt that society would not benefit from such laws until such laws were drafted to include everyone who worked.

   (B) The feminists feared such support would undermine their arguments in favor of women's suffrage.

   (C) The feminists were unaware of the contributions such laws could make to improving the quality of life of women workers.

   (D) The feminists believed that the enfranchisement of women was the quickest way to prevent the exploitation of women workers.

   (E) The feminists feared that special laws for women, however beneficial, would be a prelude to other laws that restricted women's rights.

19. The author's characterization of the views of labor historians as "class-based" (line 53) most strongly suggests that such historians

   (A) dismissed philosophical arguments deriving from concepts of individual liberty that ignore class

   (B) tended to limit their arguments to those that can be used to promote the interests of the working classes

   (C) were willing to equate gender and class by according women the status of a separate class within society

   (D) relied on historical explanations that depend on the supposed class allegiance of various individuals and groups

   (E) asserted that an unjust political and economic system was responsible for the oppression suffered by the working classes

20. According to the passage, studies by feminist historians suggest that British feminists opposed both nineteenth-century protective labor laws for women and government labor policies primarily for which one of the following reasons?

   (A) Feminist support for such laws and policies could be construed as evidence of philosophical inconsistency, given feminist arguments in favor of women's suffrage.

   (B) Such laws and policies were often intended primarily to promote the interests of male workers or the British government rather than the interests of women workers.

   (C) Women trade unionists actively solicited feminist support in the campaign against such laws and policies because they could find few allies among male trade unionists.

   (D) The potential impact of such laws and policies on women workers had not been recognized by legislators, who, according to feminists, should instead have focused on promoting women's well-being by enfranchising them.

   (E) Male trade unionists, who had previously earned feminist hostility by ignoring the demands of women trade unionists and excluding them from decision-making, favored such laws and policies.

GO ON TO THE NEXT PAGE.

Richard L. Jackson's most recent book, *Black Writers in Latin America*, continues the task of his previous project, *The Black Image in Latin American Literature*. But whereas the earlier work examined
(5) ethnic themes in the writings of both black and non-black authors, the new study examines only black writers living in Latin America (that is, African Hispanic writers). Consequently, there is a shift in emphasis. While the earlier book studied
(10) various attitudes toward black people in Latin America as revealed in a wide range of literature, the later work examines the black representation of black consciousness in Spanish American literature from the early nineteenth century to the present.
(15) In *Black Writers in Latin America*, Jackson states that "personal identification with blackness and personal experience with the black experience have a great deal to do with a black writer's choice of words, symbols, and images." He goes on to argue
(20) that only black writers have the necessary insight and mastery of the appropriate techniques to depict their situation authentically. In this regard, Jackson joins a number of other North American critics who tend to conceptualize African Hispanic literature as
(25) culturally autonomous, with its own style and themes deriving primarily from the experience of oppression in African Hispanic history. Critics influenced by the Latin American ideal of racial blending, on the other hand, believe that black and
(30) non-black writers share the same cultural context and that, given comparable talent, both are equally equipped to overcome their ethnocentrism. Although Jackson clearly embraces the North American perspective, he does concede in his
(35) introduction that most African Hispanic writers espouse integration rather than separatism.
At times Jackson's own analysis reveals the problems inherent in using ethnicity as the primary basis for critical judgment: the textual evidence he
(40) cites sometimes subverts the intent to find common tendencies among all writers of a particular racial group. For example, in his chapter on Nicolás Guillén, Jackson attempts to dissociate the black Cuban poet from the Negrista movement, claiming
(45) that "rather than associate Guillén with poetic Negrism, we should see his dramatic conversion to blackness in the late 1920s and early 1930s as a reaction against this white literary fad that was sweeping the world." Admittedly, several of
(50) Guillén's poems from the 1920s show an awareness of social ills like poverty, unemployment, and racial discrimination that is absent from the work of peers influenced by the Negrista movement. But it is difficult to argue that Guillén's portraits of black
(55) people in poems from the early 1930s such as "Canto negro" and "Rumba" are more authentic and less superficial than those in Luis Palés Matos's "Danza negra" or Emilio Ballagas's "Elegía de María Belén Chacón." This effort to distance
(60) Guillén from his Hispanic colleagues thus fails, given the very texts Jackson uses to demonstrate his points.

21. According to the passage, which one of the following is true of Jackson's earlier study of African Hispanic literature?

(A) It discusses the black experience as it is revealed in the works of African Hispanic writers exclusively.

(B) It considers diverse views about black people found in the works of both black and non-black writers.

(C) It examines the representation of black identity in almost two centuries of Spanish American literature.

(D) It focuses on the North American conception of African Hispanic literature.

(E) It emphasizes themes of integration in the works of both black and non-black writers.

22. Which one of the following, if true, would most seriously undermine Jackson's use of ethnicity as a basis for critical judgment of African Hispanic literature?

(A) Several nineteenth-century authors whose novels Jackson presents as reflecting the black experience in Latin America have been discovered to have lived in the United States before moving to Central America.

(B) Luis Palés Matos, Emilio Ballagas, and several other Hispanic poets of the Negrista movement have been shown to have plagiarized the work of African Hispanic poets.

(C) It has been discovered that African Hispanic authors in Latin America over the last two centuries usually developed as writers by reading and imitating the works of other black writers.

(D) A significant number of poems and novels in which early-twentieth-century Hispanic writers consider racial integration have been discovered.

(E) Several poems that are presented by Jackson as authentic portraits of the black experience have been discovered to be misattributed to black poets and can instead be traced to non-black poets.

23. Which one of the following best describes the organization of the second paragraph?

(A) A point of view is described and then placed in context by being compared with an opposing view.

(B) A point of view is stated, and contradictory examples are cited to invalidate it.

(C) A point of view is explained, related to the views of others, and then dismissed as untenable.

(D) A point of view is cited and, through a comparison with another view, is shown to depend on a faulty assumption.

(E) A point of view is put forward, shown to lack historical perspective, and then juxtaposed with another view.

GO ON TO THE NEXT PAGE.

24. According to the passage, which one of the following is true of some of Nicolás Guillén's poems from the 1920s?

   (A) They contain depictions of black people that are less realistic than those in the works of non-black poets.

   (B) They show greater attention to certain social ills than do poems by his contemporaries.

   (C) They demonstrate that Guillén was a leading force in the founding of the Negrista movement.

   (D) They are based on Guillén's own experience with racial discrimination, poverty, and unemployment.

   (E) They served as stylistic and thematic models for poems by Luis Palés Matos and Emilio Ballagas.

25. It can be inferred that the author of the passage would most likely agree with which one of the following statements concerning an author's capacity to depict the African Hispanic experience?

   (A) Validating only the representations of African Hispanic consciousness found in works written by black writers is a flawed approach because many of the most convincing portraits of any racial group are produced by outsiders.

   (B) African Hispanic writers, because of their personal experience with African Hispanic culture, are uniquely capable of depicting authentic black characters and experiences.

   (C) While seeking an authentic representation of the African Hispanic experience in the works of black writers may provide valuable insights, it is fallacious to attribute authenticity solely on the basis of the race of the author.

   (D) Although both black and non-black writers are equally capable of representing the African Hispanic experience, their contributions to African Hispanic literature should be considered separately.

   (E) The styles and themes relating to the African Hispanic experience that are found in writings by black authors should serve as the models by which writings by non-black authors are judged for their authenticity.

26. Which one of the following approaches to a study of Hungarian identity in painting is most analogous to the North American approach to African Hispanic literature?

   (A) Paintings by ethnic Hungarians and by foreigners living in Hungary should comprise the major focus of the study.

   (B) Paintings by ethnic Hungarians and the aspects of those paintings that make their style unique should provide the central basis for the study.

   (C) Paintings by Hungarians and non-Hungarians that are most popular with the Hungarian people should comprise the central basis for the study.

   (D) The central focus of the study should be to find ways in which ethnic Hungarian painters conform to worldwide artistic movements in their works.

   (E) The most important theme in the study should be how paintings created by ethnic Hungarians express universal human concerns.

27. Which one of the following statements best expresses the main idea of the passage?

   (A) A central feature of Jackson's approach to African Hispanic literature, shared by some other critics, can be shown to have significant weaknesses.

   (B) Jackson's reliance on the Latin American perspective of racial blending and integration in his analysis of African Hispanic literature leads him to make at least one flawed argument.

   (C) The African Hispanic authors, poets, and texts that Jackson chooses to analyze in his most recent book are unrepresentative of Spanish American literature and thus lead him to faulty conclusions.

   (D) Jackson's emphasis on black writers' contributions to African Hispanic literature in his latest book undercuts the assumptions underlying his own previous work on Spanish American literature.

   (E) Jackson's treatment of Guillén reveals a misplaced effort to integrate African Hispanic writers into worldwide literary movements.

S T O P

IF YOU FINISH BEFORE TIME IS CALLED, YOU MAY CHECK YOUR WORK ON THIS SECTION ONLY.
DO NOT WORK ON ANY OTHER SECTION IN THE TEST.

Answer Key

1. B
2. E
3. C
4. C
5. D
6. C
7. C
8. A
9. D
10. A
11. C
12. E
13. C
14. A
15. E
16. A
17. C
18. B
19. D
20. B
21. B
22. E
23. A
24. B
25. C
26. B
27. A

Reading Comprehension 13

PrepTest 19, Section III
June 1996

Reading Comprehension 13

SECTION III

Time—35 minutes

27 Questions

<u>Directions:</u> Each passage in this section is followed by a group of questions to be answered on the basis of what is <u>stated</u> or <u>implied</u> in the passage. For some of the questions, more than one of the choices could conceivably answer the question. However, you are to choose the <u>best</u> answer; that is, the response that most accurately and completely answers the question, and blacken the corresponding space on your answer sheet.

Wherever the crime novels of P. D. James are discussed by critics, there is a tendency on the one hand to exaggerate her merits and on the other to castigate her as a genre writer who is getting above
(5) herself. Perhaps underlying the debate is that familiar, false opposition set up between different kinds of fiction, according to which enjoyable novels are held to be somehow slightly lowbrow, and a novel is not considered true literature unless it is a tiny bit dull.
(10) Those commentators who would elevate James's books to the status of high literature point to her painstakingly constructed characters, her elaborate settings, her sense of place, and her love of abstractions: notions about morality, duty, pain, and
(15) pleasure are never far from the lips of her police officers and murderers. Others find her pretentious and tiresome; an inverted snobbery accuses her of abandoning the time-honored conventions of the detective genre in favor of a highbrow literary style.
(20) The critic Harriet Waugh wants P. D. James to get on with "the more taxing business of laying a tricky trail and then fooling the reader"; Philip Oakes in *The Literary Review* groans, "Could we please proceed with the business of clapping the handcuffs on the
(25) killer?"
James is certainly capable of strikingly good writing. She takes immense trouble to provide her characters with convincing histories and passions. Her descriptive digressions are part of the pleasure of her
(30) books and give them dignity and weight. But it is equally true that they frequently interfere with the story; the patinas and aromas of a country kitchen receive more loving attention than does the plot itself. Her devices to advance the story can be shameless and
(35) thin, and it is often impossible to see how her detective arrives at the truth; one is left to conclude that the detective solves crimes through intuition. At this stage in her career P. D. James seems to be less interested in the specifics of detection than in her characters'
(40) vulnerabilities and perplexities.
However, once the rules of a chosen genre cramp creative thought, there is no reason why an able and interesting writer should accept them. In her latest book, there are signs that James is beginning to feel
(45) constrained by the crime-novel genre. Here her determination to leave areas of ambiguity in the solution of the crime and to distribute guilt among the murderer, victim, and bystanders points to a conscious rebellion against the traditional neatness of detective
(50) fiction. It is fashionable, though reprehensible, for one

writer to prescribe to another. But perhaps the time has come for P. D. James to slide out of her handcuffs and stride into the territory of the mainstream novel.

1. Which one of the following best states the author's main conclusion?

    (A) Because P. D. James's potential as a writer is stifled by her chosen genre, she should turn her talents toward writing mainstream novels.

    (B) Because the requirements of the popular novel are incompatible with true creative expression, P. D. James's promise as a serious author has been diminished.

    (C) The dichotomy between popular and sophisticated literature is well illustrated in the crime novels of P. D. James.

    (D) The critics who have condemned P. D. James's lack of attention to the specifics of detection fail to take into account her carefully constructed plots.

    (E) Although her plots are not always neatly resolved, the beauty of her descriptive passages justifies P. D. James's decision to write in the crime-novel genre.

2. The author refers to the "patinas and aromas of a country kitchen" (line 32) most probably in order to

    (A) illustrate James's gift for innovative phrasing
    (B) highlight James's interest in rural society
    (C) allow the reader to experience the pleasure of James's books
    (D) explain how James typically constructs her plots
    (E) exemplify James's preoccupation with descriptive writing

GO ON TO THE NEXT PAGE.

LSAT ADVANCED STUDENTS: THIS SECTION IS ADMINISTERED AT AN IN-CLASS WORKSHOP. DO NOT USE THIS SECTION FOR PRACTICE.

Reading Comprehension 13

3. The second paragraph serves primarily to

   (A) propose an alternative to two extreme opinions described earlier
   (B) present previously mentioned positions in greater detail
   (C) contradict an assertion cited previously
   (D) introduce a controversial interpretation
   (E) analyze a dilemma in greater depth

4. The passage supports which one of the following statements about detective fiction?

   (A) There are as many different detective-novel conventions as there are writers of crime novels.
   (B) Detective fiction has been characterized by extremely high literary quality.
   (C) Detective fiction has been largely ignored by literary critics.
   (D) There is very little agreement among critics about the basic elements of a typical detective novel.
   (E) Writers of detective fiction have customarily followed certain conventions in constructing their novels.

5. The passage suggests that both Waugh and Oakes consider James's novels to have

   (A) too much material that is extraneous to the solution of the crime
   (B) too little characterization to enable the reader to solve the crime
   (C) too few suspects to generate suspense
   (D) too simple a plot to hold the attention of the reader
   (E) too convoluted a plot for the reader to understand

6. It can be inferred from the passage that, in the author's view, traditional detective fiction is characterized by

   (A) concern for the weaknesses and doubts of the characters
   (B) transparent devices to advance the plot
   (C) the attribution of intuition to the detective
   (D) the straightforward assignment of culpability for the crime
   (E) attention to the concepts of morality and responsibility

7. The author characterizes the position of some critics as "inverted snobbery" (line 17) because they hold which one of the following views?

   (A) Critics of literature must acknowledge that they are less talented than creators of literature.
   (B) Critics should hesitate to disparage popular authors.
   (C) P. D. James's novels should focus less on characters from the English landed gentry.
   (D) Detective fiction should be content to remain an unambitious literary genre.
   (E) P. D. James should be less fastidious about portraying violence.

8. Which one of the following quotations about literature best exemplifies the "familiar" attitude mentioned in lines 5–9?

   (A) "The fantasy and whimsy characteristic of this writer's novels qualify them as truly great works of literature."
   (B) "The greatest work of early English literature happens to be a highly humorous collection of tales."
   (C) "A truly great work of literature should place demands upon its readers, rather than divert them."
   (D) "Although many critics are condescending about best-selling novels, I would not wish to challenge the opinion of millions of readers."
   (E) "A novel need only satisfy the requirements of its particular genre to be considered a true work of literature."

GO ON TO THE NEXT PAGE.

Reading Comprehension 13

Many Native Americans view the archaeological excavation and museum display of ancestral skeletal remains and items buried with them as a spiritual desecration. A number of legal remedies that either
(5) prohibit or regulate such activities may be available to Native American communities, if they can establish standing in such cases. In disinterment cases, courts have traditionally affirmed the standing of three classes of plaintiffs: the deceased's heirs, the owner of the
(10) property on which the grave is located, and parties, including organizations or distant relatives of the deceased, that have a clear interest in the preservation of a particular grave. If an archaeologically discovered grave is of recent historical origin and associated with
(15) an identifiable Native American community, Native Americans are likely to establish standing in a suit to prevent disinterment of the remains, but in cases where the grave is ancient and located in an area where the community of Native Americans associated with the
(20) grave has not recently lived, they are less likely to be successful in this regard. Indeed, in most cases involving ancient graves, to recognize that Native Americans have standing would represent a significant expansion of common law. In cases where standing can
(25) be achieved, however, common law may provide a basis for some Native American claims against archaeologists and museums.

Property law, for example, can be useful in establishing Native American claims to artifacts that
(30) are retrieved in the excavation of ancient graves and can be considered the communal property of Native American tribes or communities. In *Charrier* v. *Bell*, a United States appellate court ruled that the common law doctrine of abandonment, which allows the finder
(35) of abandoned property to claim ownership, does not apply to objects buried with the deceased. The court ruled that the practice of burying items with the body of the deceased "is not intended as a means of relinquishing ownership to a stranger," and that to
(40) interpret it as such "would render a grave subject to despoliation either immediately after interment or … after removal of the descendants of the deceased from the neighborhood of the cemetery." This ruling suggests that artifacts excavated from Native American
(45) ancestral graves should be returned to representatives of tribal groups who can establish standing in such cases.

More generally, United States courts have upheld the distinction between individual and communal
(50) property, holding that an individual Native American does not have title to communal property owned and held for common use by his or her tribe. As a result, museums cannot assume that they have valid title to cultural property merely because they purchased in
(55) good faith an item that was originally sold in good faith by an individual member of a Native American community.

9. The primary purpose of the passage is to provide an answer to which on of the following questions?

(A) How should the legal protection of Native American burial grounds be enhanced?

(B) What characteristics of Native American burial grounds enhance their chances for protection by the law?

(C) In what ways does the law protect the rights of Native Americans in regard to the contents of ancestral graves?

(D) Why are the courts concerned with protecting Native American burial grounds from desecration?

(E) By what means can Native Americans establish their rights to land on which their ancestors are buried?

10. It can be inferred that a court would be most likely to deny standing in a disinterment case to which one of the following Native American plaintiffs?

(A) one who seeks, as one of several beneficiaries of his father's estate, to protect the father's burial site

(B) one who seeks to prevent tenants on her land from taking artifacts from a grave located on the property

(C) one who represents a tribe whose members hope to prevent the disinterment of remains from a distant location from which the tribe recently moved

(D) one who seeks to have artifacts that have been removed from a grave determined to be that of her second cousin returned to the grave

(E) one who seeks the return of artifacts taken from the ancient burial grounds of disparate tribes and now displayed in a museum

GO ON TO THE NEXT PAGE.

LSAT ADVANCED STUDENTS: THIS SECTION IS ADMINISTERED AT AN IN-CLASS WORKSHOP. DO NOT USE THIS SECTION FOR PRACTICE.

Reading Comprehension 13

11. According to the passage, which one of the following is true of cases involving ancient graves?

    (A) Once a plaintiff's standing has been established, such cases are usually more difficult to resolve than are cases involving more recent graves.

    (B) The distinction between individual and communal property is usually an issue in such cases.

    (C) Even when a plaintiff's standing has been established, property law cannot be used as a basis for the claims of Native Americans in most such cases.

    (D) In most such cases, common law does not currently provide a clear basis for establishing that Native Americans have standing.

    (E) Common law is rarely used as a basis for the claims of Native Americans who have established standing in such cases.

12. The passage suggests that in making the ruling in *Carrier* v. *Bell* the Court is most likely to have considered the answer to which one of the following questions?

    (A) Are the descendants of the deceased still alive?

    (B) What was the reason for burying the objects in question?

    (C) How long after interment had buried objects been claimed by a stranger?

    (D) Did the descendants of the deceased remain in the neighborhood of the cemetery?

    (E) Could the property on which buried objects were found be legally considered to be abandoned property?

13. The author uses the second paragraph to

    (A) illustrate the contention that common law may support the claims of Native Americans to the contents of ancestral graves

    (B) exemplify the difficulties that Native Americans are likely to encounter in claiming ancestral remains

    (C) introduce a discussion of the distinction between individual and communal property

    (D) confirm the contention that cases involving ancient graves present unresolved legal problems

    (E) suggest that property law is applicable in most disinterment cases.

14. Which one of the following best expresses the main idea of the passage?

    (A) Prior to an appellate court's ruling in *Carrier* vs. *Bell*, Native Americans had no legal grounds for demanding the return of artifacts excavated from ancient graves.

    (B) Property law offers the most promising remedies to Native Americans seeking to recover communally owned artifacts that were sold to museums without tribal authorization.

    (C) The older the grave, the more difficult it is for Native Americans to establish standing in cases concerning the disposition of archaeologically excavated ancestral remains.

    (D) In cases in which Native Americans can establish standing, common law can be useful in protecting ancestral remains and the artifacts buried with them.

    (E) Native Americans are unlikely to make significant progress in the recovery of cultural property until common law is significantly expanded to provide them with standing in cases involving the excavation of ancient graves.

GO ON TO THE NEXT PAGE.

Reading Comprehension 13

When the same habitat types (forests, oceans, grasslands, etc.) in regions of different latitudes are compared, it becomes apparent that the overall number of species increases from pole to equator. This
(5) latitudinal gradient is probably even more pronounced than current records indicate, since researchers believe that most undiscovered species live in the tropics.

One hypothesis to explain this phenomenon, the "time theory," holds that diverse species adapted to
(10) today's climatic conditions have had more time to emerge in the tropical regions, which, unlike the temperate and arctic zones, have been unaffected by a succession of ice ages. However, ice ages have caused less disruption in some temperate regions than in others
(15) and have not interrupted arctic conditions.

Alternatively, the species-energy hypothesis proposes the following positive correlations: incoming energy from the Sun correlated with rates of growth and reproduction; rates of growth and reproduction
(20) with the amount of living matter (biomass) at a given moment; and the amount of biomass with number of species. However, since organisms may die rapidly, high production rates can exist with low biomass. And high biomass can exist with few species. Moreover, the
(25) mechanism proposed—greater energy influx leading to bigger populations, thereby lowering the probability of local extinction—remains untested.

A third hypothesis centers on the tropics' climatic stability, which provides a more reliable supply of
(30) resources. Species can thus survive even with few types of food, and competing species can tolerate greater overlap between their respective niches. Both capabilities enable more species to exist on the same resources. However, the ecology of local communities
(35) cannot account for the origin of the latitudinal gradient. Localized ecological processes such as competition do not generate regional pools of species, and it is the total number of species available regionally for colonizing any particular area that makes the difference between
(40) for example, a forest at the equator and one at a higher latitude.

A fourth and most plausible hypothesis focuses on regional speciation, and in particular on rates of speciation and extinction. According to this hypothesis,
(45) if speciation rates become higher toward the tropics, and are not negated by extinction rates, then the latitudinal gradient would result—and become increasingly steep.

The mechanism for this rate-of-speciation
(50) hypothesis is that most new animal species, and perhaps plant species, arise because a population subgroup becomes isolated. This subgroup evolves differently and eventually cannot interbreed with members of the original population. The uneven spread
(55) of a species over a large geographic area promotes this mechanism: at the edges, small populations spread out and form isolated groups. Since subgroups in an arctic environment are more likely to face extinction than those in the tropics, the latter are more likely to survive
(60) long enough to adapt to local conditions and ultimately become new species.

15. Which one of the following most accurately expresses the main idea of the passage?

(A) At present, no single hypothesis explaining the latitudinal gradient in numbers of species is more widely accepted than any other.

(B) The tropical climate is more conducive to promoting species diversity than are arctic or temperate climates.

(C) Several explanations have been suggested for global patterns in species distribution, but a hypothesis involving rates of speciation seems most promising.

(D) Despite their differences, the various hypotheses regarding a latitudinal gradient in species diversity concur in predicting that the gradient can be expected to increase.

(E) In distinguishing among the current hypotheses for distribution of species, the most important criterion is whether a hypothesis proposes a mechanism that can be tested and validated.

16. Which one of the following situations is most consistent with the species-energy hypothesis as described in the passage?

(A) The many plants in a large agricultural tract represent a limited range of species.

(B) An animal species experiences a death rate almost as rapid as its rate of growth and reproduction.

(C) Within the small number of living organisms in a desert habitat, many different species are represented.

(D) In a tropical rain forest, a species with a large population is found to exhibit instances of local extinction.

(E) In an arctic tundra, the plants and animals exhibit a slow rate of growth and reproduction.

GO ON TO THE NEXT PAGE.

LSAT ADVANCED STUDENTS: THIS SECTION IS ADMINISTERED AT AN IN-CLASS WORKSHOP. DO NOT USE THIS SECTION FOR PRACTICE.

Reading Comprehension 13

17. As presented in the passage, the principles of the time theory most strongly support which one of the following predictions?

    (A) In the absence of additional ice ages, the number of species at high latitudes could eventually increase significantly.

    (B) No future ice ages are likely to change the climatic conditions that currently characterize temperate regions.

    (C) If no further ice ages occur, climatic conditions at high latitudes might eventually resemble those at today's tropical latitudes.

    (D) Researchers will continue to find many more new species in the tropics than in the arctic and temperate zones.

    (E) Future ice ages are likely to interrupt the climatic conditions that now characterize high-latitude regions.

18. Which one of the following, if true, most clearly weakens the rate-of-speciation hypothesis as it is described in the passage?

    (A) A remote subgroup of a tropical species is reunited with the original population and proves unable to interbreed with members of this original population.

    (B) Investigation of a small area of a tropical rain forest reveals that many competing species are able to coexist on the same range of resources.

    (C) A correlation between higher energy influx, larger populations, and lower probability of local extinction is definitively established.

    (D) Researchers find more undiscovered species during an investigation of an arctic region than they had anticipated.

    (E) Most of the isolated subgroups of mammalian life within a tropical zone are found to experience rapid extinction.

19. Which one of the following inferences about the biological characteristics of a temperate-zone grassland is most strongly supported by the passage?

    (A) It has more different species than does a tropical-zone forest.

    (B) Its climatic conditions have been severely interrupted in the past by a succession of ice ages.

    (C) If it has a large amount of biomass, it also has a large number of different species.

    (D) It has a larger regional pool of species than does an arctic grassland.

    (E) If population groups become isolated at its edges, they are likely to adapt to local conditions and become new species.

20. With which one of the following statements concerning possible explanations for the latitudinal gradient in number of species would the author be most likely to agree?

    (A) The time theory is the least plausible of proposed hypotheses, since it does not correctly assess the impact of ice ages upon tropical conditions.

    (B) The rate-of-speciation hypothesis addresses a principal objection to the climatic-stability hypothesis.

    (C) The major objection to the time theory is that it does not accurately reflect the degree to which the latitudinal gradient exists, especially when undiscovered species are taken into account.

    (D) Despite the claims of the species-energy hypothesis, a high rate of biological growth and reproduction is more likely to exist with low biomass than with high biomass.

    (E) An important advantage of the rate-of-speciation theory is that it considers species competition in a regional rather than local context.

GO ON TO THE NEXT PAGE.

Reading Comprehension 13

Two impressive studies have reexamined Eric Williams' conclusion that Britain's abolition of the slave trade in 1807 and its emancipation of slaves in its colonies in 1834 were driven primarily by economic
(5) rather than humanitarian motives. Blighted by depleted soil, indebtedness, and the inefficiency of coerced labor, these colonies, according to Williams, had by 1807 become an impediment to British economic progress.

(10) Seymour Drescher provides a more balanced view. Rejecting interpretations based either on economic interest or the moral vision of abolitionists, Drescher has reconstructed the populist characteristics of British abolitionism, which appears to have cut across lines of
(15) class, party, and religion. Noting that between 1780 and 1830 antislavery petitions outnumbered those on any other issue, including parliamentary reform, Drescher concludes that such support cannot be explained by economic interest alone, especially when
(20) much of it came from the unenfranchised masses. Yet, aside from demonstrating that such support must have resulted at least in part from widespread literacy and a tradition of political activism, Drescher does not finally explain how England, a nation deeply divided by class
(25) struggles, could mobilize popular support for antislavery measures proposed by otherwise conservative politicians in the House of Lords and approved there with little dissent.

David Eltis' answer to that question actually
(30) supports some of Williams' insights. Eschewing Drescher's idealization of British traditions of liberty, Eltis points to continuing use of low wages and Draconian vagrancy laws in the seventeenth and eighteenth centuries to ensure the industriousness of
(35) British workers. Indeed, certain notables even called for the enslavement of unemployed laborers who roamed the British countryside—an acceptance of coerced labor that Eltis attributes to a preindustrial desire≈to keep labor costs low and exports competitive.
(40) By the late eighteenth century, however, a growing home market began to alert capitalists to the importance of "want creation" and to incentives such as higher wages as a means of increasing both worker productivity and the number of consumers.
(45) Significantly, it was products grown by slaves, such as sugar, coffee, and tobacco, that stimulated new wants at all levels of British society and were the forerunners of products intended in modern capitalist societies to satisfy what Eltis describes as "nonsubsistence or
(50) psychological needs." Eltis concludes that in an economy that had begun to rely on voluntary labor to satisfy such needs, forced labor necessarily began to appear both inappropriate and counterproductive to employers. Eltis thus concludes that, while Williams
(55) may well have underestimated the economic viability of the British colonies employing forced labor in the early 1800s, his insight into the economic motives for abolition was partly accurate. British leaders became committed to colonial labor reform only when they
(60) became convinced, for reasons other than those cited

by Williams, that free labor was more beneficial to the imperial economy.

21. Which one of the following best describes the main idea of the passage?

(A) Although they disagree about the degree to which economic motives influenced Britain's abolition of slavery, Drescher and Eltis both concede that moral persuasion by abolitionists was a significant factor.

(B) Although both Drescher and Eltis have questioned Williams' analysis of the motivation behind Britain's abolition of slavery, there is support for part of Williams' conclusion.

(C) Because he has taken into account the populist characteristics of British abolitionism, Drescher's explanation of what motivated Britain's abolition of slavery is finally more persuasive than that of Eltis.

(D) Neither Eltis nor Drescher has succeeded in explaining why support for Britain's abolition of slavery appears to have cut across lines of party, class, and religion.

(E) Although flawed in certain respects, Williams' conclusions regarding the economic condition of British slave colonies early in the nineteenth century have been largely vindicated.

22. It can be inferred that Eltis cites the views of "certain notables" (line 35) in order to

(A) support the claim that British traditions of liberty were not as strong as Drescher believed them to be

(B) support the contention that a strong labor force was important to Britain's economy

(C) emphasize the importance of slavery as an institution in preindustrial Britain

(D) indicate that the laboring classes provided little support for the abolition of slavery

(E) establish that laborers in preindustrial Britain had few civil rights

GO ON TO THE NEXT PAGE.

LSAT ADVANCED STUDENTS: THIS SECTION IS ADMINISTERED AT AN IN-CLASS WORKSHOP. DO NOT USE THIS SECTION FOR PRACTICE.

Reading Comprehension 13

23. Which one of the following best states Williams' view of the primary reason for Britain's abolition of the slave trade and the emancipation of slaves in its colonies?

    (A) British populism appealed to people of varied classes, parties, and religions.
    (B) Both capitalists and workers in Britain accepted the moral precepts of abolitionists.
    (C) Forced labor in the colonies could not produce enough goods to satisfy British consumers.
    (D) The operation of colonies based on forced labor was no longer economically advantageous.
    (E) British workers became convinced that forced labor in the colonies prevented paid workers from receiving higher wages.

24. According to Eltis, low wages and Draconian vagrancy laws in Britain in the seventeenth and eighteenth centuries were intended to

    (A) protect laborers against unscrupulous employment practices
    (B) counter the move to enslave unemployed laborers
    (C) ensure a cheap and productive work force
    (D) ensure that the work force experienced no unemployment
    (E) ensure that products produced in British colonies employing forced labor could compete effectively with those produced in Britain

25. It can be inferred that the author of the passage views Drescher's presentation of British traditions concerning liberty as

    (A) accurately stated
    (B) somewhat unrealistic
    (C) carefully researched
    (D) unnecessarily tentative
    (E) superficially convincing

26. The information in the passage suggests that Eltis and Drescher agree that

    (A) people of all classes in Britain supported the abolition of slavery
    (B) the motives behind Britain's abolition of slavery were primarily economic
    (C) the moral vision of abolitionists played a vital part in Britain's abolition of slavery
    (D) British traditions of liberty have been idealized by historians
    (E) Britain's tradition of political activism was primarily responsible for Britain's abolition of slavery

27. According to the passage, Eltis argues against which one of the following contentions?

    (A) Popular support for antislavery measures existed in Britain in the early nineteenth century.
    (B) In the early nineteenth century, colonies that employed forced labor were still economically viable.
    (C) British views concerning personal liberty motivated nineteenth-century British opposition to slavery.
    (D) Widespread literacy in Britain contributed to public opposition to slavery in the early nineteenth century.
    (E) Antislavery measures proposed by conservative politicians in the early nineteenth century met with little opposition.

S T O P

IF YOU FINISH BEFORE TIME IS CALLED, YOU MAY CHECK YOUR WORK ON THIS SECTION ONLY.
DO NOT WORK ON ANY OTHER SECTION IN THE TEST.

Answer Key

1. A
2. E
3. B
4. E
5. A
6. D
7. D
8. C
9. C
10. E
11. D
12. B
13. A
14. D
15. C
16. E
17. A
18. E
19. D
20. B
21. B
22. A
23. D
24. C
25. B
26. A
27. C

Reading Comprehension 14

PrepTest 16, Section IV
September 1995

SECTION IV

Time—35 minutes

27 Questions

Directions: Each passage in this section is followed by a group of questions to be answered on the basis of what is <u>stated</u> or <u>implied</u> in the passage. For some of the questions, more than one of the choices could conceivably answer the question. However, you are to choose the <u>best</u> answer; that is, the response that most accurately and completely answers the question, and blacken the corresponding space on your answer sheet.

Three kinds of study have been performed on Byron. There is the biographical study—the very valuable examination of Byron's psychology and the events in his life; Escarpit's 1958 work is an example
(5) of this kind of study, and biographers to this day continue to speculate about Byron's life. Equally valuable is the study of Byron as a figure important in the history of ideas; Russell and Praz have written studies of this kind. Finally, there are
(10) studies that primarily consider Byron's poetry. Such literary studies are valuable, however, only when they avoid concentrating solely on analyzing the verbal shadings of Byron's poetry to the exclusion of any discussion of biographical considerations. A
(15) study with such a concentration would be of questionable value because Byron's poetry, for the most part, is simply not a poetry of subtle verbal meanings. Rather, on the whole, Byron's poems record the emotional pressure of certain moments
(20) in his life. I believe we cannot often read a poem of Byron's, as we often can one of Shakespeare's, without wondering what events or circumstances in his life prompted him to write it.

No doubt the fact that most of Byron's poems
(25) cannot be convincingly read as subtle verbal creations indicates that Byron is not a "great" poet. It must be admitted too that Byron's literary craftsmanship is irregular and often his temperament disrupts even his lax literary method
(30) (although the result, an absence of method, has a significant purpose: it functions as a rebuke to a cosmos that Byron feels he cannot understand). If Byron is not a "great" poet, his poetry is nonetheless of extraordinary interest to us because
(35) of the pleasure it gives us. Our main pleasure in reading Byron's poetry is the contact with a singular personality. Reading his work gives us illumination—self-understanding—after we have seen our weaknesses and aspirations mirrored in
(40) the personality we usually find in the poems. Anyone who thinks that this kind of illumination is not a genuine reason for reading a poet should think carefully about why we read Donne's sonnets. It is Byron and Byron's idea of himself that hold
(45) his work together (and that enthralled early-nineteenth-century Europe). Different characters speak in his poems, but finally it is usually he himself who is speaking: a far cry from the impersonal poet Keats. Byron's poetry alludes to
(50) Greek and Roman myth in the context of

contemporary affairs, but his work remains generally of a piece because of his close presence in the poetry. In sum, the poetry is a shrewd personal performance, and to shut out Byron the man is to
(55) fabricate a work of pseudocriticism.

1. Which one of the following titles best expresses the main idea of the passage?

(A) An Absence of Method: Why Byron Is Not a "Great" Poet

(B) Byron: The Recurring Presence in Byron's Poetry

(C) Personality and Poetry: The Biographical Dimension of Nineteenth-Century Poetry

(D) Byron's Poetry: Its Influence on the Imagination of Early-Nineteenth-Century Europe

(E) Verbal Shadings: The Fatal Flaw of Twentieth-Century Literary Criticism

2. The author's mention of Russell and Praz serves primarily to

(A) differentiate them from one another

(B) contrast their conclusions about Byron with those of Escarpit

(C) point out the writers whose studies suggest a new direction for Byron scholarship

(D) provide examples of writers who have written one kind of study of Byron

(E) give credit to the writers who have composed the best studies of Byron

GO ON TO THE NEXT PAGE.

3. Which one of the following would the author most likely consider to be a valuable study of Byron?

   (A) a study that compared Byron's poetic style with Keats' poetic style
   (B) a study that argued that Byron's thought ought not to be analyzed in terms of its importance in the history of ideas
   (C) a study that sought to identify the emotions felt by Byron at a particular time in his life
   (D) a study in which a literary critic argues that the language of Byron's poetry was more subtle than that of Keats' poetry
   (E) a study in which a literary critic drew on experiences from his or her own life

4. Which one of the following statements best describes the organization of the first paragraph of the passage?

   (A) A generalization is made and then gradually refuted.
   (B) A number of theories are discussed and then the author chooses the most convincing one.
   (C) Several categories are mentioned and then one category is discussed in some detail.
   (D) A historical trend is delineated and then a prediction about the future of the trend is offered.
   (E) A classification is made and then a rival classification is substituted in its place.

5. The author mentions that "Byron's literary craftsmanship is irregular" (lines 27–28) most probably in order to

   (A) contrast Byron's poetic skill with that of Shakespeare
   (B) dismiss craftsmanship as a standard by which to judge poets
   (C) offer another reason why Byron is not a "great" poet
   (D) point out a negative consequence of Byron's belief that the cosmos is incomprehensible
   (E) indicate the most-often-cited explanation of why Byron's poetry lacks subtle verbal nuances

6. According to the author, Shakespeare's poems differ from Byron's in that Shakespeare's poems

   (A) have elicited a wider variety of responses from both literary critics and biographers
   (B) are on the whole less susceptible to being read as subtle verbal creations
   (C) do not grow out of, or are not motivated by, actual events or circumstances in the poet's life
   (D) provide the attentive reader with a greater degree of illumination concerning his or her own weaknesses and aspirations
   (E) can often be read without the reader's being curious about what biographical factors motivated the poet to write them

7. The author indicates which one of the following about biographers' speculation concerning Byron's life?

   (A) Such speculation began in earnest with Escarpit's study.
   (B) Such speculation continues today.
   (C) Such speculation is less important than consideration of Byron's poetry.
   (D) Such speculation has not given us a satisfactory sense of Byron's life.
   (E) Such speculation has been carried out despite the objections of literary critics.

8. The passage supplies specific information that provides a definitive answer to which one of the following questions?

   (A) What does the author consider to be the primary enjoyment derived from reading Byron?
   (B) Who among literary critics has primarily studied Byron's poems?
   (C) Which moments in Byron's life exerted the greatest pressure on his poetry?
   (D) Has Byron ever been considered to be a "great" poet?
   (E) Did Byron exert an influence on Europeans in the latter part of the nineteenth century?

GO ON TO THE NEXT PAGE.

The United States Supreme Court has not always resolved legal issues of concern to Native Americans in a manner that has pleased the Indian nations. Many of the Court's decisions have been
(5) products of political compromise that looked more to the temper of the times than to enduring principles of law. But accommodation is part of the judicial system in the United States, and judicial decisions must be assessed with this fact in mind.

(10) Despite the "accommodating" nature of the judicial system, it is worth noting that the power of the Supreme Court has been exercised in a manner that has usually been beneficial to Native Americans, at least on minor issues, and has not
(15) been wholly detrimental on the larger, more important issues. Certainly there have been decisions that cast doubt on the validity of this assertion. Some critics point to the patronizing tone of many Court opinions and the apparent rejection
(20) of Native American values as important points to consider when reviewing a case. However, the validity of the assertion can be illustrated by reference to two important contributions that have resulted from the exercise of judicial power.

(25) First, the Court has created rules of judicial construction that, in general, favor the rights of Native American litigants. The Court's attitude has been conditioned by recognition of the distinct disadvantages Native Americans faced when
(30) dealing with settlers in the past. Treaties were inevitably written in English for the benefit of their authors, whereas tribal leaders were accustomed to making treaties without any written account, on the strength of mutual promises sealed by religious
(35) commitment and individual integrity. The written treaties were often broken, and Native Americans were confronted with fraud and political and military aggression. The Court recognizes that past unfairness to Native Americans cannot be
(40) sanctioned by the force of law. Therefore, ambiguities in treaties are to be interpreted in favor of the Native American claimants, treaties are to be interpreted as the Native Americans would have understood them, and, under the reserved rights
(45) doctrine, treaties reserve to Native Americans all rights that have not been specifically granted away in other treaties.

A second achievement of the judicial system is the protection that has been provided against
(50) encroachment by the states into tribal affairs. Federal judges are not inclined to view favorably efforts to extend states' powers and jurisdictions because of the direct threat that such expansion poses to the exercise of federal powers. In the
(55) absence of a federal statute directly and clearly allocating a function to the states, federal judges are inclined to reserve for the federal government—and the tribal governments under its charge—all those powers and rights they can be said to have
(60) possessed historically.

9. According to the passage, one reason why the United States Supreme Court "has not always resolved legal issues of concern to Native Americans in a manner that has pleased the Indian nations" (lines 1–4) is that

(A) Native Americans have been prevented from presenting their concerns persuasively
(B) the Court has failed to recognize that the Indian nations' concerns are different from those of other groups or from those of the federal government
(C) the Court has been reluctant to curtail the powers of the federal government
(D) Native Americans faced distinct disadvantages in dealing with settlers in the past
(E) the Court has made political compromises in deciding some cases

10. It can be inferred that the objections raised by the critics mentioned in line 18 would be most clearly answered by a United States Supreme Court decision that

(A) demonstrated respect for Native Americans and the principles and qualities they consider important
(B) protected the rights of the states in conflicts with the federal government
(C) demonstrated recognition of the unfair treatment Native Americans received in the past
(D) reflected consideration of the hardships suffered by Native Americans because of unfair treaties
(E) prevented repetition of inequities experienced by Native Americans in the past

GO ON TO THE NEXT PAGE.

11. It can be inferred that the author calls the judicial system of the United States "accommodating" (line 10) primarily in order to

    (A) suggest that the decisions of the United States Supreme Court have been less favorable to Native Americans than most people believe

    (B) suggest that the United States Supreme Court should be more supportive of the goals of Native Americans

    (C) suggest a reason why the decisions of the United States Supreme Court have not always favored Native Americans

    (D) indicate that the United States Supreme Court has made creditable efforts to recognize the values of Native Americans

    (E) indicate that the United States Supreme Court attempts to be fair to all parties to a case

12. The author's attitude toward the United States Supreme Court's resolution of legal issues of concern to Native Americans can best be described as one of

    (A) wholehearted endorsement
    (B) restrained appreciation
    (C) detached objectivity
    (D) cautious opposition
    (E) suppressed exasperation

13. It can be inferred that the author believes that the extension of the states' powers and jurisdictions with respect to Native American affairs would be

    (A) possible only with the consent of the Indian nations

    (B) favorably viewed by the United States Supreme Court

    (C) in the best interests of both state and federal governments

    (D) detrimental to the interests of Native Americans

    (E) discouraged by most federal judges in spite of legal precedents supporting the extension

14. The author's primary purpose is to

    (A) contrast opposing views
    (B) reevaluate traditional beliefs
    (C) reconcile divergent opinions
    (D) assess the claims made by disputants
    (E) provide evidence to support a contention

15. It can be inferred that the author believes the United States Supreme Court's treatment of Native Americans to have been

    (A) irreproachable on legal grounds
    (B) reasonably supportive in most situations
    (C) guided by enduring principles of law
    (D) misguided but generally harmless
    (E) harmful only in a few minor cases

GO ON TO THE NEXT PAGE.

When catastrophe strikes, analysts typically
blame some combination of powerful mechanisms.
An earthquake is traced to an immense instability
along a fault line; a stock market crash is blamed on
(5)   the destabilizing effect of computer trading. These
explanations may well be correct. But systems as
large and complicated as the Earth's crust or the
stock market can break down not only under the
force of a mighty blow but also at the drop of a pin.
(10) In a large interactive system, a minor event can start
a chain reaction that leads to a catastrophe.

Traditionally, investigators have analyzed large
interactive systems in the same way they analyze
small orderly systems, mainly because the methods
(15) developed for small systems have proved so
successful. They believed they could predict the
behavior of a large interactive system by studying its
elements separately and by analyzing its component
mechanisms individually. For lack of a better
(20) theory, they assumed that in large interactive
systems the response to a disturbance is
proportional to that disturbance.

During the past few decades, however, it has
become increasingly apparent that many large
(25) complicated systems do not yield to traditional
analysis. Consequently, theorists have proposed a
"theory of self-organized criticality": many large
interactive systems evolve naturally to a critical
state in which a minor event starts a chain reaction
(30) that can affect any number of elements in the
system. Although such systems produce more minor
events than catastrophes, the mechanism that leads
to minor events is the same one that leads to major
events.
(35)   A deceptively simple system serves as a
paradigm for self-organized criticality: a pile of
sand. As sand is poured one grain at a time onto a
flat disk, the grains at first stay close to the position
where they land. Soon they rest on top of one
(40) another, creating a pile that has a gentle slope. Now
and then, when the slope becomes too steep, the
grains slide down, causing a small avalanche. The
system reaches its critical state when the amount of
sand added is balanced, on average, by the amount
(45) falling off the edge of the disk.

Now when a grain of sand is added, it can start
an avalanche of any size, including a "catastrophic"
event. Most of the time the grain will fall so that no
avalanche occurs. By studying a specific area of the
(50) pile, one can even predict whether avalanches will
occur there in the near future. To such a local
observer, however, large avalanches would remain
unpredictable because they are a consequence of
the total history of the entire pile. No matter what
(55) the local dynamics are, catastrophic avalanches
would persist at a relative frequency that cannot be
altered. Criticality is a global property of the
sandpile.

16. The passage provides support for all of the following
generalizations about large interactive systems EXCEPT:

(A)   They can evolve to a critical state.
(B)   They do not always yield to traditional analysis.
(C)   They make it impossible for observers to make
any predictions about them.
(D)   They are subject to the effects of chain reactions.
(E)   They are subject to more minor events than major
events.

17. According to the passage, the criticality of a sandpile is
determined by the

(A)   size of the grains of sand added to the sandpile
(B)   number of grains of sand the sandpile contains
(C)   rate at which sand is added to the sandpile
(D)   shape of the surface on which the sandpile rests
(E)   balance between the amount of sand added to and
the amount lost from the sandpile

GO ON TO THE NEXT PAGE.

18. It can be inferred from the passage that the theory employed by the investigators mentioned in the second paragraph would lead one to predict that which one of the following would result from the addition of a grain of sand to a sandpile?

(A) The grain of sand would never cause anything more than a minor disturbance.

(B) The grain of sand would usually cause a minor disturbance, but would occasionally cause a small avalanche.

(C) The grain of sand would usually cause either a minor disturbance or a small avalanche, but would occasionally cause a catastrophic event.

(D) The grain of sand would usually cause a catastrophic event, but would occasionally cause only a small avalanche or an even more minor disturbance.

(E) The grain of sand would invariably cause a catastrophic event.

19. Which one of the following best describes the organization of the passage?

(A) A traditional procedure is described and its application to common situations is endorsed; its shortcomings in certain rare but critical circumstances are then revealed.

(B) A common misconception is elaborated and its consequences are described; a detailed example of one of these consequences is then given.

(C) A general principle is stated and supported by several examples; an exception to the rule is then considered and its importance evaluated.

(D) A number of seemingly unrelated events are categorized; the underlying processes that connect them are then detailed.

(E) A traditional method of analysis is discussed and the reasons for its adoption are explained; an alternative is then described and clarified by means of an example.

20. Which one of the following is most analogous to the method of analysis employed by the investigators mentioned in the second paragraph?

(A) A pollster gathers a sample of voter preferences and on the basis of this information makes a prediction about the outcome of an election.

(B) A historian examines the surviving documents detailing the history of a movement and from these documents reconstructs a chronology of the events that initiated the movement.

(C) A meteorologist measures the rainfall over a certain period of the year and from this data calculates the total annual rainfall for the region.

(D) A biologist observes the behavior of one species of insect and from these observations generalizes about the behavior of insects as a class.

(E) An engineer analyzes the stability of each structural element of a bridge and from these analyses draws a conclusion about the structural soundness of the bridge.

21. In the passage, the author is primarily concerned with

(A) arguing against the abandonment of a traditional approach

(B) describing the evolution of a radical theory

(C) reconciling conflicting points of view

(D) illustrating the superiority of a new theoretical approach

(E) advocating the reconsideration of an unfashionable explanation

GO ON TO THE NEXT PAGE.

Historians have long accepted the notion that women of English descent who lived in the English colonies of North America during the seventeenth and eighteenth centuries were better off than either
(5) the contemporary women in England or the colonists' own nineteenth-century daughters and granddaughters. The "golden age" theory originated in the 1920s with the work of Elizabeth Dexter, who argued that there were relatively few
(10) women among the colonists, and that all hands—male and female—were needed to sustain the growing settlements. Rigid sex-role distinctions could not exist under such circumstances; female colonists could accordingly engage in whatever
(15) occupations they wished, encountering few legal or social constraints if they sought employment outside the home. The surplus of male colonists also gave women crucial bargaining power in the marriage market, since women's contributions were vital to
(20) the survival of colonial households.

Dexter's portrait of female colonists living under conditions of rough equality with their male counterparts was eventually incorporated into studies of nineteenth-century middle-class women.
(25) The contrast between the self-sufficient colonial woman and the oppressed nineteenth-century woman, confined to her home by stultifying ideologies of domesticity and by the fact that industrialization eliminated employment
(30) opportunities for middle-class women, gained an extraordinarily tenacious hold on historians. Even scholars who have questioned the "golden age" view of colonial women's status have continued to accept the paradigm of a nineteenth-century
(35) decline from a more desirable past. For example, Joan Hoff-Wilson asserted that there was no "golden age" and yet emphasized that the nineteenth century brought "increased loss of function and authentic status for" middle-class
(40) women.

Recent publications about colonial women have exposed the concept of a decline in status as simplistic and unsophisticated, a theory that based its assessment of colonial women's status solely on
(45) one factor (their economic function in society) and assumed all too readily that a relatively simple social system automatically brought higher standing to colonial women. The new scholarship presents a far more complicated picture, one in which
(50) definitions of gender roles, the colonial economy, demographic patterns, religion, the law, and household organization all contributed to defining the circumstances of colonial women's lives. Indeed the primary concern of modern scholarship is not to
(55) generalize about women's status but to identify the specific changes and continuities in women's lives during the colonial period. For example, whereas earlier historians suggested that there was little change for colonial women before 1800, the new
(60) scholarship suggests that a three-part chronological division more accurately reflects colonial women's experiences. First was the initial period of English colonization (from the 1620s to about 1660); then a period during which patterns of family and
(65) community were challenged and reshaped (roughly from 1660 to 1750); and finally the era of revolution (approximately 1750 to 1815), which brought other changes to women's lives.

22. Which one of the following best expresses the main idea of the passage?

(A) An earlier theory about the status of middle-class women in the nineteenth century has been supported by recent scholarship.

(B) Recent studies of middle-class nineteenth century women have altered an earlier theory about the status of colonial women.

(C) Recent scholarship has exposed an earlier theory about the status of colonial women as too narrowly based and oversimplified.

(D) An earlier theory about colonial women has greatly influenced recent studies on middle-class women in the nineteenth century.

(E) An earlier study of middle-class women was based on insufficient research on the status of women in the nineteenth century.

23. The author discusses Hoff-Wilson primarily in order to

(A) describe how Dexter's theory was refuted by historians of nineteenth-century North America

(B) describe how the theory of middle-class women's nineteenth-century decline in status was developed

(C) describe an important influence on recent scholarship about the colonial period

(D) demonstrate the persistent influence of the "golden age" theory

(E) provide an example of current research on the colonial period

GO ON TO THE NEXT PAGE.

24. It can be inferred from the passage that the author would be most likely to describe the views of the scholars mentioned in line 32 as

    (A) unassailable
    (B) innovative
    (C) paradoxical
    (D) overly sophisticated
    (E) without merit

25. It can be inferred from the passage that, in proposing the "three-part chronological division" (lines 60–61), scholars recognized which one of the following?

    (A) The circumstances of colonial women's lives were defined by a broad variety of social and economic factors.
    (B) Women's lives in the English colonies of North America were similar to women's lives in seventeenth–and eighteenth-century England.
    (C) Colonial women's status was adversely affected when patterns of family and community were established in the late seventeenth century.
    (D) Colonial women's status should be assessed primarily on the basis of their economic function in society.
    (E) Colonial women's status was low when the colonies were settled but changed significantly during the era of revolution.

26. According to the author, the publications about colonial women mentioned in the third paragraph had which one of the following effects?

    (A) They undermined Dexter's argument on the status of women colonists during the colonial period.
    (B) They revealed the tenacity of the "golden age" theory in American history.
    (C) They provided support for historians, such as Wilson, who study the nineteenth century.
    (D) They established that women's status did not change significantly from the colonial period to the nineteenth century.
    (E) They provided support for earlier theories about women colonists in the English colonies of North America.

27. Practitioners of the new scholarship discussed in the last paragraph would be most likely to agree with which one of the following statements about Dexter's argument?

    (A) It makes the assumption that women's status is determined primarily by their political power in society.
    (B) It makes the assumption that a less complex social system necessarily confers higher status on women.
    (C) It is based on inadequate research on women's economic role in the colonies.
    (D) It places too much emphasis on the way definitions of gender roles affected women colonists in the colonial period.
    (E) It accurately describes the way women's status declined in the nineteenth century.

S T O P

IF YOU FINISH BEFORE TIME IS CALLED, YOU MAY CHECK YOUR WORK ON THIS SECTION ONLY.
DO NOT WORK ON ANY OTHER SECTION IN THE TEST.

Answer Key

1. B
2. D
3. C
4. C
5. C
6. E
7. B
8. A
9. E
10. A
11. C
12. B
13. D
14. E
15. B
16. C
17. E
18. A
19. E
20. E
21. D
22. C
23. D
24. C
25. A
26. A
27. B

Reading Comprehension 15

PrepTest 15, Section I
June 1995

SECTION I

Time—35 minutes

27 Questions

<u>Directions:</u> Each passage in this section is followed by a group of questions to be answered on the basis of what is <u>stated</u> or <u>implied</u> in the passage. For some of the questions, more than one of the choices could conceivably answer the question. However, you are to choose the <u>best</u> answer; that is, the response that most accurately and completely answers the question, and blacken the corresponding space on your answer sheet.

Until the 1980s, most scientists believed that noncatastrophic geological processes caused the extinction of dinosaurs that occurred approximately 66 million years ago, at the end of the Cretaceous
(5) period. Geologists argued that a dramatic drop in sea level coincided with the extinction of the dinosaurs and could have caused the climatic changes that resulted in this extinction as well as the extinction of many ocean species.
(10) This view was seriously challenged in the 1980s by the discovery of large amounts of iridium in a layer of clay deposited at the end of the Cretaceous period. Because iridium is extremely rare in rocks on the Earth's surface but common in meteorites,
(15) researchers theorized that it was the impact of a large meteorite that dramatically changed the Earth's climate and thus triggered the extinction of the dinosaurs.
Currently available evidence, however, offers
(20) more support for a new theory, the volcanic-eruption theory. A vast eruption of lava in India coincided with the extinctions that occurred at the end of the Cretaceous period, and the release of carbon dioxide from this episode of volcanism could
(25) have caused the climatic change responsible for the demise of the dinosaurs. Such outpourings of lava are caused by instability in the lowest layer of the Earth's mantle, located just above the Earth's core. As the rock that constitutes this layer is heated by
(30) the Earth's core, it becomes less dense and portions of it eventually escape upward as blobs of molten rock, called "diapirs," that can, under certain circumstances, erupt violently through the Earth's crust.
(35) Moreover, the volcanic-eruption theory, like the impact theory, accounts for the presence of iridium in sedimentary deposits; it also explains matters that the meteorite-impact theory does not. Although iridium is extremely rare on the Earth's
(40) surface, the lower regions of the Earth's mantle have roughly the same composition as meteorites and contain large amounts of iridium, which in the case of a diapir eruption would probably be emitted as iridium hexafluoride, a gas that would disperse
(45) more uniformly in the atmosphere than the iridium-containing matter thrown out from a meteorite impact. In addition, the volcanic-eruption theory may explain why the end of the Cretaceous period was marked by a gradual change in sea level.
(50) Fossil records indicate that for several hundred thousand years prior to the relatively sudden disappearance of the dinosaurs, the level of the sea gradually fell, causing many marine organisms to die out. This change in sea level might well have
(55) been the result of a distortion in the Earth's surface that resulted from the movement of diapirs upward toward the Earth's crust, and the more cataclysmic extinction of the dinosaurs could have resulted from the explosive volcanism that occurred as material
(60) from the diapirs erupted onto the Earth's surface.

1. The passage suggests that during the 1980s researchers found meteorite impact a convincing explanation for the extinction of dinosaurs, in part because

   (A) earlier theories had failed to account for the gradual extinction of many ocean species at the end of the Cretaceous period
   (B) geologists had, up until that time, underestimated the amount of carbon dioxide that would be released during an episode of explosive volcanism
   (C) a meteorite could have served as a source of the iridium found in a layer of clay deposited at the end of the Cretaceous period
   (D) no theory relying on purely geological processes had, up until that time, explained the cause of the precipitous drop in sea level that occurred at the end of the Cretaceous period
   (E) the impact of a large meteorite could have resulted in the release of enough carbon dioxide to cause global climatic change

2. According to the passage, the lower regions of the Earth's mantle are characterized by

   (A) a composition similar to that of meteorites
   (B) the absence of elements found in rocks on the Earth's crust
   (C) a greater stability than that of the upper regions
   (D) the presence of large amounts of carbon dioxide
   (E) a uniformly lower density than that of the upper regions

GO ON TO THE NEXT PAGE.

3. It can be inferred from the passage that which one of the following was true of the lava that erupted in India at the end of the Cretaceous period?

   (A) It contained less carbon dioxide than did the meteorites that were striking the Earth's surface during that period.

   (B) It was more dense than the molten rock located just above the Earth's core.

   (C) It released enough iridium hexafluoride into the atmosphere to change the Earth's climate dramatically.

   (D) It was richer in iridium than rocks usually found on the Earth's surface.

   (E) It was richer in iridium than were the meteorites that were striking the Earth's surface during that period.

4. In the passage, the author is primarily concerned with doing which one of the following?

   (A) describing three theories and explaining why the latest of these appears to be the best of the three

   (B) attacking the assumptions inherent in theories that until the 1980s had been largely accepted by geologists

   (C) outlining the inadequacies of three different explanations of the same phenomenon

   (D) providing concrete examples in support of the more general assertion that theories must often be revised in light of new evidence

   (E) citing evidence that appears to confirm the skepticism of geologists regarding a view held prior to the 1980s

5. The author implies that if the theory described in the third paragraph is true, which one of the following would have been true of iridium in the atmosphere at the end of the Cretaceous period?

   (A) Its level of concentration in the Earth's atmosphere would have been high due to a slow but steady increase in the atmospheric iridium that began in the early Cretaceous period.

   (B) Its concentration in the Earth's atmosphere would have increased due to the dramatic decrease in sea level that occurred during the Cretaceous period.

   (C) It would have been directly responsible for the extinction of many ocean species.

   (D) It would have been more uniformly dispersed than iridium whose source had been the impact of a meteorite on the Earth's surface.

   (E) It would have been more uniformly dispersed than iridium released into the atmosphere as a result of normal geological processes that occur on Earth.

6. The passage supports which one of the following claims about the volcanic-eruption theory?

   (A) It does not rely on assumptions concerning the temperature of molten rock at the lowest part of the Earth's mantle.

   (B) It may explain what caused the gradual fall in sea level that occurred for hundreds of thousands of years prior to the more sudden disappearance of the dinosaurs.

   (C) It bases its explanation on the occurrence of periods of increased volcanic activity similar to those shown to have caused earlier mass extinctions.

   (D) It may explain the relative scarcity of iridium in rocks on the Earth's surface, compared to its abundance in meteorites.

   (E) It accounts for the relatively uneven distribution of iridium in the layer of clay deposited at the end of the Cretaceous period.

7. Which one of the following, if true, would cast the most doubt on the theory described in the last paragraph of the passage?

   (A) Fragments of meteorites that have struck the Earth are examined and found to have only minuscule amounts of iridium hexafluoride trapped inside of them.

   (B) Most diapir eruptions in the geological history of the Earth have been similar in size to the one that occurred in India at the end of the Cretaceous period and have not been succeeded by periods of climatic change.

   (C) There have been several periods in the geological history of the Earth, before and after the Cretaceous period, during which large numbers of marine species have perished.

   (D) The frequency with which meteorites struck the Earth was higher at the end of the Cretaceous period than at the beginning of the period.

   (E) Marine species tend to be much more vulnerable to extinction when exposed to a dramatic and relatively sudden change in sea level than when they are exposed to a gradual change in sea level similar to the one that preceded the extinction of the dinosaurs.

GO ON TO THE NEXT PAGE.

It has become something of a truism in folklore studies that until recently the lore was more often studied than the folk. That is, folklorists concentrated on the folklore—the songs, tales, and
(5) proverbs themselves—and ignored the people who transmitted that lore as part of their oral culture. However, since the early 1970s, folklore studies have begun to regard folk performers as people of creativity who are as worthy of attention as are
(10) artists who transmit their ideas in writing. This shift of emphasis has also encouraged a growing interest in women folk performers.

Until recently, folklorists tended to collect folklore from women on only a few topics such as
(15) health and games. In other areas, as Weigle and Farrer have noted, if folklorists "had a choice between a story as told by a man or as told by a woman, the man's version was chosen." It is still too early to tell how profoundly this situation has
(20) changed, but one can point to several recent studies in which women performers play central roles. Perhaps more telling is the focus of the most recently published major folklore textbook, *The Dynamics of Folklore*. Whereas earlier textbooks
(25) gave little attention to women and their folklore, this book devotes many pages to women folk performers.

Recognition of women as important bearers of folklore is not entirely a recent phenomenon. As
(30) early as 1903, a few outstanding women folk performers were the focus of scholarly attention. But the scholarship devoted to these women tended to focus primarily on presenting the performer's repertoire. Recent works about women folk artists,
(35) however, have been more biographically oriented. Juha Pentikäinen's study of Marina Tokalo, a Finnish healer and narrator of folktales, is especially extensive and probing. Though interested in the problems of repertoire analysis, Pentikäinen
(40) gives considerable attention to the details of Tokalo's life and cultural background, so that a full picture of a woman and her folklore emerges. Another notable work is Roger Abraham's book, which presents a very clear picture of the
(45) significance of traditional singing in the life of noted ballad singer Almeda Riddle. Unfortunately, unlike Pentikäinen's study, Abraham's study contains little repertoire analysis.

These recent books reflect the current interest of
(50) folklorists in viewing folklore in context and thus answering questions about what folklore means to the people who use it. One unexpected result of this line of study has been the discovery that women may use the same folklore that men use, but for very
(55) different purposes. This realization has potential importance for future folklore studies in calling greater attention to the type of study required if a folklorist wants truly to understand the role folklore plays in a particular culture.

8. Which one of the following best describes the main point of the passage?

(A) It is only since the early 1970s that folklore studies have begun to recognize women as important bearers of folklore.

(B) A careful analysis of the repertoires of women folk performers has led to a new discovery with important implications for future folklore studies.

(C) Recent studies of women folk performers have focused primarily on the problems of repertoire analysis to the exclusion of a discussion of the culture within which the folklore was developed.

(D) The emphasis in folklore studies has shifted from a focus on the life and the cultural background of the folk performers themselves to a broader understanding of the role folklore plays in a culture.

(E) A change in the focus of folklore studies has led to increased interest in women folk performers and to a new understanding of the importance of the context in which folklore is produced.

9. The author of the passage refers to *The Dynamics of Folklore* primarily in order to

(A) support the idea that it is too soon to tell whether or not folklorists are giving greater attention to women's folklore

(B) refute Weigle and Farrer's contention that folklorists prefer to collect folklore from men rather than from women

(C) support the assertion that scholarship devoted to women folk performers tends to focus primarily on repertoire

(D) present an example of the new emphasis in folklore studies on the performer rather than on the folklore

(E) suggest that there are some signs that women folk performers are gaining increased critical attention in the field of folklore

GO ON TO THE NEXT PAGE.

10. The focus of which one of the following books would most clearly reflect the current interest of the folklorists mentioned in the last paragraph?

    (A) an anthology of tales and songs collected exclusively from women in different cultures

    (B) a compilation of tales and songs from both men and women covering a great variety of traditional and nontraditional topics

    (C) a study of the purpose and meaning of a tale or song for the men and women in a particular culture

    (D) an analysis of one particular tale or song that documents changes in the text of the folklore over a period of time

    (E) a comparison of the creative process of performers who transmit folklore with that of artists who transmit their ideas in writing

11. According to the passage, which one of the following changes has occurred in the field of folklore since the early 1970s?

    (A) increased recognition of the similar ways in which men and women use folklore

    (B) increased recognition of folk performers as creative individuals

    (C) increased emphasis on the need for repertoire analysis

    (D) less emphasis on the relationship between cultural influences and folklore

    (E) less emphasis on the individual performers and more emphasis on the meaning of folklore to a culture

12. It can be inferred from the passage that early folklorists assumed that which one of the following was true?

    (A) The people who transmitted the folklore did not play a creative role in the development of that folklore.

    (B) The people who transmitted the folklore were not consciously aware of the way in which they creatively shaped that folklore.

    (C) The text of a song or tale did not change as the folklore was transmitted from one generation to another.

    (D) Women were not involved in transmitting folklore except for songs or tales dealing with a few traditional topics.

    (E) The meaning of a piece of folklore could differ depending on whether the tale or song was transmitted by a man or by a woman.

13. Based on the information in the passage, which one of the following is most closely analogous to the type of folklore studies produced before the early 1970s?

    (A) An anthropologist studies the implements currently used by an isolated culture, but does not investigate how the people of that culture designed and used those implements.

    (B) A manufacturer hires a consultant to determine how existing equipment in a plant might be modified to improve efficiency, but does not ask employees for their suggestions on how to improve efficiency.

    (C) A historian studies different types of documents dealing with a particular historical event, but decides not to review newspaper accounts written by journalists who lived through that event.

    (D) An archaeologist studies the artifacts of an ancient culture to reconstruct the life-style of that culture, but does not actually visit the site where those artifacts were unearthed.

    (E) An architect designs a private home for a client, but ignores many of the client's suggestions concerning minor details about the final design of the home.

14. The author of the passage uses the term "context" (line 50) to refer to

    (A) a holistic assessment of a piece of folklore rather than a critical analysis of its parts

    (B) a study that examines a piece of folklore in light of earlier interpretations provided by other folklorists

    (C) the parts of a piece of folklore that can shed light on the meaning of the entire piece

    (D) the environment and circumstances in which a particular piece of folklore is used

    (E) the location in which the story line of a piece of folklore is set

15. The author's attitude toward Roger Abraham's book can best be described as one of

    (A) wholehearted approval
    (B) qualified admiration
    (C) uneasy ambivalence
    (D) extreme skepticism
    (E) trenchant criticism

GO ON TO THE NEXT PAGE.

J. G. A. Pocock's numerous investigations have all revolved around the fruitful assumption that a work of political thought can only be understood in light of the linguistic constraints to which its author
(5) was subject, for these prescribed both the choice of subject matter and the author's conceptualization of this subject matter. Only the occasional epic theorist, like Machiavelli or Hobbes, succeeded in breaking out of these bonds by redefining old terms
(10) and inventing new ones. The task of the modern commentator is to identify the "language" or "vocabulary" with and within which the author operated. While historians of literature have always been aware that writers work within particular
(15) traditions, the application of this notion to the history of political ideas forms a sharp contrast to the assumptions of the 1950s, when it was naïvely thought that the close reading of a text by an analytic philosopher was sufficient to establish its
(20) meaning, even if the philosopher had no knowledge of the period of the text's composition.

The language Pocock has most closely investigated is that of "civic humanism." For much of his career he has argued that eighteenth-century
(25) English political thought should be interpreted as a conflict between rival versions of the "virtue" central to civic humanism. On the one hand, he argues, this virtue is described by representatives of the Tory opposition using a vocabulary of public spirit and
(30) self-sufficiency. For these writers the societal ideal is the small, independent landowner in the countryside. On the other hand, Whig writers describe such virtue using a vocabulary of commerce and economic progress; for them the
(35) ideal is the merchant.

In making such linguistic discriminations Pocock has disassociated himself from historians like Namier, who deride all eighteenth-century English political language as "cant." But while
(40) Pocock's ideas have proved fertile when applied to England, they are more controversial when applied to the late-eighteenth-century United States. Pocock's assertion that Jefferson's attacks on the commercial policies of the Federalists simply echo
(45) the language of the Tory opposition in England is at odds with the fact that Jefferson rejected the elitist implications of that group's notion of virtue and asserted the right of all to participate in commercial society. Indeed, after promptings by Quentin
(50) Skinner, Pocock has admitted that a counterlanguage—one of rights and liberties—was probably as important in the political discourse of the late-eighteenth-century United States as the language of civic humanism. Fortunately, it is not
(55) necessary to rank the relative importance of all the different vocabularies in which eighteenth-century political argument was conducted. It is sufficient to recognize that any interesting text is probably a mixture of several of these vocabularies, and to
(60) applaud the historian who, though guilty of some exaggeration, has done the most to make us aware of their importance.

16. The main idea of the passage is that

(A) civic humanism, in any of its manifestations, cannot entirely explain eighteenth-century political discourse
(B) eighteenth-century political texts are less likely to reflect a single vocabulary than to combine several vocabularies
(C) Pocock's linguistic approach, though not applicable to all eighteenth-century political texts, provides a useful model for historians of political theory
(D) Pocock has more successfully accounted for the nature of political thought in eighteenth-century England than in the eighteenth-century United States
(E) Pocock's notion of the importance of language in political texts is a logical extension of the insights of historians of literature

17. According to the passage, Pocock most clearly associates the use of a vocabulary of economic progress with

(A) Jefferson
(B) Federalists
(C) English Whigs
(D) English Tories
(E) rural English landowners

18. The author's attitude toward Pocock is best revealed by which of the following pairs of words?

(A) "fruitful" (line 2) and "cant" (line 39)
(B) "sharp" (line 16) and "elitist" (line 46)
(C) "naively" (line 17) and "controversial" (line 41)
(D) "fertile" (line 40) and "applaud" (line 60)
(E) "simply" (line 44) and "importance" (line 55)

19. The passage suggests that one of the "assumptions of the 1950s" (line 17) regarding the meaning of a political text was that this meaning

(A) could be established using an approach similar to that used by literary historians
(B) could be definitively established without reference to the text's historical background
(C) could be closely read in several different ways depending on one's philosophic approach
(D) was constrained by certain linguistic preconceptions held by the text's author
(E) could be expressed most clearly by an analytic philosopher who had studied its historical context

GO ON TO THE NEXT PAGE.

20. The author of the passage would most likely agree that which one of the following is a weakness found in Pocock's work?

   (A) the use of the term "language" to describe the expressive features of several diverse kinds of discourse
   (B) the overemphatic denigration of the role of the analytic philosopher in establishing the meaning of a political, or indeed any, text
   (C) the emphasis on the overriding importance of civic humanism in eighteenth-century English political thought
   (D) the insistence on a single linguistic dichotomy to account for political thought in eighteenth-century England and the United States
   (E) the assignment of certain vocabularies to particular parties in eighteenth-century England without taking note of how these vocabularies overlapped

21. Which one of the following best describes the organization of the passage?

   (A) A description of a thesis is offered, specific cases are considered, and an evaluation is given.
   (B) A thesis is brought forward, the thesis is qualified, and evidence that calls the qualification into question is stated.
   (C) A hypothesis is described, examples that suggest it is incorrect are summarized, and supporting examples are offered.
   (D) A series of evaluations are given, concrete reasons are put forward, and a future direction for research is suggested.
   (E) Comparisons and contrasts are made, some categories of evaluation are suggested, and a framework for applying these categories is implied.

GO ON TO THE NEXT PAGE.

In 1964 the United States federal government began attempts to eliminate racial discrimination in employment and wages: the United States Congress enacted Title VII of the Civil Rights Act,
(5) prohibiting employers from making employment decisions on the basis of race. In 1965 President Johnson issued Executive Order 11,246, which prohibited discrimination by United States government contractors and emphasized direct
(10) monitoring of minority representation in contractors' work forces.

Nonetheless, proponents of the "continuous change" hypothesis believe that United States federal law had a marginal impact on the economic
(15) progress made by black people in the United States between 1940 and 1975. Instead they emphasize slowly evolving historical forces, such as long-term trends in education that improved segregated schools for black students during the 1940s and
(20) were operative during and after the 1960s. They argue that as the quality of black schools improved relative to that of white schools, the earning potential of those attending black schools increased relative to the earning potential of those attending
(25) white schools.

However, there is no direct evidence linking increased quality of underfunded segregated black schools to these improvements in earning potential. In fact, even the evidence on relative schooling
(30) quality is ambiguous. Although in the mid-1940s term length at black schools was approaching that in white schools, the rapid growth in another important measure of school quality, school expenditures, may be explained by increases in
(35) teachers' salaries, and, historically, such increases have not necessarily increased school quality. Finally, black individuals in all age groups, even those who had been educated at segregated schools before the 1940s, experienced post-1960 increases in
(40) their earning potential. If improvements in the quality of schooling were an important determinant of increased returns, only those workers who could have benefited from enhanced school quality should have received higher returns. The relative
(45) improvement in the earning potential of educated black people of all age groups in the United States is more consistent with a decline in employment discrimination.

An additional problem for continuity theorists is
(50) how to explain the rapid acceleration of black economic progress in the United States after 1964. Education alone cannot account for the rate of change. Rather, the coincidence of increased United States government antidiscrimination
(55) pressure in the mid-1960s with the acceleration in the rate of black economic progress beginning in 1965 argues against the continuity theorists' view. True, correlating federal intervention and the acceleration of black economic progress might be
(60) incorrect. One could argue that changing attitudes about employment discrimination sparked both the adoption of new federal policies and the rapid acceleration in black economic progress. Indeed, the shift in national attitude that made possible the
(65) enactment of Title VII was in part produced by the persistence of racial discrimination in the southern United States. However, the fact that the law had its greatest effect in the South, in spite of the vigorous resistance of many Southern leaders,
(70) suggests its importance for black economic progress.

22. According to the passage, Title VII of the 1964 Civil Rights Act differs from Executive Order 11,246 in that Title VII

(A) monitors employers to ensure minority representation
(B) assesses the workforces of government contractors
(C) eliminates discriminatory disparities in wages
(D) focuses on determining minority representation in government
(E) governs hiring practices in a wider variety of workplaces

23. Which one of the following statements about schooling in the United States during the mid-1940s can be inferred from the passage?

(A) School expenditures decreased for white schools.
(B) The teachers in white schools had more time to cover material during a school year than did teachers in black schools.
(C) The basic curriculum of white schools was similar to the curriculum at black schools.
(D) White schools did not change substantially in quality.
(E) Although the salaries of teachers in black schools increased, they did not keep pace with the salaries of teachers in white schools.

GO ON TO THE NEXT PAGE.

24. The primary purpose of the passage is to

(A) explain why an argument about black economic progress is incomplete

(B) describe the impact of education on black economic progress

(C) refute an argument about the factors influencing black economic progress

(D) describe black economic progress before and after the 1960s

(E) clarify the current view about the factors influencing black economic progress

25. Which one of the following best states the position of proponents of the "continuous change" hypothesis regarding the relationship between law and racial discrimination?

(A) Individuals cannot be forced by legal means to behave in nondiscriminatory ways.

(B) Discriminatory practices in education have been effectively altered by legal means.

(C) Legislation alone has had little effect on racially discriminatory behavior.

(D) Legislation is necessary, but not sufficient, to achieve changes in racial attitudes.

(E) Legislation can only exacerbate conflicts about racially discriminatory behavior.

26. The author concedes that "correlating federal intervention and the acceleration of black economic progress might be incorrect" (lines 58–60) primarily in order to

(A) strengthen the overall argument by anticipating an objection

(B) introduce another factor that may have influenced black economic progress

(C) concede a point to the continuity theorists

(D) change the overall argument in light of the views of the continuity theorists

(E) introduce a discussion about the impact of federal intervention on discrimination

27. The "continuous change" hypothesis, as it is presented in the passage, can best be applied to which one of the following situations?

(A) Homes are found for many low-income families because the government funds a project to build subsidized housing in an economically depressed area.

(B) A depressed economy does not cause the closing of small businesses in a local community because the government provides special grants to aid these businesses.

(C) Unemployed people are able to obtain jobs because private contractors receive tax incentives for constructing office buildings in an area with a high unemployment rate.

(D) A housing shortage is remedied because the changing state of the economy permits private investors to finance construction in a depressed area.

(E) A community's sanitation needs are met because neighborhood organizations lobby aggressively for government assistance.

S T O P

IF YOU FINISH BEFORE TIME IS CALLED, YOU MAY CHECK YOUR WORK ON THIS SECTION ONLY. DO NOT WORK ON ANY OTHER SECTION IN THE TEST.

Answer Key

1. C
2. A
3. D
4. A
5. D
6. B
7. B
8. E
9. E
10. C
11. B
12. A
13. A
14. D
15. B
16. C
17. C
18. D
19. B
20. D
21. A
22. E
23. B
24. C
25. C
26. A
27. D

Reading Comprehension 16

PrepTest 18, Section III
December 1992

SECTION III

Time—35 minutes

28 Questions

Directions: Each passage in this section is followed by a group of questions to be answered on the basis of what is stated or implied in the passage. For some of the questions, more than one of the choices could conceivably answer the question. However, you are to choose the best answer; that is, the response that most accurately and completely answers the question, and blacken the corresponding space on your answer sheet.

The law-and-literature movement claims to have introduced a valuable pedagogical innovation into legal study: instructing students in techniques of literary analysis for the purpose of interpreting laws
(5) and in the reciprocal use of legal analysis for the purpose of interpreting literary texts. The results, according to advocates, are not only conceptual breakthroughs in both law and literature but also more sensitive and humane lawyers. Whatever the
(10) truth of this last claim, there can be no doubt that the movement is a success: law-and-literature is an accepted subject in law journals and in leading law schools. Indeed, one indication of the movement's strength is the fact that its most distinguished critic,
(15) Richard A. Posner, paradoxically ends up expressing qualified support for the movement in a recent study in which he systematically refutes the writings of its leading legal scholars and cooperating literary critics.
(20)   Critiquing the movement's assumption that lawyers can offer special insights into literature that deals with legal matters, Posner points out that writers of literature use the law loosely to convey a particular idea, or as a metaphor for the workings
(25) of the society envisioned in their fiction. Legal questions per se, about which a lawyer might instruct readers, are seldom at issue in literature. This is why practitioners of law-and-literature end up discussing the law itself far less than one might
(30) suppose. Movement leader James White, for example, in his discussion of arguments in the Iliad, barely touches on law, and then so generally as to render himself vulnerable to Posner's devastating remark that "any argument can be analogized to a
(35) legal dispute."
     Similarly, the notion that literary criticism can be helpful in interpreting law is problematic. Posner argues that literary criticism in general aims at exploring richness and variety of meaning in texts,
(40) whereas legal interpretation aims at discovering a single meaning. A literary approach can thus only confuse the task of interpreting the law, especially if one adopts current fashions like deconstruction, which holds that all texts are inherently
(45) uninterpretable.
     Nevertheless, Posner writes that law-and-literature is a field with "promise." Why? Perhaps, recognizing the success of a movement that, in the past, has singled him out for abuse, he
(50) is attempting to appease his detractors, paying

obeisance to the movement's institutional success declaring that it "deserves a place in legal research" while leaving it to others to draw the conclusion from his cogent analysis that it is an
(55) entirely factitious undertaking, deserving of no intellectual respect whatsoever. As a result, his work stands both as a rebuttal of law-and-literature and as a tribute to the power it has come to exercise in academic circles.

1. The primary purpose of the passage is to

   (A)   assess the law-and-literature movement by examining the position of one of its most prominent critics
   (B)   assert that a mutually beneficial relationship exists between the study of law and the study of literature
   (C)   provide examples of the law-and-literature movement in practice by discussing the work of its proponents
   (D)   dismiss a prominent critic's recent study of the law-and-literature movement
   (E)   describe the role played by literary scholars in providing a broader context for legal issues

2. Posner's stated position with regard to the law-and-literature movement is most analogous to which one of the following?

   (A)   a musician who is trained in the classics but frequently plays modern music while performing on stage
   (B)   a partisan who transfers allegiance to a new political party that demonstrates more promise but has fewer documented accomplishments
   (C)   a sports fan who wholeheartedly supports the team most likely to win rather than his or her personal favorite
   (D)   an ideologue who remains committed to his or her own view of a subject in spite of compelling evidence to the contrary
   (E)   a salesperson who describes the faults in a fashionable product while conceding that it may have some value

GO ON TO THE NEXT PAGE.

KAPLAN

3. The passage suggests that Posner regards legal practitioners as using an approach to interpreting law that

   (A) eschews discovery of multiple meanings
   (B) employs techniques like deconstruction
   (C) interprets laws in light of varying community standards
   (D) is informed by the positions of literary critics
   (E) de-emphasizes the social relevance of the legal tradition

4. The passage suggests that Posner might find legal training useful in the interpretation of a literary text in which

   (A) a legal dispute symbolizes the relationship between two characters
   (B) an oppressive law is used to symbolize an oppressive culture
   (C) one of the key issues involves the answer to a legal question
   (D) a legal controversy is used to represent a moral conflict
   (E) the working of the legal system suggests something about the political character of a society

5. The author uses the word "success" in line 11 to refer to the law-and-literature movement's

   (A) positive effect on the sensitivity of lawyers
   (B) widespread acceptance by law schools and law journals
   (C) ability to offer fresh insights into literary texts
   (D) ability to encourage innovative approaches in two disciplines
   (E) response to recent criticism in law journals

6. According to the passage, Posner argues that legal analysis is not generally useful in interpreting literature because

   (A) use of the law in literature is generally of a quite different nature than use of the law in legal practice
   (B) law is rarely used to convey important ideas in literature
   (C) lawyers do not have enough literary training to analyze literature competently
   (D) legal interpretations of literature tend to focus on legal issues to the exclusion of other important elements
   (E) legal interpretations are only relevant to contemporary literature

7. According to Posner, the primary difficulty in using literary criticism to interpret law is that

   (A) the goals of the two disciplines are incompatible
   (B) there are few advocates for the law-and-literature movement in the literary profession
   (C) the task of interpreting law is too complex for the techniques of literary criticism
   (D) the interpretation of law relies heavily on legal precedent
   (E) legal scholars are reluctant to adopt the practice in the classroom

GO ON TO THE NEXT PAGE.

A recent generation of historians of science, far from portraying accepted scientific views as objectively accurate reflections of a natural world, explain the acceptance of such views in terms of the

(5) ideological biases of certain influential scientists or the institutional and rhetorical power such scientists wield. As an example of ideological bias, it has been argued that Pasteur rejected the theory of spontaneous generation not because of

(10) experimental evidence but because he rejected the materialist ideology implicit in that doctrine. These historians seem to find allies in certain philosophers of science who argue that scientific views are not imposed by reality but are free inventions of

(15) creative minds, and that scientific claims are never more than brave conjectures, always subject to inevitable future falsification. While these philosophers of science themselves would not be likely to have much truck with the recent historians,

(20) it is an easy step from their views to the extremism of the historians.

While this rejection of the traditional belief that scientific views are objective reflections of the world may be fashionable, it is deeply implausible. We

(25) now know, for example, that water is made of hydrogen and oxygen and that parents each contribute one-half of their children's complement of genes. I do not believe any serious-minded and informed person can claim that these statements are

(30) not factual descriptions of the world or that they will inevitably be falsified.

However, science's accumulation of lasting truths about the world is not by any means a straightforward matter. We certainly need to

(35) get beyond the naive view that the truth will automatically reveal itself to any scientist who looks in the right direction; most often, in fact, a whole series of prior discoveries is needed to tease reality's truths from experiment and observation.

(40) And the philosophers of science mentioned above are quite right to argue that new scientific ideas often correct old ones by indicating errors and imprecisions (as, say, Newton's ideas did to Kepler's). Nor would I deny that there are

(45) interesting questions to be answered about the social processes in which scientific activity is embedded. The persuasive processes by which particular scientific groups establish their experimental results as authoritative are themselves

(50) social activities and can be rewardingly studied as such. Indeed, much of the new work in the history of science has been extremely revealing about the institutional interactions and rhetorical devices that help determine whose results achieve prominence.

(55) But one can accept all this without accepting the thesis that natural reality never plays any part at all in determining what scientists believe. What the new historians ought to be showing us is how those doctrines that do in fact fit reality work their way

(60) through the complex social processes of scientific activity to eventually receive general scientific acceptance.

8. It can be inferred from the passage that the author would be most likely to agree with which one of the following characterizations of scientific truth?

(A) It is often implausible.
(B) It is subject to inevitable falsification.
(C) It is rarely obvious and transparent.
(D) It is rarely discovered by creative processes.
(E) It is less often established by experimentation than by the rhetorical power of scientists.

9. According to the passage, Kepler's ideas provide an example of scientific ideas that were

(A) corrected by subsequent inquiries
(B) dependent on a series of prior observations
(C) originally thought to be imprecise and then later confirmed
(D) established primarily by the force of an individual's rhetorical power
(E) specifically taken up for the purpose of falsification by later scientists

10. In the third paragraph of the passage, the author is primarily concerned with

(A) presenting conflicting explanations for a phenomenon
(B) suggesting a field for possible future research
(C) qualifying a previously expressed point of view
(D) providing an answer to a theoretical question
(E) attacking the assumptions that underlie a set of beliefs

11. The use of the words "any serious-minded and informed person" (lines 28-29) serves which one of the following functions in the context of the passage?

(A) to satirize chronologically earlier notions about the composition of water
(B) to reinforce a previously stated opinion about certain philosophers of science
(C) to suggest the author's reservations about the "traditional belief" mentioned in line 22
(D) to anticipate objections from someone who would argue for an objectively accurate description of the world
(E) to discredit someone who would argue that certain scientific assertions do not factually describe reality

GO ON TO THE NEXT PAGE.

12. It can be inferred from the passage that the author would most likely agree with which one of the following statements about the relationship between the views of "certain philosophers of science" (lines 12-13) and those of the recent historians?

    (A) These two views are difficult to differentiate.
    (B) These two views share some similarities.
    (C) The views of the philosophers ought to be seen as the source of the historians' views.
    (D) Both views emphasize the rhetorical power of scientists.
    (E) The historians explicitly acknowledge that their views are indebted to those of the philosophers.

13. Which one of the following best characterizes the author's assessment of the opinions of the new historians of science, as these opinions are presented in the passage?

    (A) They lack any credibility.
    (B) They themselves can be rewardingly studied as social phenomena.
    (C) They are least convincing when they concern the actions of scientific groups.
    (D) Although they are gross overstatements, they lead to some valuable insights
    (E) Although they are now popular, they are likely to be refuted soon.

14. In concluding the passage, the author does which one of the following?

    (A) offers a prescription
    (B) presents a paradox
    (C) makes a prediction
    (D) concedes an argument
    (E) anticipates objections

15. The author's attitude toward the "thesis" mentioned in line 56 is revealed in which one of the following pairs of words?

    (A) "biases" (line 5) and "rhetorical" (line 6)
    (B) "wield" (line 7) and "falsification" (line 17)
    (C) "conjectures" (line 16) and "truck with" (line 19)
    (D) "extremism" (line 20) and "implausible" (line 24)
    (E) "naive" (line 35) and "errors" (line 42)

GO ON TO THE NEXT PAGE.

Until recently, it was thought that the Cherokee, a Native American tribe, were compelled to assimilate Euro-American culture during the 1820s. During that decade, it was supposed, White
(5) missionaries arrived and, together with their part Cherokee intermediaries, imposed the benefits of "civilization" on Cherokee tribes while the United States government actively promoted acculturalization by encouraging the Cherokee to
(10) switch from hunting to settled agriculture. This view was based on the assumption that the end of a Native American group's economic and political autonomy would automatically mean the end of its cultural autonomy as well.

(15) William G. McLoughlin has recently argued that not only did Cherokee culture flourish during and after the 1820s, but the Cherokee themselves actively and continually reshaped their culture. Missionaries did have a decisive impact during
(20) these years, he argues, but that impact was far from what it was intended to be. The missionaries' tendency to cater to the interests of an acculturating part-Cherokee elite (who comprised the bulk of their converts) at the expense of the more
(25) traditionalist full-Cherokee majority created great intratribal tensions. As the elite initiated reforms designed to legitimize their own and the Cherokee Nation's place in the new republic of the United States, antimission Cherokee reacted by fostering
(30) revivals of traditional religious beliefs and practices. However, these revivals did not, according to McLoughlin, undermine the elitist reforms, but supplemented them with popular, traditionalist counterparts.

(35) Traditionalist Cherokee did not reject the elitist reforms outright, McLoughlin argues, simply because they recognized that there was more than one way to use the skills the missionaries could provide them. As he quotes one group as saying,
(40) "We want our children to learn English so that the White man cannot cheat us." Many traditionalist Cherokee welcomed the missionaries for another reason: they perceived that it would be useful to have White allies. In the end, McLoughlin asserts,
(45) most members of the Cherokee council, including traditionalists, supported a move which preserved many of the reforms of the part-Cherokee elite but limited the activities and influence of the missionaries and other White settlers. According to
(50) McLoughlin, the identity and culture that resulted were distinctively Cherokee, yet reflected the larger political and social setting in which they flourished.

Because his work concentrates on the nineteenth century, McLoughlin unfortunately overlooks
(55) earlier sources of influence, such as eighteenth-century White resident traders and neighbors, thus obscuring the relative impact of the missionaries of the 1820s in contributing to both acculturalization and resistance to it among the
(60) Cherokee. However, McLoughlin is undoubtedly

correct in recognizing that culture is an ongoing process rather than a static entity, and he has made a significant contribution to our understanding of how Cherokee culture changed while retaining its
(65) essential identity after confronting the missionaries.

16. Which one of the following best states the main idea of the passage?

(A) McLoughlin's studies of the impact of missionaries on Cherokee culture during the 1820s are fundamentally flawed, since McLoughlin ignores the greater impact of White resident traders in the eighteenth century.

(B) Though his work is limited in perspective, McLoughlin is substantially correct that changes in the Cherokee culture in the 1820s were mediated by the Cherokee themselves rather than simply imposed by the missionaries.

(C) Although McLoughlin is correct in asserting that cultural changes among the Cherokee were autonomous and so not the result of the presence of missionaries, he overemphasizes the role of intratribal conflicts.

(D) McLoughlin has shown that Cherokee culture not only flourished during the 1820s, but that changes in Cherokee culture during this time developed naturally from elements already present in Cherokee culture.

(E) Although McLoughlin overlooks a number of relevant factors in Cherokee culture change in the 1820s, he convincingly demonstrates that these changes were fostered primarily by missionaries.

GO ON TO THE NEXT PAGE.

17. Which one of the following statements regarding the Cherokee council in the 1820s can be inferred from the passage?

    (A) Members of the Cherokee council were elected democratically by the entire Cherokee Nation.

    (B) In order for a policy to come into effect for the Cherokee Nation, it had to have been approved by a unanimous vote of the Cherokee council.

    (C) Despite the fact that the Cherokee were dominated politically and economically by the United States in the 1820s, the Cherokee council was able to override policies set by the United States government.

    (D) Though it did not have complete autonomy in governing the Cherokee Nation, it was able to set some policies affecting the activities of White people living in tribal areas.

    (E) The proportions of traditionalist and acculturating Cherokee in the Cherokee council were determined by the proportions of traditionalist and acculturating Cherokee in the Cherokee population.

18. Which one of the following statements regarding the attitudes of traditionalist Cherokee toward the reforms that were instituted in the 1820s can be inferred from the passage?

    (A) They supported the reforms merely as a way of placating the increasingly vocal acculturating elite.

    (B) They thought that the reforms would lead to the destruction of traditional Cherokee culture but felt powerless to stop the reforms.

    (C) They supported the reforms only because they thought that they were inevitable and it was better that the reforms appear to have been initiated by the Cherokee themselves.

    (D) They believed that the reforms were a natural extension of already existing Cherokee traditions.

    (E) They viewed the reforms as a means of preserving the Cherokee Nation and protecting it against exploitation.

19. According to the passage, McLoughlin cites which one of the following as a contributing factor in the revival of traditional religious beliefs among the Cherokee in the 1820s?

    (A) Missionaries were gaining converts at an increasing rate as the 1820s progressed.

    (B) The traditionalist Cherokee majority thought that most of the reforms initiated by the missionaries' converts would corrupt Cherokee culture.

    (C) Missionaries unintentionally created conflict among the Cherokee by favoring the interests of the acculturating elite at the expense of the more traditionalist majority.

    (D) Traditionalist Cherokee recognized that only some of the reforms instituted by a small Cherokee elite would be beneficial to all Cherokee.

    (E) A small group of Cherokee converted by missionaries attempted to institute reforms designed to acquire political supremacy for themselves in the Cherokee council.

20. Which one of the following, if true, would most seriously undermine McLoughlin's account of the course of reform among the Cherokee during the 1820s?

    (A) Traditionalist Cherokee gained control over the majority of seats on the Cherokee council during the 1820s.

    (B) The United States government took an active interest in political and cultural developments within Native American tribes.

    (C) The missionaries living among the Cherokee in the 1820s were strongly in favor of the cultural reforms initiated by the acculturating elite.

    (D) Revivals of traditional Cherokee religious beliefs and practices began late in the eighteenth century, before the missionaries arrived.

    (E) The acculturating Cherokee elite of the 1820s did not view the reforms they initiated as beneficial to all Cherokee.

21. It can be inferred from the author's discussion of McLoughlin's views that the author thinks that Cherokee acculturalization in the 1820s

    (A) was reversed in the decades following the 1820s

    (B) may have been part of an already-existing process of acculturalization

    (C) could have been the result of earlier contacts with missionaries

    (D) would not have occurred without the encouragement of the United States government

    (E) was primarily a result of the influence of White traders living near the Cherokee

GO ON TO THE NEXT PAGE.

In the history of nineteenth-century landscape painting in the United States, the Luminists are distinguished by their focus on atmosphere and light. The accepted view of Luminist paintings is
(5) that they are basically spiritual and imply a tranquil mysticism that contrasts with earlier American artists' concept of nature as dynamic and energetic. According to this view, the Luminist atmosphere, characterized by "pure and constant light," guides
(10) the onlooker toward a lucid transcendentalism, an idealized vision of the world.

What this view fails to do is to identify the true significance of this transcendental atmosphere in Luminist paintings. The prosaic factors that are
(15) revealed by a closer examination of these works suggest that the glowing appearance of nature in Luminism is actually a sign of nature's domestication, its adaptation to human use. The idealized Luminist atmosphere thus seems to
(20) convey, not an intensification of human responses to nature, but rather a muting of those emotions, like awe and fear, which untamed nature elicits.

One critic, in describing the spiritual quality of harbor scenes by Fitz Hugh Lane, an important
(25) Luminist, carefully notes that "at the peak of Luminist development in the 1850s and 1860s, spiritualism in America was extremely widespread." It is also true, however, that the 1850s and 1860s were a time of trade expansion. From 1848 until his
(30) death in 1865, Lane lived in a house with a view of the harbor of Gloucester, Massachusetts, and he made short trips to Maine, New York, Baltimore, and probably Puerto Rico. In all of these places he painted the harbors with their ships—the
(35) instruments of expanding trade.

Lane usually depicts places like New York Harbor, with ships at anchor, but even when he depicts more remote, less commercially active harbors, nature appears pastoral and domesticated
(40) rather than primitive or unexplored. The ships, rather than the surrounding landscapes—including the sea—are generally the active element in his pictures. For Lane the sea is, in effect, a canal or a trade route for commercial activity, not a free,
(45) powerful element, as it is in the early pictures of his predecessor, Cole. For Lane nature is subdued, even when storms are approaching; thus, the sea is always a viable highway for the transport of goods. In sum, I consider Lane's sea simply an environment
(50) for human activity—nature no longer inviolate. The luminescence that Lane paints symbolizes nature's humbled state, for the light itself is as docile as the Luminist sea, and its tranquillity in a sense signifies no more than good conditions on
(55) the highway to progress. Progress, probably even more than transcendence, is the secret message of Luminism. In a sense, Luminist pictures are an ideological justification of the atmosphere necessary for business, if also an exaggerated,
(60) idealistic rendering of that atmosphere.

22. The passage is primarily concerned with discussing

(A) the importance of religion to the art of a particular period
(B) the way one artist's work illustrates a tradition of painting
(C) the significance of the sea in one artist's work
(D) differences in the treatment of nature as a more active or a less active force
(E) variations in the artistic treatment of light among nineteenth-century landscape painters

23. The author argues that nature is portrayed in Lane's pictures as

(A) wild and unexplored
(B) idealized and distant
(C) continually changing
(D) difficult to understand
(E) subordinate to human concerns

24. The passage contains information to suggest that the author would most probably agree with which one of the following statements?

(A) The prevailing religious principles of a given time can be reflected in the art of that time.
(B) In order to interest viewers, works of art must depict familiar subjects in detail.
(C) Because commerce is unusual as a subject in art, the painter of commercial activity must travel and observe it widely.
(D) Knowing about the environment in which an artist lived can aid in an understanding of a work by that artist.
(E) The most popular works of art at a given time are devoted to furthering economic or social progress.

GO ON TO THE NEXT PAGE.

25. According to the author, a supporter of the view of Luminism described in the first paragraph would most likely

    (A) be unimpressed by the paintings' glowing light
    (B) consider Luminist scenes to be undomesticated and wild
    (C) interpret the Luminist depiction of nature incorrectly
    (D) see Luminist paintings as practical rather than mystical
    (E) focus on the paintings' subject matter instead of on atmosphere and light

26. According to the author, the sea is significant in Lane's paintings because of its association with

    (A) exploration
    (B) commerce
    (C) canals
    (D) idealism
    (E) mysticism

27. The author's primary purpose is to

    (A) refute a new theory
    (B) replace an inadequate analysis
    (C) summarize current critics' attitudes
    (D) support another critic's evaluation
    (E) describe the history of a misinterpretation

28. The author quotes a critic writing about Lane (lines 25–27) most probably in order to

    (A) suggest that Luminism was the dominant of painting in the 1850s and 1860s
    (B) support the idea that Lane was interested in spiritualism
    (C) provide an example of the primary cultural factors that influenced the Luminists
    (D) explain why the development of Luminism coincided with that of spiritualism
    (E) illustrate a common misconception concerning an important characteristic of Lane's paintings mode

S T O P

IF YOU FINISH BEFORE TIME IS CALLED, YOU MAY CHECK YOUR WORK ON THIS SECTION ONLY.
DO NOT WORK ON ANY OTHER SECTION IN THE TEST.

Answer Key

1. A
2. E
3. A
4. C
5. B
6. A
7. A
8. C
9. A
10. C
11. E
12. B
13. D
14. A
15. D
16. B
17. D
18. E
19. C
20. D
21. B
22. B
23. E
24. D
25. C
26. B
27. B
28. E

KAPLAN

Timing Practice

Grids

Reading
Comprehension 1
Answer Grid

NAME
(Please Print)

_____ Suffix

Last Name

_____

First Name

_____

Middle Name

1 Ⓐ Ⓑ Ⓒ Ⓓ Ⓔ
2 Ⓐ Ⓑ Ⓒ Ⓓ Ⓔ
3 Ⓐ Ⓑ Ⓒ Ⓓ Ⓔ
4 Ⓐ Ⓑ Ⓒ Ⓓ Ⓔ
5 Ⓐ Ⓑ Ⓒ Ⓓ Ⓔ
6 Ⓐ Ⓑ Ⓒ Ⓓ Ⓔ
7 Ⓐ Ⓑ Ⓒ Ⓓ Ⓔ
8 Ⓐ Ⓑ Ⓒ Ⓓ Ⓔ
9 Ⓐ Ⓑ Ⓒ Ⓓ Ⓔ
10 Ⓐ Ⓑ Ⓒ Ⓓ Ⓔ
11 Ⓐ Ⓑ Ⓒ Ⓓ Ⓔ
12 Ⓐ Ⓑ Ⓒ Ⓓ Ⓔ
13 Ⓐ Ⓑ Ⓒ Ⓓ Ⓔ
14 Ⓐ Ⓑ Ⓒ Ⓓ Ⓔ
15 Ⓐ Ⓑ Ⓒ Ⓓ Ⓔ
16 Ⓐ Ⓑ Ⓒ Ⓓ Ⓔ
17 Ⓐ Ⓑ Ⓒ Ⓓ Ⓔ
18 Ⓐ Ⓑ Ⓒ Ⓓ Ⓔ
19 Ⓐ Ⓑ Ⓒ Ⓓ Ⓔ
20 Ⓐ Ⓑ Ⓒ Ⓓ Ⓔ
21 Ⓐ Ⓑ Ⓒ Ⓓ Ⓔ
22 Ⓐ Ⓑ Ⓒ Ⓓ Ⓔ
23 Ⓐ Ⓑ Ⓒ Ⓓ Ⓔ
24 Ⓐ Ⓑ Ⓒ Ⓓ Ⓔ
25 Ⓐ Ⓑ Ⓒ Ⓓ Ⓔ
26 Ⓐ Ⓑ Ⓒ Ⓓ Ⓔ
27 Ⓐ Ⓑ Ⓒ Ⓓ Ⓔ
28 Ⓐ Ⓑ Ⓒ Ⓓ Ⓔ
29 Ⓐ Ⓑ Ⓒ Ⓓ Ⓔ
30 Ⓐ Ⓑ Ⓒ Ⓓ Ⓔ

Reading Comprehension 2

Answer Grid

1 Ⓐ Ⓑ Ⓒ Ⓓ Ⓔ
2 Ⓐ Ⓑ Ⓒ Ⓓ Ⓔ
3 Ⓐ Ⓑ Ⓒ Ⓓ Ⓔ
4 Ⓐ Ⓑ Ⓒ Ⓓ Ⓔ
5 Ⓐ Ⓑ Ⓒ Ⓓ Ⓔ
6 Ⓐ Ⓑ Ⓒ Ⓓ Ⓔ
7 Ⓐ Ⓑ Ⓒ Ⓓ Ⓔ
8 Ⓐ Ⓑ Ⓒ Ⓓ Ⓔ
9 Ⓐ Ⓑ Ⓒ Ⓓ Ⓔ
10 Ⓐ Ⓑ Ⓒ Ⓓ Ⓔ
11 Ⓐ Ⓑ Ⓒ Ⓓ Ⓔ
12 Ⓐ Ⓑ Ⓒ Ⓓ Ⓔ
13 Ⓐ Ⓑ Ⓒ Ⓓ Ⓔ
14 Ⓐ Ⓑ Ⓒ Ⓓ Ⓔ
15 Ⓐ Ⓑ Ⓒ Ⓓ Ⓔ
16 Ⓐ Ⓑ Ⓒ Ⓓ Ⓔ
17 Ⓐ Ⓑ Ⓒ Ⓓ Ⓔ
18 Ⓐ Ⓑ Ⓒ Ⓓ Ⓔ
19 Ⓐ Ⓑ Ⓒ Ⓓ Ⓔ
20 Ⓐ Ⓑ Ⓒ Ⓓ Ⓔ
21 Ⓐ Ⓑ Ⓒ Ⓓ Ⓔ
22 Ⓐ Ⓑ Ⓒ Ⓓ Ⓔ
23 Ⓐ Ⓑ Ⓒ Ⓓ Ⓔ
24 Ⓐ Ⓑ Ⓒ Ⓓ Ⓔ
25 Ⓐ Ⓑ Ⓒ Ⓓ Ⓔ
26 Ⓐ Ⓑ Ⓒ Ⓓ Ⓔ
27 Ⓐ Ⓑ Ⓒ Ⓓ Ⓔ
28 Ⓐ Ⓑ Ⓒ Ⓓ Ⓔ
29 Ⓐ Ⓑ Ⓒ Ⓓ Ⓔ
30 Ⓐ Ⓑ Ⓒ Ⓓ Ⓔ

NAME
(Please Print)

_____   Suffix _____

Last Name

_____

First Name

_____

Middle Name

Reading Comprehension 3
Answer Grid

NAME
(Please Print)

_____

Last Name   Suffix

_____

First Name

_____

Middle Name

1 Ⓐ Ⓑ Ⓒ Ⓓ Ⓔ
2 Ⓐ Ⓑ Ⓒ Ⓓ Ⓔ
3 Ⓐ Ⓑ Ⓒ Ⓓ Ⓔ
4 Ⓐ Ⓑ Ⓒ Ⓓ Ⓔ
5 Ⓐ Ⓑ Ⓒ Ⓓ Ⓔ
6 Ⓐ Ⓑ Ⓒ Ⓓ Ⓔ
7 Ⓐ Ⓑ Ⓒ Ⓓ Ⓔ
8 Ⓐ Ⓑ Ⓒ Ⓓ Ⓔ
9 Ⓐ Ⓑ Ⓒ Ⓓ Ⓔ
10 Ⓐ Ⓑ Ⓒ Ⓓ Ⓔ
11 Ⓐ Ⓑ Ⓒ Ⓓ Ⓔ
12 Ⓐ Ⓑ Ⓒ Ⓓ Ⓔ
13 Ⓐ Ⓑ Ⓒ Ⓓ Ⓔ
14 Ⓐ Ⓑ Ⓒ Ⓓ Ⓔ
15 Ⓐ Ⓑ Ⓒ Ⓓ Ⓔ
16 Ⓐ Ⓑ Ⓒ Ⓓ Ⓔ
17 Ⓐ Ⓑ Ⓒ Ⓓ Ⓔ
18 Ⓐ Ⓑ Ⓒ Ⓓ Ⓔ
19 Ⓐ Ⓑ Ⓒ Ⓓ Ⓔ
20 Ⓐ Ⓑ Ⓒ Ⓓ Ⓔ
21 Ⓐ Ⓑ Ⓒ Ⓓ Ⓔ
22 Ⓐ Ⓑ Ⓒ Ⓓ Ⓔ
23 Ⓐ Ⓑ Ⓒ Ⓓ Ⓔ
24 Ⓐ Ⓑ Ⓒ Ⓓ Ⓔ
25 Ⓐ Ⓑ Ⓒ Ⓓ Ⓔ
26 Ⓐ Ⓑ Ⓒ Ⓓ Ⓔ
27 Ⓐ Ⓑ Ⓒ Ⓓ Ⓔ
28 Ⓐ Ⓑ Ⓒ Ⓓ Ⓔ
29 Ⓐ Ⓑ Ⓒ Ⓓ Ⓔ
30 Ⓐ Ⓑ Ⓒ Ⓓ Ⓔ

Reading Comprehension 4
Answer Grid

NAME
(Please Print)

_____

Last Name   Suffix

_____

First Name

_____

Middle Name

1 Ⓐ Ⓑ Ⓒ Ⓓ Ⓔ
2 Ⓐ Ⓑ Ⓒ Ⓓ Ⓔ
3 Ⓐ Ⓑ Ⓒ Ⓓ Ⓔ
4 Ⓐ Ⓑ Ⓒ Ⓓ Ⓔ
5 Ⓐ Ⓑ Ⓒ Ⓓ Ⓔ
6 Ⓐ Ⓑ Ⓒ Ⓓ Ⓔ
7 Ⓐ Ⓑ Ⓒ Ⓓ Ⓔ
8 Ⓐ Ⓑ Ⓒ Ⓓ Ⓔ
9 Ⓐ Ⓑ Ⓒ Ⓓ Ⓔ
10 Ⓐ Ⓑ Ⓒ Ⓓ Ⓔ
11 Ⓐ Ⓑ Ⓒ Ⓓ Ⓔ
12 Ⓐ Ⓑ Ⓒ Ⓓ Ⓔ
13 Ⓐ Ⓑ Ⓒ Ⓓ Ⓔ
14 Ⓐ Ⓑ Ⓒ Ⓓ Ⓔ
15 Ⓐ Ⓑ Ⓒ Ⓓ Ⓔ
16 Ⓐ Ⓑ Ⓒ Ⓓ Ⓔ
17 Ⓐ Ⓑ Ⓒ Ⓓ Ⓔ
18 Ⓐ Ⓑ Ⓒ Ⓓ Ⓔ
19 Ⓐ Ⓑ Ⓒ Ⓓ Ⓔ
20 Ⓐ Ⓑ Ⓒ Ⓓ Ⓔ
21 Ⓐ Ⓑ Ⓒ Ⓓ Ⓔ
22 Ⓐ Ⓑ Ⓒ Ⓓ Ⓔ
23 Ⓐ Ⓑ Ⓒ Ⓓ Ⓔ
24 Ⓐ Ⓑ Ⓒ Ⓓ Ⓔ
25 Ⓐ Ⓑ Ⓒ Ⓓ Ⓔ
26 Ⓐ Ⓑ Ⓒ Ⓓ Ⓔ
27 Ⓐ Ⓑ Ⓒ Ⓓ Ⓔ
28 Ⓐ Ⓑ Ⓒ Ⓓ Ⓔ
29 Ⓐ Ⓑ Ⓒ Ⓓ Ⓔ
30 Ⓐ Ⓑ Ⓒ Ⓓ Ⓔ

Reading Comprehension 5
Answer Grid

NAME
(Please Print)

_____
Last Name   Suffix

_____
First Name

_____
Middle Name

1 Ⓐ Ⓑ Ⓒ Ⓓ Ⓔ
2 Ⓐ Ⓑ Ⓒ Ⓓ Ⓔ
3 Ⓐ Ⓑ Ⓒ Ⓓ Ⓔ
4 Ⓐ Ⓑ Ⓒ Ⓓ Ⓔ
5 Ⓐ Ⓑ Ⓒ Ⓓ Ⓔ
6 Ⓐ Ⓑ Ⓒ Ⓓ Ⓔ
7 Ⓐ Ⓑ Ⓒ Ⓓ Ⓔ
8 Ⓐ Ⓑ Ⓒ Ⓓ Ⓔ
9 Ⓐ Ⓑ Ⓒ Ⓓ Ⓔ
10 Ⓐ Ⓑ Ⓒ Ⓓ Ⓔ
11 Ⓐ Ⓑ Ⓒ Ⓓ Ⓔ
12 Ⓐ Ⓑ Ⓒ Ⓓ Ⓔ
13 Ⓐ Ⓑ Ⓒ Ⓓ Ⓔ
14 Ⓐ Ⓑ Ⓒ Ⓓ Ⓔ
15 Ⓐ Ⓑ Ⓒ Ⓓ Ⓔ
16 Ⓐ Ⓑ Ⓒ Ⓓ Ⓔ
17 Ⓐ Ⓑ Ⓒ Ⓓ Ⓔ
18 Ⓐ Ⓑ Ⓒ Ⓓ Ⓔ
19 Ⓐ Ⓑ Ⓒ Ⓓ Ⓔ
20 Ⓐ Ⓑ Ⓒ Ⓓ Ⓔ
21 Ⓐ Ⓑ Ⓒ Ⓓ Ⓔ
22 Ⓐ Ⓑ Ⓒ Ⓓ Ⓔ
23 Ⓐ Ⓑ Ⓒ Ⓓ Ⓔ
24 Ⓐ Ⓑ Ⓒ Ⓓ Ⓔ
25 Ⓐ Ⓑ Ⓒ Ⓓ Ⓔ
26 Ⓐ Ⓑ Ⓒ Ⓓ Ⓔ
27 Ⓐ Ⓑ Ⓒ Ⓓ Ⓔ
28 Ⓐ Ⓑ Ⓒ Ⓓ Ⓔ
29 Ⓐ Ⓑ Ⓒ Ⓓ Ⓔ
30 Ⓐ Ⓑ Ⓒ Ⓓ Ⓔ

Reading Comprehension 6
Answer Grid

NAME
(Please Print)

_____

Last Name   Suffix

_____

First Name

_____

Middle Name

1. Ⓐ Ⓑ Ⓒ Ⓓ Ⓔ
2. Ⓐ Ⓑ Ⓒ Ⓓ Ⓔ
3. Ⓐ Ⓑ Ⓒ Ⓓ Ⓔ
4. Ⓐ Ⓑ Ⓒ Ⓓ Ⓔ
5. Ⓐ Ⓑ Ⓒ Ⓓ Ⓔ
6. Ⓐ Ⓑ Ⓒ Ⓓ Ⓔ
7. Ⓐ Ⓑ Ⓒ Ⓓ Ⓔ
8. Ⓐ Ⓑ Ⓒ Ⓓ Ⓔ
9. Ⓐ Ⓑ Ⓒ Ⓓ Ⓔ
10. Ⓐ Ⓑ Ⓒ Ⓓ Ⓔ
11. Ⓐ Ⓑ Ⓒ Ⓓ Ⓔ
12. Ⓐ Ⓑ Ⓒ Ⓓ Ⓔ
13. Ⓐ Ⓑ Ⓒ Ⓓ Ⓔ
14. Ⓐ Ⓑ Ⓒ Ⓓ Ⓔ
15. Ⓐ Ⓑ Ⓒ Ⓓ Ⓔ
16. Ⓐ Ⓑ Ⓒ Ⓓ Ⓔ
17. Ⓐ Ⓑ Ⓒ Ⓓ Ⓔ
18. Ⓐ Ⓑ Ⓒ Ⓓ Ⓔ
19. Ⓐ Ⓑ Ⓒ Ⓓ Ⓔ
20. Ⓐ Ⓑ Ⓒ Ⓓ Ⓔ
21. Ⓐ Ⓑ Ⓒ Ⓓ Ⓔ
22. Ⓐ Ⓑ Ⓒ Ⓓ Ⓔ
23. Ⓐ Ⓑ Ⓒ Ⓓ Ⓔ
24. Ⓐ Ⓑ Ⓒ Ⓓ Ⓔ
25. Ⓐ Ⓑ Ⓒ Ⓓ Ⓔ
26. Ⓐ Ⓑ Ⓒ Ⓓ Ⓔ
27. Ⓐ Ⓑ Ⓒ Ⓓ Ⓔ
28. Ⓐ Ⓑ Ⓒ Ⓓ Ⓔ
29. Ⓐ Ⓑ Ⓒ Ⓓ Ⓔ
30. Ⓐ Ⓑ Ⓒ Ⓓ Ⓔ

Reading
Comprehension 7
Answer Grid

NAME
(Please Print)

_____

Last Name   Suffix

_____

First Name

_____

Middle Name

1 Ⓐ Ⓑ Ⓒ Ⓓ Ⓔ
2 Ⓐ Ⓑ Ⓒ Ⓓ Ⓔ
3 Ⓐ Ⓑ Ⓒ Ⓓ Ⓔ
4 Ⓐ Ⓑ Ⓒ Ⓓ Ⓔ
5 Ⓐ Ⓑ Ⓒ Ⓓ Ⓔ
6 Ⓐ Ⓑ Ⓒ Ⓓ Ⓔ
7 Ⓐ Ⓑ Ⓒ Ⓓ Ⓔ
8 Ⓐ Ⓑ Ⓒ Ⓓ Ⓔ
9 Ⓐ Ⓑ Ⓒ Ⓓ Ⓔ
10 Ⓐ Ⓑ Ⓒ Ⓓ Ⓔ
11 Ⓐ Ⓑ Ⓒ Ⓓ Ⓔ
12 Ⓐ Ⓑ Ⓒ Ⓓ Ⓔ
13 Ⓐ Ⓑ Ⓒ Ⓓ Ⓔ
14 Ⓐ Ⓑ Ⓒ Ⓓ Ⓔ
15 Ⓐ Ⓑ Ⓒ Ⓓ Ⓔ
16 Ⓐ Ⓑ Ⓒ Ⓓ Ⓔ
17 Ⓐ Ⓑ Ⓒ Ⓓ Ⓔ
18 Ⓐ Ⓑ Ⓒ Ⓓ Ⓔ
19 Ⓐ Ⓑ Ⓒ Ⓓ Ⓔ
20 Ⓐ Ⓑ Ⓒ Ⓓ Ⓔ
21 Ⓐ Ⓑ Ⓒ Ⓓ Ⓔ
22 Ⓐ Ⓑ Ⓒ Ⓓ Ⓔ
23 Ⓐ Ⓑ Ⓒ Ⓓ Ⓔ
24 Ⓐ Ⓑ Ⓒ Ⓓ Ⓔ
25 Ⓐ Ⓑ Ⓒ Ⓓ Ⓔ
26 Ⓐ Ⓑ Ⓒ Ⓓ Ⓔ
27 Ⓐ Ⓑ Ⓒ Ⓓ Ⓔ
28 Ⓐ Ⓑ Ⓒ Ⓓ Ⓔ
29 Ⓐ Ⓑ Ⓒ Ⓓ Ⓔ
30 Ⓐ Ⓑ Ⓒ Ⓓ Ⓔ

Reading Comprehension 8

Answer Grid

Last Name   Suffix

First Name

Middle Name

1 Ⓐ Ⓑ Ⓒ Ⓓ Ⓔ
2 Ⓐ Ⓑ Ⓒ Ⓓ Ⓔ
3 Ⓐ Ⓑ Ⓒ Ⓓ Ⓔ
4 Ⓐ Ⓑ Ⓒ Ⓓ Ⓔ
5 Ⓐ Ⓑ Ⓒ Ⓓ Ⓔ
6 Ⓐ Ⓑ Ⓒ Ⓓ Ⓔ
7 Ⓐ Ⓑ Ⓒ Ⓓ Ⓔ
8 Ⓐ Ⓑ Ⓒ Ⓓ Ⓔ
9 Ⓐ Ⓑ Ⓒ Ⓓ Ⓔ
10 Ⓐ Ⓑ Ⓒ Ⓓ Ⓔ
11 Ⓐ Ⓑ Ⓒ Ⓓ Ⓔ
12 Ⓐ Ⓑ Ⓒ Ⓓ Ⓔ
13 Ⓐ Ⓑ Ⓒ Ⓓ Ⓔ
14 Ⓐ Ⓑ Ⓒ Ⓓ Ⓔ
15 Ⓐ Ⓑ Ⓒ Ⓓ Ⓔ
16 Ⓐ Ⓑ Ⓒ Ⓓ Ⓔ
17 Ⓐ Ⓑ Ⓒ Ⓓ Ⓔ
18 Ⓐ Ⓑ Ⓒ Ⓓ Ⓔ
19 Ⓐ Ⓑ Ⓒ Ⓓ Ⓔ
20 Ⓐ Ⓑ Ⓒ Ⓓ Ⓔ
21 Ⓐ Ⓑ Ⓒ Ⓓ Ⓔ
22 Ⓐ Ⓑ Ⓒ Ⓓ Ⓔ
23 Ⓐ Ⓑ Ⓒ Ⓓ Ⓔ
24 Ⓐ Ⓑ Ⓒ Ⓓ Ⓔ
25 Ⓐ Ⓑ Ⓒ Ⓓ Ⓔ
26 Ⓐ Ⓑ Ⓒ Ⓓ Ⓔ
27 Ⓐ Ⓑ Ⓒ Ⓓ Ⓔ
28 Ⓐ Ⓑ Ⓒ Ⓓ Ⓔ
29 Ⓐ Ⓑ Ⓒ Ⓓ Ⓔ
30 Ⓐ Ⓑ Ⓒ Ⓓ Ⓔ

Reading Comprehension 9

Answer Grid

NAME
(Please Print)

_____

Last Name   Suffix

_____

First Name

_____

Middle Name

1. Ⓐ Ⓑ Ⓒ Ⓓ Ⓔ
2. Ⓐ Ⓑ Ⓒ Ⓓ Ⓔ
3. Ⓐ Ⓑ Ⓒ Ⓓ Ⓔ
4. Ⓐ Ⓑ Ⓒ Ⓓ Ⓔ
5. Ⓐ Ⓑ Ⓒ Ⓓ Ⓔ
6. Ⓐ Ⓑ Ⓒ Ⓓ Ⓔ
7. Ⓐ Ⓑ Ⓒ Ⓓ Ⓔ
8. Ⓐ Ⓑ Ⓒ Ⓓ Ⓔ
9. Ⓐ Ⓑ Ⓒ Ⓓ Ⓔ
10. Ⓐ Ⓑ Ⓒ Ⓓ Ⓔ
11. Ⓐ Ⓑ Ⓒ Ⓓ Ⓔ
12. Ⓐ Ⓑ Ⓒ Ⓓ Ⓔ
13. Ⓐ Ⓑ Ⓒ Ⓓ Ⓔ
14. Ⓐ Ⓑ Ⓒ Ⓓ Ⓔ
15. Ⓐ Ⓑ Ⓒ Ⓓ Ⓔ
16. Ⓐ Ⓑ Ⓒ Ⓓ Ⓔ
17. Ⓐ Ⓑ Ⓒ Ⓓ Ⓔ
18. Ⓐ Ⓑ Ⓒ Ⓓ Ⓔ
19. Ⓐ Ⓑ Ⓒ Ⓓ Ⓔ
20. Ⓐ Ⓑ Ⓒ Ⓓ Ⓔ
21. Ⓐ Ⓑ Ⓒ Ⓓ Ⓔ
22. Ⓐ Ⓑ Ⓒ Ⓓ Ⓔ
23. Ⓐ Ⓑ Ⓒ Ⓓ Ⓔ
24. Ⓐ Ⓑ Ⓒ Ⓓ Ⓔ
25. Ⓐ Ⓑ Ⓒ Ⓓ Ⓔ
26. Ⓐ Ⓑ Ⓒ Ⓓ Ⓔ
27. Ⓐ Ⓑ Ⓒ Ⓓ Ⓔ
28. Ⓐ Ⓑ Ⓒ Ⓓ Ⓔ
29. Ⓐ Ⓑ Ⓒ Ⓓ Ⓔ
30. Ⓐ Ⓑ Ⓒ Ⓓ Ⓔ

Reading
Comprehension 11
Answer Grid

NAME
(Please Print)

_____
Last Name   Suffix

_____
First Name

_____
Middle Name

1 (A) (B) (C) (D) (E)
2 (A) (B) (C) (D) (E)
3 (A) (B) (C) (D) (E)
4 (A) (B) (C) (D) (E)
5 (A) (B) (C) (D) (E)
6 (A) (B) (C) (D) (E)
7 (A) (B) (C) (D) (E)
8 (A) (B) (C) (D) (E)
9 (A) (B) (C) (D) (E)
10 (A) (B) (C) (D) (E)
11 (A) (B) (C) (D) (E)
12 (A) (B) (C) (D) (E)
13 (A) (B) (C) (D) (E)
14 (A) (B) (C) (D) (E)
15 (A) (B) (C) (D) (E)
16 (A) (B) (C) (D) (E)
17 (A) (B) (C) (D) (E)
18 (A) (B) (C) (D) (E)
19 (A) (B) (C) (D) (E)
20 (A) (B) (C) (D) (E)
21 (A) (B) (C) (D) (E)
22 (A) (B) (C) (D) (E)
23 (A) (B) (C) (D) (E)
24 (A) (B) (C) (D) (E)
25 (A) (B) (C) (D) (E)
26 (A) (B) (C) (D) (E)
27 (A) (B) (C) (D) (E)
28 (A) (B) (C) (D) (E)
29 (A) (B) (C) (D) (E)
30 (A) (B) (C) (D) (E)

Reading
Comprehension 12
Answer Grid

NAME
(Please Print)

_____
Last Name

_____
First Name

_____
Middle Name

1 Ⓐ Ⓑ Ⓒ Ⓓ Ⓔ
2 Ⓐ Ⓑ Ⓒ Ⓓ Ⓔ
3 Ⓐ Ⓑ Ⓒ Ⓓ Ⓔ
4 Ⓐ Ⓑ Ⓒ Ⓓ Ⓔ
5 Ⓐ Ⓑ Ⓒ Ⓓ Ⓔ
6 Ⓐ Ⓑ Ⓒ Ⓓ Ⓔ
7 Ⓐ Ⓑ Ⓒ Ⓓ Ⓔ
8 Ⓐ Ⓑ Ⓒ Ⓓ Ⓔ
9 Ⓐ Ⓑ Ⓒ Ⓓ Ⓔ
10 Ⓐ Ⓑ Ⓒ Ⓓ Ⓔ
11 Ⓐ Ⓑ Ⓒ Ⓓ Ⓔ
12 Ⓐ Ⓑ Ⓒ Ⓓ Ⓔ
13 Ⓐ Ⓑ Ⓒ Ⓓ Ⓔ
14 Ⓐ Ⓑ Ⓒ Ⓓ Ⓔ
15 Ⓐ Ⓑ Ⓒ Ⓓ Ⓔ
16 Ⓐ Ⓑ Ⓒ Ⓓ Ⓔ
17 Ⓐ Ⓑ Ⓒ Ⓓ Ⓔ
18 Ⓐ Ⓑ Ⓒ Ⓓ Ⓔ
19 Ⓐ Ⓑ Ⓒ Ⓓ Ⓔ
20 Ⓐ Ⓑ Ⓒ Ⓓ Ⓔ
21 Ⓐ Ⓑ Ⓒ Ⓓ Ⓔ
22 Ⓐ Ⓑ Ⓒ Ⓓ Ⓔ
23 Ⓐ Ⓑ Ⓒ Ⓓ Ⓔ
24 Ⓐ Ⓑ Ⓒ Ⓓ Ⓔ
25 Ⓐ Ⓑ Ⓒ Ⓓ Ⓔ
26 Ⓐ Ⓑ Ⓒ Ⓓ Ⓔ
27 Ⓐ Ⓑ Ⓒ Ⓓ Ⓔ
28 Ⓐ Ⓑ Ⓒ Ⓓ Ⓔ
29 Ⓐ Ⓑ Ⓒ Ⓓ Ⓔ
30 Ⓐ Ⓑ Ⓒ Ⓓ Ⓔ

Reading Comprehension 13

Answer Grid

1. (A) (B) (C) (D) (E)
2. (A) (B) (C) (D) (E)
3. (A) (B) (C) (D) (E)
4. (A) (B) (C) (D) (E)
5. (A) (B) (C) (D) (E)
6. (A) (B) (C) (D) (E)
7. (A) (B) (C) (D) (E)
8. (A) (B) (C) (D) (E)
9. (A) (B) (C) (D) (E)
10. (A) (B) (C) (D) (E)
11. (A) (B) (C) (D) (E)
12. (A) (B) (C) (D) (E)
13. (A) (B) (C) (D) (E)
14. (A) (B) (C) (D) (E)
15. (A) (B) (C) (D) (E)
16. (A) (B) (C) (D) (E)
17. (A) (B) (C) (D) (E)
18. (A) (B) (C) (D) (E)
19. (A) (B) (C) (D) (E)
20. (A) (B) (C) (D) (E)
21. (A) (B) (C) (D) (E)
22. (A) (B) (C) (D) (E)
23. (A) (B) (C) (D) (E)
24. (A) (B) (C) (D) (E)
25. (A) (B) (C) (D) (E)
26. (A) (B) (C) (D) (E)
27. (A) (B) (C) (D) (E)
28. (A) (B) (C) (D) (E)
29. (A) (B) (C) (D) (E)
30. (A) (B) (C) (D) (E)

NAME
(Please Print)

_____

Last Name   Suffix

_____

First Name

_____

Middle Name

Reading Comprehension 14

Answer Grid

1 (A) (B) (C) (D) (E)
2 (A) (B) (C) (D) (E)
3 (A) (B) (C) (D) (E)
4 (A) (B) (C) (D) (E)
5 (A) (B) (C) (D) (E)
6 (A) (B) (C) (D) (E)
7 (A) (B) (C) (D) (E)
8 (A) (B) (C) (D) (E)
9 (A) (B) (C) (D) (E)
10 (A) (B) (C) (D) (E)
11 (A) (B) (C) (D) (E)
12 (A) (B) (C) (D) (E)
13 (A) (B) (C) (D) (E)
14 (A) (B) (C) (D) (E)
15 (A) (B) (C) (D) (E)
16 (A) (B) (C) (D) (E)
17 (A) (B) (C) (D) (E)
18 (A) (B) (C) (D) (E)
19 (A) (B) (C) (D) (E)
20 (A) (B) (C) (D) (E)
21 (A) (B) (C) (D) (E)
22 (A) (B) (C) (D) (E)
23 (A) (B) (C) (D) (E)
24 (A) (B) (C) (D) (E)
25 (A) (B) (C) (D) (E)
26 (A) (B) (C) (D) (E)
27 (A) (B) (C) (D) (E)
28 (A) (B) (C) (D) (E)
29 (A) (B) (C) (D) (E)
30 (A) (B) (C) (D) (E)

Reading
Comprehension 15
Answer Grid

NAME
(Please Print)

_____
Last Name   Suffix

_____
First Name

_____
Middle Name

1 Ⓐ Ⓑ Ⓒ Ⓓ Ⓔ
2 Ⓐ Ⓑ Ⓒ Ⓓ Ⓔ
3 Ⓐ Ⓑ Ⓒ Ⓓ Ⓔ
4 Ⓐ Ⓑ Ⓒ Ⓓ Ⓔ
5 Ⓐ Ⓑ Ⓒ Ⓓ Ⓔ
6 Ⓐ Ⓑ Ⓒ Ⓓ Ⓔ
7 Ⓐ Ⓑ Ⓒ Ⓓ Ⓔ
8 Ⓐ Ⓑ Ⓒ Ⓓ Ⓔ
9 Ⓐ Ⓑ Ⓒ Ⓓ Ⓔ
10 Ⓐ Ⓑ Ⓒ Ⓓ Ⓔ
11 Ⓐ Ⓑ Ⓒ Ⓓ Ⓔ
12 Ⓐ Ⓑ Ⓒ Ⓓ Ⓔ
13 Ⓐ Ⓑ Ⓒ Ⓓ Ⓔ
14 Ⓐ Ⓑ Ⓒ Ⓓ Ⓔ
15 Ⓐ Ⓑ Ⓒ Ⓓ Ⓔ
16 Ⓐ Ⓑ Ⓒ Ⓓ Ⓔ
17 Ⓐ Ⓑ Ⓒ Ⓓ Ⓔ
18 Ⓐ Ⓑ Ⓒ Ⓓ Ⓔ
19 Ⓐ Ⓑ Ⓒ Ⓓ Ⓔ
20 Ⓐ Ⓑ Ⓒ Ⓓ Ⓔ
21 Ⓐ Ⓑ Ⓒ Ⓓ Ⓔ
22 Ⓐ Ⓑ Ⓒ Ⓓ Ⓔ
23 Ⓐ Ⓑ Ⓒ Ⓓ Ⓔ
24 Ⓐ Ⓑ Ⓒ Ⓓ Ⓔ
25 Ⓐ Ⓑ Ⓒ Ⓓ Ⓔ
26 Ⓐ Ⓑ Ⓒ Ⓓ Ⓔ
27 Ⓐ Ⓑ Ⓒ Ⓓ Ⓔ
28 Ⓐ Ⓑ Ⓒ Ⓓ Ⓔ
29 Ⓐ Ⓑ Ⓒ Ⓓ Ⓔ
30 Ⓐ Ⓑ Ⓒ Ⓓ Ⓔ

Reading
Comprehension 16
Answer Grid

NAME
(Please Print)

_____
Last Name   Suffix

_____
First Name

_____
Middle Name

1 Ⓐ Ⓑ Ⓒ Ⓓ Ⓔ
2 Ⓐ Ⓑ Ⓒ Ⓓ Ⓔ
3 Ⓐ Ⓑ Ⓒ Ⓓ Ⓔ
4 Ⓐ Ⓑ Ⓒ Ⓓ Ⓔ
5 Ⓐ Ⓑ Ⓒ Ⓓ Ⓔ
6 Ⓐ Ⓑ Ⓒ Ⓓ Ⓔ
7 Ⓐ Ⓑ Ⓒ Ⓓ Ⓔ
8 Ⓐ Ⓑ Ⓒ Ⓓ Ⓔ
9 Ⓐ Ⓑ Ⓒ Ⓓ Ⓔ
10 Ⓐ Ⓑ Ⓒ Ⓓ Ⓔ
11 Ⓐ Ⓑ Ⓒ Ⓓ Ⓔ
12 Ⓐ Ⓑ Ⓒ Ⓓ Ⓔ
13 Ⓐ Ⓑ Ⓒ Ⓓ Ⓔ
14 Ⓐ Ⓑ Ⓒ Ⓓ Ⓔ
15 Ⓐ Ⓑ Ⓒ Ⓓ Ⓔ
16 Ⓐ Ⓑ Ⓒ Ⓓ Ⓔ
17 Ⓐ Ⓑ Ⓒ Ⓓ Ⓔ
18 Ⓐ Ⓑ Ⓒ Ⓓ Ⓔ
19 Ⓐ Ⓑ Ⓒ Ⓓ Ⓔ
20 Ⓐ Ⓑ Ⓒ Ⓓ Ⓔ
21 Ⓐ Ⓑ Ⓒ Ⓓ Ⓔ
22 Ⓐ Ⓑ Ⓒ Ⓓ Ⓔ
23 Ⓐ Ⓑ Ⓒ Ⓓ Ⓔ
24 Ⓐ Ⓑ Ⓒ Ⓓ Ⓔ
25 Ⓐ Ⓑ Ⓒ Ⓓ Ⓔ
26 Ⓐ Ⓑ Ⓒ Ⓓ Ⓔ
27 Ⓐ Ⓑ Ⓒ Ⓓ Ⓔ
28 Ⓐ Ⓑ Ⓒ Ⓓ Ⓔ
29 Ⓐ Ⓑ Ⓒ Ⓓ Ⓔ
30 Ⓐ Ⓑ Ⓒ Ⓓ Ⓔ